The Philosophical Imagination

An Introduction to Philosophy

The Philosophical Imagination

An Introduction to Philosophy

RAZIEL ABELSON
MARIE-LOUISE FRIQUEGNON
MICHAEL LOCKWOOD

St. Martin's Press
New York

Library of Congress Catalog Card Number: 76-28137
For information, write: St. Martin's Press, Inc.,
175 Fifth Avenue, New York, N. Y. 10010

ISBN: 312-60515-3

PREFACE

Philosophy engages both our logical skill and our creative imagination. With as much of both as we possess, each of us constructs his or her own vision of how the various bits and pieces of knowledge and experience fit together. To state the matter a little differently, philosophical questions arise out of the perplexities of human beings in dealing with the crises, impasses, and dilemmas of life; philosophical views are formed—by the rigorous exercise of reason coupled with imagination—in an effort to answer those questions and thus to resolve the human perplexities that gave rise to them.

In preparing to offer a new text for a course already served by a number of excellent books, the three of us set ourselves the following goal, and, to the extent that we may have succeeded, we believe this book will be found distinctive and even exciting: we sought, without sacrificing philosophical rigor, to focus attention on some of the ways in which philosophy is rooted in concrete and often profoundly emotional human experiences and, further, to help bring students to an appreciation of the crucial role in philosophy of imagination as well as logical analysis.

Accordingly, after a short introduction, each chapter opens with one or (occasionally) two brief literary selections that show, in dramatic human terms, how philosophical perplexity is engendered by experiences that shake our confidence in our habitual responses and beliefs. Once the central philosophical problem of the chapter has been vividly portrayed in literature, we reprint the rigorous arguments of philosophers in support of competing solutions—challenging the reader to decide among them in the process of forming his or her own philosophical vision.

There is an inescapable element of personal choice in selecting materials for an introductory textbook, particularly in a field as comprehensive as philosophy. We have chosen those areas, problems, and viewpoints that seem to us, in the light of our own teaching experiences, to be of central importance, as well as of natural interest to students. There was no compelling need to divide the first part, metaphysics, into four problems, the next two parts, epistemology and ethics, into two problems each, and to confine the parts on political philosophy and aesthetics to single chapters. We feel that the relative degrees of complexity and centrality of these five main areas of philosophy justify the space we have allotted to each, but we must warn the student reader that there are many more problems in each area than we have dealt with in this book. For example, we have not, except tangentially, gone into metaethical issues of ethics, nor problems of sense data and of necessary truth in epistemology, nor criminal justice in political philosophy, nor meaning and reality in philosophy of art, not because these topics are less important than those we have chosen to explore but because they arise less directly out of common experience. However, there is nothing to prevent the reader from going on to other books, and perhaps further courses, that delve into topics and views not included here. We hope that our book will stir the reader's own philosophical imagination and prompt him or her to do just that.

We are grateful to Joshua Halberstam for his valuable assistance in preparing this book.

R. A.
M. L. F.
M. L.

CONTENTS

The Philosophical Imagination

An Introduction to Philosophy

Introduction

The Nature and Methods of Philosophy

A distinguished philosopher, aptly named John Wisdom, once remarked that when someone asks him what he does, and he replies "philosophy," he is met with wide-eyed silence, then a sneer, and finally a change of subject. "Philosophy," like "theology," has an awesome sound to it, connoting esoteric knowledge of no practical value to daily life, but disturbingly suggestive of something of more ultimate importance. Philosophy is often praised as a vision of things unseen, and belittled as useless verbal gymnastics. The ancient Greek legend about the first philosopher, Thales, who, while gazing at the stars, fell down a well from which his servant girl had to rescue him, illustrates the popular image of the philosopher as an impractical dreamer. But another story, that Thales cornered the market in olive presses and made a fortune that he donated to the pursuit of knowledge, illustrates the equally excessive veneration accorded the philosopher for having almost supernatural understanding. The truth, as usual, lies somewhere in between the extreme stereotypes.

Philosophy began in ancient Greece 2,500 years ago as a search for general knowledge. At that time it was a mixture of natural science, religion, and psychology. Gradually, each of these disciplines became an independent specialty, although as late as the nineteenth century, physics, chemistry, and biology were still labeled natural philosophy. Nowadays, experts in mathematics, psychology, and theology have made even further inroads into the discipline. What remains as the clear-cut subject matter of philosophy is hard to say. In a way, everything; and in a way, nothing.

Philosophers consider all things to lie within their province. No subject is too commonplace or remote to be devoid of philosophical interest. Important philosophical essays have been written on sewage effluent and apple grading, as well as on time travel and witchcraft. Philosophers are professional meddlers; they look over the shoulders of scientists, theologians, artists, psychiatrists, and businesspeople and criticize their procedures. On the other hand, there is no particular area of human experience in which philosophers can claim special expertise. With respect to subject matter, they are dilettantes. What distinguishes philosophical from nonphilosophical ideas on any subject is the high degree of generality of the former. When a philosopher writes about evaluating sewage, his or her conclusions are meant to apply in evaluating anything else as well. The specific subject matter serves as an illustration of some general principle. The kinds of questions explored are very general questions about meanings of key terms, methods of reasoning, standards of evaluation, and the nature of the subject.

This universality of scope and generality of interest is characteristic of all philosophical inquiry. Nevertheless, we must distinguish between two somewhat different types of philosophical activity. On the one hand, philosophers have traditionally set themselves the task of attaining a unified view of the world and our place in it, a coherent "vision" or picture of the way things fit together. This aspect of philosophy is usually called "synthesis." The most dramatically impressive legacies of such notable figures in the history of thought as Plato, Aristotle, Thomas Aquinas, René Descartes, Immanuel Kant, and Georg Hegel are, no doubt, their syntheses of knowledge into philosophical systems. But the construction of such systems is far from being the only thing that philosophers have attempted nor, in the opinion of many, is it even the most important. Philosophers also articulate basic principles, explore the structure of our concepts and the logical relations in which they stand to one another—in short, clarify our thinking. This work, called philosophical "analysis," looms large in contemporary Anglo-American philosophy. Many contemporary philosophers are exclusively concerned with analysis and deny the validity of any attempt to present a philosophical picture of reality as a whole. But it is important to stress that even those who still regard synthesis as the ultimate goal of philosophy recognize the need for analysis as a preliminary. It is impossible to achieve a cogent vision of reality without first clarifying the concepts and principles one is employing. Most great philosophers of the past are, in fact, as well known for their analytical work as for their synthetic visions, although some—most notably Socrates, David Hume, and, in the present century, Ludwig Wittgenstein—are celebrated primarily for their analytical achievements. Our introduction to philosophy will be limited to some models of philosophical analysis because the appreciation of a philosopher's synthetic vision requires a long and intensive study of all his writings, and because system building needs to be preceded by analytic clarification.

Just as there is no distinct subject matter about which philosophers can be assumed to be better informed than nonphilosophers, there is no specific training in special skills that sets philosophers aside from others. No one can solve differential equations, or perform chemical analyses, or interpret statistical data without considerable training; but anyone can philosophize, and, for better or worse, most people do. In this respect, philosophy is more contiguous with everyday life than the specialized intellectual disciplines. Nevertheless, it can be done well or badly, and experience and instruction help. As Plato observed in the *Protagoras*, philosophy is, in this respect, like speaking or writing one's native language. There are certain natural skills involved in philosophical analysis that everyone possesses to some degree but that may be enhanced by careful study of noteworthy examples and sharpened by practice and criticism. A sense of logical consistency, an ability to imagine examples and counterexamples and also, to spot logical interconnections, and a good "ear" for precise language are among the most essential natural philosophy skills.

The Main Fields of Philosophical Interest

Philosophy is concerned with questions that have a potential bearing on all human endeavors. It seeks to know what the world as a whole is like, what difference there is between appearance and reality, what the nature of man is, whether everything has a cause, what the limits of human knowledge are, how we can distinguish good and evil, what the ideal society might be like, what standards we can apply to the appreciation of works of art, and dozens of other such inquiries. These questions fall within different major areas of philosophical discussion, traditionally called metaphysics, epistemology, ethics, political philosophy, and aesthetics. Accordingly, this book is divided into five parts, each containing essays representing philosophical answers to the above questions.

METAPHYSICS

Defining each field of philosophy is itself a philosophical task. At least one influential school of thought (logical positivism) has denounced metaphysics as a spurious substitute for science on the ground that only the sciences can provide reliable information about the structure of the world. Other philosophical schools define metaphysics more sympathetically as the study of pure being, or of the necessary conditions of possible experience, or of the evolution of absolute spirit, or of the laws of all possible worlds. We shall provisionally define metaphysics as the attempt to describe the most general features of the world, leaving open the question of whether such attempts belong to philosophy or to natural science; moreover, we shall argue later in this introduction that philosophy and science are not, in any case, sharply separable.

In order to accommodate the different emphases of the various schools of metaphysical thought, we have subdivided the subject into four specific groups of problems, each of which has been taken as central by some philosophers. Our initial question—what is the world like in its general structure—can be broken down into four specific questions: (1) Is the world governed by a divine intelligence, or is it merely a chaotic swarm of randomly moving particles? (2) Are the objects of ordinary experience the real furniture of the world, or are they mere appearances or signs of some more ultimate reality? (3) Is a human being a particularly complicated part of the system of nature, governed by the same laws as everything else, or do humans stand apart from nature as different from and superior to it? And (4) does being a person require the ability to act independently of natural forces?

The question of whether the world is governed by a divine intelligence really amounts to an inquiry about whether God exists. We come to that question naturally: the very thought of the world as a whole provokes philosophical wonder. As small children we feel the eeriness of the unlimited expanse around us. We want to know how far our world extends and what, if anything, lies beyond it. If we are told that it has no boundaries, we try in vain to visualize such a state of affairs. We wonder if and when the world began, if and when it will cease to be, and we are as puzzled if told that it has infinite duration as we are if told that it began and will end at definite dates. We want to know why there is a world, who if anyone made it, and what its purpose, if any, is. As we grow older, we may cease to ask these questions not because we have found the answers, but because we have become so preoccupied with problems of life and livelihood that we have lost our natural metaphysical curiosity. The study of philosophy helps restore it.

Why, when we first begin to think about the world as a whole, do we so naturally wonder if someone created it and governs it? We are perfectly aware that individual things like mountains and trees are not made by intelligent agents but are formed or grow by natural processes. Why should we leap to an intelligent creator when considering all such things as a whole? One motive may be wishful thinking. We would like to believe that an all-powerful, all-knowing "father" is "minding the store" and watching over us. But theologians have offered more cogent reasons. One is that the world as a totality is not the same kind of thing as a definite object like a mountain whose formation is explainable by a natural process such as an earthquake or a glacial deposit; nor is the world like an organic object such as a tree that grows from a seed. Although these familiar types of objects, with their definite shapes and sizes, develop or grow out of other things, like silt and seeds, the world as a totality includes all particular objects that ever have existed or will exist and so could not have emerged from anything at all like the objects and processes we find in it. Consequently, the type of explanation that applies to familiar objects like mountains and trees seems inapplicable to the world as a whole.

A second specific problem falling in the general area of metaphysics is that of formulating a means for distinguishing what is real from what is merely apparent. We are often enough "taken in" by appearances, so that we learn to ask whether certain flowers are real or artificial, whether a picture is a real Rembrandt or a copy, whether a table is the solid object it appears to be or is really a cloud of rapidly moving particles, and finally, whether our existence on earth is the only reality, or whether this life is merely a rehearsal for an everlasting one. Are the last two questions analogous to the first two? To answer this we must become clear about what we mean by the term "real."

One very important reason that we wonder about the fundamental nature of the world is that we want to understand ourselves and our place in the cosmic scheme. In what does our own reality consist? Is each of us just a material body, one organized system of molecules among others, that "struts and frets its hour upon the stage"? Or are we, as Descartes maintained, essentially minds mysteriously harnessed to particular swarms of molecules called bodies? Or is there yet another and more crucial element involved here, called the "soul"? If the first, then how is it that we, alone among the vast variety of things in the universe, can reflect upon our position in the universe? If the second, then why do we ordinarily think of a person as a single entity rather than as "twins" (a ghostly mental twin coupled with a robust bodily twin), and how are these two parts of us related? And if we adopt the third view, that we are trinities of body, mind, and soul, then how can we visualize the relationships between these three elements? In short, what is a person?

Whatever answer we offer to the previous question must also shed light on the problem of free will. Are we humans so different from the rest of nature that we alone can introduce unpredictable yet purposeful changes? Do we alone escape total control by the causal laws that govern everything else? Or, is our own conduct merely an especially complex process covered by the same laws that govern a falling apple? It looks, at first glance, as if we, despite our limited knowledge and power, can initiate changes in the world that could not possibly be predicted in advance nor explained by prior causes. But so strong is the modern faith in science that many philosophers support some form of determinism. They regard the appearance of uncaused activity as an illusion stemming from our ignorance of the complex processes that must be at work in even the most surprising actions of creative people.

EPISTEMOLOGY

It is a puzzling fact, if true, that of all the creatures familiar to us we humans alone know that there is a world and that we are part of it. We are thus inclined to wonder not only about the general structure of the world but also about the knowledge of it that we seem to possess. How far does our knowledge extend, how complete can it ever be, and what distinguishes it from mere opinion? What allows us to be confident that we know anything at all? In the eighteenth century Hume argued that all our presumed knowledge about the world rests on our inferences —our educated guesses—from experience. Moreover, he maintained that the principle underlying such inferences cannot be proved valid. Since then, many have tried but no one has succeeded in refuting Hume. We tend to think that what someone believes, even if it happens to be true, cannot count as knowledge unless that person can justify his or her belief. But do we really have any rational justification for our ordinary beliefs? Not according to Hume. Some philosophers have gone even further than Hume in denying that even mathematics, our favorite model of rigorous knowledge, really deserves that status, because we have no demonstrable right to be certain of its so-called laws. Others deny that a person can be said to know even what seems plainly given to the senses, such as that there is print on this page.

Such skepticism may appear to practical-minded people as an intellectual disease that calls for quarantine of its carriers. Socrates was executed by his Athenian compatriots for infecting them with more moderate doubts about their ethical principles. But the value of raising skeptical questions is that they force us to take stock of the grounds for our claims to knowledge and to see more clearly when those grounds are reasonable and when they are not. If we have a right to infer from the observed to the unobserved, what gives us that right? If we can be absolutely certain of what we see, hear, and touch, then how is it that we sometimes misperceive or fall victim to illusions and hallucinations? Descartes asked how we can be certain that we are not always dreaming. We are, of course, perfectly certain that we are not. It is one thing to ask, in the manner of Descartes, for the grounds of our certainty. But we are prepared to commit to an asylum those who seem genuinely uncertain in their behavior. The weight of public opinion is not, however, the logical force of sound reasoning. Only if we can answer the skeptic's arguments have we the logical right, rather than the mere arbitrary power, to assert claims to knowledge as distinct from mere opinion.

ETHICS

If our confidence in our knowledge of simple facts rests on shaky grounds, then our confidence in our knowledge of good and evil would seem to be built on quicksand. If we cannot even be sure there is print before us, how on earth can we make moral judgments of ourselves and others with rational assurance? Moral skepticism is much more common than skepticism about perception, for good reasons and for bad. One good reason is that there is less general agreement on moral judgments than on perceived facts. One bad reason is that moral skepticism would allow us to do anything we like. But whatever the motives of the moral skeptic, we would do well to define what we mean by right and wrong, and to state the rational grounds, if any, that justify our use of these terms in making moral judgments. Otherwise, it is difficult to see how we could claim that our moral judgments are anything more than personal prejudices. We would resemble the irritable parent who, on being asked by his or her child why something is wrong, replies "Because I say so!"

Presumably, the reason we consider an action right or wrong is that the action meets, or fails to meet, a certain standard. But now the question arises: which standard? We sometimes judge an action in terms of its intended and likely consequences, and at other times in terms of some rule that it obeys or violates. But when these two standards conflict, we may not know which one deserves priority. Is it right for a doctor to lie to an incurably ill patient who appears incapable of coping with bad news? If so, then is it equally right for an unfaithful but considerate spouse to lie for the same kind of reason? Should we permit and even encourage violations of moral rules such as "Do not lie" for the sake of beneficial consequences? Should we demand instead uniform obedience to the rules? Or, can we distinguish the conditions under which the consequences take precedence from those under which conformity to the rule is more desirable?

Besides the dilemma of rules versus consequences, there is that of morality versus self-interest. No matter how we resolve the first dilemma, we shall have to cope with the second. Whether we decide what is right in terms of rules or of consequences, we will still often face a painful choice between what is clearly right and what seems the more reasonable thing to do in one's own interest. If, for example, in rushing to put out a fire in my home, I trod across the newly sown grass of the city park, in violation of the "Keep Off" signs conspicuously displayed, I have placed my self-interest above obedience to a rule. Few would quarrel with my doing so in this instance. But what of the case of deliberately running over a dog in my haste to reach my home? Here, it seems at least doubtful that self-interest outweighs conformity to the rule that we should be considerate of animals. Even on the assumption that beneficial consequences are the proper standard of right, we may still demand to know why we should place benefit to others above benefit to ourselves, and the cases just described—of walking across the grass and of running over a dog—seem once again to call for inconsistent decisions. If self-interest may occasionally be set above either obedience to a rule or concern for the welfare of others, then we need some principle for identifying such occasions. Some tough-minded philosophers have maintained that self-interest always deserves precedence; many more have held that conformity to rules or considerations of general welfare are always overriding; and still others have argued that when self-interest, general welfare, and conformity to moral rules are adequately defined, they always coincide.

POLITICAL PHILOSOPHY

Most of us are not political leaders. We are not personally responsible for those difficult and complex political decisions that may affect the lives of thousands, even millions, of people. But we do vote. And in voting for one candidate or party rather than others we indicate the kind of society in which we prefer to live. Poiltical philosophy is the attempt to determine the best possible political and social structure and to state principles for organizing and governing society.

The most fundamental philosophical question involved in discussions of public policy concerns the primary function of government: is it to make wise laws that promote the welfare of citizens, or to protect individual rights and liberties, or to create conditions for the fuller realization of human potentialities? The answer to this bears on the degree to which we think that government should control the economic, social, and even personal activities of its citizens.

Philosophical clarification of the grounds for political policies is needed now more than ever, with the rapid increase in world population, the pollution of our natural environment and approaching exhaustion of natural resources, the constant threat of thermonuclear war, and the rapidly increasing role of government in providing for regulation of public utilities, fire, flood and pestilence control, welfare for the indigent and aged, medical care, food and drug control, and enormous military establishments. Government is nowadays becoming an ever more conspicuous and powerful factor in human life, whether one wishes it to be so or not. Hence, no question could be more urgently in need of a generally acceptable answer than that of how to shape government for the benefit of the governed.

To frame a coherent answer to this question, however, we must first agree on what is to count as a genuine benefit and who is to count as the appropriate beneficiary. Are all citizens entitled to benefit equally from the activities of government, or is each to benefit in proportion to the value of his or her services to the community, or in proportion to his or her wealth and influence? And does the benefit that comes from good government consist of fulfilling some ideal conception of what a person should be like, or of participating in a well-ordered and harmonious community, or of exercising one's individual rights and powers? Is government responsible merely for protecting each citizen against aggression by others? Or should it also impose on citizens decisions that are wiser than those they would make for themselves, or provide an environment in which they can more completely realize their potential as individuals and as social beings? Authoritarianism, libertarianism, and socialism offer us competing visions of government's function. The choice in supporting political parties and their policies is often among these three alternatives.

AESTHETICS

Profound and rapid changes provoke philosophical reflection by forcing us to reappraise our deepest beliefs and values. Like the fifth century B.C. in Greece, when agrarian monarchies were replaced by commercial democracies and tyrannies, and like the seventeenth century in western Europe, when feudalism gave way to science, industry, and commerce, our century has witnessed rapid and enormous transformations of our economic, political, and cultural institutions. Ours has been an era of totalitarian despotisms and their overthrow, world wars and genocidal campaigns, the weakening of colonialism and racism, the scientific conquest of microscopic and galactic space, the decline of sexual prudery, and the breakdown of barriers between fine art and popular culture. Of all these changes—political, social, technological, and cultural—the changes in aesthetic and sexual values have been so gradual that they have hardly been noticed. Still, their importance should not be underestimated. Although enthusiasts of the "cultural revolution" like Charles Reich (*The Greening of America*) and Herbert Marcuse (*Eros and Civilization*) may have exaggerated the impact of new aesthetic standards on social and political life, that impact has surely been considerable. Moral and religious prudery and austerity are near death. With that demise there has developed an almost universal refusal of the poor and underprivileged to accept their lowly status, with a consequent world-wide explosion of nationalism and social upheaval. The third quarter of this century has been the most culturally and socially liberating period of human history, at least outside the communist bloc of nations, and even within that sphere people are turning to the West for new styles of dress, music, dance, and personal relations.

Reflection on the changing standards of both popular culture and fine art prompts the philosophical question: What is art and, how is it to be evaluated? Was the traditional distinction between fine art and popular culture a mere prejudice of a wealthy and educated social elite, which is destined to disappear with the advance of universal education and the spread of the mass communications media? Do all products of human skill have equal intrinsic worth, regardless of their market value or the opinions of professional critics? If not, then what standards of evaluation can we rationally defend as independent of temporary fashion and personal preference?

Philosophy and Other Disciplines

Since philosophy, religion, science, and art are all products of creative imagination, the boundaries we draw between them are vague and somewhat artificial. All these activities involve our responses to the world, our attempts to understand and organize our experiences, our temperamental preferences, and the search for a truth more fundamental and more enduring than the practical knowledge of our day-to-day affairs. Philosophy, however, can be roughly distinguished from other modes of intellectual activity in both style and interest. We shall first contrast philosophy with religion, and then, successively, with science and art.

PHILOSOPHY AND RELIGION

Speculation about the structure of the world and humanity's place in it originally took a religious form. The ancient myths of all cultures offer accounts of the origins of the world and of the relation of human beings to nature and what is beyond nature. These mythical explanations were provided in poems and stories that won acceptance and belief without question, although they were often embellished by the imagination of the individual storyteller. Gradually, as methods of careful observation and scientific generalization developed, thoughtful people began to look for objective reasons for preferring one account of the world to another. Synthetic philosophy emerged as a kind of bridge between religion and science, sharing the cosmic vision of the one and the concern for rational argument of the other.

The intellectual leaders of the great religions are of two kinds: the visionaries who founded the religions—such as Moses, Jesus, Gautauma Buddha, and Mohammed—and the theologians who formulate the religious doctrines in a systematic way and argue for one interpretation over others. Synthetic philosophers resemble theologians more than visionary founders, although they are not as firmly committed to the conclusions for which they argue. Theologians employ reason to clarify and defend their faith, whereas philosophers rely upon reason alone to arrive at a unifying vision of the world. Moreover, philosophers' most general beliefs, like scientific hypotheses, are subject to refutation, although insofar as they are products of speculative imagination, their logical relations to particular facts are extremely difficult to spell out. Thus synthetic or speculative philosophy is less rationally provable than scientific theory, but more so than religious doctrine. Analytic philosophy, which aims at clarifying what is already known rather than formulating a systematic cosmic vision, aspires to the same degree of precision and rigorous proof as the most advanced fields of science. Thus, speculative philosophy lies closer to religion, while analytical philosophy has more in common with science.

PHILOSOPHY AND SCIENCE

Much of what we now think of as science, it was earlier remarked, was originally considered philosophy. The ancient Greek thinkers who initiated philosophical thinking were as much concerned with questions that are today regarded as scientific as with those still thought of as philosophical and, for that matter, as religious. One by one, astronomy, mathematics, physics, biology, and psychology split off from their parent discipline and became separate sciences. It may therefore be tempting to think of philosophy, as Bertrand Russell suggested, as "pre-science," a kind of sun that periodically throws off new disciplines like planets, depleting itself in the process. Although this account contains some truth, to regard it as the whole, or even the main, story would be a mistake. For the sun and planet picture fails to explain two essential features of philosophical inquiry. First, observable facts are not as directly linked to the solution of philosophical problems as they are to scientific problems. Second, it makes sense to go on asking philosophical questions, even when the relevant scientific evidence is agreed upon. The problem of free will provides a good example of the perennial character of a philosophical problem. If people were clear enough as to what free will is, then the question of whether some or all of us have it might well be settled by the opinion of scientific experts. But the very meaning of free will is controversial, and that is why we have a distinctively philosophical problem.

A substantial part of philosophy, the part called analytic, is concerned with such questions of conceptual clarification and is hence in no danger of being depleted by the advance of science. As for synthetic philosophy, its high degree of generality, ranging as it does over the entire universe in all its aspects, guarantees that its concerns will remain outside the scope of any specialized science. Both types of philosophy are somewhat like the general practice of medicine; the more others specialize, the more need there is for a general diagnostician to direct and coordinate the work of the specialists.

PHILOSOPHY AND ART

Philosophy, like art and religion, and unlike science, expresses attitudes and feelings as well as reasoned beliefs. Like the artist, and unlike the scientist or the religious leader, the philosopher does not claim any esoteric knowledge unavailable to others but claims only to be able to see things in a somewhat clearer way and attempts to convey that perspective to others. Imagination plays a crucial role in both art and philosophy, although the type of imaginative skill required for philosophy is more abstract than in art and in this respect resembles the talent of mathematicians. Of all the arts, literature is the closest to philosophy because it communicates through words and because it illuminates the ethical in human life. Philosophical literature—such as the plays of Shakespeare, Goethe, Shaw, and Pirandello, the epic poems of Dante and Milton, and the novels of Tolstoy, Dostoyevsky, and Thomas Mann —is a rich source of illustrations and discussions of philosophical problems, while the most eloquent philosophers, such as Kierkegaard, Nietzsche, and Ortega y Gasset, are considered literary essayists as much as philosophers. It is therefore appropriate to begin each chapter of this book with a selection from philosophical literature that sets the stage for analytical clarification and possible solutions by philosophers of a major philosophical problem.

PART ONE

Metaphysics

Chapter 1

God: Is the World Governed?

Religion and philosophy meet in metaphysical speculation about the origin and structure of the world. Did the world always exist, or did it come into existence at some moment of past time, and, if so, what was there prior to the world that produced it? Many defenders of religious belief have held that only a belief in God can provide satisfactory answers to these questions. Philosophers skeptical of these claims have argued, on the contrary, that the belief that the world always existed is just as intelligible as the belief in divine creation. Some have held that even if the creation hypothesis is true, the imperfections of this world defeat the claim that its creator is both omnipotent and benevolent.

The issue of whether or not such considerations logically compel belief or disbelief in God is the subject of what has been called "natural," or philosophical, theology, as distinct from "revealed" religion, which rests upon personal illumination or faith in scriptures. Some religious thinkers, such as Ramanuja, Tertullian, Sören Kierkegaard, and Karl Barth, have held that natural theology is a self-defeating enterprise, more likely to engender atheism than to inspire genuinely religious belief. Such belief, they maintain, is not a scientific hypothesis but an attitude of commitment and worship toward a being that transcends rational comprehension, an attitude that guides the life of a religious person. In this chapter, we shall examine the main types of philosophical arguments for and against a divine creator and governor, as well as some arguments against any use of philosophical reasoning to support religious faith.

Philosophical arguments for a divine and omnipotent creator have been of three main types, traditionally called the "cosmological," "ontological," and "teleological" arguments. The cosmological argument reasons that the world must have had a "first cause"; the ontological argument, which is the most abstract and technical, deduces the existence of God from the concept of a perfect being; and the teleological argument, also sometimes referred to as the "argument from design," holds that the high degree of order in nature manifests a purposeful design.

Immanuel Kant, the great eighteenth-century German philosopher, thought that the teleological argument was the most natural and compelling, and David Hume, a British philosopher of the same century, devoted the major portion of his *Dialogues on Natural Religion* to a painstaking consideration of all the facets of this argument. The main obstacle to this argument from design, and perhaps to the other arguments as well, is the problem of explaining evil, which was first noted by the Greek philosopher Epicurus, was worked out in thorough detail by Hume, and was most poignantly and passionately expressed by the nineteenth-century Russian writer Fyodor Dostoyevsky in the passage from *The Brothers Karamazov* with which this chapter begins. This powerful objection to belief in a providential deity challenges religion on both an intellectual and a moral level. The blood-curdling story of the sadistic murder of a child told by Ivan, Dostoyevsky's representative of religious agnosticism, holds religious optimism up to scorn as emotionally insensitive and morally blind.

Ivan's objections to belief in a creator of a world in which children are tortured seem to weigh particularly heavily against the position taken by the Hindu philosopher Ramanuja in the last selection in this chapter. Ramanuja maintains that belief in God rests on religious faith alone, not rational argumentation. If Ramanuja is wrong, and the rational weight of evidence logically compels us to recognize the existence of a divine creator, then we are not subject to Ivan's moral indictment, for we need not worship such a being nor endorse that being's cosmic purposes. But if Ramanuja is correct, and our religious faith is a voluntary personal commitment to a being beyond our understanding and a trusting acceptance of whatever comes to pass, then we are directly faced with Ivan's challenge: How can we accept the suffering of the innocent as right and good? Is not such faith morally obtuse?

A Hasidic rabbi was once asked by a student, "Why should we praise God for the evil things that happen as well as the good things?" The rabbi replied that the question was too difficult for him to answer and advised his student to consult a certain holy man who had been beaten and tortured during a pogrom. When the student located the holy man, who lay bleeding and dying, and asked him the question, the holy man replied: "I cannot answer you, because nothing evil ever happened to me."

Few can share the faith of that saint. Many religious people recognize the existence of evils but consider them justifiable punishment for sin or the inevitable outcome of human folly. Atheists regard pain, disease, and cruelty as evidence that the world is an ungoverned chaos. But there are many people who, like Ivan, find both positions unsatisfactory. Their response to the good things in life is one of gratitude. They recognize and appreciate the beauty of nature, its orderly complexity, the reliability of its laws. But they refuse to ignore the monstrous accidents, the waste and disorder of fire, flood, earthquake, and pestilence, the instinctive cruelty of predatory animals, and the deliberate cruelty of humans. Nor can they justify these evils as necessary means to the achievement of some cosmic purpose. Such people, Dostoyevsky understood, have an inclination toward religious belief but a stubborn resistance to what falls short of their moral ideals. It is this sort of "seeker of God" that theologian Paul Tillich may have had in mind when he asserted that only an atheist can be genuinely religious.

Epicurus expressed this attitude in his famous dilemma. A benevolent and omnipotent creator, according to Epicurus, would not want evil and would be able to prevent it. But there is evil. Therefore, if there is a creator, it is either malevolent or lacking in power. In either case, it is unworthy of religious worship.

Most theologians have responded to this challenge by arguing in one of two ways. They maintain (1) that what appears to be evil is really not evil because it serves a good purpose, such as punishing the wicked or tempering human character; or (2) that while there are genuine evils, they arise from the free will of humans and not from the will of God. We shall consider the possible replies to these arguments in our discussion of the selection from Hume's *Dialogues* below.

But before we decide if the creator of the world is worthy of worship, which is the question raised by the argument from evil, it will be well to make up our minds on whether the belief in any creator of the world, worthy or unworthy, is a reasonable one. The selection from St. Thomas Aquinas presents the famous "Five Ways" by which this thirteenth-century philosopher and theologian sought to show the reasonableness of this belief.

Aquinas's first "way," or proof, which was probably derived from Aristotle's theory of a Prime Mover, argues that because everything in nature is incapable of moving unless moved by something else, there must be something or someone outside of nature that provides the initial "push." His second way, which reasons that there must be a first "efficient cause," differs from the first only technically in its use of the

Aristotelian theory of four types of causality (a subject which we need not consider in detail, since the two proofs are generally recognized to stand or fall together). An interesting feature of these arguments, particularly in the first form, is that Aquinas seems to have anticipated the mechanistic model of the world that was fashioned almost four centuries later by Galileo and has guided the development of physical science in the modern age. In effect, he considers nature to be a mechanical system in which everything is a cog that moves another cog but must itself be moved by a third, and notices that there is something missing in this picture, namely, the force that moves the very first cog. That "first mover" cannot be just another cog, because a cog cannot move itself; it must therefore be an agent, like a human person but infinitely greater, who exists outside the world machine—in a word, God. The point is that this vision of the world as a finite and self-sufficient machine seems incoherent unless something, or rather someone, starts the machine going. Some machines may be said to be "self-starting"—for example, a heating system equipped with a thermostat—but this characterization would be superficial. In reality, any such mechanical system must be turned on and off by something else, whether a person or a change of temperature in the surrounding atmosphere.

Some modern philosophers who reject Aquinas's first two ways offer an escape from this difficulty. They propose an alternative mechanistic picture of the world as having existed from the infinite past, so that no cog can be considered to be the first one to move. From that it follows that there is no longer any need for an agent to move a first cog. The revised picture thus suggested is analogous to that of a freight train composed of an infinite number of boxcars, each moved by the preceding one in such a way that we will never find a locomotive that initiates the train's motion. It remains an open question whether this picture of an infinite train without a locomotive is intrinsically more plausible than the belief in a divine first mover.

Aware that many philosophers, even Aristotle, believed that the world is eternal, Aquinas formulated his third way, which does not depend on the finiteness of past time but on a distinction between "contingent being" and "necessary being." Since everything we find in nature is of limited lifespan and has to be brought into existence by something else, he argues, there must be an eternal being beyond the world, a being whose existence does not depend on anything else and that produced and sustains the world. Otherwise, Aquinas reasons, nothing at all would exist now. Why would nothing exist now if there were no such necessary being? Because, says Aquinas, "that which can not-be at some time is not. Therefore, if everything can not-be, then at one time there was nothing in existence." This reasoning seems flagrantly invalid. Granted *in deed*

that *each single thing* at some time was nonexistent, it does not follow that at some time *nothing* existed. The argument shifts from what logicians call the "distributive sense" of everything, meaning each thing taken one at a time, to the "collective sense" of nothing, meaning everything taken together and then negated.

In the subsequent selection, W. I. Matson, a contemporary American philosopher, criticizes this form of the necessary-being argument, which he calls the "crude" version. Matson maintains that it is just a restatement of the first cause argument of Aquinas's first two ways. We have already seen that there is some plausibility in the first-cause picture, which assumes a beginning to the universe, as compared with the picture of an eternal universe. Matson suggests, as a third alternative, the "big bang" theory developed by some astronomers. This theory, however, does not really provide an alternative picture. When we are told that the world as we know it emerged with a big bang from a tiny dot of immense density about 15 billion years ago, we naturally want to know what prior cause produced that big bang—God or some natural process? If the latter, then there was a material world even before the big bang, and thus *it* did not produce the universe. Matson argues that the question could just as well be asked about a divine first cause: What or who caused God? But if God's existence is necessary, in the sense that God is not dependent on anything else, then Matson's question may be ruled out of order in advance. Indeed, this is precisely the force of the necessary-being concept. Thus, the "crude" version is not so crude after all but leads us into what Matson calls the "subtle" version.

The subtle version characterizes God as the reason for the world rather than its cause in the more usual sense of that term. "Reason," according to Matson, means that God's decision or choice explains why there is a world, as, say, Leonardo da Vinci's decision to paint the Mona Lisa explains the existence of that masterpiece. Matson contends that citing a decision can provide a satisfactory explanation only if we assume that it is the best possible decision. The world that God allegedly decided to create must therefore be the best possible world he could have created if God's choice is to be self-explanatory. This interpretation links the necessary-being argument to the argument from design, which attempts to prove that this world is, in fact, the best possible one.

The fourth way argues that there must exist a being of absolute perfection to serve as a standard by which we can measure the degree of goodness of particular things. This argument, more reminiscent of Plato than of Aristotle, relies on the assumption that there can be one single standard of perfection for diverse types of things—for persons, flowers, bicycles, mountains, summers, and winters. This seems highly doubtful. It also assumes that a standard of perfection must be embodied in a real object, which seems obviously false. "Nobody's perfect," we console ourselves, after committing some blunder. We will not easily be argued into relinquishing this mode of consolation.

The fifth way argues from the recognizable order in nature to its design and governance by an infinite intelligence. This is the teleological argument, or argument from design, which will be examined in the discussion of the selection from Hume.

In the second part of the selection we have chosen from his book, *The Existence of God,* W. I. Matson provides a lucid summary, and then a critique, of the ontological argument generally credited to St. Anselm, the eleventh-century theologian and philosopher, although it had been foreshadowed by St. Augustine in the fifth century, and was rediscovered in the seventeenth century by René Descartes. The most remarkable feature of this provocative line of argument is that it deduces the existence of God without any appeal to facts of nature, but simply from the definition of God as a perfect, or greatest conceivable, being. The argument reasons that if God did not exist, we could, contrary to our definition of God, conceive of beings greater than or more perfect than God, since what exists is greater or more perfect ("greater" meaning not larger in size but having more desirable properties) than what does not exist. In criticizing the argument, Matson employs a principle (formulated by the seventeenth-century French philosopher Pierre Gassendi, but made famous a century later by Kant) that existence is not a property at all, desirable or otherwise. Thus, what exists cannot be compared with what does not exist and cannot be said to be greater. Most philosophers today agree on this principle, but cogent objections to it have been raised. The issue remains unresolved.

In the selection from Hume's *Dialogues on Natural Religion* that follows Matson's article, the necessary-being argument and the argument from design are taken together and then exposed to the withering force of the problem of evil. We have already encountered the passionate statement of the problem by Dostoyevsky. We shall now consider the rational merits of its calm and reflective statement by Hume and then by Ramanuja.

The three disputants in Hume's *Dialogues* represent three viewpoints on the relation between reason and religious belief. Cleanthes takes a position similar to that of Aquinas and Leibniz. He has cosmic optimism; his experience of nature tells him that the world is so well ordered that it must be divinely governed. Philo, the agnostic, considers the world to be so full of undeserved suffering as to require disbelief in the existence of an omnipotent and benevolent God. Demea, a proponent of faith in an unknowable deity, agrees that the world is full of inexplicable evil but insists that if only we could see the complete picture of the universe, we would find that our miseries are not really evils but necessary and justifiable elements of the cosmic design.

Many theologians, beginning with St. Augustine, have taken the position advocated by Demea but have tried to spell out in specific terms how misfortunes can be viewed as inescapable even in this "best of all possible worlds" (a phrase made famous by Leibniz and ridiculed by Voltaire in his novel, *Candide*). Moral evils such as cruelty and murder are explained as consequences of the divine gift of free will. It is better to have the freedom to choose between good and evil than to be a morally unimpeachable robot. But even conceding this point, what of the natural evils of disease, drought, fire, and flood that are not attributable to free agents? Theologians have argued that these evils, too, are necessary in order to stimulate development of moral virtues such as patience, courage, and compassion. To the rebuttal that moral virtues would not be of any use in a world without natural evil, so that appealing to their value is circular, the Augustinians reply, in turn, that this world, containing some natural calamities and some persons of moral virtue, is to be preferred to a world with neither. A rational decision between these two claims is hindered by the near impossibility of imagining what human life would be like in a world free of human and natural evils.

Another argument of the cosmic optimist is that God should be admired for having created a consistent and orderly world; thus, he cannot be constantly interfering with the laws of nature in order to forestall calamities. Hume, in the person of Philo, counters that an omnipotent creator has no need of laws of nature, and in any case need not feel bound by what he legislates for his creatures. Moreover, why could God not have constructed the world in such a way that its laws ensure that calamities never happen?

Some theologians have tried to defend belief in divine providence by explaining that natural evils are necessary for tempering the souls of human beings and testing their worthiness for salvation. However, even granting that a small amount of natural misfortune might be useful for soul testing and tempering, it is hard to see why the vast amount of evil described by Philo and Demea is needed for such a purpose. Would it not, for example, be wiser to provide a juvenile delinquent with an unloaded gun rather than a loaded one if we wanted to find out whether the youngster was capable of murder, or to expose a child to mildly cool air rather than to a wintry blizzard to develop her hardiness? And, as Ivan forcefully suggests in the selection from *The Brothers Karamazov,* the deaths of small children cannot be explained either as tempering or as testing their as yet unformed characters.

John Locke, Voltaire, and many other Deists who believed in a divine first cause, but not in divine intervention in nature, maintained that while the evils in the world count against belief in providence and miracles, the degree of lawlike orderliness in nature is sufficient to mark the world as the handiwork of a master craftsman who made a world so well designed that it runs by itself. This is the most that the argument from design could possibly establish, Philo maintains, although he remains unconvinced of even this more modest claim.

A position similar to that of Hume, but taken in defense of religious belief rather than skepticism, was developed by the celebrated Hindu philosopher, Ramanuja, in the eleventh century. Ramanuja subjected earlier Hindu natural theology to devastating criticism, and the argument from design was his main target. The favorite Hindu form of this argument had been that since the world is made up of parts, we need an explanation of why its parts fit so well together, in the way we explain why clay and paint blend well together in making a jug. Ramanuja anticipated Hume in recognizing the faulty logic of such analogies. To compare the world to an artifact like a jug, he pointed out, is to beg the question from the start. We know from perception (that is experience) that jugs are made by potters, but we do not know how worlds are made or whether they are made at all.

Furthermore, Ramanuja reasoned, even if all parts of the world are, in fact, artifacts produced by craftsmen, it does not follow they are all the handiwork of the same craftsman. There is no evidence that the rivers, trees, mountains, and other natural phenomena were brought into being at the same time; on the contrary, all the available evidence indicates that they were formed at different times by different causes. The analogy between the world and artifacts supports the conclusion that the parts of the world were produced by many causes and not by a single omniscient and omnipotent creator. However, Ramanuja accepted the traditional Hindu doctrine of karma, which holds that the souls of sentient creatures are reincarnated in new bodies, and their good or evil actions bring about rewards and punishments in their subsequent lives. Some particularly good souls become more and more "emancipated' and, Ramanuja surmised, it may well be that a group of such emancipated persons designed and gradually built the universe.

A favorite model of causality for Hindu philosophers, including Ramanuja, was the potter shaping a pot out of clay. If we carry this analogy too far, Ramanuja noted, we shall have to infer that the designer of the world has hands, feet, and, in general, a body. But if God both has a body and is eternal, then God's body, that is, the material world, is eternal and was not created at all. Moreover, the world, whether eternal or created by God, ought to be perfect. Yet it is full of imperfections. A flawed pot indicates an inept potter. Theologians are, therefore, well advised to abandon the argument from design.

Ramanuja agreed with the principle involved in Aquinas's fifth way, namely, that intelligence is essential for orderly activity. "If . . . you mean to say that all activity depends on intelligence in general, you only prove what requires no proof." But Ramanuja saw no reason to conclude that all the orderly patterns of activity throughout the cosmos require a single infinite intelligence for their explanation. His Hindu concept of nature attributed the apparent purposefulness of nature to a karmic cycle: good and evil consequences flow naturally from decisions by the imperfect sentient creatures that, for better or for worse, make things happen in the world.

According to Ramanuja, we should believe in an all-encompassing divinity not because experience logically leads us to such belief but because our sacred scriptures tell us so. If scriptures were logically incompatible with rational knowledge, they would, for Ramanuja, be unworthy of our faith; in fact, however, they provide us with a useful framework that can be flexibly enough interpreted so that it need not clash with our perceptual knowledge. He suggested a highly sophisticated interpretation of religious scripture as a set of rules of conduct, rather than true or false factual beliefs—a view of religion that leaves the description and explanation of natural phenomena to science. Ramanuja and Hume differ fundamentally in their attitude toward religion. Their intellectual differences with respect to natural theology, however, seem remarkably slight.

Now that the smoke of argument and counterargument has cleared, which side, theology or atheism, has won the day? That is for the reader to decide. It seems apparent that both sides have an almost inexhaustible stock of intellectual ammunition. Religion has shown a remarkable resilience in the face of the advance of what is often, if somewhat tendentiously, called the "scientific attitude." Yet the relative invulnerability of contemporary religious belief has, in the opinion of many, been purchased at the price of robbing traditional doctrines of most of their literal content. Religion has become so variable that it is sometimes very difficult to find a clear-cut, doctrinal issue on which the theist and the atheist can be said to disagree. But this, if true at all, is true only on an intellectual level. There remains an insurmountable emotional and moral barrier between the attitude of cosmic optimism and the tragic sense of life. The cry of rage of Dostoyevsky's Ivan refuses to be drowned out by an angelic chorus singing the praises of divine providence.

GOD AND EVIL

Fyodor Dostoyevsky

"I must make you one confession," Ivan began. "I could never understand how one can love one's neighbors. It's just one's neighbors, to my mind, that one can't love, though one might love those at a distance. I once read somewhere of John the Merciful, a saint, that when a hungry, frozen beggar came to him, he took him into his bed, held him in his arms, and began breathing into his mouth, which was putrid and loathsome from some awful disease. I am convinced that he did that from 'self-laceration,' from the self-laceration of falsity, for the sake of the charity imposed by duty, as a penance laid on him. For any one to love a man, he must be hidden, for as soon as he shows his face, love is gone."

"Father Zossima has talked of that more than once," observed Alyosha; "he, too, said that the face of a man often hinders many people not practiced in love, from loving him. But yet there's a great deal of love in mankind, and almost Christ-like love. I know that myself, Ivan."

"Well, I know nothing of it so far, and can't understand it, and the innumerable mass of mankind are with me there. The question is, whether that's due to men's bad qualities or whether it's inherent in their nature. To my thinking, Christ-like love for men is a miracle impossible on earth. He was God. But we are not gods. Suppose I, for instance, suffer intensely. Another can never know how much I suffer, because he is another and not I. And what's more, a man is rarely ready to admit another's suffering (as though it were a distinction). Why won't he admit it, do you think? Because I smell unpleasant, because I have a stupid face, because I once trod on his foot. Besides there is suffering and suffering; degrading, humiliating suffering such as humbles me— hunger, for instance—my benefactor will perhaps allow me; but when you come to higher suffering—for an idea, for instance—he will very rarely admit that, perhaps because my face strikes him as not at all what he fancies a man should have who suffers for an idea. And so he de-

FROM *The Brothers Karamazov*, book 5, chapter 4, translated by Constance Garnett. Published by Random House, Inc.

prives me instantly of his favor, and not at all from badness of heart. Beggars, especially genteel beggars, ought never to show themselves, but to ask for charity through the newspapers. One can love one's neighbors in the abstract, or even at a distance, but at close quarters it's almost impossible. If it were as on the stage, in the ballet, where if beggars come in, they wear silken rags and tattered lace and beg for alms dancing gracefully, then one might like looking at them. But even then we should not love them. But enough of that. I simply wanted to show you my point of view. I meant to speak of the suffering of mankind generally, but we had better confine ourselves to the sufferings of the children. That reduces the scope of my argument to a tenth of what it would be. Still we'd better keep to the children, though it does weaken my case. But, in the first place, children can be loved even at close quarters, even when they are dirty, even when they are ugly (I fancy, though, children never are ugly). The second reason why I don't speak of grown-up people is that, besides being disgusting and unworthy of love, they have a compensation—they've eaten the apple and know good and evil, and they have become 'like god.' They go on eating it still. But the children haven't eaten anything, and are so far innocent. Are you fond of children, Alyosha? I know you are, and you will understand why I prefer to speak of them. If they, too, suffer horribly on earth, they must suffer for their fathers' sins, they must be punished for their fathers, who have eaten the apple; but that reasoning is of the other world and is incomprehensible for the heart of man here on earth. The innocent must not suffer for another's sins, and especially such innocents! You may be surprised at me, Alyosha, but I am awfully fond of children, too. And observe, cruel people, the violent, the rapacious, the Karamazovs are sometimes very fond of children. Children while they are quite little—up to seven, for instance—are so remote from grown-up people; they are different creatures, as it were, of a different species. I knew a criminal in prison who had, in the course of his career as a burglar, murdered whole families, including several children. But when he was in prison, he had a strange affection for them. He spent all his time at his window, watching the children playing in the prison yard. He trained one little boy to come up to his window and made great friends with him. . . . You don't know why I am telling you all this, Alyosha? My head aches and I am sad."

"You speak with a strange air," observed Alyosha uneasily, "as though you were not quite yourself."

"By the way, a Bulgarian I met lately in Moscow," Ivan went on, seeming not to hear his brother's words, "told me about the crimes committed by Turks and Circassians in all parts of Bulgaria through fear of a general rising of the Slavs. They burn villages, murder, outrage women and children, they nail their prisoners by the ears to the fences, leave them so till morning, and in the morning they hang them—all sorts of things you can't imagine. People talk sometimes of bestial cruelty, but that's a great injustice and insult to the beasts; a beast can never be so cruel as a man, so artistically cruel. The tiger only tears and gnaws, that's all he can do. He would never think of nailing people by the ears, even if he were able to do it. These Turks took a pleasure in torturing children, too; cutting the unborn child from the mother's womb, and tossing babies up in the air and catching them on the points of their bayonets before their mother's eyes. Doing it before the mother's eyes was what gave zest to the amusement. Here is another scene that I thought very interesting. Imagine a trembling mother with her baby in her arms, a circle of invading Turks around her. They've planned a diversion; they pet the baby, laugh to make it laugh. They succeed, the baby laughs. At that moment a Turk points a pistol four inches from the baby's face. The baby laughs with glee, holds out its little hands to the pistol, and he pulls the trigger in the baby's face and blows out its brains. Artistic, wasn't it? By the way, Turks, are particularly fond of sweet things, they say."

"Brother, what are you driving at?" asked Alyosha.

"I think if the devil doesn't exist, but man has created him, he has created him in his own image and likeness."

"Just as he did God, then?" observed Alyosha.

" 'It's wonderful how you can turn words,' as Polonius says in *Hamlet*," laughed Ivan. "You turn my words against me. Well, I am glad. Yours must be a fine God, if man created Him in His image and likeness. You asked just now what I was driving at. You see, I am fond of collecting certain facts, and, would you believe, I even copy anecdotes of a certain sort from newspapers and books, and I've already got a fine collection. The Turks, of course, have gone into it, but they are foreigners. I have specimens from home that are even better than the Turks. You know we prefer beating—rods and scourges—that's our national institution. Nailing ears is unthinkable for us, for we are, after all, Europeans. But the rod and the scourge we have always with us and they cannot be taken from us. Abroad now they scarcely do any beating. Manners are more humane, or laws have been passed, so that they don't dare to flog men now. But they make up for it another way just as national as ours. And so national that it would be practically impossible among us, though I believe we are being inoculated with it, since the religious movement began in our aristocracy. I have a charming pamphlet, translated from the French, describing how, quite recently, five years ago, a murderer, Richard, was executed—a young man, I believe, of three and twenty, who repented and was converted to the

Christian faith at the very scaffold. This Richard was an illegitimate child who was given as a child of six by his parents to some shepherds on the Swiss mountains. They brought him up to work for them. He grew up like a little wild beast among them. The shepherds taught him nothing, and scarcely fed or clothed him, but sent him out at seven to herd the flock in cold and wet, and no one hesitated or scrupled to treat him so. Quite the contrary, they thought they had every right, for Richard had been given to them as a chattel, and they did not even see the necessity of feeding him. Richard himself describes how in those years, like the Prodigal Son in the Gospel, he longed to eat of the mash given to the pigs, which were fattened for sale. But they wouldn't even give him that, and beat him when he stole from the pigs. And that was how he spent all his childhood and his youth, till he grew up and was strong enough to go away and be a thief. The savage began to earn his living as a day laborer in Geneva. He drank what he earned, he lived like a brute, and finished by killing and robbing an old man. He was caught, tried, and condemned to death. They are not sentimentalists there. And in prison he was immediately surrounded by pastors, members of Christian brotherhoods, philanthropic ladies, and the like. They taught him to read and write in prison, and expounded the Gospel to him. They exhorted him, worked upon him, drummed at him incessantly, till at last he solemnly confessed his crime. He was converted. He wrote to the court himself that he was a monster, but that in the end God had vouchsafed him light and shown grace. All Geneva was in excitement about him—all philanthropic and religious Geneva. All the aristocratic and well-bred society of the town rushed to the prison, kissed Richard and embraced him; 'You are our brother, you have found grace.' And Richard does nothing but weep with emotion, 'Yes, I've found grace! All my youth and childhood I was glad of pigs' food, but now even I have found grace. I am dying in the Lord.' 'Yes, Richard, die in the Lord; you have shed blood and must die. Though it's not your fault that you knew not the Lord, when you coveted the pig's food and were beaten for stealing it (which was very wrong of you, for stealing is forbidden); but you've shed blood and you must die.' And on the last day, Richard, perfectly limp, did nothing but cry and repeat every minute: 'This is my happiest day. I am going to the Lord.' 'Yes,' cry the pastors and the judges and philanthropic ladies. 'This is the happiest day of your life, for you are going to the Lord!' They all walk or drive to the scaffold in procession behind the prison van. At the scaffold they call to Richard: 'Die, brother, die in the Lord, for even thou has found grace!' And so, covered with his brothers' kisses, Richard is dragged on to the scaffold, and led to the guillotine. And they chopped off his head in brotherly fashion, because he had found grace. Yes, that's characteristic. That pamphlet is translated into Russian by some Russian philanthropists of aristocratic rank and evangelical aspirations, and has been distributed gratis for the enlightenment of the people. The case of Richard is interesting because it's national. Though to us it's absurd to cut off a man's head, because he has become our brother and has found grace, yet we have our own specialty, which is all but worse. Our historical pastime is the direct satisfaction of inflicting pain. There are lines in Nekrassov describing how a peasant lashes a horse on the eyes, 'on its meek eyes,' every one must have seen it. It's peculiarly Russian. He describes how a feeble little nag had foundered under too heavy a load and cannot move. The peasant beats it, beats it savagely, beats it at last not knowing what he is doing in the intoxication of cruelty, thrashes it mercilessly over and over again. 'However weak you are, you must pull, if you die for it.' The nag strains, and then he begins lashing the poor defenseless creature on its weeping, on its 'meek eyes.' The frantic beast tugs and draws the load, trembling all over, gasping for breath, moving sideways, with a sort of unnatural spasmodic action—it's awful in Nekrassov. But that's only a horse, and God has given horses to be beaten. So the Tatars have taught us, and they left us the knout as a remembrance of it. But men, too, can be beaten. A well-educated, cultured gentleman and his wife beat their own child with a birch-rod; a girl of seven. I have an exact account of it. The papa was glad that the birch was covered with twigs. 'It stings more,' said he, and so he began stinging his daughter. I know for a fact there are people who at every blow are worked up to sensuality, to literal sensuality, which increases progressively at every blow they inflict. They beat for a minute, for five minutes, for ten minutes, more often and more savagely. The child screams. At last the child cannot scream, it gasps, 'Daddy, daddy!' By some diabolical unseemly chance the case was brought into court. A counsel is engaged. The Russian people have long called a barrister 'a conscience for hire.' The counsel protests in his client's defense. 'It's such a simple thing,' he says, 'an everyday domestic event. A father corrects his child. To our shame be it said, it is brought into court.' The jury, convinced by him, give a favorable verdict. The public roars with delight that the torturer is acquitted. Ah, pity I wasn't there! I would have proposed to raise a subscription in his honor! . . . Charming pictures.

"But I've still better things about children. I've collected a great, great deal about Russian children, Alyosha. There was a little girl of five who was hated by her father and mother, 'most worthy and respectable people, of good education and breeding.' You see, I must repeat again, it is a peculiar characteristic of many people, this love of torturing children, and children only. To all other types of humanity these torturers behave mildly and benevolently, like cultivated and humane Europeans; but they are very fond of tormenting children, even fond of children themselves in that sense. It's just their defenselessness that tempts the tormentor, just the angelic confidence of the child who has no refuge and no appeal, that sets his vile blood on fire. In every man, of course, a demon lies hidden—the demon of rage, the demon of lustful heat at the screams of the tortured victim, the demon of lawlessness let off the chain, the demon of diseases that follow on vice, gout, kidney disease, and so on.

"This poor child of five was subjected to every possible torture by those cultivated parents. They beat her, thrashed her, kicked her for no reason till her body was one bruise. Then, they went to greater refinements of cruelty—shut her up all night in the cold and frost in a privy, and because she didn't ask to be taken up at night (as though a child of five sleeping its angelic, sound sleep could be trained to wake and ask), they smeared her face and filled her mouth with excrement, and it was her mother, her mother did this. And that mother could sleep, hearing the poor child's groans! Can you understand why a little creature, who can't even understand what's done to her, should beat her little aching heart with her tiny fist in the dark and the cold, and weep her meek unresentful tears to dear, kind God to protect her? Do you understand that, friend and brother, you pious and humble novice? Do you understand why this infamy must be and is permitted? Without it, I am told, man could not have existed on earth, for he could not have known good and evil. Why should he know that diabolical good and evil when it costs so much? Why, the whole world of knowledge is not worth that child's prayer to 'dear, kind God'! I say nothing of the sufferings of grown-up people, they have eaten the apple, damn them, and the devil take them all! But these little ones! I am making you suffer, Alyosha, you are not yourself. I'll leave off if you like."

"Never mind. I want to suffer too," muttered Alyosha.

"One picture, only one more, because it's so curious, so characteristic, and I have only just read it in some collection of Russian antiquities. I've forgotten the name. I must look it up. It was in the darkest days of serfdom at the beginning of the century, and long live the Liberator of the People! There was in those days a general of aristocratic connections, the owner of great estates, one of those men—somewhat exceptional, I believe, even then—who, retiring from the service into a life of leisure, are convinced that they've earned absolute power over the lives of their subjects. There were such men then. So our general, settled on his property of two thousand souls, lives in pomp, and domineers over his poor neighbors as though they were dependents and buffoons. He has kennels of hundreds of hounds and nearly a hundred dog-boys—all mounted, and in uniform. One day a serf boy, a little child of eight, threw a stone in play and hurt the paw of the general's favorite hound. 'Why is my favorite dog lame?' He is told that the boy threw a stone that hurt the dog's paw. 'So you did it.' The general looked the child up and down. 'Take him.' He was taken —taken from his mother and kept shut up all night. Early that morning the general comes out on horseback, with the hounds, his dependents, dog-boys, and huntsmen, all mounted around him in full hunting parade. The servants are summoned for their edification, and in front of them all stands the mother of the child. The child is brought from the lock-up. It's a gloomy cold, foggy autumn day, a capital day for hunting. The general orders the child to be undressed; the child is stripped naked. He shivers, numb with terror, not daring to cry! . . . 'Make him run,' commands the general. 'Run! run!' shout the dog-boys. The boy runs. . . . 'At him!' yells the general, and he sets the whole pack of hounds on the child. The hounds catch him, and tear him to pieces before his mother's eyes! . . . I believe the general was afterward declared incapable of administering his estates. Well—what did he deserve? To be shot? To be shot for the satisfaction of our moral feelings? Speak, Alyosha!"

"To be shot," murmured Alyosha, lifting his eyes to Ivan with a pale, twisted smile.

"Bravo!" cried Ivan delighted. "If even you say so . . . You're a pretty monk! So there is a little devil sitting in your heart, Alyosha Karamazov!"

"What I said was absurd, but——"

"That's just the point that 'but'!" cried Ivan. "Let me tell you, novice, that the absurd is only too necessary on earth. The world stands on absurdities, and perhaps nothing would have come to pass in it without them. We know what we know!"

"What do you know?"

"I understand nothing," Ivan went on, as though in delirium. "I don't want to understand anything now. I want to stick to the fact. I made up my mind long ago not to understand. If I try to understand anything, I shall be false to the fact and I have determined to stick to the fact."

"Why are you trying me?" Alyosha cried, with sudden distress. "Will you say what you mean at last?"

"Of course, I will; that's what I've been leading up to. You are dear to me, I don't want to let you go, and I won't give you up to your Zossima."

Ivan for a minute was silent, his face became all at once very sad.

"Listen! I took the case of children only to make my case clearer. Of the other tears of humanity with which the earth is soaked from its crust to its center, I will say nothing. I have narrowed my subject on purpose. I am a bug, and I recognize in all humility that I cannot understand why the world is arranged as it is. Men are themselves to blame, I suppose; they were given paradise, they wanted freedom, and stole fire from heaven, though they knew they would become unhappy, so there is no need to pity them. With my pitiful, earthly, Euclidian understanding, all I know is that there is suffering and that there are none guilty; that cause follows effect, simply and directly; that every-thing flows and finds its level—but that's only Euclidian nonsense, I know that, and I can't consent to live by it! What comfort is it to me that there are none guilty and that cause follows effect simply and directly, and that I know it—I must have justice, or I will destroy myself. And not justice in some remote infinite time and space, but here on earth, and that I could see myself. I have believed in it. I want to see it, and if I am dead by then, let me rise again, for if it all happens without me, it will be too unfair. Surely I haven't suffered, simply that I, my crimes and my sufferings, may manure the soil of the future harmony for somebody else. I want to see with my own eyes the hind lie down with the lion and the victim rise up and embrace his murderer. I want to be there when every one suddenly understands what it has all been for. All the religions of the world are built on this longing, and I am a believer. But then there are the children, and what am I to do about them? That's a question I can't answer. For the hundredth time I repeat, there are numbers of questions, but I've only taken the children, because in their case what I mean is so unanswerably clear. Listen! If all must suffer to pay for the eternal harmony, what have children to do with it, tell me, please? It's beyond all comprehension why they should suffer, and why they should pay for the harmony. Why should they, too, furnish material to enrich the soil for the harmony of the future? I understand solidarity in sin among men. I understand solidarity in retribution, too; but there can be no such solidarity with children. And if it is really true that they must share responsibility for all their fathers' crimes, such a truth is not of this world and is beyond my comprehension. Some jester will say, perhaps, that the child would have grown up and have sinned, but you see he didn't grow up, he was torn to pieces by the dogs, at eight years old. Oh, Alyosha, I am not blaspheming! I understand, of course, what an upheaval of the universe it will be, when everything in heaven and earth blends in one hymn of praise and everything that lives and has lived cries aloud: 'Thou are just, O Lord, for Thy ways are revealed.'

When the mother embraces the fiend who threw her child to the dogs, and all three cry aloud with tears, 'Thou art just, O Lord!' then, of course, the crown of knowledge will be reached and all will be made clear. But what pulls me up here is that I can't accept that harmony. And while I am on earth, I make haste to take my own measures. You see, Alyosha, perhaps it really may happen that if I live to that moment, or rise again to see it, I, too, perhaps, may cry aloud with the rest, looking at the mother embracing the child's torturer, 'Thou art just, O Lord!' but I don't want to cry aloud then. While there is still time, I hasten to protect myself and so I renounce the higher harmony altogether. It's not worth the tears of that one tortured child who beat itself on the breast with its little fist and prayed in its stinking outhouse, with its unexpiated tears to 'dear, kind God'! It's not worth it, because those tears are unatoned for. They must be atoned for, or there can be no harmony. But how? How are you going to atone for them? Is it possible? By their being avenged? But what do I care for avenging them? What do I care for a hell for oppressors? What good can hell do, since those children have already been tortured? And what becomes of harmony, if there is hell? I want to forgive. I want to embrace. I don't want more suffering. And if the sufferings of children go to swell the sum of sufferings which was necessary to pay for truth, then I protest that the truth is not worth such a price. I don't want the mother to embrace the oppressor who threw her son to the dogs! She dare not forgive him! Let her forgive him for herself, if she will, let her forgive the torturer for the immeasurable suffering of her mother's heart. But the sufferings of her tortured child she has no right to forgive; she dare not forgive the torturer, even if the child were to forgive him! And if that is so, if they dare not forgive, what becomes of harmony? Is there in the whole world a being who would have the right to forgive and could forgive? I don't want harmony. From love for humanity I don't want it. I would rather be left with the unavenged suffering. I would rather remain with my unavenged suffering and unsatisfied indignation, *even if I were wrong*. Besides, too high a price is asked for harmony; it's beyond our means to pay so much to enter on it. And so I hasten to give back my entrance ticket, and if I am an honest man I am bound to give it back as soon as possible. And that I am doing. It's not God that I don't accept, Alyosha, only I most respectfully return Him the ticket."

"That's rebellion," murmured Alyosha, looking down.

"Rebellion? I am sorry you call it that," said Ivan earnestly. "One can hardly live in rebellion, and I want to live. Tell me yourself, I challenge you—answer. Imagine that you are creating a fabric of human destiny with the object of making men happy in the end, giving them peace and rest at last, but that it was essential and inevitable to torture to death only one tiny creature—that baby beating its breast with its fist, for instance—and to found that edifice on its unavenged tears, would you consent to be the architect on those conditions? Tell me, and tell the truth."

"No, I wouldn't consent," said Alyosha softly.

THE FIVE WAYS

St. Thomas Aquinas

Whether God Exists?

OBJECTION 1. It seems that God does not exist; because if one of two contraries be infinite, the other would be altogether destroyed. But the name God means that He is infinite goodness. If, therefore, God existed, there would be no evil discoverable; but there is evil in the world. Therefore God does not exist.

OBJ. 2. Further, it is superfluous to suppose that what can be accounted for by a few principles has been produced by many. But it seems that everything we see in the world can be accounted for by other principles, supposing God did not exist. For all natural things can be reduced to one principle, which is nature; and all voluntary things can be reduced to one principle, which is human reason, or will. Therefore there is no need to suppose God's existence.

On the contrary, it is said in the person of God: I am Who am [Exod. 3:14].

I answer that, The existence of God can be proved in five ways.

The first and more manifest way is the argument from motion. It is certain, and evident to our senses, that in the world some things are in motion. Now whatever is moved is moved by another, for nothing can be moved except it is in potentiality to that toward which it is moved; whereas a thing moves inasmuch as it is in act. For motion is nothing else than the reduction of something from potentiality to actuality. But nothing can be reduced from potentiality to actuality, except by something in a state of actuality. Thus that which is actually hot, as fire, makes wood, which is potentially hot, to be actually hot, and thereby moves and changes it. Now it is not possible that the same thing should be at once in actuality and potentiality in the same respect, but only in different respects. For what is actually hot cannot simultaneously be potentially hot; but it is simultaneously potentially cold.

FROM "Summa Theologica" in *Basic Writings of St. Thomas Aquinas*, edited by Anton C. Pegis. Reprinted by permission of Random House, Inc.

It is therefore impossible that in the same respect and in the same way a thing should be both mover and moved, i.e., that it should move itself. Therefore, whatever is moved must be moved by another. If that by which it is moved be itself moved, then this also must needs be moved by another, and that by another again. But this cannot go on to infinity, because then there would be no first mover, and, consequently, no other mover, seeing that subsequent movers move only inasmuch as they are moved by the first mover; as the staff moves only because it is moved by the hand. Therefore it is necessary to arrive at a first mover, moved by no other; and this everyone understands to be God.

The second way is from the nature of efficient cause. In the world of sensible things we find there is an order of efficient causes. There is no case known (neither is it, indeed, possible) in which a thing is found to be the efficient cause of itself; for so it would be prior to itself, which is impossible. Now in efficient causes it is not possible to go on to infinity, because in all efficient causes following in order, the first is the cause of the intermediate cause, and the intermediate is the cause of the ultimate cause, whether the intermediate cause be several, or one only. Now to take away the cause is to take away the effect. Therefore, if there be no first cause among efficient causes, there will be no ultimate, nor any intermediate, cause. But if in efficient causes it is possible to go on to infinity, there will be no first efficient cause, neither will there be an ultimate effect, nor any intermediate efficient causes; all of which is plainly false. Therefore it is necessary to admit a first efficient cause, to which everyone gives the name of God.

The third way is taken from possibility and necessity, and runs thus. We find in nature things that are possible to be and not to be, since they are found to be generated, and to be corrupted, and consequently, it is possible for them to be and not to be. But it is impossible for these always to exist, for that which can not-be at some time is not. Therefore, if everything can not-be, then at one time there was nothing in existence. Now if this were true, even now there would be nothing in existence, because that which does not exist begins to exist only through something already existing. Therefore, if at one time nothing was in existence, it would have been impossible for anything to have begun to exist; and thus even now nothing would be in existence—which is absurd. Therefore, not all beings are merely possible, but there must exist something the existence of which is necessary. But every necessary thing either has its necessity caused by another, or not. Now it is impossible to go on to infinity in necessary things which have their necessity caused by another, as has been already proved in regard to efficient causes. Therefore we cannot but admit the existence of some being having of itself its own necessity, and not receiving it from another, but rather causing in others their necessity. This all men speak of as God.

The fourth way is taken from the gradation to be found in things. Among beings there are some more and some less good, true, noble, and the like. But *more* and *less* are predicated of different things according as they resemble in their different ways something which is the maximum, as a thing is said to be hotter according as it more nearly resembles that which is hottest; so that there is something which is truest, something best, something noblest, and, consequently, something which is most being, for those things that are greatest in truth are greatest in being, as it is written in Metaph. ii. [a book of Aristotle]. Now the maximum in any genus is the cause of all in that genus, as fire, which is the maximum of heat, is the cause of all hot things, as is said in the same book. Therefore there must also be something which is to all beings the cause of their being, goodness, and every other perfection; and this we call God.

The fifth way is taken from the governance of the world. We see that things which lack knowledge, such as natural bodies, act for an end, and this is evident from their acting always, or nearly always, in the same way, so as to obtain the best result. Hence it is plain that they achieve their end, not fortuitously, but designedly. Now whatever lacks knowledge cannot move toward an end, unless it be directed by some being endowed with knowledge and intelligence; as the arrow is directed by the archer. Therefore some intelligent being exists by whom all natural things are directed to their end; and this being we call God.

REPLY OBJ. 1. As Augustine says: Since God is the highest good, He would not allow any evil to exist in His works, unless His omnipotence and goodness were such as to bring good even out of evil. This is part of the infinite goodness of God, that He should allow evil to exist, and out of it produce good.

REPLY OBJ. 2. Since nature works for a determinate end under the direction of a higher agent, whatever is done by nature must be traced back to God as to its first cause. So likewise whatever is done voluntarily must be traced back to some higher cause other than human reason and will, since these can change and fail; for all things that are changeable and capable of defect must be traced back to an immovable and self-necessary first principle, as has been shown.

THE EXISTENCE OF GOD

W. I. Matson

The Ontological Argument

Discussions of the traditional arguments for the existence of God usually begin with an account of the ontological argument (argument from the concept of being), as formulated by St. Anselm of Canterbury (1033–1109). The gist of it is this:

"God" means "the perfect Being." "Perfect Being" means "Being combining perfect power, perfect goodness, etc., *and perfect reality*." Hence to say "God does not exist" amounts to uttering the contradiction "The Being which is (among other attributes) perfectly real is not real." Therefore the statement "God exists" is necessarily true. Indeed, it is inconceivable that God should not exist, as it is inconceivable that there should be a round square or that there should not be a prime number greater than 29, though one might (mistakenly) think that he conceives it, entertains the possibility.

This argument has had a perennial fascination for philosophers. Some of the greatest, including Descartes and Leibniz, have defended it. At one time, even Bertrand Russell thought it valid:

I remember the precise moment, one day in 1894, as I was walking along Trinity Lane, when I saw in a flash (or thought I saw) that the ontological argument is valid. I had gone out to buy a tin of tobacco; on my way back, I suddenly threw it up in the air, and exclaimed as I caught it: "Great Scott, the ontological argument is sound."

Philosophers—especially those, like the three just named, who are also mathematicians—are intrigued by the argument because it purports to bridge the gap between the realms of mathematical and factual truths. If it is valid, then there is at least one truth of fact, one true statement about what exists "out there," that is demonstrable by procedures like those used in mathematical reasoning, and that shares, moreover, in the absolute certainty (inconceivability of the opposite) that attaches to the theorems of logic and mathematics. Pure reason in an armchair can then tell us something—something of the last importance—about what there is. Mathematical statements do not have this character; though it is certain that two apples and two more apples make four apples, one cannot infer from this alone that there are any apples: cf. "two unicorns and two more unicorns make four unicorns."

One might suppose that theologians would be equally enthusiastic. For this argument, alone among the traditional three, is such that if it proves anything at all, it patently proves just what theologians are concerned to prove: the existence of God, the perfect Being, the Being than which a greater cannot be conceived—not perhaps merely a big bang or a limited universe-artificer. Yet very few theologians have espoused the argument. On its first appearance it was severely criticized by the monk Gaunilo, who pointed out that *something* must be wrong with it, for if not, then by similar reasoning one ought to be able to define into existence a perfect island. Subsequently St. Thomas Aquinas rejected it; and thus the matter has stood to this day. Perhaps this bespeaks the greater skepticism of theologians as compared with philosophers.

ST. ANSELM'S FORMULATION OF THE ARGUMENT

Anselm's writings are among the most charming to be found on the theological shelf. Particularly attractive is the passage in the *Proslogium* in which the ontological argument is set out. It is in the form of a commentary on the words of the Psalmist, "The fool hath said in his heart, There is no god." Anselm sets out to show that such a one in very truth is a fool, since what he utters is a contradiction.

In the following presentation, I preserve Anselm's words as far as possible, only abridging and altering the order slightly. (GCB = Being than which a greater cannot be conceived.)

1. Whatever is understood exists in the understanding.
2. When the fool hears of the GCB, he understands what he hears.
3. Therefore something exists in the understanding, at least, than which nothing greater can be conceived.
4. Suppose the GCB exists in the understanding alone: then it can be conceived to exist in reality;
5. which is greater.
6. Therefore if that than which nothing greater can be conceived exists in the understanding alone, the very Being than which nothing greater can be conceived is one than which a greater can be conceived.

7. Obviously this is impossible.
8. Assuredly that than which nothing greater can be conceived cannot exist in the understanding alone.
9. There is no doubt that there exists a Being than which nothing greater can be conceived, and it exists both in the understanding and in reality. (This is God.)

CRITICISM OF THE ARGUMENT

There are many ways of showing what is wrong with this reasoning. The most famous is Kant's doctrine that existence is not a predicate. When we say, "God is good," we predicate goodness of God, that is, we assert that God has the property of being good. Anselm assumes that in a similar way, when we say, "God is real," we ascribe a property, reality, to God. However (Kant objects), reality adds nothing to our conception of anything: "A hundred imaginary thalers have all the predicates of a hundred real thalers." If they did not, we should never be able to compare our conception with the object, to see whether our conception was *realized*. Before Kant, Hume had made the same point:

To reflect on any thing simply, and to reflect on it as existent, are nothing different from each other. That idea, when conjoin'd with the idea of any object, makes no addition to it. Whatever we conceive, we conceive to be existent. Any idea we please to form is the idea of a being; and the idea of a being is any idea we please to form.

This refutation, however, is not definitive principally because the question "Is *x* a property?" has a precise and unambiguous answer only in the context of an ideal (completely formalized) language; and neither English, nor German, nor medieval Latin is such an ideal language. It is always open to a partisan of Anselm to reply: "Existence *is* a property—though admittedly of a unique kind; but every property is unique in some respect."

I shall try to criticize the argument in the spirit of Kant without invoking this somewhat dubious and controversial doctrine as self-evident. I shall take each premise of the argument, translate it into a synonymous expression not containing the word "exists," and see what happens then.

A minimum of apparatus must first be developed: the distinction between use and mention of a word, and the concept of denoting.

Suppose we overhear someone saying: "Schmidt understands horses," and we hear no more of the conversation. Then we cannot tell whether the speaker meant (a) Schmidt is knowledgeable about horses: easily senses their moods, knows what pleases them and what makes them nervous, can tell the skittish ones at a glance, and so on; or (b) Schmidt is making progress in English; he has just learned that the English for "Pferde" is "horses."

Context normally settles easily in which sense the sentence is to be taken. If it is *written* correctly, the ambiguity cannot arise in the first place, for sense (b) requires quotation marks around "horses." These marks serve to indicate that it is the *word* "horses" that is being talked about, not the animals to which the word refers. The word "horses" is being *mentioned* (talked about or written about), not *used* (to refer to nonlinguistic entities).

It is important to note that although in "Schmidt understands horses," the word "horses" is used to refer to animals that exist in the real world, a word can be used even when there is no actual object named by the word: e.g., "Unicorns are rare" contains a use-occurrence of "unicorns."

Suppose, now, that we utter the true sentence: "Unicorns don't exist." Since it is clearly not the *word* "unicorn" the existence of which we are denying, we must class this occurrence of the word as a use. This leads us to the question: What *is* the use of "unicorn" in this sentence? Some philosophers have supposed that the only kind of use a word has (at any rate, the only kind of use a noun has) is to refer; hence, since "unicorn" is not a meaningless noise, and is successfully used in the sentence, there must be some sort of thing—an idea, a Subsistent Entity —that is the referent.

Such metaphysics, however, can be avoided. First, the somewhat misleading term "use" should be nontendentiously defined as "successful linguistic employment other than mention." Second, we note that the meaning we convey in the sentence "Unicorns don't exist" can be just as well expressed by saying, "The word 'unicorn' doesn't denote anything." Here "denote" has this sense: " 'W' denotes W's" means "The word 'W' is the name of objects of the W-kind." Then "W's don't exist," "W's aren't real," "There aren't any W's" are all expressions that come to the same as " 'W' doesn't denote anything." Here we have erected a kind of bridge between use and mention: sentences asserting (or denying) existence, in which the word designating what is said (or denied) to exist is used, can be exactly rephrased as sentences asserting (or denying) that the same word, but now mentioned, has a denotation.

We can now return to the argument.

The first three premises constitute a subargument to show that the GCB "exists in the understanding." We can concede this, with the proviso that "exists in the understanding" means no more than "is understood." If anyone objects to this, it is incumbent on him to formulate a set of circumstances in which it could be truly said that some x

existed in the understanding without being understood by anyone; or else, someone understood *x,* but *x* did not exist in the understanding.

The occurrences of "GCB" in the second and third premises are mentions. What the fool understands "when he hears of the GCB" is the *phrase;* it is clear at any rate that this is all that Anselm claims.

We can then paraphrase these premises as follows:

1′. Whatever is understood is understood.
2′. Someone understands "GCB."
3′. Therefore someone understands "GCB."

True, the paraphrase is trivial. But that is no serious objection, either to Anselm or to the translation. Anselm's purpose in these sentences was to elucidate his meaning of "exist in the understanding"; ours is better served by emphasizing the identity in meaning of this phrase with "be understood"; we accomplish this by reducing both terms to the same one.

The second premise, which is the same as the conclusion, is a factual statement to the effect that somebody (nearly everybody) understands the meaning of the phrase "Being than which a greater cannot be conceived." Some critics have objected that this premise is false, since the Being in question = God, and nobody understands (has adequate knowledge of) God. But this complaint seems to miss the point. We must grant that no one understands God, if to understand Him means to understand His motives, have His wisdom, etc. In this sense I do not understand the President of France, nor do I understand the phrase "richest man in the world" in the sense of knowing what it would feel like to be in that position. I certainly understand the words though, in the sense of knowing what the criteria are for identifying the occupants of these positions. Now it seems sufficient for Anselm's argument that the fool should understand "GCB" in this less grandiose sense: that the GCB should be the wisest, most powerful, best, etc., Being imaginable; and certainly one can understand what is intended by a phrase like "wisest possible" without being oneself as wise as possible. In fact, our own requirement is more stringent than is necessary. All that is needed for the argument is the concession that "GCB" should not be meaningless; and this condition may be met, even if one cannot specify criteria for applying the term to an object. "Most beautiful statue ever carved" is a meaningful phrase, though I do not know how to go about identifying its referent.

We come now to the meatier premises. The fourth consists of two clauses, the first being "Suppose the GCB exists in the understanding alone." In accordance with our rule for translating such expressions, the part of this not containing the word "alone" should be rendered

"Suppose 'GCB' is understood," while the force of "alone" is to deny that GCB "exists in reality." And since this comes to asserting that " 'GCB' does not denote anything," the whole "Suppose . . ." clause becomes: "Suppose 'GCB' is understood, but 'GCB' does not denote anything."

The second clause is "then it [the GCB] can be conceived to exist in reality." This is translated as "then 'GCB' can be conceived to denote something"; and the translation of the entire premise is:

4'. Suppose "GCB" is understood, but "GCB" does not denote anything: then "GCB" can be conceived to denote something;

This is the point at which Hume and Kant attack the argument, on the ground that there is no difference between conceiving and conceiving to denote; since, moreover, conceiving does not appear to differ from understanding, at least in the context of this argument, the premise reduces to the triviality:

4''. Suppose "GCB" is understood, but "GCB" does not denote anything: then "GCB" can be understood;

and the argument collapses.

Anselm, however, clearly believed that there was a difference between conceiving merely, and conceiving to denote; and this is a prima facie reason to think there is some difference. But if we ask ourselves what the difference could be, we must conclude that it is one in attitude toward a conception, not in the conception itself; and this is to concede the Kant-Hume objection. Although just idly thinking about mermaids is not the same as believing that there are mermaids, the difference does not lie in the conception. "Mermaid" means "half-woman half-fish" for believer and unbeliever alike; the image conjured up when the word is pronounced is the same; the difference is that the believer believes this image to correspond to something of flesh and blood, whereas the unbeliever does not.

In any event, the argument can hardly survive scrutiny of its next premise:

5. which is greater.

The "which" refers to "existing in reality" (sc. the GCB), so that our paraphrase must be:

5'. "GCB" denoting something is greater than "GCB" not denoting anything.

The trouble with this rendering is that it does not appear to have any intelligible meaning. If the rephrasing is at fault, then there must be something wrong with our previous analysis of the equivalence between "X exists" and " 'X' denotes something." That may be; it is up to the objector to investigate the possibility.

Anselm's meaning is perhaps something like this: thinking of mermaids is different from not thinking at all; ergo, when one hears of mermaids, and understands what one hears, one is conceiving of *something:* to wit, something imaginary. But imaginary mermaids are poor thin things—just barely objects—as compared with (say) hippopotamuses of flesh and blood. Similarly, when one hears of the Greatest Conceivable Being, and understands what one hears, one is conceiving *something*—at worst, something imaginary, just barely an object. But it would be ludicrous to suppose that such a wraith could really be the Greatest Conceivable Being:

> 6. Therefore if that than which nothing greater can be conceived exists in the understanding alone, the very being than which nothing greater can be conceived is one than which a greater can be conceived.
> 7. Obviously this is impossible.

The if clause of premise 6 is easily put as "if 'GCB' is understood but does not denote anything"; but the remainder defies this treatment. At first sight it looks as if it should be rendered, "then the GCB is not the GCB" (in which "GCB," for the first time in the argument, *is used*). If so, however, the whole premise would be a glaring non sequitur, and besides, the then clause and premise 7 would beg the question; for it is only "obviously impossible" for an *existent thing* not to be identical with itself. Let us suppose, then, that the two occurrences of "GCB" in the then clause are mentions: "then 'GCB' is not identical with 'GCB.'" This is an improvement, as it does not beg the question; but it is still a non sequitur. A concept cannot be self-contradictory just because it denotes nothing. Reality does not come in different grades, qualities, or concentrations.

Even if we grant Anselm his fundamental assumption of grades of reality, his argument is still invalid. Let us assume for the sake of argument that there are two species of existence, a higher and a lower, and that by the very nature of the concept, "GCB" must partake of the higher. We grant even that it is part of the concept that GCB must exist in reality, not merely in the understanding. It still does not follow that there exists in reality the Greatest Conceivable Being. All that can be concluded is that *if* there is a GCB, it must be real—a trivial and harmless inference.

We show this in the following way. The ontological argument can be abbreviated thus:

> 1. "GCB" means, among other things, "perfectly Real Being."

2. Therefore the following statement is self-contradictory: "The GCB is not real."
3. Therefore the GCB *is* real.

Consider now the parallel argument:

1. "Myriagon" means "10,000-sided plane figure."
2. Therefore the following statement is self-contradictory: "The myriagon does not have 10,000 sides."
3. Therefore there is a myriagon with 10,000 sides.

This latter argument is easily seen to be fallacious. All that follows from the premises is that *if* anything is a myriagon, then necessarily it has 10,000 sides, neither more nor less. In exactly the same way, all that follows from the premises of the ontological argument is that *if* anything is the GCB, then necessarily that thing is real. There is no way of getting rid of the *if* by logic alone. If we grant that "unreal GCB" is a contradiction in terms, all we can infer is the Irish conclusion that "if it's unreal it can't be the GCB."

CONSEQUENCE OF THE FAILURE OF THE ONTOLOGICAL ARGUMENT

If this short refutation (which is also to be found in Kant) is sufficient to dispose of the matter, then was not the long discussion of the existence-is-not-a-predicate business superfluous? No, because one point of great importance can be derived from the latter but not from the former: "logically necessary being" is a phrase without meaning. The shorter refutation suffices to show that the concept cannot guarantee the existence of its own referent; but it leaves open the possibility that God's essence entails His existence in the logical sense of entailment. In that case, the statement "God exists" would have not merely factual but logical certainty. If, however, denotation can, as a matter of logic, never be contained in a concept, then nothing—not even God—can have existence logically guaranteed it. There is not then, nor can there be, anything the nonexistence of which is inconceivable or involves contradiction. . . .

The Cosmological Argument

All versions of the cosmological argument have this general form: the universe, regarded as a whole, cannot be self-sufficient; for it to exist there must be, outside it and prior to it, some real Being of such a kind as to constitute the reason for the existence of the universe; such a Being must be God.

While the cosmological argument contains a factual premise, to wit, *something exists,* it contains only this noncontroversial reference to matter of fact. All the rest of the edifice is constructed of and by pure reason. If, as we have suggested, it is particularly appropriate that God's existence should be demonstrable by the intellect unaided by the senses, it would be overly nice to complain that this argument does not completely fulfill that requirement.

There *is* something—at the very least, as St. Augustine and Descartes pointed out, there is indubitably the intellect of the reasoner. But why should there be something rather than nothing? The argument regards this as a legitimate question, to which the only ultimately satisfactory answer is: Because of God.

There are two main forms of the argument, accordingly as the relation of God to the universe is conceived to be that of a first cause in time—God as instigator of the first event; or that of reason for nature— God as reason to which we should inevitably be led, whether or not the cosmos had a beginning in time. I shall call these the crude and subtle cosmological arguments, respectively.

FIRST CAUSE ARGUMENT

This argument is implied in the common rhetorical question "If there is no God, then who or what made the world?" Put explicitly, it is as follows:

1. Everything has a cause. For everything that exists (E), there is some other thing (C), which existed before E came into existence; and C produced E—that is, without C there would have been no E. C itself was produced by a pre-existing C' and so on.
2. But not ad infinitum: the series of causes and effects must have a beginning.
3. The first cause must have been a Being capable of producing everything else in the series. For the effect cannot exceed the cause; if it did, that part which exceeded it would be uncaused.
4. Such a Being must be an infinite Being, i.e., God.

REFUTATION OF THE FIRST CAUSE ARGUMENT

Every premise of this argument is vulnerable. If the universe, however great, is finite, then we cannot legitimately infer an infinite Being as its cause; the argument at most proves a deity, not God. But perhaps not even that: in the absence of further argumentation, we are left with the possibility that the "big bang," supposed by astrophysicists to have occurred eleven billion years ago, was the first cause: a mere event, lacking (for all we know) personality and intelligence. Furthermore, the notion of "cause" assumed in the argument is somewhat dubious.

All these defects are remediable; but we shall postpone discussion of the remedies until we come to the subtle cosmological argument and the argument from design. For the second premise of the present argument is incurable.

This second premise is to be interpreted, not as asserting that as a matter of fact the universe happens to have had a beginning in time, but that as a matter of logical necessity it must have had one. Now we had best pause a moment to illustrate this distinction, crucial in all forms of the cosmological argument, between matter of fact and matter of logical necessity.

This distinction is illustrated in the following instances:

(1) "If this boulder is pushed over the edge of the precipice, it *must* fall into the gorge."
(2) "If there are two boulders here, and two more over there, then there *must be* four boulders altogether."

In (1) the "must" means "cannot but; there is no physically possible alternative." If asked for the reasons for our expectation, we would reply that that is the way boulders always behave; perhaps we might cite also the universal law of gravitation. We might be tempted to say that it would be inconceivable for the boulder not to fall. But that would be rhetorical exaggeration; we can very easily conceive of what it would be like for the boulder, after being pushed over the brink, to remain suspended in mid-air, to explode, to vanish in a puff of smoke, or to take wing and fly away.

In (2), however, the "must be" means "could not conceivably be more or less than." And here "conceivably" is to be taken literally. One cannot form any conception of what it would be like for a certain collection to contain just two couples, and at the same time, in the same respect, have (say) five members altogether. It is not hard to see why this is so: "2" means "1 + 1," and "4" means "1 + 1 + 1 + 1." Hence "2 + 2 = 4" means "1 + 1 + 1 + 1 = 1 + 1 + 1 + 1"—that is, the ideas symbolized by the marks on the left and right of the "=" are identical. And the rule for the use of the symbol "=" is such that we do not know what it would be like for a quantity not to be equal to itself.

Hence if someone says, "I pushed a boulder over a precipice, and you know what? It just hung there in mid-air!" we will not believe him, though we understand what he is saying. But if he says, "There were two boulders there, and two more, and just those; and do you know what? There were five boulders in all!" we do not know what he means. If he means anything, he must be using the words in some private senses, different from their usual ones.

Now let us get back to the second premise of the first cause argument: "The series of causes and effects must have a beginning." The "must" indicates that logical necessity is being claimed. For if not, all that is claimed is that as a matter of fact the series has a beginning, though it could have been otherwise. In that case, factual evidence for the conclusion would need to be supplied. It is clear, however, that the proponents of the argument have nothing like this in mind. They mean that it is self-evident that the series has a beginning, in the way, say, that it is self-evident that a whole cannot be less than the sum of its parts.

This contention is defensible only if it is logically impossible for a series to have no first member; and the existence of many series, such as the series of all negative integers

$$\ldots, -8, -7, -6, -5, -4, -3, -2, -1$$

shows that there is no such impossibility. When we say that the series of negative integers has no beginning, what we mean is that it is impossible to select a member of the series which has no predecessor; for if it is suggested that some number $-N$ has no predecessor, we can always counter the suggestion by producing the predecessor, namely, $-N-1$.

To be sure, the series of negative integers is an intellectual construction, and the argument concerns things and events "out there" in the world. But to repeat: the argument is not about what happened to exist, but about what *must* have existed. There is nothing logically inconsistent in the notion of a (numerical) series without a first member; therefore there is nothing logically inconsistent in the notion of a series of events, forming a causal chain, and such that at least one event in the chain is associated with each number in the beginningless series.

The attempt has been made to rebut this refutation by arguing in this way: Events are *now* occurring. If there is no beginning to the causal series to which these present events belong, then an infinite series has been already run through. But it is impossible to run through, enumerate successively every member of, an infinite series; therefore the causal series cannot be infinite.

This rejoinder begs the question, since it is only impossible to run through an infinite series in a finite time. Probably what accounts for the plausibility of the argument is the supposition that if the causal series had no beginning, then some event must have occurred infinitely long ago—in the sense that the number of hours between that event and (say) the bombing of Hiroshima is not a finite number, however large. But the conception of an infinite series does not entail that there should be any two given members of that series that are not a finite distance apart in the series; on the contrary, the series of integers is infinite, although the difference between any two given integers is always finite. All that is required for a causal series to be infinite is that however remote two events in the series may be from each other, there are other events remoter still.

Careful thinkers, Christians included, have been aware of these considerations. Those who have held the Judeo-Christian doctrine of a creation of nature out of nothing have followed St. Thomas Aquinas in holding that its truth can be known only by revelation: that as far as the unaided reason can say, the world may or may not have a beginning. Neither views leads to contradiction.

One more observation and we shall be done with this argument. To the common question "If there is no God, then who made the world?" the common retort "Well, who made God?" is a fair one. The first premise of the argument is that everything must have a cause; the conclusion, surprisingly, is its contradictory: some thing, namely God, does *not* have a cause. And those who produce this argument have no ground for objecting to calling God a "thing," for as far as the argument goes, God, the first cause, is just one more member of the totality.

THE SUBTLE COSMOLOGICAL ARGUMENT

The version of the cosmological argument which attempts to show that God must exist as a *reason* for nature, whether nature is finite or infinite in duration, is less well known than the popular version we have just considered. Its essentials were formulated by Plato and Aristotle. Leibniz's version, which our presentation will follow in its main outlines, states it probably as well as it is capable of being put.

A brief preliminary summary of the argument is this: If the world is intelligible, then God exists. But the world is intelligible. Therefore God exists.

"Intelligibility" is defined in terms of the principle of sufficient reason: "There is a Sufficient Reason why everything that is, is so and not otherwise." That is to say, a mere fact, of itself in isolation, is not intelligible, understandable; it becomes intelligible when it is explained —when it is put into a context enabling us to see not just *that* it is, but *why* it is "so and not otherwise."

There are, I am told, at least ninety-three different kinds of explanation; and though I think that that is an exaggeration, there is admittedly danger in talking, as I am about to do, in terms of only two kinds: mechanical and purposive. These two may be considered, however, as genera embracing many particular species. If they do not jointly exhaust the field, they very nearly do so; and at any rate, it does not seem that anyone has proposed a different kind of explanation that could qualify as universal or cosmic.

A mechanical explanation is one in terms of causes, regularities, laws of nature. It is the type of explanation usually—though as I shall point out in a moment, perhaps not always—encountered in the natural sciences. Explanations of how an airplane works, or why it failed and crashed, are mechanical. Life, or the evolution of a galaxy, is explained mechanically if states at one time are related to states at another via laws, which in the more sophisticated sciences take the form of differential equations; in the less developed disciplines these laws may be no more than statements to the effect that one kind of occurrence has been observed always to be followed by another (cause-effect).

The kind of account we naturally give of why a rational creature is engaged in a certain activity is purposive or teleological. Such explanations commonly include references to motives, choices, deliberations, reasons, not to mention emotions and passions.

The contrast between these types of explanation will be in the focus of our attention throughout this part, and indeed for the rest of this book. At present it will be sufficient to make the following points concerning them:

1. Both mechanical and purposive explanations are in everyday use. Why did the lights go out last night? Because there was a storm up-country, as a consequence of which a tree was uprooted and fell across a power line. (Mechanical.) Why are there so few doors in this house? Because the architect was an enthusiast for togetherness; moreover his client wanted to cut expenses as far as possible. (Purposive.)

2. As we see from the examples just given, both types are, in certain contexts, answers to questions of the form "Why is . . . ?" It is sometimes said that mechanical explanations are responses only to "how" questions; but this is not the case. For the present, we content ourselves with defending the last statement merely on the ground that the English language happens to be used this way. To be sure, the "why" in the question about the lights going out could be replaced by the locution "How did it come about that . . . ?" But this is equally true of the question about the doors.

3. Causal and purposive explanations are not always incompatible and are sometimes complementary. Why is Jones in the prison hospital? (a) Because a train hit the car in which he was riding and dragged it

300 yards. (b) Because he thought to avoid the police by crossing the intersection just in front of the train. Although either (a) or (b) might sensibly be offered as an answer to the question, it may be maintained that strictly speaking (b) presupposes (a), or (a) is an incomplete explanation, or (a) and (b) are relevant in different contexts. All this may be true. And the more specific we make our question, the more completely determined is the type of explanation that will be appropriate. Where animate agencies are involved, causal and purposive explanations may intertwine. A caused B, because C, wishing D, set E into operation. Moreover, C wished D because F caused him to wish it. Briefly, purposes *are* causes, and are themselves the effects of other causes—sometimes, not always, of other purposes.

4. We note the corollary that it is not obvious which, if either, type of explanation is ultimate. As we have just seen, when we explain some event more and more fully, purposive and causal explanations may oscillate in such a way that there is no clear answer to the question "Yes, but what is the real reason why it happened: cause or purpose?" The question itself is not clear, and may not even have any meaning. In a famous passage in Plato's *Phaedo,* Socrates ridicules the causal (physiological) explanation that might be put forth of his sitting in prison and insists that the true explanation must be in terms of what he and the Athenians "thought best." We may admit that he was right as far as he went; still it would not have been inappropriate to inquire why he and the Athenians thought as they did. The answer to this question might be a causal one, involving economics, climate, gene mutations, or what not.

5. It is not to be taken for granted that scientific explanation is exclusively of the mechanical type. Many scientific advances, especially in the last five centuries, have consisted in producing causal explanations for phenomena previously "explained" in purposive terms: comets, plagues, paranoia, etc. And it is permissible to speculate that eventually science will find it possible to dispense with purposive explanations altogether, in every field of inquiry including the distinctively human. However, if by "scientific" we refer to the actual practices of present-day scientists, we find that certainly psychology and the social sciences have not yet arrived at this point. It still counts as science when one explains that Jones devotes his leisure and his riches to the Society for the Suppression of Vice because he wants to punish himself for his incestuous cravings. (Unconsciously, to be sure—and it is a nice question whether an "unconscious wish" is to be regarded as a cause or a purpose.) In any event, the aim of science is to understand—and science is in no position to determine in advance what the ultimate categories of understanding may turn out to be. For various reasons, it is generally

more convenient and fruitful to investigate causes rather than purposes: first, because in some cases there may really be no purpose operating, except possibly very remotely, to produce the phenomenon being investigated, for instance, the appearance of a comet; second, even where a purposive agent (man or animal) is known to be involved, it always operates via causes. But these are dictates of convenience; there is nothing obviously unscientific in the belief that in the last analysis everything happens as it does because God wills it, and that science studies merely the "second causes" whereby He attains His ends.

To return to the principle of sufficient reason: it is just the claim that there are no brute facts, that everything has an explanation—though we may not be able to find out what it is. The principle thus includes the causal principle, that everything has a cause; but it is broader. It says that everything has a cause, or serves a purpose, or both.

But then, why should we accept the principle—if we should? This is a curious question: is there a sufficient reason for accepting the principle of sufficient reason? We shall not face it squarely in this book. It might be maintained that the principle is an assumption that we are obliged to make if our attempts to understand the world are not to be pointless. That is to say, our efforts to explain particular things presuppose that there is some explanation. We do not know what the cause of cancer is, but the biochemist does not for a moment entertain the possibility that cancer has no cause at all. The psychoanalyst does not know what the pattern of his patient's behavior is in all its details; but however "irrational" and apparently meaningless the actions, psychoanalysis is committed to the assumption that there is a meaning to be found in them. Furthermore, the principle does not let us down; our successes in finding reasons why things are "so and not otherwise" are so many confirmations of it, and our failures we ascribe to the difficulty, not the impossibility, of understanding. These may not be adequate reasons for accepting the principle; but we shall simply assume it in what follows.

"So *and not otherwise*." This boulder is here in this gorge; but it "might just as well" have been somewhere else? So it might, considered just in itself. But it used to be on the edge of the precipice above, and someone pushed it; that is why it is here, why it has to be here. But then, why could it not have flown through the air when pushed? Well, heavy bodies near the surface of the earth, fall when unsupported. This, then, is just a brute fact? No, it follows from the property of matter that bodies attract one another. But why . . . ?

Someone pushed it? He "might just as well' not have pushed it. But inasmuch as unfriendly Indians were pursuing him up the gorge. . . .

Explanation, the finding of sufficient reasons, we see to be a process of ruling out alternative possibilities. Without an explanation we do not know why the boulder should not be in just any old place. The explanation tells us why it is here rather than there—why just this possibility, out of the indefinite or infinite number of conceivable ones, was realized. We know further why it was pushed by this man at just this time; and so on.

We say that a thing or event is *contingent* if the reason why it is what it is, and not otherwise, is not ascertainable without looking beyond the thing or event itself. To be contingent is just to be dependent on something else, to be the effect of something else. The opposite of "contingent" in this sense is "necessary." Something is necessary if it is what it is no matter what else is the case—if it is something entirely independent, in its existence and all its properties, of the existence and properties of everything else.

We have now defined the term "necessary being." The question is whether there is any reason to believe that a necessary Being exists. (We might as well use capitals, as it will not have escaped the reader that such a Being = God.) The argument proceeds:

It is obvious that there is no necessary Being in nature. This is just another way of saying that everything in nature has a cause. There is no particular thing that would not have been otherwise if something else had been otherwise. Now one may be tempted to say that although this is true of particular things—objects and events—at any rate the laws of nature are exceptions. There might have been more or fewer boulders in this gorge, but the law of gravitation must be what it is. We should note, however, that science explains laws as well as particulars. In Kepler's day, it was one brute fact that heavy bodies near the earth fall when unsupported, another brute fact that smoke goes up, and a third that the planets move around the sun. Newton exhibited the sufficient reason for these in terms of a more comprehensive generalization: given that all matter has the property of gravitating, it follows that all these things must behave as they do and not otherwise. But as to why bodies gravitate, Newton himself knew not, "and [he said] I frame no hypotheses." Before Newton there were the three brute laws we have mentioned, plus a lot of others; after Newton, just one. What are to us, today, the brute laws of gravitation, electromagnetism, nuclear forces, etc., await their explanation in, presumably, a general field theory. Once physicists enunciate such a theory, the number of separate brute facts will be again reduced. But even so, at least one will remain: we shall not know why the general field equation is what it is, and not otherwise. We will be able to imagine other possibilities, and we shall not know why just this one is realized. It will be contingent, but we shall not know on what it is contingent. Or so it appears.

Thus not only is there no necessary thing in nature, but there is no necessary characteristic of nature either. Given that some things in nature are what they are, we understand how it is necessary (relative to them) that other parts of nature are as they are. Given that nature has certain characteristics, we understand why necessarily (relative to them) nature must have certain other characteristics also. But nowhere in nature is there a thing, or a characteristic, of which we can say: This is as it is, and could not be otherwise than it is, no matter what else were to change.

Not only is this last statement true of things in, and characteristics of, nature: nature as a whole is not a necessary Being. The world—the totality of everything that was and is and will be—is only one among an infinitude of possible worlds. By a "possible world" is meant any assemblage of coherently describable things and occurrences. Thus for example one possible world is that in which everything is exactly the same as in this one, with the single exception that there is a misprint in this line of this book. (More grammatically: it is possible that there should be such a world.) It is possible that your parents might never have met, and in consequence that you would not have existed: we have described another possible world. Still another is inhabited by unicorns, mermaids, and centaurs. This is not to say that such creatures are biologically possible; only that no contradiction is involved in supposing that they could exist were the laws of biology different from what they are. Novelists and painters, including surrealists, describe possible worlds. The only limitation on imagining them—and it is not really a limitation—is that a possible world cannot be such that description of it would involve logical contradiction. Thus there is no possible world containing round squares.

This world that we live in, then, is not the only possible world; but it is the only real or actual world. Now when one state of affairs, out of a plurality of possibilities, is realized, there must be a sufficient reason why just that one exists. Yet it is clear that the sufficient reason for this world's existence cannot be contained within it, in nature.

Must we then abandon the principle of sufficient reason? Each part of nature has its sufficient reason in some other part of nature: in its cause at least, perhaps also in its purpose if it has one. And that sufficient reason has its sufficient reason in some other part; and so on . . . ad infinitum? It appears that if we stay within nature, we must either come in the end to at least one brute fact (maybe the "big bang" of the astrophysicists) or one "brute law" (maybe a unified field theory); or else we are confronted with an infinite regress of sufficient reasons, such that no reason is absolutely sufficient, only relatively so. In any case, as we have just seen, nature cannot contain within itself the sufficient reason for its own being, considered as a whole: in particular, why should there not have been just nothing at all? If we confine ourselves within nature in our search for a reason for nature, assuredly we shall find none; the totality of things will have to be taken as one stupendous brute fact; and as a brute fact it will be unintelligible, irrational.

Perhaps it is so. Perhaps the principle breaks down. Perhaps existence, at base, is absurd, and there is not use trying to adequate it to the intellect. Perhaps we must make shift to comprehend only the parts, never the whole.

However, let us not give up so easily. Let us at least ask ourselves what a sufficient reason for the whole might be like, if there were one.

We see immediately that it could not be a cause in the mechanical sense. The attempt to explain everything, whether piecemeal or all at once, in terms of a cause obviously leads us into an infinite regress— just what we are trying to escape. There remains for investigation, then, the possibility of finding a sufficient reason that is a choice.

Are we not faced here at the outset with the same difficulty of infinite regress? For we have already admitted that choices have causes. So that if the sufficient reason for the world were a choice, we could still ask for the cause of the choice; and so on.

But, after all, the choices that we are familiar with are made by limited, contingent beings. We must not be led too hastily to generalize on the sole basis of them. Rather, let us consider, within the sphere of human activities, what are the criteria by which we judge the adequacy of any explanation made in terms of a choice. That is, if we are told that X is as it is because P chose it to be that way, we may demand a further explanation of the choice—the choice itself may puzzle us. But perhaps not always: maybe sometimes this kind of answer is satisfying in itself.

Now it seems that we go on the following principle: we assume that a person makes the best choice he can. If his choice does not strike us as being the best possible, we wonder why it was not, and we search for reasons for the failure; but insofar as it is the best, we demand no further explanation. For the choice seems to us perfectly rational. Let me illustrate.

Someone builds a house of cheap materials, in a run-down neighborhood, not even taking advantage of the best available site on his lot; the rooms are poorly arranged and ventilated; the style is grotesque. We ask: Why did he do this? We answer: He couldn't afford anything better; he is not clever at design, and he was brought up by an ignorant and vulgar aunt. In view of his limitations, that was the best he could do. If a wealthy, ingenious, and well-educated person built such a house, we should perhaps have to conclude that he was not quite sane; we should think it fruitless to search for reasons for such behavior, and should engage in a clinical investigation of the causes of his psychosis.

If, however, a man of wealth and taste builds a convenient and beautiful mansion, we are not puzzled at all. That is just what one would expect; that is the rational thing to do. No doubt, there are causes of his being wealthy and tasteful; but those causes, whatever they are, are of only secondary relevance at most in explaining the house. It is sufficient that the house is the result of a rational choice.

Now let us suppose, for the sake of argument, that the world is the outcome of a choice. Is there any kind of choice that would in itself put an end to all puzzlement—that would not tempt us to ask further questions about the causes of the choice?

If we follow our homely example, it seems that this condition could be satisfied only if the choice were an absolutely rational one. And to be absolutely rational, to be self-sufficient as an explanation, the choice would have to be made by a Being subject to no limitations. If the chooser lacked power to produce whatever he wished to produce, we should want to know what prevented him. If he lacked the knowledge of all the alternatives, we should need to explain this lack. If, having complete knowledge and power, he nevertheless did not make the best choice, that would be most puzzling of all; we should call his behavior irrational and demand a cause. But if the chooser were subject to no limitations of power, if he chose in full knowledge of all the alternatives (all the logically possible ones), and chose the best—then this choice would be absolutely rational and would in itself constitute the sufficient reason for the world's being so and not otherwise. Since we have eliminated causes, and choices not fulfilling these conditions, only such a choice by an omnipotent, omniscient, and benevolent Being could be the sufficient reason for the universe.

Therefore if nature is rational, God exists. But there is good reason to believe that nature is rational: to wit, all of science and the rest of experience. Therefore there is good reason to believe that God exists.

This completes the exposition of the subtle cosmological argument, which in ingenuity and elegance perhaps marks the high point of rational theology. A few points concerning it remain to be noted:

First, it is not appropriate to ask, "Who made God?" and "What are the causes of the infinite Being?" in this context. God, as sufficient reason for nature—chooser of its laws as well as of its furniture—must be outside nature; but it is only within nature, i.e., within a framework of causal presuppositions, that it makes sense to ask for causes.

Second, God is the necessary Being in the sense of our definition of this term: a Being not dependent on the existence of anything else for His existence; not such that He could be otherwise in any respect, whatever else were the case. This is not to say that God's existence is logically necessary, in the sense that His nonexistence is inconceivable. One can conceive of there being no universe at all and no God. One can (perhaps) also conceive of the universe being irrational, hence either the result of the choice of some small-g god or of no choice. The argument claims only that God, as the source of all being, including all causation, cannot conceivably be Himself limited by any causes—in other words, there cannot be any cause (or indeed any resaon) why He should not exist. Only in this sense does His essence entail His existence.

Third, the word "choice" in this context must of course not be supposed to carry with it any connotation of an act in time. The choice of "the best" by God is not to be thought of as the result of long and painful deliberation; this would be inconsistent with omnipotence. Hence the argument is neutral with respect to the issue whether nature has a beginning or not. (Or is this quite true? Theologians since St. Augustine have been aware of the difficulty involved in the notion of a temporal world brought into existence by a timeless Being: if the sufficient reason for the world is eternal, must not the world be eternal? If not, there must have been a time when the sufficient reason existed, but what it was the sufficient reason *for* did not. This is still another problem that we shall pass by as not relevant to our main concern.)

Fourth, as Leibniz noted, it follows as a corollary that this is the best of all possible worlds. The reader is begged to withhold his Voltairean laughter, pending discussion in due course. . . .

DESIGN AND EVIL

David Hume

It is my opinion, I own, replied Demea, that each man feels, in a manner, the truth of religion within his own breast, and, from a consciousness of his imbecility and misery rather than from any reasoning, is led to seek protection from that Being on whom he and all nature is dependent. So anxious or so tedious are even the best scenes of life that futurity is still the object of all our hopes and fears. We incessantly look forward and endeavor, by prayers, adoration, and sacrifice, to appease those unknown powers whom we find, by experience, so able to afflict and oppress us. Wretched creatures that we are! What resource for us amidst the innumerable ills of life did not religion suggest some methods of atonement, and appease those terrors with which we are incessantly agitated and tormented?

I am indeed persuaded, said Philo, that the best and indeed the only method of bringing everyone to a due sense of religion is by just representations of the misery and wickedness of men. And for that purpose a talent of eloquence and strong imagery is more requisite than that of reasoning and argument. For is it necessary to prove what everyone feels within himself? It is only necessary to make us feel it, if possible, more intimately and sensibly.

The people, indeed, replied Demea, are sufficiently convinced of this great and melancholy truth. The miseries of life, the unhappiness of man, the general corruptions of our nature, the unsatisfactory enjoyment of pleasures, riches, honors—these phrases have become almost proverbial in all languages. And who can doubt of what all men declare from their own immediate feeling and experience?

In this point, said Philo, the learned are perfectly agreed with the vulgar; and in all letters, *sacred* and *profane,* the topic of human misery has been insisted on with the most pathetic eloquence that sorrow and melancholy could inspire. The poets, who speak from sentiment, without a system, and whose testimony has therefore the more authority, abound

FROM *Dialogues Concerning Natural Religion,* part 5. Copyright 1948 by Hafner Publishing Co., Inc. and reprinted by permission of Macmillan, Inc.

in images of this nature. From Homer down to Dr. Young, the whole inspired tribe have ever been sensible that no other representation of things would suit the feeling and observation of each individual.

As to authorities, replied Demea, you need not seek them. Look round this library of Cleanthes. I shall venture to affirm that, except authors of particular sciences, such as chemistry or botany, who have no occasion to treat of human life, there is scarce one of those innumerable writers from whom the sense of human misery has not, in some passage or other, extorted a complaint and confession of it. At least, the chance is entirely on that side; and no one author has ever, so far as I can recollect, been so extravagant as to deny it.

There you must excuse me, said Philo: Leibniz has denied it, and is perhaps the first who ventured upon so bold and paradoxical an opinion; at least, the first who made it essential to his philosophical system.

And by being the first, replied Demea, might he not have been sensible of his error? For is this a subject in which philosophers can propose to make discoveries especially in so late an age? And can any man hope by a simple denial (for the subject scarcely admits of reasoning) to bear down the united testimony of mankind, founded on sense and consciousness?

And why should man, added he, pretend to an exemption from the lot of all other animals? The whole earth, believe me, Philo, is cursed and polluted. A perpetual war is kindled amongst all living creatures. Necessity, hunger, want stimulate the strong and courageous; fear, anxiety, terror agitate the weak and infirm. The first entrance into life gives anguish to the new-born infant and to its wretched parent; weakness, impotence, distress attend each stage of that life, and it is, at last, finished in agony and horror.

Observe, too, says Philo, the curious artifices of nature in order to embitter the life of every living being. The stronger prey upon the weaker and keep them in perpetual terror and anxiety. The weaker, too, in their turn, often prey upon the stronger, and vex and molest them without relaxation. Consider that innumerable race of insects, which either are bred on the body of each animal or, flying about, infix their stings in him. These insects have others still less than themselves which torment them. And thus on each hand, before and behind, above and below, every animal is surrounded with enemies which incessantly seek his misery and destruction.

Man alone, said Demea, seems to be, in part, an exception to this rule. For by combination in society he can easily master lions, tigers, and bears, whose greater strength and agility naturally enable them to prey upon him.

On the contrary, it is here chiefly, cried Philo, that the uniform and equal maxims of nature are most apparent. Man, it is true, can, by combination, surmount all his *real* enemies and become master of the whole animal creation; but does he not immediately raise up to himself *imaginary* enemies, the demons of his fancy, who haunt him with superstitious terrors and blast every enjoyment of life? His pleasure, as he imagines, becomes in their eyes a crime; his food and repose give them umbrage and offense; his very sleep and dreams furnish new materials to anxious fear; and even death, his refuge from every other ill, presents only the dread of endless and innumerable woes. Nor does the wolf molest more the timid flock than superstition does the anxious breast of wretched mortals.

Besides, consider, Demea: This very society by which we surmount those wild beasts, our natural enemies, what new enemies does it not raise to us? What woe and misery does it not occasion? Man is the greatest enemy of man. Oppression, injustice, contempt, contumely, violence, sedition, war, calumny, treachery, fraud—by these they mutually torment each other, and they would soon dissolve that society which they had formed were it not for the dread of still greater ills which must attend their separation.

But though these external insults, said Demea, from animals, from men, from all the elements, which assault us form a frightful catalogue of woes, they are nothing in comparison of those which arise within ourselves, from the distempered condition of our mind and body. How many lie under the lingering torment of diseases? Hear the pathetic enumeration of the great poet.

> Intestine stone and ulcer, colic-pangs,
> Demoniac frenzy, moping melancholy,
> And moon-struck madness, pining atrophy,
> Marasmus, and wide-wasting pestilence,
> Dire was the tossing, deep the groans: *Despair*
> Tended the sick, busiest from couch to couch.
> And over them triumphant *Death* his dart
> Shook: but delay'd to strike, though oft invok'd
> With vows, as their chief good and final hope.

The disorders of the mind, continued Demea, though more secret, are not perhaps less dismal and vexatious. Remorse, shame, anguish, rage, disappointment, anxiety, fear, dejection, despair—who has ever passed through life without cruel inroads from these tormentors? How many have scarcely ever felt any better sensations? Labor and poverty, so abhorred by everyone, are the certain lot of the far greater number; and those few privileged persons who enjoy ease and opulence never reach contentment or true felicity. All the goods of life united would not make a very happy man, but all the ills united would make a wretch indeed; and any one of them almost (and who can be free from every one?), nay, often the absence of one good (and who can possess all?) is sufficient to render life ineligible.

Were a stranger to drop on a sudden into this world, I would show him, as a specimen of its ills, a hospital full of diseases, a prison crowded with malefactors and debtors, a field of battle strewed with carcases, a fleet foundering in the ocean, a nation languishing under tyranny, famine, or pestilence. To turn the gay side of life to him and give him a notion of its pleasures—whither should I conduct him? To a ball, to an opera, to court? He might justly think that I was only showing him a diversity of distress and sorrow.

There is no evading such striking instances, said Philo, but by apologies which still further aggravate the charge. Why have all men, I ask, in all ages, complained incessantly of the miseries of life? . . . They have no just reason, says one: these complaints proceed only from their discontented, repining, anxious disposition. . . . And can there possibly, I reply, be a more certain foundation of misery than such a wretched temper?

But if they were really as unhappy as they pretend, says my antagonist, why do they remain in life? . . .

> Not satisfied with life, afraid of death—

this is the secret chain, say I, that holds us. We are terrified, not bribed to the continuance of our existence.

It is only a false delicacy, he may insist, which a few refined spirits indulge, and which has spread these complaints among the whole race of mankind. . . . And what is this delicacy, I ask, which you blame? Is it anything but a greater sensibility to all the pleasures and pains of life? And if the man of a delicate, refined temper, by being so much more alive than the rest of the world, is only so much more unhappy, what judgment must we form in general of human life?

Let men remain at rest, says our adversary, and they will be easy. They are willing artificers of their own misery. . . . No! reply I: an anxious languor follows their repose; disappointment, vexation, trouble, their activity and ambition.

I can observe something like what you mention in some others, replied Cleanthes, but I confess I feel little or nothing of it in myself, and hope that it is not so common as you represent it.

If you feel not human misery yourself, cried Demea, I congratulate you on so happy a singularity. Others, seemingly the most prosperous, have not been ashamed to vent their complaints in the most melancholy strains. Let us attend to the great, the fortunate emperor, Charles V, when, tired with human grandeur, he resigned all his extensive dominions into the hands of his son. In the last harangue which he made on that memorable occasion, he publicly avowed *that the greatest prosperities which he had ever enjoyed had been mixed with so many adversities that he might truly say he had never enjoyed any satisfaction or contentment.* But did the retired life in which he sought for shelter afford him any greater happiness? If we may credit his son's account, his repentance commenced the very day of his resignation.

Cicero's fortune, from small beginnings, rose to the greatest luster and renown; yet what pathetic complaints of the ills of life do his familiar letters, as well as philosophical discourses, contain? And suitably to his own experience, he introduces Cato, the great, the fortunate Cato protesting in his old age that had he a new life in his offer he would reject the present.

Ask yourself, ask any of your acquaintance, whether they would live over again the last ten or twenty years of their life. No! but the next twenty, they say, will be better:

> And from the dregs of life, hope to receive
> What the first sprightly running could not give.

Thus, at last, they find (such is the greatness of human misery, it reconciles even contradictions) that they complain at once of the shortness of life and of its vanity and sorrow.

And is it possible, Cleanthes, said Philo, that after all these reflections, and infinitely more which might be suggested, you can still persevere in your anthropomorphism, and assert the moral attributes of the Deity, his justice, benevolence, mercy, and rectitude, to be of the same nature with these virtues in human creatures? His power, we allow, is infinite; whatever he wills is executed; but neither man nor any other animal is happy; therefore, he does not will their happiness. His wisdom is infinite; he is never mistaken in choosing the means to any end; but the course of nature tends not to human or animal felicity; therefore, it is not established for that purpose. Through the whole compass of human knowledge there are no inferences more certain and infallible than these. In what respect, then, do his benevolence and mercy resemble the benevolence and mercy of men?

Epicurus' old questions are yet unanswered.

Is he willing to prevent evil, but not able? then is he impotent. Is he able, but not willing? then is he malevolent. Is he both able and willing? whence then is evil?

You ascribe, Cleanthes, (and I believe justly) a purpose and intention to nature. But what, I beseech you, is the object of that curious artifice and machinery which she has displayed in all animals—the preservation alone of individuals, and propagation of the species? It seems enough for her purpose, if such a rank be barely upheld in the universe, without any care or concern for the happiness of the members that compose it. No resource for this purpose: no machinery in order merely to give pleasure or ease; no fund of pure joy and contentment; no indulgence without some want or necessity accompanying it. At least, the few phenomena of this nature are overbalanced by opposite phenomena of still greater importance.

Our sense of music, harmony, and indeed beauty of all kinds, gives satisfaction, without being absolutely necessary to the preservation and propagation of the species. But what racking pains, on the other hand, arise from gouts, gravels, megrims, toothaches, rheumatisms, where the injury to the animal machinery is either small or incurable? Mirth, laughter, play, frolic seem gratuitous satisfactions which have no further tendency; spleen, melancholy, discontent, superstition are pains of the same nature. How then does the Divine benevolence display itself, in the sense of you anthropomorphites? None but we mystics, as you were pleased to call us, can account for this strange mixture of phenomena, by deriving it from attributes infinitely perfect but incomprehensible.

And have you, at last, said Cleanthes smiling, betrayed your intentions, Philo? Your long agreement with Demea did indeed a little surprise me, but I find you were all the while erecting a concealed battery against me. And I must confess that you have now fallen upon a subject worthy of your noble spirit of opposition and controversy. If you can make out the present point, and prove mankind to be unhappy or corrupted, there is an end at once of all religion. For to what purpose establish the natural attributes of the Deity, while the moral are still doubtful and uncertain?

You take umbrage very easily, replied Demea, at opinions the most innocent and the most generally received, even amongst the religious and devout themselves; and nothing can be more surprising than to find a topic like this—concerning the wickedness and misery of man—charged with no less than atheism and profaneness. Have not all pious divines and preachers who have indulged their rhetoric on so fertile a subject, have they not easily, I say, given a solution of any difficulties which may attend it? This world is but a point in comparison of the universe; this life but a moment in comparison of eternity. The present evil phenomena, therefore, are rectified in other regions, and in some future period of existence. And the eyes of men, being then opened to larger views of things, see the whole connection of general laws, and trace, with adoration, the benevolence and rectitude of the Deity through all the mazes and intricacies of his providence.

No! replied Cleanthes, no! These arbitrary suppositions can never be admitted, contrary to matter of fact, visible and uncontroverted. Whence can any cause be known but from its known effects? Whence can any hypothesis be proved but from the apparent phenomena? To establish one hypothesis upon another is building entirely in the air; and the utmost we ever attain by these conjectures and fictions is to ascertain the bare possibility of our opinion, but never can we, upon such terms, establish its reality.

The only method of supporting Divine benevolence—and it is what I willingly embrace—is to deny absolutely the misery and wickedness of man. Your representations are exaggerated; your melancholy views mostly fictitious; your inferences contrary to fact and experience. Health is more common than sickness; pleasure than pain; happiness than misery. And for one vexation which we meet with, we attain, upon computation, a hundred enjoyments.

Admitting your position, replied Philo, which yet is extremely doubtful, you must at the same time allow that, if pain be less frequent than pleasure, it is infinitely more violent and durable. One hour of it is often able to outweigh a day, a week, a month of our common insipid enjoyments; and how many days, weeks, and months are passed by several in the most acute torments? Pleasure, scarcely in one instance, is ever able to reach ecstasy and rapture; and in no one instance can it continue for any time at its highest pitch and altitude. The spirits evaporate, the nerves relax, the fabric is disordered, and the enjoyment quickly degenerates into fatigue and uneasiness. But pain often, good God, how often! rises to torture and agony; and the longer it continues, it becomes still more genuine agony and torture. Patience is exhausted, courage languishes, melancholy seizes us, and nothing terminates our misery but the removal of its cause or another event which is the sole cure of all evil, but which, from our natural folly, we regard with still greater horror and consternation.

But not to insist upon these topics, continued Philo, though most obvious, certain, and important, I must use the freedom to admonish you, Cleanthes, that you have put the controversy upon a most dangerous issue, and are unawares introducing a total scepticism into the most essential articles of natural and revealed theology. What! no method of fixing a just foundation for religion unless we allow the happiness of human life, and maintain a continued existence even in this world, with all our present pains, infirmities, vexations, and follies, to be eligible and desirable! But this is contrary to everyone's feeling and experience; it is contrary to an authority so established as nothing can subvert. No decisive proofs can ever be produced against this authority; nor is it possible for you to compute, estimate, and compare all the pains and all the pleasures in the lives of all men and of all animals; and thus, by your resting the whole system of religion on a point which, from its very nature, must for ever be uncertain, you tacitly confess that that system is equally uncertain.

But allowing you what never will be believed, at least, what you never possibly can prove, that animal or, at least, human happiness in this life exceeds its misery, you have yet done nothing; for this is not, by any means, what we expect from infinite power, infinite wisdom, and infinite goodness. Why is there any misery at all in the world? Not by chance, surely. From some cause then. Is it from the intention of the Deity? But he is perfectly benevolent. Is it contrary to his intention? But he is almighty. Nothing can shake the solidity of this reasoning, so short, so clear, so decisive, except we assert that these subjects exceed all human capacity, and that our common measures of truth and falsehood are not applicable to them—a topic which I have all along insisted on, but which you have, from the beginning, rejected with scorn and indignation.

But I will be contented to retire still from this intrenchment, for I deny that you can ever force me in it. I will allow that pain or misery in man is *compatible* with infinite power and goodness in the Deity, even in your sense of these attributes; what are you advanced by all these concessions? A mere possible compatibility is not sufficient. You must *prove* these pure, unmixed, and uncontrollable attributes from the present mixed and confused phenomena, and from these alone. A hopeful undertaking! Were the phenomena ever so pure and unmixed, yet, being finite, they would be insufficient for that purpose. How much more, where they are also so jarring and discordant!

Here, Cleanthes, I find myself at ease in my argument. Here I triumph. Formerly, when we argued concerning the natural attributes of intelligence and design, I needed all my skeptical and metaphysical subtlety to elude your grasp. In many views of the universe and of its parts, particularly the latter, the beauty and fitness of final causes strike us with such irresistible force that all objections appear (what I believe they really are) mere cavils and sophisms; nor can we then imagine how it was ever possible for us to repose any weight on them. But there is no view of human life or of the condition of mankind from which, without the greatest violence, we can infer the moral attributes or learn that infinite benevolence, conjoined with infinite power and infinite wisdom, which we must discover by the eyes of faith alone. It is your turn now to tug the laboring oar, and to support your philosophical subtleties against the dictates of plain reason and experience.

COMMENTARY ON THE VEDÂNTA SÛTRAS

Ramanuja

Because Brahman, being raised above all contact with the senses, is not an object of perception and the other means of proof, but to be known through Scripture only; therefore the text "Whence these creatures are born," etc., has to be accepted as instructing us regarding the true nature of Brahman.—But, our opponent points out, Scripture cannot be the source of our knowledge of Brahman, because Brahman is to be known through other means. For it is an acknowledged principle that Scripture has a meaning only with regard to what is not established by other sources of knowledge.—But what, to raise a prima facie counter objection, are those other sources of knowledge? It cannot, in the first place, be Perception. Perception is twofold, being based either on the sense-organs or on extraordinary concentration of mind (yoga). Of Perception of the former kind there are again two sub-species, according as Perception takes place either through the outer sense-organs or the internal organ (manas). Now the outer sense-organs produce knowledge of their respective objects, in so far as the latter are in actual contact with the organs, but are quite unable to give rise to the knowledge of the special object constituted by a supreme Self that is capable of being conscious of and creating the whole aggregate of things. Nor can internal perception give rise to such knowledge; for only purely internal things, such as pleasure and pain, fall within its cognizance, and it is incapable of relating itself to external objects apart from the outer sense-organs. Nor, again, perception based on Yoga; for although such perception—which springs from intense imagination—implies a vivid presentation of things, it is, after all, nothing more than a reproduction of objects perceived previously, and does not therefore rank as an instrument of knowledge; for it has no means of applying itself to objects other than those perceived previously. And

FROM *The Vedânta-Sûtras,* translated by George Thibaut. Published in 1966 by Motilal Banarsidass, India.

if, after all, it does so, it is (not a means of knowledge but) a source of error.—Nor also inference either of the kind which proceeds on the observation of special cases or of the kind which rests on generalizations. Not inference of the former kind, because such inference is not known to relate to anything lying beyond the reach of the senses. Nor inference of the latter kind, because we do not observe any characteristic feature that is invariably accompanied by the presence of a supreme Self capable of being conscious of, and constructing, the universe of things.—But there *is* such a feature, viz. the world's being an effected thing; it being a matter of common experience that whatever is an effect or product, is due to an agent who possesses a knowledge of the material cause, the instrumental cause, the final end, and the person meant to make use of the thing produced. It further is a matter of experience that whatever consists of non-sentient matter is dependent on, or ruled by, a single intelligent principle. The former generalization is exemplified by the case of jars and similar things, and the latter by a living body in good health, which consists of non-intelligent matter dependent on an intelligent principle. And that the body is an effected thing follows from its consisting of parts.—Against this argumentation also objections may be raised. What, it must be asked, do you understand by this dependence on an intelligent principle? Not, we suppose, that the origination and subsistence of the non-intelligent thing should be dependent on the intelligent principle; for in that case your example would not help to prove your contention. Neither the origin nor the subsistence of a person's healthy body depends on the intelligent soul of that person alone; they rather are brought about by the merit and demerit of all those souls which in any way share the fruition of that body—the wife, e.g. of that person, and others. Moreover, the existence of a body made up of parts means that body's being connected with its parts in the way of so-called intimate relation (samavâya), and this requires a certain combination of the parts but not a presiding intelligent principle. The existence of animated bodies, moreover, has for its characteristic mark the process of breathing, which is absent in the case of the earth, sea, mountains, etc.—all of which are included in the class of things concerning which you wish to prove something— and we therefore miss a uniform kind of existence common to all those things.—Let us then understand by the dependence of a non-intelligent thing on an intelligent principle, the fact of the motion of the former depending on the latter!—This definition, we rejoin, would comprehend also those cases in which heavy things, such as carriages, masses of stone, trees, etc., are set in motion by several intelligent beings (while what you want to prove is the dependence of a moving thing on one intelligent principle). If, on the other hand, you mean to say that all motion depends on intelligence in general, you only prove what requires no proof.—Another alternative, moreover, here presents itself. As we both admit the existence of individual souls, it will be the more economical hypothesis to ascribe to them the agency implied in the construction of the world. Nor must you object to this view on the ground that such agency cannot belong to the individual souls because they do not possess the knowledge of material causes, etc., as specified above; for all intelligent beings are capable of direct knowledge of material causes, such as earth and so on, and instrumental causes, such as sacrifices and the like. Earth and other material substances, as well as sacrifices and the like, are directly perceived by individual intelligent beings at the present time (and were no doubt equally perceived so at a former time when this world had to be planned and constructed). Nor does the fact that intelligent beings are not capable of direct insight into the unseen principle—called "apûrva," or by similar names—which resides in the form of a power in sacrifices and other instrumental causes, in any way preclude their being agents in the construction of the world. Direct insight into powers is nowhere required for undertaking work: what *is* required for that purpose is only direct presentative knowledge of the things endowed with power, while of power itself it suffices to have some kind of knowledge. Potters apply themselves to the task of making pots and jars on the strength of the direct knowledge they possess of the implements of their work—the wheel, the staff, etc.— without troubling about a similar knowledge of the powers inherent in those implements; and in the same way intelligent beings may apply themselves to their work (to be effected by means of sacrifices, etc.), if only they are assured by sacred tradition of the existence of the various powers possessed by sacrifices and the like.—Moreover, experience teaches that agents having a knowledge of the material and other causes must be inferred only in the case of those effects which can be produced, and the material and other causes of which can be known: such things, on the other hand, as the earth, mountains, and oceans, can neither be produced, nor can their material and other causes ever be known; we therefore have no right to infer for them intelligent producers. Hence the quality of being an effected thing can be used as an argument for proving the existence of an intelligent causal agent, only where that quality is found in things, the production of which, and the knowledge of the causes of which, is possible at all.— Experience further teaches that earthen pots and similar things are produced by intelligent agents possessing material bodies, using implements, not endowed with the power of a Supreme Lord, limited in knowledge and so on; the quality of being an effect therefore supplies a reason for inferring an intelligent agent of the kind described only, and thus is opposed to the inference of attributes of a contrary nature, viz. omniscience, omnipotence, and those other attributes that belong to the highest Soul, whose existence you wish to establish.—Nor does this (as might be objected) imply an abandonment of all inference. Where the thing to be inferred is known through other means of proof also, any qualities of an opposite nature which may be suggested by the inferential mark (linga) are opposed by those other means of proof, and therefore must be dropped. In the case under discussion, however, the thing to be inferred is something not guaranteed by any other means of proof, viz. a person capable of constructing the entire universe: here there is nothing to interfere with the ascription to such a person of all those qualities which, on the basis of methodical inference, necessarily belong to it.—The conclusion from all this is that, apart from Scripture, the existence of a Lord does not admit of proof.

Against all this the Pûrvapakshin now restates his case as follows:— It cannot be gainsaid that the world is something effected, for it is made up of parts. We may state this argument in various technical forms. "The earth, mountains, etc., are things effected, because they consist of parts; in the same way as jars and similar things." "The earth, seas, mountains, etc., are effects, because, while being big (i.e. non-atomic), they are capable of motion; just as jars and the like." "Bodies, the world, etc., are effects, because, while being big, they are solid (mûrtta); just as jars and the like."—But, an objection is raised, in the case of things made up of parts we do not, in addition to this attribute of consisting of parts, observe any other aspect determining that the thing is an effect—so as to enable us to say "this thing is effected, and that thing is not"; and, on the other hand, we do observe it as an indispensable condition of something being an effect, that there should be the possibility of such an effect being brought about, and of the existence of such knowledge of material causes, etc. (as the bringing about of the effect presupposes).—Not so, we reply. In the case of a cause being inferred on the ground of an effect, the knowledge and power of the cause must be inferred in accordance with the nature of the effect. From the circumstance of a thing consisting of parts we know it to be an effect, and on this basis we judge of the power and knowledge of the cause. A person recognizes pots, jars and the like, as things produced, and therefrom infers the constructive skill and knowledge of their maker; when, after this, he sees for the first time a kingly palace with all its various wonderful parts and structures, he concludes from the special way in which the parts are joined that this also is an effected thing, and then makes an inference as to the architect's manifold knowledge and skill. Analogously, when a living body and the world have once been recognized to be effects, we infer—as their maker—some special intelligent being, possessing direct insight into their nature and skill to construct them.—Pleasure and pain, moreover, by which men are requited for their merit and demerit, are themselves of a non-intelligent nature, and hence cannot bring about their results unless they are controlled by an intelligent principle, and this also compels us to assume a being capable of allotting to each individual soul a fate corresponding to its deserts. For we do not observe that non-intelligent implements, such as axes and the like, however much they may be favored by circumstances of time, place, and so on, are capable of producing posts and pillars unless they be handled by a carpenter. And to quote against the generalization on which we rely the instance of the seed and sprout and the like can only spring from an ignorance and stupidity which may be called truly demoniac. The same remark would apply to pleasure and pain if used as a counter instance. (For in all these cases the action which produces an effect must necessarily be guided by an intelligent principle.)—Nor may we assume, as a "less complicated hypothesis," that the guiding principle in the construction of the world is the individual souls, whose existence is acknowledged by both parties. For on the testimony of observation we must deny to those souls the power of seeing what is extremely subtle or remote in time or place (while such power must necessarily be ascribed to a world-constructing intelligence). On the other hand, we have no ground for concluding that the Lord is, like the individual souls, destitute of such power; hence it cannot be said that other means of knowledge make it impossible to infer such a Lord. The fact rather is that as his existence is proved by the argument that any definite effect presupposes a causal agent competent to produce that effect, he is proved at the same time as possessing the essential power of intuitively knowing and ruling all things in the universe.—The contention that from the world being an effect it follows that its maker does not possess lordly power and so on, so that the proving reason would prove something contrary to the special attributes (belonging to a supreme agent, viz. omnipotence, omniscience, etc.), is founded on evident ignorance of the nature of the inferential process. For the inference clearly does not prove that there exist in the thing inferred all the attributes belonging to the proving collateral instances, including even those attributes which stand in no causal relation to the effect. A certain effect which is produced by some agent presupposes just so much power and knowledge on the part of that agent as is requisite for the production of the effect, but in no way presupposes any incapability or ignorance on the part of that agent with regard to things other than the particular effect; for such incapability and ignorance do not stand toward that effect in any causal relation. If the origination of the effect can be accounted for on the basis of the agent's capability of bringing it about, and of his knowledge of the special material and instrumental causes, it would be unreasonable to ascribe causal agency to his (altogether irrelevant) incapabilities and ignorance with regard to other things, only because those incapabilities, etc., are observed to exist together with his special capability and knowledge. The question would arise moreover whether such want of capability and knowledge (with regard to things others than the one actually effected) would be helpful toward the bringing about of that one effect, in so far as extending to all other things or to some other things. The former alternative is excluded because no agent, a potter e.g., is quite ignorant of all other things but his own special work; and the second alternative is inadmissible because there is no definite rule indicating that there should be certain definite kinds of want of knowledge and skill in the case of all agents, and hence exceptions would arise with regard to every special case of want of knowledge and skill. From this it follows that the absence of lordly power and similar qualities which (indeed is observed in the case of ordinary agents but) in no way contributes toward the production of the effects (to which such agents give rise) is not proved in the case of that which we wish to prove (i.e. a Lord, creator of the world), and that hence Inference does not establish qualities contrary (to the qualities characteristic of a Lord).

A further objection will perhaps be raised, viz. that as experience teaches that potters and so on direct their implements through the mediation of their own bodies, we are not justified in holding that a bodiless Supreme Lord directs the material and instrumental causes of the universe.—But in reply to this we appeal to the fact of experience, that evil demons possessing men's bodies, and also venom, are driven or drawn out of those bodies by mere will power. Nor must you ask in what way the volition of a bodiless Lord can put other bodies in motion; for volition is not dependent on a body. The cause of volitions is not the body but the internal organ (manas), and such an organ we ascribe to the Lord also, since what proves the presence of an internal organ endowed with power and knowledge is just the presence of effects.—But volitions, even if directly springing from the internal organ, can belong to embodied beings only, such only possessing internal organs!—This objection also is founded on a mistaken generalization: the fact rather is that the internal organ is permanent, and exists also in separation from the body. The conclusion, therefore, is that—as the individual souls with their limited capacities and knowledge, and their dependence on merit and demerit, are incapable of giving rise to things so variously and wonderfully made as worlds and animated bodies are—inference directly leads us to the theory that there is a supreme intelligent agent, called the Lord, who possesses unfathomable, unlimited powers and wisdom, is capable of constructing the entire world, is without a body, and through his mere volition brings about the infinite expanse of this entire universe so variously and wonderfully planned. As Brahman may thus be ascertained by means of knowledge other than revelation, the text quoted under the preceding Sûtra cannot be taken to convey instruction as to Brahman. Since, moreover, experience demonstrates that material and instrumental causes always are things absolutely distinct from each other, as e.g. the clay and the potter with his implements; and since, further, there are substances not made up of parts, as e.g. ether, which therefore cannot be viewed as effects; we must object on these grounds also to any attempt to represent the one Brahman as the universal material and instrumental cause of the entire world.

Against all this we now argue as follows:—The Vedânta-text declaring the origination, etc., of the world does teach that there is a Brahman possessing the characteristics mentioned; since Scripture alone is a means for the knowledge of Brahman. That the world is an effected thing because it consists of parts; and that, as all effects are observed to have for their antecedents certain appropriate agents competent to produce them, we must infer a causal agent competent to plan and construct the universe, and standing toward it in the relation of material and operative cause—this would be a conclusion altogether unjustified. There is no proof to show that the earth, oceans, etc., although things produced, were created at one time by one creator. Nor can it be pleaded in favor of such a conclusion that all those things have one uniform character of being effects, and thus are analogous to one single jar; for we observe that various effects are distinguished by difference of time of production, and difference of producers. Nor again may you maintain the oneness of the creator on the ground that individual souls are incapable of the creation of this wonderful universe, and that if an additional principle be assumed to account for the world—which manifestly is a product—it would be illegitimate to assume more than one such principle. For we observe that individual beings acquire more and more extraordinary powers in consequence of an increase of religious merit; and as we may assume that through an eventual supreme degree of merit they may in the end qualify themselves for producing quite extraordinary effects, we have no right to assume a highest soul of infinite merit, different from all individual souls. Nor also can it be proved that all things are destroyed and produced all at once; for no such thing is observed to take place, while it is, on the other hand, observed that things are produced and destroyed in succession; and if we infer that all things are produced and destroyed because they are effects, there is no reason why this production and destruction should not take place in a way agreeing with ordinary experience. If, therefore, what it is desired to prove is the agency of one intelligent being, we are met by the difficulty that the proving reason (viz. the circumstance of something being an effect) is not invariably connected with what it is desired to prove; there, further, is the fault of qualities not met with in experience being attributed to the subject about which something has to be proved; and lastly there is the fault of the proving collateral instances being destitute of what has to be proved—for experience does not exhibit to us one agent capable of producing everything. If, on the other hand, what you wish to prove is merely the existence of an intelligent creative agent, you prove only what is proved already (not contested by any one).—Moreover, if you use the attribute of being an effect (which belongs to the totality of things) as a means to prove the existence of one omniscient and omnipotent creator, do you view this attribute as belonging to all things in so far as produced together, or in so far as produced in succession? In the former case the attribute of being an effect is not established (for experience does not show that all things are produced together); and in the latter case the attribute would really prove what is contrary to the hypothesis of one creator (for experience shows that things produced in succession have different causes). In attempting to prove the agency of one intelligent creative being only, we thus enter into conflict with Perception and Inference, and we moreover contradict Scripture, which says that "the potter is born" and "the cartwright is born" (and thus declares a plurality of intelligent agents). Moreover, as we observe that all effected things, such as living bodies and so on, are connected with pleasure and the like, which are the effects of sattva (goodness) and the other primary constituents of matter, we must conclude that effected things have sattva and so on for their causes. Sattva and so on—which constitute the distinctive elements of the causal substance—are the causes of the various nature of the effects. Now those effects can be connected with their causes only in so far as the internal organ of a person possessing sattva and so on undergoes modifications. And that a person possesses those qualitie is due to karman. Thus, in order to account for the origination of different effects we must necessarily assume the connection of an intelligent agent with karman, whereby alone he can become the cause of effects; and moreover the various character of knowledge and power (which the various effects presuppose) has its reason in karman. And if it be said that it is (not the various knowledge, etc., but) the mere wish of the agent that causes the origination of effects, we point out that the wish, as being specialized by its particular object, must be based on sattva and so on, and hence is necessarily connected with karman. From all this it follows that individual souls only can be causal agents: no legitimate inference leads to a Lord different from them in nature.—This admits of various expressions in technical form. "Bodies, worlds, etc., are effects due to the causal energy of individual souls, just as pots are"; "the Lord is not a causal agent, because he has no aims; just as the released souls have none"; "the Lord is not an agent, because he has no body; just as the released souls have none." (This last argumentation cannot be objected to on the ground that individual souls take possession of bodies; for in their case there exists a beginningless subtle body by means of which they enter into gross bodies).—"Time is never devoid of created worlds; because it is time, just like the present time (which has its created world)."

Consider the following point also. Does the Lord produce his effects, with his body or apart from his body? Not the latter; for we do not observe causal agency on the part of an bodiless being: even the activities of the internal organ are found only in beings having a body, and although the internal organ be eternal we do not know of its producing any effects in the case of released disembodied souls. Nor again is the former alternative admissible; for in that case the Lord's body would either be permanent or non-permanent. The former alternative would imply that something made up of parts is eternal; and if we once admit this we may as well admit that the world itself is eternal, and then there is no reason to infer a Lord. And the latter alternative is inadmissible because in that case there would be no cause of the body, different from it (which would account for the origination of the body). Nor could the Lord himself be assumed as the cause of the body, since a bodiless being cannot be the cause of a body. Nor could it be maintained that the Lord can be assumed to be "embodied" by means of some other body; for this leads us into a *regressus in infinitum* [infinite regress].—Should we, moreover, represent to ourselves the Lord (when productive) as engaged in effort or not?—The former is inadmissible, because he is without a body. And the latter alternative is excluded because a being not making an effort does not produce effects. And if it be said that the effect, i.e. the world, has for its causal agent one whose activity consists in mere desire, this would be to ascribe to the subject of the conclusion (i.e. the world) qualities not known from experience; and moreover the attribute to be proved would be absent in the case of the proving instances (such as jars, etc., which are not the work of agents engaged in mere wishing). Thus the inference of a creative Lord which claims to be in agreement with observation is refuted by reasoning which itself is in agreement with observation, and we hence conclude that Scripture is the only source of knowledge with regard to a supreme soul that is the Lord of all and constitutes the highest Brahman. What Scripture tells us of is a being which comprehends within itself infinite, altogether unsurpassable excellences such as omnipotence and so on, is antagonistic to all evil, and totally different in character from whatever is cognized by the other means of knowledge: that to such a being there should attach even the slightest imperfection due to its similarity in nature to the things known by the ordinary means of knowledge, is thus altogether excluded.—The Pûrvapakshin had remarked that the oneness of the instrumental and the material cause is neither a matter of observation nor capable of proof, and that the same holds good with regard to the theory that certain non-composite substances such as ether are created things; that these points also are in no way contrary to reason, we shall show later on. . . .

The conclusion meanwhile is that since Brahman does not fall within the sphere of the other means of knowledge, and is the topic of Scripture only, the text "from whence these creatures," etc., *does* give authoritative information as to a Brahman possessing the characteristic qualities so often enumerated. Here terminates the adhikarana [chapter] of "Scripture being the source."

Questions for Discussion

1. Some philosophers, including J. S. Mill and William James, recognizing the force of the argument from evil, concluded that if God exists, He is limited in power to prevent evil. Why would this be an unsatisfactory solution from the standpoint of Western monotheism?
2. Aquinas says that nothing moves unless it is moved by something else. Is the motion of the stars evidence against this claim? Why or why not?
3. "If everything can not-be, then at one time there was nothing," Aquinas wrote. What is the reasoning behind this assertion? Compare: "If everyone can sneeze, then at one time everyone was sneezing." Why is this reasoning unsound?
4. Aquinas claims that insentient natural objects nearly always act to achieve the best result. What does he mean by "best result"—the best for humankind, for nature, or for God?
5. Matson points out that a monk named Gaunilo tried to refute Anselm's ontological argument by maintaining that the same reasoning could prove the existence of a greatest conceivable island. What was Anselm's reply? Who was right? Is there a difference, that matters to the argument, between the concept of an island and that of a necessary being?
6. Matson translates "The GCB exists" into "The word 'GCB' denotes."

Explain why this does or does not help to show what is wrong with the ontological argument. Matson also claims that no concept can guarantee its own denotation. Is he begging the question?

7. It is often claimed that Darwin's theory of evolution can explain the high degree of order or design in nature as due to natural selection. Does this undercut Aquinas's argument for a cosmic designer in the fifth way? Or does evolution itself require a purposive explanation? Explain.

8. Hume argues that God should be able to interfere with causal processes in a way so subtle that it would not frighten us. Is Hume underestimating the power of science to detect violations of laws of nature?

9. According to Ramanuja, "there is no proof that the earth, oceans, etc. were created at one time by a single creator. Nor can it be pleaded in favor of such a conclusion that all those things have one uniform character of being effects and thus are analogous to one single jar; for we observe that various effects are distinguished by time of production and difference of producers." Is this consideration—that different processes may have produced oceans, planets, and so forth at different times—relevant to the question of the origin of the universe *as a totality?* Explain.

10. Comment on Ramanuja's remark that "if . . . you mean to say that all motion depends on intelligence in general, you only prove what requires no proof." Compare this with Aquinas's notion that the "first cog" must be moved by an intelligent agent to get things started.

Selected Readings

AQUINAS, THOMAS, ST. *Summa Theologica.* Translated by Dominican Fathers. New York: Benziger Brothers, 1925. The main source of natural theology.

AUGUSTINE, AURELIUS, ST. *The City of God.* Translated by M. Dods. New York: Modern Library, 1950. The systematic theology of early Christianity.

BARTH, K. *Theology and Church.* Translated by C. P. Smith. New York: Harper & Row, 1962. Criticizes rational theology in favor of faith.

BURRILL, D., ed. *The Cosmological Arguments.* Encino, California: Dickenson, 1971. Essays for and against the first cause argument.

DOSTOYEVSKY, F. *The Brothers Karamazov.* Translated by Constance Garnett. New York: Random House, 1925. The argument from evil.

FLEW, A., AND MACINTYRE, A. *New Essays in Philosophical Theology.* New York: Macmillan, 1955. Essays attacking and defending religious belief.

FREUD, S. *The Future of an Illusion.* Translated by W. Robson-Scott. New York: Liveright, 1955. A devastating criticism of religion.

HEPBURN, R. *Christianity and Paradox.* London: Watts, 1958. A critical study of existential and neo-orthodox theology.

HERBERG, W., ed. *Four Existentialist Theologians*. Garden City, New York: Anchor, 1958. Selections from Nicholas Berdiaev, Martin Buber, Paul Tillich, and Jacques Maritain.

HICK, J., ed. *The Existence of God*. New York: Macmillan, 1964. The major arguments for and against religious belief.

HUME, DAVID. *Dialogues Concerning Natural Religion*. New York: Liberal Arts Press, 1947. The classic argument from evil.

KIERKEGAARD, S. *Authority and Revelation*. Translated by W. Laurie. Princeton, New Jersey: Princeton University Press, 1955. On the irrelevance of proofs of God's existence.

MATSON, W. I. *The Existence of God*. Ithaca, New York: Cornell University Press, 1965.

MUNITZ, M. K., ed. *Theories of the Universe*. Glencoe, Illinois: Free Press, 1957. Religious and scientific theories of the origin of the universe.

MURCHLAND, B., ed. *The Meaning of the Death of God*. New York: Random House, 1967. Various interpretations of "God is dead" theology.

PHILLIPS, D. Z., ed. *Religion and Understanding*. New York: Macmillan, 1967. Philosophical defenses of religious belief.

PIKE, N., ed. *God and Evil*. Englewood Cliffs, New Jersey: Prentice-Hall, 1964. Essays debating the problem of evil.

PLANTINGS, A., ed. *The Ontological Argument*. Garden City, New York: Anchor, 1965. Classical and modern essays on the ontological argument.

RAMANUJA. *The Vedânta-Sûtras*, pp. 161–174. Translated by George Thibaut. Delhi, India: Motilal Banarsidass, 1966.

ROSS, J. F. *Philosophical Theology*. Indianapolis, Indiana: Bobbs-Merrill, 1960. A sophisticated defense of the necessary-being argument.

SHEED, F. *Theology and Sanity*. New York: Sheed and Ward, 1964. A defense of the theology of St. Thomas Aquinas.

SMART, N. *Doctrine and Argument in Indian Philosophy*. London: Allen & Unwin, 1969. Expositions of Hindu and Buddhist theology.

VOLTAIRE, F. *Philosophical Dictionary*. Translated by P. Gay. New York: Basic Books, 1962. Commonsense arguments for Deism.

Chapter 2

Reality: Is There a Higher Realm?

In order to survive in this world and to be accepted as sane, we must learn quite early in life to distinguish our fantasies from reality. Most of us undergo this gradual and sometimes painful educational process without noticeable difficulty. We come to realize that fairies and goblins, dream events and fantasies are neither to be relied upon nor feared but are to be set aside as "unreal," unlike the objects and events in everyday life. We soon take it for granted that we know what is real and what is unreal, so long as others do not seriously question our judgment. When, therefore, we find philosophers who engage in speculative metaphysics questioning the reality of what we have learned, we are likely to be disturbed by their doubts. They tell us that the real things of everyday life stand to certain higher or deeper or more ultimate things somewhat as our fantasies stand to commonsense facts. Should we be persuaded to unravel the protective garment of the reality we have so carefully woven and expose ourselves to new doubts about what is actual and what appearance? Why isn't the ordinary reality that regularly satisfies our expectations and that we share in common with our neighbors not good enough for these starry-eyed metaphysicians? What are they looking for that is missing from our familiar picture of the world?

Some people tell us that there is a better world awaiting us, where we will be immeasurably happier than in this world because we will have absolute power to shape things to our purposes. If only we open the right "door," they contend, we will find and enter that world.

Some maintain that we can accomplish this feat by means of hallucinogenic drugs, others offer a regimen of exercise and meditation, still others advise us to undo the learning process we went through from infancy to maturity and return to the unspoiled experience of infancy. The philosophers whom we shall study in this chapter advise us to think hard and apply rigorously the intellectual standards that already guide our judgments to a considerable degree.

Still, it is easy to see why metaphysical speculation by such philosophers gets confused in the popular mind with all sorts of claims to occult magical powers. Both the occultist and the metaphysical philosopher assure us that our commonsense distinctions between the real and unreal are false. Both maintain that there is a better world or higher reality that is accessible to us. In this sense, both appear to be mystics.

But there are more disimilarities than likenesses between the two. The occultist tells us to abandon our hard-won practical and scientific methods of reasoning and to restore our infantile capacity for wishful thinking and self-delusion. He or she believes that the only way to the better world is to escape from the confines of the overintellectualized world of adulthood and recapture the delights of childlike gratification. The methods employed involve abandoning the standards of precise description, logical consistency, and explanatory simplicity that guide us in practical life.

The rational metaphysician, on the other hand, attempts to steer us in the opposite direction. He or she insists that if we apply our intellectual standards more rigorously than ever, we shall find that commonsense reality fails to satisfy these standards adequately. But, if we push on resolutely in the same direction, searching for what can be described with absolute precision, consistency, and explanatory simplicity, we shall find something still more reliable than the objects of practical life—a higher reality.

Even if the rational metaphysician is incorrect in the notion that a higher reality can be found, the quest can have some value in teaching us to be less satisfied with what we cannot reliably prove. We must be on our guard, however, that in questioning the rational standards of evidence, we do not accept a delusory surrogate for the world of everyday experience.

We begin our study with a fanciful story by the Nobel Prize-winning South American novelist and poet, Jorge Luis Borges. "Tlön, Uqbar, Orbis Tertius" describes a distant planet, Tlön, where the relation between appearance and reality is the opposite of what we usually take it to be. The inhabitants of Tlön are idealists who believe that space and matter are illusory appearances and that only transient states of mind really exist. Their language which contains mostly verbs and adjectives and very few nouns, reflects this metaphysical view. they consider it logically puzzling that coins seem to remain where they fall rather than just disappearing like any thoughts.

Borges, a witty and learned satirist of modern culture, is not serious in his detailed descriptions of this bizarre world, but he does mean to suggest that our insistence on the reality of what we happen to find most convenient to believe is a local prejudice as arbitrary as the Tlön insistence that coins cannot continue to exist when unperceived. His own view would seem to be a kind of metaphysical relativism, which holds that there is no objective reality at all, or else that there are as many realities as there are coherent systems of belief. While this viewpoint fosters intellectual tolerance, it might be hard to maintain consistently in practice without losing one's sanity. For example, what would banking or fire-department procedures be like if objects were not considered to exist when unseen? Nevertheless, speculative views such as this challenge us to produce the rational grounds for our own distinctions between appearance and reality.

It may be instructive to compare Borges's purely intellectual experiment in thought, which parodies the speculations of the rational metaphysicians we shall subsequently consider, with the intensely serious inversion of the commonsense view of fantasy and reality explored by Dr. Carlos Castaneda in his widely read series of books on Yaqui sorcery. In *The Confessions of Don Juan, A Separate Reality, Journey to Ixtlan,* and *Tales of Power,* Castaneda describes his extraordinary experiences, at first under the influence of hallucinogenic drugs, in undergoing preliminary training to achieve the magical powers of a sorcerer by penetrating to a higher realm called the *nagual.* In *Tales of Power* Castaneda is approaching mastery and is introduced by his mentor, Don Juan, to the higher realm. The climactic scene in a restaurant, where Don Juan for the first time gives a general characterization of the nature of sorcery, is a literary gem that combines vividly realistic and commonplace detail with an abstract discussion of metaphysics. Whether one believes Don Juan's claims or not, one can appreciate the stark and poignant contrast Castaneda draws between the way Don Juan appears to a conventional outsider and the way he appears to his reverential disciple. Don Juan, described as a small, frail, uncultivated Mexican Indian, overdressed in his holiday suit, unable to command even minimum respect from the waiter, nevertheless exercises hypnotic power over a well-educated anthropologist, and dismisses the abstruse doctrines of Western metaphysics and theology as superficial compared to his own intuitive insight into the higher reality of the *nagual:*

"This is my *tonal*," Don Juan said, rubbing his hands on his chest.

"Your suit?"

"No. My person." . . . He pounded his chest and his thighs and the side of his ribs.

He explained that every human being has two sides, two separate entities, two counterparts which became operative at the moment of birth; one was called the *tonal* and the other the *"nagual."*

"The *tonal* is an island," he explained. "The best way of describing it is to say that the *tonal* is this." He ran his hand over the table top.

". . . This island is, in fact, the world."

". . . What then is the *nagual?*"

". . . The *nagual* is the part of us for which there is no description— no words, no names, no feelings, no knowledge."

"Would you say that the *nagual* is the mind?"

"No. The mind is an item on the table. . . . Let's say that the mind is the chili sauce."

"Is the *nagual* the soul?"

"No. The soul is also on the table. Let's say that the soul is the ashtray."

"Is the *nagual* the supreme being, the Almighty God?" I asked.

"No. God is also on the table. Let's say that God is the tablecloth."

Castaneda is convinced of this higher reality, after years of training. But our own studies of more rational systems of metaphysics may help us to decide whether his procedure is a way to truth or to self-delusion.

The philosophers explored in this chapter also claim to reveal to us a higher reality, but they are not, like the sorcerer, interested in achieving omnipotence by the revelation. What they want is to be able to understand the world in an intellectually satisfactory way. By applying more rigorously than most people the intellectual standards implicit in our everyday reasoning, they bring to our attention certain baffling paradoxes, inconsistencies, and ambiguities of which most of us are unaware. Far from attempting to achieve and provide others with magical powers over their environment, they are most likely to despair of ever controlling or even adequately understanding the world. Goethe's character Faust complains that he has long studied philosophy and yet is no wiser or happier than he was before. He summons the devil to provide him with the power he mistakenly sought from philosophy. Thus, Faust confuses metaphysics with the practice of magic.

We have chosen, for our first philosophical selection in this chapter, a passage from the writings of Nagarjuna, a Buddhist sage of the second century A.D. Eastern mystical thought has some features in common with occultism and some features in common with Western metaphysics; it may therefore serve us as a bridge between the two. Like the occultist, Nagarjuna seeks to achieve a state of psychic well-being and self-mastery, which the Buddhists call "nirvana," by penetrating beyond the limits of ordinary experience and conventional modes of thought. But like the rational metaphysician, he insists on strict conformity to the standards of precise language and consistent reasoning. His arguments against the reality of the objects of ordinary experience and scientific reasoning are designed to show that the ecstatic state of nirvana achieved through the Buddhist practice of meditation is the only true reality.

Nagarjuna tries to prove that our most confident beliefs about the world are so full of inconsistencies and paradoxes that the world they describe cannot possibly exist. His method of establishing this radical claim is to uncover certain logical difficulties in such fundamental concepts as that of causality, in an attempt to demonstrate that all relations, except that of identity, are unreal. If identity is the only relation that can exist between things, then it follows that each individual thing is the same as everything else; in brief, all things are one. This is the fundamental thesis of the mystical tradition, both Oriental and Western. Elsewhere in his writings, Nagarjuna calls this solitary reality the "void" because all characterization of it would imply differences between things and would thus fail to capture its true nature; this reality can only be described negatively, by denying that any particular features belong to it. When the void becomes known to us through meditation, we achieve the ecstatic state of nirvana. We need not here concern ourselves with the truth of Nagarjuna's positive claims about the transcendent value of nirvana, anymore than with the truth of Castaneda's claims about the powers of sorcery. What is of interest to us in our study of rational metaphysics and its quest for ultimate reality is Nagarjuna's attack on the reality of relations, most prominently the relation of causality. He argues that relations are unreal on the ground that they fail to satisfy the standards of precision and consistency.

Most of our knowledge of the world extends beyond what we immediately experience and rests upon our inferences from effects to causes or from causes to effects. Nagarjuna argues that the concept of causality is hopelessly paradoxical. If the cause must precede the effect, as we usually assume, then it cannot exist when the effect exists. But in that case it cannot be the real cause, for the real cause must be present to produce the effect. One might try to avoid the thrust of this argument by holding, as some of Nagarjuna's predecessors did, that cause and effect are identical. But this would imply that a thing produces itself, which he considered to be an absurdity.

According to Nagarjuna, all discourse about production or causation is absurd because, if the alleged effect already exists, then it does not have to be produced; conversely, if it must be produced, then it does not yet exist, and we are back to the earlier difficulty. Thus, if cause and effect are in any way separate in time or space, then there is no connection between them by means of which one can directly affect the other.

Similar arguments have been directed against the general concept of relation. In *The Encyclopedia of Philosophy,* Professor Ninian Smart has summarized them as follows: "Relation is a contradictory concept since a real relation between entities implies that they have an inner connection (and so are in a sense identical). But it also implies that there are two terms, and thus the entities have to be different."

What Nagarjuna seems to have had in mind, as Smart interprets him, is something very similar to certain modern theories of causality. According to such theories a truly causal relation, as distinct from an accidental regularity, involves some part of the cause being transferred to the effect, such as one billiard ball transferring its motion to another, or a warm object transferring its heat to a cold object. In this sense, it might be held that the cause is partially identical with, but partly different from, the effect.

If this is what Nagarjuna was driving at, it may not be difficult to defend causality and other relations against his attack, which seems to confuse part with whole. It seems reasonable to suggest that part of a complex causal process is transferred to another complex process called the effect and is thus identical with part of it, but that the entire cause is not identical with the entire effect. A similar defense could be made for relations in general, along the line that the entities related can have something in common without having everything in common, and thus without actually being identical to each other, but this solution has yet to be worked out.

Nagarjuna's twofold emphasis (1) on logical consistency as an intellectual standard to be respected and (2) on the practical goal of self-discipline, culminating in mystical ecstasy, places him midway between the practitioner of occult sorcery and the rational metaphysician. He employs logic to test the consistency of our commonsense beliefs. When they fail his tests, he rejects them in favor of mystical experience. Whether or not we follow him toward nirvana, he calls to our attention the fact that we are not as clear as we should be about the logic of our fundamental concepts, and that our general beliefs about the world may stand in need of radical revision.

Zeno of Elea, a Greek philosopher of the fifth century B.C., disclosed similar difficulties in our common beliefs in order to give support to the mysticism of his teacher, Parmenides. Parmenides, like Nagarjuna, believed that reality is one undifferentiated unity. He called knowledge of this higher reality the "Way of Truth," as contrasted with everyday knowledge, which he did not reject but relegated to the inferior level of the "Way of Opinion." Zeno devoted himself to refuting critics of Parmenides with arguments designed to show that our beliefs in plurality and change lead to contradictions. In constructing these arguments he formulated paradoxes that philosophers have been engaged in trying to resolve ever since. Although only small fragments of Zeno's own writings have been preserved, and most of what we know of Zeno is derived from Aristotle's summaries, it appears likely that he was less concerned than Nagarjuna with the religious significance of a higher reality, and more interested in bringing to light problems of logical analysis. We have reprinted W. C. Guthrie's lucid accounts both of Zeno's paradoxes of motion and of Aristotle's proposed solutions to them. More sophisticated solutions than those of Aristotle, but along the same basic lines, have been advanced in modern times since the invention of the differential calculus and the subsequent development of general mathematical analysis.

Zeno's paradoxes purport to show that motion is unreal on the ground that the concept of motion involves inescapable contradictions. If Zeno is correct, then all change is illusory, since motion seems to be involved in all processes of change. If change is illusory, then our commonsense beliefs about the world stand as delusory beliefs. The higher reality to which Zeno and his teacher Parmenides aspired was a reality that can be known and described with absolute verbal precision and logical consistency. In insisting on these rigorous standards of knowledge, they spurred the development of logical theory as well as of rational metaphysics.

The theory of forms developed by Plato in the fourth and fifth centuries B.C. was the culmination of the metaphysical search for ultimate reality in ancient Greek thought. Earlier Greek thinkers had looked for an unchanging physical substance underlying the variety of nature. Thales suggesting it was water, Anaximenes air, Heraclitus fire, and Empedocles proposed four basic elements—air, water, fire, and earth. Parmenides and Zeno had criticized these materialist theories as naive and logically inconsistent since they assumed that there is something that both changes and yet remains the same. They argued that what is ultimately real cannot be visible or tangible, because whatever is subject to sense perception undergoes change and, for the reasons we have already considered, cannot be described with precision and consistency. Plato appreciated equally the contributions to natural science of the early materialists and the recognition of the demands of logic of Parmenides and Zeno. He did not agree with the latter that nothing at all can be known and described with demonstrable certainty because he thought he had found such rational certainty in mathematics, and he believed, following his teacher, Socrates, that equal certainty could eventually be achieved in ethics.

In our selection from his dialogue *The Republic,* Plato offers an account of knowledge and its objects. He wanted to make clear the superiority of mathematics and ethics to everyday practical knowledge and even to natural science and to show that the reason for their superiority was the greater reality and perfection of their objects. Plato illustrates his distinctions with an unequally divided line. The lower segment, again divided into two unequal parts, represents our beliefs about shadows and images and our more reliable opinions about material objects. The smaller (because inferior) division represents fantasy and art, both of which, he maintained, provide us with beliefs about mere shadows and images of things. The second division represents practical knowledge and the rudimentary natural science of his time. Their objects are more real than shadows and images but less real than the objects of the higher main segment of the line, which represent knowledge of mathematical and ethical forms. Material objects, he suggested, are imperfect "copies" of these forms, somewhat as pictures and images are imperfect copies of material objects. The realm of forms, culminating in the form of "the Good," is the higher reality sought by his predecessors.

Parmenide's distinction between the Way of Truth and the Way of Opinion is echoed in this passage of Plato; the form of the Good, from which all other forms stem, retains some resemblance to the mystical One that Parmenides and the Buddhists postulated. But Plato's account has the great advantage of providing for a plurality of real things, which his predecesors denied. It also affords us some degree of understanding of the relation between ultimate reality and the objects of everyday experience. While he did not make this relation clear enough even by his own standards, and later criticized it mercilessly in his dialogue *Parmenides,* he at least worked out a fairly well-articulated explanation of why we naturally tend to be satisfied with our inadequate knowledge of objects of experience and why we get into logical difficulties if we fail to press onward to the more rigorous knowledge of forms. The famous analogy of the cave in the second part of our selection portrays in a vivid manner the metaphysical theory that was more abstractly, but also more literally and precisely formulated in the passage on the divided line.

Although Plato succeeded in showing the rigorous precision and consistency of mathematics, he failed to demonstrate how ethics can become an equally rigorous science. By deliberately rejecting the practical concern that motivates both the person in his "cave" and the practitioner of the occult—namely, the concern for increasing one's control over one's environment—he also failed to give a proper place to the role of science. Writing at a time when natural science was in its infancy, Plato had little interest in the enormous technological power over nature that science was potentially capable of giving us—a power spectacularly realized in modern times.

If Plato had been aware of this potentiality he might have argued, as some modern Platonists have done, that the advance of scientific knowledge is made possible mainly by the application of mathematical laws to the description of nature, so that where science increases its insight into reality it does so by redescribing reality in mathematical terms. But his allegory of the cave suggests that he might not have welcomed the application of mathematics to experimental physics and chemistry as a road upward toward reality. Instead, he might have criticized applied mathematics as a debasement of pure mathematics, too concerned with practical accomplishments and too little concerned with precision and consistency.

Modern anti-Platonists have argued that pure mathematical relations are not real objects of knowledge but constructions of the mind, providing formal rules governing symbolic operations rather than true descriptions of real objects or events. It is difficult for us to take pure mathematics as the picture of ultimate reality merely on the ground that it satisfies rigorous intellectual standards. The objects of our experience, the things that we see and touch and fear and enjoy, have too strong a claim on our interest and our belief to be set aside as mere shadowy copies of mathematical laws.

George Berkeley, an eighteenth-century Irish bishop and philosopher, led the rebellion of commonsense practicality against the excessive intellectualism of the metaphysical tradition. He attacked not Plato, but the dualistic metaphysics of René Descartes and John Locke that had been inspired by the success of modern physics. However, the main feature of metaphysical dualism that Berkeley singled out for his assault was a carryover from Plato's doctrine of forms—the claim that reality consists of mathematically describable entities, such as absolute space, absolute time, and material substance, entities that are known through abstract intuition rather than through perceptual experience. Berkeley insisted on returning to the commonsense reliance on what we can see, taste, and touch as the fundamental criterion of what is real. He recognized, however, that our intellectual standards of precision and coherence must be satisfied as well. These considerations led him to develop what is called an "empiricist" theory of knowledge, which bases all knowledge on perception, and an "idealist" theory of reality, which identifies the objects of perception as mental states. Subsequent philosophers accepted his empiricism but rejected his idealism.

The first of Berkeley's three *Dialogues Between Hylas and Philonous,* from which our selection is taken, unleashes an attack on any view that places reality beyond the limits of sense perception. Its immediate target is Locke's claim that the measurable properties studied by physicists, such as weight, size, and velocity, together with the "material substance" which underlies these properties, are objects that make up the so-called external world. If that is what the external world is supposed to be, Berkeley argues, then there simply is no external world. Reality is within the mind.

Berkeley's attack proceeds in three main stages: (1) arguments to prove that "secondary" qualities, the qualities that we directly feel, taste, see, and smell, are states of mind that he calls "sensations"; (2) arguments to prove that the measurable properties studied by physics, which Locke called "primary," are just as mental and subjective as secondary qualities; and (3) arguments to prove that the concepts of pure matter, space, time, and motion are self-contradictory, so that if these nonentities are all that is left of what is supposed to exist outside the mind, then reality is to be found within.

Berkeley's first battery of arguments consists of examples of how our judgments of secondary qualities such as color, warmth, tastes, odors, and pleasure and pain vary with conditions of observation. These examples succeed in demonstrating that such qualities involve relations between the object and the observer. But does it follow that they are subjective as well as relative, in the sense that they exist only in the mind of the person experiencing them? This, even if true, remains to be shown. His arguments to prove that primary qualities such as size, figure, and motion are, like secondary qualities, relative to a person's experience of them seem somewhat less convincing. Granted that we cannot measure primary qualities without employing clues involving the secondary qualities—that, for example, we cannot measure length without observing the color of both the measuring tape and the object—it does not clearly follow that the length we measure is identical with our procedure for measuring it.

Berkeley's arguments against the coherence and meaningfulness of the concepts of physical (or "real") time, space, motion, and substance similarly employ the crucial principle that a concept is intelligible only if it represents what can be perceived or at least visualized. His chief argument against material substance is that it is a contradiction to claim that we can conceive of something as existing unperceived. But this seems to rely on making *con*ceiving and *per*ceiving equivalent, which again stands in need of proof.

These arguments against materialist and dualist metaphysics, while perhaps not as conclusive as Berkeley believed, are at least plausible challenges to any theory that places reality outside the limits of direct perception. Up to this point it would seem as if Berkeley's protagonist, Philonous, is merely vindicating, as Philonous himself insists, the commonsense belief that reality is what we perceive (or, as we might say, "seeing is believing"). However, Berkeley does not stop there but goes on to explain that what exists in only one person's mind is a figment of the imagination, but what exists in reality is implanted in the minds of all by God. He defines mind as an immaterial substance that actively creates illusory ideas and that passively receives and stores true ideas from the mind of God, which he considers the ultimate source of all reality.

This bizarre explanation of the continued existence of things when we are not perceiving them (due not to their being objective properties of matter but to their presence in the mind of God), has been parodied by Ronald Knox in a notorious limerick:

> There was a young man who said "God
> Must think it exceedingly odd
>   If he finds that this tree
>   Continues to be
> When there's no one about in the Quad."
>
>   (Reply)
>
> Dear Sir:
> Your astonishment's odd.
> *I* am always about in the Quad
>   And that's why the tree
>   Continues to be,
> Since observed by
>
> Yours faithfully,
God

Berkeley's concept of mind as spiritual substance exposes him to the same objections that he so effectively raised against material substance, in particular, the objection that spiritual substance is unobservable and even unimaginable. Beginning with David Hume, empiricists have considered such objections to be conclusive and have therefore rejected Berkeley's "higher reality" of the divine mind while accepting his vindication of the "lower reality" of the familiar objects of sense experience.

Hugh Elliot, a British philosopher of the late nineteenth and early twentieth centuries, applauded Berkeley's attack on the metaphysical concept of substance and agreed with Berkeley's empiricist principle that all knowledge depends upon the senses. Nevertheless, Elliot claimed that scientific philosophy, unlike speculative metaphysics, can inform us about a deeper reality consisting of unobservable processes that underlie and explain the sense data (color, weight, etc.) that we perceive directly. He maintained that natural science, in successfully explaining an enormous variety of our experiences in terms of a few fundamental laws, has provided philosophy with a sound basis for answering the question that speculative metaphysics has tried in vain to answer: What is ultimately real? The correct answer, Elliot argued, is that matter and energy and their fundamental properties such as mass, position, and velocity constitute reality because they explain everything else and enable us to predict and control events.

In the selection reprinted here from his book, *Modern Science and Materialism,* Elliot defines what has become known as "scientific materialism" in terms of three principles: (1) the uniformity of law, which holds that every event is explainable in terms of antecedent events according to laws; (2) the denial of teleology, which rules out purposive explanations (i.e., appeals to the divine causality) of natural events on the empiricist ground that purposes other than our own are unobservable and cannot be related to events by causal laws; and (3) materialistic "monism," which rejects any substance other than mass-energy as unnecessary for scientific explanation. According to Elliot, science has made its most dramatic advances when it has rejected hypotheses about invisible minds and purposes. This has even occurred, he maintains, in the field of psychology, where successful explanation of behavior has only recently been made possible by the identification of mind with the activity of the central nervous system.

Elliot makes an extremely plausible case for the view that there is indeed a higher or more ultimate reality than what we find in everyday life, and that the most advanced theories of science are the long-sought door to that reality. His view has the great merit of satisfying both the intellectual standards insisted on by speculative metaphysics and the pragmatic standards of practitioners of the occult. He tells us, in effect, and with considerable truth, that modern scientists are both successful metaphysicians and successful sorcerers because their theories both explain our experience precisely and coherently and also increase our power over nature.

Is this case for scientific materialism conclusive? Is the problem of reality solved once and for all? It would be rash to jump to that conclusion. What the latest scientific theories tell us can hardly be the last word on what is real since theories are constantly being revised and are sometimes replaced by new theories. The very Newtonian system of physics that Elliot took to be the ultimate truth about reality has been replaced by relativity theory and quantum mechanics. The American pragmatist C. S. Pierce defined reality as the ideal limit toward which scientific inquiry tends to move by a self-corrective process. If reality is determined by what science tells us, then reality must be what science *will* tell us at some infinitely distant future time. It cannot be what science *now* tells us, on pain of lapsing into the mistakes of past speculative metaphysics once again.

If we are really to avoid such mistakes, then perhaps we should stop thinking and talking about reality in general and concern ourselves only with explanations of specific types of phenomena, which is what scientists do. Yet Elliot, who recommends such a course, himself engages in generalities about reality by insisting that matter and its physical properties are the fundamental reality. Although he holds that his assertions are grounded in science, he recognizes that they are philosophical, not scientific, assertions. He seems to shrink from outright admission that they are *metaphysical* but we need not be as finicky as he. Once we recognize that materialism is one metaphysical theory among others, it becomes clear that the issue of what is ultimately real remains undecided.

TLÖN, UQBAR, ORBIS TERTIUS

Jorge L. Borges

Some limited and waning memory of Herbert Ashe, an engineer of the southern railways, persists in the hotel at Adrogué, amongst the effusive honeysuckles and in the illusory depths of the mirrors. In his lifetime, he suffered from unreality, as do so many Englishmen; once dead, he is not even the ghost he was then. He was tall and listless and his tired rectangular beard had once been red. I understand he was a widower, without children. Every few years he would go to England, to visit (I judge from some photographs he showed us) a sundial and a few oaks. He and my father had entered into one of those close (the adjective is excessive) English friendships that begin by excluding confidences and very soon dispense with dialogue. They used to carry out an exchange of books and newspapers and engage in taciturn chess games . . . I remember him in the hotel corridor, with a mathematics book in his hand, sometimes looking at the irrecoverable colors of the sky. One afternoon, we spoke of the duodecimal system of numbering (in which twelve is written as 10). Ashe said that he was converting some kind of tables from the duodecimal to the sexagesimal system (in which sixty is written as 10). He added that the task had been entrusted to him by a Norwegian, in Rio Grande do Sul. We had known him for eight years and he had never mentioned his sojourn in that region . . . We talked of country life, of the *capangas,* of the Brazilian etymology of the word *gaucho* (which some old Uruguayans still pronounce *gaúcho*) and nothing more was said—may God forgive me— of duodecimal functions. In September of 1937 (we were not at the hotel), Herbert Ashe died of a ruptured aneurysm. A few days before, he had received a sealed and certified package from Brazil. It was a book in large octavo. Ashe left it at the bar, where—months later—I found it. I began to leaf through it and experienced an astonished and airy feeling of vertigo which I shall not describe, for this is not the story of my emotions but of Uqbar and Tlön and Orbis Tertius. On one of the nights of Islam called the Night of Nights, the secret doors of heaven open wide and the water in the jars becomes sweeter; if those doors opened, I would not feel what I felt that afternoon. The book was written in English and contained 1001 pages. On the yellow leather back I read these curious words which were repeated on the title page: *A First Encyclopaedia of Tlön. Vol. XI. Hlaer to Jangr.* There was no indication of date or place. On the first page and on a leaf of silk paper that covered one of the color plates there was stamped a blue oval with this inscription: *Orbis Tertius.* Two years before I had discovered, in a volume of a certain pirated encyclopedia, a superficial description of a nonexistent country; now chance afforded me something more precious and arduous. Now I held in my hands a vast methodical fragment of an unknown planet's entire history, with its architecture and its playing cards, with the dread of its mythologies and the murmur of its languages, with its emperors and its seas, with its minerals and its birds and its fish, with its algebra and its fire, with its theological and metaphysical controversy. And all of it articulated, coherent, with no visible doctrinal intent or tone of parody.

In the "Eleventh Volume" which I have mentioned, there are allusions to preceding and succeeding volumes. In an article in the *N. R. F.* which is now classic, Néstor Ibarra has denied the existence of those companion volumes; Ezequiel Martínez Estrada and Drieu La Rochelle have refuted that doubt, perhaps victoriously. The fact is that up to now the most diligent inquiries have been fruitless. In vain we have upended the libraries of the two Americas and of Europe. Alfonso Reyes, tired of these subordinate sleuthing procedures, proposes that we should all undertake the task of reconstructing the many and weighty tomes that are lacking: *ex ungue leonem.* He calculates, half in earnest and half jokingly, that a generation of *tlönistas* should be sufficient. This venturesome computation brings us back to the fundamental problem: Who are the inventors of Tlön? The plural is inevitable, because the hypothesis of a lone inventor—an infinite Leibniz laboring away darkly and modestly—has been unanimously discounted. It is conjectured that this brave new world is the work of a secret society of astronomers, biologists, engineers, metaphysicians, poets, chemists, algebraists, moralists, painters, geometers . . . directed by an obscure man of genius. Individuals mastering these diverse disciplines are abundant, but not so those capable of inventiveness and less so those capable of subordinating that inventiveness to a rigorous and systematic plan. This plan is so vast that each writer's contribution is infinitesimal. At first it was believed that Tlön was a mere chaos, an irresponsible license of the imagination; now it is known that it is a cosmos and that the intimate laws which govern it have been formulated, at least provisionally. Let it suffice for me to recall that the apparent contradictions of the Eleventh Volume are the fundamental basis for the proof that the other volumes exist, so lucid and exact is the order observed in it. The popular magazines, with pardonable excess, have spread news of the zoology and topography of Tlön; I think its transparent tigers and towers of blood perhaps do not merit the continued attention of *all* men. I shall venture to request a few minutes to expound its concept of the universe.

Hume noted for all time that Berkeley's arguments did not admit the slightest refutation nor did they cause the slightest conviction. This dictum is entirely correct in its application to the earth, but entirely false in Tlön. The nations of this planet are congenitally idealist. Their language and the derivations of their language—religion, letters, metaphysics—all presuppose idealism. The world for them is not a concourse of objects in space; it is a heterogeneous series of independent acts. It is successive and temporal, not spatial. There are no nouns in Tlön's conjectural *Ursprache,* from which the "present" languages and the dialects are derived: there are impersonal verbs, modified by monosyllabic suffixes (or prefixes) with an adverbial value. For example: there is no word corresponding to the word "moon," but there is a verb which in English would be "to moon" or "to moonate." "The moon rose above the river" is *hlör u fang axaxaxas mlö,* or literally: "upward behind the onstreaming it mooned."

The preceding applies to the languages of the southern hemisphere. In those of the northern hemisphere (on whose *Ursprache* there is very little data in the Eleventh Volume) the prime unit is not the verb, but the monosyllabic adjective. The noun is formed by an accumulation of adjectives. They do not say "moon," but rather "round airy-light on dark" or "pale-orange-of-the-sky" or any other such combination. In the example selected the mass of adjectives refers to a real object, but this is purely fortuitous. The literature of this hemisphere (like Meinong's subsistent world) abounds in ideal objects, which are convoked and dissolved in a moment, according to poetic needs. At times they are determined by mere simultaneity. There are objects composed of two terms, one of visual and another of auditory character: the color of the rising sun and the faraway cry of a bird. There are objects of many terms: the sun and the water on a swimmer's chest, the vague tremulous rose color we see with our eyes closed, the sensation of being carried along by a river and also by sleep. These second-dgree objects can be combined with others; through the use of certain abbreviations, the process is practically infinite. There are famous poems made up of one enormous word. This word forms a *poetic object* created by the author. The fact that no one believes in the reality of nouns paradoxically causes their number to be unending. The languages of Tlön's northern hemisphere contain all the nouns of the Indo-European languages—and many others as well.

It is no exaggeration to state that the classic culture of Tlön comprises only one discipline: psychology. All others are subordinated to it. I have said that the men of this planet conceive the universe as a series of mental processes which do not develop in space but successively in time. Spinoza ascribes to his inexhaustible divinity the attributes of extension and thought; no one in Tlön would understand the juxtaposition of the first (which is typical only of certain states) and the second—which is a perfect synonym of the cosmos. In other words, they do not conceive that the spatial persists in time. The perception of a cloud of smoke on the horizon and then of the burning field and then of the half-extinguished cigarette that produced the blaze is considered an example of association of ideas.

This monism or complete idealism invalidates all science. If we explain (or judge) a fact, we connect it with another; such linking, in Tlön, is a later state of the subject which cannot affect or illuminate the previous state. Every mental state is irreducible: the mere fact of naming it—i.e., of classifying it—implies a falsification. From which it can be deduced that there are no sciences on Tlön, not even reasoning. The paradoxical truth is that they do exist, and in almost uncountable number. The same thing happens with philosophies as happens with nouns in the northern hemisphere. The fact that every philosophy is by definition a dialectical game, a *Philosophie des Als Ob,* has caused them to multiply. There is an abundance of incredible systems of pleasing design or sensational type. The metaphysicians of Tlön do not seek for the truth or even for verisimilitude, but rather for the astounding. They judge that metaphysics is a branch of fantastic literature. They know that a system is nothing more than the subordination of all aspects of the universe to any one such aspect. Even the phrase "all aspects" is rejectable, for it supposes the impossible addition of the present and of all past moments. Neither is it licit to use the plural "past moments," since it supposes another impossible operation . . . One of the schools of Tlön goes so far as to negate time: it reasons that the present is indefinite, that the future has no reality other than as a present hope, that the past has no reality other than as a present memory. Another school declares that *all time* has already transpired and that our life is only the crepuscular and no doubt falsified and mutilated memory or reflection of an irrecoverable process. Another, that the history of the universe—

and in it our lives and the most tenuous detail of our lives—is the scripture produced by a subordinate god in order to communicate with a demon. Another, that the universe is comparable to those cryptographs in which not all the symbols are valid and that only what happens every three hundred nights is true. Another, that while we sleep here, we are awake elsewhere and that in this way every man is two men.

Amongst the doctrines of Tlön, none has merited the scandalous reception accorded to materialism. Some thinkers have formulated it with less clarity than fervor, as one might put forth a paradox. In order to facilitate the comprehension of this inconceivable thesis, a heresiarch of the eleventh century devised the sophism of the nine copper coins, whose scandalous renown is in Tlön equivalent to that of the Eleatic paradoxes. There are many versions of this "specious reasoning," which vary the number of coins and the number of discoveries; the following is the most common:

On Tuesday, X crosses a deserted road and loses nine copper coins. On Thursday, Y finds in the road four coins, somewhat rusted by Wednesday's rain. On Friday, Z discovers three coins in the road. On Friday morning, X finds two coins in the corridor of his house. The heresiarch would deduce from this story the reality—i.e., the continuity —of the nine coins which were recovered. *It is absurd* (he affirmed) *to imagine that four of the coins have not existed between Tuesday and Thursday, three between Tuesday and Friday afternoon, two between Tuesday and Friday morning. It is logical to think that they have existed —at least in some secret way, hidden from the comprehension of men— at every moment of those three periods.*

The language of Tlön resists the formulation of this paradox; most people did not even understand it. The defenders of common sense at first did no more than negate the veracity of the anecdote. They repeated that it was a verbal fallacy, based on the rash application of two neologisms not authorized by usage and alien to all rigorous thought: the verbs "find" and "lose," which beg the question, because they presuppose the identity of the first and of the last nine coins. They recalled that all nouns (man, coin, Thursday, Wednesday, rain) have only a metaphorical value. They denounced the treacherous circumstance "somewhat rusted by Wednesday's rain," which presupposes what is trying to be demonstrated: the persistence of the four coins from Tuesday to Thursday. They explained that *equality* is one thing and *identity* another, and formulated a kind of *reductio ad absurdum:* the hypothetical case of nine men who on nine successive nights suffer a severe pain. Would it not be ridiculous—they questioned—to pretend that this pain is one and the same? They said that the heresiarch was prompted only by the blasphemous intention of attributing the divine category of *being* to some simple coins and that at times he negated plurality and at other times did not. They argued: if equality implies identity, one would also have to admit that the nine coins are one.

Unbelievably, these refutations were not definitive. A hundred years after the problem was stated, a thinker no less brilliant than the heresiarch but of orthodox tradition formulated a very daring hypothesis. This happy conjecture affirmed that there is only one subject, that this indivisible subject is every being in the universe and that these beings are the organs and masks of the divinity. X is Y and is Z. Z discovers three coins because he remembers that X lost them; X finds two in the corridor because he remembers that the others have been found . . . The Eleventh Volume suggests that three prime reasons determined the complete victory of this idealist pantheism. The first, its repudiation of solipsism; the second, the possibility of preserving the psychological basis of the sciences; the third, the possibility of preserving the cult of the gods. Schopenhauer (the passionate and lucid Schopenhauer) formulates a very similar doctrine in the first volume of *Parerga und Paralipomena.*

The geometry of Tlön comprises two somewhat different disciplines: the visual and the tactile. The latter corresponds to our own geometry and is subordinated to the first. The basis of visual geometry is the surface, not the point. This geometry disregards parallel lines and declares that man in his movement modifies the forms which surround him. The basis of its arithmetic is the notion of indefinite numbers. They emphasize the importance of the concepts of greater and lesser, which our mathematicians symbolize as $>$ and $<$. They maintain that the operation of counting modifies quantities and converts them from indefinite into definite sums. The fact that several individuals who count the same quantity should obtain the same result is, for the psychologists, an example of association of ideas or of a good exercise of memory. We already know that in Tlön the subject of knowledge is one and eternal.

In literary practices the idea of a single subject is also all-powerful. It is uncommon for books to be signed. The concept of plagiarism does not exist: it has been established that all works are the creation of one author, who is atemporal and anonymous. The critics often invent authors: they select two dissimilar works—the *Tao Te Ching* and the *1001 Nights,* say—attribute them to the same writer and then determine most scrupulously the psychology of this interesting *homme de lettres* . . .

Their books are also different. Works of fiction contain a single plot, with all its imaginable permutations. Those of a philosophical nature invariably include both the thesis and the antithesis, the rigorous pro and con of a doctrine. A book which does not contain its counterbook is considered incomplete.

Centuries and centuries of idealism have not failed to influence reality. In the most ancient regions of Tlön, the duplication of lost objects is not infrequent. Two persons look for a pencil; the first finds it and says nothing; the second finds a second pencil, no less real, but closer to his expectations. These secondary objects are called *hrönir* and are, though awkward in form, somewhat longer. Until recently, the *hrönir* were the accidental products of distraction and forgetfulness. It seems unbelievable that their methodical production dates back scarcely a hundred years, but this is what the Eleventh Volume tells us. The first efforts were unsuccessful. However, the *modus operandi* merits description. The director of one of the state prisons told his inmates that there were certain tombs in an ancient river bed and promised freedom to whoever might make an important discovery. During the months preceding the excavation the inmates were shown photographs of what they were to find. This first effort proved that expectation and anxiety can be inhibitory; a week's work with pick and shovel did not manage to unearth anything in the way of a *hrön* except a rusty wheel of a period posterior to the experiment. But this was kept in secret and the process was repeated later in four schools. In three of them the failure was almost complete; in the fourth (whose director died accidentally during the first excavations) the students unearthed—or produced—a gold mask, an archaic sword, two or three clay urns and the moldy and mutilated torso of a king whose chest bore an inscription which it has not yet been possible to decipher. Thus was discovered the unreliability of witnesses who knew of the experimental nature of the search . . . Mass investigations produce contradictory objects; now individual and almost improvised jobs are preferred. The methodical fabrication of *hrönir* (says the Eleventh Volume) has performed prodigious services for archaeologists. It has made possible the interrogation and even the modification of the past, which is now no less plastic and docile than the future. Curiously, the *hrönir* of second and third degree—the *hrönir* derived from another *hrön,* those derived from the *hrön* of a *hrön*—exaggerate the aberrations of the initial one; those of fifth degree are almost uniform; those of ninth degree become confused with those of the second; in those of the eleventh there is a purity of line not found in the original. The process of cyclical: the *hrön* of twelfth degree begins to fall off in quality. Stranger and more pure than any *hrön* is, at times, the *ur:* the object produced through suggestion, educed by hope. The great golden mask I have mentioned is an illustrious example.

Things become duplicated in Tlön; they also tend to become effaced and lose their details when they are forgotten. A classic example is the doorway which survived so long as it was visited by a beggar and disappeared at his death. At times some birds, a horse, have saved the ruins of an amphitheater.

Postscript (1947). I reproduce the preceding article just as it appeared in the *Anthology of Fantastic Literature* (1940), with no omission other than that of a few metaphors and a kind of sarcastic summary which now seems frivolous. So many things have happened since then . . . I shall do no more than recall them here.

In March of 1941 a letter written by Gunnar Erfjord was discovered in a book by Hinton which had belonged to Herbert Ashe. The envelope bore a cancellation from Ouro Preto; the letter completely elucidated the mystery of Tlön. Its text corroborated the hypotheses of Martínez Estrada. One night in Lucerne or in London, in the early seventeenth century, the splendid history has its beginning. A secret and benevolent society (amongst whose members were Dalgarno and later George Berkeley) arose to invent a country. Its vague initial program included "hermetic studies," philanthropy and the cabala. From this first period dates the curious book by Andreä. After a few years of secret conclaves and premature syntheses it was understood that one generation was not sufficient to give articulate form to a country. They resolved that each of the masters should elect a disciple who would continue his work. This hereditary arrangement prevailed; after an interval of two centuries the persecuted fraternity sprang up again in America. In 1824, in Memphis (Tennessee), one of its affiliates conferred with the ascetic millionaire Ezra Buckley. The latter, somewhat disdainfully, let him speak—and laughed at the plan's modest scope. He told the agent that in America it was absurd to invent a country and proposed the invention of a planet. To this gigantic idea he added another, a product of his nihilism: that of keeping the enormous enterprise secret. At that time the twenty volumes of the *Encyclopaedia Britannica* were circulating in the United States; Buckley suggested that a methodical encyclopedia of the imaginary planet be written. He was to leave them his mountains of gold, his navigable rivers, his pasture lands roamed by cattle and buffalo, his Negroes, his brothels and his dollars, on one condition: "The work will make no pact with the impostor Jesus Christ." Buckley did not believe in God, but he wanted to demonstrate to this nonexistent God that mortal man was capable of conceiving a world. Buckley was poisoned in Baton Rouge in 1828; in 1914 the society delivered to its collaborators, some three hundred in number, the last volume of the First Encyclopedia of Tlön. The edition was a secret one; its forty volumes (the vastest undertaking ever carried out by man) would be the basis for another more detailed edition, written not in English but in one of the languages of Tlön. This revision of an illusory world, was called, provisionally, *Orbis Tertius* and one of its modest demiurgi was Herbert Ashe, whether as an agent of Gunnar Erfjord or as an affiliate, I do not know. His having received a copy of the Eleventh Volume would seem to favor the latter assumption. But what about the others?

In 1942 events became more intense. I recall one of the first of these with particular clarity and it seems that I perceived then something of its premonitory character. It happened in an apartment on Laprida Street, facing a high and light balcony which looked out toward the sunset. Princess Faucigny Lucinge had received her silverware from Poitiers. From the vast depths of a box embellished with foreign stamps, delicate immobile objects emerged: silver from Utrecht and Paris covered with hard heraldic fauna, and a samovar. Amongst them—with the perceptible and tenuous tremor of a sleeping bird—a compass vibrated mysteriously. The Princess did not recognize it. Its blue needle longed for magnetic north; its metal case was concave in shape; the letters around its edge corresponded to one of the alphabets of Tlön. Such was the first intrusion of this fantastic world into the world of reality.

I am still troubled by a stroke of chance which made me the witness of the second intrusion as well. It happened some months later, at a country store owned by a Brazilian in Cuchilla Negra. Amorim and I were returning from Sant' Anna. The River Tacuarembó had flooded and we were obliged to sample (and endure) the proprietor's rudimentary hospitality. He provided us with some creaking cots in a large room cluttered with barrels and hides. We went to bed, but were kept from sleeping until dawn by the drunken ravings of an unseen neighbor, who intermingled inextricable insults with snatches of *milongas*—or rather with snatches of the same *milonga*. As might be supposed, we attributed this insistent uproar to the store owner's fiery cane liquor. By daybreak, the man was dead in the hallway. The roughness of his voice had deceived us: he was only a youth. In his delirium a few coins had fallen from his belt, along with a cone of bright metal, the size of a die. In vain a boy tried to pick up this cone. A man was scarcely able to raise it from the ground. I held it in my hand for a few minutes; I remember that its weight was intolerable and that after it was removed, the feeling of oppressiveness remained. I also remember the exact circle it pressed into my palm. This sensation of a very small and at the same time extremely heavy object produced a disagreeable impression of repugnance and fear. One of the local men suggested we throw it into the swollen river; Amorim acquired it for a few pesos. No one knew anything about the dead man, except that "he came from the border." These small, very heavy cones (made from a metal which is not of this world) are images of the divinity in certain regions of Tlön.

Here I bring the personal part of my narrative to a close. The rest is in the memory (if not in the hopes or fears) of all my readers. Let it suffice for me to recall or mention the following facts, with a mere brevity of words which the reflective recollection of all will enrich or amplify. Around 1944, a person doing research for the newspaper *The American* (of Nashville, Tennessee) brought to light in a Memphis library the forty volumes of the First Encyclopedia of Tlön. Even today there is a controversy over whether this discovery was accidental or whether it was permitted by the directors of the still nebulous *Orbis Tertius*. The latter is most likely. Some of the incredible aspects of the Eleventh Volume (for example, the multiplication of the *hrönir*) have been eliminated or attenuated in the Memphis copies; it is reasonable to imagine that these omissions follow the plan of exhibiting a world which is not too incompatible with the real world. The dissemination of objects from Tlön over different countries would complement this plan . . . The fact is that the international press infinitely proclaimed the "find." Manuals, anthologies, summaries, literal versions, authorized re-editions and pirated editions of the Greatest Work of Man flooded and still flood the earth. Almost immediately, reality yielded on more than one account. The truth is that it longed to yield. Ten years ago any symmetry with a semblance of order—dialectical materialism, anti-Semitism, Nazism—was sufficient to entrance the minds of men. How could one do other than submit to Tlön, to the minute and vast evidence of an orderly planet? It is useless to answer that reality is also orderly. Perhaps it is, but in accordance with divine laws—I translate: inhuman laws—which we never quite grasp. Tlön is surely a labyrinth, but it is a labyrinth devised by men, a labyrinth destined to be deciphered by men.

The contact and the habit of Tlön have disintegrated this world. Enchanted by its rigor, humanity forgets over and again that it is a rigor of chess masters, not of angels. Already the schools have been invaded by the (conjectural) "primitive language" of Tlön; already the teaching of its harmonious history (filled with moving episodes) has wiped out the one which governed in my childhood; already a fictitious past occupies in our memories the place of another, a past of which we know nothing with certainty—not even that it is false. Numismatology, pharmacology and archaeology have been reformed. I understand that biology and mathematics also await their avatars . . . A scattered dynasty of solitary men has changed the face of the world. Their task continues. If our forecasts are not in error, a hundred years from now someone will discover the hundred volumes of the Second Encyclopedia of Tlön.

Then English and French and mere Spanish will disappear from the globe. The world will be Tlön. I pay no attention to all this and go on revising, in the still days at the Adrogué hotel, an uncertain Quevedian translation (which I do not intend to publish) of Browne's *Urn Burial*.

THE UNITY OF BEING

Nagarjuna

Thus it is that Buddha wished to put in a strong light [the principle of relativity, i.e.,] the fact that entities are produced only in the sense of being coordinated. He therefore maintains that they neither are produced at random, nor from a unique cause, nor from a variety of causes; he denies that they are identical with their causes, that they are different from them, or that they are both [partly identical and partly non-identical]. By this negative method he discloses the true relative character of all the relative entities [of everyday life]. This is relative existence or dependent origination, because nothing really new is produced. From the transcendentalist's point of view it is a condition where nothing disappears [nor something new appears], etc., and in which there is no motion. It is a condition characterized by the eight above-mentioned characteristics, "nothing disappears," etc. The whole of this treatise is intended by its author to prove that the condition of interdependence [or the principle of relativity] does not allow for something in the universe to disappear, or for something new to appear.

The principle of relativity [being the central law of all existence] can be characterized by an infinite number of finite characteristics, but only eight have been selected, because they are predominant in the sense of having given opportunity for discussion.

It is also called [nirvāṇa] the quiescence [or equalization] of all plurality, because when it is critically realized there is for the philosopher absolutely no differentiation of existence to which our words [and concepts] could be applied. That very essence of relativity is called [nirvāṇa] the quiescence of plurality, for which there are no words.

Thoughts and feelings do not arise in this [undifferentiated whole], there is no subject and no object of knowledge, there is [consequently] no turmoil like birth, old age, and death, there is eternal bliss. . . .

FROM *The Conception of Buddhist Nirvana,* translated by Th. Stcherbatsky. Published by the Academy of Sciences of the U.S.S.R.

DEDICATION

The Perfect Buddha,
The foremost of all Teachers I salute.
He has proclaimed
The principle of [universal] relativity,
'Tis like blissful [*nirvāṇa*],
Quiescence of plurality.
There nothing disappears,
Nor anything appears;
Nothing has an end,
Nor is anything eternal;
Nothing is identical [with itself],
Nor is there anything differentiated;
Nothing moves,
Neither hither nor thither.

I.   There absolutely are no things,
Nowhere and none, that arise [anew],
Neither out of themselves, nor out of non-self,
Nor out of both, nor at random.

II.   Four can be the conditions
[Of everything produced],
Its cause, its object, its foregoing moment,
Its most decisive factor.

III.   In these conditions we can find
No self-existence of the entities.
Where self-existence is deficient,
Relational existence also lacks.

IV.   No energies in causes,
Nor energies outside them.
No causes without energies,
Nor causes that possess them.

V.   Let those facts be causes
With whom coordinated other facts arise.
Non-causes will they be,
So far the other facts have not arisen.

VI.   Neither non-*ens* nor *ens*
Can have a cause.
If non-*ens*, whose the cause?
If *ens*, what for the cause?

VII. Neither an *ens* nor a non-*ens*,
      Nor any *ens*-non-*ens*,
      No element is really turned out.
      How can we then assume
      The possibility of a producing cause?

VIII. A mental *ens* is reckoned as an element,
      Separately from its objective [counterpart].
      Now, if it [begins] by having no objective counterpart,
      How can it get one afterward?

IX.   If [separate] elements do not exist,
      Nor is it possible for them to disappear.
      The moment which immediately precedes
      Is thus impossible. And if 'tis gone,
      How can it be a cause?

X.   If entities are relative,
      They have no real existence.
      The [formula] "this being, that appears"
      Then loses every meaning.

XI.   Neither in any of the single causes
      Nor in all of them together
      Does the [supposed] result reside.
      How can you out of them extract
      What in them never did exist?

XII. Supposing from these causes does appear
      What never did exist in them,
      Out of non-causes, then,
      Why does it not appear?

XIII. The result is cause-possessor,
      But causes are not even self-possessors.
      How can result be cause-possessor,
      If of non-self-possessors it be a result?

XIV. There is, therefore, no cause-possessor,
      Nor is there an effect without a cause.
      If altogether no effect arises,
      [How can we then distinguish]
      Between the causes and non-causes?

I. If every thing is relative,
    No [real] origination, no [real] annihilation,
    How is *nirvāṇa*, then, conceived?
    Through what deliverance, through what annihilation?

II. Should every thing be real in substance,
    No [new] creation, no [new] destruction,
    How would *nirvāṇa*, then, be reached?
    Through what deliverance, through what annihilation?

III. What neither is released, nor is it ever reached,
    What neither is annihilation, nor is it eternality,
    What never disappears, nor has it been created,
    This is *nirvāṇa*. It escapes precision.

IV. *Nirvāṇa*, first of all, is not a kind of *ens*,
    It would then have decay and death.
    There altogether is no *ens*
    Which is not subject to decay and death.

V. If *nirvāṇa* is *ens*,
    It is produced by causes,
    Nowhere and none the entity exists
    Which would not be produced by causes.

VI. If *nirvāṇa* is *ens*,
    How can it lack substratum?
    There whatsoever is no *ens*
    Without any substratum.

VII. If *nirvāṇa* is not an *ens*,
    Will it be, then, a non-*ens*?
    Wherever there is found no *ens*,
    There neither is a [corresponding] non-*ens*.

VIII. Now, if *nirvāṇa* is a non-*ens*,
    How can it, then, be independent?
    For sure, an independent non-*ens*
    Is nowhere to be found.

IX. Coordinated here or caused are [separate things],
    We call this world phenomenal;
    But just the same is called *nirvāṇa*,
    When from causality abstracted.

x. The Buddha has declared
That *ens* and non-*ens* should be both rejected.
Neither as *ens* nor as a non-*ens*
Nirvāṇa therefore is conceived.

xi. If *nirvāṇa* were both *ens* and non-*ens,*
Final deliverance would be also both
Reality and unreality together.
This never could be possible!

xii. If *nirvāṇa* were both *ens* and non-*ens,*
Nirvāṇa could not be uncaused.
Indeed the *ens* and the non-*ens*
Are both dependent on causation.

xiii. How can *nirvāṇa* represent
An *ens* and a non-*ens* together?
Nirvāṇa is, indeed, uncaused;
Both *ens* and non-*ens* are productions.

xiv. How can *nirvāṇa* represent
[The place] of *ens* and of non-*ens* together,
As light and darkness [in one spot]
They cannot simultaneously be present.

xv. If it were clear, indeed,
What an *ens* means, and what a non-*ens,*
We could then understand the doctrine
About *nirvāṇa* being neither *ens* nor non-*ens.*

xvi. If *nirvāṇa* is neither *ens* nor non-*ens,*
No one can really understand
This doctrine which proclaims at once
Negation of them both together.

xvii. What is the Buddha after his *nirvāṇa?*
Does he exist or does he not exist,
Or both, or neither?
We never will conceive it!

xviii. What is the Buddha, then, at lifetime?
Does he exist, or does he not exist,
Or both, or neither?
We never will conceive it!

xix. There is no difference at all
Between *nirvāṇa* and *saṁsāra.*

There is no difference at all
Between *saṃsāra* and *nirvāṇa.*

XX. What makes the limit of *nirvāṇa*
Is also then the limit of *saṃsāra.*
Between the two we cannot find
The slightest shade of difference.

XXI. [Insoluble are antinomic] views
Regarding what exists beyond *nirvāṇa,*
Regarding what the end of this world is,
Regarding its beginning.

XXII. Since everything is relative [we do not know],
What is finite and what is infinite?
What means finite and infinite at once?
What means negation of both issues?

XXIII. What is identity, and what is difference?
What is eternity, what non-eternity?
What means eternity and non-eternity together?
What means negation of both issues?

XXIV. The bliss consists in the cessation of all thought,
In the quiescence of plurality.
No [separate] reality was preached at all,
Nowhere and none by Buddha!

In this case how can the reproach made above affect us! Our view
is that *nirvāṇa* represents quiescence, i.e., the non-applicability of all
the variety of names and [non-existence of] particular objects. This very
quiescence, so far as it is the natural [genuine] quiescence [of the world],
is called bliss. The quiescence of plurality is also a bliss because of the
cessation of speech or because of the cessation of thought. It is also a
bliss because, by putting an end to all defiling agencies, all individual
existences are stopped. It is also a bliss because, by quenching all defiling
forces, all instinct [and habits of thought] have been extirpated without
residue. It is also a bliss because, since all the objects of knowledge
have died away, knowledge itself has also died.

PARADOXES

Zeno

Motion

Late authorities give a general argument of Zeno's against motion, to the effect that if anything moves, it must move either in the place where it is or in the place where it is not. The latter is impossible (nothing can act or be acted upon where it isn't), and where a thing *is,* it must be at rest. This, however, is very similar to the paradox of the flying arrow (no. 3 below), and may be only a condensation of it. The arguments against motion, as given by Aristotle in his *Physics* and amplified by the Greek commentators, are four. These constitute the famous paradoxes of Zeno on which the attention of philosophers and mathematicians has chiefly been focused.

1. *The dichotomy.* Motion is impossible because an object moving between any two points *A* and *B* must always cover half the distance before it gets to the end. But before covering half the distance it must cover the half of the half, and so *ad infinitum*. Thus to traverse any distance at all it must cover an infinite number of points, which is impossible in any finite time.

Aristotle criticizes this argument by pointing out that "infinite" has two senses: to be infinite in divisibility is not the same as to be infinite in extent. Any continuum is infinitely divisible, and this applies to time as well as to space. Hence it is perfectly possible to traverse in a finite time a space which is infinite in divisibility, though not in extent. Later in the *Physics* however he returns to the point and admits that although this is a sufficient argument *ad hominem* against Zeno, it does not fully and satisfactorily account for the facts.

If [he says] one leaves out of account the distance and the question whether it is possible to traverse an infinite number of distances in a finite time, and asks the same questions about time itself (for time contains an infinite number of divisions), this solution will no longer be adequate.

FROM *History of Greek Philosophy* by W. C. K. Guthrie. Reprinted by permission of Cambridge University Press.

This second attack on the problem shows that Aristotle was not unaware of its deeper significance, and this awareness, together with his claim that the earlier answer was sufficient for Zeno, makes it improbable that (as some recent writers have claimed) Zeno himself saw all the implications and Aristotle simply failed to catch his meaning. Aristotle's own solution involves recourse to the distinction between potential and actual (one of his own major contributions to thought): "In a continuum there is an infinite number of halves, but only potentially, not actually."

2. *Achilles and the tortoise.* The fleet-footed Achilles will never overtake a tortoise if he gives it any start at all. To do so, he must first reach the point from which it started, but by that time the tortoise will have moved further. When he has covered that further distance the tortoise will again have moved on, and so on. As in the dichotomy, Achilles will have to pass through an infinite number of points to catch up to the tortoise, and this is assumed to be impossible. Aristotle treats this argument as essentially the same as the dichotomy, and vulnerable to the same criticism. The only difference is that the dichotomy involved successive division into equal halves, whereas this involves division into decreasing portions corresponding to the relative speeds of the runners.

3. *The flying arrow.* The two previous arguments depended on the assumption that a spatial length could not be reduced to minimal units but was infinitely divisible. This one, on the other hand, is only effective on the premise that time consists of indivisible minimal instants.

The text of the paradox in Aristotle is obscure in detail, and is probably corrupt and incomplete, but its general tenor is plain enough and a restoration is possible with the aid of fuller statements in the Greek commentators. Zeno seems to have argued that an arrow which appears to be flying is really stationary because everything that occupies a space equal to itself must be at rest in that space, and at any given instant of its flight (literally, every "now") an arrow can only occupy a space equal to itself; therefore at every instant of its flight it is motionless.

After stating this argument, Aristotle disposes of it by denying that time is composed of separate moments. Earlier in the *Physics* he had argued more fully that it is meaningless to talk of either motion or rest as taking place in a "now." It is true that if we try to describe the state of the arrow at one instant only, we cannot say that it is either in motion or at rest, for an instant (in the sense of an indivisible and durationless unit of time corresponding to a point in geometrical space) is not a reality but a mental construct.

4. *The stadium.* In the stadium are three rows, each containing an equal number of equal-sized objects or bodies, arranged initially as follows:

A A A A

B B B B→

←C C C C

The *A*s are stationary, the *B*s and *C*s begin to move in opposite directions at the same time and with equal velocity, until all three rows are opposite each other.

A A A A

B B B B

C C C C

The leading *B* has now passed two *A*s while the leading *C* has passed four *B*s. Now, says Zeno, bodies moving with equal velocity must take the same time to pass an equal number of bodies of the same size. Therefore (since *A*s, *B*s and *C*s are all equal), $4A = 2A$, or alternatively half a given time is equal to the whole. The conclusion, like that of the other arguments, was a reiteration of Parmenides's thesis that motion is unreal.

This argument ignores the obvious fact that some of the bodies involved are moving and some are at rest, and that, says Aristotle, was Zeno's mistake: "The fallacy lies in assuming that a body takes an equal time to pass with equal velocity a body that is in motion and a body of equal size at rest." This judgment of Aristotle is the most controversial point in modern interpretations of Zeno. Since Tannery it has been commonly thought that he could not possibly have been guilty of such an elementary logical howler. Zeller however (who argues against Tannery in a footnote) thought it rash to assume that because the fallacy is obvious at sight to the least philosophical of us now, it would not be taken seriously by Zeno. The error of assuming that the space traversed by a body is measured by the size of the body it passes, whether the latter is stationary or in motion, "might well escape the first man to reflect on the laws of motion in this universal way, and all the more easily if, like Zeno, he set out with the conviction that his examination of them would lead to contradictions." This view has been revived by N. B. Booth, who writes: "There is no evidence to support the view that Zeno never made blunders which seem elementary to us now; this is a dogma of modern thinkers, who fail to take into account either the numerous other blunders of the Eleatic philosophers or the limitations of the times."

Those who believe that in this matter Zeno must have been wronged by Aristotle defend him on the ground that he was arguing against opponents who denied the infinite divisibility of matter. If the *onkoi* (bodies) represent indivisible minima, then his argument is valid, and moreover the arguments fall neatly into two pairs, the first two arguing on the assumption of infinite divisibility and the last two on the contrary assumption (applied first to time and then to space). We say that because the *C*'s are also moving, the first *B* can press two *C*'s in the time in which it passes one stationary *A*. But if so, there must be a period in which it passes one *C*, and in that period it will pass half an *A*. Common sense would say that is exactly what it does; but the opponents whom Zeno has in mind cannot say so, because for them each *A* is an indivisible minimum passed in an indivisible instant of time.

Such an argument, as Raven says, would certainly be useful against the Pythagoreans who were still confusing indivisible arithmetical units with the points in infinitely divisible geometrical magnitudes, and tacitly assuming (as Zeno assumed for dialectical purposes) that everything that exists has some physical size. Indeed if he intended it, it considerably strengthens the case of those who believe that in formulating his arguments he had the Pythagoreans chiefly in mind. It is of course possible that Aristotle misrepresented Zeno's thought; but unfortunately we are in his hands and those of his commentators, since we have no information from any other source. And they give no hint that any such further argument occurred, at least explicitly, in his book. There is no evidence for it, and since they had the whole book and we have only what they choose to tell us, we are in a weak position to dispute the point with them. Moreover the considerations adduced by Zeller and Booth have some weight.

Place

Still following his plan of assisting Parmenides not by positive arguments in favor of his theses but by showing their contraries to be impossible and absurd, Zeno disposes of the notion of place or space in addition of those of plurality and motion. Like his other arguments this one too is made possible by the peculiar philosophical situation in his time. No one, that is, had yet conceived the idea of incorporeal being, although both Heraclitus and Parmenides had in their different ways brought thought to a stage where it needed such a conception if it was not to be at the mercy of paradox and absurdity. The argument, which again we owe in the first place to Aristotle, is simple. Everything that exists exists in a place (or occupies a space). Therefore if place exists, it also exists in a place, and so on *ad infinitum*. This is absurd, therefore place does not exist.

THE REALM OF FORMS

Plato

What, he said, is there a knowledge still higher than this—higher than justice and the other virtues?

Yes, I said, there is. And of the virtues too we must behold not the outline merely, as at present—nothing short of the most finished picture should satisfy us. When little things are elaborated with an infinity of pains, in order that they may appear in their full beauty and utmost clearness, how ridiculous that we should not think the highest truths worthy of attaining the highest accuracy!

A right noble thought; but do you suppose that we shall refrain from asking you what is this highest knowledge?

Nay, I said, ask if you will; but I am certain that you have heard the answer many times, and now you either do not understand me or, as I rather think, you are disposed to be troublesome; for you have often been told that the idea of good is the highest knowledge, and that all other things become useful and advantageous only by their use of this. You can hardly be ignorant that of this I was about to speak, concerning which, as you have often heard me say, we know so little; and, without which, any other knowledge or possession of any kind will profit us nothing. Do you think that the possession of all other things is of any value if we do not possess the good? or the knowledge of all other things if we have no knowledge of beauty and goodness?

Assuredly not.

You are further aware that most people affirm pleasure to be the good, but the finer sort of wits say it is knowledge?

Yes.

And you are aware too that the latter can not explain what they mean by knowledge, but are obliged after all to say knowledge of the good?

How ridiculous!

Yes, I said, that they should begin by reproaching us with our ignorance of the good, and then presume our knowledge of it—for the

FROM "The Republic," Book VII, in *The Dialogues of Plato,* translated by Benjamin Jowett (1892).

good they define to be knowledge of the good, just as if we understood them when they use the term "good"—this is of course ridiculous.

Most true, he said.

And those who make pleasure their good are in equal perplexity; for they are compelled to admit that there are bad pleasures as well as good.

Certainly.

And therefore to acknowledge that bad and good are the same?

True.

There can be no doubt about the numerous difficulties in which this question is involved.

There can be none.

Further, do we not see that many are willing to do or to have or to seem to be what is just and honorable without the reality; but no one is satisfied with the appearance of good—the reality is what they seek; in the case of the good, appearance is despised by every one.

Very true, he said.

Of this then, which every soul of man pursues and makes the end of all his actions, having a presentiment that there is such an end, and yet hesitating because neither knowing the nature nor having the same assurance of this as of other things, and therefore losing whatever good there is in other things—of a principle such and so great as this ought the best men in our State, to whom everything is entrusted, to be in the darkness of ignorance?

Certainly not, he said.

I am sure, I said, that he who does not know how the beautiful and the just are likewise good will be but a sorry guardian of them; and I suspect that no one who is ignorant of the good will have a true knowledge of them.

That, he said, is a shrewd suspicion of yours.

And if we only have a guardian who has this knowledge our State will be perfectly ordered?

Of course, he replied; but I wish that you would tell me whether you conceive this supreme principle of the good to be knowledge or pleasure, or different from either?

Aye, I said, I knew all along that a fastidious gentleman like you would not be contented with the thoughts of other people about these matters.

True, Socrates; but I must say that one who like you has passed a lifetime in the study of philosophy should not be always repeating the opinions of others, and never telling his own.

Well, but has any one a right to say positively what he does not know?

Not, he said, with the assurance of positive certainty; he has no right to do that: but he may say what he thinks, as a matter of opinion.

And do you not know, I said, that all mere opinions are bad, and the best of them blind? You would not deny that those who have any true notion without intelligence are only like blind men who feel their way along the road?

Very true.

And do you wish to behold what is blind and crooked and base, when others will tell you of brightness and beauty?

Still, I must implore you, Socrates, said Glaucon, not to turn away just as you are reaching the goal; if you will only give such an explanation of the good as you have already given of justice and temperance and the other virtues, we shall be satisfied.

Yes, my friend, and I shall be at least equally satisfied, but I can not help fearing that I shall fail, and that my indiscreet zeal will bring ridicule upon me. No, sweet sirs, let us not at present ask what is the actual nature of the good, for to teach what is now in my thoughts would be an effort too great for me. But of the child of the good who is likest him, I would fain speak, if I could be sure that you wished to hear—otherwise, not.

By all means, he said, tell us about the child, and you shall remain in our debt for the account of the parent.

I do indeed wish, I replied, that I could pay, and you receive, the account of the parent, and not, as now, of the offspring only; take, however, this latter by way of interest, and at the same time have a care that I do not render a false account, although I have no intention of deceiving you.

Yes, we will take all the care that we can: proceed.

Yes, I said, but I must first come to an understanding with you, and remind you of what I have mentioned in the course of this discussion, and at many other times.

What?

The old story, that there is a many beautiful and a many good, and so of other things which we describe and define; to all of them the term "many" is applied.

True, he said.

And there is an absolute beauty and an absolute good, and of other things to which the term "many" is applied there is an absolute; for they may be brought under a single idea, which is called the essence of each.

Very true.

The many, as we say, are seen but not known, and the ideas are known but not seen.

Exactly.

And what is the organ with which we see the visible things?

The sight, he said.

And with the hearing, I said, we hear, and with the other senses perceive the other objects of sense?

True.

But have you remarked that sight is by far the most costly and complex piece of workmanship which the artificer of the senses ever contrived?

No, I never have, he said.

Then reflect: has the ear or voice need of any third or additional nature in order that the one may be able to hear and the other to be heard?

Nothing of the sort.

No, indeed, I replied; and the same is true of most, if not all, the other senses—you would not say that any of them requires such an addition?

Certainly not.

But you see that without the addition of some other nature there is no seeing or being seen?

How do you mean?

Sight being, as I conceive, in the eyes, and he who has eyes wanting to see; color being also present in them, still unless there be a third nature specially adapted to the purpose, the owner of the eyes will see nothing and the colors will be invisible.

Of what nature are you speaking?

Of that which you term light, I replied.

True, he said.

Noble, then, is the bond which links together sight and visibility, and great beyond other bonds by no small difference of nature; for light is their bond, and light is no ignoble thing?

Nay, he said, the reverse of ignoble.

And which, I said, of the gods in heaven would you say was the lord of this element? Whose is that light which makes the eye to see perfectly and the visible to appear?

You mean the sun, as you and all mankind say.

May not the relation of sight to this deity be described as follows? How?

Neither sight nor the eye in which sight resides is the sun?

No.

Yet of all the organs of sense the eye is the most like the sun?

By far the most like.

And the power which the eye possesses is a sort of effluence which is dispensed from the sun?

Exactly.

Then the sun is not sight, but the author of sight who is recognized by sight?

True, he said.

And this is he whom I call the child of the good, whom the good begat in his own likeness, to be in the visible world, in relation to sight and the things of sight, what the good is in the intellectual world in relation to mind and the things of mind:

Will you be a little more explicit? he said.

Why, you know, I said, that the eyes, when a person directs them toward objects on which the light of day is no longer shining, but the moon and stars only, see dimly, and are nearly blind; they seem to have no clearness of vision in them?

Very true.

But when they are directed toward objects on which the sun shines, they see clearly and there is sight in them?

Certainly.

And the soul is like the eye: when resting upon that on which truth and being shine, the soul perceives and understands, and is radiant with intelligence; but when turned toward the twilight of becoming and perishing, then she has opinion only, and goes blinking about, and is first of one opinion and then of another, and seems to have no intelligence?

Just so.

Now, that which imparts truth to the known and the power of knowing to the knower is what I would have you term the idea of good, and this you will deem to be the cause of science, and of truth in so far as the latter becomes the subject of knowledge; beautiful too, as are both truth and knowledge, you will be right in esteeming this other nature as more beautiful than either; and, as in the previous instance, light and sight may be truly said to be like the sun, and yet not to be the sun, so in this other sphere, science and truth may be deemed to be like the good, but not the good; the good has a place of honor yet higher.

What a wonder of beauty that must be, he said, which is the author of science and truth, and yet surpasses them in beauty; for you surely can not mean to say that pleasure is the good?

God forbid, I replied; but may I ask you to consider the image in another point of view?

In what point of view?

You would say, would you not, that the sun is not only the author of visibility in all visible things, but of generation and nourishment and growth, though he himself is not generation?

Certainly.

In like manner the good may be said to be not only the author of knowledge to all things known, but of their being and essence, and yet the good is not essence, but far exceeds essence in dignity and power.

Glaucon said, with a ludicrous earnestness: By the light of heaven, how amazing!

Yes, I said, and the exaggeration may be set down to you; for you made me utter my fancies.

And pray continue to utter them; at any rate let us hear if there is anything more to be said about the similitude of the sun.

Yes, I said, there is a great deal more.

Then omit nothing, however slight.

I will do my best, I said; but I should think that a great deal will have to be omitted.

I hope not, he said.

You have to imagine, then, that there are two ruling powers, and that one of them is set over the intellectual world, the other over the visible. I do not say heaven, lest you should fancy that I am playing upon the name. May I suppose that you have this distinction of the visible and intelligible fixed in your mind?

I have.

Now take a line which has been cut into two unequal parts, and divide each of them again in the same proportion, and suppose the two main divisions to answer, one to the visible, and the other to the intelligible, and then compare the subdivisions in respect of their clearness and want of clearness, and you will find that the first section in the sphere of the visible consists of images. And by images I mean, in the first place, shadows, and in the second place, reflections in water and in solid, smooth and polished bodies and the like: Do you understand?

Yes, I understand.

Imagine, now, the other section, of which this is only the resemblance, to include the animals which we see, and everything that grows or is made.

Very good.

Would you not admit that both the sections of this division have different degrees of truth, and that the copy is to the original as the sphere of opinion is to the sphere of knowledge?

Most undoubtedly.

Next proceed to consider the manner in which the sphere of the intellectual is to be divided.

In what manner?

Thus—There are two subdivisions, in the lower of which the soul uses the figures given by the former division as images; the inquiry can only be hypothetical, and instead of going upwards to a principle descends to the other end; in the higher of the two, the soul passes out of hypotheses, and goes up to a principle which is above hypotheses, making no use of images as in the former case, but proceeding only in and through the ideas themselves.

I do not quite understand your meaning, he said.

Then I will try again; you will understand me better when I have made some preliminary remarks. You are aware that students of geometry, arithmetic, and the kindred sciences assume the odd and the even and the figures and three kinds of angles and the like in their several branches of science; these are their hypotheses, which they and everybody are supposed to know, and therefore they do not deign to give any account of them either to themselves or others; but they begin with them, and go on until they arrive at last, and in a consistent manner, at their conclusion?

Yes, he said, I know.

And do you not know also that although they make use of the visible forms and reason about them, they are thinking not of these, but of the ideals which they resemble; not of the figures which they draw, but of the absolute square and the absolute diameter, and so on—the forms which they draw or make, and which have shadows and reflections in water of their own, are converted by them into images, but they are really seeking to behold the things themselves, which can only be seen with the eye of the mind?

That is true.

And of this I spoke as the intelligible, although in the search after it the soul is compelled to use hypotheses; not ascending to a first principle, because she is unable to rise above the region of hypothesis, but employing the objects of which the shadows below are resemblances in their turn as images, they having in relation to the shadows and reflections of them a greater distinctness, and therefore a higher value.

I understand, he said, that you are speaking of the province of geometry and the sister arts.

And when I speak of the other division of the intelligible, you will understand me to speak of that other sort of knowledge which reason herself attains by the power of dialectic, using the hypotheses not as first principles, but only as hypotheses—that is to say, as steps and points of departure into a world which is above hypotheses, in order that she may soar beyond them to the first principle of the whole; and clinging to this and then to that which depends on this, by successive steps she descends again without the aid of any sensible object, from ideas, through ideas, and in ideas she ends.

I understand you, he replied; not perfectly, for you seem to me to be describing a task which is really tremendous; but, at any rate, I understand you to say that knowledge and being, which the science of dialectic contemplates, are clearer than the notions of the arts, as they are termed, which proceed from hypotheses only: these are also contemplated by the understanding, and not by the senses: yet, because they start from hypotheses and do not ascend to a principle, those who contemplate them appear to you not to exercise the higher reason upon them, although when a first principle is added to them they are cognizable by the higher reason. And the habit which is concerned with geometry and the cognate sciences I suppose that you would term understanding and not reason, as being intermediate between opinion and reason.

You have quite conceived my meaning, I said; and now, corresponding to these four divisions, let there be four faculties in the soul—reason answering to the highest, understanding to the second, faith (or conviction) to the third, and perception of shadows to the last—and let there be a scale of them, and let us suppose that the several faculties have clearness in the same degree that their objects have truth.

I understand, he replied, and give my assent, and accept your arrangement.

.   .   .   .

And now, I said, let me show in a figure how far our nature is enlightened or unenlightened:—Behold! human beings living in an underground den, which has a mouth open toward the light and reaching all along the den; here they have been from their childhood, and have their legs and necks chained so that they can not move, and can only see before them, being prevented by the chains from turning round their heads. Above and behind them a fire is blazing at a distance, and between the fire and the prisoners there is a raised way; and you will see, if you look, a low wall built along the way, like the screen which marionette players have in front of them, over which they show the puppets.

I see.

And do you see, I said, men passing along the wall carrying all sorts of vessels, and statues and figures of animals made of wood and stone and various materials, which appear over the wall? Some of them are talking, others silent.

You have shown me a strange image, and they are strange prisoners.

Like ourselves, I replied; and they see only their own shadows, or the shadows of one another, which the fire throws on the opposite wall of the cave?

True, he said; how could they see anything but the shadows if they were never allowed to move their heads?

And of the objects which are being carried in like manner they would only see the shadows?

Yes, he said.

And if they were able to converse with one another, would they not suppose that they were naming what was actually before them?

Very true.

And suppose further that the prison had an echo which came from the other side, would they not be sure to fancy when one of the passers-by spoke that the voice which they heard came from the passing shadow?

No question, he replied.

To them, I said, the truth would be literally nothing but the shadows of the images.

That is certain.

And now look again, and see what will naturally follow if the prisoners are released and disabused of their error. At first, when any of them is liberated and compelled suddenly to stand up and turn his neck round and walk and look toward the light, he will suffer sharp pains; the glare will distress him, and he will be unable to see the realities of which in his former state he had seen the shadows; and then conceive some one saying to him, that what he saw before was an illusion, but that now, when he is approaching nearer to being and his eye is turned toward more real existence, he has a clearer vision—what will be his reply? And you may further imagine that his instructor is pointing to the objects as they pass and requiring him to name them—will he not be perplexed? Will he not fancy that the shadows which he formerly saw are truer than the objects which are now shown to him?

Far truer.

And if he is compelled to look straight at the light, will he not have a pain in his eyes which will make him turn away to take refuge in the objects of vision which he can see, and which he will conceive to be in reality clearer than the things which are now being shown to him?

True, he said.

And suppose once more, that he is reluctantly dragged up a steep and rugged ascent, and held fast until he is forced into the presence of the sun himself, is he not likely to be pained and irritated? When he approaches the light his eyes will be dazzled, and he will not be able to see anything at all of what are now called realities.

Not all in a moment, he said.

He will require to grow accustomed to the sight of the upper world. And first he will see the shadows best, next the reflections of men and other objects in the water, and then the objects themselves; then he will gaze upon the light of the moon and the stars and the spangled heaven; and he will see the sky and the stars by night better than the sun or the light of the sun by day?

Certainly.

Last of all he will be able to see the sun, and not mere reflections of him in the water, but he will see him in his own proper place, and not in another; and he will contemplate him as he is.

Certainly.

He will then proceed to argue that this is he who gives the season and the years, and is the guardian of all that is in the visible world, and in a certain way the cause of all things which he and his fellows have been accustomed to behold?

Clearly, he said, he would first see the sun and then reason about him.

And when he remembered his old habitation, and the wisdom of the den and his fellow-prisoners, do you not suppose that he would felicitate himself on the change, and pity them?

Certainly, he would.

And if they were in the habit of conferring honors among themselves on those who were quickest to observe the passing shadows and to remark which of them went before, and which followed after, and which were together; and who were therefore best able to draw conclusions as to the future, do you think that he would care for such honors and glories, or envy the possessors of them? Would he not say with Homer,

Better to be the poor servant of a poor master

and to endure anything, rather than think as they do and live after their manner?

Yes, he said, I think that he would rather suffer anything than entertain these false notions and live in this miserable manner.

Imagine once more, I said, such a one coming suddenly out of the sun to be replaced in his old situation; would he not be certain to have his eyes full of darkness?

To be sure, he said.

And if there were a contest, and he had to compete in measuring the shadows with the prisoners who had never moved out of the den, while his sight was still weak, and before his eyes had become steady (and the time which would be needed to acquire this new habit of sight might be very considerable), would he not be ridiculous? Men would say of him that up he went and down he came without his eyes; and that it was better not even to think of ascending; and if any one tried to loose another and lead him up to the light, let them only catch the offender, and they would put him to death.

No question, he said.

This entire allegory, I said, you may now append, dear Glaucon, to the previous argument; the prison-house is the world of sight, the light of the fire is the sun, and you will not misapprehend me if you interpret the journey upwards to be the ascent of the soul into the intellectual world according to my poor belief, which, at your desire, I have expressed—whether rightly or wrongly God knows. But, whether true or false, my opinion is that in the world of knowledge the idea of good appears last of all, and is seen only with an effort; and, when seen, is also inferred to be the universal author of all things beautiful and right, parent of light and of the lord of light in this visible world, and the immediate source of reason and truth in the intellectual; and that this is the power upon which he who would act rationally either in public or private life must have his eye fixed.

I agree, he said, as far as I am able to understand you.

Moreover, I said, you must not wonder that those who attain to this beatific vision are unwilling to descend to human affairs; for their souls are ever hastening into the upper world where they desire to dwell; which desire of theirs is very natural, if our allegory may be trusted.

Yes, very natural.

And is there anything surprising in one who passes from divine contemplations to the evil state of man, misbehaving himself in a ridiculous manner; if, while his eyes are blinking and before he has become accustomed to the surrounding darkness, he is compelled to fight in courts of law, or in other places, about the images or the shadows of images of justice, and is endeavoring to meet the conceptions of those who have never yet seen absolute justice?

Anything but surprising, he replied.

Any one who has common sense will remember that the bewilderments of the eyes are of two kinds, and arise from two causes, either from coming out of the light or from going into the light, which is true of the mind's eye, quite as much as of the bodily eye; and he who remembers this when he sees any one whose vision is perplexed and weak, will not be too ready to laugh; he will first ask whether that soul of man has come out of the brighter life, and is unable to see because unaccustomed to the dark, or having turned from darkness to the day is dazzled by excess of light. And he will count the one happy in his condition and state of being, and he will pity the other; or, if he have a mind to laugh at the soul which comes from below into the light, there will be more reason in this than in the laugh which greets him who returns from above out of the light into the den.

That, he said, is a very just distinction.

But then, if I am right, certain professors of education must be wrong when they say that they can put a knowledge into the soul which was not there before, like sight into blind eyes.

They undoubtedly say this, he replied.

Whereas, our argument shows that the power and capacity of learning exists in the soul already; and that just as the eye was unable to turn from darkness to light without the whole body, so too the instrument of knowledge can only by the movement of the whole soul be turned from the world of becoming into that of being, and learn by degrees to endure the sight of being, and of the brightest and best of being, or in other words, of the good.

Very true.

And must there not be some art which will effect conversion in the easiest and quickest manner; not implanting the faculty of sight, for that exists already, but has been turned in the wrong direction, and is looking away from the truth?

Yes, he said, such an art may be presumed.

And whereas the other so-called virtues of the soul seem to be akin to bodily qualities, for even when they are not originally innate they can be implanted later by habit and exercise, the virtue of wisdom more than anything else contains a divine element which always remains, and by this conversion is rendered useful and profitable; or, on the other hand, hurtful and useless. Did you never observe the narrow intelligence flashing from the keen eye of a clever rogue—how eager he is, how clearly his paltry soul sees the way to his end; he is the reverse of blind, but his keen eye-sight is forced into the service of evil, and he is mischievous in proportion to his cleverness?

Very true, he said.

But what if there had been a circumcision of such natures in the days of their youth; and they had been severed from those sensual pleasures, such as eating and drinking, which, like leaden weights, were attached to them at their birth, and which drag them down and turn the vision of their souls upon the things that are below—if, I say, they had been released from these impediments and turned in the opposite direction, the very same faculty in them would have seen the truth as keenly as they see what their eyes are turned to now.

Very likely.

Yes, I said; and there is another thing which is likely, or rather a necessary inference from what has preceded, that neither the uneducated and uninformed of the truth, nor yet those who never make an end of their education, will be able ministers of State; not the former, because they have no single aim of duty which is the rule of all their actions, private as well as public; nor the latter, because they will not act at all except upon compulsion, fancying that they are already dwelling apart in the islands of the blest.

Very true, he replied.

Then, I said, the business of us who are the founders of the State will be to compel the best minds to attain that knowledge which we have already shown to be the greatest of all—they must continue to ascend until they arrive at the good; but when they have ascended and seen enough we must not allow them to do as they do now.

What do you mean?

I mean that they remain in the upper world: but this must not be allowed; they must be made to descend again among the prisoners in the den, and partake of their labors and honors, whether they are worth having or not.

ALL THINGS ARE IDEAS

George Berkeley

PHILONOUS. Good morrow, Hylas: I did not expect to find you abroad so early.

HYLAS. It is indeed something unusual; but my thoughts were so taken up with a subject I was discoursing of last night, that finding I could not sleep, I resolved to rise and take a turn in the garden.

PHIL. It happened well, to let you see what innocent and agreeable pleasures you lose every morning. Can there be a pleasanter time of the day, or a more delightful season of the year? That purple sky, those wild but sweet notes of birds, the fragrant bloom upon the trees and flowers, the gentle influence of the rising sun, these and a thousand nameless beauties of nature inspire the soul with secret transports; its faculties too being at this time fresh and lively, are fit for those meditations, which the solitude of a garden and tranquillity of the morning naturally dispose us to. But I am afraid I interrupt your thoughts; for you seemed very intent on something.

HYL. It is true, I was, and shall be obliged to you if you will permit me to go on in the same vein; not that I would by any means deprive myself of your company, for my thoughts always flow more easily in conversation with a friend, than when I am alone; but my request is, that you would suffer me to impart my reflections to you.

PHIL. With all my heart, it is what I should have requested myself if you had not prevented me.

HYL. I was considering the odd fate of those men who have in all ages, through an affectation of being distinguished from the vulgar, or some unaccountable turn of thought, pretended either to believe nothing at all, or to believe the most extravagant things in the world. This however might be borne, if their paradoxes and scepticism did not draw after them some consequences of general disadvantage to mankind. But the mischief lieth here; that when men of less leisure see them who are supposed to have spent their whole time in the

FROM the first dialogue in *Three Dialogues between Hylas and Philonous,* first published in 1713.

pursuits of knowledge professing an entire ignorance of all things, or advancing such notions as are repugnant to plain and commonly receive principles, they will be tempted to entertain suspicions concerning the most important truths, which they had hitherto held sacred and unquestionable.

PHIL.   I entirely agree with you, as to the ill tendency of the affected doubts of some philosophers, and fantastical conceits of others. I am even so far gone of late in this way of thinking, that I have quitted several of the sublime notions I had got in their schools for vulgar opinions. And I give it you on my word; since this revolt from metaphysical notions to the plain dictates of nature and common sense, I find my understanding strangely enlightened, so that I can now easily comprehend a great many things which before were all mystery and riddle.

HYL.   I am glad to find there was nothing in the accounts I heard of you.

PHIL.   Pray, what were those?

HYL.   You were represented, in last night's conversation, as one who maintained the most extravagant opinion that ever entered into the mind of man, to wit, that there is no such thing as *material substance* in the world.

PHIL.   That there is no such thing as what *philosophers* call *material substance,* I am seriously persuaded: but, if I were made to see anything absurd or skeptical in this, I should then have the same reason to renounce this that I imagine I have now to reject the contrary opinion.

HYL.   What! can anything be more fantastical, more repugnant to Common Sense, or a more manifest piece of Skepticism, than to believe there is no such thing as *matter?*

PHIL.   Softly, good Hylas. What if I should prove that you, who hold there is, are, by virtue of that opinion, a greater skeptic, and maintain more paradoxes and repugnances to Common Sense, than I who believe no such thing?

HYL.   You may as soon persuade me, the part is greater than the whole, as that, in order to avoid absurdity and Skepticism, I should ever be obliged to give up my opinion in this point.

PHIL.   Well then, are you content to admit that opinion for true, which upon examination shall appear most agreeable to Common Sense, and remote from Skepticism?

HYL.   With all my heart. Since you are for raising disputes about the plainest things in nature, I am content for once to hear what you have to say.

PHIL.   Pray, Hylas, what do you mean by a *skeptic?*

HYL. I mean what all men mean—one that doubts of everything.

PHIL. He then who entertains no doubt concerning some particular point, with regard to that point cannot be thought a skeptic.

HYL. I agree with you.

PHIL. Whether doth doubting consist in embracing the affirmative or negative side of a question?

HYL. In neither; for whoever understands English cannot but know that *doubting* signifies a suspense between both.

PHIL. He then that denies any point, can no more be said to doubt of it, then he who affirmeth it with the same degree of assurance.

HYL. True.

PHIL. And, consequently, for such his denial is no more to be esteemed a skeptic than the other.

HYL. I acknowledge it.

PHIL. How cometh it to pass then, Hylas, that you pronounce me a *skeptic,* because I deny what you affirm, to wit, the existence of Matter? Since, for aught you can tell, I am as peremptory in my denial, as you in your affirmation.

HYL. Hold, Philonous, I have been a little out in my definition; but every false step a man makes in discourse is not to be insisted on. I said indeed that a *skeptic* was one who doubted of everything; but I should have added, or who denies the reality and truth of things.

PHIL. What things? Do you mean the principles and theorems of sciences? But these you know are universal intellectual notions, and consequently independent of Matter. The denial therefore of this doth not imply the denying them.

HYL. I grant it. But are there no other things? What think you of distrusting the senses, of denying the real existence of sensible things, of pretending to know nothing of them. Is not this sufficient to denominate a man a *skeptic?*

PHIL. Shall we therefore examine which of us it is that denies the reality of sensible things, or professes the greatest ignorance of them; since, if I take you rightly, he is to be esteemed the greatest *skeptic?*

HYL. That is what I desire.

PHIL. What mean you by Sensible Things?

HYL. Those things which are perceived by the senses. Can you imagine that I mean anything else?

PHIL. Pardon me, Hylas, if I am desirous clearly to apprehend your notions, since this may much shorten our inquiry. Suffer me then to ask you this farther question. Are those things only perceived by the senses which are perceived immediately? Or, may those things properly be said to be *sensible* which are perceived mediately, or not without the intervention of others?

HYL. I do not sufficiently understand you.

PHIL. In reading a book, what I immediately perceive are the letters; but mediately, or by means of these, are suggested to my mind the notions of God, virtue, truth, etc. Now, that the letters are truly sensible things, or perceived by sense, there is no doubt: but I would know whether you take the things suggested by them to be so too.

HYL. No, certainly: it were absurd to think *God* or *virtue* sensible things; though they may be signified and suggested to the mind by sensible marks, with which they have an arbitrary connection.

PHIL. It seems then, that by *sensible things* you mean those only which can be perceived *immediately* by sense?

HYL. Right.

PHIL. Doth it not follow from this, that though I see one part of the sky red, and another blue, and that my reason doth thence evidently conclude there must be some cause of that diversity of colors, yet that cause cannot be said to be a sensible thing, or perceived by the sense of seeing?

HYL. It doth.

PHIL. In like manner, though I hear variety of sounds, yet I cannot be said to hear the causes of those sounds?

HYL. You cannot.

PHIL. And when by my touch I perceive a thing to be hot and heavy, I cannot say, with any truth or propriety, that I feel the cause of its heat or weight?

HYL. To prevent any more questions of this kind, I tell you once and for all, that by *sensible things* I mean those only which are perceived by sense; and that in truth the senses perceive nothing which they do not perceive *immediately:* for they make no inferences. The deducing therefore of causes or occasions from effects and appearances, which alone are perceived by sense, entirely relates to reason.

PHIL. This point then is agreed between us—That *sensible things are those only which are immediately perceived by sense.* You will further inform me, whether we immediately perceive by sight anything beside light, and colors, and figures; or by hearing, anything but sounds; by the palate, anything beside taste; by the smell, beside odors; or by the touch, more than tangible qualities.

HYL. We do not.

PHIL. It seems, therefore, that if you take away all sensible qualities, there remains nothing sensible?

HYL. I grant it.

PHIL. Sensible things therefore are nothing else but so many sensible qualities, or combinations of sensible qualities?

HYL. Nothing else.

PHIL. *Heat* then is a sensible thing?

HYL. Certainly.

PHIL. Doth the *reality* of sensible things consist in being perceived? or, is it something distinct from their being perceived, and that bears no relation to the mind?

HYL. To *exist* is one thing, and to be *perceived* is another.

PHIL. I speak with regard to sensible things only. And of these I ask, whether by their real existence you mean a subsistence exterior to the mind, and distinct from their being perceived?

HYL. I mean a real absolute being, distinct from, and without any relation to, their being perceived.

PHIL. Heat therefore, if it be allowed a real being, must exist without the mind?

HYL. It must.

PHIL. Tell me, Hylas, is this real existence equally compatible to all degrees of heat, which we perceive; or is there any reason why we should attribute it to some, and deny it to others? And if there be, pray let me know that reason.

HYL. Whatever degree of heat we perceive by sense, we may be sure the same exists in the object that occasions it.

PHIL. What! the greatest as well as the least?

HYL. I tell you, the reason is plainly the same in respect of both. They are both perceived by sense; nay, the greater degree of heat is more sensibly perceived; and consequently, if there is any difference, we are more certain of its real existence than we can be of the reality of a lesser degree.

PHIL. But is not the most vehement and intense degree of heat a very great pain?

HYL. No one can deny it.

PHIL. And is any unperceiving thing capable of pain or pleasure?

HYL. No, certainly.

PHIL. Is your material substance a senseless being, or a being endowed with sense and perception?

HYL. It is senseless without doubt.

PHIL. It cannot therefore be the subject of pain?

HYL. By no means.

PHIL. Nor consequently of the greatest heat perceived by sense, since you acknowledge this to be no small pain?

HYL. I grant it.

PHIL. What shall we say then of your external object; is it a material substance, or no?

HYL. It is a material substance with the sensible qualities inhering in it.

PHIL.   How then can a great heat exist in it, since you own it cannot in a material substance? I desire you would clear this point.

HYL.   Hold, Philonous, I fear I was out in yielding intense heat to be a pain. It should seem rather, that pain is something distinct from heat, and the consequence or effect of it.

PHIL.   Upon putting your hand near the fire, do you perceive one simple uniform sensation, or two distinct sensations?

HYL.   But one simple sensation.

PHIL.   Is not the heat immediately perceived?

HYL.   It is.

PHIL.   And the pain?

HYL.   True.

PHIL.   Seeing therefore they are both immediately perceived at the same time, and the fire affects you only with one simple or uncompounded idea, it follows that this same simple idea is both the intense heat immediately perceived, and the pain; and, consequently, that the intense heat immediately perceived is nothing distinct from a particular sort of pain.

HYL.   It seems so.

PHIL.   Again, try in your thoughts, Hylas, if you can conceive a vehement sensation to be without pain or pleasure.

HYL.   I cannot.

PHIL.   Or can you frame to yourself an idea of sensible pain or pleasure in general, abstracted from every particular idea of heat, cold, tastes, smells, etc.?

HYL.   I do not find that I can.

PHIL.   Doth it not therefore follow, that sensible pain is nothing distinct from those sensations or ideas, in an intense degree?

HYL.   It is undeniable; and, to speak the truth, I begin to suspect a very great heat cannot exist but in a mind perceiving it.

PHIL.   What! are you then in that skeptical state of suspense between affirming and denying?

HYL.   I think I may be positive in the point. A very violent and painful heat cannot exist without the mind.

PHIL.   It hath not therefore, according to you, any *real* being?

HYL.   I own it.

PHIL.   Is it therefore certain, that there is no body in nature really hot?

HYL.   I have not denied there is any real heat in bodies. I only say, there is no such thing as an intense real heat.

PHIL.   But, did you not say before that all degrees of heat were equally real; or, if there was any difference, that the greater were more undoubtedly real than the lesser?

HYL. True: but it was because I did not then consider the ground there is for distinguishing between them, which I now plainly see. And it is this: because intense heat is nothing else but a particular kind of painful sensation; and pain cannot exist but in a perceiving being; it follows that no intense heat can really exist in an unperceiving corporeal substance. But this is no reason why we should deny heat in an inferior degree to exist in such a substance.

PHIL. But how shall we be able to discern those degrees of heat which exist only in the mind from those which exist without it?

HYL. That is no difficult matter. You know the least pain cannot exist unperceived; whatever, therefore, degree of heat is a pain exists only in the mind. But, as for all other degrees of heat, nothing obliges us to think the same of them.

PHIL. I think you granted before that no unperceiving being was capable of pleasure, any more than of pain.

HYL. I did.

PHIL. And is not warmth, or a more gentle degree of heat than what causes uneasiness, a pleasure?

HYL. What then?

PHIL. Consequently, it cannot exist without the mind in an unperceiving substance, or body.

HYL. So it seems.

PHIL. Since, therefore, as well those degrees of heat that are not painful, as those that are, can exist only in a thinking substance; may we not conclude that external bodies are absolutely incapable of any degree of heat whatsoever?

HYL. On second thoughts, I do not think it so evident that warmth is a pleasure as that a great degree of heat is a pain.

PHIL. I do not pretend that warmth is as great a pleasure as heat is a pain. But, if you grant it to be even a small pleasure, it serves to make good my conclusion.

HYL. I could rather call it an *indolence*. It seems to be nothing more than a privation of both pain and pleasure. And that such a quality or state as this may agree to an unthinkable substance, I hope you will not deny.

PHIL. If you are resolved to maintain that warmth, or a gentle degree of heat, is no pleasure, I know not how to convince you otherwise than by appealing to your own sense. But what think you of cold?

HYL. The same that I do of heat. An intense degree of cold is a pain; for to feel a very great cold, is to perceive a great uneasiness; it cannot therefore exist without the mind; but a lesser degree of cold may, as well as a lesser degree of heat.

PHIL. Those bodies, therefore, upon whose application to our own, we perceive a moderate degree of heat, must be concluded to have a moderate degree of heat or warmth in them; and those, upon whose application we feel a like degree of cold, must be thought to have cold in them.

HYL. They must.

PHIL. Can any doctrine be true that necessarily leads a man into an absurdity?

HYL. Without doubt it cannot.

PHIL. Is it not an absurdity to think that the same thing should be at the same time both cold and warm?

HYL. It is.

PHIL. Suppose now one of your hands hot, and the other cold, and that they are both at once put into the same vessel of water, in an intermediate state; will not the water seem cold to one hand, and warm to the other?

HYL. It will.

PHIL. Ought we not therefore, by your principles, to conclude it is really both cold and warm at the same time, that is, according to your own concession, to believe an absurdity?

HYL. I confess it seems so.

PHIL. Consequently, the principles themselves are false, since you have granted that no true principle leads to an absurdity.

HYL. But, after all, can anything be more absurd than to say, *there is not heat in the fire?*

PHIL. To make the point still clearer; tell me whether, in two cases exactly alike, we ought not to make the same judgment?

HYL. We ought.

PHIL. When a pin pricks your finger, doth it not rend and divide the fibers of your flesh?

HYL. It doth.

PHIL. And when a coal burns your finger, doth it any more?

HYL. It doth not.

PHIL. Since, therefore, you neither judge the sensation itself occasioned by the pin, nor anything like it to be in the pin; you should not, conformably to what you have now granted, judge the sensation occasioned by the fire, or anything like it, to be in the fire.

HYL. Well, since it must be so, I am content to yield this point, and acknowledge that heat and cold are only sensations existing in our minds. But there still remain qualities enough to secure the reality of external things.

PHIL. But what will you say, Hylas, if it shall appear that the case is the same with regard to all other sensible qualities, and that they can no more be supposed to exist without the mind, than heat and cold?

HYL. Then indeed you will have done something to the purpose; but that is what I despair of seeing proved.

PHIL. Let us examine them in order. What think you of *tastes*—do they exist without the mind, or no?

HYL. Can any man in his senses doubt whether sugar is sweet, or wormwood bitter?

PHIL. Inform me, Hylas. Is a sweet taste a particular kind of pleasure or pleasant sensation, or is it not?

HYL. It is.

PHIL. And is not bitterness some kind of uneasiness or pain?

HYL. I grant it.

PHIL. If therefore sugar and wormwood are unthinking corporeal substances existing without the mind, how can sweetness and bitterness, that is, pleasure and pain, agree to them?

HYL. Hold, Philonous, I now see what it was deluded me all this time. You asked whether heat or cold, sweetness and bitterness, were not particular sorts of pleasure and pain; to which I answered simply, that they were. Whereas I should have thus distinguished—those qualities, as perceived by us, are pleasures or pains; but not as existing in the external objects. We must not therefore conclude absolutely, that there is no heat in the fire, or sweetness in the sugar, but only that heat or sweetness, as perceived by us, are not in the fire or sugar. What say you to this?

PHIL. I say it is nothing to the purpose. Our discourse proceeded altogether concerning sensible things, which you defined to be, *the things we immediately perceive by our senses.* Whatever other qualities, therefore, you speak of, as distinct from these, I know nothing of them, neither do they at all belong to the point in dispute. You may, indeed, pretend to have discovered certain qualities which you do not perceive, and assert those insensible qualities exist in fire and sugar. But what use can be made of this to your present purpose, I am at a loss to conceive. Tell me then once more, do you acknowledge that heat and cold, sweetness and bitterness (meaning those qualities which are perceived by the senses), do not exist without the mind?

HYL. I see it is to no purpose to hold out, so I give up the cause as to those mentioned qualities. Though I profess it sounds oddly, to say that sugar is not sweet.

PHIL. But, for your further satisfaction, take this along with you: that which at other times seems sweet, shall, to a distempered palate, appear bitter. And, nothing can be plainer than that diverse persons perceive different tastes in the same food; since that which one man delights in, another abhors. And how could this be, if the taste was something really inherent in the food?

HYL. I acknowledge I know not how.

PHIL. In the next place, *odors* are to be considered. And, with regard to these, I would fain know whether what hath been said of tastes doth not exactly agree to them? Are they not so many pleasing or displeasing sensations?

HYL. They are.

PHIL. Can you then conceive it possible that they should exist in an unperceiving thing?

HYL. I cannot.

PHIL. Or, can you imagine that filth and ordure affect those brute animals that feed on them out of choice, with the same smells which we perceive in them?

HYL. By no means.

PHIL. May we not therefore conclude of smells, as of the other forementioned qualities, that they cannot exist in any but a perceiving substance or mind?

HYL. I think so.

PHIL. Then as to *sounds,* what must we think of them: are they accidents really inherent in external bodies, or not?

HYL. That they inhere not in the sonorous bodies is plain from hence: because a bell struck in the exhausted receiver of an air-pump sends forth no sound. The air, therefore, must be thought the subject of sound.

PHIL. What reason is there for that, Hylas?

HYL. Because, when any motion is raised in the air, we perceive a sound greater or lesser, according to the air's motion; but without some motion in the air, we never hear any sound at all.

PHIL. And granting that we never hear a sound but when some motion is produced in the air, yet I do not see how you can infer from thence, that the sound itself is in the air.

HYL. It is this very motion in the external air that produces in the mind the sensation of *sound.* For, striking on the drum of the ear, it causeth a vibration, which by the auditory nerves being communicated to the brain, the soul is thereupon affected with the sensation called *sound.*

PHIL. What! is sound then a sensation?

HYL. I tell you, as perceived by us, it is a particular sensation in the mind.

PHIL. And can any sensation exist without the mind?

HYL. No, certainly.

PHIL. How then can sound, being a sensation, exist in the air, if by the *air* you mean a senseless substance existing without the mind?

HYL. You must distinguish, Philonous, between sound as it is perceived by us, and as it is in itself; or (which is the same thing) between the sound we immediately perceive, and that which exists without us. The former, indeed, is a particular kind of sensation, but the latter is merely a vibrative or undulatory motion in the air.

PHIL. I thought I had already obviated that distinction, by the answer I gave when you were applying it in a like case before. But, to say no more of that, are you sure then that sound is really nothing but motion?

HYL. I am.

PHIL. Whatever therefore agrees to real sound, may with truth be attributed to motion?

HYL. It may.

PHIL. It is then good sense to speak of *motion* as of a thing that is *loud, sweet, acute, or grave.*

HYL. I see you are resolved not to understand me. Is it not evident those accidents or modes belong only to sensible sound, or *sound* in the common acceptation of the word, but not to *sound* in the real and philosophic sense; which, as I just now told you, is nothing but a certain motion of the air?

PHIL. It seems then there are two sorts of sound—the one vulgar, or that which is heard, the other philosophical and real?

HYL. Even so.

PHIL. And the latter consists in motion?

HYL. I told you so before.

PHIL. Tell me, Hylas, to which of the senses, think you, the idea of motion belongs? to the hearing?

HYL. No, certainly; but to the sight and touch.

PHIL. It should follow then, that, according to you, real sounds may possibly be *seen* or *felt*, but never *heard*.

HYL. Look you, Philonous, you may, if you please, make a jest of my opinion, but that will not alter the truth of things. I own, indeed, the inferences you draw me into sound something oddly; but common language, you know, is framed by, and for the use of the vulgar: we must not therefore wonder if expressions adapted to exact philosophic notions seem uncouth and out of the way.

PHIL. Is it come to that? I assure you, I imagine myself to have gained no small point, since you make so light of departing from common phrases and opinions; it being a main part of our inquiry, to examine whose notions are wildest of the common road, and most repugnant to the general sense of the world. But, can you think it no more than a philosophical paradox, to say that *real sounds are never heard,* and that the idea of them is obtained by some other sense? And is there nothing in this contrary to nature and the truth of things?

HYL.　To deal ingenuously, I do not like it. And, after the concessions already made, I had as well grant that sounds too have no real being without the mind.

PHIL.　And I hope you will make no difficulty to acknowledge the same of *colors.*

HYL.　Pardon me: the case of colors is very different. Can anything be plainer than that we see them on the objects?

PHIL.　The objects you speak of are, I suppose, corporeal Substances existing without the mind?

HYL.　They are.

PHIL.　And have true and real colors inhering in them?

HYL.　Each visible object hath that color which we see in it.

PHIL.　How! is there anything visible but what we perceive by sight?

HYL.　There is not.

PHIL.　And, do we perceive anything by sense which we do not perceive immediately?

HYL.　How often must I be obliged to repeat the same thing? I tell you, we do not.

PHIL.　Have patience, good Hylas; and tell me once more, whether there is anything immediately perceived by the senses, except sensible qualities. I know you asserted there was not; but I would now be informed, whether you still persist in the same opinion.

HYL.　I do.

PHIL.　Pray, is your corporeal substance either a sensible quality, or made up of sensible qualities?

HYL.　What a question that is! who ever thought it was?

PHIL.　My reason for asking was, because in saying, *each visible object hath that color which we see in it,* you make visible objects to be corporeal substances; which implies either that corporeal substances are sensible qualities, or else that there is something beside sensible qualities perceived by sight: but, as this point was formerly agreed between us, and is still maintained by you, it is a clear consequence, that your *corporeal substance* is nothing distinct from *sensible qualities.*

HYL.　You may draw as many absurd consequences as you please, and endeavor to perplex the plainest things; but you shall never persuade me out of my senses. I clearly understand my own meaning.

PHIL.　I wish you would make me understand it too. But, since you are unwilling to have your notion of corporeal substance examined,

I shall urge that point no farther. Only be pleased to let me know, whether the same colors which we see exist in external bodies, or some other.

HYL. The very same.

PHIL. What! are then the beautiful red and purple we see on yonder clouds really in them? Or do you imagine they have in themselves any other form than that of a dark mist or vapor?

HYL. I must own, Philonous, those colors are not really in the clouds as they seem to be at this distance. They are only apparent colors.

PHIL. Apparent call you them? How shall we distinguish these apparent colors from real?

HYL. Very easily. Those are to be thought apparent which, appearing only at a distance, vanish upon a nearer approach.

PHIL. And those, I suppose, are to be thought real which are discovered by the most near and exact survey.

HYL. Right.

PHIL. Is the nearest and exactest survey made by the help of a microscope, or by the naked eye?

HYL. By a microscope, doubtless.

PHIL. But a microscope often discovers colors in an object different from those perceived by the unassisted sight. And, in case we had microscopes magnifying to any assigned degree, it is certain that no object whatsoever, viewed through them, would appear in the same color which it exhibits to the naked eye.

HYL. And what will you conclude from all this? You cannot argue that there are really and naturally no colors on objects: because by artificial managements they may be altered, or made to vanish.

PHIL. I think it may evidently be concluded from your own concessions, that all the colors we see with our naked eyes are only apparent as those on the clouds, since they vanish upon a more close and accurate inspection which is afforded us by a microscope. Then, as to what you say by way of prevention: I ask you whether the real and natural state of an object is better discovered by a very sharp and piercing sight, or by one which is less sharp?

HYL. By the former without doubt.

PHIL. Is it not plain from *Dioptrics* that microscopes make the sight more penetrating, and represent objects as they would appear to the eye in case it were naturally endowed with a most exquisite sharpness?

HYL. It is.

PHIL. Consequently the microscopical representation is to be thought that which best sets forth the real nature of the thing, or what it is in itself. The colors, therefore, by it perceived are more genuine and real than those perceived otherwise.

HYL.   I confess there is something in what you say.

PHIL.   Besides, it is not only possible but manifest, that there actually are animals whose eyes are by nature framed to perceive those things which by reason of their minuteness escape our sight. What think you of those inconceivably small animals perceived by glasses? Must we suppose they are all stark blind? Or, in case they see, can it be imagined their sight hath not the same use in preserving their bodies from injuries, which appears in that of all other animals? And if it hath, is it not evident they must see particles less than their own bodies; which will present them with a far different view in each object from that which strikes our senses? Even our own eyes do not always represent objects to us after the same manner. In the jaundice every one knows that all things seem yellow. Is it not therefore highly probable those animals in whose eyes we discern a very different texture from that of ours, and whose bodies abound with different humors, do not see the same colors in every object that we do? From all which, should it not seem to follow that all colors are equally apparent, and that none of those which we perceive are really inherent in any outward object?

HYL.   It should.

PHIL.   The point will be past all doubt, if you consider that, in case colors were real properties or affections inherent in external bodies, they could admit of no alteration without some change wrought in the very bodies themselves: but, is it not evident from what hath been said that, upon the use of microscopes, upon a change happening in the humors of the eye, or a variation of distance, without any manner of real alteration in the thing itself, the colors of any object are either changed, or totally disappear? Nay, all other circumstances remaining the same, change but the situation of some objects, and they shall present different colors to the eye. The same thing happens upon viewing an object in various degrees of light. And what is more known than that the same bodies appear differently colored by candlelight from what they do in the open day? Add to these the experiment of a prism which, separating the heterogeneous rays of light, alters the color of any object, and will cause the whitest to appear of a deep blue or red to the naked eye. And now tell me whether you are still of the opinion that every body hath its true real color inhering in it; and, if you think it hath, I would fain know further from you, what certain distance and position of the object, what peculiar texture and formation of the eye, what degree or kind of light is necessary for ascertaining that true color, and distinguishing it from apparent ones.

HYL.   I own myself entirely satisfied, that they are all equally apparent, and that there is no such thing as color really inhering in external bodies, but that it is altogether in the light. And what confirms me in this opinion is, that in proportion to the light colors are still more or less vivid; and if there be no light, then are there no colors perceived. Besides, allowing there are colors on external objects, yet, how is it possible for us to perceive them? For no external body affects the mind, unless it acts first on our organs of sense. But the only action of bodies is motion; and motion cannot be communicated otherwise than by impulse. A distant object therefore cannot act on the eye; nor consequently make itself or its properties perceivable to the soul. Whence it plainly follows that it is immediately some contiguous substance, which, operating on the eye, occasions a perception of colors: and such is light.

PHIL.   How! is light then a substance?

HYL.   I tell you, Philonous, external light is nothing but a thin fluid substance, whose minute particles being agitated with a brisk motion, and in various manners reflected from the different surfaces of outward objects to the eyes, communicate different motions to the optic nerves; which, being propagated to the brain, cause therein various impressions; and these are attended with the sensations of red, blue, yellow, etc.

PHIL.   It seems then the light doth no more than shake the optic nerves.

HYL.   Nothing else.

PHIL.   And consequent to each particular motion of the nerves, the mind is affected with a sensation, which is some particular color.

HYL.   Right.

PHIL.   And these sensations have no existence without the mind.

HYL.   They have not.

PHIL.   How then do you affirm that colors are in the light; since by *light* you understand a corporeal substance external to the mind?

HYL.   Light and colors, as immediately perceived by us, I grant cannot exist without the mind. But in themselves they are only the motions and configurations of certain insensible particles of matter.

PHIL.   Colors then, in the vulgar sense, or taken for the immediate objects of sight, cannot agree to any but a perceiving substance.

HYL.   That is what I say.

PHIL.   Well then, since you give up the point as to those sensible qualities which are alone thought colors by all mankind beside, you may hold what you please with regard to those invisible ones of the philosophers. It is not my business to dispute about *them;* only I would advise you to bethink yourself, whether, considering the inquiry we are upon, it be prudent for you to affirm—*the red and blue which we see are not real colors, but certain unknown motions and figures which no man ever did or can see are truly so.* Are not these shocking notions, and are not they subject to as many ridiculous inferences, as those you were obliged to renounce before in the case of sounds?

HYL.   I frankly own, Philonous, that it is in vain to stand out any longer. Colors, sounds, tastes, in a word all those termed *secondary qualities,* have certainly no existence without the mind. But by this acknowledgment I must not be supposed to derogate anything from the reality of Matter, or external objects; seeing it is no more than several philosophers maintain, who nevertheless are the furthest imaginable from denying Matter. For the clearer understanding of this, you must know sensible qualities are by philosophers divided into *Primary* and *Secondary.* The former are Extension, Figure, Solidity, Gravity, Motion, and Rest; and these they hold exist really in bodies. The latter are those above enumerated; or, briefly, *all sensible qualities beside the Primary;* which they assert are only so many sensations or ideas existing nowhere but in the mind. But all this, I doubt not, you are apprised of. For my part, I have been a long time sensible there was such an opinion current among philosophers, but was never thoroughly convinced of its truth until now.

PHIL.   You are still then of the opinion that *extension* and *figures are* inherent in external unthinking substances?

HYL.   I am.

PHIL.   But what if the same arguments which are brought against Secondary Qualities will hold good against these also?

HYL.   Why then I shall be obliged to think, they too exist only in the mind.

PHIL.   Is it your opinion the very figure and extension which you perceive by sense exist in the outward object or material substance?

HYL.   It is.

PHIL.   Have all other animals as good grounds to think the same of the figure and extension which they see and feel?

HYL.   Without doubt, if they have any thought at all.

PHIL.   Answer me, Hylas. Think you the senses were bestowed upon all animals for their preservation and well-being in life? or were they given to men alone for this end?

HYL.   I make no question but they have the same use in all other animals.

PHIL.   If so, is it not necessary they should be enabled by them to perceive their own limbs, and those bodies which are capable of harming them?

HYL.   Certainly.

PHIL.   A mite therefore must be supposed to see his own foot, and things equal or even less than it, as bodies of some considerable dimension; though at the same time they appear to you scarce discernible, or at best as so many visible points?

HYL. I cannot deny it.

PHIL. And to creatures less than the mite they will seem yet larger?

HYL. They will.

PHIL. Insomuch that what you can hardly discern will to another extremely minute animal appear as some huge mountain?

HYL. All this I grant.

PHIL. Can one and the same thing be at the same time in itself of different dimensions?

HYL. That were absurd to imagine.

PHIL. But, from what you have laid down it follows that both the extension by you perceived, and that perceived by the mite itself, as likewise all those perceived by lesser animals, are each of them the true extension of the mite's foot; that is to say, by your own principles you are led into an absurdity.

HYL. There seems to be some difficulty in the point.

PHIL. Again, have you not acknowledged that no real inherent property of any object can be changed without some change in the thing itself?

HYL. I have.

PHIL. But, as we approach to or recede from an object, the visible extension varies, being at one distance ten or a hundred times greater than at another. Doth it not therefore follow from hence likewise that it is not really inherent in the object?

HYL. I own I am at a loss what to think.

PHIL. Your judgment will soon be determined, if you will venture to think as freely concerning this quality as you have done concerning the rest. Was it not admitted as a good argument, that neither heat nor cold was in the water, because it seemed warm to one hand and cold to the other?

HYL. It was.

PHIL. Is it not the very same reasoning to conclude, there is no extension or figure in an object, because to one eye it shall seem little, smooth, and round, when at the same time it appears to the other, great, uneven, and angular?

HYL. The very same. But does this latter fact ever happen?

PHIL. You may at any time make the experiment, by looking with one eye bare, and with the other through a microscope.

HYL. I know not how to maintain it; and yet I am loath to give up *extension*, I see so many odd consequences following upon such a concession.

PHIL. Odd, say you? After the concessions already made, I hope you will stick at nothing for its oddness. But, on the other hand, should it not seem very odd, if the general reasoning which includes all other sensible qualities did not also include extension? If it be allowed that no idea, nor anything like an idea, can exist in an unperceiving substance, then surely it follows that no figure, or mode of extension, which we can either perceive, or imagine, or have any idea of, can be really inherent in Matter; not to mention the peculiar difficulty there must be in conceiving a material substance, prior to and distinct from extension, to be the *substratum* of extension. Be the sensible quality what it will—figure, or sound, or color, it seems alike impossible it should subsist in that which doth not perceive it.

HYL. I give up the point for the present, reserving still a right to retract my opinion, in case I shall hereafter discover any false step in my progress to it.

PHIL. That is a right you cannot be denied. Figures and extension being dispatched, we proceed next to *motion.* Can a real motion in any external body be at the same time both very swift and very slow?

HYL. It cannot.

PHIL. Is not the motion of a body swift in a reciprocal proportion to the time it takes up in describing any given space? Thus a body that describes a mile in an hour moves three times faster than it would in case it described only a mile in three hours.

HYL. I agree with you.

PHIL. And is not time measured by the succession of ideas in our minds?

HYL. It is.

PHIL. And is it not possible ideas should succeed one another twice as fast in your mind as they do in mine, or in that of some spirit of another kind?

HYL. I own it.

PHIL. Consequently the same body may to another seem to perform its motion over any space in half the time that it doth to you. And the same reasoning will hold as to any other proportion: that is to say, according to your principles (since the motions perceived are both really in the object) it is possible one and the same body shall be really moved the same way at once, both very swift and very slow. How is this consistent either with common sense, or with what you just now granted?

HYL. I have nothing to say to it.

PHIL. Then as for *solidity;* either you do not mean any sensible quality by that word, or so it is beside our inquiry: or if you do, it must be either hardness or resistance. But both the one and the other are plainly relative to our senses: it being evident that what seems hard to one animal may appear soft to another, who hath greater force and firmness of limbs. Nor is it less plain that the resistance I feel is not in the body.

HYL. I own the very *sensation* of resistance, which is all you immediately perceive, is not in the body; but the *cause* of that sensation is.

PHIL. But the causes of our sensations are not things immediately perceived, and therefore are not sensible. This point I thought had been already determined.

HYL. I own it was; but you will pardon me if I seem a little embarrassed: I know not how to quit my old notions.

PHIL. To help you out, do but consider that if *extension* be once acknowledged to have no existence without the mind, the same must necessarily be granted of motion, solidity, and gravity; since they all evidently suppose extension. It is therefore superfluous to inquire particularly concerning each of them. In denying extension, you have denied them all to have any real existence.

HYL. I wonder, Philonous, if what you say be true, why those philosophers who deny the Secondary Qualities any real existence should yet attribute it to the Primary. If there is no difference between them, how can this be accounted for?

PHIL. It is not my business to account for every opinion of the philosophers. But, among other reasons which may be assigned for this, it seems probable that pleasure and pain being rather annexed to the former than the latter may be one. Heat and cold, tastes and smells, have something more vividly pleasing or disagreeable than the ideas of extension, figure, and motion affect us with. And, it being too visibly absurd to hold that pain or pleasure can be in an unperceiving Substance, men are more easily weaned from believing the external existence of the Secondary than the Primary Qualities. You will be satisfied there is something in this, if you recollect the difference you made between an intense and more moderate degree of heat; allowing the one a real existence, while you denied it to the other. But, after all, there is no rational ground for that distinction; for, surely an indifferent sensation is as truly a *sensation* as one more pleasing or painful; and consequently should not any more than they be supposed to exist in an unthinking subject.

HYL. It is just come into my head, Philonous, that I have somewhere heard of a distinction between absolute and sensible extension. Now, though it be acknowledged that *great* and *small,* consisting merely in the relation which other extended beings have to the parts of our own bodies, do not really inhere in the substances themselves; yet nothing obliges us to hold the same with regard to *absolute extension,* which is something abstracted from *great* and *small,* from this or that particular magnitude or figure. So likewise as to motion; *swift* and *slow* are altogether relative to the succession of ideas in our own minds. But, it doth not follow, because those modifications of motion exist not without the mind, that therefore absolute motion abstracted from them doth not.

PHIL. Pray what is it that distinguishes one motion, or one part of extension, from another? It is not something sensible, as some degree of swiftness or slowness, some certain magnitude or figure peculiar to each?

HYL. I think so.

PHIL. These qualities, therefore, stripped of all sensible properties, are without all specific and numerical differences, as the schools call them.

HYL. They are.

PHIL. That is to say, they are extension in general, and motion in general.

HYL. Let it be so.

PHIL. But it is a universally received maxim that *Everything which exists is particular.* How then can motion in general, or extension in general, exist in any corporeal substance?

HYL. I will take time to solve your difficulty.

PHIL. But I think the point may be speedily decided. Without doubt you can tell whether you are able to frame this or that idea. Now I am content to put our dispute on this issue. If you can frame in your thoughts a distinct *abstract idea* of motion or extension, divested of all those sensible modes, as swift and slow, great and small, round and square, and the like, which are acknowledged to exist only in the mind, I will then yield the point you contend for. But if you cannot, it will be unreasonable on your side to insist any longer upon what you have no notion of.

HYL. To confess ingenuously, I cannot.

PHIL. Can you even separate the ideas of extension and motion from the ideas of all those qualities which they who make the distinction term *secondary?*

HYL. What! is it not an easy matter to consider extension and motion by themselves, abstracted from all other sensible qualities? Pray how do the mathematicians treat of them?

PHIL. I acknowledge, Hylas, it is not difficult to form general propositions and reasonings about those qualities, without mentioning any other; and, in this sense, to consider or treat of them abstractedly. But, how doth it follow that, because I can pronounce the word *motion* by itself, I can form the idea of it in my mind exclusive of body? or, because theorems may be great of extension and figures, without any mention of *great* or *small,* or any other sensible mode of quality, that therefore it is possible such an abstract idea of extension, without any particular size or figure, or sensible quality, should be distinctly formed, and apprehended by the mind? Mathematicians treat of quantity, without regarding what other sensible qualities it is attended with, as being altogether indifferent to their demonstrations. But, when laying aside the words, they contemplate the bare ideas, I believe you will find, they are not the pure abstracted ideas of extension.

HYL. But what say you to *pure intellect?* May not abstracted ideas be framed by that faculty?

PHIL. Since I cannot frame abstract ideas at all, it is plain I cannot frame them by the help of *pure intellect,* whatsoever faculty you understand by those words. Besides, not to inquire into the nature of pure intellect and its spiritual objects, as *virtue, reason, God,* or the like, this much seems manifest—that sensible things are only to be perceived by sense, or represented by the imagination. Figures, therefore, and extension, being originally perceived by sense, do not belong to pure intellect: but, for your further satisfaction, try if you can frame the idea of any figure, abstracted from all particularities of size, or even from other sensible qualities.

HYL. Let me think a little—I do not find that I can.

PHIL. And can you think it possible that should really exist in nature which implies a repugnancy in its conception?

HYL. By no means.

PHIL. Since therefore it is impossible even for the mind to disunite the ideas of extension and motion from all other sensible qualities, doth it not follow, that where the one exist there necessarily the other exist likewise?

HYL. It should seem so.

PHIL. Consequently, the very same arguments which you admitted as conclusive against the Secondary Qualities are, without any further application of force, against the Primary too. Besides, if you will trust your senses, is it not plain all sensible qualities coexist, or to them appear as being in the same place? Do they ever represent a motion, or figure, as being divested of all other visible and tangible qualities?

HYL. You need say no more on this head. I am free to own, if there be no secret error or oversight in our proceedings hitherto, that *all* sensible qualities are alike to be denied existence without the mind. But, my fear is that I have been too liberal in my former concessions, or overlooked some fallacy or other. In short, I did not take time to think.

PHIL. For that matter, Hylas, you may take what time you please in reviewing the progress of our inquiry. You are at liberty to recover any slips you might have made, or offer whatever you have omitted which makes for your first opinion.

HYL. One great oversight I take to be this—that I did not sufficiently distinguish the *object* from the *sensation*. Now, though this latter may not exist without the mind, yet it will not thence follow that the former cannot.

PHIL. What object do you mean? the object of the senses?

HYL. The same.

PHIL. It is then immediately perceived?

HYL. Right.

PHIL. Make me to understand the difference between what is immediately perceived and a sensation.

HYL. The sensation I take to be an act of the mind perceiving; besides which, there is something perceived; and this I call the *object*. For example, there is red and yellow on that tulip. But then the act of perceiving those colors is in me only, and not in the tulip.

PHIL. What tulip do you speak of? Is it that which you see?

HYL. The same.

PHIL. And what do you see beside color, figure, and extension?

HYL. Nothing.

PHIL. What you would say then is that the red and yellow are coexistent with extension; is it not?

HYL. That is not all; I would say they have a real existence without the mind, in some unthinking substance.

PHIL. That the colors are really in the tulip which I see is manifest. Neither can it be denied that this tulip may exist independent of your mind or mine; but, that any immediate object of the senses—that is, any idea, or combination of ideas—should exist in an unthinking substance, or exterior to *all* minds, is in itself an evident contradiction. Nor can I imagine how this follows from what you said just now, to wit, that the red and yellow were on the tulip *you saw,* since you do not pretend to *see* that unthinking substance.

HYL. You have an artful way, Philonous, of diverting our inquiry from the subject.

PHIL. I see you have no mind to be pressed that way. To return then to your distinction between *sensation* and *object;* if I take you right, you distinguish in every perception two things, the one an action of the mind, the other not.

HYL. True.

PHIL. And this action cannot exist in, or belong to, any unthinking thing; but, whatever beside is implied in a perception may?

HYL. That is my meaning.

PHIL. So that if there was a perception without any act of the mind, it were possible such a perception should exist in an unthinking substance?

HYL. I grant it. But it is impossible there should be such a perception.

PHIL. When is the mind said to be active?

HYL. When it produces, puts an end to, or changes, anything.

PHIL. Can the mind produce, discontinue, or change anything, but by an act of the will?

HYL. It cannot.

PHIL. The mind therefore is to be accounted *active* in its perceptions so far forth as *volition* is included in them?

HYL. It is.

PHIL. In plucking this flower I am active; because I do it by the motion of my hand, which was consequent upon my volition; so likewise in applying it to my nose. But is either of these smelling?

HYL. No.

PHIL. I act too in drawing the air through my nose; because my breathing so rather than otherwise is the effect of my volition. But neither can this be called *smelling:* for, if it were, I should smell every time I breathed in that manner?

HYL. True.

PHIL. Smelling then is somewhat consequent to all this?

HYL. It is.

PHIL. But I do not find my will concerned any further. Whatever more there is—as that I perceive such a particular smell, or any smell at all—this is independent of my will, and therein I am altogether passive. Do you find it otherwise with you, Hylas?

HYL. No, the very same.

PHIL. Then, as to seeing, is it not in your power to open your eyes, or keep them shut; to turn them this or that way?

HYL. Without doubt.

PHIL. But, doth it in like manner depend on *your* will that in looking on this flower you perceive *white* rather than any other color? Or, directing your open eyes toward yonder part of the heaven, can you avoid seeing the sun? Or is light or darkness the effect on your volition?

HYL. No, certainly.

PHIL. You are then in these respects altogether passive?

HYL. I am.

PHIL. Tell me now, whether *seeing* consists in perceiving light and colors, or in opening and turning the eyes?

HYL. Without doubt, in the former.

PHIL.   Since therefore you are in the very perception of light and colors altogether passive, what is become of that action you were speaking of as an ingredient in every sensation? And doth it now follow from your own concessions, that the perception of light and colors, including no action in it, may exist in an unperceiving substance? And is not this a plain contradiction?

HYL.   I know not what to think of it.

PHIL.   Besides, since you distinguish the *active* and *passive* in every perception, you must do it in that of pain. But how is it possible that pain, be it as little active as you please, should exist in an unperceiving substance? In short, do but consider the point, and then confess ingenuously, whether light and colors, tastes, sounds, etc., are not all equally passions or sensations in the soul. You may indeed call them *external objects,* and give them in words what subsistence you please. But, examine your own thoughts, and then tell me whether it be not as I say?

HYL.   I acknowledge, Philonous, that upon a fair observation of what passes in my mind, I can discover nothing else but that I am a thinking being, affected with a variety of sensations; neither is it possible to conceive how a sensation should exist in an unperceiving substance.—But then, on the other hand, when I look on sensible things in a different view, considering them as so many modes and qualities, I find it necessary to suppose a *material substratum,* without which they cannot be conceived to exist.

PHIL.   *Material substratum* call you it? Pray, by which of your senses came you acquainted with that being?

HYL.   It is not itself sensible; its modes and qualities only being perceived by the senses.

PHIL.   I presume then it was by reflection and reason you obtained the idea of it?

HYL.   I do not pretend to any proper positive *idea* of it. However, I conclude it exists, because qualities cannot be conceived to exist without a support.

PHIL.   It seems then you have only a relative *notion* of it, or that you conceive it not otherwise than by conceiving the relation it bears to sensible qualities?

HYL.   Right.

PHIL.   Be pleased therefore to let me know wherein that relation consists.

HYL.   Is it not sufficiently expressed in the term *substratum,* or *substance?*

PHIL.   If so, the word *substratum* should import that it is spread under the sensible qualities or accidents?

HYL. True.

PHIL. And consequently under extension?

HYL. I own it.

PHIL. It is therefore somewhat in its own nature entirely distinct from extension?

HYL. I tell you, extension is only a mode, and Matter is something that supports modes. And is it not evident the thing supported is different from the thing supporting?

PHIL. So that something distinct from, and exclusive of, extension is supposed to be the *substratum* of extension?

HYL. Just so.

PHIL. Answer me, Hylas. Can a thing be spread without extension? or is not the idea of extension necessarily included in *spreading?*

HYL. It is.

PHIL. Whatsoever therefore you suppose spread under anything must have in itself an extension distinct from the extension of that thing under which it is spread?

HYL. It must.

PHIL. Consequently, every corporeal substance, being the *substratum* of extension, must have in itself another extension, by which it is qualified to be a *substratum:* and so on to infinity? And I ask whether this be not absurd in itself, and repugnant to what you granted just now, to wit, that the *substratum* was something distinct from and exclusive of extension?

HYL. Aye but, Philonous, you take me wrong. I do not mean that Matter is *spread* in a gross literal sense under extension. The word *substratum* is used only to express in general the same thing with *substance.*

PHIL. Well then, let us examine the relation implied in the term *substance.* Is it not that it stands under accidents?

HYL. The very same.

PHIL. But, that one thing may stand under or support another, must it not be extended?

HYL. It must.

PHIL. Is not therefore this supposition liable to the same absurdity with the former?

HYL. You still take things in a strict literal sense. That is not fair, Philonous.

PHIL. I am not for imposing any sense on your words: you are at liberty to explain them as you please. Only, I beseech you, make me understand something by them. You tell me Matter supports or stands under accidents. How! is it as your legs support your body?

HYL. No; that is the literal sense.

PHIL. Pray let me know any sense, literal or not literal, that you understand it in.—How long must I wait for an answer, Hylas?

HYL. I declare I know not what to say. I once thought I understood well enough what was meant by Matter's supporting accidents. But now, the more I think on it the less can I comprehend it: in short I find that I know nothing of it.

PHIL. It seems then you have no idea at all, neither relative nor positive, of Matter; you know neither what it is in itself, nor what relation it bears to accidents?

HYL. I acknowledge it.

PHIL. And yet you asserted that you could not conceive how qualities or accidents should really exist, without conceiving at the same time a material support of them?

HYL. I did.

PHIL. That is to say, when you conceive the *real* existence of qualities, you do withal conceive Something which you cannot conceive?

HYL. It was wrong, I own. But still I fear there is some fallacy or other. Pray what think you of this? It is just come into my head that the ground of all our mistake lies in your treating of each quality by itself. Now, I grant that each quality cannot singly subsist without the mind. Color cannot without extension, neither can figure without some other sensible quality. But, as the several qualities united or blended together form entire sensible things, nothing hinders why such things may not be supposed to exist without the mind.

PHIL. Either, Hylas, you are jesting, or have a very bad memory. Though indeed we went through all the qualities by name one after another, yet my arguments, or rather your concessions, nowhere tend to prove that the Secondary Qualities did not subsist each alone by itself; but, that they were not *at all* without the mind. Indeed, in treating of figure and motion we concluded they could not exist without the mind, because it was impossible even in thought to separate them from all secondary qualities, so as to conceive them existing by themselves. But then this was not the only argument made use of upon that occasion. But (to pass by all that hath been hitherto said, and reckon it for nothing, if you will have it so) I am content to put the whole upon this issue. If you can conceive it possible for any mixture or combination of qualities, or any sensible object whatever, to exist without the mind, then I will grant it actually to be so.

HYL. If it comes to that the point will soon be decided. What more easy than to conceive a tree or house existing by itself, independent of, and unperceived by, any mind whatsoever? I do at this present time conceive them existing after that manner.

PHIL. How say you, Hylas, can you see a thing which is at the same time unseen?

HYL. No, that were a contradiction.

PHIL. Is it not as great a contradiction to talk of *conceiving* a thing which is *unconceived?*

HYL. It is.

PHIL. The tree or house therefore which you think of is conceived by you?

HYL. How should it be otherwise?

PHIL. And what is conceived is surely in the mind?

HYL. Without question, that which is conceived is in the mind.

PHIL. How then came you to say, you conceived a house or tree existing independent and out of all minds whatsoever?

HYL. That was I own an oversight; but stay, let me consider what led me into it.—It is a pleasant mistake enough. As I was thinking of a tree in a solitary place, where no one was present to see it, methought that was to conceive a tree as existing unperceived or unthought of; not considering that I myself conceived it all the while. But now I plainly see that all I can do is to frame ideas in my own mind. I may indeed conceive in my own thoughts the idea of a tree, or a house, or a mountain, but that is all. And this is far from proving that I can conceive them *existing out of the minds of all Spirits.*

PHIL. You acknowledge then that you cannot possibly conceive how any one corporeal sensible thing should exist otherwise than in a mind?

HYL. I do.

PHIL. And yet you will earnestly contend for the truth of that which you cannot so much as conceive?

HYL. I profess I know not what to think; but still there are some scruples remain with me. Is it not certain I *see things at a distance?* Do we not perceive the stars and moon, for example, to be a great way off? Is not this, I say, manifest to the senses?

PHIL. Do you not in a dream too perceive those or the like objects?

HYL. I do.

PHIL. And have they not then the same appearance of being distant?

HYL. They have.

PHIL. But you do not thence conclude the apparitions in a dream to be without the mind?

HYL. By no means.

PHIL. You ought not therefore to conclude that sensible objects are without the mind, from their appearance, or manner wherein they are perceived.

HYL. I acknowledge it. But doth not my sense deceive me in those cases?

PHIL. By no means. The idea or thing which you immediately perceive, neither sense nor reason informs you that *it* actually exists without the mind. By sense you only know that you are affected with such certain sensations of light and colors, etc. And these you will not say are without the mind.

HYL. True: but, beside all that, do you not think the sight suggests something of *outness* or *distance?*

PHIL. Upon approaching a distant object, do the visible size and figure change perpetually, or do they appear the same at all distances?

HYL. They are in a continual change.

PHIL. Sight therefore doth not suggest, or any way inform you, that the visible object you immediately perceive exists at a distance, or will be perceived when you advance farther onward; there being a continued series of visible objects succeeding each other during the whole time of your approach.

HYL. It doth not; but still I know, upon seeing an object, what object I shall perceive after having passed over a certain distance: no matter whether it be exactly the same or no: there is still something of distance suggested in the case.

PHIL. Good Hylas, do but reflect a little on the point, and then tell me whether there be any more in it than this: From the ideas you actually perceive by sight, you have by experience learned to collect what other ideas you will (according to the standing order of nature) be affected with, after such a certain succession of time and motion.

HYL. Upon the whole, I take it to be nothing else.

PHIL. Now, is it not plain that if we suppose a man born blind was on a sudden made to see, he could at first have no experience of what may be *suggested* by sight?

HYL. It is.

PHIL. He would not then, according to you, have any notion of distance annexed to the things he saw; but would take them for a new set of sensations, existing only in his mind?

HYL. It is undeniable.

PHIL. But, to make it still more plain: is not *distance* a line turned endwise to the eye?

HYL. It is.

PHIL. And can a line so situated be perceived by sight?

HYL. It cannot.

PHIL. Doth it not therefore follow that distance is not properly and immediately perceived by sight?

HYL. It should seem so.

PHIL. Again, is it your opinion that colors are at a distance?

HYL. It must be acknowledged they are only in the mind.

PHIL. But do not colors appear to the eye as coexisting in the same place with extension and figures?

HYL. They do.

PHIL. How can you then conclude from sight that figures exist without, when you acknowledge colors do not; the sensible appearance being the very same with regard to both?

HYL. I know not what to answer.

PHIL. But, allowing that distance was truly and immediately perceived by the mind, yet it would not thence follow it existed out of the mind. For, whatever is immediately perceived is an idea: and can any idea exist out of the mind?

HYL. To suppose that were absurd: but, inform me, Philonous, can we perceive or know nothing beside our ideas?

PHIL. As for the rational deducing of causes from effects, that is beside our inquiry. And, by the senses you can best tell whether you perceive anything which is not immediately perceived. And I ask you, whether the things immediately perceived are other than your own sensations or ideas? You have indeed more than once, in the course of this conversation, declared yourself on those points; but you seem, by this last question, to have departed from what you then thought.

MODERN SCIENCE
AND MATERIALISM

Hugh Elliot

The main purpose of the present work is to defend the doctrine of materialism. It is, indeed, a materialism infinitely different from that of the ancients, for it makes vast concessions to Agnosticism, and it concedes the whole foundation of knowledge to idealism. Yet it remains materialism; for I shall endeavor to show that the whole of the positive knowledge available to mankind can be embraced within the limits of a single materialistic system. The outlines of this system are not new; the main features of it, indeed, have been admittedly associated with scientific progress for centuries past. An age of science is necessarily an age of materialism; ours is a scientific age, and it may be said with truth that we are all materialists now. The main principles which I shall endeavor to emphasize are three.

1. The uniformity of law. In early times events appeared to be entirely hazardous and unaccountable, and they still seem so, if we confine attention purely to the passing moment. But as science advances, there is disclosed a uniformity in the procedure of Nature. When the conditions at any one moment are precisely identical with those which prevailed at some previous moment, the results flowing from them will also be identical. It is found, for instance, that a body of given mass attracts some other body of given mass at a given distance with a force of a certain strength. It is found that when the masses, distances, and other conditions are precisely repeated, the attraction between the bodies is always exactly the same. It is found, further, that when the distance between the bodies is increased the force of their attraction is diminished in a fixed proportion, and this again is found to hold true at all distances at which they may be placed. The force of their attraction again varies in a different but still constant proportion to their masses. And hence results the law of gravitation, by which the force of attraction

FROM *Modern Science and Materialism,* chapters 5 and 6. Reprinted by permission of Longman Group Limited.

can be precisely estimated from a knowledge of the masses and distances between any two bodies whatever. A uniformity is established which remains absolute within the experience of Man, and to an equivalent extent the haphazard appearance of events is found to be only an appearance. Innumerable other laws of a similar character are gradually discovered, establishing a sort of nexus between every kind of event. If oxygen and hydrogen in the proportion by weight of eight to one are mixed together, and an electric spark is passed through them, water is formed; and on every occasion where precisely the same conditions are realized precisely the same result ensues. This truth is the basis of the experimental method. If from similar conditions it were possible that dissimilar results should follow on various occasions, then experiments would be useless for advancing knowledge.

. This uniformity of sequence confers the power of prophecy; and the more we learn about the nexus of natural phenomena, the greater becomes our power of prophesying future events. Such prophecies are made and fulfilled at the present day in all departments of knowledge where the data or conditions are sufficiently few and simple to be dealt with by calculation, as, for instance, in many astronomical problems. They are made even when the data are numerous and complicated, though with much less accuracy. We can foretell at what minute on what day an eclipse of the Sun will begin to take place. We can equally foretell that a rise in the bank-rate will, under normal conditions, cause an influx of gold; but precisely how much gold we cannot tell. With a larger knowledge of the conditions, we could arrive at a closer approximation to the amount of the influx. With an absolute knowledge of all the conditions at work, we could prophesy the exact number of ounces of gold that any specified rise of bank-rate would divert into this country. Such a knowledge, of course, is for ever impossible, since the factors concerned are innumerable and severally minute; to apply mathematical analysis to them, even if they could all be collected, would infinitely transcend our powers. Nevertheless, we shall be led to adopt the proposition of Laplace, to the effect that if we knew the precise disposition at any moment of all the matter and energy existing in the Universe, and the direction of motion of every moving particle, and if we were armed with a mathematics of infinite power, we should be able to prophesy the exact disposition of all the matter and energy in the Universe at any future time. Any being who possessed such powers, and who, a myriad ages ago, had acquired absolute knowledge at some moment of the nebula from which the solar system arose, would have been able to prophesy that at this present moment there would exist a being identical with myself who would be writing the words that are now flowing from my pen; he would have been able to prophesy that a little later other beings, identical with my readers, would be perusing those words, and he would be aware of what emotions would be excited within them by the perusal. In other words, the uniformity of Nature and the paramountcy of law are universal and without exception.

2. The denial of teleology. Scientific materialism warmly denies that there exists any such thing as purpose in the Universe, or that events have any ulterior motive or goal to which they are striving. It asserts that all events are due to the interaction of matter and motion acting by blind necessity in accordance with those invariable sequences to which we have given the name of laws. This is an important bond of connection between the materialism of the ancient Greeks and that of modern science. Among all peoples not highly cultivated there reigns a passionate conviction, not only that the Universe as a whole is working out some pre-determined purpose, but that every individual part of it subserves some special need in the fulfillment of this purpose. Needless to say, the purpose has always been regarded as associated with human welfare. The Universe, down to its smallest parts, is regarded by primitive superstition as existing for the special benefit of man. To such extreme lengths has this view been carried that even Bernardin de Saint-Pierre, who only died last century, argued that the reason why melons are ribbed is that they may be eaten more easily by families.

The reason for this early teleology is obvious. We all of us survey the Universe from the standpoint of our own centrality. Subjectively we all do stand actually at the center of the Universe. Our entire experience of the Universe is an experience of it as it affects ourselves; for if it does not affect ourselves, we know of it only indirectly, and in primitive stages we do not know of it at all. As our education endows us with a wider outlook and a wider knowledge, we come to see that the objective Universe is very different from our own private subjective Universe. At first we discover that we as individuals are not the center of the Universe, as appears to uncorrected experience, but that we are merely one individual among many others of equal status constituting a nation or society. We then perhaps regard our own society as the center of the Universe, as many primitive peoples do, such, for instance, as the ancient Romans and the modern Chinese. Or we may regard our own sex as the purposed product of the Universe, as in many Mohammedan peoples, who hold that women have not souls like men, and that they exist purely for the benefit or use of men, in the same way that cattle exist in order to be eaten, or that melons are ribbed to indicate the proper amount of one portion.

With still further cultivation, the entire human species becomes regarded as the center and object of all events in the Universe. This is the stage now reached by the masses in modern civilizations. Just as the existence of one particular individual has not the world-wide or cosmic importance that that individual is apt to suppose; just as the existence of a particular tribe or society is not of the profound historic import that that tribe or society very commonly imagines; so too the human species as a whole is far from being, as it too often believes, the sole object for which the Universe was created, with all things in it, great and small. The human species is, indeed, a mere incident in the universal redistribution of matter and motion; its existence has not the smallest cosmic significance. Our species is biologically very modern. Neither in numbers nor in antiquity can it compare with infinitely numerous species of other animals inhabiting the Earth. The Earth itself is one of the smaller planets, revolving round a minor star. The entire solar system, of which the Earth is so insignificant a portion, is itself a system of contemptible minuteness, set among other luminaries and other systems which surpass it many times in magnitude, in brightness, and in every other ascertainable quality that we are accustomed to admire.

When it is alleged that the Universe is purposive, it is assumed that humanity is intimately connected with the purpose. Without that assumption, none but the most transcendental of philosophers would have any interest in maintaining teleology. As the anthropocentric doctrine falls, therefore, the doctrine of teleology must fall with it. This, at all events, is the position taken up by scientific, as indeed by all materialism; it is the position that I hope I shall have little difficulty in defending in the following pages. Nevertheless, however obvious its truth, we must recognize that it involves a profound alteration in the existing mental point of view of the majority of mankind; for most men have as yet not shaken off the habit, which all men necessarily start from, that they themselves, or their family, nation or kind, are in fact, as in appearance, the very center of the cosmos.

3. The denial of any form of existence other than those envisaged by physics and chemistry, that is to say, other than existences that have some kind of palpable material characteristics and qualities. It is here that modern materialism begins to part company with ancient materialism, and it is here that I expect the main criticisms of opponents to be directed. The modern doctrine stands in direct opposition to a belief in any of those existences that are vaguely classed as "spiritual." To this category belong not only ghosts, gods, souls, *et hoc genus omne* [and others of this type], for these have long been rejected from the beliefs of most advanced thinkers. The time has now come to include also in the condemned list that further imaginary entity which we call "mind," "consciousness," etc., together with its various sub-

species of intellect, will, feeling, etc., in so far as they are supposed to be independent or different from material existences or processes.

I beg that the reader will not hastily repudiate a suggestion which, until rightly understood, must appear almost as absurd as did Berkeley's original formulation of idealism. It seems to the ordinary observer that nothing can be more remotely and widely separated than some so-called "act of consciousness" and a material object. An act of consciousness or mental process is a thing of which we are immediately and indubitably aware: so much I admit. But that it differs in any sort of way from a material process, that is to say, from the ordinary transformations of matters and energy, is a belief which I very strenuously deny, and which I propose to discuss and elucidate at length in my final chapter. The proposition which I here desire to advance is that every event occurring in the Universe, including those events known as mental processes, and all kinds of human action or conduct, are expressible purely in terms of matter and motion. If we assume in the primeval nebula of the solar system no other elementary factors beyond those of matter and energy or motion, we can theoretically, as above remarked, deduce the existing Universe, including mind, consciousness, etc., without the introduction of any new factor whatsoever. The existing Universe and all things and events therein may be theoretically expressed in terms of matter and energy, undergoing continuous redistribution in accordance with the ordinary laws of physics and chemistry. If all manifestations within our experience can be thus expressed, as has for long been believed by men of science, what need is there for the introduction of any new entity of spiritual character, called mind? It has no part to play; it is impotent in causation. According to Huxley's theory it accompanies certain physical processes as a shadow, without any power, or any reason, or any use. The world, as Huxley and the great majority of physiologists affirm, would be just the same without it. Now there is an ancient logical precept which retains a large validity: *entia non sunt multiplicanda praeter necessitatem* [don't postulate more entities than you need]. It is sometimes referred to as William of Occam's razor, which cuts off and rejects from our theories all factors or entities which are superfluous in guiding us to an explanation. "Mind" as a separate entity is just such a superfluity. I will not deny—indeed I cordially affirm—that it is a direct datum of experience; but there is no direct datum of experience to the effect that it is anything different from certain cerebral processes. If uneducated experience seems to deny the identity, the denial rests upon an inference or deduction which is just as faulty as was the denial of Berkeley's theory that what we call matter is no more than sense-impressions. In passing, I may point out the difference here disclosed between modern scientific materialism and the crude materialism of the ancients. They agree in declaring the uniformity of law; they agree in denying the doctrine of teleology; they agree that all existences are of a material character. But they disagree in their treatment of the alleged spiritual and unseen world. The ancient materialists believed to a certain extent in an unseen world; they believed even in the existence of souls. They asserted their materialism only by the theory that these entities were material in character. Democritus conceived the soul as consisting of smooth, round, material particles. The scientific materialist of today does not believe in any separate existence of this kind whatever. He regards what is called soul or mind as *identical* with certain physical processes passing in a material brain, processes of which the ancient Greeks knew nothing, and, indeed, which are still entirely unknown to all who have not acquired some smattering of physiology.

That materialism is the basis of all *science* is a proposition that many, if not most, philosophers would admit. That it is the basis of all *knowledge* is a more comprehensive proposition, which the majority of philosophers would certainly deny. Yet this more comprehensive proposition follows necessarily from the first, if once it is admitted that there can be no knowledge save that derived from the ordinary methods of natural science—observation and experiment. A materialist may, and indeed must, admit that "feeling" or some "conscious" state is the original material of the whole of our experience, when analyzed down to its extreme depths. He must further admit that matter is not, like feeling, an elementary datum of experience, but that it is built up by invariable associations of conscious elements. In short, matter is made of feeling, as Berkeley said; matter is clotted consciousness; it is a derivative of acquired experience, precisely of the same order as time and space. It may be regarded, like time and space, as a form of thought. With them it is the foundation of all that vast body of associations and inter-relations that we call knowledge, and when more highly organized, science. I do not for a moment defend materialism in a metaphysical sense, as would be the case if I were to affirm that matter is an ultimate fact, reducible to no lower or more recondite elements. Far from it. Idealism holds the field, but scientific materialism *does not conflict with it,* as crude materialism has always done. Out of the raw and meaningless "experiences" of the infant, there gradually evolve a set of constant associations which in course of time swell up and form the sum-total of the individual's knowledge. This set of associations is based upon those very early ones in which sensations of color, touch, etc., are combined to yield the generalized idea which is called "matter." To this any one may assent. The peculiarity of the materialist is to affirm that no new knowledge can be acquired except by association of new experiences with the great sphere of associations already established on the basis of matter, time and space. There cannot be isolated wisps of knowledge, wholly unassociated with the main body, any more than there can exist in an animal a single elementary reflex-arc, not integrated up with the nervous system; and the comparison is far more than a mere analogy. I must, however, leave this difficult subject for the present.

The materialism which I shall advocate, therefore, is centered round three salient points: the uniformity of law, the exclusion of purpose, and the assertion of monism; that is to say, that there exists no kind of spiritual substance or entity of a different nature from that of which matter is composed.

The first of these propositions, otherwise called the Law of Universal Causation, affirms that nothing happens without a cause, and that the same causes under the same conditions always produce the same effects. In order to gain a true comprehension of this law, we have to define what we mean by "cause" and "effect," and what is the nature of the nexus between them. The conception of the Universe from which we start is that of a great system of matter and motion undergoing redistribution according to fixed sequences, which in the terminology of science are called laws. The matter is constantly undergoing transformation from one of its forms into another, and the energy is redistributed and transformed in a corresponding manner. From this primary conception alone, we are able to derive a precise definition of what is meant by cause, a problem which is almost insuperable from any other standpoint. Mill defined one event as being the cause of another when the first event is found invariably in experience to be followed by the second. In cause and effect he saw nothing further than an invariable sequence. His view was at once demolished when he was asked whether he considered that day was the cause of night, for this also is a sequence invariable in our experience. But if we apply analysis, the difficulty vanishes. If we regard an event as a momentary phase in the redistribution of matter and motion, then the cause of the event is found in the immediately preceding state of distribution of that same matter and motion. Let us ask, for instance, what is the cause of the sudden appearance of a new fixed star in the heavens. Supposing that there were previously two extinct suns moving rapidly toward each other and coming into collision, we should be making a statement of events which would be recognized as a possibly true "cause." The second event, or "effect," is represented exclusively in terms of matter and motion by the idea of two coalesced and volatilized bodies giving rise to vast quantities of heat and light. And the cause is given merely by stating the previous distribution of that matter and energy which is concerned in the production of the event. The *matter* concerned in the event consisted of two solid bodies at a rapidly diminishing distance from one another. The *energy* consisted of half the product of their momentum and velocity. By the collision the matter contained in the solid bodies underwent that redistribution involved in passing into a gaseous state, with the decomposition of many of its molecules, that is to say, with a rearrangement or redistribution of its atoms. The energy of motion previously contained in the solid bodies underwent at the same time a transformation into heat and light. The sudden light, therefore, is explained, or derives its cause, merely by furnishing a statement of the previous distribution of the matter and energy concerned in its production.

Let me now take a slightly more complex instance, that, namely, of a specifiç bacillus as the cause of tuberculosis. What is the cause of tuberculosis? The disease is characterized by lesions of a specific type, which may occur in very various parts of the body. The effect, therefore, or the tuberculous condition, may be analyzed into a particular arrangement of matter and energy. The arrangement, indeed, is very similar to that which prevails in, and constitutes, a healthy organism; but here and there the matter and energy are somewhat differently located, so as to constitute what is called a tuberculous organism.

Before infection, the matter and energy of the organism were normally distributed. At the moment of infection there is an addition of a minute quantity of other matter and energy specifically distributed into a number of little bodies, which we call bacilli; and their matter and energy, combined with the matter and energy of the healthy organism, undergo further redistribution, resulting ultimately in that new arrangement which is characteristic of the disease. All this works by inevitable laws, just those same laws which control the unceasing redistribution of matter and motion in every part of the Universe. The cause of any phenomenon is found when we have described the antecedent state of distribution of the matter and energy which are combined to constitute that phenomenon.

It happens, however, that in practical life we are commonly interested only in one element out of the numerous constituent parts that go to make up a phenomenon. From the objective point of view this element is very often extremely insignificant, yet we confine the appellation of cause to it alone. In the example above cited, the objective or absolute cause of a tubercular lung is furnished only by an account of the origin or previous state of distribution of the matter and energy constituting the lung, as well as of that constituting the bacilli. But we are in the habit of taking the lung for granted, and referring to the bacilli as the cause of the disease. The reason of this is, that the matter and energy of the healthy lung undergo transformation normally in a uniform and regular manner: the organ undergoes what is called a healthy metabolism. Matter and energy are unceasingly being introduced from without, to take the place of that used up. We are only interested in the breach of that uniformity, and the assumption of a new kind of distribution. Although, therefore, the unceasing supply of abundance of new matter and new energy is as essential to the continued existence of a diseased lung as of a healthy lung, and although this abundance is objectively the predominant factor in the production of a tuberculous lung, yet we do not speak of it as the cause of the tuberculous lung, because we take it for granted, and concentrate our interest on the new and unusual factor. From other points of view, we might take just the same facts, originating in just the same way, and yet assign equally correctly another quite different, though, of course, not conflicting, cause, simply because our interest is differently orientated. Suppose, for instance, that we knew nothing of men or any animals, but were entirely wrapped in the lives and history of bacilli. We may be watching a little colony of bacilli which have, for many of their generations, led an uneventful or somewhat precarious existence, perhaps in milk or dried up in dust, etc. Our attention being fixed exclusively on them, we may be startled to find that the colony suddenly becomes inexplicably prosperous. The bacilli become fat and healthy, they reproduce in enormous numbers, having by chance become transferred to a favorable environment, viz. a susceptible lung. The state of affairs is that which has already been described—a lung swarming with bacilli. What is the cause of this state of affairs? Fixing our interest now on the sudden prosperity of the bacilli, we must assign as a cause the favorable nutritive condition supplied by the lung. From the point of view of the bacilli, that particular distribution of matter and energy which we called a tubercular lung, is due to the continued supply of nutritive material through the blood of the infected organism. To the man, the cause of the phenomenon in question is the supply of bacilli to the lung. To the bacilli, the cause of the phenomenon is the supply of a succulent lung. Both are true and essential causes; yet we only call by the name of cause the particular factor, out of innumerable others, in which we happen to be interested. All the others we name "conditions." In that particular collocation of matter and energy known as a lung swarming with bacilli, the man takes the lung with its metabolic processes for granted, and ascribes the cause of the phenomenon to the invasion of foreign bacilli; the bacilli take themselves for granted, and ascribe the cause of the phenomenon to the food supply constantly furnished to the lung.

The notion of cause has, therefore, both an objective and a subjective element. Objectively, the cause of any phenomenon is the preceding state of distribution of the matter and energy concerned in that phenomenon. From this point of view, it is plain that the efficient cause of the existing state of the Universe at any one moment is its state at the moment immediately preceding. Subjectively, we are interested, however, only in the evolution of some part of the component matter and energy, and we are in the habit of conferring the name of cause only on that particular factor in the evolution that happens to interest us, while designating the other factors conditions.

The above definition of cause at once clears up the problem of the difference between "how" and "why." Many men of science, following Mach and Karl Pearson, have affirmed that science can never explain more than "how" events occur: it can never touch the problem of "why" they occur. On this second point humanity must always rest ignorant. They have thus set up a deep and fundamental distinction between "how" and "why" which a very moderate amount of analysis suffices altogether to dispel. I must ask the reader once more to visualize the Universe as consisting of a fixed sum of matter and energy undergoing redistribution. Consider some momentary and circumscribed phase of that evolution, which in ordinary language is called an event, and let us see how we should answer the two questions "how" and "why" this event comes about. Clearly we describe "how" it comes about, when we render a complete statement of the immediately preceding history of all the matter and energy engaged in it. "How" corresponds to the purely objective definition of cause given above. Now let us ask "why" the event occurs. The answer is given by naming the immediately preceding history, not of all the matter and motion engaged, but of that part of it *in which we happen to be interested*. "Why" corresponds to that final definition of cause, offered above, in which both objective and subjective elements are included. In fact, "why" is simply a limited "how"; it covers less ground; it demands the history, not of the whole of the matter and energy engaged in the event, but only of a particular section of it which happens to arouse special interest.

It follows from the above that, whereas to the question "how" an event takes place there can be but one complete answer, to the question "why" it takes place there may be many answers, and all equally true. For, in order to give a complete answer to "how," we have to describe the preceding history of the entire sum of the matter and energy involved; whereas in order to give a complete answer to "why," we only have to describe the preceding history of one selected element in the sum of matter and motion, and we may choose at random many elements, describing one after another, to satisfy the interest of the inquirer, thus offering a number of true, though different, answers to the same question. To answer the question "how," we must describe all the conditions which led up to the event. To answer the question "why," we name one of these conditions. This one condition, in which special interest happens to be taken, is then called "cause." With a different interest, we should have selected some other of the conditions, and this one would then be referred to as the cause. A few instances will make the matter clear.

Suppose that a locomotive engine linked up to a train is standing at a railway station, and that it suddenly begins to move off. Suppose that the question is asked "why" it has moved. A great variety of answers, all equally true, might be given, and if we did not know the special interest of the inquirer, we should be altogether at a loss how to answer him. We may reply that it moved off because it was timed to go at that hour, or because the guard waved his flag, or because the last passenger had just got in, or because the signal had gone down, or because the engine-driver pulled a lever, or because a sudden pressure within the cylinder had forced forward the piston, or because the friction between the wheels and the lines exceeded the inertia to be overcome, or because some fault in the machinery which had hitherto prevented its moving had at length been remedied. Similarly, when the train stops at the next station, we may analyze the question "why" it stops. We may reply, to enable passengers to get out, or because the engine-driver pulled a lever, etc., etc. And in neither case should we know which of the numerous possible answers to give, unless we were acquainted with the motives of the questioner. Each of these answers names one of the antecedent conditions to the motion of the train, and we cannot know which particular antecedent condition will satisfy the question "why" unless we know something about the purpose with which the questioner is animated. If we had no such knowledge, it would be necessary, to cover all possibilities, to give a recital of the entire sum of antecedent conditions, and these would speedily be found to throw roots far back into the past, and to multiply further the more we followed them, exemplifying the truth that all things in the Universe are bound together by an indissoluble nexus, and that every event is the product, not of one or two single causes, but of the general distribution of matter and energy throughout the Universe at preceding periods of time.

The subject seems so important that I venture to cite one further example. Suppose the question asked is, "Why is the moon full tonight?" A great variety of true answers may be offered, when we are ignorant of the questioner's special interest in the matter. The moon is full because it is placed on the opposite side of the Earth from the Sun;

because it has a surface which reflects light; because a month has elapsed since last full moon; because it is a little out of the direct straight line with the Sun and Earth; because the Sun is shining upon that half of its surface turned toward the Earth; because rays of light can traverse space, etc., etc. Our answer to a child would be different from our answer to an astronomer; for the former would be interested in different features of the process from the latter. But in order to furnish a comprehensive answer to the question *how* or by what process the full moon occurs, all these factors one after another would have to be enumerated. The "why" of phenomena is no more than a special case of the "how"; and all questions "why" certain phenomena occur are answered, if at all, only by relating how they occur; nor can they be answered in any other way; nor has the interrogative "why" any other significance that is conceivable to mankind. In explaining why some phenomenon occurs, we merely have to exercise an eclectic discrimination in deciding which of the numerous factors concerned in the process is most likely to satisfy the curiosity of the inquirer. And all those factors, under analysis, may be resolved into a graphical or historical account of the changes undergone from moment to moment by the matter and energy engaged in the production of the phenomenon.

Not only is there no transcendental difference between how and why, as Professor Karl Pearson imagines, but, in the loose and imperfect language of ordinary life, their meanings insensibly grade into one another, and they may even be used indiscriminately. The questions how he got tuberculosis and why he got tuberculosis are very slightly, if at all, different. In other cases the difference is greater, as, for instance, in the questions how he traveled up to London, and why he traveled up to London. The first question would be understood to refer to the more obvious and palpable redistributions of matter concerned in the process, and would be sufficiently answered by replying that he traveled up in a train. The second question, why he traveled, refers to his motive; that is to say, to one special factor antecedent to the process of traveling, a factor to which particular interest attaches.

And this leads me to the second problem which I have here to deal with, the problem of teleology. I have hitherto endeavored to represent the notion of cause and effect in purely materialistic terms, to the exclusion of all metaphysical transcendentalism; to state the relation of cause and effect in terms of the redistribution of matter and motion. I now have to perform the same task for the conception of purpose, and more particularly of human purpose, in order to show how purposiveness may be translated into purely materialistic and mechanical terms; that is to say, how it, too, may be expressed as a phase of the normal process of redistribution of matter and motion under fixed and invariable laws.

At the outset of this inquiry, we have to notice that the word purpose is involved in the same vagueness of significance that attends almost all words used in popular speech. In general a word in popular use has to be defined and limited to some precise meaning before it is fit for employment in a philosophical discussion. In the present case the word is commonly employed in at least two meanings, which differ greatly from each other; and this duality of meaning leads to a duality in the derivative conceptions of "teleology," "finalism," "end," etc., which has not infrequently given rise to confusion and error. The two significations may be roughly grouped as intelligent purposiveness and unintelligent purposiveness, and the reduction of each of these to mechanistic terms involves two different lines of analysis. I shall deal first with unintelligent purposiveness.

In this case, the word is usually applied to a certain kind of organic reactions that bear an obvious relation to the requirements of the reacting organism. An *Amoeba* in the water throws out pseudopodia at random in all directions. When one of these pseudopodia comes into contact with some substance suitable for food, the protoplasm streams round and encloses the particle, which is thus incorporated in the body of the *Amoeba* and there digested. The reaction is purposive in the sense that a somewhat complicated series of movements is carried out, which leads to the preservation of the active organism.

In just the same way, when we ascend the animal scale, the sea-anemone spreads its tentacles at large under the surface of the water. On contact with any substance suitable for food the tentacles contract around the substance and draw it into the interior of the sea-anemone. This action is similarly purposive in that it procures the continued existence of the animal. In all animals the common movements and reactions are predominantly of this purposive type. If an object suddenly appears close to our eyes, we involuntarily close them for an instant, and this reaction is obviously purposive, as directed toward the protection of the eyes.

All these instinctive actions are purposive in character, yet equally, without doubt, they are all of the nature of reflex action, working blindly and inevitably to their conclusion. On contact with the tentacle of a sea-anemone, the stimulus thus applied to that tentacle sets up by entirely mechanical procedure organic processes which necessarily result in the observed contractions. Similarly, in the case of the human being, the sudden appearance of a near object causes an impulse to be conveyed down the optic nerve, which immediately and mechanically propagates its effect to the efferent nerves which lead to the muscles that close the eyelids. The same kind of reaction is characteristic of the functions in plants. The turning of flowers toward the light, and all the processes of absorption, transpiration, etc., are, on the one hand, subservient to the life and prosperity of the plant, while, on the other hand, they are blind mechanical reactions to stimuli.

Seeing that a single action may thus be at the same time both purposive and mechanical, it is plain that there can be no antithesis between the two; but that the difference between purpose and blind mechanism arises simply from our point of view, and not from any difference of objective character. Purposive reactions are not different from mechanical reactions, but they *are* mechanical reactions of a certain kind. Not all mechanical reactions are purposive, but all purposive reactions are mechanical; and it remains to determine *what* mechanical reactions may be correctly described as purposive, and what are simply blind and meaningless.

The distinction is entirely one of convention. I have represented all events in the light of a redistribution of matter and energy under fixed mechanical laws. Certain particular phases in this redistribution, certain particular collocations of the evolving matter and energy, happen to possess for us a very special interest, and we watch with peculiar attention the material developments and antecedents which give rise to those particular collocations that concern us. Of such collocations, the most enthralling is the maintenance of that moving equilibrium which we call the life of an organism. This equilibrium is due to a succession of stimuli from without, met by "adapted" reactions on the part of the organism; and it is to that particular item of the universal mechanism called an adapted organic reaction, that we apply the name of purpose.

The material origin of all purposive reactions would be adequately explained by the theory of Natural Selection. We must suppose that, at the origin of life, the primeval little speck of organic matter would respond in any haphazard kind of way to the stimuli affecting it from without. These organisms or pre-organisms would in every case give a blind response, due to the chemical or material constitution of their protoplasm. By the ordinary laws of chance, the vast majority of these reactions would not be such as to promote the continuance of life, and in many cases would be such as immediately to destroy life. But again, by the ordinary laws of chance, it would happen in some cases that the response to external stimuli would be such as in some way or other to favor the continuance of life. Pre-organisms, the chemical constitution of whose protoplasm was of this type, would flourish and be perpetuated, while all other types of incipient life would be extinguished. The reactions of the surviving pre-organisms are what we should call "purposive." In this sense, therefore, we mean by purpose those reactions of organic matter which happen to promote the continued existence of that organic matter. By the mechanical process of Natural Selection, all varieties of organic matter that respond unpurposively—that is, whose responses do not happen to promote their continued existence—perish, with the result that either the whole or the larger part of every animal's activities are purposive in character. At first, therefore, Natural Selection is the great teleological agent. The net result of this analysis is that purpose is a name given to certain material phenomena which fulfill some arbitrarily chosen condition, and withheld from all other material phenomena which do not fulfill that condition. The condition usually taken in simple cases is the maintenance of life, and among the factors in this maintenance of life are commonly selected those which involve organic activity. All such organic activity is then said to be purposive.

The point specially to be noticed is that purpose is purely arbitrary and subjective; it corresponds to nothing in outer nature, nor are purposive acts in any way objectively different from random acts. By selecting a new set of conditions to be satisfied, or a new standard, it is possible to represent any kind of mechanical event as being purposive. Supposing, for instance, that the condition to be fulfilled was that the planets of our solar system should revolve round the Sun in the orbits that they actually do; supposing that we had a great personal interest in their doing so, and anxiously watched all material developments in the primeval nebula which appeared to lead to such a consummation; supposing that we can transfer ourselves to this cosmic point of view, we might then rightly affirm that gravitation is purposive, just as we now affirm that Natural Selection is purposive. The one leads to the moving equilibrium of the solar system, the other leads to the moving equilibrium of a living organism. Extinguish gravitation, so that the planets move at hazard, and the solar system will not survive. Extinguish Natural Selection, so that organisms react at hazard, and those organisms will not survive. The parallel is complete; and there is no more *a priori* objection to calling the movements of the planets purposive than there is to calling the movements of animals purposive. The former are "adapted" to the continued maintenance of the solar system, the latter to the continued maintenance of vital manifestations. If we do not call the cosmic manifestations purposive, but do call vital manifestations purposive, it is because we are intensely interested in the latter, and but slightly interested in the former. The continuance of life, the satisfaction of needs, etc., are conditions that appear to us so important as to demand a special name for the most prominent group of factors concerned in them; whereas the continuance of the solar system, and the unfailing adherence of the planets to their present orbits, is not a subject of such overweening importance, or of such unceasing allusion in common life, as to require the establishment of a special name. A purposive movement, therefore, is an ordinary case of the redistribution of matter and energy. The name is used in those cases where the matter and energy are knotted up into that structure which we call a living organism, and is applied to such activities of the organism as conduce to its own continued existence.

I now come to the second class of activities to which the name of purpose is applied, that is to say, cases of activity which bear reference to an end consciously and intelligently foreseen, such as the acts inspired by the conscious will in human beings. These activities are commonly regarded as being in a higher degree teleological than the unintelligent reactions hitherto considered; and in many uses of the word "purpose," reference is intended exclusively to these intelligent anticipations of future events, and to the activities carried out in consequence of such anticipations. In this sense purpose is allied to will, and purposive actions are more or less synonymous with voluntary actions. The question before us, therefore, is whether the will can be comprised in the materialistic scheme which governs all other natural phenomena, or whether it is something outside and independent, knowing no laws, and therefore not amenable to scientific discussion. And this question, again, is nothing more than the problem of free-will and determinism; of vitalism and mechanism; of spritualism and materialism; according to the standpoint from which we approach it.

The exclusion of the will from materialistic laws is refuted by considerations of every kind, and refuted with equal facility from many different points of view: from biology, from physiology, from psychology, and even from logic alone. Any one of these sciences can furnish overwhelming refutation of the hypothesis of the independence of the will, a hypothesis which never could have obtained any attention from philosophers were it not that it harmonizes so well with the ignorant prejudices and superstitions of the multitude, and thus, being refuted time after time, was constantly pressed anew on their attention.

. . . There is no qualitative difference between the simpler reflex action and the highest or most complicated reactions that the developed nervous system is capable of evincing. In the lowest animals, the nervous system is adapted simply for conveying impulses from the outer surface to some nerve-center, whence proceeds a new impulse along another nerve back to the periphery, causing a contraction or some other movement. The whole procedure is purely mechanical. Now the most developed known nervous system arises by evolution in gradual stages from this most elementary form, and the mode of development consists in the compounding of reflex action. From the simple reflex-arc arise multitudinous other reflex-arcs, integrated together into one great nervous system. Instead of one nerve running from periphery to center, many nerves run; a corresponding multiplication occurs in the outgoing nerves. The center likewise increases beyond recognition in elaboration and complexity. It is broken up into a number of constituent parts, themselves connected by bundles of nerve-fibers, and higher centers grow up, which receive impulses from the lower centers, and send back others. But the simple reflex-arc remains the unit of functional activity and of structural form. However infinite the complication of the developed system, it is still based on the simple reflex-arc, and, indeed, consists of innumerable reflex-arcs compounded together in every variety. The reflex-arc is mechanical in function; hence the developed nervous system is mechanical in function. Nowhere is there any break in development, at which we might suppose that a new and non-mechanical factor makes its appearance.

The relation between the highly compounded nervous system of a man to the elementary reflex-arc corresponds to the relation between the intelligent purposiveness now under discussion and the unintelligent purposiveness analyzed above. We now have to consider which of the reactions of the nervous system are to be called purposive, and which are to be looked upon as merely random.

One of the most striking features of the developed nervous system as compared with the primitive system is that a stimulus does not give immediate rise to an action. In the elementary animal, stimulus is promptly followed by contraction. In the highly developed animal, the stimulus may simply take effect on the nervous system without causing any external response. The nervous system, however, is to some degree affected by the stimulus, so that at future times different actions will arise from it from those that would have arisen if no such stimulus had ever been experienced. So, too, the nervous system may initiate an action without any immediately preceding external stimulus. Instead of the primitive arrangement by which a stimulus elicits a simple and immediate response, a stimulus may now impinge upon the nervous system and leave its effects stored up there. It buries itself, and is lost in the complex maze of nervous tissue; in so doing it causes some modification of that tissue, which will thereafter affect the responses to stimuli upon it. The sequence of stimulus and response is obscured. In a highly developed nervous system, the stimuli incessantly entering no longer bear any immediate relation with the responses incessantly given out. The brain provides a great storehouse and clearing-ground for nervous impulses, so that the impressions entering and the impulses departing from it lose a great part of their immediate connection. The incoming currents spend themselves in effecting some rearrangement of the matter and energy belonging to the brain. Outgoing currents are similarly due in very many cases to rearrangements occurring in the brain, the product of a number of elements internal and external, rather than to any individual external stimulus. To this is due what appears to an outside observer as the initiating power of the brain, and all those kind of activities known to psychologists as choice, will, etc.

We are now in a position to appreciate the true meaning of those acts which are described as intelligently purposive. Being deliberate and reasoned activities, they are as far as possible removed from the simple type of reflex action in which response follows immediately on external stimulus. They belong to the category in which the immediate stimulus is in the brain itself, and is to be regarded as consisting of rearrangements of the matter and energy contained in the nervous substance of the brain. The brain during consciousness can never be still, and its unceasing activities supply the stimulus, not only for purposive, but for all actions of an intellectual character. Now this permanent cerebral activity can be divided into a number of different types, known psychologically by such names as memory, imagination, reason, etc. Although nervous physiology has not yet advanced far enough to enable us to say what are the different kinds of material processes in the brain corresponding to these psychical processes, yet there is no doubt that the psychical distinction is based upon some actual distinction in the corresponding activities occurring in the brain. Among these cerebral processes is that which is known psychologically as a desire for some external object or event, a visualization of some external phenomenon as an end or purpose to be attained. This desire may then act upon efferent nerves and give rise to the activities which we know as purposive. The essence of a purposive action, and the standard by which it is distinguished from other kinds of actions, is that the "end" to which the action leads was previously represented in the brain of the agent, and composes the stimulus of action. The compound stimulus arises, as I have said, from the composition of large numbers of elementary stimuli previously received. It consists psychologically of a faint representation of the sensation which would be vividly presented by the realization of some outward occurrence. And when this faint representation actually functions as a stimulus which innervates the muscles whose contraction brings about the external occurrence represented, we have what is called an action of intelligent purpose.

Hereafter the analysis is identical with that employed in the description of unintelligent purpose. The only difference is that the stimulus which in the latter case consisted of a simple external contact, is replaced by a complex cerebral pattern, based upon, and produced by, a large number of these stimuli acquired at various former periods, and of course determined by the structure of the brain. It may be asked by what process it happens that a faint psychical (or cerebral) representation of some desired sensation can give rise to just that complicated series of muscular activities needed for the actual realization of this sensation. The answer is the same as in the case of unintelligent purpose, when we inquired how the stimulus provided by contact of a food-particle set up just the right contractions for absorbing that particle into the substance of the organism. The answer suggested was *Natural Selection*. In all cases where the complex cerebral stimulus causes a muscular activity that does not happen to meet the end in view, the organism is extinguished. Only that small minority survive in which the correct muscular activity is brought about. A new factor is indeed introduced, owing to the circumstances that the brain is functionally (and therefore in some way histologically) excessively pliable, and owes more of its ultimate development to education and environmental influences than is the case with the nervous apparatus of inferior organisms. To this extent Natural Selection is replaced by a less rigid discipline. Error need not result in extinction, but merely in pain or in privation of the end desired. This pain or privation constitutes a new stimulus, which combines with the many other elements in the previous cerebral pattern, and suffices to intermit further muscular activity of the kind which has been injurious. In proportion as the animal's educability is developed, the rigorous consequences of Natural Selection are mitigated. The old process of trial and error continues, but it is no longer a process of immediate life and death. Education itself, or the information gained from the knowledge and experience of others, largely contributes the elements of that complex cerebral pattern which acts as the stimulus to purposive activities.

Intelligent purposes, like unintelligent purpose, is then only a name given to a particular kind of incident in the midst of the eternal redistribution of matter and motion under blind mechanical laws. It is in perfect harmony with that materialistic scheme; it can be stated in terms of the purest mechanism. As the matter and motion undergo their invariable and unalterable redistribution, we naturally find ourselves more interested in some phases of it than in others; and in one class of evolving events we are so interested and we have such frequent occasion to refer to them, that we denominate them by a special name— the name of purposive. By this name we designate the majority of those redistributions which issue from the little whirlpools of matter and energy called organisms, and those factors in particular by which the immediate continuance of such whirlpools is ensured.

I have now dealt with the law of universal causation, and with the doctrine of teleology. It remains only to say a few preliminary words about the third main pillar of materialism—the assertion of monism, that is, that there are not two kinds of fundamental existences, material and spiritual, but one kind only. . . . For simplifying the discussion, it will be as well at once to dismiss from consideration all those kinds of spiritual entities imagined by religious believers. The Victorian writers said on this subject nearly all that could be said, and interest now attaches only to those problems of matter and spirit which they left unsolved. I shall, therefore, confine myself to an attempt to reduce the last stronghold of dualism; to ascertain the relation between mind and body; to show that mental manifestations and bodily manifestations are not two different things, as generally supposed, but one and the same thing appearing under different aspects. I shall not attempt to deal with any of the so-called "non-material" existences with the exception of mind; for if mind can be identified with matter, all other kinds of non-material entities must lapse, even those described by religious systems.

It has often been observed that the progress of knowledge has involved strong tendencies toward monism and away from all kinds of dualism. The early philosophers were fond of establishing fundamental antitheses, such as between wet and dry, hot and cold, light and dark, male and female, etc. Organic and inorganic, animal and plant, were likewise regarded as being in radical opposition. These bi-polar theories have all given way to monistic conceptions in modern science. The same evolution has occurred in our ideas both of energy and of matter. Heat, light, sound, motion, etc., were formerly regarded as being so many independent manifestations; now they are known to be fundamentally the same, and any one kind of energy can, at all events in theory, be transformed into any other kind of energy. So with reference to matter. The chemical elements, formerly regarded as wholly distinct from one another, are now looked upon as being all developed from one common type. It is therefore altogether in accordance with what we should expect from the evolution of knowledge, that the rigid distinction previously drawn between mind and matter should be found untenable, and that these two, apparently opposed, manifestations should be seen to have a common basis. With recognition of this truth, complete continuity and uniformity will be established between all classes of phenomena, and philosophical discussion can only turn on what particular kind of monism we are to accept. . . .

At present we have shown how the law of causation and how the conception of purpose are essentially materialistic phenomena. The prevailing confusion as regards causation is due to an intrusion of the subjective method into a purely objective problem. There is no transcendental difference between "how" and "why." When we say "why" an event occurs, we are merely describing one element in the total story as to "how" it occurred—that element which for the moment excites our subjective attention. Regarding all processes in the Universe as a redistribution of matter and energy, the *cause* of any event is found by naming the antecedent distribution of the matter and energy involved in that event. In practical life, we usually refer only to one aspect of this total "cause," and we then use the word "cause" in the limited sense suggested by our present interest.

So, also, the difficulty as regards teleology is due to confusion between the subjective and the objective. In the continuous flow of matter and energy, we single out those items which chance to have a special bearing on our own existence, and call them purposive. If interpreted by Natural Selection, they are seen at once to be purely mechanistic. Not that it is *necessary* to invoke. Natural Selection for such an explanation; purposive results may be achieved by mechanistic methods other than Natural Selection, and Darwin's theory in the foregoing discussion has merely been used as a convenient illustration of *one* way in which purpose can be rendered in terms of mechanism.

As regards intelligent purpose, as evinced by human beings, the same principle holds good. In this case, some definite desired end is attained by an act of definite will. The chain of material sequences lies mainly in the brain of the agent. The final consummation is preceded by particular cerebral states known as desires and will. All those sequences into which these states enter at some stage are termed intelligently purposive. Sequences into which they do not enter are regarded as mechanical. Yet there is between them no objective difference. The difference is purely subjective, and relative to ourselves. All confusion arises from the old anthropocentric fallacy—the supreme difficulty of taking up a wholly external and objective attitude toward ourselves. Just as the savage supposes the whole Universe to be specially created for the benefit of himself or his tribe; just as the more civilized man supposes the Universe to be specially subservient to the human race; so in the most recondite problems of philosophy our arguments tend to be vitiated by infusion of the subjective element, in such a way that we read into external nature the human interests and egocentric habits which belong to our own minds.

Questions for Discussion

1. Does the following passage in the story by Borges imply that time is illusory? "The present is indefinite, the future has no reality other than as a present hope . . . the past has no reality other than as a present memory."

2. Nagarjuna argues that since a cause must precede its effect, nothing can cause anything else because the cause would cease to exist before the effect began, and thus would no longer be able to exert any influence. Is this reasoning sound? Why can a cause not be simultaneous with its effect?

3. Gilbert Ryle, a contemporary British philosopher, has compared Zeno's problem of Achilles and the tortoise to the problem of a mother slicing a cake for an infinite number of children. Theoretically, Ryle points out, so long as the mother makes each slice half the thickness of the previous slice, she can go on slicing forever. But in reality, the thickness of the knife would soon put an end to her slicing. In what sense does this analogy provide a solution to Zeno's paradox?

4. In the arrow paradox, Zeno argues that at every instant the arrow must be in a definite space equal to its length. What do you suppose Zeno means by "instant?" Does it refer to an actual span of time or an artificial notion invented by mathematicians?

5. What does Plato mean by "the child of the good?" Why "child" rather than "twin?" Comment on the relation between this "child" and its parent.

6. A philosopher has written that he considers Cervantes's literary character Don Quixote more real than most of the people he meets in real life. What do you suppose he may have meant by this assertion? Would Plato have agreed? Explain.

7. In arguing that we must be guided by secondary qualities like color in judging primary qualities like distance or speed, and that primary qualities are therefore no more external to the mind than secondary ones, Berkeley has been accused of equating evidence with what it is evidence *for*. The photographs of the Mars landscape depended for their existence on the camera in the Viking landing vessel. Does it follow that the Mars landscape depended for its existence on that camera? Is Berkeley making that kind of inference? Explain.

8. "Is it not . . . a contradiction to talk of *conceiving* a thing which is unconceived?" asks Philonous. What criticism of material substance is Berkeley making here? Does "conceive" mean the same in both occurrences in the quoted sentence? If not, explain the difference.

9. "The human species is, indeed, a mere incident in the universal redistribution of matter and motion; its existence has not the slightest significance," asserts Hugh Elliot. Is his conclusion a matter of science, as he claims, or a matter of ethics that one might reject without denying any facts of science? Compare this argument with the following: "A bullet in a small part of the brain is a mere incident in the redistribution of the matter and motion of a human body; its occurrence has not the slightest significance." Is this a fair analogy? Why or why not?

10. Elliot cites Occam's Razor (the principle that entities should not be postulated without necessity) in arguing that a mind distinct from a nervous system is an unnecessary entity, on the ground that anything that can reasonably be said about the mind can be translated into an

equivalent statement about the nervous system. Is he right about this? How would he (or you) translate "John is daydreaming about Mary" into a statement about John's nervous system?

Selected Readings

ARISTOTLE. *Metaphysics*. Translated by J. Warrington. London: Everyman, 1956. One of the classic works in metaphysics, with solutions to Zeno's paradoxes.

BERKELEY, G. *Dialogues between Hylas and Philonous*. Cleveland: World Publishing Co., 1963. The main arguments for idealism.

BORGES, J. L. *Labyrinths, Selected Stories, and Other Writings*. New York: New Directions, 1969. Short stories, including "Tlön, Uqbar, Orbis Tertius."

CAMPBELL, K. *Metaphysics*. Encino, California: Dickenson, 1976. A good introduction to metaphysics.

CASTANEDA, C. *Confessions of Don Juan: A Yaqui Way of Knowing*. Berkeley: University of California Press, 1968.

———. *Journey to Ixtlan*. New York: Simon & Schuster, 1972.

———. *A Separate Reality*. New York: Simon & Schuster, 1971.

———. *Tales of Power*. New York: Simon & Schuster, 1974.

Descriptions of Yaqui sorcery and claims to a higher reality.

ELLIOT, H. *Modern Science and Materialism*. London: Longman's Green, 1919. A detailed argument to prove that natural science is the key to reality.

GUTHRIE, W. K. *The Greek Philosophers from Thales to Aristotle*. London: Methuen, 1950. Contains a clear and thorough discussion of Zeno's paradoxes.

KENNICK, W., AND LAZEROWITZ, M. *Metaphysics*. Englewood Cliffs, New Jersey: Prentice-Hall, 1966. An introductory anthology.

LANGE, F. A. *History of Materialism*. 3 vols. Boston: Houghton Osgood, 1880. The most thorough account of the evolution of materialist metaphysics.

LOCKE, J. *Essay Concerning Human Understanding*. Book II, chaps. 7–9. New York: Dover, 1974. Arguments for the reality of the primary qualities of physics.

PLATO. *Republic; Parmenides*. In *The Dialogues of Plato*. Translated by B. Jowett. London: Methuen, 1892. The Platonic doctrine of forms and Plato's own criticisms of it.

RUSSELL, B. *History of Western Philosophy*. New York: Simon & Schuster, 1945. Incisive expositions and criticisms of classical metaphysics.

RYLE, G. *Dilemmas*. London: Cambridge University Press, 1959. A new solution to Zeno's paradoxes.

SMART, J. J. C. *Between Science and Philosophy*. New York: Random House, 1968. A sophisticated defense of scientific materialism.

SMART, N. *Doctrine and Argument in Indian Philosophy*. London: Allen & Unwin, 1969. Idealism, dualism, and materialism in ancient Hindu and Buddhist thought.

TAYLOR, A. E. *Plato; The Man and His Works*. London: Methuen, 1949. A very clear exposition of Plato's dialogues.

TAYLOR, R. *Metaphysics*. Englewood Cliffs, New Jersey: Prentice-Hall, 1963. A readable introduction to the subject.

WARNOCK, G. J., *Berkeley*. Baltimore: Pelican, 1953. A clear account and criticism of Berkeley's idealism.

WHITEHEAD, A. N. *Science and the Modern World*. New York: Macmillan, 1925. A critique of materialism by a physicist and philosopher.

Chapter 3
Mind and Body: What Is a Person?

Man, wrote the German existential philosopher, Martin Heidegger, is the being who places being in question. A reflective person wants to know what the world in which he or she lives is really like, and whether there is a higher reality beyond everyday experience. For this reason there is, as we have seen, a natural human tendency to engage in metaphysical speculation. Equally, there is a natural human desire to know what *we,* as persons, are really like, what the essential nature of a person is, and whether there is in ourselves, as well as in the world, a higher or deeper reality that is not directly observable. Is a person a pure center of consciousness, or a spiritual substance (soul), or merely a complex organic body, or a mind plus a body, or a bundle of experiences?

Idealism, the view for which Berkeley argued in the previous chapter, holds that a person is really a spiritual substance and that one's bodily features exist only in one's own mind and in the minds of others. Materialism holds that nothing exists but matter and its properties; consequently, either minds do not exist at all, or they are special properties of complex organic bodies. A person, on this view, is a living body equipped with a highly developed nervous system. This view flatly rules out reincarnation, the possibility of our moving from our present bodies into others while remaining the same person.

Dualism offers a compromise between idealism and materialism, although it is usually strongly tilted toward idealism. For the dualist, a person is an embodied mind, but most dualists consider the mind more essential to personal identity than the body. While admitting that a disembodied individual is significantly different from an embodied one (perhaps for the better, perhaps for the worse), and that a reincarnated person is not exactly the same as a previous embodiment of that person, the dualist usually maintains that in such cases of bodily transfer a person is still *basically* the same person, dramatically changed, of course, but still recognizable at least to himself or herself. The "accidents" of that person are different, but not the "essence." Thus on this view, a person is really a mind that happens to inhabit a certain body for a relatively brief period of its eternal existence.

The "bundle theory" of the self, first advanced in Western thought by David Hume in the eighteenth century but suggested centuries earlier by Buddhist thinkers, denies that any substance, whether mental or physical, is required to unify and support the data of experience. On this view a person is a sequence of experiences, and both minds and bodies are, in British philosopher Bertrand Russell's phrase, "logical constructions" out of experiences of the appropriate types. The mind is that bundle of experiences most subject to one's control, and the body is that bundle that obeys the laws of natural science.

François de Voltaire, the most influential spokesman for the eighteenth-century Enlightenment in France, ridiculed the pretensions of human beings to their being unique possessors of minds. These complacent pretensions, he believed, were the fault of church theologians. Science in the previous century had succeeded in explaining both terrestrial and celestial phenomena according to precise laws, and it seemed reasonable to Voltaire to assume that human nature would also eventually be explained in accordance with the same laws. The mind was not, as religion thought, a divine element in humans, but a natural propensity to behave in certain ways shared with other complex organisms.

The impact of the scientific assault on the traditional religious picture of the human race as the center and uniquely favored inhabitant of the cosmos can be clearly recognized in Voltaire's science-fiction fantasy, *Micromegas*. In this story Voltaire describes titanic creatures who come to earth from outer space, dwarfing humanity morally and intellectually as well as physically. We humans appear to these giants as the tiniest of insects appear to us, and as more quarrelsome, vain, and foolish. Philosophers of various schools try, with dubious success, to define the soul for the giants, until a theologian recklessly provokes them to laughter by asserting that God created the entire universe for the exclusive benefit of humankind.

Voltaire took no clear position on the nature of mind and its relation to the body, but his story is clearly intended to illustrate the folly of regarding mind as a unique and divine gift to the human species. The visiting titans obviously have minds that are far superior to those of the human theologian and his colleagues. Voltaire seems to be suggesting that mind can be understood in terms of bodily behavior and that no ghostly spiritual substance needs to be postulated. Thus, the story seems to support some form of materialism. The philosopher of whom Voltaire approves remarks: "That it is impossible for God to communicate the faculty of thinking to matter, I doubt very much." Voltaire was not clear about his views on metaphysics, but his commonsense naturalism inclined him toward materialism.

For the most persuasive philosophical argument for dualism, weighted strongly in favor of the mental component of the mind-body duality, we turn to René Descartes, a seventeenth-century thinker and the first influential philosopher of the modern age. Descartes accepted the view of the physical world as a kind of machine, which grew out of the spectacular success of Galilean physics, but he exempted God and the human mind (which he identified with the soul) from the laws of natural science. Mind and body, for Descartes, were entirely distinct substances having no properties in common. A person is a *res cogitans,* a thinking being, that temporarily inhabits and controls a particular body but in no way depends on it for existence.

Descartes's argument for this view is contained in his work *Meditations.* The second Meditation presents a powerful challenge, perhaps never yet adequately answered, to scientific materialism. After systematically doubting all his beliefs in the first Meditation, Descartes arrives, in the second, at the conclusion that one proposition—the proposition "I exist"—is immune from doubt, since his very attempt at doubting entails that he exists as the doubter. But what sort of entity, he asks, am I that thinks and doubts? I must be the sort of entity that is capable of doubting and thus of thinking, namely, a mind or *res cogitans.* Thus he knows with certainty that he exists as a mind, though he does not yet know whether he has a body. He is able to assure himself of the existence of his body only later on, in his sixth Meditation, and even then, the reasoning involved is less certain than this immediate inference to the existence of his mind. From these facts Descartes concludes that a person is first and essentially a mind and only secondarily a material being. This reasoning provides him with confidence in the immortality of the mind or soul with which he identifies himself.

The most serious difficulty that faces a Cartesian dualist is how to explain the obvious interdependence of mind and body, such as the loss of consciousness resulting from a blow on the head, or the agitation of the body when the mind is disturbed. A related difficulty is how to explain the intimate relation of a particular mind to a particular body, since normally we identify other persons, if not ourselves, by observation of their bodily features. And, in exactly what way can we say that a mind "inhabits" a body, if mind has no spatial location and dimensions? Descartes wrestled with these aspects of what has come to be called the "mind-body problem," in his essay *On the Passions of the Soul*. He concluded that the focus of interaction between a particular mind and its corresponding body is in the pineal gland, lying between the frontal lobes of the brain. He thereby granted materialists that the mind is most intimately associated with the central nervous system. But he was unable to explain further just how a nonspatial mind can affect or be affected by a physical object such as the pineal gland.

John Locke, the seventeenth-century British philosopher, accepted Descartes's contention that mind and matter are distinct substances, but he realized the difficulties in identifying a person with pure mind. He therefore distinguished between the soul or mental substance and the person or self. Persons, he suggested, are rational beings who can identify themselves as individuals by means of the continuity of their particular memories. This view required him to hold (1) that a single mind or soul may animate more than one person, and (2) that a person ceases to exist when he or she loses consciousness, and a new person awakens. For practical purposes, so long as these successive selves remain similar, we regard them as one person, but in reality they are different persons.

Joseph Butler, an eighteenth-century bishop of the Anglican church, offered a devastating criticism of Locke's account of personal identity in order to defend the Christian doctrine of personal immortality. Butler maintained, in opposition to Locke, that we have a direct and infallible awareness of our personal identity and that "person," "self," "mind," and "soul" are equivalent terms for one indivisible and indestructible entity. He argued that Locke confused the *evidence* for personal identity, in the form of one's memory of past experiences, with that for which it is evidence, namely, the soul.

Butler distinguished a "loose and popular" sense of identity, according to which we call a tree the same tree years later, even though every particle of the earlier tree has been replaced by a new particle, from the "strict and philosophical" sense, according to which only an unchanging entity like the soul can be said to remain the same over time.

In opposing Locke, Butler was surely right. In view of the many gaps in memory, if continuity of consciousness is taken as the defining condition of personal identity, then "no one can remain the same person two moments together . . . and . . . it is a fallacy to charge our present selves with anything we did." In short, Locke's account of what it is to be a person leads to the absurd result that what we normally call a person is really a succesion of persons closely associated with each other, like the beads of a necklace.

In his work *A Treatise of Human Nature,* David Hume was still more skeptical than Locke about the notion of a person as a spiritual substance. Locke had identified a person as a triad of a mind, a body, and a sequence of experiences made continuous by memory. Hume's bundle theory of personal identity jettisoned the mind and body components in Locke's account, leaving only experiences unified by their temporal connectedness in memory. When consciousness is discontinuous, as when we sleep or suffer from amnesia, we close the gaps fictitiously by simply assuming continuity. Thus, the concept of personal or self-identity is *always* a "loose and popular" concept, and never a "strict and philosophical" one, in Butler's phraseology. It is simply not the case, according to Hume, that we have, as Butler claimed, an infallible awareness of ourselves:

When I enter intimately into what I call *myself,* I always stumble on some particular perception or other, of heat or cold, light or shade, love or hatred, pain or pleasure. I never can catch *myself* at any time without a perception, and never can observe anything but the perception. When my perceptions are removed for any time, as by sound sleep, so long am I insensible of *myself,* and may truly be said not to exist. And were all my perceptions removed by death, and could I neither think, or feel, nor see, nor love, nor hate, after the dissolution of my body, I should be entirely annihilated, nor do I conceive what is further requisite to make me a perfect non-entity. If anyone, upon serious and unprejudiced reflection, thinks he has a different notion of *himself,* I must confess I can no longer reason with him. . . .

But setting aside some metaphysicians of this kind, I may venture to affirm of the rest of mankind that they are nothing but a bundle of different perceptions, which succeed each other with an inconceivable rapidity. . . .

The identity, which we ascribe to the mind of man, is only a fictitious one, and of a like kind with that which we ascribe to vegetable and animal bodies.

Hume's critique of the notion of a mental substance was anticipated by Buddhist thinkers such as the legendary Nagasena and, in fact, was a cornerstone of Buddhist philosophical religion. The selection from the *Questions of King Milinda* reprinted in this chapter shows Nagasena comparing a person with a carriage. Just as a carriage is a bundle of wheels, frame, ropes, and yoke, a person is a bundle of bodily parts, perceptions, and thoughts. Thus, "there is no permanent individuality involved in the matter."

But King Milinda is not easily convinced of Nagasena's view, and his initial objection may be more perceptive than Nagasena seems to have recognized. "If that be so," King Milinda protests (very much in the spirit of Butler's objection to Locke), if there is no single person who possesses bodily and mental parts, then "there is neither merit nor demerit; there is neither doer nor causer of good or evil deeds." It would be absurd, the king argues, to attribute responsibility for good or evil deeds to a mere collection of bodily parts and states of consciousness, rather than to an enduring person who possesses those parts and states. A carriage may indeed be identified with the collection of its parts. But carriages are not persons; they are not held responsible for actions. Nor are carriages aware of themselves or answerable to their names. Even Nagasena, despite his denial that he is a single entity, admits to being Nagasena and to continuing to be Nagasena, no matter how much his bodily parts and mental states may change. Nagasena could perhaps, like Hume, acknowledge this fact and then explain that such continuing identity is a convenient fiction that we are entitled to employ for practical purposes. But as the Scottish philosopher Thomas Reid argued, in criticizing Hume, nothing seems to us more real and less fictitious than our own unity and identity as persons. Therefore, the burden of proof of the fictitiousness of our enduring selves lies with the skeptic.

Neither Nagasena nor Hume could find the self among their perceptions. But should they have looked for it in that direction? Is the self the sort of thing that we should expect to be able to observe either outwardly, like a table, or introspectively, like a pain? Dualists, bundle theorists, and materialists all seem to agree that it is. The contemporary British philosopher, B. A. O. Williams, a materialist, argues that a person or self is a conscious human organism, and that the fundamental criterion of personal identity (what makes an individual a person) is the continuity in space and time of the body. That is the same criterion that serves us in identifying any material object over time, despite the changes it undergoes.

Williams takes up the "change of body" problem that Locke considered a conclusive argument for dualism. Suppose a man, Charles, wakes up one fine morning and remembers having been Guy Fawkes, the notorious rebel who is burned in effigy once a year in England. And suppose Charles now behaves exactly like Guy Fawkes and reports facts that it seems only Guy Fawkes would have known. Has the person of Guy Fawkes entered Charles's body, as Locke's criterion of self (and Hume's and Nagasena's as well) implies? Williams observes that personality traits are as dependent on the body as physical traits, so that "when we are asked to distinguish a man's personality from his body, we do not really know what to distinguish from what." We should therefore say, in the Charles–Guy Fawkes case, that, assuming no tricks nor even honest mistakes were involved, Charles has inexplicably become just like Guy Fawkes but is not identical with that unsavory person.

Each of the views considered has both merits and difficulties as compared with its competitors that might be worth reviewing. Dualism seems closest to common belief in that we often speak of someone as having a weak mind and a strong body or vice versa, and the prospect of injury to one's mind is even more frightening than the prospect of bodily injury. Moreover, it seems possible to imagine finding oneself inside a completely different body, like Gregor, in Franz Kafka's short story "Metamorphosis," who awakes one morning to find that he has turned into a grotesque insect. And we seem capable of visualizing some kind of disembodied existence to judge from the popularity of beliefs in an afterlife. But the major, perhaps fatal, defect of dualism is that it makes the relation between mind and body an inexplicable mystery.

An additional defect of Descartes's dualistic account of a person as primarily a mind and secondarily a body is that since we have no way of identifying a pure mind, we could not identify persons if they were really only minds. Locke realized this and so concluded that a person must be as much a body as a mind. Yet he was still puzzled by the problem of identification because of Descartes's argument that we can identify ourselves independently of our bodies. He therefore thought it necessary to consider memory the most important means of self-identification. But this conclusion exposed him to Butler's objection that we must then regard the person who wakes up in the morning as someone other than the one who went to sleep the night before. On the other hand, Butler's return to Descartes's claim that we know ourselves infallibly and intuitively as mental substances exposes him equally to Locke's objection that we do not thereby know which particular entity we are. Thus, for all I know, my body may house the reincarnation of the soul of Socrates, although neither I nor anyone else would for a moment believe that I *am* Socrates. The point is that even if there is such a thing as a soul, we know of no feature or mark that makes that soul different from any other. It does not, so far as we can see, have the individuality of a person.

Bundle theorists such as Nagasena and Hume escape the problem of identification of individual persons involved in the mental substance theory by proposing that "person" is a convenient shorthand for a related group of bodily parts and mental states, and "self" is shorthand for one's own mental states. But this view faces two other difficulties. One such difficulty as noted above, is that a bundle of parts does not seem to amount to an agent, so that it is hard to see how it can be praised or blamed. This difficulty may not be insuperable. The bundle theorist might reply that the difference between a person and his or her parts or momentary stages is that the person is a historical sequence of such parts and stages, and that it is this historical sequence (which we call character) that we praise and blame.

But a more serious defect is that the bundle theorist cannot easily—perhaps cannot possibly—explain just which experiences and parts belong to one bundle, or person, rather than another. The bundle theorist relies on the continuity of memory to identify his or her *own* bundle. However, even aside from the fact that memory sometimes lapses or plays us false, how can my memory enable me to identify the bundles that constitue persons other than myself? Nagasena was able to identify his own experiences and features and to distinguish them from those of King Milinda. But *how* did he know which were his and which were King Milinda's? That which unites successive states of mind or body as belonging to one person rather than another cannot be their mere connectedness, since connectedness can hold between the successive experiences and states of different persons when they are involved in the same situation.

Materialists like Williams seem to hold the strongest cards with respect to identifying persons other than oneself, since the most reliable grounds we have discovered for deciding such matters in practice are physical traits, such as fingerprints and birthmarks, that imply bodily continuity from birth to death. For persons to preexist their births and/or survive their bodily deaths may seem possible or even likely to many, but it may well be that we can no more coherently entertain these possibilities than we can entertain square circles or frictionless machines, although there may be countless people who think they can.

The main stumbling block of the materialist view is the problem of accounting for knowledge of one's own identity, which Descartes brought to our attention by arguing that he knew of his existence independently of any knowledge of his body. Some writers have tried to blunt the edge of this objection to materialism by contending that one's awareness of oneself as the subject of one's own experiences does not present the problem for materialism that Descartes and subsequent dualists have supposed, because identifying another person is simply not on a par with self-identification. For me to know that I exist is not to know any special fact about myself, but simply to be able to use the first-person pronoun "I"; and to be aware of my identity with the subject of certain past experiences is nothing more complicated than simply remembering those experiences. The point is that to use the pronoun "I" correctly is not to make any meaningful identification of oneself. It is not like knowing the name of another person or identifying him by means of a description such as "the eldest son of the present pretender to the throne." The orphan left on the doorstep of a foundling home may not have the foggiest notion of who he is, yet he can use the first-person pronoun as well as anyone. In order to find out who he is, he would have to resort to the bodily clues that detectives employ, such as fingerprints and birthmarks.

Yet Descartes's argument is not so easily outflanked. It seems an almost incontrovertible fact that we know ourselves better than we know others, not only because we can use the first-person pronoun without fear of error, but more importantly because we can testify to our own states of mind and feeling with more certainty than we can report states of our bodies or states of the bodies or minds of others. We seem to have what has been termed "privileged access" to our own states of mind, which tempts us to conclude that our minds are more intimately ourselves than our bodies.

When we as individuals are in a certain state such as fear or joy, we automatically know that we are in that state, without looking or inquiring to find out. We only have to *be* in a certain mental state to know that we are in it. This is not the case with respect to our knowledge of our own bodies or the minds and bodies of other persons. This asymmetry between knowledge of one's own mind and knowledge of one's body and of other persons has been the main problem that the various theories we have considered were designed to solve. Is the peculiarly privileged access involved in self-knowledge sufficient reason to conclude that persons are radically different from the rest of nature, so different that they must be thought of as spiritual substances or as bundles of experience, rather than as complex physical organisms? This is what idealists, dualists, and bundle theorists maintain in common. But the new problem with which they then saddle themselves is that of explaining how we can identify either spiritual substances or bundles other than ourselves and acquire any kind of knowledge of other persons.

Materialists, in contrast, insist that persons are not all that different from the rest of nature; they are merely more complex systems of molecules, capable of more complex behavior than other creatures. Knowledge of other persons is quite unproblematic for the materialists, since it parallels our knowledge of all material objects through observation. But the materialist has the converse problem of accounting for the curiously self-guaranteeing nature of self-knowledge.

It was noted in the commentary to the previous chapter that we may not automatically infer, as Plato seemed to do, from differences in knowledge to differences in the nature of the objects of knowledge. It may well have been an error on the part of Descartes to have reasoned that there must be an entity called the "self" that corresponds to the peculiar kind of knowledge that we have of ourselves through introspection and that is distinct from anything that is accessible to public observation. But this said, self-knowledge, with its strangely self-certifying character, remains an embarrassingly unexplained—perhaps inexplicable—datum. As long as this extraordinary fact about ourselves remains unexplained, we must acknowledge that we do not yet know quite what we are, nor do we know our place in the cosmic scheme.

MICROMEGAS

Voltaire

The Conversation Between Micromegas and the Inhabitant of Saturn

His excellency having laid himself down, and the secretary approached his nose:

"It must be confessed," said Micromegas, "that nature is full of variety."

"Yes," replied the Saturnian, "nature is like a parterre, whose flowers—"

"Pshaw!" cried the other, "a truce with your parterres."

"It is," resumed the secretary, "like an assembly of fair and brown women, whose dresses—"

"What a plague have I to do with your brunettes?" said our traveler.

"Then it is like a gallery of pictures, the strokes of which—"

"Not at all," answered Micromegas, "I tell you once for all, nature is like nature, and comparisons are odious."

"Well, to please you," said the secretary—

"I won't be pleased," replied the Sirian, "I want to be instructed; begin, therefore, without further preamble, and tell me how many senses the people of this world enjoy."

"We have seventy and two," said the academician, "but we are daily complaining of the small number, as our imagination transcends our wants, for, with the seventy-two senses, our five moons and ring, we find ourselves very much restricted; and notwithstanding our curiosity, and the no small number of those passions that result from these few senses, we have still time enough to be tired of idleness."

"I sincerely believe what you say," cried Micromegas, "for, though we Sirians have near a thousand different senses, there still remains a certain vague desire, an unaccountable inquietude incessantly admonishing us of our own unimportance, and giving us to understand that

FROM Voltaire's *Collected Works*.

there are other beings who are much our superiors in point of perfection. I have traveled a little, and seen mortals both above and below myself in the scale of being, but I have met with none who had not more desire than necessity, and more want than gratification. Perhaps I shall one day arrive in some country where nought is wanting, but hitherto I have had no certain information of such a happy land."

The Saturnian and his guest exhausted themselves in conjectures upon this subject, and after abundance of argumentation equally ingenious and uncertain, were fain to return to matter of fact.

"To what age do you commonly live?" said the Sirian.

"Lack-a-day! a mere trifle," replied the little gentleman.

"It is the very same case with us," resumed the other, "the shortness of life is our daily complaint, so that this must be a universal law in nature."

"Alas!" cried the Saturnian, "few, very few on this globe outlive five hundred great revolutions of the sun (these, according to our way of reckoning, amount to about fifteen thousand years). So, you see, we in a manner begin to die the very moment we are born: our existence is no more than a point, our duration an instant, and our globe an atom. Scarce do we begin to learn a little, when death intervenes before we can profit by experience. For my own part, I am deterred from laying schemes when I consider myself as a single drop in the midst of an immense ocean. I am particularly ashamed, in your presence, of the ridiculous figure I make among my fellow-creatures."

To this declaration, Micromegas replied:

"If you were not a philosopher, I should be afraid of mortifying your pride by telling you that the term of our lives is seven hundred times longer than the date of your existence: but you are very sensible that when the texture of the body is resolved, in order to reanimate nature in another form, which is the consequence of what we call death—when that moment of change arrives, there is not the least difference betwixt having lived a whole eternity, or a single day. I have been in some countries where the people live a thousand times longer than with us, and yet they murmured at the shortness of their time. But one will find everywhere some few persons of good sense, who know how to make the best of their portion, and thank the author of nature for his bounty. There is a profusion of variety scattered through the universe, and yet there is an admirable vein of uniformity that runs through the whole: for example, all thinking beings are different among themselves, though at bottom they resemble one another in the powers and passions of the soul. Matter, though interminable, hath different properties in every sphere. How many principal attributes do you reckon in the matter of this world?"

"If you mean those properties," said the Saturnian, "without which we believe this our globe could not subsist, we reckon in all three hundred, such as extent, impenetrability, motion, gravitation, divisibility, et cetera."

"That small number," replied the traveler, "probably answers the views of the creator on this your narrow sphere. I adore his wisdom in all his works. I see infinite variety, but everywhere proportion. Your globe is small; so are the inhabitants. You have few sensations; because your matter is endued with few properties. These are the works of unerring providence. Of what color does your sun appear when accurately examined?"

"Of a yellowish white," answered the Saturnian, "and in separating one of his rays we find it contains seven colors."

"Our sun," said the Sirian, "is of a reddish hue, and we have no less than thirty-nine original colors. Among all the suns I have seen there is no sort of resemblance, and in this sphere of yours there is not one face like another."

After diverse questions of this nature, he asked how many substances, essentially different, they counted in the world of Saturn; and understood that they numbered but thirty: such as God; space; matter; beings endowed with sense and extension; beings that have extension, sense, and reflection; thinking beings who have no extension; those that are penetrable; those that are impenetrable, and also all others. But this Saturnian philosopher was prodigiously astonished when the Sirian told him they had no less than three hundred, and that he himself had discovered three thousand more in the course of his travels. In short, after having communicated to each other what they knew, and even what they did not know, and argued during a complete revolution of the sun, they resolved to set out together on a small philosophical tour.

The Voyage of These Inhabitants of Other Worlds

Our two philosophers were just ready to embark for the atmosphere of Saturn, with a large provision of mathematical instruments, when the Saturnian's mistress, having got an inkling of their design, came all in tears to make her protests. She was a handsome brunette, though not above six hundred and three-score fathoms high; but her agreeable attractions made amends for the smallness of her stature.

"Ah! cruel man," cried she, "after a courtship of fifteen hundred years, when at length I surrendered, and became your wife, and scarce have passed two hundred more in thy embraces, to leave me thus, before the honeymoon is over, and go a rambling with a giant of another world!

Go, go, thou art a mere virtuoso, devoid of tenderness and love! If thou wert a true Saturnian, thou wouldst be faithful and invariable. Ah! whither art thou going? what is thy design? Our five moons are not so inconstant, nor our ring so changeable as thee! But take this along with thee, henceforth I ne'er shall love another man."

The little gentleman embraced and wept over her, notwithstanding his philosophy; and the lady, after having swooned with great decency, went to console herself with more agreeable company.

Meanwhile our two virtuosi set out, and at one jump leaped upon the ring, which they found pretty flat, according to the ingenious guess of an illustrious inhabitant of this our little earth. From thence they easily slipped from moon to moon; and a comet changing to pass, they sprang upon it with all their servants and apparatus. Thus carried about one hundred and fifty million of leagues, they met with the satellites of Jupiter, and arrived upon the body of the planet itself, where they continued a whole year; during which they learned some very curious secrets, which would actually be sent to the press, were it not for fear of the gentlemen inquisitors, who have found among them some corollaries very hard of digestion.

But to return to our travelers. When they took leave of Jupiter, they traversed a space of about one hundred millions of leagues, and coasting along the planet Mars, which is well known to be five times smaller than our little earth, they descried two moons subservient to that orb, which have escaped the observation of all our astronomers. I know Castel will write, and that pleasantly enough, against the existence of these two moons; but I entirely refer myself to those who reason by analogy. Those worthy philosophers are very sensible that Mars, which is at such a distance from the sun, must be in a very uncomfortable situation, without the benefit of a couple of moons. Be that as it may, our gentlemen found the planet so small, that they were afraid they should not find room to take a little repose; so that they pursued their journey like two travelers who despise the paltry accommodation of a village, and push forward to the next market town. But the Sirian and his companion soon repented of their delicacy; for they journeyed a long time without finding a resting place, till at length they discerned a small speck, which was the Earth. Coming from Jupiter, they could not but be moved with compassion at the sight of this miserable spot, upon which, however, they resolved to land, lest they should be a second time disappointed. They accordingly moved toward the tail of the comet, where, finding an Aurora Borealis ready to set sail, they embarked, and arrived on the northern coast of the Baltic on the fifth day of July, new style, in the year 1737.

What Befell Them upon This Our Globe

Having taken some repose, and being desirous of reconnoitering the narrow field in which they were, they traversed it at once from north to south. Every step of the Sirian and his attendants measured about thirty thousand royal feet, whereas, the dwarf of Saturn, whose stature did not exceed a thousand fathoms, followed at a distance quite out of breath; because, for every single stride of his companion, he was obliged to make twelve good steps at least. The reader may figure to himself (if we are allowed to make such comparisons) a very little rough spaniel dodging after a captain of the Prussian grenadiers.

As those strangers walked at a good pace, they compassed the globe in six and thirty hours; the sun, it is true, or rather the earth, describes the same space in the course of one day; but it must be observed that it is much easier to turn upon an axis than to walk a-foot. Behold them then returned to the spot from whence they had set out, after having discovered that almost imperceptible sea which is called the Mediterranean; and the other narrow pond that surrounds this mole-hill, under the denomination of the great ocean; in wading through which the dwarf had never wet his mid-leg, while the other scarce moistened his heel. In going and coming through both hemispheres, they did all that lay in their power to discover whether or not the globe was inhabited. They stooped, they lay down, they groped in every corner; but their eyes and hands were not at all proportioned to the small beings that crawl upon this earth and, therefore, they could not find the smallest reason to suspect that we and our fellow-citizens of this globe had the honor to exist.

The dwarf, who sometimes judged too hastily, concluded at once that there were no living creatures upon earth; and his chief reason was, that he had seen nobody. But Micromegas, in a polite manner, made him sensible of the unjust conclusion:

"For," said he, "with your diminutive eyes you cannot see certain stars of the fiftieth magnitude, which I easily perceive; and do you take it for granted that no such stars exist?"

"But I have groped with great care," replied the dwarf.

"Then your sense of feeling must be bad," said the other.

"But this globe," said the dwarf, "is ill contrived; and so irregular in its form as to be quite ridiculous. The whole together looks like a chaos. Do but observe these little rivulets; not one of them runs in a straight line: and these ponds which are neither round, square, nor oval, nor indeed of any regular figure; together with these sharp pebbles (meaning the mountains) that roughen the whole surface of the globe, and have torn all the skin from my feet. Besides, pray take notice of the shape of the whole, how it flattens at the poles, and turns round the sun in an awkward oblique manner, so as that the polar circles cannot possibly be cultivated. Truly, what makes me believe there is no inhabitant on this sphere, is a full persuasion that no sensible being would live in such a disagreeable place."

"What then?" said Micromegas, "perhaps the beings that inhabit it come not under that denomination; but, to all appearance, it was not made for nothing. Everything here seems to you irregular; because you fetch all your comparisons from Jupiter or Saturn. Perhaps this is the very reason of the seeming confusion which you condemn; have I not told you, that in the course of my travels I have always met with variety?"

The Saturnian replied to all these arguments; and perhaps the dispute would have known no end, if Micromegas, in the heat of the contest, had not luckily broken the string of his diamond necklace, so that the jewels fell to the ground; they consisted of pretty small unequal karats, the largest of which weighed four hundred pounds, and the smallest fifty. The dwarf, in helping to pick them up, perceived, as they approached his eye, that every single diamond was cut in such a manner as to answer the purpose of an excellent microscope. He therefore took up a small one, about one hundred and sixty feet in diameter, and applied it to his eye, while Micromegas chose another of two thousand five hundred feet. Though they were of excellent powers, the observers could perceive nothing by their assistance, so they were altered and adjusted. At length, the inhabitant of Saturn discerned something almost imperceptible moving between two waves in the Baltic. This was no other than a whale, which, in a dexterous manner, he caught with his little finger, and, placing it on the nail of his thumb, showed it to the Syrian, who laughed heartily at the excessive smallness peculiar to the inhabitants of this our globe. The Saturnian, by this time convinced that our world was inhabited, began to imagine we had no other animals than whales; and being a mighty debater, he forthwith set about investigating the origin and motion of this small atom, curious to know whether or not it was furnished with ideas, judgment, and free will. Micromegas was very much perplexed upon this subject. He examined the animal with the most patient attention, and the result of his inquiry was, that he could see no reason to believe a soul was lodged in such a body. Two travelers were actually inclined to think there was no such thing as mind in this our habitation, when, by the help of their microscope, they perceived something as large as a whale floating upon the surface of the sea. It is well known that, at this period, a flight of philosophers were upon their return from the polar circle, where they had been making observations, for which nobody has hitherto been the wiser. The gazettes record that their vessel ran ashore on the coast of Bothnia and that they with great difficulty saved their lives; but in this world one can never dive to the bottom of things. For my own part, I will ingenuously recount the transaction just as it happened, without any addition of my own; and this is no small effort in a modern historian.

The Travelers Capture a Vessel

Micromegas stretched out his hand gently toward the place where the object appeared, and advanced two fingers, which he instantly pulled back, for fear of being disappointed, then opening softly and shutting them all at once, he very dexterously seized the ship that contained those gentlemen, and placed it on his nail, avoiding too much pressure, which might have crushed the whole in pieces.

"This," said the Saturnian dwarf, "is a creature very different from the former."

Upon which the Sirian placing the supposed animal in the hollow of his hand, the passengers and crew, who believed themselves thrown by a hurricane upon some rock, began to put themselves in motion. The sailors having hoisted out some casks of wine, jumped after them into the hand of Micromegas: the mathematicians having secured their quadrants, sectors, and Lapland servants, went overboard at a different place, and made such a bustle in their descent, that the Sirian at length felt his fingers tickled by something that seemed to move. An iron bar chanced to penetrate about a foot deep into his forefinger; and from this prick he concluded that something had issued from the little animal he held in his hand; but at first he suspected nothing more: for the microscope, that scarce rendered a whale and a ship visible, had no effect upon an object so imperceptible as man.

I do not intend to shock the vanity of any person whatever; but here I am obliged to beg your people of importance to consider that, supposing the stature of a man to be about five feet, we mortals make just such a figure upon the earth, as an animal the sixty thousandth part of a foot in height would exhibit upon a bowl ten feet in circumference. When you reflect upon a being who could hold this whole earth in the palm of his hand, and is provided with organs proportioned to those we possess, you will easily conceive that there must be a great variety of created substances—and pray, what must such beings think of those battles by which a conqueror gains a small village, to lose it again in the sequel?

I do not at all doubt, but if some captain of grenadiers should chance to read this work, he would add two large feet at least to the caps of his company; but I assure him his labor will be in vain; for, do what he will, he and his soldiers will never be other than infinitely diminutive and inconsiderable.

What wonderful address must have been inherent in our Sirian philosopher that enabled him to perceive those atoms of which we have been speaking. When Leuwenhock and Hartsoecker observed the first rudiments of which we are formed, they did not make such an astonishing discovery. What pleasure, therefore, was the portion of Micromegas, in observing the motion of those little machines, in examining all their pranks, and following them in all their operations! With what joy did he put his microscope into his companion's hand; and with what transport did they both at once exclaim:

"I see them distinctly—don't you see them carrying burdens, lying down and rising up again?"

So saying, their hands shook with eagerness to see, and apprehension to lose such uncommon objects. The Saturnian, making a sudden transition from the most cautious distrust to the most excessive credulity, imagined he saw them engaged in their devotions and cried aloud in astonishment.

Nevertheless, he was deceived by appearances: a case too common, whether we do or do not make use of microscopes.

What Happened in Their Intercourse with Men

Micromegas being a much better observer than the dwarf, perceived distinctly that those atoms spoke; and made the remark to his companion, who was so much ashamed of being mistaken in his first suggestion, that he would not believe such a puny species could possibly communicate their ideas: for, though he had the gift of tongues, as well as his companion, he could not hear those particles speak; and therefore supposed they had no language.

"Besides, how should such imperceptible beings have the organs of speech? and what in the name of Jove can they say to one another? In order to speak, they must have something like thought, and if they think, they must surely have something equivalent to a soul. Now, to attribute anything like a soul to such an insect species appears a mere absurdity."

"But just now," replied the Sirian, "you believed they were engaged in devotional exercises; and do you think this could be done without thinking, without using some sort of language, or at least some way of making themselves understood? Or do you suppose it is more difficult to advance an argument than to engage in physical exercise? For my own part, I look upon all faculties as alike mysterious."

"I will no longer venture to believe or deny," answered the dwarf: "in short I have no opinion at all. Let us endeavor to examine these insects, and we will reason upon them afterward."

"With all my heart," said Micromegas, who, taking out a pair of scissors which he kept for paring his nails, cut off a paring from his thumb nail, of which he immediately formed a large kind of speaking trumpet, like a vast tunnel, and clapped the pipe to his ear: as the circumference of this machine included the ship and all the crew, the most feeble voice was conveyed along the circular fibers of the nail; so that, thanks to his industry, the philosopher could distinctly hear the buzzing of our insects that were below. In a few hours he distinguished articulate sounds, and at last plainly understood the French language. The dwarf heard the same, though with more difficulty.

The astonishment of our travelers increased every instant. They heard a nest of mites talk in a very sensible strain: and that . . . seemed to them inexplicable. You need not doubt but the Sirian and his dwarf glowed with impatience to enter into conversation with such atoms. Micromegas being afraid that his voice, like thunder, would deafen and confound the mites, without being understood by them, saw the necessity of diminishing the sound; each, therefore, put into his mouth a sort of small toothpick, the slender end of which reached to the vessel. The Sirian setting the dwarf upon his knees, and the ship and crew upon his nail, held down his head and spoke softly. In fine, having taken these and a great many more precautions, he addressed himself to them in these words:

"O ye invisible insects, whom the hand of the Creator hath deigned to produce in the abyss of infinite littleness! I give praise to his goodness, in that he hath been pleased to disclose unto me those secrets that seemed to be impenetrable."

If ever there was such a thing as astonishment, it seized upon the people who heard this address, and who could not conceive from whence it proceeded. The chaplain of the ship repeated exorcisms, the sailors swore, and the philosophers formed a system: but, notwithstanding all their systems, they could not divine who the person was that spoke to them. Then the dwarf of Saturn, whose voice was softer than that of Micromegas, gave them briefly to understand what species of beings they had to do with. He related the particulars of their voyage from Saturn, made them acquainted with the rank and quality of Monsieur Micromegas; and, after having pitied their smallness, asked if they had always been in that miserable state so near akin to annihilation;

and what their business was upon that globe which seemed to be the property of whales. He also desired to know if they were happy in their situation? if they were inspired with souls? and put a hundred questions of the like nature.

A certain mathematician on board, braver than the rest, and shocked to hear his soul called in question, planted his quadrant, and having taken two observations of this interlocutor, said: "You believe then, Mr. what's your name, that because you measure from head to foot a thousand fathoms——"

"A thousand fathoms!" cried the dwarf, "good heavens! How should he know the height of my stature? A thousand fathoms! My very dimensions to a hair. What, measured by a mite! This atom, forsooth, is a geometrician, and knows exactly how tall I am: while I, who can scarce perceive him through a microscope, am utterly ignorant of his extent!"

"Yes, I have taken your measure," answered the philosopher, "and I will now do the same by your tall companion."

The proposal was embraced: his excellency reclined upon his side; for, had he stood upright, his head would have reached too far above the clouds. Our mathematicians planted a tall tree near him, and then, by a series of triangles joined together, they discovered that the object of their observation was a strapping youth, exactly one hundred and twenty thousand royal feet in length. In consequence of this calculation, Micromegas uttered these words:

"I am now more than ever convinced that we ought to judge of nothing by its external magnitude. O God! who hast bestowed understanding upon such seemingly contemptible substances, thou canst with equal ease produce that which is infinitely small, as that which is incredibly great: and if it be possible, that among thy works there are beings still more diminutive than these, they may nevertheless, be endued with understanding superior to the intelligence of those stupendous animals I have seen in heaven, a single foot of whom is larger than this whole globe on which I have alighted."

One of the philosophers assured him that there were intelligent beings much smaller than men, and recounted not only Virgil's whole fable of the bees; but also described all that Swammerdam hath discovered, and Reaumur dissected. In a word, he informed him that there are animals which bear the same proportion to bees, that bees bear to man; the same as the Sirian himself compared to those vast beings whom he had mentioned; and as those huge animals as to other substances, before whom they would appear like so many particles of dust. Here the conversation became very interesting, and Micromegas proceeded in these words:

"O ye intelligent atoms, in whom the Supreme Being hath been pleased to manifest his omniscience and power, without all doubt your joys on this earth must be pure and exquisite: for, being unencumbered with matter, and, to all appearance, little else than soul, you must spend your lives in the delights of pleasure and reflection, which are the true enjoyments of a perfect spirit. True happiness I have no where found; but certainly here it dwells."

At this harangue all the philosophers shook their heads, and one among them, more candid than his brethren, frankly owned, that expecting a very small number of inhabitants who were very little esteemed by their fellows, all the rest were a parcel of knaves, fools, and miserable wretches.

"We have matter enough," said he, "to do abundance of mischief, if mischief comes from matter; and too much understanding, if evil flows from understanding. You must know, for example, that at this very moment, while I am speaking, there are one hundred thousand animals of our own species, covered with hats, slaying an equal number of their fellow-creatures, who wear turbans; at least they are either slaying or being slain; and this hath usually been the case all over the earth from time immemorial."

The Sirian, shuddering at this information, begged to know the cause of those horrible quarrels among such a puny race; and was given to understand that the subject of the dispute was a pitiful mole-hill [called Palestine] no larger than his heel. Not that any one of those millions who cut one another's throats pretends to have the least claim to the smallest particle of that clod. The question is, whether it shall belong to a certain person who is known by the name of Sultan, or to another whom (for what reason I know not) they dignify with the appellation of King. Neither the one nor the other has seen or ever will see the pitiful corner in question; and probably none of these wretches, who so madly destroy each other, ever beheld the ruler on whose account they are so mercilessly sacrificed!

"Ah, miscreants!" cried the indignant Sirian, "such excess of desperate rage is beyond conception. I have a good mind to take two or three steps, and trample the whole nest of such ridiculous assassins under my feet."

"Don't give yourself the trouble," replied the philosopher, "they are industrious enough in procuring their own destruction. At the end of ten years the hundredth part of those wretches will not survive; for you must know that, though they should not draw a sword in the cause they have espoused, famine, fatigue, and intemperance, would sweep almost all of them from the face of the earth. Besides, the punishment should not be inflicted upon them, but upon those sedentary and slothful barbarians, who, from their palaces, give orders for murdering a million of men and then solemnly thank God for their success."

Our traveler was moved with compassion for the entire human race, in which he discovered such astonishing contrast. "Since you are of the small number of the wise," said he, "and in all likelihood do not engage yourselves in the trade of murder for hire, be so good as to tell me your occupation."

"We anatomize flies," replied the philosopher, "we measure lines, we make calculations, we agree upon two or three points which we understand, and dispute upon two or three thousand that are beyond our comprehension."

"How far," said the Sirian, "do you reckon the distance between the great star of the constellation Gemini and that called Canicula?"

To this question all of them answered with one voice: "Thirty-two degrees and a half."

"And what is the distance from hence to the moon?"

"Sixty semi-diameters of the earth."

He then thought to puzzle them by asking the weight of the air; but they answered distinctly, that common air is about nine hundred times specifically lighter than an equal column of the lightest water, and nineteen hundred times lighter than current gold. The little dwarf of Saturn, astonished at their answers, was now tempted to believe those people sorcerers, who, but a quarter of an hour before, he would not allow were inspired with souls.

"Well," said Micromegas, "since you know so well what is without you, doubtless you are still more perfectly acquainted with that which is within. Tell me what is the soul, and how do your ideas originate?"

Here the philosophers spoke altogether as before; but each was of a different opinion. The eldest quoted Aristotle; another pronounced the name of Descartes; a third mentioned Malebranche; a fourth Leibniz; and a fifth Locke. An old peripatecian, lifting up his voice, exclaimed with an air of confidence: "The soul is perfection and reason, having power to be such as it is, as Aristotle expressly declares, page 633, of the Louvre edition.

"I am not very well versed in Greek," said the giant.

"Nor I either," replied the philosophical mite.

"Why then do you quote that same Aristotle in Greek?" resumed the Sirian.

"Because," answered the other, "it is but reasonable we should quote what we do not comprehend in a language we do not understand."

Here the Cartesian interposing: "The soul," said he, "is a pure spirit or intelligence, which hath received before birth all the metaphysical ideas; but after that event it is obliged to go to school and learn anew the knowledge which it hath lost."

"So it was necessary," replied the animal of eight leagues, "that thy soul should be learned before birth, in order to be so ignorant when thou hast got a beard upon thy chin. But what dost thou understand by spirit?"

"I have no idea of it," said the philosopher, "indeed it is supposed to be immaterial."

"At least, thou knowest what matter is?" resumed the Sirian.

"Perfectly well," answered the other. "For example: that stone is gray, is of a certain figure, has three dimensions, specific weight, and divisibility."

"I want to know," said the giant, "what that object is, which, according to thy observation, hath a gray color, weight, and divisibility. Thou seest a few qualities, but dost thou know the nature of the thing itself?"

"Not I, truly," answered the Cartesian.

Upon which the Sirian admitted that he also was ignorant in regard to this subject. Then addressing himself to another sage, who stood upon his thumb, he asked "what is the soul? and what are her functions?"

"Nothing at all," replied this disciple of Malebranche; "God hath made everything for my convenience. In him I see everything, by him I act; he is the universal agent, and I never meddle in his work."

"This is being a nonentity indeed," said the Sirian sage; and then, turning to a follower of Leibniz, he exclaimed: "Hark ye, friend, what is thy opinion of the soul?"

"In my opinion," answered this metaphysician, "the soul is the hand that points at the hour, while my body does the office of the clock; or, if you please, the soul is the clock, and the body is the pointer; or again, my soul is the mirror of the universe, and my body the frame. All this is clear and incontrovertible."

A little partisan of Locke who chanced to be present, being asked his opinion on the same subject, said: "I do not know by what power I think; but well I know that I should never have thought without the assistance of my senses. That there are immaterial and intelligent substances I do not at all doubt; but that it is impossible for God to communicate the faculty of thinking to matter, I doubt very much. I revere the eternal power, to which it would ill become me to prescribe bounds. I affirm nothing, and am contented to believe that many more things are possible than are usually thought so."

The Sirian smiled at this declaration, and did not look upon the author as the least sagacious of the company: and as for the dwarf of Saturn, he would have embraced this adherent of Locke, had it not been for the extreme disproportion in their respective sizes. But unluckily there was another animalcule in a square cap, who, taking the word from all his philosophical brethren, affirmed that he knew the whole secret. He surveyed the two celestial strangers from top to toe, and maintained to their faces that their persons, their fashions, their suns and their stars, were created solely for the use of man. At this wild assertion our two travelers were seized with a fit of that uncontrollable laughter, which (according to Homer) is the portion of the immortal gods: their bellies quivered, their shoulders rose and fell, and, during these convulsions, the vessel fell from the Sirian's nail into the Saturnian's pocket, where these worthy people searched for it a long time with great diligence. At length, having found the ship and set everything to rights again, the Sirian resumed the discourse with those diminutive mites, and promised to compose for them a choice book of philosophy which would demonstrate the very essence of things. Accordingly, before his departure, he made them a present of the book, which was brought to the Academy of Sciences at Paris, but when the old secretary came to open it he saw nothing but blank paper.

"Ay, ay," said he, "this is just what I suspected."

THAT I EXIST

René Descartes

Yesterday's Meditation has filled my mind with so many doubts that it is no longer in my power to forget them. Nor do I yet see how I will be able to resolve them; I feel as though I were suddenly thrown into deep water, being so disconcerted that I can neither plant my feet on the bottom nor swim on the surface. I shall nevertheless make every effort to conform precisely to the plan commenced yesterday and put aside every belief in which I could imagine the least doubt, just as though I knew that it was absolutely false. And I shall continue in this manner until I have found something certain, or at least, if I can do nothing else, until I have learned with certainty that there is nothing certain in this world. Archimedes, to move the earth from its orbit and place it in a new position, demanded nothing more than a fixed and immovable fulcrum; in a similar manner I shall have the right to entertain high hopes if I am fortunate enough to find a single truth which is certain and indubitable.

I suppose, accordingly, that everything that I see is false; I convince myself that nothing has ever existed of all that my deceitful memory recalls to me. I think that I have no senses; and I believe that body, shape, extension, motion, and location are merely inventions of my mind. What then could still be thought true? Perhaps nothing else, unless it is that there is nothing certain in the world.

But how do I know that there is not some entity, of a different nature from what I have just judged uncertain, of which there cannot be the least doubt? Is there not some God or some other power who gives me these thoughts? But I need not think this to be true, for possibly I am able to produce them myself. Then, at the very least, am I not an entity myself? But I have already denied that I had any senses or any body. However, at this point I hesitate, for what follows from

FROM "Second Meditation," in *Meditations on First Philosophy,* translated by Laurence J. La Fleur. Copyright © 1951, 1960 by the Liberal Arts Press, Inc. Reprinted by permission of the Liberal Arts Division of the Bobbs-Merrill Company.

that? Am I so dependent upon the body and the senses that I could not exist without them? I have just convinced myself that nothing whatsoever existed in the world, that there was no sky, no earth, no minds, and no bodies; have I not thereby convinced myself that I did not exist? Not at all; without doubt I existed if I was convinced [or even if I thought anything], Even though there may be a deceiver of some sort, very powerful and very tricky, who bends all his efforts to keep me perpetually deceived, there can be no slightest doubt that I exist, since he deceives me; and let him deceive me as much as he will, he can never make me be nothing as long as I think that I am something. Thus, after having thought well on this matter, and after examining all things with care, I must finally conclude and maintain that this proposition: *I am, I exist,* is necessarily true every time that I pronounce it or conceive it in my mind.

But I do not yet know sufficiently clearly what I am, I who am sure that I exist. So I must henceforth take very great care that I do not incautiously mistake some other thing for myself, and so make an error even in that knowledge which I maintain to be more certain and more evident than all other knowledge [that I previously had]. That is why I shall now consider once more what I thought myself to be before I began these last deliberations. Of my former opinions I shall reject all that are rendered even slightly doubtful by the arguments that I have just now offered, so that there will remain just that part alone which is entirely certain and indubitable.

What then have I previously believed myself to be? Clearly, I believed that I was a man. But what is a man? Shall I say a rational animal? Certainly not, for I would have to determine what an "animal" is and what is meant by "rational"; and so, from a single question, I would find myself gradually enmeshed in an infinity of others more difficult [and more inconvenient], and I would not care to waste the little time and leisure remaining to me in disentangling such difficulties. I shall rather pause here to consider the ideas which previously arose naturally and of themselves in my mind whenever I considered what I was. I thought of myself first as having a face, hands, arms, and all this mechanism composed of [bone and flesh and] members, just as it appears in a corpse, and which I designated by the name of "body." In addition, I thought of the fact that I consumed nourishment, that I walked, that I perceived and thought, and I ascribed all these actions to the soul. But either I did not stop to consider what this soul was or else, if I did, I imagined that it was something very rarefied and subtle, such as a wind, a flame, or a very much expanded air which [penetrated into and] was infused throughout my grosser components. As for what body was, I did not realize that there could be any doubt about it, for I thought that

I recognized its nature very distinctly. If I had wished to explain it according to the notions that I then entertained, I would have described it somewhat in this way: by "body" I understand all that can be bounded by some figure; that can be located in some place and occupy space in such a way that every other body is excluded from it; that can be perceived by touch or sight or hearing or taste or smell; that can be moved in various ways, not by itself but by some other object by which it is touched [and from which it receives an impulse]. For to possess the power to move itself, and also to feel or to think, I did not believe at all that these are attributes of corporeal nature; on the contrary, rather, I was astonished to see a few bodies possessing such abilities.

But I, what am I, on the basis of the present hypothesis that there is a certain spirit who is extremely powerful and, if I may dare to say so, malicious [and tricky], and who uses all his abilities and efforts in order to deceive me? Can I be sure that I possess the smallest fraction of all those characteristics which I have just now said belonged to the nature of body? I pause to consider this attentively. I pass and repass in review in my mind each one of all these things—it is not necessary to pause to take the time to list them—and I do not find any one of them which I can pronounce to be part of me. Is it characteristic of me to consume nourishment and to walk? But if it is true that I do not have a body, these also are nothing but figments of the imagination. To perceive? But once more, I cannot perceive without the body, except in the sense that I have thought I perceived various things during sleep, which I recognized upon waking not to have been really perceived. To think? Here I find the answer. Thought is an attribute that belongs to me; it alone is inseparable from my nature.

I am, I exist—that is certain; but for how long do I exist? For as long as I think; for it might perhaps happen, if I totally ceased thinking, that I would at the same time completely cease to be. I am now admitting nothing except what is necessarily true. I am therefore, to speak precisely, only a thinking being, that is to say, a mind, an understanding, or a reasoning being, which are terms whose meaning was previously unknown to me.

I am something real and really existing, but what thing am I? I have already given the answer: a thing which thinks. And what more? I will stimulate my imagination [to see if I am not something else beyond this]. I am not this assemblage of members which is called a human body; I am not a rarefied and penetrating air spread throughout all these members; I am not a wind, [a flame,] a breath, a vapor, or anything at all that I can imagine and picture to myself—since I have supposed that all that was nothing, and since, without abandoning this supposition, I find that I do not cease to be certain that I am something.

But perhaps it is true that those same things which I suppose not to exist because I do not know them are really no different from the self which I do know. As to that I cannot decide; I am not discussing that question at the moment, since I can pass judgment only upon those things which are known to me: I know that I exist and I am seeking to discover what I am, that "I" that I know to be. Now it is very certain that this notion [and knowledge of my being], thus precisely understood, does not depend on things whose existence is not yet known to me; and consequently [and even more certainly], it does not depend on any of those things that I [can] picture in my imagination. And even these terms, "picture" and "imagine," warn me of my error. For I would be imagining falsely indeed were I to picture myself as something; since to imagine is nothing else than to contemplate the shape or image of a bodily entity, and I already know both that I certainly exist and that it is altogether possible that all these images, and everything in general which is involved in the nature of body, are only dreams [and illusions]. From this I see clearly that there was no more sense in saying that I would stimulate my imagination to learn more distinctly what I am than if I should say: I am now awake, and I see something real and true; but because I do not yet perceive it sufficiently clearly, I will go to sleep on purpose, in order that my dreams will show it to me with more truth and evidence. And thus I know manifestly that nothing of all that I can understand by means of the imagination is pertinent to the knowledge which I have of myself, and that I must remember this and prevent my mind from thinking in this fashion, in order that it may clearly perceive its own nature.

But what then am I? A thinking being. What is a thinking being? It is a being which doubts, which understands, [which conceives,] which affirms, which denies, which wills, which rejects, which imagines also, and which perceives. It is certainly not a trivial matter if all these things belong to my nature. But why should they not belong to it? Am I not that same person who now doubts almost everything, who nevertheless understands [and conceives] certain things, who [is sure of and] affirms the truth of this one thing alone, who denies all the others, who wills and desires to know more about them, who rejects error, who imagines many things, sometimes even against my will, and who also perceives many things, as through the medium of the senses [for the organs of the body]? Is there anything in all that which is not just as true as it is certain that I am and that I exist, even though I were always asleep and though the one who created me directed all his efforts to deluding me? And is there any one of these attributes which can be distinguished from my thinking or which can be said to be separable from my nature? For it is so obvious that it is I who doubt, understand, and desire, that nothing could be added to make it more evident. And I am also certainly the same one who imagines for once more, even though it could happen that the things I imagine are not true, nevertheless this power of imagining cannot fail to be real, and it is part of my thinking. Finally I am the same being which perceives—that is, which observes certain objects as though by means of the sense organs, because I do really see light, hear noises, feel heat. Will it be said that these appearances are false and that I am sleeping? [Let it be so; yet at the very least] it is certain that it seems to me that I see light, hear noises, and feel heat. This much cannot be false, and it is this, properly considered, which in my nature is called perceiving, and that, again speaking precisely, is nothing else but thinking.

As a result of these considerations, I begin to recognize what I am somewhat better [and with a little more clarity and distinctness] than heretofore. But nevertheless it still seems to me, and I cannot keep myself from believing that corporeal things, images of which are formed by thought and which the senses themselves examine, are much more distinctly known than that indescribable part of myself which cannot be pictured by the imagination. Yet it would truly be very strange to say that I know and comprehend more distinctly things whose existence seems doubtful to me, that are unknown to me and do not belong to me, than those of whose truth I am persuaded, which are known to me, and which belong to my real nature—to say, in a word, that I know them better than myself. But I see well what is the trouble: my mind is a vagabond who likes to wander and is not yet able to stay within the strict bounds of truth. Therefore, let us [give it the rein once more and] allow it every kind of liberty, [permitting it to consider the objects which appear to be external,] so that when a little later we come to restrain it [gently and] at the right time and force it to the consideration of its own nature and of the things that it finds in itself, it will more readily permit itself to be ruled and guided.

Let us now consider the [commonest] things, which are commonly believed to be the most distinctly known [and the easiest of all to know], namely, the bodies which we touch and see. I do not intend to speak of bodies in general, for general notions are usually somewhat more confused; let us rather consider one body in particular. Let us take, for example, this bit of wax which has just been taken from the hive. It has not yet completely lost the sweetness of the honey it contained; it still retains something of the odor of the flowers from which it was collected; its color, shape, and size are apparent; it is hard and cold; it can easily be touched; and, if you knock on it, it will give out some sound. Thus everything which can make a body distinctly known are found in this example.

But now while I am talking I bring it close to the fire. What remains of the taste evaporates; the odor vanishes; its color changes; its shape is lost; its size increases; it becomes liquid; it grows hot; one can hardly touch it; and although it is knocked upon, it will give out no sound. Does the same wax remain after this change? We must admit that it does; no one denies it, no one judges otherwise. What is it then in this bit of wax that we recognize with so much distinctness? Certainly it cannot be anything that I observed by means of the senses, since everything in the field of taste, smell, sight, touch, and hearing are changed, and since the same wax nevertheless remains.

The truth of the matter perhaps, as I now suspect, is that this wax was neither that sweetness of honey, nor that [pleasant] odor of flowers, nor that whiteness, nor that shape, nor that sound, but only a body which a little while ago appeared to my senses under these forms and which now makes itself felt under others. But what is it, to speak precisely, that I imagine [when I conceive it] in this fashion? Let us consider it attentively and, rejecting everything that does not belong to the wax, see what remains. Certainly nothing is left but something extended, flexible, and movable. But what is meant by flexible and movable? Does it consist in my picturing that this wax, being round, is capable of becoming square and of passing from the square into a triangular shape? Certainly not; [it is not that,] since I conceive it capable of undergoing an infinity of similar changes, and I could not compass this infinity in my imagination. Consequently this conception that I have of the wax is not achieved by the faculty of imagination.

Now what is this extension? Is it not also unknown? For it becomes greater in the melting wax, still greater when it is completely melted, and much greater again when the heat increases still more. And I would not conceive [clearly and] truthfully what wax was if I did not think that even this bit of wax is capable of receiving more variations in extension than I have ever imagined. We must therefore agree that I cannot even conceive what this bit of wax is by means of the imagination, and that there is nothing but my understanding alone which does conceive it. I say this bit of wax in particular, for as to wax in general, it is still more evident. But what is this bit of wax which cannot be comprehended except by [the understanding, or by] the mind? Certainly it is the same as the one that I see, that I touch, that I imagine; and finally it is the same as I always believed it to be from the beginning. But what is here important to notice is that perception [, or the action by which we perceive,] is not a vision, a touch, nor an imagination, and has never been that, even though it formerly appeared so; but is solely an inspection by the mind, which can be imperfect and confused as it was formerly, or clear and distinct as it is at present, as I attend more or less to the things [which are in it and] of which it is composed.

Now I am truly astonished when I consider [how weak my mind is and] how apt I am to fall into error. For even though I consider all this in my mind without speaking, still words impede me, and I am nearly deceived by the terms of ordinary language. For we say that we see the same wax if it is present, and not that we judge that it is the same from the fact that it has the same color or shape. Thus I might be tempted to conclude that one knows the wax by means of eyesight, and not uniquely by the perception of the mind. So I may by chance look out of a window and notice some men passing in the street, at the sight of whom I do not fail to say that I see men, just as I say that I see wax; and nevertheless what do I see from this window except hats and cloaks which might cover [ghosts, or] automata [which move only by springs]? But I judge that they are men, and thus I comprehend, solely by the faculty of judgment which resides in my mind, that which I believed I saw with my eyes.

A person who attempts to improve his understanding beyond the ordinary ought to be ashamed to go out of his way to criticize the forms of speech used by ordinary men. I prefer to pass over this matter and to consider whether I understood what wax was more evidently and more perfectly when I first noticed it and when I thought I knew it by means of the external senses, or at the very least by common sense, as it is called, or the imaginative faculty; or whether I conceive it better at present, after having more carefully examined what it is and how it can be known. Certainly it would be ridiculous to doubt the superiority of the latter method of knowing. For what was there in that first perception which was distinct [and evident]? What was there which might not occur similarly to the senses of the lowest of the animals? But when I distinguished the real wax from its superficial appearances, and when, just as though I had removed its garments, I consider it all naked, it is certain that although there might still be some error in my judgment, I could not conceive it in this fashion without a human mind.

And now what shall I say of the mind, that is to say, of myself? For so far I do not admit in myself anything other than the mind. Can it be that I, who seem to perceive this bit of wax so [clearly and] distinctly, do not know my own self, not only with much more truth and certainty, but also much more distinctly and evidently? For if I judge that the wax exists because I see it, certainly it follows much more evidently that I exist myself because I see it. For it might happen that what I see is not really wax; it might also happen that I do not even possess eyes to see anything; but it could not happen that, when I see, or what amounts to the same thing, when I think I see, I who think am not something. For a similar reason, if I judge that the wax exists because I touch it, the same conclusion follows once more, namely, that I am. And if I hold to this judgment because my imagination, or whatever other entity it might be, persuades me of it, I will still reach the same conclusion. And what I have said here about the wax can be applied to all other things which are external to me.

Furthermore, if the idea or knowledge of the wax seems clearer and more distinct to me after I have investigated it, not only by sight or touch, but also in many other ways, with how much more [evidence,] distinctness [and clarity] must it be admitted that I now know myself; since all the reasons which help me to know and conceive the nature of the wax, or of any other body whatsoever, serve much better to show the nature of my mind! And we also find so many other things in the mind itself which can contribute to the clarification of its nature, that those which depend on the body, such as the ones I have just mentioned, hardly deserve to be taken into account.

And at last here I am, having insensibly returned to where I wished to be; for since it is at present manifest to me that even bodies are not properly known by the senses nor by the faculty of imagination, but by the understanding alone; and since they are not known in so far as they are seen or touched, but only in so far as they are understood by thinking, I see clearly that there is nothing easier for me to understand than my mind. But since it is almost impossible to rid oneself so soon of an opinion of long standing, it would be wise to stop a while at this point, in order that, by the length of my meditation, I may impress this new knowledge more deeply upon my memory.

SOUL AND SELF

John Locke

1. Another occasion the mind often takes of comparing, is the very being of things, when, considering anything as existing at any determined time and place, we compare it with itself existing at another time, and thereon form the ideas of *identity* and *diversity*. When we see anything to be in any place in any instant of time, we are sure (be it what it will) that it is that very thing, and not another which at that same time exists in another place, how like and undistinguishable soever it may be in all other respects: and in this consists *identity*, when the ideas it is attributed to vary not at all from what they were that moment wherein we consider their former existence, and to which we compare the present. For we never finding, nor conceiving it possible, that two things of the same kind should exist in the same place at the same time, we rightly conclude, that, whatever exists anywhere at any time, excludes all of the same kind, and is there itself alone. When therefore we demand whether anything be the same or no, it refers always to something that existed such a time in such a place, which it was certain, at that instant, was the same with itself, and no other. From whence it follows, that one thing cannot have two beginnings of existence, nor two things one beginning; it being impossible for two things of the same kind to be or exist in the same instant, in the very same place; or one and the same thing in different places. That, therefore, that had one beginning, is the same thing; and that which had a different beginning in time and place from that, is not the same, but diverse. That which has made the difficulty about this relation has been the little care and attention used in having precise notions of the things to which it is attributed.

2. We have the ideas but of three sorts of substances: (1) *God*. (2) *Finite intelligences*. (3) *Bodies*.

First, *God* is without beginning, eternal, unalterable, and everywhere, and therefore concerning his identity there can be no doubt.

FROM *An Essay Concerning Human Understanding*, Book I (1690).

Secondly, *Finite spirits* having had each of its determinate time and place of beginning to exist, the relation to that time and place will always determine to each of them its identity, as long as it exists.

Thirdly, The same will hold of every *particle of matter,* to which no addition or subtraction of matter being made, it is the same. For, though these three sorts of substances, as we term them, do not exclude one another out of the same place, yet we cannot conceive but that they must necessarily each of them exclude any of the same kind out of the same place: or else the notions and names of identity and diversity would be in vain, and there could be no such distinctions of substances, or anything else one from another. For example: could two bodies be in the same place at the same time; then those two parcels of matter must be one and the same, take them great or little.

All other things being but modes or relations ultimately terminated in substances, the identity and diversity of each particular existence of them too will be by the same way determined: only as to things whose existence is in succession, such as are the actions of finite beings, e.g. *motion* and *thought,* both which consist in a continued train of succession, concerning their diversity there can be no question; because each perishing the moment it begins, they cannot exist in different times, or in different places, as permanent beings can at different times exist in distant places; and therefore no motion or thought, considered as at different times, can be the same, each part thereof having a different beginning of existence.

3. From what has been said, it is easy to discover what is so much inquired after, the *principium individuationis* [individuating principle]; and that, it is plain, is existence itself; which determines a being of any sort to a particular time and place, incommunicable to two beings of the same kind. This, though it seems easier to conceive in simple substances or modes; yet, when reflected on, is not more difficult in compound ones, if care be taken to what it is applied: e.g. let us suppose an atom, i.e. a continued body under one immutable superficies, existing in a determined time and place; it is evident, that, considered in any instant of its existence, it is in that instant the same with itself. For, being at that instant what it is, and nothing else, it is the same, and so must continue as long as its existence is continued; for so long it will be the same, and no other. In like manner, if two or more atoms be joined together into the same mass, every one of those atoms will be the same, by the foregoing rule: and whilst they exist united together, the mass, consisting of the same atoms, must be the same mass, or the same body, let the parts be ever so differently jumbled. But if one of these atoms be taken away, or one new one added, it is no longer the same mass or the same body. In the state of living creatures, their

identity depends not on a mass of the same particles, but on something else. For in them the variation of great parcels of matter alters not the identity: an oak growing from a plant to a great tree, and then lopped, is still the same oak; and a colt grown up to a horse, sometimes fat, sometimes lean, is all the while the same horse: though, in both these cases, there may be a manifest change of the parts; so that truly they are not either of them the same masses of matter, though they be truly one of them the same oak, and the other the same horse. The reason whereof is, that, in these two cases—a *mass of matter* and a *living body* —identity is not applied to the same thing.

4, 5. We must therefore consider wherein an oak differs from a mass of matter, and that seems to me to be in this, that the one is only the cohesion of particles of matter any how united, the other such a disposition of them as constitutes the parts of an oak; and such an organization of those parts as is fit to receive and distribute nourishment, so as to continue and frame the wood, bark, and leaves, etc., of an oak, in which consists the vegetable life. For this organization, being at any one instant in any one collection of matter, is in that particular concrete distinguished from all other, and *is* that individual life. The case is not so much different in *brutes* but that any one may hence see what makes an animal and continues it the same.

6. This also shows wherein the identity of the same *man* consists; viz. in nothing but a participation of the same continued life, by constantly fleeting particles of matter, in succession vitally united to the same organized body. He that shall place the identity of man in anything else but, like that of other animals, in one fitly organized body, taken in any one instant, and from thence continued, under one organization of life, in several successively fleeting particles of matter united to it, will find it hard to make an embryo, one of years, mad and sober, the *same* man, by any supposition that will not make it possible for Seth, Ishmael, Socrates, Pilate, St. Augustine, and Caesar Borgia, to be the same man. For if the identity of *soul alone* makes the same *man;* and there be nothing in the nature of matter why the same individual spirit may not be united to different bodies, it will be possible that those men, living in distant ages, and of different tempers, may have been the same man: which way of speaking must be from a very strange use of the word man, applied to an idea out of which body and shape are excluded.

7, 8. It is not therefore unity of substance that comprehends all sorts of identity, or will determine it in every case; but to conceive and judge of it aright, we must consider what idea the word it is applied to stands for: it being one thing to be the same *substance,* another the same *man,* and a third the same *person,* if *person, man,* and *substance* are three names standing for three different ideas—for such as is the idea belonging to that name, such must be the identity. For I presume it is not the idea of a thinking or rational being alone that makes the *idea of a man* in most people's sense: but of a body, so and so shaped, joined to it; and if that be the idea of a man, the same successive body not shifted all at once must, as well as the same immaterial spirit, go to the making of the same man.

9. To find wherein personal identity consists, we must consider what *person* stands for; which, I think, is a thinking intelligent being, that has reason and reflection, and can consider itself as itself, the same thinking thing, in different times and places; which it does only by that *consciousness* which is inseparable from thinking, and, as it seems to me, essential to it: it being impossible for any one to perceive without *perceiving* that he does perceive. When we see, hear, smell, taste, feel, meditate, or will anything, we know that we do so. Thus it is always as to our present sensations and perceptions: and by this every one is to himself that which he calls *self*.

10. But it is further inquired, whether it be the same identical substance. That which seems to make the difficulty is this, that *consciousness* being interrupted always by forgetfulness, there being no moment of our lives wherein we have the whole train of all our past actions before our eyes in one view, but even the best memories losing the sight of one part whilst they are viewing another; and we sometimes, and that the greatest part of our lives, not reflecting on our past selves, being intent on our present thoughts, and in sound sleep having no thoughts at all, or at least none with that consciousness which remarks our waking thoughts—I say, in all these cases, our *consciousness* being interrupted, and we losing the sight of our past selves, doubts are raised whether we are the same thinking thing, i.e. the same *substance,* or no. Which, however reasonable or unreasonable, concerns not *personal* identity at all: the question being what makes the same person; and not whether it be the same identical substance, which always thinks in the same person, which, in this case, matters not at all: different substances, by the same consciousness (where they do partake in it) being united into one person, as well as different bodies by the same life are united into one animal, whose identity is preserved in that change of substances by the unity of one continued life. For, it being the same consciousness that makes a man be himself to himself, personal identity depends on that only, whether it be annexed solely to one individual substance, or can be continued in a succession of several substances.

11. That this is so, we have some kind of evidence in our very bodies, all whose particles, whilst vitally united to this same thinking conscious

self, so that *we feel* when they are touched, and are affected by, and conscious of, good or harm that happens to them, are a part of ourselves; i.e. of our thinking conscious self. Thus, the limbs of his body are to every one a part of himself; he sympathizes and is concerned for them. Cut off a hand, and thereby separate it from that consciousness he had of its heat, cold, and other affections, and it is then no longer a part of that which is himself, any more than the remotest part of matter. Thus, we see the *substance* whereof personal self consisted at one time may be varied at another, without the change of personal identity; there being no question about the same person, though the limbs, which but now were a part of it, be cut off.

12. But the question is, Whether, if the same substance which thinks be changed, it can be the same person; or, remaining the same, it can be different persons.

And to this I answer: First, This can be no question at all to those who place thought in a purely material animal constitution, void of an immaterial substance. For, whether their supposition be true or no, it is plain they conceive personal identity preserved in something else than identity of substance; as animal identity is preserved in identity of life, and not of substance. And therefore those who place thinking in an immaterial substance only, before they can come to deal with these men, must show why personal identity cannot be preserved in the change of immaterial substances, or variety of particular immaterial substances, as well as animal identity is preserved in the change of material substances, or variety of particular bodies: unless they will say, it is one immaterial spirit that makes the same life in brutes, as it is one immaterial spirit that makes the same person in men; which the Cartesians at least will not admit, for fear of making brutes thinking things too.

13. But next, as to the first part of the question, whether, if the same thinking substance (supposing immaterial substances only to think) be changed, it can be the same person. I answer: That cannot be resolved but by those who know what kind of substances they are that do think; and whether the consciousness of past actions can be transferred from one thinking substance to another. I grant, were the same consciousness the same individual action, it could not: but it being a present representation of a past action, why it may not be possible that that may be represented to the mind to have been which really never was, will remain to be shown. And therefore how far the consciousness of past actions is annexed to any individual agent, so that another cannot possibly have it, will be hard for us to determine, till we know what kind of action it is that cannot be done without a reflex act of

perception accompanying it, and how performed by thinking substances, who cannot think without being conscious of it. But that which we call the same consciousness, not being the same individual act, why one intellectual substance may not have represented to it, as done by itself, what *it* never did, and was perhaps done by some other agent—why, I say, such a representation may not possibly be without reality of matter of fact, as well as several representations in dreams are, which yet whilst dreaming we take for true—will be difficult to conclude from the nature of things. And that it never is so, will by us, till we have clearer views of the nature of thinking substances, be best resolved into the goodness of God; who, as far as the happiness or misery of any of his sensible creatures is concerned in it, will not, by a fatal error of theirs, transfer from one to another that consciousness which draws reward or punishment with it. How far this may be an argument against those who would place thinking in a system of fleeting animal spirits, I leave to be considered. But yet, to return to the question before us, it must be allowed, that, if the same consciousness (which, as has been shown, is quite a different thing from the same numerical figure or motion in body) can be transferred from one thinking substance to another, it will be possible that two thinking substances may make but one person. For the same consciousness being preserved, whether in the same or different substances, the personal identity is preserved.

14. As to the second part of the question, whether, the same immaterial substance remaining, there may be two distinct persons; which question seems to me to be built on this: whether the same immaterial being, being conscious of the action of its past duration, may be wholly stripped of all the consciousness of its past existence, and lose it beyond the power of ever retrieving it again; and so as it were beginning a new account from a new period, have a consciousness that *cannot* reach beyond this new state. All those who hold pre-existence are evidently of this mind; since they allow the soul to have no remaining consciousness of what it did in that pre-existent state, either wholly separate from body, or informing any other body; and if they should not, it is plain experience would be against them. So that, personal identity reaching no further than consciousness reaches, a pre-existent spirit not having continued so many ages in a state of silence, must needs make different persons. I once met with one who was persuaded his had been the *soul* of Socrates (how reasonably I will not dispute; this I know, that in the post he filled, which was no inconsiderable one, he passed for a very rational man, and the press has shown that he wanted not parts or learning); would any one say, that he, being not conscious of any of Socrates' actions or thoughts, could be the same *person* with Socrates? Let any one reflect upon himself, and conclude that he has in himself

an immaterial spirit, which is that which thinks in him, and in the constant change of his body keeps him the same, and is that which he calls *himself:* let him also suppose it to be the same soul that was in Nestor or Thersites, at the siege of Troy (for souls being, as far as we know anything of them, in their nature indifferent to any parcel of matter, the supposition has no apparent absurdity in it), which it may have been, as well as it is now the soul of any other man: but he now having no consciousness of any of the actions either of Nestor or Thersites, does or can he conceive himself the same person with either of them? Can he be concerned in either of their actions? attribute them to himself, or think them his own, more than the actions of any other men that ever existed? So that, this consciousness not reaching to any of the actions of either of those men, he is no more one *self* with either of them than if the soul or immaterial spirit that now informs him had been created, and began to exist, when it began to inform his present body; though it were never so true, that the same *spirit* that informed Nestor's or Thersites' body were numerically the same that now informs his. For this would no more make him the same person with Nestor, than if some of the particles of matter that were once a part of Nestor were now a part of this man; the same immaterial substance, without the same consciousness, no more making the same person, by being united to any body, than the same particle of matter, without consciousness, united to any body, makes the same person. But let him once find himself conscious of any of the actions of Nestor, he then finds himself the same person with Nestor.

15. And thus may we be able, without any difficulty, to conceive the same person at the resurrection, though in a body not exactly in make or parts the same which he had here—the same consciousness going along with the soul that inhabits it. But yet the soul alone, in the change of bodies, would scarce to any one but to him that makes the soul the man, be enough to make the same man. For should the soul of a prince, carrying with it the consciousness of the prince's past life, enter and inform the body of a cobbler, as soon as deserted by his own soul, every one sees he would be the same *person* with the prince, accountable only for the prince's actions: but who would say it was the same *man?*

16. But though the same immaterial substance or soul does not alone, wherever it be, in whatsoever state, make the same *man;* yet it is plain, consciousness, as far as ever it can be extended—should it be to ages past—unites existences and actions very remote in time into the same *person,* as well as it does the existences and actions of the immediately preceding moment: so that whatever has the consciousness of present and past actions, is the same person to whom they both belong. Had I

the same consciousness that I saw the ark and Noah's flood, as that I saw an overflowing of the Thames last winter, or as that I write now, I could no more doubt that I who write this now, that saw the Thames overflowed last winter, and that viewed the flood at the general deluge, was the same *self*—place that self in what *substance* you please—than that I who write this am the same *myself* now whilst I write (whether I consist of all the same substance, material or immaterial, or no) that I was yesterday. For as to this point of being the same self, it matters not whether this present self be made up of the same or other substances— I being as much concerned and as justly accountable for any action that was done a thousand years since, appropriated to me now by this self-consciousness, as I am for what I did the last moment.

17. *Self* is that conscious thinking thing—whatever substance made up of (whether spiritual or material, simple or compounded, it matters not)—which is sensible or conscious of pleasure and pain, capable of happiness or misery, and so is concerned for itself, as far as that consciousness extends. Thus every one finds that, whilst comprehended under that consciousness, the little finger is as much a part of himself as what is most so. Upon separation of this little finger, should this consciousness go along with the little finger, and leave the rest of the body, it is evident the little finger would be the person, the same person; and self then would have nothing to do with the rest of the body. As in this case it is the consciousness that goes along with the substance, when one part is separate from another, which makes the same person, and constitutes this inseparable self: so it is in reference to substances remote in time. That with which the consciousness of this present thinking thing *can* join itself, makes the same person, and is one self with it, and with nothing else; and so attributes to itself and owns all the actions of that thing as its own, as far as that consciousness reaches, and no further; as every one who reflects will perceive.

18. In this personal identity is founded all the right and justice of reward and punishment; happiness and misery being that for which every one is concerned for *himself,* and not mattering what becomes of any *substance,* not joined to, or affected with, that consciousness. For, as it is evident in the instance I gave but now, if the consciousness went along with the little finger when it was cut off, that would be the same self which was concerned for the whole body yesterday, as making part of itself, whose actions then it cannot but admit as its own now. Though, if the same body should still live, and immediately from the separation of the little finger have its own peculiar consciousness, whereof the little finger knew nothing, it would not at all be concerned for it, as a part of itself, or could own any of its actions, or have any of them imputed to him.

19. This may show us wherein personal identity consists: not in the identity of substance, but, as I have said, in the identity of consciousness, wherein if Socrates and the present mayor of Queenborough agree, they are the same person: if the same Socrates waking and sleeping do not partake of the same consciousness, Socrates waking and sleeping is not the same person. And to punish Socrates waking for what sleeping Socrates thought, and waking Socrates was never conscious of, would be no more of right, than to punish one twin for what his brother-twin did, whereof he knew nothing, because their outsides were so like, that they could not be distinguished; for such twins have been seen.

20. But yet possibly it will still be objected: Suppose I wholly lose the memory of some parts of my life, beyond a possibility of retrieving them, so that perhaps I shall never be conscious of them again; yet am I not the same person that did those actions, had those thoughts that I once was conscious of, though I have now forgot them. To which I answer, that we must here take notice what the word *I* is applied to; which, in this case, is the *man* only. And the same man being presumed to be the same person, I is easily here supposed to stand also for the same person. But if it be possible for the same man to have distinct incommunicable consciousness at different times, it is past doubt the same man would at different times make different persons; which, we see, is the sense of mankind in the solemnest declaration of their opinions, human laws not punishing the mad man for the sober man's actions, nor the sober man for what the mad man did—thereby making them two persons: which is somewhat explained by our way of speaking in English when we say such an one is "not himself," or is "beside himself"; in which phrases it is insinuated, as if those who now, or at least first used them, thought that self was changed; the self-same person was no longer in that man.

21. But yet it is hard to conceive that Socrates, the same individual man, should be two persons. To help us a little in this, we must consider what is meant by Socrates, or the same individual *man*.

First, it must be either the same individual, immaterial, thinking substance; in short, the same numerical soul, and nothing else.

Secondly, or the same animal, without any regard to an immaterial soul.

Thirdly, or the same immaterial spirit united to the same animal.

Now, take which of these suppositions you please, it is impossible to make personal identity to consist in anything but consciousness; or reach any further than that does.

For, by the first of them, it must be allowed possible that a man born of different women, and in distant times, may be the same man. A way of speaking which, whoever admits, must allow it possible for the same man to be two distinct persons, as any two that have lived in different ages without the knowledge of one another's thoughts.

By the second and third, Socrates, in this life and after it, cannot be the same man any way but by the same consciousness; and so making human identity to consist in the same thing wherein we place personal identity, there will be no difficulty to allow the same man to be the same person. But then they who place human identity in consciousness only, and not in something else, must consider how they will make the infant Socrates the same man with Socrates after the resurrection. But whatsoever to some men makes a man, and consequently the same individual man, wherein perhaps few are agreed, personal identity can by us be placed in nothing but consciousness (which is that alone which makes what we call *self*), without involving us in great absurdities.

22. But is not a man drunk and sober the same person? Why else is he punished for the fact he commits when drunk, though he be never afterward conscious of it? Just as much the same person as a man that walks and does other things in his sleep, is the same person, and is answerable for any mischief he shall do in it. Human laws punish both, with a justice suitable to *their* way of knowledge; because, in these cases, they cannot distinguish certainly what is real, what counterfeit: and so the ignorance in drunkenness or sleep is not admitted as a plea. For, though punishment be annexed to personality, and personality to consciousness, and the drunkard perhaps be not conscious of what he did, yet human judicatures justly punish him; because the fact is proved against him, but want of consciousness cannot be proved for him. But in the Great Day, wherein the secrets of all hearts shall be laid open, it may be reasonable to think, no one shall be made to answer for what he knows nothing of; but shall receive his doom, his conscience accusing or excusing him.

23. Nothing but consciousness can unite remote existences into the same person: the identity of substance will not do it; for whatever substance there is, however framed, without consciousness there is no person: and a carcass may be a person, as well as any sort of substance be so, without consciousness.

Could we suppose two distinct incommunicable consciousnesses acting the same body, the one constantly by day, the other by night; and, on the other side, the same consciousness, acting by intervals, two distinct bodies: I ask, in the first case, whether the day and the night man would not be two as distinct persons as Socrates and Plato? And whether, in the second case, there would not be one person in two distinct bodies, as much as one man is the same in two distinct clothings?

Nor is it at all material to say, that this same and this distinct consciousness, in the cases above mentioned, is owing to the same and distinct immaterial substances, bringing it with them to those bodies; which, whether true or no, alters not the case: since it is evident the personal identity would equally be determined by the consciousness, whether that consciousness were annexed to some individual immaterial substance or no. For, granting that the thinking substance in man must be necessarily supposed immaterial, it is evident that immaterial thinking thing may sometimes part with its past consciousness, and be restored to it again: as appears in the forgetfulness men often have of their past actions; and the mind many times recovers the memory of a past consciousness, which it had lost for twenty years together. Make these intervals of memory and forgetfulness to take their turns regularly by day and night, and you have two persons with the same immaterial spirit, as much as in the former instance two persons with the same body. So that self is not determined by identity or diversity of substance, which it cannot be sure of, but only by identity of consciousness.

24, 25. Indeed it may conceive the substance whereof it is now made up to have existed formerly, united in the same conscious being: but, consciousness removed, that substance is no more itself, or makes no more a part of it, than any other substance. For, whatsoever any substance has thought or done, which I cannot recollect, and by my consciousness make my own thought and action, it will no more belong to me, whether a part of me thought or did it, than if it had been thought or done by any other immaterial being anywhere existing. I agree, the more probable opinion is, that this consciousness is annexed to, and the affection of, one individual immaterial substance. Any substance vitally united to the present thinking being is a part of that very same self which now is; anything united to it by a consciousness of former actions, makes also a part of the same self, which is the same both then and now.

26. *Person,* as I take it, is the name for this self. Wherever a man finds what he calls himself, there, I think, another may say is the same person. It is a forensic term, appropriating actions and their merit; and so belongs only to intelligent agents, capable of a law, and happiness, and misery. This personality extends itself beyond present existence to what is past, only by consciousness; whereby it becomes concerned and accountable; owns and imputes to itself past actions, just upon the same ground and for the same reason as it does the present. All which is founded in a concern for happiness, the unavoidable concomitant of consciousness; that which is conscious of pleasure and pain, desiring that that self that is conscious should be happy. And therefore whatever

past actions it cannot reconcile or *appropriate* to that present self by consciousness, it can be no more concerned in than if they had never been done: and to receive pleasure or pain, i.e. reward or punishment, on the account of any such action, is all one as to be made happy or miserable in its first being, without any demerit at all.

OF PERSONAL IDENTITY

Joseph Butler

Whether we are to live in a future state, as it is the most important question which can possibly be asked, so it is the most intelligible one which can be expressed in language. Yet strange perplexities have been raised about the meaning of that identity or sameness of person, which is implied in the notion of our living now and hereafter, or in any two successive moments. And the solution of these difficulties hath been stranger than the difficulties themselves. For, personal identity has been explained so by some, as to render the inquiry concerning a future life of no consequence at all to us the persons who are making it. And though few men can be misled by such subtleties; yet it may be proper a little to consider them.

Now when it is asked, wherein personal identity consists, the answer should be the same, as if it were asked, wherein consists similitude, or equality; that all attempts to define would but perplex it. Yet there is no difficulty at all in ascertaining the idea. For as, upon two triangles being compared or viewed together, there arises to the mind the idea of similitude; or upon twice two and four, the idea of equality: so likewise, upon comparing the consciousness of one's self, or one's own existence, in any two moments, there as immediately arises to the mind the idea of personal identity. And as the two former comparisons not only give us the ideas of similitude and equality; but also show us, that two triangles are alike, and twice two and four are equal: so the latter comparison not only gives us the idea of personal identity, but also shows us the identity of ourselves in those two moments; the present, suppose, and that immediately past; or the present, and that a month, a year, or twenty years past. Or in other words, by reflecting upon that, which is my self now, and that, which was my self twenty years ago, I discern they are not two, but one and the same self.

But though consciousness of what is past does thus ascertain our personal identity to ourselves, yet to say, that it makes personal identity,

FROM "On Personal Identity," reprinted in *Works,* edited by W. E. Gladstone (1896).

or is necessary to our being the same persons, is to say, that a person has not existed a single moment, nor done one action, but what he can remember; indeed none but what he reflects upon. And one should really think it self-evident, that consciousness of personal identity presupposes, and therefore cannot constitute, personal identity; any more than knowledge, in any other case, can constitute truth, which it presupposes.

This wonderful mistake may possibly have arisen from hence; that to be endued with consciousness is inseparable from the idea of a person, or intelligent being. For, this might be expressed inaccurately thus, that consciousness makes personality: and from hence it might be concluded to make personal identity. But though present consciousness of what we at present do and feel is necessary to our being the persons we now are; yet present consciousness of past actions or feelings is not necessary to our being the same persons who performed those actions, or had those feelings.

The inquiry, what makes vegetables the same in the common acceptation of the word, does not appear to have any relation to this of personal identity: because, the word *same,* when applied to them and to persons, is not only applied to different subjects, but it is also used in different senses. For when a man swears to the same tree, as having stood fifty years in the same place, he means only the same as to all the purposes of property and uses of common life, and not that the tree has been all that time the same in the strict philosophical sense of the word. For he does not know, whether any one particle of the present tree be the same with any one particle of the tree which stood in the same place fifty years ago. And if they have not one common particle of matter, they cannot be the same tree in the proper philosophic sense of the word *same:* it being evidently a contradiction in terms, to say they are, when no part of their substance, and no one of their properties is the same: no part of their substance, by the supposition: no one of their properties, because it is allowed, that the same property cannot be transferred from one substance to another. And therefore, when we say the identity or sameness of a plant consists in a continuation of the same life, communicated under the same organization, to a number of particles of matter, whether the same or not; the word *same,* when applied to life and to organization, cannot possibly be understood to signify, what it signifies in this very sentence, when applied to matter. In a loose and popular sense then, the life and the organization and the plant are justly said to be the same, notwithstanding the perpetual change of the parts. But in a strict and philosophical manner of speech, no man, no being, no mode of being, no anything, can be the same with that, with which it hath indeed nothing the same. Now sameness is used in this latter sense, when applied to persons. The identity of these, therefore, cannot subsist with diversity of substance.

The thing here considered, and demonstratively, as I think, determined, is proposed by Mr. Locke in these words, *Whether* it, i.e., the same self or person, *be the same identical substance?* And he has suggested what is a much better answer to the question, than that which he gives it in form. For he defines Person, *a thinking intelligent being,* etc., and personal identity, *the sameness of a rational being.* The question then is, whether the same rational being is the same substance; which needs no answer, because Being and Substance, in this place, stand for the same idea. The ground of the doubt, whether the same person be the same substance, is said to be this; that the consciousness of our own existence, in youth and in old age, or in any two joint successive moments, is not the *same individual action,* i.e., not the same consciousness, but different successive consciousnesses. Now it is strange that this should have occasioned such perplexities. For it is surely conceivable, that a person may have a capacity of knowing some object or other to be the same now, which it was when he contemplated it formerly: yet in this case, where, by the supposition, the object is perceived to be the same, the perception of it in any two moments cannot be one and the same perception. And thus though the successive consciousnesses, which we have of our own existence, are not the same, yet are they consciousnesses of one and the same thing or object; of the same person, self, or living agent. The person, of whose existence the consciousness is felt now, and was felt an hour or a year ago, is discerned to be, not two persons, but one and the same person; and therefore is one and the same.

Mr. Locke's observations upon this subject appear hasty: and he seems to profess himself dissatisfied with suppositions, which he has made relating to it. But some of those hasty observations have been carried to a strange length by others, whose notion, when traced and examined to the bottom, amounts, I think, to this: "That personality is not a permanent, but a transient thing: that it lives and dies, begins and ends continually: that no one can any more remain one and the same person two moments together, than two successive moments can be one and the same moment: that our substance is indeed continually changing; but whether this be so or not, is, it seems, nothing to the purpose; since it is not substance, but consciousness alone, which constitutes personality; which consciousness, being successive, cannot be the same in any two moments, nor consequently the personality constituted by it." And from hence it must follow, that it is a fallacy upon ourselves, to charge our present selves with any thing we did, or to imagine our present selves interested in any thing which befell us yesterday; or that our present self will be interested in what will befall us tomorrow: since our present self is not, in reality, the same with the self of yesterday, but another like self or person coming in its room, and mistaken for it; to which another self will succeed tomorrow. This, I say, must follow: for if the self or person of today, and that of tomorrow, are not the same, but only like persons; the person of today is really no more interested in what will befall the person of tomorrow, than in what will befall any other person. It may be thought, perhaps, that this is not a just representation of the opinion we are speaking of: because those who maintain it allow, that a person is the same as far back as his remembrance reaches. And indeed they do use the *words, identity* and *same person*. Nor will language permit these words to be laid aside; since if they were, there must be I know not what ridiculous periphrasis substituted in the room of them. But they cannot, consistently with themselves, mean, that the person is really the same. For it is self-evident, that the personality cannot be really the same, if, as they expressly assert, that in which it consists is not the same. And as, consistently with themselves, they cannot, so, I think it appears, they do not, mean, that the person is *really* the same, but only that he is so in a fictitious sense: in such a sense only as they assert, for this they do assert, that any number of persons whatever may be the same person. The bare unfolding this notion, and laying it thus naked and open, seems the best confutation of it. However, since great stress is said to be put upon it, I add the following things.

First, this notion is absolutely contradictory to that certain conviction, which necessarily and every moment rises within us, when we turn our thoughts upon ourselves, when we reflect upon what is past, and look forward upon what is to come. All imagination of a daily change of that living agent which each man calls himself, for another, or of any such change throughout our whole present life, is entirely borne down by our natural sense of things. Nor is it possible for a person in his wits to alter his conduct, with regard to his health or affairs, from a suspicion, that, though he should live tomorrow, he should not, however, be the same person he is today. And yet, if it be reasonable to act, with respect to a future life, upon this notion, that personality is transient; it is reasonable to act upon it, with respect to the present.

Here then is a notion equally applicable to religion and to our temporal concerns; and every one sees and feels the inexpressible absurdity of it in the latter case. If, therefore, any can take up with it in the former, this cannot proceed from the reason of the thing, but must be owing to an inward unfairness, and secret corruption of heart.

Secondly, it is not an idea, or abstract notion, or quality but a being only, which is capable of life and action, of happiness and misery. Now all beings confessedly continue the same, during the whole time of their existence. Consider then a living being now existing, and which has existed for any time alive: this living being must have done and suffered and enjoyed, what it has done and suffered and enjoyed formerly (this living being, I say, and not another), as really as it does and suffers and enjoys, what it does and suffers and enjoys this instant. All these successive actions, enjoyments, and sufferings, are actions, enjoyments, and sufferings, of the same living being. And they are so, prior to all consideration of its remembering or forgetting: since remembering or forgetting can make no alteration in the truth of past matter of fact. And suppose this being endued with limited powers of knowledge and memory, there is no more difficulty in conceiving it to have a power of knowing itself to be the same living being which it was some time ago, of remembering some of its actions, sufferings, and enjoyments, and forgetting others, than in conceiving it to know or remember or forget any thing else.

Thirdly, every person is conscious, that he is now the same person or self he was as far back as his remembrance reaches: since when any one reflects upon a past action of his own, he is just as certain of the person who did that action, namely, himself, the person who now reflects upon it, as he is certain that the action was at all done. Nay, very often a person's assurance of an action having been done, of which he is absolutely assured, arises wholly from the consciousness that he himself did it. And this he, person, or self, must either be a substance, or the property of some substance. If he, if person, be a substance; then consciousness that he is the same person is consciousness that he is the same substance. If the person, or he, be the property of a substance, still consciousness that he is the same property is as certain a proof that his substance remains the same, as consciousness that he remains the same substance would be: since the same property cannot be transferred from one substance to another.

But though we are thus certain, that we are the same agents, living beings, or substances, now, which we were as far back as our remembrance reaches; yet it is asked, whether we may not possibly be deceived in it? And this question may be asked at the end of any demonstration whatever: because it is a question concerning the truth of perception by memory. And he who can doubt, whether perception by memory can in this case be depended upon, may doubt also, whether perception by deduction and reasoning, which also include memory, or indeed whether intuitive perception can. Here then we can go no further. For it is ridiculous to attempt to prove the truth of those perceptions, whose truth we can not otherwise prove, than by other perceptions of exactly the same kind with them, and which there is just the same ground to suspect; or to attempt to prove the truth of our faculties, which can not otherwise be proved, than by the use or means of those very suspected faculties themselves.

On a Future Life

But the states of life in which we ourselves existed formerly in the womb and in our infancy, are almost as different from our present in mature age, as it is possible to conceive any two states or degrees of life can be. Therefore, that we are to exist hereafter in a state as different (suppose) from our present, as this is from our former, is but according to the analogy of nature; according to a natural order or appointment of the very same kind, with what we have already experienced.

We know we are endued with capacities of action, of happiness and misery: for we are conscious of acting, of enjoying pleasure and suffering pain. Now that we have these powers and capacities before death, is a presumption that we shall retain them through and after death; indeed a probability of it abundantly sufficient to act upon, unless there be some positive reason to think that death is the destruction of those living powers: because there is in every case a probability, that all things will contine as we experience they are, in all respects, except those in which we have some reason to think they will be altered. This is that *kind* of presumption or probability from analogy, expressed in the very word *continuance,* which seems our only natural reason for believing the course of the world will continue tomorrow, as it has done so far as our experience or knowledge of history can carry us back. Nay, it seems our only reason for believing, that any one substance now existing will continue to exist a moment longer; the self-existent substance only excepted. Thus if men were assured that the unknown event, death, was not the destruction of our faculties of perception and of action, there would be no apprehension, that any other power or event unconnected with this of death, would destroy these faculties just at the instant of each creature's death; and therefore no doubt but that they would remain after it: which shows the high probability that our living powers will continue after death, unless there be some ground to think that death is their destruction. For, if it would be in a manner certain that we should survive death, provided it were certain that death would not be our destruction, it must be highly probable we shall survive it, if there be no ground to think death will be our destruction.

Now though I think it must be acknowledged, that prior to the natural and moral proofs of a future life commonly insisted upon, there would arise a general confused suspicion, that in the great shock and alteration which we shall undergo by death, we, i.e., our living powers, might be wholly destroyed; yet even prior to those proofs, there is really no particular distinct ground or reason for this apprehension at all, so far as I can find. If there be, it must arise either from *the reason of the thing,* or from *the analogy of nature.*

But we cannot argue from *the reason of the thing,* that death is the destruction of living agents, because we know not at all what death is in itself; but only some of its effects, such as the dissolution of flesh, skin, and bones. And these effects do in no wise appear to imply the destruction of a living agent. And besides, as we are greatly in the dark, upon what the exercise of our living powers depends, so we are wholly ignorant what the powers themselves depend upon; the powers themselves as distinguished, not only from their actual exercise, but also from the present capacity of exercising them: and as opposed to their destruction: for sleep, or however a swoon, shows us, not only that these powers exist when they are not exercised, as the massive power of motion does in inanimate matter: but shows also that they exist, when there is no present capacity of exercising them: or that the capacities of exercising them for the present, as well as the actual exercise of them, may be suspended, and yet the powers themselves remain undestroyed. Since then we know not at all upon what the existence of our living powers depends, this shows further, there can no probability be collected from the reason of the thing, that death will be their destruction: because their existence may depend upon somewhat in no degree affected by death; upon somewhat quite out of the reach of this king of terrors. So that there is nothing more certain, than that *the reason of the thing* shows us no connection between death, and the destruction of living agents.

Nor can we find any thing throughout the whole *analogy of nature,* to afford us even the slightest presumption, that animals ever lose their living powers; much less, if it were possible, that they lose them by death: for we have no faculties wherewith to trace any beyond or through it, so as to see what becomes of them. This event removes them from our view. It destroys the *sensible* proof, which we had before their death, of their being possessed of living powers, but does not appear to afford the least reason to believe that they are, then, or by that event, deprived of them. . . .

All presumption of death's being the destruction of living beings, must go upon supposition that they are compounded; and so, discerptible. But since consciousness is a single and indivisible power, it should seem that the subject in which it resides must be so too. For were the motion of any particle of matter absolutely one and indivisible, so as that it should imply a contradiction to suppose part of this motion to exist, and part not to exist, i.e., part of this matter to move, and part to be at rest; then its power of motion would be indivisible; and so also would the subject in which the power inheres, namely, the particle of matter: for if this could be divided into two, one part might be moved and the other at rest, which is contrary to the supposition. In like manner it has been argued, and, for any thing appearing to the contrary, justly, that since the perception or consciousness, which we have of our own existence, is indivisible, so as that it is a contradiction to suppose one part of it should be here and the other there; the perceptive power, or the power of consciousness, is indivisible too: and consequently the subject in which it resides; i.e., the conscious being.

Now upon supposition that the living agent each man calls himself, is thus a single being, which there is at least no more difficulty in conceiving than in conceiving it to be a compound, and of which there is the proof now mentioned; it follows, that our organized bodies are no more ourselves or part of our selves, than any other matter around us. And it is as easy to conceive, how matter, which is no part of ourselves, may be appropriated to us in the manner which our present bodies are; as how we can receive impressions from, and have power over any matter. It is as easy to conceive, that we may exist out of bodies, as in them; that we might have animated bodies of any other organs and senses wholly different from these now given us, and that we may hereafter animate these same or new bodies variously modified and organized; as to conceive how we can animate such bodies as our present. And lastly, the dissolution of all these several organized bodies, supposing ourselves to have successively animated them, would have no more conceivable tendency to destroy the living beings ourselves, or deprive us of living faculties, the faculties of perception and of action, than the dissolution of any foreign matter, which we are capable of receiving impressions from, and making use of for the common occasions of life.

The simplicity and absolute oneness of a living agent cannot indeed, from the nature of the thing, be properly proved by experimental observations. But as these *fall in* with the supposition of its unity, so they plainly lead us to *conclude* certainly, that our gross organized bodies, with which we perceive the objects of sense, and with which we act, are no part of ourselves; and therefore show us, that we have no reason to believe their destruction to be ours: even without determining whether our living substances be material or immaterial. For we see by experience, that men may lose their limbs, their organs of sense, and even the greatest part of these bodies and yet remain the same living agents. And persons can trace up the existence of themselves to a time, when the bulk of their bodies was extremely small, in comparison of what it is in mature age: and we cannot but think, that they might then have lost a considerable part of that small body, and yet have remained the same living agents; as they may now lose great part of their present body, and remain so. . . .

And thus our finding, that the dissolution of matter, in which living beings were most nearly interested, is not their dissolution; and that the destruction of several of the organs and instruments of perception and of motion belonging to them, is not their destruction; shows demonstratively, that there is no ground to think that the dissolution of any other matter, or destruction of any other organs and instruments, will be the dissolution or destruction of living agents, from the like kind of relation. And we have no reason to think we stand in any other kind of relation to any thing which we find dissolved by death. . . .

Human creatures exist at present in two states of life and perception, greatly different from each other; each of which has its own peculiar laws, and its own peculiar enjoyments and sufferings. When any of our senses are affected or appetites gratified with the objects of them, we may be said to exist or live in a state of sensation. When none of our senses are affected or appetites gratified, and yet we perceive, and reason, and act; we may be said to exist or live in a state of reflection. Now it is by no means certain, that any thing which is dissolved by death, is any way necessary to the living being in this its state of reflection, after ideas are gained. For, though, from our present constitution and condition of being, our external organs of sense are necessary for conveying in ideas to our reflecting powers, as carriages, and levers, and scaffolds are in architecture: yet when these ideas are brought in, we are capable of reflecting in the most intense degree, and of enjoying the greatest pleasure, and feeling the greatest pain, by means of that reflection, without any assistance from our senses; and without any at all, which we know of, from that body which will be dissolved by death. It does not appear then, that the relation of this gross body to the reflecting being is, in any degree, necessary to thinking; to our intellectual enjoyments or sufferings: nor, consequently, that the dissolution or alienation of the former by death, will be the destruction of those present powers, which render us capable of this state of reflection.

Further, there are instances of mortal diseases, which do not at all affect our present intellectual powers; and this affords a presumption, that those diseases will not destroy these present powers. Indeed, from the observations made above, it appears, that there is no presumption, from their mutually affecting each other, that the dissolution of the body is the destruction of the living agent. And by the same reasoning, it must appear too, that there is no presumption, from their mutually affecting each other, that the dissolution of the body is the destruction of our present reflecting powers: but instances of their not affecting each other, afford a presumption of the contrary. Instances of mortal diseases not impairing our present reflecting powers, evidently turn our thoughts even from imagining such diseases to be the destruction of them. Several things indeed greatly affect all our living powers, and at length suspend the exercise of them; as for instance drowsiness, increasing till it ends in sound sleep: and from hence we might have imagined it would destroy them, till we found by experience the weakness of this way of judging. But in the diseases now mentioned, there is not so much as this shadow of probability, to lead us to any such conclusion, as to the reflecting powers which we have at present. For in those diseases, persons the moment before death appear to be in the highest vigor of life. They discover apprehension, memory, reason, all entire; with the utmost force of affection; sense of a character, of shame and honor; and the highest mental enjoyments and sufferings, even to the last gasp: and these surely prove even greater vigor of life than bodily strength does. Now what pretense is there for thinking, that a progressive disease when arrived to such a degree, I mean that degree which is mortal, will destroy those powers, which were not impaired, which were not affected by it, during its whole progress quite up to that degree? And if death by diseases of this kind is not the destruction of our present reflecting powers, it will scarce be thought that death by any other means is. . . .

Death may, in some sort, and in some respects, answer to our birth; which is not a suspension of the faculties which we had before it, or a total change of the state of life in which we existed when in the womb; but a continuation of both, with such and such great alterations.

Nay, for ought we know of ourselves, of our present life and of death; death may immediately, in the natural course of things, put us into a higher and more enlarged state of life, as our birth does; a state in which our capacities, and sphere of perception and of action, may be much greater than at present. For as our relation to our external organs of sense, renders us capable of existing in our present state of sensation; so it may be the only natural hindrance to our existing, immediately and of course, in a higher state of reflection. The truth is, reason does not at all show us, in what state death naturally leaves us.

These observations together may be sufficient to show, how little presumption there is, that death is the destruction of human creatures. However, there is the shadow of an analogy, which may lead us to imagine it is; the supposed likeness which is observed between the decay of vegetables, and of living creatures. And this likeness is indeed sufficient to afford the poets very apt allusions to the flowers of the field, in their pictures of the frailty of our present life. But in reason, the analogy is so far from holding, that there appears no ground even for the comparison, as to the present question: because one of the two subjects compared is wholly void of that, which is the principal and chief thing in the other, the power of perception and of action; and which is the only thing we are inquiring about the continuance of. So that the destruction of a vegetable is an event not similar or analogous to the destruction of a living agent.

But if, as was above intimated, leaving off the delusive custom of substituting imagination in the room of experience, we would confine ourselves to what we do know and understand; if we would argue only from that, and from that form our expectations; it would appear at first sight, that as no probability of living beings ever ceasing to be so, can be concluded from the reason of the thing; so none can be collected from the analogy of nature; because we cannot trace any living beings beyond death. But as we are conscious that we are endued with capacities of perception and of action, and are living persons; what we are to go upon is, that we shall continue so, till we foresee some accident or event, which will endanger those capacities, or be likely to destroy us: which death does in no wise appear to be.

ON THE SELF

Anonymous

Now Milinda the king went up to where the venerable Nāgasena was, and addressed him with the greetings and compliments of friendship and courtesy, and took his seat respectfully apart. And Nāgasena reciprocated his courtesy, so that the heart of the king was propitiated.

And Milinda began by asking, "How is your Reverence known, and what, Sir, is your name?"

"I am known as Nāgasena, O king, and it is by that name that my brethren in the faith address me. But although parents, O king, give such a name as Nāgasena, or Sūrasena, or Virasena, or Sihasena, yet this, Sire—Nāgasena and so on—is only a generally understood term, a designation in common use. For there is no permanent individuality (no soul) involved in the matter."

Then Milinda called upon the Yonakas and the brethren to witness: "This Nāgasena says there is no permanent individuality (no soul) implied in his name. Is it now even possible to approve him in that?" And turning to Nāgasena, he said: "If, most reverend Nāgasena, there be no permanent individuality (no soul) involved in the matter, who is it, pray, who gives to your members of the Order your robes and food and lodging and necessaries for the sick? Who is it who enjoys such things when given? Who is it who lives a life of righteousness? Who is it who devotes himself to meditation? Who is it who attains to the goal of the Excellent Way, to the Nirvāna of Arahatship? And who is it who destroys living creatures? who is it who takes what is not his own? who is it who lives an evil life of worldly lusts, who speaks lies, who drinks strong drink, who (in a word) commits any one of the five sins which work out their bitter fruit even in this life? If that be so there is neither merit nor demerit; there is neither doer nor causer of good or evil deeds; there is neither fruit nor result of good or evil Karma.—If, most reverend Nāgasena, we are to think that were

FROM "The Questions of King Milinda," translated by T. W. Rhys Davids, in *Sacred Books of the East,* vol. 35, edited by F. Max Muller (1890). Reprinted by permission of Oxford University Press.

a man to kill you there would be no murder, then it follows that there are no real masters or teachers in your Order, and that your ordinations are void.—You tell me that your brethren in the Order are in the habit of addressing you as Nāgasena. Now what is that Nāgasena? Do you mean to say that the hair is Nāgasena?"

"I don't say that, great king."

"Or the hairs on the body, perhaps?"

"Certainly not."

"Or is it the nails, the teeth, the skin, the flesh, the nerves, the bones, the marrow, the kidneys, the heart, the liver, the abdomen, the spleen, the lungs, the larger intestines, the lower intestines, the stomach, the feces, the bile, the phlegm, the pus, the blood, the sweat, the fat, the tears, the serum, the saliva, the mucus, the oil that lubricates the joints, the urine, or the brain, or any or all of these, that is Nāgasena?"

And to each of these he answered no.

"Is it the outward form then (Rūpa) that is Nāgasena, or the sensations (Vedanā), or the ideas (Saññā), or the confections (the constituent elements of character, Samkhārā), or the consciousness (Viññāna), that is Nāgasena?"

And to each of these he also answered no.

"Then it is all these Skandhas [bodily and mental components] combined that are Nāgasena?"

"No! great king."

"But is there anything outside the five Skandhas that is Nāgasena?"

And still he answered no.

"Then thus, ask as I may, I can discover no Nāgasena. Nāgasena is a mere empty sound. Who then is the Nāgasena that we see before us? It is a falsehood that your reverence has spoken, an untruth!"

And the venerable Nāgasena said to Milinda the king: "You, Sire, have been brought up in great luxury, as beseems your noble birth. If you were to walk this dry weather on the hot and sandy ground, trampling under foot the gritty, gravelly grains of the hard sand, your feet would hurt you. And as your body would be in pain, your mind would be disturbed, and you would experience a sense of bodily suffering. How then did you come, on foot, or in a chariot?"

"I did not come, Sir, on foot. I came in a carriage."

"Then if you came, Sire, in a carriage, explain to me what that is. Is it the pole that is the chariot?"

"I did not say that."

"Is it the axle that is the chariot?"

"Certainly not."

"Is it the wheels, or the framework, or the ropes, or the yoke, or the spokes of the wheels, or the goad, that are the chariot?"

And to all these he still answered no.

"Then is it all these parts of it that are the chariot?"

"No, Sir."

"But is there anything outside them that is the chariot?"

And still he answered no.

"Then thus, ask as I may, I can discover no chariot. Chariot is a mere empty sound. What then is the chariot you say you came in? It is a falsehood that your Majesty has spoken, an untruth! There is no such thing as a chariot! You are king over all India, a mighty monarch. Of whom then are you afraid that you speak untruth? And he called upon the Yonakas and the brethren to witness, saying: "Milinda the king here has said that he came by carriage. But when asked in that case to explain what the carriage was, he is unable to establish what he averred. Is it, forsooth, possible to approve him in that?"

When he had thus spoken the five hundred Yonakas shouted their applause, and said to the king: "Now let your Majesty get out of that if you can?"

And Milinda the king replied to Nāgasena, and said: "I have spoken no untruth, reverend Sir. It is on account of its having all these things —the pole, and the axle, the wheels, and the framework, the ropes, the yoke, the spokes, and the goad—that it comes under the generally understood term, the designation in common use, of "chariot."

"Very good! Your Majesty has rightly grasped the meaning of "chariot." And just even so it is on account of all those things you questioned me about—the thirty-two kinds of organic matter in a human body, and the five constituent elements of being—that I come under the generally understood term, the designation in common use, of "Nāgasena." For it was said, Sire, by our Sister Vagirā in the presence of the Blessed One:

" 'Just as it is by the condition precedent of the coexistence of its various parts that the word "chariot" is used, just so is it that when the Skandhas are there we talk of a "being".' "

"Most wonderful. Nāgasena, and most strange. Well has the puzzle put to you, most difficult though it was, been solved. Were the Buddha himself here he would approve your answer. Well done, well done, Nāgasena.!"

ON TRANSFER OF BODIES

Bernard Williams

There is a special problem about personal identity for two reasons. The first is self-consciousness—the fact that there seems to be a peculiar sense in which a man is conscious of his own identity. . . . The second reason is that a question of personal identity is evidently not answered merely by deciding the identity of a certain physical body. If I am asked whether the person in front of me is the same person as one uniquely present at place *a* at time *t,* I shall not necessarily be justified in answering "yes" merely because I am justified in saying that this human body is the same as that present at *a* at *t.* Identity of body is at least not a sufficient condition of personal identity, and other considerations, of personal characteristics and, above all, memory, must be invoked.

Some have held, further, that bodily identity is not a necessary condition of personal identity. This, however, is ambiguous, and yields either a weak or a strong thesis, depending on one's view of the necessity and sufficiency of the other conditions. The weaker thesis asserts merely that at least one case can be consistently constructed in which bodily identity fails, but in which the other conditions will be sufficient for an assertion of personal identity; even though there may be some other imaginable case in which, some other condition failing, bodily identity *is* a necessary condition of personal identity. The stronger thesis asserts that there is no conceivable situation in which bodily identity would be necessary, some other conditions being always both necessary and sufficient. I take it that Locke's theory is an example of this latter type.

I shall try to show that bodily identity is always a necessary condition of personal identity, and hence that both theses fail. In this connection I shall discuss in detail a case apparently favorable to the weaker thesis. I shall also be concerned with the stronger thesis, or rather with something that follows from it—the idea that we can give a sense to the concept of a *particular personality* without reference to a body. . . . The criterion of bodily identity itself I take for granted. I assume that

FROM *Problems of the Self,* chapter 1. Reprinted by permission of Cambridge University Press.

it includes the notion of spatio-temporal continuity, however that notion is to be explained.

In discussions of this subject, it is easy to fall into ways of speaking that suggest that "bodily" and other considerations are easily divorced. I have regrettably succumbed to this at some points, but I certainly do not believe that this easy divorce is possible; I hope that both the general tenor of my thesis and some more direct remarks on the subject will show why.

Deciding Another's Identity

Suppose someone undergoes a sudden and violent change of character. Formerly quiet, deferential, church-going and home-loving, he wakes up one morning and has become, and continues to be, loud-mouthed, blasphemous and bullying. Here we might ask the question

(a) Is he the same person as he used to be?

There seem to be two troubles with the formulation of this question, at least as an *identity* question. The first is a doubt about the reference of the second "he": if asked the question "as *who* used to be?" we may well want to say "this person," which answers the original question (a) for us. This is not a serious difficulty, and we can easily avoid it by rephrasing the question in some such way as

(b) Is this person the same as the person who went to sleep here last night?

We do not, however, *have* to rephrase the question in any such way; we can understand (a) perfectly well, and avoid paradox, because our use of personal pronouns and people's names is malleable. It is a reflection of our concept of "a person" that some references to *him* cannot be understood as references to his body or to parts of it, and that others can; and that these two sorts of reference can readily occur in one statement. ("He was embarrassed and went red.") In the case of (a), the continuity of reference for "he" can be supplied by the admitted continuity of reference of "his body," and the more fundamental identity question can be discussed in these terms without any serious puzzlement.

The second difficulty with (a) is that it is too readily translated into

(c) Is he the same sort of person as he used to be? or possibly

(d) Has he the same personality as he used to have? But (c) and (d) are not identity questions in the required sense. For on any interpretation, "sort of person," and on one interpretation, "personality," are quality-terms, and we are merely asking whether the same subject now has different qualities, which is too easy to answer.

But this is only one interpretation of "personality." It corresponds interestingly to a loose sense of "identity," which is found for instance in Nigel Dennis' novel *Cards of Identity*. There "identity" is often used to mean "a set of characteristics," and "giving someone an identity" means "convincing someone that he is a certain sort of person." It does not, however, only mean this; for Dennis' Identity Club do not stop at giving someone a new character—they give him a new background as well, and a local sponger is made by their persuasive methods not just into a submissive old-style butler, but into such a butler who used to be at sea and has deserted his wife.

We might feel that this was the point at which something specially uncanny was beginning to happen, and that this was the kind of anomalous example we were really looking for—the uncanniness of someone's acquiring a new past is connected with our increasing reluctance to describe the situation as one in which the same man has acquired a new set of qualities. Here we have one powerful motive for the introduction of memory. It can be put by saying that there are, or we can imagine, cases where we want to use some term like "personality" in such a way that it is not a type-expression, meaning "set of characteristics," but is a particular term meaning something like *individual* personality. It may seem that this particularity is attained by reference to memory—the possession of a particular past. Thus we are concerned here with cases more drastic than those in which for instance people say "it has made a new man of him," or even "he is not the same person as he used to be" in the sense suggested by a change of character; these cases we can too readily redescribe. Thus we may put our question in the barbarous form

(*e*) Is the (particular) personality he has now the same as the one he had before?
We must now see whether we can make sense, in terms of memory, of the idea of a particular personality; and whether there can be personal identity without bodily identity.

In doing this, two obvious but important features of memory have to be borne in mind.

(I) To say "A remembers *x*," without irony or inverted commas, is to imply that *x* really happened; in this respect "remember" is parallel to know."

(II) It does not follow from this, nor is it true, that all claims to remember, any more than all claims to know, are veridical; or, not everything one seems to remember is something one really remembers.
So much is obvious, although Locke was forced to invoke the providence of God to deny the latter. These points have been emphasized by Flew in his discussion of Locke's views on personal identity. In formulating

Locke's thesis, however, Flew makes a mistake; for he offers Locke's thesis in the form "if X can remember Y's doing such-and-such, then X and Y are the same person." But this obviously will not do, even for Locke, for we constantly say things like "I remember my brother joining the army" without implying that I and my brother are the same person. So if we are to formulate such a criterion, it looks as though we have to say something like "if X remembers doing such-and-such, then he is the person who did that thing." But since "remembers doing" means "remembers himself doing," this is trivially tautologous, and moreover lends color to Butler's famous objection that memory, so far from constituting personal identity, presupposed it. Hence the criterion should rather run: "if X claims to remember doing such-and-such . . ." We must now ask how such a criterion might be used.

Suppose the man who underwent the radical change of character—let us call him Charles—claimed, when he woke up, to remember witnessing certain events and doing certain actions which earlier he did not claim to remember; and that under questioning he could not remember witnessing other events and doing other actions which earlier he did remember. Would this give us grounds for saying that he now was or had, in some particular sense, a different personality? An argument to show that it did give us such grounds might be constructed on the following lines.

Any token event E, and any token action A, are by definition particulars. Moreover, the description "the man who did the action A" necessarily individuates some one person; for it is logically impossible that two persons should do the same *token* action. In the case of events, it is possible that two persons should witness the same token event; but nevertheless the description "the man who witnessed E" may happen to individuate some one person, and "the man who witnessed $E_1, E_2 . . . E_n$" has a proportionately greater chance of so doing. Thus if our subject Charles now claims to remember doing certain actions A_1, A_2, etc., and witnessing certain events E_1, E_2, etc., which are themselves suitably identified, we have good grounds for saying that he is some particular person or has some particular personality.

Now by principle (II), we have no reason without corroborative evidence of some kind to believe Charles when he new claims to remember A or E; so we must set about checking. How are we to do this in the present case? Ordinarily if some person X claims to have witnessed E, and we wish to check this, we must find out whether there is any record, or anyone has any memory, of X's witnessing E. This is evidently inapplicable to the present case. For either the evidence shows that Charles was *bodily* present at E, or it does not. If it does, then Charles is remembering in the ordinary way, which is contrary to the hypothesis. If it does not, then there is no corroboration. Here we have a first important step. We are trying to pry apart "bodily" and "mental" criteria; but we find that the normal operation of one "mental" criterion involves the "bodily" one.

However, the situation may not be quite as desperate as this makes it appear. We can examine Charles' putative memories, and we may find that he can offer detailed information which there is no reason to believe he would ordinarily have known, and which strongly suggests the reports of an eye-witness of some particular events. What we can do with this information in the present case depends on a number of considerations. I shall now examine these, first in connection with events, and then with actions. Events can in principle be witnessed by any number of persons, or by none. Some of the events which Charles claims to remember witnessing may be events of which we have other eye-witness accounts; others may be events which we believe to have occurred, though we do not know whether or not anyone witnessed them; others again may be events which we believe to have occurred, but which we believe no one to have witnessed.

For all these, there is an hypothesis about—or, perhaps, description of—Charles' present condition which has nothing to do with a change of personality: the hypothesis of clairvoyance (together, of course, with the loss of his real memories). To describe Charles as clairvoyant is certainly not to advance very far toward an *explanation* of his condition; it amounts to little more than saying that he has come to know, by no means, what other people know by evidence. But so long as Charles claimed to remember events which were supposedly or certainly unwitnessed, such a description might be the best we could offer. We might do better than this, however, if the events Charles claimed to remember were witnessed; in this case we could begin to advance to the idea that Charles had a new identity, because we would have the chance of finding someone for him to be identical *with*. Thus if the events were witnessed, we might say that Charles was (now) identical with a witness of these events. This is ambiguous; it might mean that he was identical with anyone who witnessed the events, or with some particular person who witnessed the events. The former of these is no advance, since it comes to a roundabout way of saying that he claims to have witnessed the events, i.e. is possibly clairvoyant. The situation is different, however, if we can identify some one person who, it is plausible to suppose, witnessed all the events that Charles now claims to remember. That this should be possible is, indeed, a necessary condition of describing what has happened to Charles as *a change of identity;* I shall return to this point a little later.

If we now turn to actions, it looks as though we can find even better grounds for describing the case in terms of a change of identity. While there can be unwitnessed token events, there can be no unwitnessed token actions; moreover, as we noticed above, each token action can be performed by only one person. So if we can find out who performed the actions that Charles now claims to remember performing, it looks as if we can find out who he now is. These supposed advantages, however, are largely illusory. We may say, crudely, that there are many features of actions in which they are just like events—which, from another point of view, they indeed are. What differentiates actions from events are rather certain features of the agent, such as his intentions. In a particular case, some of these latter features may be known to, or inferred by, observers, while others may remain private to the agent. In neither case, however, do these special features of actions much help our investigation of Charles' identity. In so far as these special features may be known to observers, they are still, for the purposes of the investigation, in the class of events, and Charles' claim to remember them may still be plausibly described as clairvoyance; and in so far as these features remain private to the performer of the actions in question, we can have no ground for saying whether Charles' claims to remember them are even correct.

Again, the logical truth that a description of the form "the person who did the (token) action A" individuates some one person, does not give unfailing help. How much help it gives depends on how effectively, and by what means, we can identify the action in question. Suppose that several men at a certain time and place are each sharpening a pencil. In these circumstances the description "the man sharpening a pencil" fails to individuate: the action of sharpening a pencil is common to them all. If, however, the pencils were of different colors, I might be able to identify a particular pencil, and through this a token action of sharpening; thus "the man sharpening the red pencil" may individuate. But such methods of identifying token actions are not always available. In particular, there are some cases in which a token action can be effectively identified only through a reference to the agent. Thus if several men were all dancing the czardas, I might be able to identify a token dancing only as e.g. *"Josef's* dancing of the czardas." In such a case reference to a token action cannot help in identifying its agent, since I must identify him in order to identify it.

However, we often can effectively identify actions without actually identifying the agents, and so have a use for descriptions like "the person who murdered the Duchess, whoever it was." It is obvious that such descriptions can play a peculiarly useful role in an inquiry into identity; and this role may, for several reasons, be more useful than that played by descriptions like "the man who witnessed the event E." For, first, granted that I have identified *an action,* the description cannot fail of reference because there is no such agent; while the mere fact that I have identified a certain event E of course does not guarantee the description "the man who *witnessed* the event E" against failure of reference. Secondly, it is inherently less likely that the description referring to an action should fail of unique reference because of multiplicity, than it is that the description referring to an event should so fail. For it is in general less probable that a certain action should have been co-operatively undertaken than that a certain event should have been multiply witnessed; and, as we noticed above, for every description of a co-operative action, we can produce a series of descriptions of constituent actions which have progressively greater chance of unique reference. Last, knowledge of a particular action can give one knowledge not only of the location, but of the character, of its agent, but knowledge of a particular event will standardly give one knowledge only of the location of its witnesses.

Let us now go back to the case of Charles. We may suppose that our inquiry has turned out in the most favorable possible way, and that all the events he claims to have witnessed and all the actions he claims to have done point unanimously to the life-history of some one person in the past—for instance, Guy Fawkes. Not only do all Charles' memory-claims that can be checked fit the pattern of Fawkes' life as known to historians, but others that cannot be checked are plausible, provide explanations of unexplained facts, and so on. Are we to say that Charles is now Guy Fawkes, that Guy Fawkes has come to life again in Charles' body, or some such thing?

Certainly the temptation to say something on this pattern is very strong. It is difficult to insist that we *couldn't* say that Charles (or sometime Charles) had become Guy Fawkes; this is certainly what the newspapers would say if they heard of it. But newspapers are prone to exaggeration, and this might be an exaggeration. For why shouldn't we say that Charles had, except for his body, become just like Guy Fawkes used to be; or perhaps that Charles clairvoyantly—i.e., mysteriously—knows all about Guy Fawkes and his *ambiance?* In answer to this, it will be argued that this is just what memory was introduced to rule out; granted that we need similar personal characteristics, skills, and so on as necessary conditions of the identification, the final—and, granted these others, sufficient—condition is provided by memories of seeing just *this,* and doing just *that,* and it is these that pick out a particular man. But perhaps this point is fundamentally a logical trick. Granted that in a certain context the expressions "the man who did A," "the man who saw *E*," do effectively individuate, it is logically impossible that two different persons should (correctly) remember being the man who did *A* or saw *E*; but it is not logically impossible that two different persons should *claim* to remember being this man, and this is the most we can get.

This last argument is meant to show only that we are not forced to accept the description of Charles' condition as his being identical with Guy Fawkes. I shall now put forward an argument to strengthen this contention and to suggest that we should not be justified in accepting this description. If it is logically possible that Charles should undergo the changes described, then it is logically possible that some other man should simultaneously undergo the same changes; e.g. that both Charles and his brother Robert should be found in this condition. What should we say in that case? They cannot both be Guy Fawkes; if they were, Guy Fawkes would be in two places at once, which is absurd. Moreover, if they were both identical with Guy Fawkes, they would be identical with each other, which is also absurd. Hence we could not say that they were both identical with Guy Fawkes. We might instead say that one of them was identical with Guy Fawkes, and that the other was just like him; but this would be an utterly vacuous maneuver, since there would be *ex hypothesi* [by that hypothesis] no principle determining which description was to apply to which. So it would be best, if anything, to say that both had mysteriously become like Guy Fawkes, clairvoyantly knew about him, or something like this. If this would be the best description of each of the two, why would it not be the best description of Charles if Charles alone were changed?

Perhaps this last rhetorical question too readily invites an answer. It might be said that there is a relevant difference between the case in which two persons are changed and the case in which only one is changed, the difference being just this difference in numbers; and that there is no guarantee that what we would say in one of these situations would be the same as what we would say in the other. In the more complicated situation our linguistic and conceptual resources would be taxed even more severely than in the simpler one, and we might not react to the demands in the same way. Moreover, there is a reason why we should not react in the same way. The standard form of an identity question is "Is this *x* the same *x* as that *x* which . . . ?" and in the simpler situation we are at least presented with just the materials for constructing such a question; but in the more complicated situation we are baffled even in asking the question, since both the transformed persons are equally good candidates for being its subject, and the question "Are these two *x*'s the same (*x*?) as the *x* which . . . ?" is not a recognizable form of identity question. Thus, it might be argued, the fact that we could not speak of identity in the latter situation is no kind of proof that we could not do so in the former.

Certainly it is not a proof. Yet the argument does indicate that to speak of identity in the simpler case would be at least quite vacuous. The point can be made clearer in the following way. In the case of material objects, we can draw a distinction between identity and exact similarity; it is clearly not the same to say that two men live in the same house, and that they live in exactly similar houses. This notion of identity is given to us primarily, though not completely, by the notion of spatio-temporal continuity. In the case of character, however, this distinction cannot be drawn, for to say that A and B have the same character is just to say that A's character is exactly similar to B's. Nor can this distinction be drawn in the case of memories—if you could say that two men had the same memories, this would be to say that their memories were exactly similar. There is, however, an extreme difficulty in saying these things about memories at all; it is unclear what it would mean to say that there were two men who had exactly similar, or the same, memories, since to call them real memories is to imply their correctness. Thus if we are to describe Charles's relations to Guy Fawkes in terms of *exact similarity* of everything except the body, we are going to have difficulty in finding a suitable description in these terms of his memory claims. We cannot say that he has the same memories as Guy Fawkes, as this is to imply, what we want to deny, that he really is Guy Fawkes; nor can we say that the memory claims he makes are the same as those made by Guy Fawkes, as we have little idea of what memory claims Fawkes in fact made, or indeed of how much he at various times remembered. All we actually know is that Charles' claims fit Fawkes' life.

These difficulties, in applying the concept of exact similarity in the matter of the supposed memories, are (I suspect) a motive for the thought that we *must* describe the situation in terms of identity. This is where the reduplicated situation of Charles and Robert gives some help. In that situation it is quite obvious that the idea of identity cannot be applied, and that we must fall back on similarity; and that one respect in which the trio are similar is—however we are to express it—that of "memory." (If the situation sometimes occurred, we might find an expression; we might speak of "similarity of one's supposed past.") This eases the way for doing the same thing in the case of Charles alone, whose relation to Fawkes in his unique case is exactly the same as both his and Robert's in the reduplicated one. We can then say that Charles has the same character, and the same supposed past, as Fawkes, which is just the same as to say that they are in these respects exactly similar. This is not to say that they are identical at all. The only case in which identity and exact similarity could be distinguished, as we have just seen, is that of the body—"same body" and "exactly similar body" really do mark a difference. Thus I should claim that the omission of the body takes away all content from the idea of personal *identity*.

I should like to make one last point about this example. This turns on the fact, mentioned before, that in order to describe Charles' change of identity, we must be able to identify some one person who might plausibly be supposed to have seen and done all the things that Charles now claims to remember having seen and done; otherwise there would be nothing to pin down Charles' memory claims as other than random feats of clairvoyance. We succeeded in doing this, just by discovering that Charles' memory claims fitted Fawkes' life. This could be done only by knowing what Fawkes did, and what Fawkes did could be known only by reference to witnesses of Fawkes' activities, and these witnesses must have seen Fawkes' body. In order for their accounts to be connected into the history of one person, it is necessary to reply on the continuity of this body.

Now the fact that Fawkes is in this sense identified through his body does not rule out the possibility that Charles should later be identified with Fawkes without reference to a body; i.e. this fact does not rule out the weaker thesis about the non-necessity of bodies. To illustrate this, one might compare the case of someone's going to a crowded party, where he sees a girl who is very like all the other girls at the party except that she has red hair. This girl sings various songs and quarrels with the band; she is easily identified on each occasion by the color of her hair. The man later meets a platinum blonde who recalls singing songs at a party and quarreling with the band. He can identify her as the red-haired girl at the party, even though she has changed the color of her hair in the meantime. There is an important difference, however, between this case and that of Fawkes. If the girl had remarkably changed the color of her hair between songs and before the quarrel, identifying her at the various stages of the party would have been more difficult, but not in principle impossible; but if the Fawkes-personality changed bodies frequently, identification would become not just difficult but impossible. For the only other resource would be the memory criterion, and the operation of this would once more make exactly the same requirements. Hence it is a necessary condition of making the supposed identification on non-bodily grounds that at some stage identifications should be made on bodily grounds. Hence any claim that bodily considerations can be absolutely omitted from the criteria of personal identity must fail; i.e. these facts do rule out the stronger thesis.

Some Remarks on Bodily Interchange

Anyone who believed that personalities could be identified without reference to bodies might be expected to make sense of the idea of bodily interchange; and anyone who thought that they might always be identified in this way would presumably require that for any two contemporaneous persons we should be able to make sense of the idea that their bodies should be interchanged. It is worth considering how far we can make sense of it, if we look at it closely.

Suppose a magician is hired to perform the old trick of making the emperor and the peasant become each other. He gets the emperor and the peasant in one room, with the emperor on his throne and the peasant in the corner, and then casts the spell. What will count as success? Clearly not that after the smoke has cleared the old emperor should be in the corner and the old peasant on the throne. That would be a rather boring trick. The requirement is presumably that the emperor's body, with the peasant's personality, should be on the throne, and the peasant's body with the emperor's personality, in the corner. What does this mean? In particular, what has happened to the voices? The voice presumably ought to count as a bodily function; yet how would the peasant's gruff blasphemies be uttered in the emperor's cultivated tones, or the emperor's witticisms in the peasant's growl? A similar point holds for the features; the emperor's body might include the sort of face that just could not express the peasant's morose suspiciousness, the peasant's a face no expression of which could be taken for one of fastidious arrogance. These could's are not just empirical—such expressions on these features might be unthinkable.

The point need not be elaborated; I hope I have said enough to suggest that the concept of bodily interchange cannot be taken for granted, and that there are even logical limits to what we should be prepared to say in this direction. What these limits are, cannot be foreseen—one has to consider the cases, and for this one has to see the cases. The converse is also true, that it is difficult to tell in advance how far certain features may suddenly seem to express something quite unexpected. But there are limits, and when this is recognized, the idea of the interchange of personalities seems very odd. There might be something like a logical impossibility of the magician's trick's succeeding. However much of the emperor's past the sometime peasant now claimed to remember, the trick would not have succeeded if he could not satisfy the simpler requirement of being the same *sort* of person as the sometime emperor. Could he do this, if he could not smile royally? Still less, could he be the same person, if he could not smile the characteristic smile of the emperor?

These considerations are relevant to the present question in two ways. First, the stronger view about the identification implies that an interchange is always conceivable; but there are many cases in which it does not seem to be conceivable at all. Secondly, there is connected with this the deeper point, that when we are asked to distinguish a man's personality from his body, we do not really know what to distinguish from what. I take it that this was part of what Wittgenstein meant when he said that the best picture of the human soul was the human body.

Questions for Discussion

1. Which of the phiosophers in "Micromegas" does Voltaire consider most reasonable; which does he consider most foolish, and why?
2. Bertrand Russell once said that Descartes did not have a right to conclude that he, Descartes, existed as a thinking being, but only that his thoughts existed. Comment on this assertion. What sense, if any, can you give to the notion of thoughts as existing all by themselves, without a thinking person?
3. In a passage from Locke's *Essay Concerning Human Understanding* that is not included in our selection, the philosopher described a cobbler who woke up with the memories and personality of a prince, and a prince who woke up with the memories and personality of the cobbler. According to Locke, the two persons involved may be said to have mysteriously changed bodies. How would Nagasena and B. A. O. Williams describe what happened? How would you describe it?
4. The contemporary American philosopher, Roderick Chisholm, has envisioned a person, A, splitting like an ameba into two persons, B and C, in such a way that B retains the memories of A while C does not. Would B be the same person as A? If both B and C retained the memories and personality of A, would they both be the same person as A? Would they then be identical with each other?
5. Is it true, as Locke implies, that someone who sustained total amnesia would be a completely different person, in effect, a new person? Do the laws governing inheritance support this view? If not, should the laws be changed?
6. King Milinda argues that if Nagasena's hair is not Nagasena, and his nails, teeth, and other bodily parts are not Nagasena, then he "can discern no Nagasena." Is Milinda a materialist? Is he committing the fallacy of assuming that what is true of a totality must be true also of its parts?
7. Butler asserts: "Nor can we find anything throughout the whole analogy of nature to afford us even the slightest presumption that animals ever lose their living powers . . . by death." By what reasoning does he arrive at this bizarre conclusion? Evaluate his reasons.

8. According to Williams, what ambiguity is there to the question, "Is he the same person he used to be?" Why does the question in this form appear silly, and how could it be translated so as to make good sense?

9. Williams considers it absurd to suggest that two people could be identical persons, even if they had the same experiences and memories. Locke maintained that such a possibility is not at all absurd. Suppose two Siamese twins have exactly the same thoughts, feeelings, and memories. Would they be one person or two? Would it matter whether they remained bodily joined or were surgically separated in deciding to consider them one person or two?

10. The most serious difficulty faced by dualists such as Descartes and Butler is to explain how mental states can affect or be affected by bodily states. Why is this not a difficulty for the materialist Williams or the bundle theorists Nagasena and Hume?

Selected Readings

ABELSON, R. *Persons.* London: Macmillan, 1977. A new form of dualism called "conceptual dualism."

ARMSTRONG, D. M. *A Materialist Theory of Mind.* New York: Humanities Press, 1968. A strong argument for reductive materialism.

AYER, A. J. *The Concept of a Person.* New York: St. Martin's Press, 1963. A critique of behaviorism.

BROAD, C. D. *The Mind and Its Place in Nature.* New York: Harcourt Brace Jovanovich, 1925. A strong case for dualism.

BUTLER, J. "Of Personal Identity." In *Works,* edited by W. Gladstone. Oxford: Oxford University Press, 1896. A critique of the bundle theory and an argument for the soul as substance.

DESCARTES, R. *Meditations.* Translated by L. J. La Fleur. Meditation II. New York: Liberal Arts Press, 1960. Classic statement of dualism.

———. *On the Passions of the Soul.* Vol. I. Translated by E. Haldane and G. Ross. Cambridge: Cambridge University Press, 1911. An attempt to explain mind-body interaction.

GUSTAFSON, D., ed. *Essays in Philosophical Psychology.* Garden City, New York: Anchor, 1964. Discussions of Gilbert Ryle's behaviorism.

HUME, D. *A Treatise of Human Nature.* Part IV, Book I. Oxford: Clarendon Press, 1975. A classic statement of the bundle theory.

LOCKE, J. *Essay Concerning Human Understanding.* Book II, Chap. 27. New York: Dover, 1974. Argues for continuity of memory as the criterion of personal identity.

METTRIE, DE LA, J. *Man a Machine.* Translated by G. Bussey. Chicago: Open Court, 1927. A classic statement of materialism.

MILINDA, KING. *Milindipanha.* Translated by T. Davids. New York: Dover, 1963. Presents a bundle theory similar to Hume.

PARFIT, D. "Personal Identity." *Philosophical Review,* 80 (1971). A subtle analysis of the concept of a person as not reducible to either mind or body.

PENELHUM, T. *Survival and Disembodied Existence.* New York: Humanities Press, 1969. A detailed criticism of dualism and survival after death.

REID, T. *Essay on the Intellectual Powers of Man.* Cambridge, Massachusetts: M.I.T. Press, 1969. A critique of Hume's bundle theory.

RYLE, G. *The Concept of Mind.* New York: Barnes & Noble, 1949. A critique of Cartesian dualism and an argument for materialist behaviorism.

SHOEMAKER, S. *Self Knowledge and Self Identity.* Ithaca, New York: Cornell University Press, 1963. Criticizes substance theory, bundle theory, and memory theory and argues for materialism.

STRAWSON, P. F. *Individuals.* Chap. 3. London: Methuen, 1959. Argues that the concept of person is not reducible to mind or body or both.

WIGGINS, D. *Identity and Spatio-Temporal Continuity.* Oxford: Oxford University Press, 1967. Offers a technical analysis of identity and an argument for materialism.

WILLIAMS, B. A. O. *Problems of the Self.* London: Cambridge University Press, 1973. Argues that the bodily criterion for personal identity is primary and memory secondary.

WISDOM, J. *Problems of Mind and Matter.* Cambridge: Cambridge University Press, 1934. Attempts to show how the mind-body problem results from conceptual confusion.

Chapter 4

Free Will and Determinism: Is Freedom an Illusion?

Are our virtues and vices, our achievements and failures, our sacrifices and our sins thrust upon us by forces beyond our control, or are they manifestations of our freely chosen decisions for which we can be praised or blamed? Or is this question improperly phrased, implying that our actions and characters cannot be products of causal processes and yet also be our own responsibility? In short, do we have free will and, if so, is it compatible with causality?

In *Walden Two,* the eminent psychologist B. F. Skinner has described a utopian society whose members have been "conditioned" to act peacefully and cooperatively. Are they acting freely, or are they being manipulated by a benevolently despotic psychologist? The visitor in the story politely refuses to join the community because he feels that the right to choose freely between good and evil depends on being capable of either choice, and that this freedom is surrendered when one subjects oneself to the conditioning techniques employed by the utopian community's director. Is he right in believing that an individual can be so thoroughly manipulated by another person? If so, then in refusing to join, is he protecting a real possession called free will, or is he simply a product of another form of social conditioning that has produced in him an irrational fear of submitting to the authority of a superior person?

At first glance our next selection, "Learning Theory," a science-fiction story by another psychologist, James McConnell, seems to refute Skinner's concept of complete human conditioning. It illustrates how a person knowledgeable in the techniques of behavioral psychology can defeat the purposes of those who attempt to govern him. But the author stacks the cards, so to speak, by picturing his psychologists from outer space as seriously underestimating the intelligence and knowledge of the human being they have selected for their experiments. What if they realized that their human subject was familiar with their methods of conditioning and was capable of resisting them? Could they not then modify their procedures so as to turn his very efforts at resistance into additional reinforcing factors? Is the failure of these extraterrestrial Skinnerians due merely to imperfections of their techniques and knowledge, or does their human subject possess a power known as "free will," which would enable him to defeat any attempt, by however sophisticated an experimenter, to mold his behavior in accordance with the experimenter's own purposes?

The determinist and the libertarian give different answers to the question: "Is it ever possible for a person to do anything different, in a given situation, from what he actually does?" The libertarian says "Yes" on what are, essentially, commonsense grounds. We are constantly faced with situations that call for choosing from a range of alternative actions, all of which are possible before we actually act.

But then are we really correct in thinking that those courses of action that we end up rejecting are really in our power to begin with? Libertarians insist that the appearance of genuine choice would be illusory if the "choice" a person actually makes were (at least in principle) predictable in advance on the basis of knowledge of causal factors that determine that choice. Some philosophers, whom the American philosopher William James called "hard determinists," agree with the libertarians that genuine free choice is incompatible with causal determinism, and so conclude that free will is illusory. Many, however, take what James called a "soft" position, that freely willed choice can be reasonably defined so as not to rule out determination of one's choice by prior causes.

Neither hard nor soft determinists deny the phenomenon that we call "choosing what to do." But both reject the interpretation that libertarians place upon this phenomenon. Considered purely as a psychological occurrence, the reality of "choice" is beyond dispute; however, the appearance of genuine alternatives may be an illusion. For when a person does what we call "choosing to perform action X," he or she cannot claim to know that it really would have been possible to have chosen Y instead. As the eighteenth-century German philosopher Baron d'Holbach points out, in the selection below, our tendency to assume that alternative courses of action are open to us may simply result from our limited knowledge of our own inner workings and the manner in which these are influenced by external stimuli. In Holbach's words, it may just be because "the mechanism of . . .

sensations, . . . perceptions, and the manner they engrave ideas on the brain of man, are not known to him; because he is unable to unravel all these motions; because he cannot perceive the chain of operations in his soul, or the motive principle that acts within him that he supposes himself a free agent." Thus, although I may think that it is possible for me either to go to a movie tonight or to stay home and watch television, I may in fact simply be unaware of all the forces operating within me, or impinging upon me from outside, that pretermine my decision, say, to stay home.

Of course, these considerations—even if sound—do not by themselves constitute a case for hard determinism. At best they serve to discredit somewhat our natural tendency to believe in free will. What positive arguments do the determinists have at their disposal? Setting aside those thinkers, such as St. Augustine and John Calvin, who have argued for determinism on the strength of the supposed omniscience of God, most determinists seem to regard their position as a natural corollary of the scientific outlook. There are both empirical and methodological reasons for this position. On the methodological side, it is often felt to be essential to the scientific approach to assume that events can be causally explained—at least until the most strenuous and thorough search for such a scientific explanation has proved fruitless.

As for the empirical arguments for determinism, these are really of two kinds. On the one hand, there is the materialist argument. Philosophers of Holbach's time were immensely impressed with the success of Newtonian physics in accounting for the motions of material bodies. Given any "closed" system of particles (that is, one that is free from outside interference), it seemed that the positions and momenta of these particles at any one instant, when expressed numerically, could be shown to be a mathematical function of their positions and momenta at any other time. Thus, to cite the standard example, if we set a group of billiard balls in motion, the balls will (so the theory goes) change place in a manner that is rigidly determined by their initial positions, masses, and velocities, the shape of the table, and so on. And even if we then bring in such external influences as billiard cues, these in turn will affect the positions and momenta of the balls in a way that can be predicted. Thus, the change of motion due to a cue striking a ball will itself be dependent on the momentum of the cue and its point of impact.

In the light of modern knowledge, the laws of physics are now thought to be neither as simple nor, when we come to consider the subatomic realm, quite as rigidly deterministic as Newton believed. But with respect to observable reality, more and more properties of matter are becoming incorporated into mathematical laws of this kind, so that, for example, chemical reactions and electromagnetic processes may now be regarded as pursuing predetermined courses. Indeed, we have every reason to suppose that—at what physicists call the "macroscopic level" —ordinary material objects are completely subject to such laws.

The question that naturally follows from this is: "Why should the human organism be any exception?" From a certain point of view the human body is, after all, just a very complicated chunk of matter whose workings, when subjected to scientific scrutiny, appear to be nothing more than a network of complex physicochemical reactions. Take, for example, my simplest action—say, that of waving to a friend. From the standpoint of physical science, the motion of my arm is immediately caused by a muscular contraction induced by nerve impulses transmitted electrochemically from one neuron to the next, leading back to the brain; and the process is ultimately triggered, presumably, by similar impulses transmitted to the brain from the retinas of my eyes when I see my friend. Now admittedly one cannot prove that, at each stage, what occurs is what is bound to occur given the prior circumstances and the relevant physicochemical laws. As with weather forecasting, the whole set-up is so complex that precisely measuring all the relevant data, and computing the implications of the operative laws, is totally impractical. (In addition, no one knows for certain what factors are relevant to begin with.) But to insist that the matter composing the human body is somehow exempt from the laws obtaining elsewhere in nature, or that these laws are limited in scope, permitting human organisms a kind of causal license denied to material objects in general, seems both arbitrary and counter to all available neurological and biochemical evidence.

This is one argument. But sometimes the determinist contends not so much that human behavior is subject to the same *physical* laws as apply to inanimate matter, but rather that human actions are in principle subject to *psychological* explanations that imply determinism. Holbach, like most hard determinists, is a materialist; he insists that "the will . . . is a modification of the brain." Yet when he comes to argue the hard determinist case in detail, he appeals not to physics or chemistry but to a crude psychological theory that uses Newtonian mechanics merely as an analogy. This is evident in his example of the man who, parched with thirst, first abstains from drinking poisoned water but finally succumbs to the temptation as his thirst increases. Here, says Holbach, "the human will . . . finds itself in the same situation as a bowl, which, although it has received an impulse that drives it forward in a straight line, is deranged in its course whenever a force superior to the first obliges it to change its direction." Holbach pictures here a sort of internal tug-of-war between conflicting desires; the final action is, mathematically speaking, the vector sum of these opposing forces.

Admittedly, Holbach's notion of how actions are brought about is not a very sophisticated one. And doubtless contemporary psychology, whether psychoanalytic or behavioristic, has far greater explanatory power. Even so, our present ability to predict human actions seems only marginally superior, if at all, to informed common sense. But the validity of the determinist's outlook does not stand or fall on the success of any *particular* psychological theory, much less on that of any that has yet been devised. Once again, the weather-forecasting anology may be helpful here. The extreme complexity of both weather and human behavior makes it unlikely that an effective science will be readily attainable for either; moreover, human beings, like local climates, are both individually unique and in a process of constant mutual interaction.

There are thus two things that the determinist finds implausible about free will in the sense employed by the libertarian: (1) the fact that it seems to set humans apart from the rest of nature, implying that the human body is to some extent free from the causal bonds to which matter is elsewhere subject; and (2) the fact that it seems to entail the existence of events that are, in principle, causally inexplicable. To qualify as a genuine libertarian, as opposed merely to a soft determinist, a philosopher must be prepared to accept both these consequences.

One highly influential thinker who does so qualify is Jean-Paul Sartre, the leading proponent of existentialist philosophy. Sartre reminds us that there is at least one respect in which a human being quite obviously *is* set apart from inanimate nature—in the possession of consciousness, and more specifically, reflective consciousness. This reflective consciousness is identified by Sartre as the human capacity to stand back, as it were, from one's objective situation—to make oneself an object of thought, to evaluate, or, as Sartre puts it, to question the state and circumstances in which one finds oneself. To the extent that a person is able to step back from and reflect upon his or her objective circumstances, which Sartre calls "facticity," he or she cannot also stand in complete causal bondage to these circumstances, Sartre argues. Reflective consciousness, for Sartre, means the capacity to "transcend" one's facticity, and this in turn means that a person is "condemned to be free." In Sartre's own words:

It is essential therefore that the questioner have the permanent possibility of dissociating himself from the causal series which constitutes being and which can produce only being. If we admitted that the question is determined in the questioner by universal determinism the question would thereby become unintelligible and even inconceivable. . . . Thus, insofar as the questioner must be able to effect in relation to the questioned a kind of nihilating withdrawal he is not subject to the causal order of the world; he detaches himself from being.

When Sartre speaks of a person as questioning or effecting a "nihilating withdrawal" from his objective situation, he is not thinking merely of that person's external circumstances. For no determinist would deny that, of two workers whose external circumstances were (in all relevant respects) identical, one might bear his burden in silence, and the other initiate protest action, merely because of a difference in the respective psychological make-up of the two individuals. But Sartre insists that "no factual state whatever it may be (the political and economic structure of society, the *psychological* 'state' etc.) is capable by itself of motivating any act whatsover." Thus two workers might be equally exploited and underpaid (i.e., be subject to the same *external circumstances*), and both might be equally afraid to act (i.e., be in the same psychological state); and yet one, by what Sartre calls "a pure wrenching away from himself," might act in spite of his fear, while the other might use it to justify his own inaction.

A person's past is part of his or her facticity, inasmuch as it is fixed and beyond anyone's power to affect in any way. But, for a being capable of reflection, the past cannot, Sartre maintains, completely determine the future. One individual, who has been raised in the slums, who has never had a decent education, and whose father and peers have all taken to a life of crime, may attempt to justify his own criminality by saying: "How could I have become anything else but a criminal, given my background and lack of opportunities?" But another, raised in identical circumstances, may "wrench himself away from his past," and cite these very same circumstances as having provided the challenge to overcome these initial handicaps, to work his way through college, and, by becoming, say, a social worker, to try to improve the social conditions in which he grew up. Thus, according to Sartre, "Man is without excuse." A person cannot claim, in good faith, to be the slave of circumstances while possessing the capacity to question or reflect upon them.

The trouble with all this is that it is very difficult to see what such highly metaphorical language really comes down to. It may be true (on one level) that the circumstances that a person characteristically cites to explain his or her motive for acting in a particular way constitute a motive only insofar as he or she considers them so. To cite a rather trivial example, the fact that the grass on my lawn is over an inch tall will motivate me to mow the lawn only insofar as I judge it a bad thing to have grass of this height. But then why should the fact that I consider the height of the grass sufficient motive to act stop a scientist from explaining my act as the consequence of my genetic inheritance and the conditioning I received while living in middle-class suburban society?

Sartre's reason for thinking that such a determinist account must be impossible is that my desire to initiate a change invariably involves perceiving a *lack* of something, what Sartre calls a *negatité*. It means seeing, in the actual situation, the *absence* of some ideal or preferred state of affairs. Sartre's argument, then, seems to be this: Objectively regarded—regarded in the way that the scientist would regard them in order to make them the basis of a causal explanation—states of affairs are not intrinsically lacking or deficient; they simply are as they are. They become imbued with this lack only when they are compared to an ideal state of affairs, *which has no existence at all.* Without being compared to ideal states—as I might compare my overgrown grass to the well-trimmed lawn it might become if I mowed it—actual states of affairs, even states of the individual's own mind, cannot motivate. Yet, at the same time, there is nothing about an objective state of affairs that forces a person to judge it according to a particular ideal, or to act to realize this ideal. Sartre apparently has this in mind when he insists that "what is can in no way determine what is not."

But, if we understand him correctly, Sartre is here guilty of confusing causal necessity with logical necessity. It is perfectly true that no objective description of how things actually are can logically entail how things ought to be—a point stressed by David Hume when he observed that "an 'ought' cannot be derived from an 'is'." That is to say, some additional evaluative premise is invariably called for, in order to render the inference valid. But the fact that a person has in mind a certain concept of how things ought to be and judges the present situation deficient in the light of this concept is not itself a value judgment. It may be a perfectly objective present fact about that person. And, as such, it is difficult to see how any of the considerations Sartre mentions would preclude a fully deterministic explanation of how he or she came by this concept and was prompted to act upon it. Even though the evaluation of the situation upon which a person acts is not a *logical* consequence of any objective characterization of the situation, that does not mean that the individual came to make that evaluation and act upon it free from the *causal* influences of his or her heredity and environment.

Although Sartre's attempts to refute determinism outright are unconvincing, there is nevertheless much in his analysis of human action that commands attention and might at least give the determinist pause. As Sartre points out, what many determinists (including Holbach) object to most strongly is the notion of actions that have no reason or motive. But, as Sartre quite rightly observes, to supply a reason or motive for an action is not—on the face of it, at least—the same as providing a cause, as the determinists maintain. Supplying a reason means explaining the purpose of the action, or saying what it was done *for.* And this form of explanation is teleological rather than causal; that is to say, the explanation is in terms of the projected *future* states of affairs aimed at in the action, rather than in terms of some past set of conditions of which the action was an inevitable effect. As Sartre puts it, explanation, here, is a matter not so much of relating the action to a prior determining cause as of showing how the action makes sense in the context of the agent's "projects."

The question of the relation between explanation in terms of reasons and purposes and explanation in terms of causes is debated widely among contemporary philosophers (and is touched on, briefly, in the second of our two selections from A. J. Ayer). Some philosophers think that explanation in terms of reasons is actually a type of causal explanation; others think that the first form of explanation at least presupposes the possibility of the second; others again see the two forms of explanation as incompatible; and some hold the more complicated view that actions may be explained only in terms of reasons (a claim, incidentally, which Sartre endorses), but that the physical movements that actions involve may be explained causally (a claim that Sartre denies).

In any case, Sartre has a still more telling objection against determinism, which has special bearing on situations involving conflicting desires. In cases of this kind, determinists such as Holbach tend, as we have seen, to appeal to the greater force or strength of the one desire as opposed to the other in giving a causal explanation of why an agent acts as he or she does. Admittedly, the decision will usually involve a process of deliberation, seen by the determinist as a process of weighing alternative desires as though they were, as Sartre puts it, "entirely transcendent things which I balance in my hands like weights and which possess weight as a permanent property." But is this really so? Can one desire or feeling really be regarded, in general, as having more weight than another, other than by reference to the agent's actual decision? Sartre's skepticism on this point emerges clearly in his essay "Existentialism Is a Humanism" (see chap. 8), in which he discusses the case of a young Frenchman during the Nazi occupation who was undecided as to whether he should stay with his mother or leave for England to join the Free French forces. As Sartre reports it:

When I saw him he said, "In the end, it is feeling that counts; the direction in which it is really pushing me is the one I ought to choose. If I feel that I love my mother enough to sacrifice everything else for her—my will to be avenged, all my longings for action and adventure—then I stay with her. If, on the contrary, I feel that my love for her is not enough, I go." But how does one estimate the strength of a feeling? The value of his feeling for his mother was determined precisely by the fact that he was standing by her. I may say that I love a certain friend enough to sacrifice such and such a sum of money for him, but I cannot prove that unless I have done it. I may say, "I love my mother enough to remain with her," if actually I have remained with her. I can only estimate the strength of this affection if I have performed an action by which it is defined and ratified. But if I then appeal to this affection to justify my action, I find myself drawn into a vicious circle.

Sartre is here concerned with the moral justification of an action rather than its causal explanation. But plainly, if what Sartre says is correct, any determinist who thinks that a person's decision to act is the result of the relative forces of his or her desires will be open to the charge of circular reasoning. If it is true, as Sartre maintains, that it makes sense to speak of one desire as stronger than another only insofar as a person has already decided to act upon the first rather than the second, then clearly it cannot also be true that it is *because* one feeling is stronger that the agent makes that decision. Whether or not Sartre is correct in his basic claim is another matter, of which the reader must be the judge.

Enough has been said to indicate that, in rejecting determinism, the libertarian is not necessarily implying that actions are inexplicably capricious. Nevertheless, in the eyes of many philosophers, it seems an extremely unsatisfactory feature of libertarianism that it places prior limits on the scope of scientific explanation. Somehow it just does not seem plausible to suppose that philosophical reflection alone should enable us to assert that the attempt to give a causal account of human behavior is bound, at some stage, to break down. This point has been forcefully expressed by the contemporary British philosopher P. F. Strawson, who remarks in this context: "It seems to me sheer folly for any philosopher to declare, about any scientific aim that can intelligibly be stated, that the aim is in principle unattainable for philosophical reasons." So the question naturally arises: Is it really necessary, as Sartre and others seem to assume, to deny causal determinism in order to defend the existence of free will? Can we come up with a plausible definition of "free will," which will allow us to say of someone both that he or she is genuinely exercising free will in performing a certain action, and that his or her action is in principle causally explainable?

A variety of attempts have been made to supply such a definition. Some philosophers maintain that for an action to be free, it must be the case that the agent could have acted otherwise; but the phrase "could have acted otherwise" does not, as the determinist assumes, mean "could, consistently with prior circumstances and the laws of nature, have acted otherwise." Rather, it means *"would have acted otherwise if he or she (the agent) had so desired."* This view concedes that the action may have been causally inevitable, given the actual desires of the agent, and that the agent could not help having the desires he or she did. Nevertheless, the action may still have been free precisely because it sprang from the agent's own wishes and because the agent would have acted differently if he or she had had different desires.

This line is taken by the contemporary British Philosopher A. J. Ayer in his essay, "Freedom and Necessity," which represents the soft determinist position in this volume. Ayer argues that for a person's action to count as free, it need not be uncaused; rather it must have the right kind of causal explanation. Thus, behavior occasioned by physical force, behavior evoked by subjecting the agent to extreme psychological pressure (by placing a gun to one's head or using or threatening to use torture), behavior resulting from neurotic compulsion or occurring under the influence of certain drugs or posthypnotic suggestion—all of these differ significantly from actions that issue from the desires of a person in full command of his faculties and under no duress whatsoever. And the agent may be held to be acting freely only in the latter case. But this is not because the latter behavior is any less subject to causal determination; it, too, is a consequence of external stimuli and the agent's inner make-up, which, in turn, is a product of heredity and environment. The point is rather that such behavior is free from constraint. And on this view, it is constraint, not causal necessity, that is opposed to free will. There remains, of course, the problem of distinguishing between those causes of behavior that "constrain" and those that do not.

Another variant of the soft determinist position that deserves mention builds its case on the distinction, discussed earlier, between explanation in terms of reasons and explanation in terms of causes. Most philosophers believe that these two forms of explanation do not exclude one another, so that we will not be prejudging the issue of determinism if we define free actions as those that can be explained in terms of reasons. One problem with this formulation, however, is that many, perhaps most, of our actions are performed impulsively, by force of habit or simply without thinking, and hence may not, strictly speaking, have any reasons behind them at all. Yet it seems wrong to regard them, merely on that score, as unfree. A more promising suggestion, therefore, may be to define an action as free if, in performing it, the agent is *open to reason*—that is, if the agent would have acted differently on being presented with cogent reasons, consistent with his or her beliefs and desires, for doing so. This, incidentally, is also a significant improvement upon the earlier suggestion that a person could have acted otherwise, and was hence acting freely, if he would have acted otherwise, had he so desired. For, according to that proposal, we would be obliged to say of alcoholics and kleptomaniacs that they are free not to drink and not to steal—for doubtless they would not do so if they lacked the desire. But then surely it is precisely because they do have such compulsive desires that we judge their behavior unfree. It is, however, characteristic of compulsive behavior that the agent is not open to reason, in the sense just given. The chronic alcoholic who, as a result of her drinking, neglects her family and is threatened with abandonment by her spouse has, even as she views the situation, overwhelming reasons for not drinking; but these considerations simply fail to affect her action in the rationally appropriate manner.

Theories of this kind certainly have considerable initial appeal. But it still seems questionable whether the concept of "free" action that the soft determinist offers us is compatible with the traditional notion of free will. It is, after all, basic to our ordinary notion of free will that a person may justly be held responsible for actions that are performed freely. And this, in turn, means that those actions may be deemed worthy of praise or blame, things for which the agent may legitimately take credit or feel guilty. But, can the soft determinist—that is, someone who holds that an action can be both free and causally explained—really do justice to this notion of responsibility? It seems the soft determinist can do so only by jettisoning the following very plausible principle: if a person is not responsible for a given set of circumstances, then neither can he or she be held responsible for anything that is an inevitable causal consequence of those circumstances. We apply this principle unhesitatingly in everyday affairs. If a doctor is not responsible for a patient's having contracted a certain disease, and is not responsible for the same patient's having failed to take the medication that was prescribed, and the combination of these two factors leads inevitably to the patient's death, then no one would hold the doctor responsible for the death of the patient. But now apply this same principle to, say, a bank robber. His action, in robbing a bank, may be free by all the soft determinist's criteria: performed in accordance with his sane, considered wishes; fully premeditated; something he would not have done had it been made worth his while not to do so; and so forth. But if the robbery is nevertheless an inevitable causal consequence of his hereditary nature and the sum of environmental influences that have operated upon him, then— in view of the fact that he can scarcely be held responsible for his heredity and upbringing—how can he *really* be held responsible for the robbery either? It is far from clear how the soft determinist can meet this challenge.

Ayer himself has, in recent years, had second thoughts about the soft determinism that he championed in "Freedom and Necessity," for reasons that he outlined in a later article on fatalism, part of which is included here. This latter article provides, in addition, a lucid critical survey of the contemporary free will–determinism debate. It is worth stressing that Ayer himself is to be classified as an antilibertarian rather than a determinist, properly speaking. He feels that the question of whether human behavior may ever be brought fully within the orbit of causal laws is essentially a scientific question, which it is not the business of philosophers to prejudge one way or the other. He is, however, inclined to reject libertarianism on the grounds that it would not be reasonable to hold someone responsible for an uncaused action, which he rather tendentiously characterizes as "a matter of pure chance." Libertarians retort that an action that cannot be *causally* explained may still be adequately explained in terms of *purpose*—in which case it would be incorrect to label the act "merely accidental" or "a purely chance occurrence." In his later article, Ayer shows himself well aware of this potential line of rebuttal but argues that it is inadequate.

Leaving open the question of whether determinism is a defensible doctrine, it is worth considering, finally, what the practical consequences of seriously entertaining it would be. In the first place, belief in determinism does not provide any rational support for a so called "fatalistic attitude toward life—the attitude that whatever will be must be, so that there is really no point in trying to bring about what one desires. On this point, however, there has been much confusion. Thus Sir Arthur Eddington, the British physicist, has argued that determinism does entail fatalism. He therefore asks:

What significance is there in my mental struggle tonight whether I shall or shall not give up smoking, if the laws which govern the matter of the physical universe already preordain for the morrow a configuration of matter consisting of pipe, tobacco, and smoke connected with my lips?

This might be a reasonable argument if determinists were committed to holding that "effort" or "trying" was useless, but they are committed to no such thing. On the contrary, they will admit, in accordance with common sense, that if a person does succeed in giving up smoking, this will most likely be caused by his or her mental struggle. It is just that whether he or she will struggle, or struggle sufficiently hard, is itself something that is predetermined, according to determinists. Determinism in no way entails that effort is, in any sense, pointless.

On the other hand, hard determinism does entail that it is somehow inappropriate to feel remorse or guilt about the way we act, or conversely, to take personal credit for past accomplishments. For it is perverse to feel guilt over an action we could not help doing. And it is baseless egotism to take credit for our accomplishments if, as Skinner put it in a recent interview, "I am merely a locus at which certain effects come together." In one sense, this change of attitudes might be beneficial. Few of us suffer from a surfeit of humility; and many of us do suffer from an excess of regret of the kind, "If only I had done such-and-such instead."

There might be some consolation to be gained from the thought that we could not really have acted any differently from the way we did.

On the other hand, we must not ignore the value of guilt and pride in providing important negative and positive incentives. This connects up with the activities of praise and blame. If hard determinism is true, no one can be justly praised or blamed for any action, although, as Ayer points out, the activities of praising and blaming people may still be very useful. In Skinner's terminology, praise and blame may serve as powerful "positive and negative reinforcements." Skinner himself is a great believer in the value of assigning credit to people for those activities we wish to encourage (while pointedly observing that we tend, in practice, to award credit for an action in inverse proportion to the *conspicuousness* of its causes). It may be important to point out that the efficacy of praise and blame might be less if these activities ceased to evince in people pride or remorse. But, in any case, as we stressed at the start, the question of whether widespread or universal belief in hard determinism would or would not have social benefits has no bearing whatever on the question of whether the doctrine is true.

A final word should be said about Skinner's belief that free will is an illusion since we are all ultimately slaves to the haphazard positive and negative reinforcements of our social and natural environment, so that we have nothing to lose and much to gain by trading in this "natural" conditioning for a conditioning that is scientifically engineered to make us happier. Although there is some plausibility in this, there is also a potential fallacy in the argument. Compare it with the case of human genetics. Does it follow from the fact that our natures are largely determined by our heredity that the present haphazard method of reproduction should be replaced by scientifically controlled eugenic breeding? Not necessarily. For this assumes that we know in advance which, of all the various possible genetic combinations, are the most desirable ones. The truth, however, is that only a tiny fraction of all the available options have been mentally surveyed. The one great virtue of a process that constantly generates new combinations, more or less haphazardly, is that every now and then it produces unexpectedly advantageous results.

It also seems that Skinner confuses freedom in a sociopolitical sense with free will, and assumes that if the latter is an illusion, the former must be an illusion as well. But, even granted the nonexistence of free will, is it not possible that political or social freedom is a virtue that a humanistic hard determinist should recognize? It all depends, of course, on just what "freedom" is taken to mean in a political context. But this leads on to thoughts concerning the good society that properly belong to a later chapter.

WALDEN TWO

B. F. Skinner

Castle got his chance to take up "general issues" that afternoon. A walk to the summit of Stone Hill had been planned for a large party, which included Mr. and Mrs. Meyerson and three or four children. It seemed unlikely that any serious discussion would be possible. But a storm had been threatening all morning, and at lunch we heard it break. The afternoon was again open. I detected a certain activity in the dining room as plans were changed. As we were finishing dinner two young people approached our table and spoke to Rodge, Steve, and the girls.

"Do you play? Concert, sax, trombone? We're getting up a concert. We even have a lonely tuba."

"You play, Steve," said Mary.

"Steve was the best little old trombone in the Philippines," said Rodge.

"Good! Anybody else? It's strictly amateur."

It appeared that Barbara could play popular tunes on the piano, mostly by ear, and it was thought that something might be arranged. They departed for the theater to look over the common stock of instruments, and Frazier, Castle, and I were left alone.

Castle immediately began to warm up his motors. He picked up an empty cigarette package which Barbara had left on the table, tore it in two, placed the halves together, and tore them again. Various husky noises issued from his throat. It was obvious that something was about to happen, and Frazier and I waited in silence.

"Mr. Frazier," Castle said at last, in a sudden roar, "I accuse you of one of the most diabolical machinations in the history of mankind!" He looked as steadily as possible at Frazier, but he was trembling, and his eyes were popping.

"Shall we go to my room?" Frazier said quietly.

It was a trick of Frazier's to adopt a contrasting tone of voice, and in this instance it was devastating. Castle came down to earth with a

FROM *Walden Two,* chapter 29. Copyright © 1960 by Macmillan, Inc. and reprinted with their permission.

humiliating bump. He had prepared himself for a verbal battle of heroic dimensions, but he found himself humbly carrying his tray to the service window and trailing Frazier along the Walk.

I was not sure of the line Castle was going to take. Apparently he had done some thinking since morning, probably during the service, but I could not guess the result. Frazier's manner was also puzzling. His suggestion that we go to his room had sounded a little as if he were inviting a truculent companion to "step outside and say that again!" He had apparently expected the attack from Castle and had prepared .the defenses to his satisfaction.

When we had settled ourselves in Frazier's room, with Frazier full-length on the bed, over which he had hastily pulled a cover, Castle began again in an unsuccessful attempt to duplicate the surprise and force of his first assault.

"A modern, mechanized, managerial Machiavelli—that is my final estimate of you, Mr. Frazier," he said, with the same challenging stare.

"It must be gratifying to know that one has reached a 'final estimate,'" said Frazier.

"An artist in power," Castle continued, "whose greatest art is to conceal art. The silent despot."

"Since we are dealing in 'M's,' why not sum it all up and say 'Mephistophelian'?" said Frazier, curiously reviving my fears of the preceding afternoon.

"I'm willing to do that!" said Castle. "And unless God is very sure of himself, I suspect He's by no means easy about this latest turn in the war of the angels. So far as I can see, you've blocked every path through which man was to struggle upward toward salvation. Intelligence, initiative—you have filled their places with a sort of degraded instinct, engineered compulsion. Walden Two is a marvel of efficient coordination—as efficient as an anthill!"

"Replacing intelligence with instinct—" muttered Frazier. "I had never thought of that. It's an interesting possibility. How's it done?" It was a crude maneuver. The question was a digression, intended to spoil Castle's timing and to direct our attention to practical affairs in which Frazier was more at home.

"The behavior of your members is carefully shaped in advance by a Plan," said Castle, not to be taken in, "and it's shaped to perpetuate that Plan. Intellectually Walden Two is quite as incapable of a spontaneous change of course as the life within a beehive."

"I see what you mean," said Frazier distantly. But he returned to his strategy. "And have you discovered the machinery of my power?"

"I have, indeed. We were looking in the wrong place. There's no *current* contact between you and the members of Walden Two. You threw us off the track very skillfully on that point last night. But you were behaving as a despot when you first laid your plans—when you designed the social structure and drew up the contract between community and member, when you worked out your educational practices and your guarantees against despotism—What a joke! Don't tell me you weren't in control *then!* Burris saw the point. What about your career as organizer? *There* was leadership! And the most damnable leadership in history, because you were setting the stage for the withdrawal of yourself as a personal force, knowing full well that everything that happened would still be your doing. Hundreds—you predicted millions —of unsuspecting souls were to fall within the scope of your ambitious scheme."

Castle was driving his arguement home with great excitement, but Frazier was lying in exaggerated relaxation, staring at the ceiling, his hands cupped behind his head.

"Very good, Mr. Castle," he said softly. "I gave you the clue, of course, when we parted last night."

"You did, indeed. And I've wondered why. Were you led into that fatal error by your conceit? Perhaps that's the ultimate answer to your form of despotism. No one could enjoy the power you have seized without wishing to display it from time to time."

"I've admitted neither power nor despotism. But you're quite right in saying that I've exerted an influence and in one sense will continue to exert it forever. I believe you called me a *primum mobile* [prime mover] —not quite correctly, as I found upon looking the term up last night. But I did plan Walden Two—not as an architect plans a building, but as a scientist plans a long-term experiment, uncertain of the conditions he will meet but knowing how he will deal with them when they arise. In a sense, Walden Two is predetermined, but not as the behavior of a beehive is determined. Intelligence, no matter how much it may be shaped and extended by our educational system, will still function as intelligence. It will be used to puzzle out solutions to problems to which a beehive would quickly succumb. What the plan does is to keep intelligence on the right track, for the good of society rather than of the intelligent individual—or for the eventual rather than the immediate good of the individual. It does this by making sure that the individual will not forget his personal stake in the welfare of society."

"But you are forestalling many possibly useful acts of intelligence which aren't encompassed by your plan. You have ruled out points of view which may be more productive. You are implying that T. E. Frazier, looking at the world from the middle of the twentieth century, understands the best course for mankind forever."

"Yes, I suppose I do."

"But that's absurd!"

"Not at all. I don't say I foresee the course man will take a hundred years hence, let alone forever, but I know which he should take now."

"How can you be sure of it? It's certainly not a question you have answered experimentally."

"I think we're in the course of answering it," said Frazier. "But that's beside the point. There's no alternative. We must take that course."

"But that's fantastic. You who are taking it are in a small minority."

Frazier sat up.

"And the majority are in a big quandary," he said. "They're not on the road at all, or they're scrambling back toward their starting point, or sidling from one side of the road to the other like so many crabs. What do you think two world wars have been about? Something as simple as boundaries or trade? Nonsense. The world is trying to adjust to a new conception of man in relation to men."

"Perhaps it's merely trying to adjust to despots whose ideas are incompatible with the real nature of man."

"Mr. Castle," said Frazier very earnestly, "let me ask you a question. I warn you, it will be the most terrifying question of your life. *What would you do if you found yourself in possession of an effective science of behavior?* Suppose you suddenly found it possible to control the behavior of men as you wished. What would you do?"

"That's an assumption?"

"Take it as one if you like. *I* take it as a fact. And apparently you accept it as a fact too. I can hardly be as despotic as you claim unless I hold the key to an extensive practical control."

"What would I do?" said Castle thoughtfully. "I think I would dump your science of behavior in the ocean."

"And deny men all the help you could otherwise give them?"

"And give them the freedom they would otherwise lose forever!"

"How could you give them freedom?"

"By refusing to control them!"

"But you would only be leaving the control in other hands."

"Whose?"

"The charlatan, the demagogue, the salesman, the ward heeler, the bully, the cheat, the educator, the priest—all who are now in possession of the techniques of behavioral engineering."

"A pretty good share of the control would remain in the hands of the individual himself."

"That's an assumption, too, and it's your only hope. It's your only possible chance to avoid the implications of a science of behavior. If man is free, then a technology of behavior is impossible. But I'm asking you to consider the other case."

FREE WILL AND DETERMINISM: IS FREEDOM AN ILLUSION? 267

"Then my answer is that your assumption is contrary to fact and any further consideration idle."

"And your accusations—?"

"—were in terms of intention, not of possible achievement."

Frazier sighed dramatically.

"It's a little late to be proving that a behavioral technology is well advanced. How can you deny it? Many of its methods and techniques are really as old as the hills. Look at their frightful misuse in the hands of the Nazis! And what about the techniques of the psychological clinic? What about education? Or religion? Or practical politics? Or advertising and salesmanship? Bring them all together and you have a sort of rule-of-thumb technology of vast power. No, Mr. Castle, the science is there for the asking. But its techniques and methods are in the wrong hands—they are used for personal aggrandizement in a competitive world or, in the case of the psychologist and educator, for futilely corrective purposes. My question is, have you the courage to take up and wield the science of behavior for the good of mankind? You answer that you would dump it in the ocean!"

"I'd want to take it out of the hands of the politicians and advertisers and salesmen, too."

"And the psychologists and educators? You see, Mr. Castle, you can't have that kind of cake. The fact is, we not only *can* control human behavior, we *must*. But who's to do it, and what's to be done?"

"So long as a trace of personal freedom survives, I'll stick to my position," said Castle, very much out of countenance.

"Isn't it time we talked about freedom?" I said. "We parted a day or so ago on an agreement to let the question of freedom ring. It's time to answer, don't you think?"

"My answer is simple enough," said Frazier. "I deny that freedom exists at all. I must deny it—or my program would be absurd. You can't have a science about a subject matter which hops capriciously about. Perhaps we can never *prove* that man isn't free; it's an assumption. But the increasing success of a science of behavior makes it more and more plausible."

"On the contrary, a simple personal experience makes it untenable," said Castle. "The experience of freedom. I *know* that I'm free."

"It must be quite consoling," said Frazier.

"And what's more—you do, too," said Castle hotly. "When you deny your own freedom for the sake of playing with a science of behavior, you're acting in plain bad faith. That's the only way I can explain it." He tried to recover himself and shrugged his shoulders. "At least you'll grant that you *feel* free."

"The 'feeling of freedom' should deceive no one," said Frazier. "Give me a concrete case."

"Well, right now," Castle said. He picked up a book of matches. "I'm free to hold or drop these matches."

"You will, of course, do one or the other," said Frazier. "Linguistically or logically there seem to be two possibilities, but I submit that there's only one in fact. The determining forces may be subtle but they are inexorable. I suggest that as an orderly person you will probably hold—ah! you drop them! Well, you see, that's all part of your behavior with respect to me. You couldn't resist the temptation to prove me wrong. It was all lawful. You had no choice. The deciding factor entered rather late, and naturally you couldn't foresee the result when you first held them up. There was no strong likelihood that you would act in either direction, and you said you were free."

"That's entirely too glib," said Castle. "It's easy to argue lawfulness after the fact. But let's see you predict what I will do in advance. Then I'll agree there's law."

"I didn't say that behavior is always predictable, any more than the weather is always predictable. There are often too many factors to be taken into account. We can't measure them all accurately, and we couldn't perform the mathematical operations needed to make a prediction if we had the measurements. The legality is usually an assumption —but none the less important in judging the issue at hand."

"Take a case where there's no choice, then," said Castle. "Certainly a man in jail isn't free in the sense in which I am free now."

"Good! That's an excellent start. Let us classify the kinds of determiners of human behavior. One class, as you suggest, is physical restraint—handcuffs, iron bars, forcible coercion. These are ways in which we shape human behavior according to our wishes. They're crude, and they sacrifice the affection of the controllee, but they often work. Now, what other ways are there of limiting freedom?"

Frazier had adopted a professorial tone and Castle refused to answer.

"The threat of force would be one." I said.

"Right. And here again we shan't encourage any loyalty on the part of the controllee. He has perhaps a shade more of the feeling of freedom, since he can always 'choose to act and accept the consequences,' but he doesn't feel exactly free. He knows his behavior is being coerced. Now what else?"

I had no answer.

"Force or the threat of force—I see no other possibility," said Castle after a moment.

"Precisely," said Frazier.

"But certainly a large part of my behavior has no connection with force at all. There's my freedom!" said Castle.

"I wasn't agreeing that there was no other possibility—merely that *you* could see no other. Not being a good behaviorist—or a good Christian, for that matter—you have no feeling for a tremendous power of a different sort."

"What's that?"

"I shall have to be technical," said Frazier. "But only for a moment. It's what the science of behavior calls 'reinforcement theory.' The things that can happen to us fall into three classes. To some things we are indifferent. Other things we like—we want them to happen, and we take steps to make them happen again. Still other things we don't like—we don't want them to happen and we take steps to get rid of them or keep them from happening again.

"Now," Frazier continued earnestly, "if it's in our power to create any of the situations which a person likes or to remove any situation he doesn't like, we can control his behavior. When he behaves as we want him to behave, we simply create a situation he likes, or remove one he doesn't like. As a result, the probability that he will behave that way again goes up, which is what we want. Technically it's called 'positive reinforcement.'

"The old school made the amazing mistake of supposing that the reverse was true, that by removing a situation a person likes or setting up one he doesn't like—in other words by punishing him—it was possible to *reduce* the probability that he would behave in a given way again. That simply doesn't hold. It has been established beyond question. What is emerging at this critical stage in the evolution of society is a behavioral and cultural technology based on positive reinforcement alone. We are gradually discovering—at an untold cost in human suffering—that in the long run punishment doesn't reduce the probability that an act will occur. We have been so preoccupied with the contrary that we always take 'force' to mean punishment. We don't say we're using force when we send shiploads of food into a starving country, though we're displaying quite as much *power* as if we were sending troops and guns."

"I'm certainly not an advocate of force," said Castle. "But I can't agree that it's not effective."

"It's *temporarily* effective, that's the worst of it. That explains several thousand years of bloodshed. Even nature has been fooled. We 'instinctively' punish a person who doesn't behave as we like—we spank him if he's a child or strike him if he's a man. A nice distinction! The immediate effect of the blow teaches us to strike again. Retribution and revenge are the most natural things on earth. But in the long run the man we strike is no less likely to repeat his act."

"But he won't repeat it if we hit him hard enough," said Castle.

"He'll still *tend* to repeat it. He'll *want* to repeat it. We haven't really altered his potential behavior at all. That's the pity of it. If he doesn't repeat it in our presence, he will in the presence of someone else. Or it will be repeated in the disguise of a neurotic symptom. If we hit hard enough, we clear a little place for ourselves in the wilderness of civilization, but we make the rest of the wilderness still more terrible.

"Now, early forms of government are naturally based on punishment. It's the obvious technique when the physically strong control the weak. But we're in the throes of a great change to positive reinforcement—from a competitive society in which one man's reward is another man's punishment, to a cooperative society in which no one gains at the expense of anyone else.

"The change is slow and painful because the immediate, temporary effect of punishment overshadows the eventual advantage of positive reinforcement. We've all seen countless instances of the temporary effect of force, but clear evidence of the effect of not using force is rare. That's why I insist that Jesus, who was apparently the first to discover the power of refusing to punish, must have hit upon the principle by accident. He certainly had none of the experimental evidence which is available to us today, and I can't conceive that it was possible, no matter what the man's genius, to have discovered the principle from casual observation."

"A touch of revelation, perhaps?" said Castle.

"No, accident. Jesus discovered one principle because it had immediate consequences, and he got another thrown in for good measure."

I began to see light.

"You mean the principle of 'love your enemies'?" I said.

"Exactly! To 'do good to those who despitefully use you' has two unrelated consequences. You gain the peace of mind we talked about the other day. Let the stronger man push you around—at least you avoid the torture of your own rage. *That's* the immediate consequence. What an astonishing discovery it must have been to find that in the long run you could *control the stronger man* in the same way!"

"It's generous of you to give so much credit to your early colleague," said Castle, "but why are we still in the throes of so much misery? Twenty centuries should have been enough for one piece of behavioral engineering."

"The conditions which made the principle difficult to discover made it difficult to teach. The history of the Christian Church doesn't reveal many cases of doing good to one's enemies. To inoffensive heathens, perhaps, but not enemies. One must look outside the field of organized religion to find the principle in practice at all. Church governments are devotees of *power,* both temporal and bogus."

"But what has all this got to do with freedom?" I said hastily.

Frazier took time to reorganize his behavior. He looked steadily toward the window, against which the rain was beating heavily.

"Now that we *know* how positive reinforcement works and why negative doesn't," he said at last, "we can be more deliberate, and hence more successful, in our cultural design. We can achieve a sort of control under which the controlled, though they are following a code much more scrupulously than was ever the case under the old system, nevertheless *feel free.* They are doing what they want to do, not what they are forced to do. That's the source of the tremendous power of positive reinforcement—there's no restraint and no revolt. By a careful cultural design, we control not the final behavior, but the *inclination* to behave—the motive, the desires, the wishes.

"The curious thing is that in that case *the question of freedom never arises.* Mr. Castle was free to drop the matchbook in the sense that nothing was preventing him. If it had been securely bound to his hand he wouldn't have been free. Nor would he have been quite free if I'd covered him with a gun and threatened to shoot him if he let it fall. The question of freedom arises when there is restraint—either physical or psychological.

"But restraint is only one sort of control, and absence of restraint isn't freedom. It's not control that's lacking when one feels 'free,' but the objectionable control of force. Mr. Castle felt free to hold or drop the matches in the sense that he felt no restraint—no threat of punishment in taking either course of action. He neglected to examine his positive reasons for holding or letting go, in spite of the fact that these were more compelling in this instance than any threat of force."

LEARNING THEORY

James McConnell

I am writing this because I presume He wants me to. Otherwise He would not have left paper and pencil handy for me to use. And I put the word "He" in capitals because it seems the only thing to do. If I am dead and in hell, then this is only proper. However, if I am merely a captive somewhere, then surely a little flattery won't hurt matters.

As I sit here in this small room and think about it, I am impressed most of all by the suddenness of the whole thing. At one moment I was out walking in the woods near my suburban home. The next thing I knew, here I was in a small featureless room, naked as a jaybird, with only my powers of rationalization to stand between me and insanity. When the "change" was made (whatever the change was), I was not conscious of so much as a momentary flicker between walking in the woods and being here in this room. Whoever is responsible for all of this is to be complimented—either He has developed an instantaneous anesthetic or He has solved the problem of instantaneous transportation of matter. I would prefer to think it the former, for the latter leads to too much anxiety.

As I recall, I was immersed in the problem of how to teach my class in beginning psychology some of the more abstruse points of Learning Theory when the transition came. How far away life at the University seems at the moment: I must be forgiven if now I am much more concerned about where I am and how to get out of here than about how freshmen can be cajoled into understanding Hull or Tolman.

Problem #1: Where am I? For an answer, I can only describe this room. It is about twenty feet square, some twelve feet high, with no windows, but with what might be a door in the middle of one of the walls. Everything is of a uniform gray color, and the walls and ceiling emit a fairly pleasant achromatic light. The walls themselves are of some hard material which might be metal since it feels slightly cool to the touch. The floor is of a softer, rubbery material that yields a little when I walk on it. Also, it has a rather "tingly" feel to it, suggesting that it may be in constant vibration. It is somewhat warmer than the walls, which is all to the good since it appears I must sleep on the floor.

The only furniture in the room consists of what might be a table and what passes for a chair. They are not quite that, but they can be made to serve this purpose. On the table I found the paper and the pencil. No, let me correct myself. What I call paper is a good deal rougher and thicker than I am used to, and what I call a pencil is nothing more than a thin round stick of graphite which I have sharpened by rubbing one end of it on the table.

And that is the sum of my surroundings. I wish I knew what He has done with my clothes. The suit was an old one, but I am worried about the walking boots. I was very fond of those boots—they were quite expensive and I would hate to lose them.

The problem still remains to be answered, however, as to just where in the hell I am—if not hell itself!

Problem #2 is a knottier one—Why am I here? Were I subject to paranoid tendencies, I would doubtless come to the conclusion that my enemies had kidnapped me. Or perhaps that the Russians had taken such an interest in my research that they had spirited me away to some Siberian hideout and would soon appear to demand either cooperation or death. Sadly enough, I am too reality oriented. My research was highly interesting to me, and perhaps to a few other psychologists who like to dabble in esoteric problems of animal learning, but it was scarcely startling enough to warrant such attention as kidnapping.

So I am left as baffled as before. Where am I, and why?

And who is He?

I have decided to forego all attempts at keeping this diary according to "days" or "hours." Such units of time have no meaning in my present circumstances, for the light remains constant all the time I am awake. The human organism is not possessed of as neat an internal clock as some of the lower species. Far too many studies have shown that a human being who is isolated from all external stimulation soon loses his sense of time. So I will merely indicate breaks in the narrative and hope that He will understand that if He wasn't bright enough to leave me with my wristwatch, He couldn't expect me to keep an accurate record.

Nothing much has happened. I have slept, been fed and watered, and have emptied my bladder and bowels. The food was waiting on the table when I awoke last time. I must say that He has little of the gourmet in Him. Protein balls are not my idea of a feast royal. However, they will serve to keep body and soul together (presuming, of course, that they *are* together at the moment). But I must object to my source of liquid refreshment. The meal made me very thirsty, and I was in the process of cursing Him and everybody else when I noticed a small nipple which had appeared in the wall while I was asleep. At first I thought that perhaps Freud was right after all, and that my libido had taken over control of my imagery. Experimentation convinced me, however, that the thing was real, and that it is my present source of water. If one sucks on the thing, it delivers a slightly cool and somewhat sweetish flow of liquid. But really, it's a most undignified procedure. It's bad enough to have to sit around all day in my birthday suit. But for a full professor to have to stand on his tip-toes and suck on an artificial nipple in order to obtain water is asking a little too much. I'd complain to the Management if only I knew to whom to complain!

Following eating and drinking, the call to nature became a little too strong to ignore. Now, I was adequately toilet-trained with indoor plumbing, and the absence of same is most annoying. However, there was nothing much to do but choose a corner of the room and make the best of a none too pleasant situation. (As a side-thought, I wonder if the choosing of a corner was in any way instinctive?) However, the upshot of the whole thing was my learning what is probably the purpose of the vibration of the floor. For the excreted material disappeared through the floor not too many minutes later. The process was a gradual one. Now I will be faced with all kinds of uncomfortable thoughts concerning what might possibly happen to me if I slept too long!

Perhaps this is to be expected, but I find myself becoming a little paranoid after all. In attempting to solve my Problem #2, why I am here, I have begun to wonder if perhaps some of my colleagues at the University are not using me as a subject in some kind of experiment. It would be just like McCleary to dream up some fantastic kind of "human-in-isolation" experiment and use me as a pilot observer. You would think that he'd have asked my permission first. However, perhaps it's important that the subject not know what's happening to him. If so, I have one happy thought to console me. If McCreary *is* responsible for this, he'll have to take over the teaching of my classes for the time being. And how he hates teaching Learning Theory to freshmen!

You know, this place seems dreadfully quiet to me.

Suddenly I have solved two of my problems. I know both where I am and who He is. And I bless the day that I got interested in the perception of motion.

I should say to begin with that the air in this room seems to have more than the usual concentration of dust particles. This didn't seem particularly noteworthy until I noticed that most of them seemed to pile up along the floor against one wall in particular. For a while I was sure that this was due to the ventilation system—perhaps there was an out-going airduct there where this particular wall was joined to the floor. However, when I went over and put my hand to the floor there, I could feel no breeze whatsoever. Yet even as I held my hand along the dividing line between the wall and the floor, dust motes covered my hand with a thin coating. I tried this same experiment everywhere else in the room to no avail. This was the only spot where the phenomenon occurred, and it occurred along the entire length of this one wall.

But if ventilation was not responsible for the phenomenon, what was? All at once there popped into my mind some calculations I had made when the rocket boys had first proposed a manned satellite station. Engineers are notoriously naive when it comes to the performance of a human being in most situations, and I remembered that the problem of the perception of the satellite's rotation seemingly had been ignored by the slip-stick crowd. They had planned to rotate the doughnut-shaped satellite in order to substitute centrifugal force for the force of gravity. Thus the outer shell of the doughnut would appear to be "down" to anyone inside the thing. Apparently they had not realized that man is at least as sensitive to angular rotation as he is to variations in the pull of gravity. As I figured the problem then, if a man aboard the doughnut moved his head as much as three or four feet outwards from the center of the doughnut, he would have become fairly dizzy! Rather annoying it would have been, too, to have been hit by a wave of nausea every time one sat down in a chair. Also, as I pondered the problem, it became apparent that dust particles and the like would probably show a tendency to move in a direction opposite to the direction of the rotation, and hence pile up against any wall or such that impeded their flight.

Using the behavior of the dust particles as a clue, I then climbed atop the table and leapt off. Sure enough, my head felt like a mule had kicked it by the time I landed on the floor. My hypothesis was confirmed.

So I am aboard a spaceship!

The thought is incredible, but in a strange way comforting. At least now I can postpone worrying about heaven and hell—and somehow I find the idea of being in a spaceship much more to the liking of a confirmed agnostic. I suppose I owe McCleary an apology—I should have known he would never have put himself in a position where he would have to teach freshmen all about learning!

And, of course, I know who "He" is. Or rather, I know who He *isn't,* which is something else again. Surely, though, I can no longer think of

Him as being human. Whether I should be consoled at this or not, I have no way of telling.

I still have no notion of *why* I am here, however, nor why this alien chose to pick me of all people to pay a visit to His spaceship. What possible use could I be? Surely if He were interested in making contact with the human race, He would have spirited away a politician. After all, that's what politicians are for! Since there has been no effort made to communicate with me, however, I must reluctantly give up any cherished hopes that His purpose is that of making contact with *genus homo*.

Or perhaps He's a galactic scientist of some kind, a biologist of sorts, out gathering specimens. Now, that's a particularly nasty thought. What if he turned out to be a physiologist, interested in cutting me open eventually, to see what makes me tick? Will my innards be smeared over a glass slide for scores of youthful Hims to peer at under a microscope? Brrrr! I don't mind giving my life to Science, but I'd rather do it a little at a time.

If you don't mind, I think I'll go do a little repressing for a while.

Good God! I should have known it! Destiny will play her little tricks, and all jokes have their cosmic angles. He is a *psychologist!* Had I given it due consideration, I would have realized that whenever you come across a new species, you worry about behavior first, physiology second. So I have received the ultimate insult—or the ultimate compliment. I don't know which. I have become a specimen for an alien psychologist!

This thought first occurred to me when I awoke after my latest sleep (which was filled, I must admit, with most frightening dreams). It was immediately obvious that something about the room had changed. Almost at once I noticed that one of the walls now had a lever of some kind protruding from it, and to one side of the lever, a small hole in the wall with a container beneath the hole. I wandered over to the lever, inspected it a few moments, then accidentally depressed the thing. At once there came a loud clicking noise, and a protein ball popped out of the hole and fell into the container.

For just a moment a frown crossed my brow. This seemed somehow so strangely familiar. Then, all at once, I burst into wild laughter. The room had been changed into a gigantic Skinner Box! For years I had been studying animal learning by putting white rats in a Skinner Box and following the changes in the rats' behavior. The rats had to learn to press the lever in order to get a pellet of food, which was delivered to them through just such an apparatus as is now affixed to the wall of my cell. And now, after all of these years, and after all of the learning studies I had done, to find myself trapped like a rat in a Skinner Box! Perhaps this was hell after all, I told myself, and the Lord High Executioner's admonition to "let the punishment fit the crime" was being followed.

Frankly, this sudden turn of events has left me a little shaken.

I seem to be performing according to theory. It didn't take me long to discover that pressing the lever would give me food some of the time, while at other times all I got was the click and no protein ball. It appears that approximately every twelve hours the thing delivers me a random number of protein balls—the number has varied from five to fifteen so far. I never know ahead of time how many pellets—I mean protein balls—the apparatus will deliver, and it spews them out intermittently. Sometimes I have to press the lever a dozen times or so before it will give me anything, while at other times it gives me one ball for each press. Since I don't have a watch on me, I am never quite sure when the twelve hours have passed, so I stomp over to the lever and press it every few minutes when I think it's getting close to time to be fed. Just like my rats always did. And since the pellets are small and I never get enough of them, occasionally I find myself banging away on the lever with all the compulsion of a stupid animal. But I missed the feeding time once and almost starved to death (so it seemed) before the lever delivered food the next time. About the only consolation to my wounded pride is that at this rate of starvation, I'll lose my bay window in short order.

At least He doesn't seem to be fattening me up for the kill. Or maybe he just likes lean meat!

I have been promoted. Apparently He in his infinite alien wisdom has decided that I'm intelligent enough to handle the Skinner-type apparatus, so I've been promoted to solving a maze. Can you picture the irony of the situation? All of the classic Learning Theory methodology is practically being thrown in my face. If only I could communicate with Him! I don't mind being subjected to tests nearly as much as I mind being underestimated. Why, I can solve puzzles hundreds of times more complex than what He's throwing at me. But how can I tell Him?

As it turns out, the maze is much like our standard T-mazes, and is not too difficult to learn. It's a rather long one, true, with some 23 choice points along the way. I spent the better part of half an hour wandering through the thing the first time I found myself in it. Surprisingly enough, I didn't realize the first time out what I was in, so I made no conscious attempt to memorize the correct turns. It wasn't until I reached the final turn and found food waiting for me that I recognized what I was expected to do. The next time through the maze my performance was a good deal better, and I was able to turn in a perfect performance in not too long a time. However, it does not do my ego any good to realize that my own white rats could have learned the maze a little sooner than I did.

My "home cage," so to speak, still has the Skinner apparatus in it, but the lever delivers food only occasionally now. I still give it a whirl now and again, but since I'm getting a fairly good supply of food at the end of the maze each time, I don't pay the lever much attention.

Now that I am very sure of what is happening to me, quite naturally my thoughts have turned to how I can get out of this situation. Mazes I can solve without too much difficulty, but how to escape apparently is beyond my intellectual capacity. But then, come to think of it, there was precious little chance for my own experimental animals to get out of my clutches. And assuming that I am unable to escape, what then? After He has finished putting me through as many paces as He wishes, where do we go from there? Will He treat me as I treated most of my nonhuman subjects—that is, will I get tossed into a jar containing chloroform? "Following the experiment, the animals were sacrificed," as we so euphemistically report in the scientific literature. This doesn't appeal to me much, as you can imagine. Or maybe if I seem particularly bright to Him, He may use me for breeding purposes, to establish a colony of His own. Now, that might have possibilities . . .

Oh, damn Freud anyhow!

And damn Him too! I had just gotten the maze well learned when He upped and changed things on me. I stumbled about like a bat in the sunlight for quite some time before I finally got to the goal box. I'm afraid my performance was pretty poor. What He did was just to reverse the whole maze so that it was a mirror image of what it used to be. Took me only two trials to discover the solution. Let Him figure that one out if He's so smart!

My performance on the maze reversal must have pleased Him, because now He's added a new complication. And again I suppose I could have predicted the next step if I had been thinking along the right direction. I woke up a few hours ago to find myself in a totally different room. There was nothing whatsoever in the room, but opposite me were two doors in the wall—one door a pure white, the other jet black. Between me and the doors was a deep pit, filled with water. I didn't like the looks of the situation, for it occurred to me right away that He had devised a kind of jumping stand for me. I had to choose which of the doors was open and led to food. The other door would be locked. If I jumped at the wrong door, and found it locked, I'd fall in the water. I needed a bath, that was for sure, but I didn't relish getting it in this fashion.

While I stood there watching, I got the shock of my life. I meant it quite literally. The bastard had thought of everything. When I used to run rats on jumping stands, to overcome their reluctance to jump, I used to shock them. He's following exactly the same pattern. The floor in this room is wired but good. I howled and jumped about and showed all the usual anxiety behavior. It took me less than two seconds to come to my senses and make a flying leap at the white door, however.

You know something? That water is ice cold!

I have now, by my own calculations solved no fewer than 87 different problems on the jumping stand, and I'm getting sick and tired of it. Once I got angry and just pointed at the correct door—and got shocked for not going ahead and jumping. I shouted bloody murder, cursing Him at the top of my voice, telling Him if He didn't like my performance, He could damn well lump it. All He did, of course, was to increase the shock.

Frankly, I don't know how much longer I can put up with this. It's not that the work is difficult. If He were giving me half a chance to show my capabilities, I wouldn't mind it. I suppose I've contemplated a thousand different means of escaping, but none of them is worth mentioning. But if I don't get out of here soon, I shall go stark raving mad!

For almost an hour after it happened, I sat in this room and just wept. I realize that it is not the style in our culture for a grown man to weep, but there are times when cultural taboos must be forgotten. Again, had I thought much about the sort of experiments He must have had in mind, I most probably could have predicted the next step. Even so, I most likely would have repressed the knowledge.

One of the standard problems which any learning psychologist is interested in is this one—will an animal learn something if you fail to reward him for his performance? There are many theorists, such as Hull and Spence, who believe that reward (or "reinforcement," as they call it) is absolutely necessary for learning to occur. This is mere stuff and nonsense, as anyone with a grain of sense knows, but nonetheless the "reinforcement" theory has been dominant in the field for years now. We fought a hard battle with Spence and Hull, and actually had them with their backs to the wall at one point, when suddenly they came up with the concept of "secondary reinforcement." That is, anything associated with a reward takes on the ability to act as a reward itself. For example, the mere sight of food would become a reward in and of itself—almost as much a reward, in fact, as is the eating of the food. The *sight* of food, indeed! But nonetheless, it saved their theories for the moment.

For the past five years now, I have been trying to design an experiment that would show beyond a shadow of a doubt that the *sight* of a reward was not sufficient for learning to take place. And now look at what has happened to me!

I'm sure that He must lean towards Hull and Spence in His theorizing, for earlier today, when I found myself in the jumping stand room, instead of being rewarded with my usual protein balls when I made the correct jump, I—I'm sorry, but it is difficult to write about even now. For when I made the correct jump and the door opened and I started toward the food though, I found it had been replaced with a photograph. A calendar photograph. You know the one. Her name, I think, is Monroe.

I sat on the floor and cried. For five whole years I have been attacking the validity of the secondary reinforcement theory, and now I find myself giving Him evidence that the theory is correct! For I cannot help "learning" which of the doors is the correct one to jump through. I refuse to stand on the apparatus and have the life shocked out of me, and I refuse to pick the wrong door all the time and get an icy bath time after time. It isn't fair! For He will doubtless put it all down to the fact that the mere *sight* of the photograph is functioning as a reward, and that I am learning the problems merely to be able to see Miss What's-her-name in her bare skin!

I can just see Him now, sitting somewhere else in this spaceship, gathering in all the data I am giving Him, plotting all kinds of learning curves, chortling to Himself because I am confirming all of His pet theories. I just wish . . .

Almost an hour has gone by since I wrote the above section. It seems longer than that, but surely it's been only an hour. And I have spent the time deep in thought. For I have discovered a way out of this place, I think. The question is, dare I do it?

I was in the midst of writing that paragraph about His sitting and chortling and confirming His theories, when it suddenly struck me that theories are born of the equipment that one uses. This has probably been true throughout the history of all science, but perhaps most true of all in psychology. If Skinner had never invented his blasted box, if the maze and the jumping stand had not been developed, we probably would have entirely different theories of learning today than we now have. For if nothing else, the type of equipment that one uses drastically reduces the type of behavior that one's subjects can show, and one's theories have to account only for the type of behavior that appears in the laboratories.

It follows from this also that any two cultures that devise the same sort of experimental procedures will come up with almost identical theories.

Keeping all this in mind, it's not hard for me to believe that He is an iron-clad reinforcement theorist, for He uses all of the various paraphernalia that they use, and uses it in exactly the same way.

My means of escape is therefore obvious. He expects from me confirmation of all His pet theories. Well, he won't get it any more! I know all of His theories backwards and forwards, and this means I know how to give Him results that will tear His theories right smack in half!

I can almost predict the results. What does any learning theorist do with an animal that won't behave properly, that refuses to give the results that are predicted? One gets rid of the beast, quite naturally. For one wishes to use only healthy, normal animals in one's work, and any animal that gives "unusual" results is removed from the study but quickly. After all, if it doesn't perform as expected, it must be sick, abnormal, or aberrant in one way or another . . .

There is no guarantee, of course, what method He will employ to dispose of my now annoying presence. Will He "sacrafice" me? Or will He just return me to the "permanent colony"? I cannot say. I know only that I will be free from what is now an intolerable situation.

Just wait until He looks at His results from now on!

FROM: Experimenter-in-Chief, Interstellar Labship PSYCH-145
To: Director, Bureau of Science

Thlan, my friend, this will be an informal missive. I will send the official report along later, but I wanted to give you my subjective impressions first.

The work with the newly discovered species is, for the moment, at a standstill. Things went exceedingly well at first. We picked what seemed to be a normal, healthy animal and smattered it into our standard test apparatus. I may have told you that this new species seemed quite identical to our usual laboratory animals, so we included a couple of the "toys" that our home animals seem so fond of—thin pieces of material made from woodpulp and a tiny stick of graphite. Imagine our surprise, and our pleasure, when this new specimen made exactly the same use of the materials as have all of our home colony specimens. Could it be that there are certain innate behavior patterns to be found throughout the universe in the lower species?

Well, I merely pose the question. The answer is of little importance to a Learning Theorist. Your friend Verpk keeps insisting that the use of these "toys" may have some deeper meaning to it, and that perhaps we should investigate further. At his insistence, then, I include with this informal missive the materials used by our first subject. In my opinion, Verpk is guilty of gross anthropomorphism, and I wish to have nothing further to do with the question. However, this behavior did give us hope that our newly discovered colony would yield subjects whose performances would be exactly in accordance with standard theory.

And, in truth, this is exactly what seemed to be the case. The animal solved the Bfian Box problem in short order, yielding as beautiful data as I have ever seen. We then shifted it to maze, maze-reversal and jumping stand problems, and the results could not have confirmed our theories better had we rigged the data. However, when we switched the animal to secondary reinforcement problems, it seemed to undergo a strange sort of change. No longer was its performance up to par. In fact, at times it seemed to go quite berserk. For part of the experiment, it would perform superbly. But then, just as it seemed to be solving whatever problem we set it to, its behavior would subtly change into patterns that obviously could not come from a normal specimen. It got worse and worse, until its behavior departed radically from that which our theories predicted. Naturally, we knew then that something had happened to the animal, for our theories are based upon thousands of experiments with similar subjects, and hence our theories must be right. But our theories hold only for normal subjects, and for normal species, so it soon became apparent to us that we had stumbled upon some abnormal type of animal.

Upon due consideration, we returned the subject to its home colony. However, we also voted almost unanimously to request from you permission to take steps to destroy the complete colony. It is obviously of little scientific use to us, and stands as a potential danger that we must take adequate steps against. Since all colonies are under your protection, we therefore request permission to destroy it.

I must report, by the way, that Verpk's vote was the only one which was cast against this procedure. He has some silly notion that one should study behavior as one finds it. Frankly, I cannot understand why you have seen fit to saddle me with him on this expedition, but perhaps you have your own reasons.

Verpk's vote notwithstanding, however, the rest of us are of the considered opinion that this whole new colony must be destroyed, and quickly. For it is obviously diseased or some such—as reference to our theories has proven. And should it by some chance come in contact with our other colonies, and infect our other animals with whatever disease or aberration it has, we would never be able to predict their behavior again. I need not carry the argument further, I think.

May we have your permission to destroy the colony as soon as possible, then, so that we may search out yet other colonies and test our theories against other healthy animals? For it is only in this fashion that science progresses.

Respectfully yours,

Iowyy

THE DETERMINATION
OF THE WILL

Baron d'Holbach

In whatever manner man is considered, he is connected to universal nature, and submitted to the necessary and immutable laws that she imposes on all the beings she contains, according to their peculiar essences or to the respective properties with which, without consulting them, she endows each particular species. Man's life is a line that nature commands him to describe upon the surface of the earth, without his ever being able to swerve from it, even for an instant. He is born without his own consent; his organization does in nowise depend upon himself; his ideas come to him involuntarily; his habits are in the power of those who cause him to contract them; he is unceasingly modified by causes, whether visible or concealed, over which he has no control, which necessarily regulate his mode of existence, give the hue to his way of thinking, and determine his manner of acting. He is good or bad, happy or miserable, wise or foolish, reasonable or irrational, without his will being for anything in these various states. Nevertheless, in spite of the shackles by which he is bound, it is pretended he is a free agent, or that independent of the causes by which he is moved, he determines his own will, and regulates his own condition.

However slender the foundation of this opinion, of which everything ought to point out to him the error, it is current at this day and passes for an incontestable truth with a great number of people, otherwise extremely enlightened; it is the basis of religion, which, supposing relations between man and the unknown being she has placed above nature, has been incapable of imagining how man could merit reward or deserve punishment from this being, if he was not a free agent. Society has been believed interested in this system; because an idea has gone abroad, that if all the actions of man were to be contemplated as neces-

FROM *Freedom: Its History, Nature, and Varieties* by R. Dewey and J. Gould.

sary, the right of punishing those who injure their associates would no longer exist. At length human vanity accommodated itself to a hypothesis which, unquestionably, appears to distinguish man from all other physical beings, by assigning to him the special privilege of a total independence of all other causes, but of which a very little reflection would have shown him the impossibility. . . .

The will, as we have elsewhere said, is a modification of the brain, by which it is disposed to action, or prepared to give play to the organs. This will is necessarily determined by the qualities, good or bad, agreeable or painful, of the object or the motive that acts upon his senses, or of which the idea remains with him, and is resuscitated by his memory. In consequence, he acts necessarily, his action is the result of the impulse he receives either from the motive, from the object, or from the idea which has modified his brain, or disposed his will. When he does not act according to this impulse, it is because there comes some new cause, some new motive, some new idea, which modifies his brain in a different manner, gives him a new impulse, determines his will in another way, by which the action of the former impulse is suspended: thus, the sight of an agreeable object, or its idea, determines his will to set him in action to procure it; but if a new object or a new idea more powerfully attracts him, it gives a new direction to his will, annihilates the effect of the former, and prevents the action by which it was to be procured. This is the mode in which reflection, experience, reason, necessarily arrests or suspends the action of man's will: without this he would of necessity have followed the anterior impulse which carried him toward a then desirable object. In all this he always acts according to necessary laws from which he has no means of emancipating himself.

If when tormented with violent thirst, he figures to himself in idea, or really perceives a fountain, whose limpid streams might cool his feverish want, is he sufficient master of himself to desire or not to desire the object competent to satisfy so lively a want? It will no doubt be conceded, that it is impossible he should not be desirous to satisfy it; but it will be said—if at this moment it is announced to him that the water he so ardently desires is poisoned, he will, notwithstanding his vehement thirst, abstain from drinking it: and it has, therefore, been falsely concluded that he is a free agent. The fact, however, is, that the motive in either case is exactly the same: his own conservation. The same necessity that determined him to drink before he knew the water was deleterious upon this new discovery equally determined him not to drink; the desire of conserving himself either annihilates or suspends the former impulse; the second motive becomes stronger than the preceding, that is, the fear of death, or the desire of preserving himself, necessarily prevails over the painful sensation caused by his eagerness to drink: but, it will be said, if the thirst is very parching, an inconsiderate man without regarding the danger will risk swallowing the water. Nothing is gained by this remark: in this case, the anterior impulse only regains the ascendency; he is persuaded that life may possibly be longer preserved, or that he shall derive a greater good by drinking the poisoned water than by enduring the torment, which, to his mind, threatens instant dissolution; thus the first becomes the strongest and necessarily urges him on to action. Nevertheless, in either case, whether he partakes of the water, or whether he does not, the two actions will be equally necessary; they will be the effect of that motive which finds itself most puissant; which consequently acts in the most coercive manner upon his will.

This example will serve to explain the whole phenomenon of the human will. This will, or rather the brain, finds itself in the same situation as a bowl, which, although it has received an impulse that drives it forward in a straight line, is deranged in its course whenever a force superior to the first obliges it to change its direction. The man who drinks the poisoned water appears a madman; but the actions of fools are as necessary as those of the most prudent individuals. The motives that determine the voluptuary and the debauchee to risk their health, are as powerful, and their actions are as necessary, as those which decide the wise man to manage his. But, it will be insisted, the debauchee may be prevailed on to change his conduct: this does not imply that he is a free agent; but that motives may be found sufficiently powerful to annihilate the effect of those that previously acted upon him; then these new motives determine his will to the new mode of conduct he may adopt as necessarily as the former did to the old mode. . . .

The errors of philosophers on the free agency of man, have arisen from their regarding his will as the *primum mobile,* the original motive of his actions; for want of recurring back, they have not perceived the multiplied, the complicated causes which, independently of him, give motion to the will itself; or which dispose and modify his brain, whilst he himself is purely passive in the motion he receives. Is he the master of desiring or not desiring an object that appears desirable to him? Without doubt it will be answered, no: but he is the master of resisting his desire, if he reflects on the consequences. But, I ask, is he capable of reflecting on these consequences, when his soul is hurried along by a very lively passion, which entirely depends upon his natural organization, and the causes by which he is modified? Is it in his power to add to these consequences all the weight necessary to counterbalance his desire? Is he the master of preventing the qualities which render an object desirable from residing in it? I shall be told: he ought to have learned to resist his passions; to contract a habit of putting a curb on his desires. I agree to it without any difficulty. But in reply, I again ask, is his nature susceptible of this modification? Does his boiling blood, his unruly imagination, the igneous fluid that circulates in his veins, permit him to make, enable him to apply true experience in the moment when it is wanted? And even when his temperament has capacitated him, has his education, the examples set before him, the ideas with which he has been inspired in early life, been suitable to make him contract this habit of repressing his desires? Have not all these things rather contributed to induce him to seek with avidity, to make him actually desire those objects which you say he ought to resist?

The *ambitious man* cries out: you will have me resist my passion; but have they not unceasingly repeated to me that rank, honors, power, are the most desirable advantages in life? Have I not seen my fellow citizens envy them, the nobles of my country sacrifice every thing to obtain them? In the society in which I live, am I not obliged to feel, that if I am deprived of these advantages, I must expect to languish in contempt; to cringe under the rod of oppression?

The *miser* says: you forbid me to love money, to seek after the means of acquiring it: alas! does not every thing tell me that, in this world, money is the greatest blessing; that it is amply sufficient to render me happy? In the country I inhabit, do I not see all my fellow citizens covetous of riches? but do I not also witness that they are little scrupulous in the means of obtaining wealth? As soon as they are enriched by the means which you censure, are they not cherished, considered and respected? By what authority, then, do you defend me from amassing treasure? What right have you to prevent my using means, which, although you call them sordid and criminal, I see approved by the sovereign? Will you have me renounce my happiness?

The *voluptuary* argues: you pretend that I should resist my desires; but was I the maker of my own temperament, which unceasingly invites me to pleasure? You call my pleasures disgraceful; but in the country in which I live, do I not witness the most dissipated men enjoying the most distinguished rank? Do I not behold that no one is ashamed of adultery but the husband it has outraged? Do not I see men making trophies of their debaucheries, boasting of their libertinism, rewarded with applause?

The *choleric man* vociferates: you advise me to put a curb on my passions, and to resist the desire of avenging myself: but can I conquer my nature? Can I alter the received opinions of the world? Shall I not be forever disgraced, infallibly dishonored in society, if I do not wash out in the blood of my fellow creatures the injuries I have received?

The *zealous enthusiast* exclaims: you recommend me mildness; you advise me to be tolerant; to be indulgent to the opinions of my fellow men; but is not my temperament violent? Do I not ardently love my God? Do they not assure me, that zeal is pleasing to him; that sanguinary inhuman persecutors have been his friends? As I wish to render myself acceptable in his sight, I therefore adopt the same means.

In short, the actions of man are never free; they are always the necessary consequence of his temperament, of the received ideas, and of the notions, either true or false, which he has formed to himself of happiness; of his opinions, strengthened by example, by education, and by daily experience. So many crimes are witnessed on the earth only because every thing conspires to render man vicious and criminal; the religion he has adopted, his government, his education, the examples set before him, irresistibly drive him on to evil: under these circumstances, morality preaches virtue to him in vain. In those societies where vice is esteemed, where crime is crowned, where venality is constantly recompensed, where the most dreadful disorders are punished only in those who are too weak to enjoy the privilege of committing them with impunity, the practice of virtue is considered nothing more than a painful sacrifice of happiness. Such societies chastise, in the lower orders, those excesses which they respect in the higher ranks; and frequently have the injustice to condemn those in the penalty of death, whom public prejudices, maintained by constant example, have rendered criminal.

Man, then, is not a free agent in any one instant of his life; he is necessarily guided in each step by those advantages, whether real or fictitious, that he attaches to the objects by which his passions are roused: these passions themselves are necessary in a being who unceasingly tends towards his own happiness; their energy is necessary, since that depends on his temperament; his temperament is necessary, because it depends on the physical elements which enter into his composition; the modification of this temperament is necessary, as it is the infallible and inevitable consequence of the impulse he receives from the incessant action of moral and physical beings.

In spite of these proofs of the want of free agency in man, so clear to unprejudiced minds, it will, perhaps be insisted upon with no small feeling of triumph, that if it be proposed to any one, to move or not to move his hand, an action in the number of those called indifferent, he evidently appears to be the master of choosing; from which it is concluded that evidence has been offered of free agency. The reply is, this example is perfectly simple; man in performing some action which he is resolved on doing, does not by any means prove his free agency: the very desire of displaying this quality, excited by the dispute, becomes a necessary motive, which decides his will either for the one or the other of these actions: What deludes him in this instance, or that which persuades him he is a free agent at this moment, is, that he does not discern the true motive which sets him in action, namely, the desire of convincing his opponent: if in the heat of the dispute he insists and asks, "Am I not the master of throwing myself out of the window?" I shall answer him, no; that whilst he preserves his reason there is no probability that the desire of proving his free agency, will become a motive sufficiently powerful to make him sacrifice his life to the attempt: if, notwithstanding this, to prove he is a free agent, he should actually precipitate himself from the window, it would not be a sufficient warranty to conclude he acted freely, but rather that it was the violence of his temperament which spurred him on to this folly. Madness is a state, that depends upon the heat of the blood, not upon the will. A fanatic or a hero, braves death as necessarily as a more phlegmatic man or coward flies from it.

There is, in point of fact, no difference between the man that is cast out of the window by another, and the man who throws himself out of it, except that the impulse in the first instance comes immediately from without whilst that which determines the fall in the second case, springs from within his own peculiar machine, having its more remote cause also exterior. When Mutius Scaevola held his hand in the fire, he was as much acting under the influence of necessity (caused by interior motives) that urged him to this strange action, as if his arm had been held by strong men: pride, despair, the desire of braving his enemy, a wish to astonish him, and anxiety to intimidate him, etc., were the invisible chains that held his hand bound to the fire. The love of glory, enthusiasm for their country, in like manner caused Codrus and Decius to devote themselves for their fellow-citizens. The Indian Colanus and the philosopher Peregrinus were equally obliged to burn themselves, by desire of exciting the astonishment of the Grecian assembly.

It is said that free agency is the absence of those obstacles competent to oppose themselves to the actions of man, or to the exercise of his faculties: it is pretended that he is a free agent whenever, making use of these faculties, he produces the effect he has proposed to himself. In reply to this reasoning, it is sufficient to consider that it in nowise depends upon himself to place or remove the obstacles that either determine or resist him; the motive that causes his action is no more in his own power than the obstacle that impedes him, whether this obstacle or motive be within his own machine or exterior of his person: he is not master of the thought presented to his mind, which determines his will; this thought is excited by some cause independent of himself.

To be undeceived on the system of his free agency, man has simply to recur to the motive by which his will is determined; he will always find this motive is out of his own control. It is said: that in consequence of an idea to which the mind gives birth, man acts freely if he encounters no obstacle. But the question is, what gives birth to this idea in his brain? was he the master either to prevent it from presenting itself, or from renewing itself in his brain? Does not this idea depend either upon objects that strike him exteriorly and in despite of himself, or upon causes, that without his knowledge, act within himself and modify his brain? Can he prevent his eyes, cast without design upon any object whatever, from giving him an idea of this object, and from moving his brain? He is not more master of the obstacles; they are the necessary effects of either interior or exterior causes, which always act according to their given properties. A man insults a coward; this necessarily irritates him against his insulter; but his will cannot vanquish the obstacle that cowardice places to the object of his desire, because his natural conformation, which does not depend upon himself, prevents his having courage. In this case, the coward is insulted in spite of himself; and against his will is obliged patiently to brook the insult he has reecived.

The partisans of the system of free agency appear ever to have confounded constraint with necessity. Man believes he acts as a free agent, every time he does not see any thing that places obstacles to his actions; he does not perceive that the motive which causes him to will, is always necessary and independent of himself. A prisoner loaded with chains is compelled to remain in prison; but he is not a free agent in the desire to emancipate himself; his chains prevent him from acting, but they do not prevent him from willing; he would save himself if they would loose his fetters; but he would not save himself as a free agent; fear or the idea of punishment would be sufficient motives for his action.

Man may, therefore, cease to be restrained, without, for that reason, becoming a free agent: in whatever manner he acts, he will act necessarily, according to motives by which he shall be determined. He may be compared to a heavy body that finds itself arrested in its descent by any obstacle whatever: take away this obstacle, it will gravitate or continue to fall; but who shall say this dense body is free to fall or not? Is not its descent the necessary effect of its own specific gravity? The virtuous Socrates submitted to the laws of his country, although they were unjust; and though the doors of his jail were left open to him, he would not save himself; but in this he did not act as a free agent: the invisible chains of opinion, the secret love of decorum, the inward respect for the laws, even when they were iniquitous, the fear of tarnishing his glory, kept him in his prison; they were motives sufficiently powerful with this enthusiast for virtue, to induce him to wait death with tranquility; it was not in his power to save himself, because he could find no potential motive to bring him to depart, even for an instant, from those principles to which his mind was accustomed.

Man, it is said, frequently acts against his inclination, from whence it is falsely concluded he is a free agent; but when he appears to act contrary to his inclination, he is always determined to it by some motive sufficiently efficacious to vanquish this inclination. A sick man, with a view to his cure, arrives at conquering his repugnance to the most disgusting remedies: the fear of pain, or the dread of death, then become necessary motives; consequently this sick man cannot be said to act freely.

When it is said, that man is not a free agent, it is not pretended to compare him to a body moved by a simple impulsive cause: he contains within himself causes inherent to his existence; he is moved by an interior organ, which has its own peculiar laws, and is itself necessarily determined in consequence of ideas formed from perception resulting from sensation which it receives from exterior objects. As the mechanism of these sensations, of these perceptions, and the manner they engrave ideas on the brain of man, are not known to him; because he is unable to unravel all these motions; because he cannot perceive the chain of operations in his soul, or the motive principle that acts within him, he supposes himself a free agent; which literally translated, signifies, that he moves himself by himself; that he determines himself without cause: when he rather ought to say, that he is ignorant of how or why he acts in the manner he does. It is true the soul enjoys an activity peculiar to itself: but it is equally certain that this activity would never be displayed, if some motive or some cause did not put it in a condition to exercise itself: at least it will not be pretended that the soul is able either to love or to hate without being moved, without knowing the objects, without having some idea of their qualities. Gunpowder has unquestionably a particular activity, but this activity will never display itself, unless fire be applied to it; this, however, immediately sets it in motion.

It is the great complication of motion in man, it is the variety of his action, it is the multiplicity of causes that move him, whether simultaneously or in continual succession, that persuades him he is a free agent: if all his motions were simple, if the causes that move him did not confound themselves with each other, if they were distinct, if his machine were less complicated, he would perceive that all his actions were necessary, because he would be enabled to recur instantly to the cause that made him act. A man who should be always obliged to go toward the west, would always go on that side; but he would feel that, in so going, he was not a free agent: if he had another sense, as his actions or his motion, augmented by a sixth, would be still more varied and much more complicated, he would believe himself still more a free agent than he does with his five senses.

It is then, for want of recurring to the causes that move him; for want of being able to analyze, from not being competent to decompose the complicated motion of his machine, that man believes himself a free agent: it is only upon his own ignorance that he founds the profound yet deceitful notion he has of his free agency; that he builds those opinions which he brings forward as a striking proof of his pretended freedom of action. If, for a short time, each man was willing to examine his own peculiar actions, search out their true motives to discover their concatenation, he would remain convinced that the sentiment he has of his natural free agency, is a chimera that must speedily be destroyed by experience.

Nevertheless it must be acknowledged that the multiplicity and diversity of the causes which continually act upon man, frequently without even his knowledge, render it impossible, or at least extremely difficult for him to recur to the true principles of his own peculiar actions, much less the actions of others: they frequently depend upon causes so fugitive, so remote from their effects, and which, superficially examined, appear to have so little analogy, so slender a relation with them, that it requires singular sagacity to bring them into light. This is what renders the study of the moral man a task of such difficulty; this is the reason why his heart is an abyss, of which it is frequently impossible for him to fathom the depth. . . .

If he understood the play of his organs, if he were able to recall to himself all the impulsions they have received, all the modifications they have undergone, all the effects they have produced, he would perceive that all his actions are submitted to that fatality, which regulates his own particular system, as it does the entire system of the universe: no one effect in him, any more than in nature, produces itself by chance; this, as has been before proved, is word void of sense. All that passes in him; all that is done by him; as well as all that happens in nature, or that is attributed to her, is derived from necessary causes, which act according to necessary laws, and which produce necessary effects from whence necessarily flow others.

Fatality, is the eternal, the immutable, the necessary order, established in nature; or the indispensable connection of causes that act, with the effects they operate. Conforming to this order, heavy bodies fall: light bodies rise; that which is analogous in matter reciprocally attracts; that which is heterogeneous mutually repels; man congregates himself in society, modifies each his fellow; becomes either virtuous or wicked; either contributes to his mutual happiness, or reciprocates his misery;

either loves his neighbor, or hates his companion necessarily, according to the manner in which the one acts upon the other. From whence it may be seen, that the same necessity which regulates the physical, also regulates the moral world, in which every thing is in consequence submitted to fatality. Man, in running over, frequently without his own knowledge, often in spite of himself, the route which nature has marked out for him, resembles a swimmer who is obliged to follow the current that carries him along: he believes himself a free agent, because he sometimes consents, sometimes does not consent, to glide the stream, which, notwithstanding, always hurries him forward; he believes himself the master of his condition, because he is obliged to use his arms under the fear of sinking. . . .

ABSOLUTE FREEDOM

Jean-Paul Sartre

It is strange that philosophers have been able to argue endlessly about determinism and free-will, to cite examples in favor of one or the other thesis without ever attempting first to make explicit the structures contained in the very idea of *action*. The concept of an act contains, in fact, numerous subordinate notions which we shall have to organize and arrange in a hierarchy: to act is to modify the *shape* of the world; it is to arrange means in view of an end; it is to produce an organized instrumental complex such that by a series of concatenations and connections the modification effected on one of the links causes modifications throughout the whole series and finally produces an anticipated result. But this is not what is important for us here. We should observe first that an action is on principle *intentional*. The careless smoker who has through negligence caused the explosion of a powder magazine has not *acted*. On the other hand the worker who is charged with dynamiting a quarry and who obeys the given orders has acted when he has produced the expected explosion; he knew what he was doing or, if you prefer, he intentionally realized a conscious project.

This does not mean, of course, that one must foresee all the consequences of his act. The emperor Constantine when he established himself at Byzantium, did not foresee that he would create a center of Greek culture and language, the appearance of which would utimately provoke a schism in the Christian Church and which would contribute to weakening the Roman Empire. Yet he performed an act just in so far as he realized his project of creating a new residence for emperors in the Orient. Equating the result with the intention is here sufficient for us to be able to speak of action. But if this is the case, we establish that the action necessarily implies as its condition the recognition of a "desideratum"; that is, of an objective lack or again of a *négatité*

FROM "An Existentialist's View of Freedom" in *Being and Nothingness,* translated by Hazel E. Barnes. Reprinted by permission of Sanford J. Greenburger Associates, Inc.

the action necessarily implies as its condition the recognition of a [negativity]. The intention of providing a rival for Rome can come to Constantine only through the apprehension of an objective lack: Rome lacks a counterweight; to this still profoundly pagan city ought to be opposed a Christian city which at the moment *is missing*. Creating Constantinople is understood as an act only if first the conception of a new city has preceded the action itself or at least if this conception serves as an organizing theme for all later steps. But this conception cannot be the pure representation of the city as *possible*. It apprehends the city in its essential characteristic, which is to be a *desirable* and not yet realized possible.

This means that from the moment of the first conception of the act, consciousness has been able to withdraw itself from the full world of which it is consciousness and to leave the level of being in order frankly to approach that of non-being. Consciousness in so far as it is considered exclusively in its being, is perpetually referred from being to being and can not find in being any motive for revealing non-being. The imperial system with Rome as its capital functions positively and in a certain real way which can be easily discovered. Will someone say that the taxes are collected badly, that Rome is not secure from invasions, that it does not have the geographical location which is suitable for the capital of a Mediterranean empire which is threatened by barbarians, that its corrupt morals make the spread of the Christian religion difficult? How can anyone fail to see that all these considerations are *negative;* that is, that they aim at what is not, not at what is. To say that sixty per cent of the anticipated taxes have been collected can pass, if need be for a positive appreciation of the situation *such at it is*. To say that they are *badly* collected is to consider the situation across a situation which is posited as an absolute end but which precisely *is not*. To say that the corrupt morals at Rome hinder the spread of Christianity is not to consider this diffusion for what it is; that is, for a propagation at a rate which the reports of the clergy can enable us to determine. It is to posit the diffusion in itself as insufficient; that is, as suffering from a secret nothingness. But it appears as such only if it is surpassed toward a limiting-situation posited *a priori* as a value (for example, toward a certain rate of religious conversions, toward a certain mass morality). This limiting-situation can not be conceived in terms of the simple consideration of the real state of things; for the most beautiful girl in the world can offer only what she *has,* and in the same way the most miserable situation can by itself be designated only as it *is* without any reference to an ideal nothingness.

In so far as man is immersed in the historical situation, he does not even succeed in conceiving of the failures and lacks in a political organization or determined economy; this is not, as is stupidly said, because he "is accustomed to it," but because he apprehends it in its plenitude of being and because he can not even imagine that he can exist in it otherwise. For it is necessary here to reverse common opinion and on the basis of what it is not, to acknowledge the harshness of a situation or the sufferings which it imposes, both of which are motives for conceiving of another state of affairs in which things would be better for everybody. It is on the day that we can conceive of a different state of affairs that a new light falls on our troubles and our suffering and that we *decide* that these are unbearable. A worker in 1830 is capable of revolting if his salary is lowered, for he easily conceives of a situation in which his wretched standard of living would be not as low as the one which is about to be imposed on him. But he does not represent his sufferings to himself as unbearable; he adapts himself to them not through resignation but because he lacks the education and reflection necessary for him to conceive of a social state in which these sufferings would not exist. Consequently *he* does not act. Masters of Lyon following a riot, the workers at Croix-Rousse do not know what to do with their victory; they return home bewildered, and the regular army has no trouble in overcoming them. Their misfortunes do not appear to them "habitual" but rather *natural;* they *are,* that is all, and they constitute the worker's condition. They are not detached; they are not seen in the clear light of day, and consequently they are integrated by the worker with his being. He suffers without considering his suffering and without conferring value upon it. To suffer and to *be* are one and the same for him. His suffering is the pure affective tenor of his non-positional consciousness, but he does not contemplate it. Therefore this suffering can not be in itself a *motive* for his acts. Quite the contrary, it is after he has formed the project of changing the situation that it will appear intolerable to him. This means that he will have had to give himself room, to withdraw in relation to it, and will have to have effected a double nihilation: on the one hand, he must posit an ideal state of affairs as a pure *present* nothingness; on the other hand, he must posit the actual situation as nothingness in relation to this state of affairs. He will have to conceive of a happiness attached to his class as a pure possible—that is, presently as a certain nothingness—and on the other had, he will return to the present situation in order to illuminate it in the light of this nothingness and in order to nihilate it in turn by declaring: "I *am not* happy."

Two important consequences result. (1) No factual state whatever it may be (the political and economic structure of society, the psychological "state," *etc.*) is capable by itself of motivating any act whatsoever. For an act is a projection of the for-itself toward what is not, and what is can in no way determine by itself what is not. (2) No factual state can determine consciousness to apprehend it as a *négatité* or as a lack. Better yet no factual state can determine consciousness to define it and to circumscribe it since, as we have seen, Spinoza's statement, "Omnis determinatio est negatio" [All determination is a negation], remains profoundly true. Now every action has for its express condition not only the discovery of a state of affairs as "lacking in—," *i.e.*, as a *négatité*—but also, and before all else, the constitution of the state of things under consideration into an isolated system. There is a factual state—satisfying or not—only by means of the nihilating power of the for-itself. But this power of nihilation can not be limited to realizing a simple *withdrawal* in relation to the world. In fact in so far as consciousness is "invested" by being, in so far as it simply suffers what is, it must be included in being. It is the organized form—worker-finding-his-suffering-natural—which must be surmounted and denied in order for it to be able to form the object of a revealing contemplation. This means evidently that it is by a pure wrenching away from himself and the world that the worker can posit his suffering as unbearable suffering and consequently can *make of it the motive* for his revolutionary action. This implies for consciousness the permanent possibility of effecting a rupture with its own past, of wrenching itself away from its past so as to be able to consider it in the light of a non-being and so as to be able to confer on it the meaning which *it has* in terms of the project of a meaning which it *does not have*. Under no circumstances can the past in any way by itself produce *an act;* that is, the positing of an end which turns back upon itself so as to illuminate it. This is what Hegel caught sight of when he wrote that "the mind is the negative," although he seems not to have remembered this when he came to presenting his own theory of action and of freedom. In fact as soon as one attributes to consciousness this negative power with respect to the world and itself, as soon as the nihilation forms an integral part of the *positing* of an end, we must recognize that the indispensable and fundamental condition of all action is the freedom of the acting being.

Thus at the outset we can see what is lacking in those tedious discussions between determinists and the proponents of free will. The latter are concerned to find cases of decision for which there exists no prior cause, or deliberations concerning two opposed acts which are equally possible and possess causes (and motives) of exactly the same weight. To which the determinists may easily reply that there is no action without a *cause* and that the most insignificant gesture (raising the right hand rather than the left hand, *etc.*) refers to causes and motives which confer its meaning upon it. Indeed the case could not be otherwise since every action must be *intentional;* each action must, in fact, have an end, and the end in turn is referred to a cause. Such indeed is the unity of the three temporal ekstases; the end or temporalization of my future implies a cause (or motive); that is, it points toward my past, and the present is the upsurge of the act. To speak of an act without a cause is to speak of an act which would lack the intentional structure of every act; and the proponents of free will by searching for it on the level of the act which is in the process of being performed can only end up by rendering the act absurd. But the determinists in turn are weighing the scale by stopping their investigation with the mere designation of the cause and motive. The essential question in fact lies beyond the complex organization "cause-intention-act-end"; indeed we ought to ask how a cause (or motive) can be constituted as such.

Now we have just seen that if there is not act without a cause, this is not in the sense that we can say that there is no phenomenon without a cause. In order to be a *cause,* the *cause* must be *experienced* as such. Of course this does not mean that it is to be thematically conceived and made explicit as in the case of deliberation. But at the very least it means that the for-itself must confer on it its value as cause or motive. And, as we have seen, this constitution of the cause as such can not refer to another real and positive existence; that is, to a prior cause. For otherwise the very nature of the act as engaged intentionally in non-being would disappear. The motive is understood only by the end; that is, by the non-existent. It is therefore in itself a *négatité.* If I accept a niggardly salary it is doubtless because of fear; and fear is a motive. But it is *fear of dying from starvation;* that is, this fear has meaning only outside itself in an end ideally posited, which is the preservation of a life which I apprehend as "in danger." And this fear is understood in turn only in relation to the *value which I* implicitly give to this life; that is, it is referred to that hierarchal system of ideal objects which are values. Thus the motive makes itself understood as what it is by means of the ensemble of beings which "are not," by ideal existences, and by the future. Just as the future turns back upon the present and the past in order to elucidate them, so it is the ensemble of my projects which turns back in order to confer upon the *motive* its structure as a motive. It is only because I escape the in-itself by nihilating myself toward my possibilities that this in-itself can take on value as cause or motive. Causes and motives have meaning only inside a projected ensemble which is precisely an ensemble of non-existents. And this ensemble is ultimately myself as transcendence; it is Me in so far as I have to be myself outside of myself.

If we recall the principle which we established earlier—namely that it is the apprehension of a revolution as possible which gives to the workman's suffering its value as a motive—we must thereby conclude that it is by fleeing a situation toward our possibility of changing it that we organize this situation into complexes of causes and motives. The nihilation by which we achieve a withdrawal in relation to the situation is the same as the ekstasis by which we project ourselves toward a modification of this situation. The result is that it is in fact impossible to find an act without a motive but that this does not mean that we must conclude that the motive causes the act; the motive is an integral part of the act. For as the resolute project toward a change is not distinct from the act, the motive, the act, and the end are all constituted in a single upsurge. Each of these three structures claims the two others as its meaning. But the organized totality of the three is no longer explained by any particular structure, and its upsurge as the pure temporalizing nihilation of the in-itself is one with freedom. It is the act which decides its ends and its motives, and the act is the expression of freedom. . . .

In our attempt to reach to the heart of freedom we may be helped by the few observations which we have made on the subject in the course of this work and which we must summarize here. . . . We established the fact that if negation comes into the world through human-reality, the latter must be a being who can realize a nihilating rupture with the world and with himself; and we established that the permanent possibility of this rupture is the same as freedom. But on the other hand, we stated that this permanent possibility of nihilating what I am in the form of "having-been" implies for man a particular type of existence. We were able then to determine by means of analyses like that of bad faith that human reality is its own nothingness. For the for-itself, to be is to nihilate the in-itself which it is. Under these conditions freedom can be nothing other than this nihilation. It is through this that the for-itself escapes its being as its essence; it is through this that the for-itself is always something other than what can be said of it. For in the final analysis the for-itself is the one which escapes this very denomination, the one which is already beyond the name which is given to it, beyond the property which is recognized in it. To say that the for-itself has to be what it is, to say that it is what it is not while not being what it is, to say that in it existence precedes and conditions essence or inversely according to Hegel, that for it "Wesen ist was gewesen ist" [Essence is what was]—all this is to say one and the same thing: to be aware that man is free. Indeed by the sole fact that I am conscious of the causes which inspire my action, these causes are already transcendent objects for my consciousness; they are outside. In vain shall I seek to catch hold of them; I escape them by my very existence. I am condemned to exist forever beyond my essence, beyond the causes and motives of my act. I am condemned to be free. This means that no limits to my freedom can be found except freedom itself or, if you prefer, that we are not free to cease being free. To the extent that the for-itself wishes to hide its own nothingness from itself and to incorporate the in-itself as its true mode of being, it is trying also to hide its freedom from itself.

The ultimate meaning of determinism is to establish within us an unbroken continuity of existence in itself. The motive conceived as a psychic fact—*i.e.,* as a full and given reality—is, in the deterministic view, articulated without any break with the decision and the act, both of which are equally conceived as psychic givens. The in-itself has got hold of all these "data"; the motive provokes the act as the physical cause its effect; everything is real, everything is full. Thus the refusal of freedom can be conceived only as an attempt to apprehend oneself as being-in-itself; it amounts to the same thing. Human reality may be defined as a being such that in its being its freedom is at stake because human reality perpetually tries to refuse to recognize its freedom. Psychologically in each one of us this amounts to trying to take the causes and motives as *things.* We try to confer permanence upon them. We attempt to hide from ourselves that their nature and their weight depend each moment on the meaning which I give to them; we take them for constants. This amounts to considering the meaning which I gave to them just now or yesterday—which is irremediable because it is *past* —and extrapolating from it a character fixed still in the present. I attempt to persuade myself that the cause *is* as it was. Thus it would pass whole and untouched from my past consciousness to my present consciousness. It would inhabit my consciousness. This amounts to trying to give an essence to the for-itself. In the same way people will posit ends as transcendences, which is not an error. But instead of seeing that the transcendences there posited are maintained in their being by my own transcendence, people will assume that I encounter them upon my surging up in the world; they come from God, from nature, from "my" nature, from society. These ends ready made and pre-human will therefore define the meaning of my act even before I conceive it, just as causes as pure psychic givens will produce it without my even being aware of them.

Cause, act, and end constitute a *continuum,* a *plenum.* These abortive attempts to stifle freedom under the weight of being (they collapse with the sudden upsurge of anguish before freedom) show sufficiently that freedom in its foundation coincides with the nothingness which is at the heart of man. Human-reality is free because it *is not enough.* It is free because it is perpetually wrenched away from itself and because it has been separated by a nothingness from what it is and from what it will be. It is free, finally, because its present being is itself a nothingness in the form of the "reflection-reflecting." Man is free because he is not himself but presence to himself. The being which is what it is can not be free. Freedom is precisely the nothingness which *is made-to-be* at the heart of man and which forces human-reality *to make itself* instead of to be. As we have seen, for human reality, to be is to *choose oneself;* nothing comes to it either from the outside or from within which it can *receive or accept.* Without any help whatsoever, it is entirely abandoned to the intolerable necessity of making itself be—down to the slightest detail. Thus freedom is not *a* being; it is *the being* of man —*i.e.,* his nothingness of being. If we start by conceiving of man as a plenum, it is absurd to try to find in him afterwards moments or psychic regions in which he would be free. As well look for emptiness in a container which one has filled beforehand up to the brim! Man can not be sometimes slave and sometimes free; he is wholly and forever free or he is not free at all.

These observations can lead us, if we know how to use them, to new discoveries. They will enable us first to bring to light the relations between freedom and what we call the "will." There is a fairly common tendency to seek to identify free acts with voluntary acts and to restrict the deterministic explanation to the world of the passions. In short the point of view of Descartes. The Cartesian will is free, but there are "passions of the soul." Again Descartes will attempt a physiological interpretation of these passions. Later there will be an attempt to instate a purely psychological determinism. Intellectualistic analyses such as Proust, for example, attempts with respect to jealousy or snobbery can serve as illustration for this concept of the passional "mechanism." In this case it would be necessary to conceive of man as simultaneously free and determined, and the essential problem would be that of the relations between this unconditioned freedom and the determined processes of the psychic life: how will it master the passions, how will it utilize them for its own benefit? A wisdom which comes from ancient times—the wisdom of the Stoics—will teach us to come to terms with these passions so as to master them; in short it will counsel us how to conduct ourselves with regard to affectivity as man does with respect to nature in general when he obeys it in order better to control it. Human reality therefore appears as a free power besieged by an ensemble of determined processes. One will distinguish wholly free acts, determined processes over which the free will has power, and processes which on principle escape the human-will.

It is clear that we shall not be able to accept such a conception. But let us try better to understand the reasons for our refusal. There is one objection which is obvious and which we shall not waste time in developing; this is that such a trenchant duality is inconceivable at the heart of the psychic unity. How in fact could we conceive of a being which could be *one* and which nevertheless on the one hand would be constituted as a series of facts determined by one another—hence existents in exteriority—and which on the other hand would be constituted as a spontaneity determining itself to be and revealing only itself? *A priori* this spontaneity would be capable of no action on a determinism already *constituted*. On what could it act? On the object itself (the present psychic fact)? But how could it modify an in-itself which by definition is and can be only what it is? On the actual law of the process? This is self-contradictory. On the antecedents of the process? But it amounts to the same thing whether we act on the present psychic fact in order to modify it in itself or act upon it in order to modify its consequences. And in each case we encounter the same impossibility which we pointed out earlier. Moreover, what instrument would this spontaneity have at its disposal? If the hand can clasp, it is because it can be clasped. Spontaneity, since by definition it is *beyond reach* can not in turn *reach;* it can produce only itself. And if it could dispose of a special instrument, it would then be necessary to conceive of this as of an intermediary nature between free will and determined passions—which is not admissible. For different reasons the passions could get no hold upon the will. Indeed it is impossible for a determined process to act upon a spontaneity, exactly as it is impossible for objects to act upon consciousness. Thus any synthesis of two types of existents is impossible; they are not homogeneous; they will remain each one in its incommunicable solitude. The only bond which a nihilating spontaneity could maintain with mechanical process would be the fact that it *produces itself by an internal negation directed toward these existents.* But then the spontaneity will exist precisely only in so far as it denies concerning itself that it is these passions. Henceforth the ensemble of the determined pathos will of necessity be apprehended by spontaneity as a pure transcendent; that is, as what is necessarily *outside,* as what *is* not it. This internal negation would therefore have for its effect only the dissolution of the pathos in the world, and the pathos would exist as some sort of object in the midst of the world for a free spontaneity which would be simultaneously will and consciousness. This discussion shows that two solutions and only two are possible: either man is wholly determined (which is inadmissible, especially because a determined consciousness—*i.e.,* a consciousness externally motivated—becomes itself pure exteriority and ceases to be consciousness) or else man is wholly free. . . .

But this is not all: the will, far from being the unique or at least the privileged manifestation of freedom, actually—like every event of the for-itself—must presuppose the foundation of an original freedom in order to be able to constitute itself as will. The will in fact is posited as a reflective decision in relation to certain ends. But it does not create these ends. It is rather a mode of being in relation to them: it decrees that the pursuit of these ends will be reflective and deliberative. Passion can posit the same ends. For example, if I am threatened, I can run away at top speed because of my fear of dying. This passional fact nevertheless posits implicitly as a supreme end the value of life. Another person in the same situation will, on the contrary, understand that he must remain at his post even if resistance at first appears more dangerous than flight; he "will stand firm." But his goal, although better understood and explicitly posited, remains the same as in the case of the emotional reaction. It is simply that the methods of attaining it are more clearly conceived; certain of them are rejected as dubious or inefficacious, others are more solidly organized. The difference here depends on the choice of means and on the degree of reflection and of making explicit, not on the end. Yet the one who flees is said to be "passionate," and we reserve the term "voluntary" for the man who resists. Therefore the question is of a difference of subjective attitude in relation to a transcendent end. But if we wish to avoid the error which we denounced earlier and not consider these transcendent ends as pre-human and as an *a priori* limit to our transcendence then we are indeed compelled to recognize that they are the temporalizing projection of our freedom. Human reality can not receive its ends, as we have seen, either from outside or from a so-called inner "nature." It chooses them and by this very choice confers upon them a transcendent existence as the external limit of its projects. From this point of view—and if it is understood that the existence of the *Dasein* [person] precedes and commands its essence—human reality in and through its very upsurge decides to define its own being by its ends. It is therefore the positing of my ultimate ends which characterizes my being and which is identical with the sudden thrust of the freedom which is mine. And this thrust is an *existence;* it has nothing to do with an essence or with a property of a being which would be engendered conjointly with an idea.

Thus since freedom is identical with my existence, it is the foundation of ends which I shall attempt to attain either by the will or by passionate efforts. Therefore it can not be limited to voluntary acts. Volitions, on the contrary, like passions are certain subjective attitudes by which we attempt to attain the ends posited by original freedom. By original freedom, of course, we should not understand a freedom which would be *prior* to the voluntary or passionate act but rather a foundation which is strictly contemporary with the will or the passion and which these *manifest,* each in its own way. Neither should we oppose freedom to the will or to passion as the "profound self" of Bergson is opposed to the superficial self; the for-itself is wholly selfness and can not have a "profound self," unless by this we mean certain transcendent structures of the psyche. Freedom is nothing but the *existence* of our will or of our passions in so far as this existence is the nihilation of facticity; that is, the existence of being which is its being in the mode of having to be it. We shall return to this point. In any case let us remember that the will is determined within the compass of motives and ends already posited by the for-itself in a transcendent projection of itself toward its possibles. If this were not so, how could we understand deliberation, which is an evaluation of means in relation to already existing ends?

If these ends are already posited, then what remains to be decided at each moment is the way in which I shall conduct myself with respect to them; in other words, the attitude which I shall assume. Shall I act by volition or by passion? Who can decide except me? In fact, if we admit that circumstances decide for me (for example, I can act by volition when faced with a minor danger but if the peril increases, I shall fall into passion), we thereby suppress all freedom. It would indeed be absurd to declare that the will is autonomous when it appears but that external circumstances strictly determine the moment of its appearance. But, on the other hand, how can it be maintained that a will which does not yet exist can suddenly decide to shatter the chain of the passions and suddenly stand forth on the fragments of these chains? Such a conception would lead us to consider the will as a *power* which sometimes would manifest itself to consciousness and at other times would remain hidden, but which would in any case possess the permanence and the existence "in-itself" of a property. This is precisely what is inadmissible. It is, however, certain that common opinion conceives of the moral life as a struggle between a will-thing and passion-substances. There is here a sort of psychological Manichaeism which is absolutely insupportable.

Actually it is not enough to will; it is necessary to will to will. Take, for example, a given situation: I can react to it emotionally. We have shown elsewhere that emotion is not a physiological tempest; it is a reply adapted to the situation; it is a type of conduct, the meaning and form of which are the object of an intention of consciousness which aims at attaining a particular end by particular means. In fear, fainting and cataplexie aim at suppressing the danger by suppressing the consciousness of the danger. There is an *intention* of losing consciousness in order to do away with the formidable world in which consciousness is engaged and which comes into being through consciousness. Therefore we have to do with magical behavior provoking the symbolic satisfactions of our desires and revealing by the same stroke a magical stratum of the world. In contrast to this conduct voluntary and rational conduct will consider the situation scientifically, will reject the magical, and will apply itself to realizing determined series and instrumental complexes which will enable us to resolve the problems. It will organize a system of means by taking its stand on instrumental determinism. Suddenly it will reveal a technical world; that is, a world in which each instrumental-complex refers to another larger complex and so on. But what will make me decide to choose the magical aspect or the technical aspect of the world? It can not be the world itself, for this in order to be manifested waits to be discovered. Therefore it is necessary that the for-itself in its project must choose being the one by whom the world is revealed as magical or rational; that is, the for-itself must as a free project of itself give to itself magical or rational existence. It is responsible for either one, for the for-itself can *be* only if it has chosen itself. Therefore the for-itself appears as the free foundation of its emotions as of its volitions. My fear *is* free and manifests my freedom; I have put all my freedom into my fear, and I have chosen myself as fearful in this or that circumstance. Under other circumstances I shall exist as deliberate and courageous, and I shall have put all my freedom into my courage. In relation to freedom there is no privileged psychic phenomenon. All my "modes of being" manifest freedom equally since they are all ways of being my own nothingness. . . .

Yet if the motive is transcendent, if it is only the irremediable being which we have to be in the mode of the "was," if like all our past it is separated from us by a breadth of nothingness, then it can act only if it is *recovered;* in itself it is without force. It is therefore by the very thrust of the engaged consciousness that a value and a weight will be conferred on motives and on prior causes. What they have been does not depend on consciousness, but consciousness has the duty of maintaining them in their existence in the past. I have willed this or that: here is what remains irremediable and which even constitutes my essence, since my essence is what I have been. But the meaning held for me by this desire, this fear, these objective considerations of the world when presently I project myself toward my futures—this must be decided by me alone. I determine them precisely and only by the very act by which I project myself toward my ends. The recovery of former motives—or the rejection or new appreciation of them—is not distinct from the project by which I assign new ends to myself and by which in the light of these ends I apprehend myself as discovering a supporting cause in the world. Past motives, past causes, present motives and causes, future ends, all are organized in an indissoluble unity by the very upsurge of a freedom which is beyond causes, motives, and ends.

The result is that a voluntary deliberation is always a deception. How can I evaluate causes and motives on which I myself confer their value before all deliberation and by the very choice which I make of myself? The illusion here stems from the fact that we endeavor to take causes and motives for entirely transcendent things which I balance in my hands like weights and which possess a weight as a permanent property. Yet on the other hand we try to view them as contents of consciousness, and this is self-contradictory. Actually causes and motives have only the weight which my project—*i.e.,* the free production of the end and of the known act to be realized—confers upon them. When I deliberate, the chips are down. And if I am brought to the point of deliberating, this is simply because it is a part of my original project to realize motives by means of *deliberation* rather than by some other form of discovery (by passion, for example, or simply by action, which reveals to me the organized ensemble of causes and of ends as my language informs me of my thought). There is therefore a choice of deliberation as a procedure which will make known to me what I project and consequently what I am. And *the choice* of deliberation is organized with the ensemble motives-causes and end by free spontaneity. When the will intervenes, the decision is taken, and it has no other value than that of making the announcement. . . .

The essential consequence of our earlier remarks is that man being condemned to be free carries the weight of the whole world on his shoulders; he is responsible for the world and for himself as a way of being. We are taking the word "responsibility" in its ordinary sense as "consciousness (of) being the incontestable author of an event or of an object." In this sense the responsibility of the for-itself is overwhelming since he is the one by whom it happens that there is a world; since he is also the one who makes himself be, then whatever may be the situation in which he finds himself, the for-itself must wholly assume this situation with its peculiar coefficient of adversity, even though it be insupportable. He must assume the situation with the proud consciousness of being the author of it, for the very worst disadvantages or the worst threats which can endanger my person have meaning only in and through my project; and it is on the ground of the engagement which I am that they appear. It is therefore senseless to think of complaining since nothing foreign has decided what we feel, what we live, or what we are.

Furthermore this absolute responsibility is not resignation; it is simply the logical requirement of the consequences of our freedom. What happens to me happens through me, and I can neither affect myself with it nor revolt against it nor resign myself to it. Moreover everything which happens to me is *mine*. By this we must understand first of all that I am always equal to what happens to me *qua* man, for what happens to a man through other men and through himself can be only human. The most terrible situations of war, the worst tortures do not create a non-human state of things; there is no non-human situation. It is only through fear, flight, and recourse to magical types of conduct that I shall decide on the non-human, but this decision is human, and I shall carry the entire responsibility for it. But in addition the situation is *mine* because it is the image of my free choice of myself, and everything which it presents to me is *mine* in that this represents me and symbolizes me. Is it not I who decide the coefficient of adversity in things and even their unpredictability by deciding myself?

Thus there are no *accidents* in a life; a community event which suddenly bursts forth and involves me in it does not come from the outside. If I am mobilized in a war, this war is *my* war; it is in my image and I deserve it. I deserve it first because I could always get out of it by suicide or by desertion; these ultimate possibles are those which must always be present for us when there is a question of envisaging a situation. For lack of getting out of it, I have *chosen* it. This can be due to inertia, to cowardice in the face of public opinion, or because I prefer certain other values to the value of the refusal to join in the war (the good opinion of my relatives, the honor of my family, etc.). Anyway you look at it, it is a matter of a choice. This choice will be repeated later on again and again without a break until the end of the war. Therefore we must agree with the statement by J. Romains, "In war there are no innocent victims." If therefore I have preferred war to death or to dishonor, everything takes place as if I bore the entire responsibility for this war. Of course others have declared it, and one might be tempted perhaps to consider me as a simple accomplice. But this notion of complicity has only a juridical sense, and it does not hold here. For it depended on me that for me and by me this war should not exist, and I have decided that it does exist. There was no compulsion here, for the compulsion could have got no hold on a freedom. I did not have any excuse; for as we have said repeatedly in this book, the peculiar character of human-reality is that it is without excuse. Therefore it remains for me only to lay claim to this war.

But in addition the war is *mine* because by the sole fact that it arises in a situation which I cause to be and that I can discover it there only by engaging myself for or against it, I can no longer distinguish at present the choice which I make of myself from the choice which I make of the war. To live this war is to choose myself through it and to choose it through my choice of myself. There can be no question of considering it as "four years of vacation" or as a "reprieve," as a "recess," the essential part of my responsibilities being elsewhere in my married, family, or professional life. In this war which I have chosen I choose myself from day to day, and I make it mine by making myself. If it is going to be four empty years, then it is I who bear the responsibility for this.

Finally, as we pointed out earlier, each person is an absolute choice of self from the standpoint of a world of knowledges and of techniques which this choice both assumes and illumines; each person is an absolute upsurge at an absolute date and is perfectly unthinkable at another date. It is therefore a waste of time to ask what I should have been if this war had not broken out, for I have chosen myself as one of the possible meanings of the epoch which imperceptibly led to war. I am not distinct from this same epoch; I could not be transported to another epoch without contradiction. Thus *I am* this war which restricts and limits and makes comprehensible the period which preceded it. In this sense we may define more precisely the responsibility of the for-itself if to the earlier quoted statement, "There are no innocent victims," we add the words, "We have the war we deserve." Thus, totally free, undistinguishable from the period for which I have chosen to be the meaning, as profoundly responsible for the war as if I had myself declared it, unable to live without integrating it in *my* situation, engaging myself in it wholly and stamping it with my seal, I must be without remorse or regrets as I am without excuse; for from the instant of my upsurge into being, I carry the weight of the world by myself alone without anything or any person being able to lighten it.

Yet this responsibility is of a very particular type. Someone will say, "I did not ask to be born." This is a naive way of throwing greater emphasis on our facticity. I am responsible for everything, in fact, except for my very responsibility, for I am not the foundation of my being. Therefore everything takes place as if I were compelled to be responsible. I am *abandoned* in the world, not in the sense that I might remain abandoned and passive in a hostile universe like a board floating on the water, but rather in the sense that I find myself alone and without help, engaged in a world for which I bear the whole responsibility without being able, whatever I do, to tear myself away from this responsibility for an instant. For I am responsible for my very desire of fleeing responsibilities. To make myself passive in the world, to refuse to act upon things and upon others is still to choose myself, and suicide is one mode among others of being-in-the-world. Yet I find an absolute responsibility for the fact that my facticity (here the fact of my birth) is directly inapprehensible and even inconceivable, for this fact of my birth never appears as a brute fact but always across a projective re-construction of my for-itself. I am ashamed of being born or I am astonished at it or I rejoice over it, or in attempting to get rid of my life I affirm that I live and I assume this life as bad. Thus in a certain sense I *choose* being born. This choice itself is integrally affected with facticity since I am not able not to choose, but this facticity in turn will appear only in so far as I surpass it toward my ends. Thus facticity is everywhere but inapprehensible; I never encounter anything except my responsibility. That is why I can not ask, "*Why* was I born?" or curse the day of my birth or declare that I did not ask to be born, for these various attitudes toward my birth—*i.e.,* toward the *fact* that I realize a presence in the world—are absolutely nothing else but ways of assuming this birth in full responsibility and of making it *mine.* Here again I encounter only myself and my projects so that finally my abandonment —*i.e.,* my facticity—consists simply in the fact that I am condemned to be wholly responsible for myself. I am the being which is in such a way that in its being its being is in question. And this "is" of my being *is* as present and inapprehensible.

Under these conditions since every event in the world can be revealed to me only as an *opportunity* (an opportunity made use of, lacked, neglected, *etc.*), or better yet since everything which happens to us can be considered as a *chance* (i.e., can appear to us only as a way of realizing this being which is in question in our being) and since others as transcendences-transcended are themselves only *opportunities* and *chances,* the responsibility of the for-itself extends to the entire world as a peopled-world. It is precisely thus that the for-itself apprehends itself in anguish; that is, as a being which is neither the foundation of its own being nor of the Other's being nor of the in-itselfs which form the world, but a being which is compelled to decide the meaning of being— within it and everywhere outside of it. The one who realizes in anguish his condition as *being* thrown into a responsibility which extends to his very abandonment has no longer either remorse or regret or excuse; he is no longer anything but a freedom which perfectly reveals itself and whose being resides in this very revelation. But as we pointed out at the beginning of this work, most of the time we flee anguish in bad faith.

FREEDOM AND NECESSITY

A. J. Ayer

When I am said to have done something of my own free will it is implied that I could have acted otherwise; and it is only when it is believed that I could have acted otherwise that I am held to be morally responsible for what I have done. For a man is not thought to be morally responsible for an action that it was not in his power to avoid. But if human behavior is entirely governed by causal laws, it is not clear how any action that is done could ever have been avoided. It may be said of the agent that he would have acted otherwise if the causes of his action had been different, but they being what they were, it seems to follow that he was bound to act as he did. Now it is commonly assumed both that men are capable of acting freely, in the sense that is required to make them morally responsible, and that human behavior is entirely governed by causal laws: and it is the apparent conflict between these two assumptions that gives rise to the philosophical problem of the freedom of the will.

Confronted with this problem, many people will be inclined to agree with Dr. Johnson: "Sir, we *know* our will is free, and *there's* an end on't." But, while this does very well for those who accept Dr. Johnson's premise, it would hardly convince anyone who denied the freedom of the will. Certainly, if we do know that our wills are free, it follows that they are so. But the logical reply to this might be that since our wills are not free, it follows that no one can know that they are: so that if anyone claims, like Dr. Johnson, to know that they are, he must be mistaken. What is evident, indeed, is that people often believe themselves to be acting freely; and it is to this "feeling" of freedom that some philosophers appeal when they wish, in the supposed interests of morality, to prove that not all human action is causally determined. But if these philosophers are right in their assumption that a man cannot be acting freely if his action is causally determined, then the fact that someone feels free to do, or not to do, a certain action does not

FROM *Philosophical Essays*. Reprinted by permission of St. Martin's Press, Inc. and Macmillan Ltd.

prove that he really is so. It may prove that the agent does not himself know what it is that makes him act in one way rather than another: but from the fact that a man is unaware of the causes of his action, it does not follow that no such causes exist.

So much may be allowed to the determinist; but his belief that all human actions are subservient to causal laws still remains to be justified. If, indeed, it is necessary that every event should have a cause, then the rule must apply to human behavior as much as to anything else. But why should it be supposed that every event must have a cause? The contrary is not unthinkable. Nor is the law of universal causation a necessary presupposition of scientific thought. The scientist may try to discover causal laws, and in many cases he succeeds; but sometimes he has to be content with statistical laws, and sometimes he comes upon events which, in the present state of his knowledge, he is not able to subsume under any law at all. In the case of these events he assumes that if he knew more he would be able to discover some law, whether causal or statistical, which would enable him to account for them. And this assumption cannot be disproved. For however far he may have carried his investigation, it is always open to him to carry it further; and it is always conceivable that if he carried it further he would discover the connection which had hitherto escaped him. Nevertheless, it is also conceivable that the events with which he is concerned are not systematically connected with any others: so that the reason why he does not discover the sort of laws that he requires is simply that they do not obtain.

Now in the case of human conduct the search for explanations has not in fact been altogether fruitless. Certain scientific laws have been established; and with the help of these laws we do make a number of successful predictions about the ways in which different people will behave. But these predictions do not always cover every detail. We may be able to predict that in certain circumstances a particular man will be angry, without being able to prescribe the precise form that the expression of his anger will take. We may be reasonably sure that he will shout, but not sure how loud his shout will be, or exactly what words he will use. And it is only a small proportion of human actions that we are able to forecast even so precisely as this. But that, it may be said, is because we have not carried our investigations very far. The science of psychology is still in its infancy and, as it is developed, not only will more human actions be explained, but the explanations will go into greater detail. The ideal of complete explanation may never in fact be attained: but it is theoretically attainable. Well, this may be so: and certainly it is impossible to show *a priori* that it is not so: but equally it cannot be shown that it is. This will not, however, discourage the scientist who, in the field of human behavior, as elsewhere, will continue to formulate theories and test them by the facts. And in this he is justified. For since he has no reason *a priori* to admit that there is a limit to what he can discover, the fact that he also cannot be sure that there is no limit does not make it unreasonable for him to devise theories, nor, having devised them, to try constantly to improve them.

But now suppose it to be claimed that, so far as men's actions are concerned, there is a limit: and that this limit is set by the fact of human freedom. An obvious objection is that in many cases in which a person feels himself to be free to do, or not to do, a certain action, we are even now able to explain, in causal terms, why it is that he acts as he does. But it might be argued that even if men are sometimes mistaken in believing that they act freely, it does not follow that they are always so mistaken. For it is not always the case that when a man believes that he has acted freely we are in fact able to account for his action in causal terms. A determinist would say that we should be able to account for it if we had more knowledge of the circumstances, and had been able to discover the appropriate natural laws. But until those discoveries have been made, this remains only a pious hope. And may it not be true that, in some cases at least, the reason why we can give no causal explanation is that no causal explanation is available; and that this is because the agent's choice was literally free, as he himself felt it to be?

The answer is that this may indeed be true, inasmuch as it is open to anyone to hold that no explanation is possible until some explanation is actually found. But even so it does not give the moralist what he wants. For he is anxious to show that men are capable of acting freely in order to infer that they can be morally responsible for what they do. But if it is a matter of pure chance that a man should act in one way rather than another, he may be free but he can hardly be responsible. And indeed when a man's actions seem to us quite unpredictable, when, as we say, there is no knowing what he will do, we do not look upon him as a moral agent. We look upon him rather as a lunatic.

To this it may be objected that we are not dealing fairly with the moralist. For when he makes it a condition of my being morally responsible that I should act freely, he does not wish to imply that it is purely a matter of chance that I act as I do. What he wishes to imply is that my actions are the result of my own free choice: and it is because they are the result of my own free choice that I am held to be morally responsible for them.

But now we must ask how it is that I come to make my choice. Either it is an accident that I choose to act as I do or it is not. If it is an accident, then it is merely a matter of chance that I did not choose other-wise; and if it is merely a matter of chance that I did not choose other-wise, it is surely irrational to hold me morally responsible for choosing as I did. But if it is not an accident that I choose to do one thing rather than another, then presumably there is some causal explanation of my choice: and in that case we are led back to determinism.

Again, the objection may be raised that we are not doing justice to the moralist's case. His view is not that it is a matter of chance that I choose to act as I do, but rather that my choice depends upon my character. Nevertheless he holds that I can still be free in the sense that he requires; for it is I who am responsible for my character. But in what way am I responsible for my character? Only, surely, in the sense that there is a causal connection between what I do now and what I have done in the past. It is only this that justifies the statement that I have made myself what I am: and even so this is an over-simplification, since it takes no account of the external influences to which I have been subjected. But, ignoring the external influences, let us assume that it is in fact the case that I have made myself what I am. Then it is still legitimate to ask how it is that I have come to make myself one sort of person rather than another. And if it be answered that it is a matter of my strength of will, we can put the same question in another form by asking how it is that my will has the strength that it has and not some other degree of strength. Once more, either it is an accident or it is not. If it is an accident, then by the same argument as before, I am not morally responsible, and if it is not an accident we are led back to determinism.

Furthermore, to say that my actions proceed from my character or, more colloquially, that I act in character, is to say that my behavior is consistent and to that extent predictable: and since it is, above all, for the actions that I perform in character that I am held to be morally responsible, it looks as if the admission of moral responsibility, so far from being incompatible with determinism, tends rather to presuppose it. But how can this be so if it is a necessary condition of moral respon-sibility that the person who is held responsible should have acted freely? It seems that if we are to retain this idea of moral responsibility, we must either show that men can be held responsible for actions which they do not do freely, or else find some way of reconciling determinism with the freedom of the will.

It is no doubt with the object of effecting this reconciliation that some philosophers have defined freedom as the consciousness of neces-sity. And by so doing they are able to say not only that a man can be acting freely when his action is causally determined, but even that his action must be causally determined for it to be possible for him to be acting freely. Nevertheless this definition has the serious disadvantage that it gives to the word "freedom" a meaning quite different from any that it ordinarily bears. It is indeed obvious that if we are allowed to give the word "freedom" any meaning that we please, we can find a meaning that will reconcile it with determinism: but this is no more a solution of our present problem than the fact that the word "horse" could be arbitrarily used to mean what is ordinarily meant by "sparrow" is a proof that horses have wings. For suppose that I am compelled by another person to do something "against my will." In that case, as the word "freedom" is ordinarily used, I should not be said to be acting freely: and the fact that I am fully aware of the constraint to which I am subjected makes no difference to the matter. I do not become free by becoming conscious that I am not. It may, indeed, be possible to show that my being aware that my action is causally determined is not incompatible with my acting freely: but it by no means follows that it is in this that my freedom consists. Moreover, I suspect that one of the reasons why people are inclined to define freedom as the consciousness of necessity is that they think that if one is conscious of necessity one may somehow be able to master it. But this is a fallacy. It is like some-one's saying that he wishes he could see into the future, because if he did he would know what calamities lay in wait for him and so would be able to avoid them. But if he avoids the calamities then they don't lie in the future and it is not true that he foresees them. And similarly if I am able to master necessity, in the sense of escaping the operation of a necessary law, then the law in question is not necessary. And if the law is not necessary, then neither my freedom nor anything else can consist in my knowing that it is.

Let it be granted, then, that when we speak of reconciling freedom with determinism we are using the word "freedom" in an ordinary sense. It still remains for us to make this usage clear: and perhaps the best way to make it clear is to show what it is that freedom, in this sense, is contrasted with. Now we began with the assumption that freedom is contrasted with causality: so that a man cannot be said to be acting freely if his action is causally determined. But this assumption has led us into difficulties and I now wish to suggest that it is mistaken. For it is not, I think, causality that freedom is to be contrasted with, but con-straint. And while it is true that being constrained to do an action entails being caused to do it, I shall try to show that the converse does not hold. I shall try to show that from the fact that my action is causally determined it does not necessarily follow that I am constrained to do it: and this is equivalent to saying that it does not necessarily follow that I am not free.

If I am constrained, I do not act freely. But in what circumstances can I legitimately be said to be constrained? An obvious instance is the case in which I am compelled by another person to do what he wants. In a case of this sort the compulsion need not be such as to deprive one of the power of choice. It is not required that the other person should have hypnotized me, or that he should make it physically impossible for me to go against his will. It is enough that he should induce me to do what he wants by making it clear to me that, if I do not, he will bring about some situation that I regard as even more undesirable than the consequences of the action that he wishes me to do. Thus, if the man points a pistol at my head I may still choose to disobey him: but this does not prevent its being true that if I do fall in with his wishes he can legitimately be said to have compelled me. And if the circumstances are such that no reasonable person would be expected to choose the other alternative, then the action that I am made to do is not one for which I am held to be morally responsible.

A similar, but still somewhat different, case is that in which another person has obtained an habitual ascendancy over me. Where this is so, there may be no question of my being induced to act as the other person wishes by being confronted with a still more disagreeable alternative: for if I am sufficiently under his influence this special stimulus will not be necessary. Nevertheless I do not act freely, for the reason that I have been deprived of the power of choice. And this means that I have acquired so strong a habit of obedience that I no longer go through any process of deciding whether or not to do what the other person wants. About other matters I may still deliberate; but as regards the fulfillment of this other person's wishes, my own deliberations have ceased to be a causal factor in my behavior. And it is in this sense that I may be said to be constrained. It is not, however, necessary that such constraint should take the form of subservience to another person. A kleptomaniac is not a free agent, in respect of his stealing, because he does not go through any process of deciding whether or not to steal. Or rather, if he does go through such a process, it is irrelevant to his behavior. Whatever he resolved to do, he would steal all the same. And it is this that distinguishes him from the ordinary thief.

But now it may be asked whether there is any essential difference between these cases and those in which the agent is commonly thought to be free. No doubt the ordinary thief does go through a process of deciding whether or not to steal, and no doubt it does affect his behavior. If he resolved to refrain from stealing, he could carry his resolution out. But if it be allowed that his making or not making this resolution is causally determined, then how can he be any more free than the kleptomaniac? It may be true that unlike the kleptomaniac he could refrain from stealing if he chose: but if there is a cause, or set of causes, which necessitate his choosing as he does, how can he be said to have the power of choice? Again, it may be true that no one now compels me to get up and walk across the room: but if my doing so can be causally explained in terms of my history or my environment, or whatever it may be, then how am I any more free than if some other person had compelled me? I do not have the feeling of constraint that I have when a pistol is manifestly pointed at my head; but the chains of causation by which I am bound are no less effective for being invisible.

The answer to this is that the cases I have mentioned as examples of constraint do differ from the others: and they differ just in the ways that I have tried to bring out. If I suffered from a compulsion neurosis, so that I got up and walked across the room, whether I wanted to or not, or if I did so because somebody else compelled me, then I should not be acting freely. But if I do it now, I shall be acting freely, just because these conditions do not obtain; and the fact that my action may nevertheless have a cause is, from this point of view, irrelevant. For it is not when my action has any cause at all, but only when it has a special sort of cause, that it is reckoned not to be free.

But here it may be objected that, even if this distinction corresponds to ordinary usage, it is still very irrational. For why should we distinguish, with regard to a person's freedom, between the operations of one sort of cause and those of another? Do not all causes equally necessitate? And is it not therefore arbitrary to say that a person is free when he is necessitated in one fashion but not when he is necessitated in another?

That all causes equally necessitate is indeed a tautology, if the word "necessitate" is taken merely as equivalent to "cause": but if, as the objection requires it is taken as equivalent to "constrain" or "compel," then I do not think that this proposition is true. For all that is needed for one event to be the cause of another is that, in the given circumstances, the event which is said to be the effect would not have occurred if it had not been for the occurrence of the event which is said to be the cause, or vice versa, according as causes are interpreted as necessary, or sufficient, conditions: and this fact is usually deductible from some causal law which states that whenever an event of the one kind occurs then, given suitable conditions, an event of the other kind will occur in a certain temporal or spatio-temporal relationship to it. In short, there is an invariable concomitance between the two classes of events; but there is no compulsion, in any but a metaphorical sense. Suppose, for example, that a psychoanalyst is able to account for some aspect of my behavior by referring it to some lesion that I suffered in my childhood. In that case, it may be said that my childhood experience, together with certain other events, necessitates my behaving as I do. But all that this involves is that it is found to be true in general that when people have had certain experiences as children, they subsequently behave in certain specifiable ways; and my case is just another instance of this general law. It is in this way indeed that my behavior is explained. But from the fact that my behavior is capable of being explained, in the sense that it can be subsumed under some natural law, it does not follow that I am acting under constraint.

If this is correct, to say that I could have acted otherwise is to say, first, that I should have acted otherwise if I had so chosen; secondly, that my action was voluntary in the sense in which the actions, say, of the kleptomaniac are not; and thirdly, that nobody compelled me to choose as I did: and these three conditions may very well be fulfilled. When they are fulfilled, I may be said to have acted freely. But this is not to say that it was a matter of chance that I acted as I did, or, in other words, that my action could not be explained. And that my actions should be capable of being explained is all that is required by the postulate of determinism.

If more than this seems to be required it is, I think, because the use of the very word "determinism" is in some degree misleading. For it tends to suggest that one event is somehow in the power of another, whereas the truth is merely that they are factually correlated. And the same applies to the use, in this context, of the word "necessity" and even of the word "cause" itself. Moreover, there are various reasons for this. One is the tendency to confuse causal with logical necessitation, and so to infer mistakenly that the effect is contained in the cause. Another is the uncritical use of a concept of force which is derived from primitive experiences of pushing and striking. A third is the survival of an animistic conception of causality, in which all causal relationships are modeled on the example of one person's exercising authority over another. As a result we tend to form an imaginative picture of an unhappy effect trying vainly to escape from the clutches of an overmastering cause. But, I repeat, the fact is simply that when an event of one type occurs, an event of another type occurs also, in a certain temporal or spatio-temporal relation to the first. The rest is only metaphor. And it is because of the metaphor, and not because of the fact, that we come to think that there is an antithesis between causality and freedom.

Nevertheless, it may be said, if the postulate of determinism is valid, then the future can be explained in terms of the past: and this means that if one knew enough about the past one would be able to predict the future. But in that case what will happen in the future is already decided. And how then can I be said to be free? What is going to happen is going to happen and nothing that I do can prevent it. If the determinist is right, I am the helpless prisoner of fate.

But what is meant by saying that the future course of events is already decided? If the implication is that some person has arranged it, then the proposition is false. But if all that is meant is that it is possible, in principle, to deduce it from a set of particular facts about the past, together with the appropriate general laws, then, even if this is true, it does not in the least entail that I am the helpless prisoner of fate. It does not even entail that my actions make no difference to the future: for they are causes as well as effects; so that if they were different their consequences would be different also. What it does entail is that my behavior can be predicted: but to say that my behavior can be predicted is not to say that I am acting under constraint. It is indeed true that I cannot escape my destiny if this is taken to mean no more than that I shall do what I shall do. But this is a tautology, just as it is a tautology that what is going to happen is going to happen. And such tautologies as these prove nothing whatsoever about the freedom of the will.

FREEDOM AND NECESSITY: A REAPPRAISAL

A. J. AYER

. . . The [fatalistic] position becomes less clear when it is assumed that there is a God who not only has foreknowledge of everything that is going to happen but also has foreordained it. And indeed it would seem that we need some such further assumption in order to give any substance to the doctrine of fatalism. The fact that what will be will be is incontestable, but also . . . innocuous. On the other hand, if it were the case that some agency, whether benevolent or not, had planned everything that was going to be, then there might be some ground for our regarding ourselves as puppets in its hands. Can those who believe in such an agency consistently regard themselves as free, in any interesting sense?

. . . I am not concerned here with examining the status of this belief. I do not in fact think that there is any way in which it can be justified. I see no reason to regard the universe as a goal-directed system, neither do I think that the analogy which some natural theologians have attempted to draw between its workings and the workings of human artifacts is capable of supporting an argument from design. But the objections to this form of argument are well known, and I have nothing fresh to add to them. The question which I now wish to raise is whether it leads to fatalism. Even for those who disbelieve in the existence of an Arch-Designer, this question should be of theoretical interest, if only because of its historical bearing upon the stubborn problem of free-will.

One difficulty in answering this question is that the assumption which gives rise to it may take different forms. If it is held that everything that happens, including everything that any of us does, is planned in every detail, then I do not see how it can be denied that if the responsibility for what we do can be assigned to anyone at all, it must ultimately fall upon the planner rather than ourselves. We may still make choices but, in the last resort, we are no more responsible for them, or for the actions which flow from them, than if we had been hypnotized. For someone who takes this view, the doctrine of predestination does seem irresistible; and even so it would appear rather unjust that we should be rewarded or punished simply for playing our allotted part.

On the other hand, it might be held that while the course of events was designed in the main, some elements were left to chance. If these elements included human actions, or human actions were dependent on them, then the responsibility for human actions could not be attributed to the deity. But could it be attributed to their agents either? If the actions are due, directly or indirectly, to chance, it would seem that no one is responsible.

I suppose, however, that the most prevalent view is neither of these. It is assumed that there is a grand design, but that it does not cover every detail. Some things happen, perhaps, by chance, and some are the result of the exercise of human will. There are, indeed, limitations to what can be achieved by the human will, but within these limits it operates freely. God gives us the power to do this or that, but whether we do it and how we do it is our own concern. Therefore, we are accountable for what we do not only to one another but to him.

Given its presuppositions, how far is this a tenable theory? It is not suggested that we act as we do by chance; for this would appear to imply that we are not responsible. It is held rather, that our actions proceed from our characters, and that our characters are to some extent of our own making. We start with certain dispositions for good or evil and it depends upon our own free choice which of these dispositions are actualized and to what degree. But how do we come to make these choices? Through the exercise of our wills. But what does this mean? The picture which is presented is that of the will as a sort of crane hovering over a storehouse of motives, shuffling them around, and picking one or other of them out. It operates on its own or else, perhaps, it is directed by a crane-man, called the self. Some of the instruments are more powerful than others, and some of the crane-men have a firmer hand upon the levers. But how does it come about that some of the instruments are more powerful or that some of their operators are more resolute and skilled? Were they made so, or did it just happen? If they were made so, the responsibility would seem to fall upon their maker. If it just happened, it would seem that no one is responsible.

It can now be seen that this problem goes beyond the theoretical framework in which I have so far presented it. It is possibly more acute for theists because it is a recognized ground for disclaiming reponsibility that one has been no more than the instrument of another's will; but even if I am right in thinking that we have no good reason to accept this idea of a Creator, the fatalistic argument can still be presented in a slightly different form. It again runs very simply. Either human actions are entirely governed by causal laws or they are not. If they are, then they are necessary: given our heredity and environment we could not act otherwise than as we do; if they are not, then to the extent that they are not caused they must occur by chance: if they occur by chance they are indeed not necessary, but equally we have no control over them. In neither case can we help ourselves.

The response which many philosophers now make to this argument is that it presents a false dilemma. It is not true that the only alternative to explaining human actions in casual terms is to regard them as occurring by chance. To speak of an action as occurring by chance suggests that it is done at random. But what an action which is done at random is properly contrasted with is not an action which lacks a cause, in the sense of a sufficient condition, but an action which lacks a purpose. The alternative to explaining human actions in terms of their causes is to explain them in terms of the reasons for which they are done. What was the agent's intention? What end did he have in view? When we account for actions in this way, we do not have to conclude either that they are necessary or that they occur by chance.

I think that this answer makes an important point. We do normally explain people's actions in terms of reasons rather than in terms of causes, and it is a perfectly legitimate form of explanation. The distinction between reason and cause is tenable at this level, since the fact that the agent has such and such a motive or intention need not consist in his having some particular experience which would be a sufficient, or even a necessary condition of the action which ensued. Nevertheless, I doubt if this answer really opens up a way of escape between the horns of the dilemma. For it can still be asked how it comes about that the agent has these purposes, and how it comes about that he does or does not seek to realize them. If he inhibits them, we may say that he does so for a reason, but then again what supplies him with this reason, and how does it come to work more strongly on him than the purposes which it overrides? Is there a causal explanation of these things, or do they just happen to be so? In either case, it is tempting to conclude that in the last resort the agent is not responsible.

Considering the extent to which it goes against our habitual mode of thought, this is not a conclusion to be accepted lightly, and various means have been suggested which would enable us to avoid it. The course which I have hitherto favored is to argue that when we say that an action was done freely we are not implying that it cannot be given any sort of causal explanation. On this view, we have to distinguish between causation and constraint. To say that an action is subject to a causal law need mean no more than that it can be fitted into some regular pattern, that under conditions of this kind an action of this sort always does occur, and this in itself is not destructive of the agent's freedom. It is only if the cause is of a certain special type that the agent is constrained and so not responsible for what he does: if, for example, he is drugged or hypnotized or suffering from certain forms of mental disease. Generally speaking the cases in which he is not responsible are those in which his will is, as it were, bypassed. They are contrasted with the cases in which the agent's choice, though it can be accounted for in causal terms, is still itself a causal factor.

I still think that a theory of this kind may be tenable, but it is by no means so obviously true as some of its advocates have assumed. The main objections to it are that the boundaries of constraint are not at all easy to draw with any precision; and that even if they could be drawn at all precisely, the distinction for which they are needed seems rather arbitrary. Why should a man be praised or blamed if his actions are brought about in one way, and acquitted of all responsibility if they are brought about in another? In either case they are equally the product of his heredity and environment.

An answer which is sometimes given to this objection is that the distinction can be justified on utilitarian grounds. The cases in which we hold an agent responsible are those in which we judge that the stimulus of praise or blame, reward or punishment, will have some effect upon him. If the action is one which we regard as socially undesirable, and the consequences of doing it are made painful to the agent, then we may hope that their effect on him will be such that his inclination to repeat the action will be inhibited. On the other hand, if the action is one that he has been constrained to do, these stimuli are likely to be ineffective. Given the constraining factor, the application of them would not cause him to act differently on a subsequent occasion. There is therefore no point in holding him responsible.

Again, I think that this view may be tenable. Though it might be rather difficult in practice to discriminate between the cases in which the stimulus of praise or blame would be effective and those in which it would not, the theoretical basis of the distinction is clear enough. At the same time I think it has to be admitted that this is not so much an analysis as a transformation of our ordinary notion of responsibility. It is true that when we have to decide how much or in what way we should reward or punish someone, we are influenced by considerations of utility. But the primary ground for rewarding or punishing a man at all is that he *deserves* it; and this is understood to imply that the actions on which his merit is assessed were not necessitated. It is assumed that he need not have done them, not merely in the sense that he could, or would, have avoided doing them if the circumstances had been different, but that he could have avoided doing them, the circumstances being exactly as they were. Now the claim that our actions are avoidable in this sense is hard to interpret, let alone to justify, and it may well be false or even incoherent. In that case the ordinary notion of desert falls with it, and a great deal of our moral thinking will have to be revised. I do not say that this would be a bad thing, even on moral grounds, but only that it would be a much more far-reaching step than utilitarians commonly admit.

A quite different line of argument, which has recently come somewhat into favor, is that the teleological form of explanation, an explanation in terms of reasons rather than in terms of causes, is the only one that is appropriate to human conduct. The actions for which a man is held responsible are motivated, but not necessitated. He could have acted otherwise just in the sense that there is no causal law from which it follows, given the circumstances in question, that he must have acted as he did. How this could be is a question which we still have to examine. For the sake of argument, however, let us assume that it is so. What we must not then do is fall on the second horn of the dilemma by inferring that in that case it is just a matter of chance that the man acts for the reasons that he does. For not only are the actions of a rational agent not haphazard, his motives are not haphazard either. We can explain how he comes to have them, but the explanation will be in terms of the rational inter-connection of his purposes, and not in terms of their causal origin. His actions become intelligible to us in the light of our general understanding of his character, just as a work of art becomes intelligible to us when we grasp its general plan. To insist on asking whether or not it is a matter of chance that he has this character is beside the point, just as it would be beside the point to ask whether it was a matter of chance that Rembrandt painted his mother, or Beethoven composed his last quartets, in the manner that they did.

The difficulty with this view is that it is not at all clear why we should not be allowed to ask these questions. If we are anxious to understand a work of art, or even a person's character, it may not be very profitable to try to account for it in purely causal terms; but this is not to say that the attempt to do so is illegitimate. Neither is it clear why the problem of free-will should be solved merely through making the assumption that such an attempt is bound to be unsuccessful. And in any case what right have we to make this assumption? How can we be so sure that the behavior of a rational agent is not susceptible of a purely causal explanation?

Let us begin, however, by approaching this question from the other side. What reasons are there for supposing that all human conduct is governed by causal laws? Many people believe that this is so, but mostly, it would seem, on *a priori* grounds. That is, they deduce it from some general doctrine of determinism. Nowadays this most commonly takes the form of maintaining that every event, and in consequence every human action, is theoretically predictable. Admittedly, the number of human actions which we are in fact capable of predicting is very small: but this, it is claimed, is only because we do not know enough. The factors involved are so numerous and so complex that it is not practically possible to take account of them all. Nevertheless the fact remains that if we did know all the relevant initial conditions, and all the relevant laws, we could deduce exactly what any given person would think or feel or do; and the same would apply of course, on the hypothesis of complete determinism, to every other type of event.

But let us consider what this claim amounts to. The first point to note is that it is not even logically possible that every event should actually be predicted, if only because this would lead to an infinite regress. The making of each prediction would itself have to be predicted and so *ad infinitum*. However, this does not exclude the possibility that every event is actually predictable in the sense that if one were required to predict some individual event, there is none of them that would not be a candidate. But even this is not certain. For it might be a necessary condition of the occurrence of certain events that they were not in fact predicted, or at any rate that they were not predicted by a given person. In one's own case, for example, there may well be actions which one would not in fact perform, if one had predicted that one was going to perform them. And here there is no refuge in the argument that to say that the action is foreseen entails that it will occur. For the point is just that there are actions which the agent cannot foresee. The mere fact that he made the prediction would ensure that it was false.

No doubt the determinist has a reply to this. He will argue that the most that such examples can prove is that it is causally impossible that certain actions should actually be predicted; it still does not follow that they are not predictable in principle, and this is all that he is claiming. But what is meant by saying that an event is predictable in principle? Presumably just that there are some events antecedent to it with which it is connected by a natural law; so that the materials which would permit it to be predicted are available, even if for some special reason the prediction cannot actually be made. But if this is what is being claimed, it is unnecessary, and indeed rather misleading, to couch it in terms of prediction. The thesis of determinism is just that every occurrence is governed by some natural law.

This sounds well enough, but what exactly does it come to? If the contention is merely that there is always some true generalization from which, given the appropriate initial conditions, the occurrence of a given event can be deduced, it is correct but trivial. For every set of events must fit into some pattern, if no restriction is placed upon its complexity; even if the event is of a type of which it is the only instance it can still be linked by a generalization to any other unique event; if each kind of event occurs only once, then, however they are spatiotemporally related, it will be universally true that no event of either kind occurs except in that relation to the other. It may indeed be objected that what we understand by a natural law is something stronger than a mere *de facto* generalization, but while there may be some ground for this distinction, it is not at all easy to see what it can be. My own view that the difference does not lie in the character of the generalizations, so much as in our attitude toward them: the generalizations which we treat as natural laws are those which we are the most confident of being able to extrapolate successfully. But, if this is correct, is is idle to speculate in the abstract about the subjection of events to natural laws. It is a truism that every event falls under some generalization or other; whether the generalization is one to which we should be prepared to accord the status of a natural law is a question to which there can be no answer unless we know what the generalization is.

The thesis of determinism has lived very largely on the credit of classical mechanics. Given that one knew the position and velocity of every physical particle in the universe at a given instant, the laws of classical mechanics enabled one to calculate exactly what would be the position and velocity of these particles at any other instant. The deterministic empire was then erected on the assumption that everything that happened could ultimately be accounted for in terms of the motion of these physical particles. If determinism is now said to have broken down in quantum physics, the reason is that one of the conditions which underlay its classical formulation cannot be fulfilled; it is not possible to fix exactly both the position and momentum of a microscopic particle at any given instant; indeed, the prevalent view is that it makes no sense to say of such particles that they simultaneously have an exact position and momentum. What this shows is that the causal scheme which was found to work in the domain of classical mechanics cannot be simply transferred to the domain of quantum physics. It does not show that the behavior of microscopic particles is entirely lawless, and it leaves it an open question what laws may hold in other fields. So, if we wish to discover how far human actions are subject to natural law, we have to pursue our investigations at the appropriate level.

To some extent this has already been done. The biological and social sciences do enable us to account for human actions to a certain extent. Admittedly the predictions which we draw from them are not very far-reaching and, for the most part, not very precise. We can foretell that a man will be angry if such and such things are said or done to him, but probably not the precise form that the expression of his anger will take; a psycho-analyst may predict in certain favorable circumstances that his patient will exhibit neurotic symptoms, a physiologist that as the result of a brain operation the patient's powers of perception or his moral character will deteriorate, but the range of behavior which such predictions cover is wide: they come a long way short of pin-pointing the events which are said to verify them. We are rather more successful at explaining human conduct *ex post facto* [after the fact], but still in a way that fits the facts rather loosely. Moreover the type of explanation which prevails in historical studies is that of explanation in terms of reasons rather than in terms of causes.

Nevertheless, I do not think that we can exclude the possibility of discovering a causal scheme into which human behavior can be made to fit, not only in outline but even in detail. For example, it is believed by many physiologists that the sufficient condition of every conscious state or action is to be found in some state of the agent's body, and primarily in the functioning of his brain. They would, therefore, claim that every facet of human behavior could be adequately accounted for in physiological terms. This is, indeed, only an ideal which is still very far from being fulfilled. Our knowledge of the mechanism of the brain is still imperfect, and no dictionary has been compiled which would serve to match variations in brain processes with variations in conscious states. It may be that such a dictionary never will be compiled, perhaps even that it never could be, on scientific grounds. On the other hand, there seems to be no logical reason why it should not be: so far as I can see, this is not a possibility that we are entitled to rule out *a priori*. I am, therefore, suspicious of any philosophical theory which is based on the assumption that a program of this kind cannot be fulfilled.

Now suppose that it were fulfilled; suppose that we had a physiological theory which gave content to the thesis that all human actions were determined, and that this theory were reasonably well established: how would this affect the problems which we have been discussing? In particular how far would it lend support to any form of fatalism?

In answering this question, we must distinguish between the practical consequences of applying such a theory and the logical consequences of the theory itself. If it came to the point where we had the means of knowing what was going on in a person's brain and could use this as a basis for predicting what he would do, and if this knowledge extended to our own future conduct, it is unlikely that our present view of life would remain the same. As I have remarked before, the making of these predictions would itself be a causal factor; they would inhibit the emotional responses to an action which depend upon its being unexpected: in the long run certain forms of conduct would themselves be inhibited. But it is idle to pursue these speculations in the abstract, especially as the practical difficulties of applying such a thory would be so great that the predictions which it yielded would probably not be very far-reaching. And it is from our actual success in making such predictions that these consequences would result, rather than from the mere acceptance of the view that human action was physiologically determined.

One practical consequence which the acceptance of this view would itself be likely to have would be a weakening of our belief in the justice of retributive punishment, if only on the principle that the better we understand the more we are inclined to forgive. It might even be held that this was not merely a practical, but a logical consequence. For, as I have already said, it is at least very doubtful whether a deterministic view of this kind can be logically reconciled with our current notion of moral responsibility. As we have seen, this does not imply that we could not then operate with any notion of moral responsibility at all, but only that we should have to fall back upon a utilitarian notion which would differ, at least in one important respect, from that which most people now appear to have. The difference, as I have already suggested, would be that we should have to abandon, or at least to modify, the prevalent concept of moral desert. For if I am right in what I said about this concept, the conditions for its application would not be satisfied.

On the other hand, I do not think that the fact that human behavior was governed by causal laws, in any such way as we have been imaginging, would entail that human beings were merly puppets or that their aspirations were futile, or any fatalistic conclusion of that sort. A person is said to become a puppet when he is made the hapless instrument of another person's will, but unless we make certain theistic assumptions, for which there appears to be no reasonable warrant, our mere subjection to natural law would not put us in this position. Neither would it follow that our actions could not be purposive, or that our lives would pursue their courses independently of our purposes. The important point here is that acting for a reason is not incompatible with acting from a cause. The two forms of explanation are not exclusive.

It does not cease to be true that an action is consciously directed toward an end, even if the agent's choice of the end in question and his selection of the means to attain it are explicable in purely causal terms.

An argument which is sometimes put forward against the hypothesis that all human behavior is governed by causal laws is that it is self-defeating. For we ought not to accept a hypothesis unless we have some reason to believe it. But, it is argued, if this hypothesis were true, we could have no reason to believe it. We have reason to believe a hypothesis when we are able to see that it is supported by evidence which we also have reason to trust. But if the sort of hypothesis which we have been considering were true, whether or not we believed a hypothesis would depend simply on the condition of our brains, or whatever else was the determinant factor. It might indeed happen that the belief which so resulted was true, but this would be the fruit of one's good fortune, not of one's rational judgement: had one's brain been in a different condition one might just as inevitably have been led to a belief which was false. In neither case would the rational assessment of the evidence play any part.

I think that this argument is fallacious, just because it rests on the assumption that to act for a reason is incompatible with acting from a cause. The statement that one believes a given proposition on such and such rational grounds, and the statement that one believes it because such and such processes are occurring in one's brain can, both of them, be true. The word "because" is used in a different sense in either case, but these senses are not destructive of each other. The fact that there was a causal explanation for my advancing these views, that I should, for example, be thinking differently if my brain were differently constituted, would not prove that I do not genuinely hold them, or that I hold them for any other *reasons* than the reasons which I give; neither would it have any bearing on the question whether the reasons are good or bad. This is illustrated even by the example of a calculating machine. The way the machine operates depends on the way in which it has been constructed, but it is also true that it operates in accordance with certain logical rules. From the fact that its operations are causally explicable it does not follow that they are not logically valid. However loose the analogy between human beings and machines, if this libertarian argument breaks down in the one case, it breaks down in the other.

I have not been maintaining that the case for regarding human conduct as causally determined has been made out: the most that I have tried to show is that it cannot be refuted on purely logical grounds. It is an empirical question which, in the present state of our knowledge, we are not in a position to decide. If we were able to decide it in favor of determinism, we might still attempt to avoid drawing a fatalistic conclusion. We might argue that the fact that our actions fitted into a causal pattern did not imply that they could not be purposive or that we had no command over our own fortunes. However they might be accounted for, our choices would still themselves be causal factors. It is true that if our actions are determined, there is a sense in which they are not avoidable. But from our own point of view as agents, this makes no more serious difference than the logical truism that the future will be what it will.

I think that this attitude could be maintained so long as the theory which was taken as justifying the belief in the causal determination of our actions was not one which we could easily employ to make concrete predictions. If its application were virtually limited to explaining human behavior *ex post facto,* we should still be faced in practice with the responsibility of coming to decisions; and we should not cease to regard these decisions as being efficacious, even though we believed that they could all be given a physiological explanation. On the other hand, if the theory were actually used to predict human behavior with a fair degree of precision, I think that our view of ourselves as agents might be radically changed. We should not have the same use for the concept of human action, if we had this scientific means of knowing what we were going to do and what the results would be. The important point here is not so much that our conduct would be foreseen, but that it would be foreseen without any account being taken of our intentions, except as the correlates of certain physiological states. If this were to happen, we might well come to think of ourselves, not as living our lives in the way we now do, but rather as spectators of a process over which we had no effective control. But while I think that this is a possibility, I do not think that it is one with which we have to reckon very seriously. For not only is the case for determinism, in respect of human behavior, not yet established; but even if it were established, the practical consequences would not be likely to extend very far. The chances that we could actually use a physiological, or even a psychological, theory to plot the course of our destinies in detail appear very small.

Questions for Discussion

1. Who is more genuinely exercising freedom of the will, the inhabitants of the ideal community in *Walden Two* or the captive human psychologist in "Learning Theory"? How do you think Holbach, Sartre, and Ayer, respectively, would answer this question?
2. If you provided a complete causal explanation as to why a person did

something, would it follow that you had given him or her a perfect excuse for doing it? What if one component of that causal explanation was the fact that he or she wanted to do it?

3. "He is a slave to his desires." According to Holbach, this phrase fits everyone. What problem, if any, does this present for Holbach's theory?

4. Does it make sense to suppose that someone could know in advance what you are going to do even though you are acting with complete freedom? Does it make a difference if the person who knows what you will do is (a) a close friend, or (b) God? If so, why?

5. What do we mean by "strength of will" and "weakness of will"? Are strong-willed people more free than weak-willed people? Explain.

6. Is it literally possible for someone to act out of character? If it is, what is the right way to conceive of such action?

7. The contemporary American philosopher, Sidney Hook, once wrote of a defendant in a murder case who pleaded for clemency on the ground that his heredity and upbringing made it inevitable that he would commit his crimes. The judge replied that his own heredity and upbringing made it impossible for him to grant clemency. Hook took this story to support determinism. Discuss, indicating your opinion.

8. "I could do no other," said Martin Luther. Sartre claims that such a statement must always be made in bad faith? Do you agree?

9. According to Sartre, we are "condemned to be free." What do you suppose he means? Could a person meaningfully be said to have a choice between being free and not being free?

10. Of the three writers—Holbach, Sartre, and Ayer—which one is best able to account for the *degrees* of responsibility that we assign to people in everyday life? Why?

Selected Readings

ABELSON, R. *Persons*. Chaps. 3, 5. London: Macmillan, 1977. Arguments against determinism.

AUGUSTINE, AURELIUS, ST. *On Free Will*. In *Augustine's Earlier Writings*, translated by J. Burleigh. Philadelphia: Westminster Press, 1955. A religious form of soft determinism.

AYER, A. J. *The Concept of a Person*. New York: St. Martin's Press, 1963.
———. *Philosophical Essays*. New York: St. Martin's Press, 1954. Arguments for determinism, both soft and hard.

BEROFSKY, B. *Determinism*. Princeton, New Jersey: Princeton University Press, 1971. A precise definition of determinism and a defense.
———, ed. *Free Will and Determinism*. New York: Harper & Row, 1966. Classical and modern essays pro and con free will.

BRAND, M., ed. *The Nature of Human Action*. Glenview, Illinois: Scott, Foresman, 1970. An anthology of essays on the concept of action and its relation to free will.

CARE, N., and LANDESMAN, C. *Readings in the Theory of Action.* Blooming-ton: Indiana University Press, 1968. Essays on action and free will.

CAMPBELL, C. A. *On Selfhood and Godhood.* New York: Macmillan, 1957. A religious form of libertarianism.

DANTO, A. *An Analytical Philosophy of Action.* Cambridge: Cambridge University Press, 1973. A dualistic defense of determinism.

DWORKIN, G., ed. *Determinism, Freedom and Moral Responsibility.* Engle-wood Cliffs, New Jersey: Prentice-Hall, 1970. Essays for and against free will.

EDDINGTON, A. *The Philosophy of Physical Science.* Chap. 11. New York: Macmillan, 1939. Critique of scientific determinism.

EDWARDS, J. *Freedom of the Will.* New Haven, Connecticut: Yale University Press, 1957. A neo-Augustinian argument for the compatibility of free will and divine predestination.

FARRER, A. *The Freedom of the Will.* New York: Scribner's, 1958. A well-written defense of libertarianism in the tradition of ordinary language analysis.

HOLBACH, BARON D'. *The System of Nature.* Chaps. 11–12. Translated by H. Robinson. New York: Burt Franklin, 1970. The classic statement of determinism.

HOOKS, S., ed. *Determinism and Freedom in an Age of Modern Science.* New York: New York University Press, 1957. Essays on determinism, pro and con, by contemporary philosophers.

HUME, D. *Enquiry Concerning Human Understanding,* Sec. IV, VII.
———. "On Liberty and Necessity." In *A Treatise of Human Nature.* The classical arguments for soft determinism.

JAMES, W. "The Dilemma of Determinism." In *Essays in Pragmatism.* New York: Hafner, 1948. The classic defense of free will.

LEHRER, K., ed. *Freedom and Determinism.* New York: Random House, 1966. Precise and technical contemporary essays for and against free will.

MELDEN, A. I. *Free Action.* New York: Humanities Press, 1961. A careful analysis of the concept of action indicating that causal explanation is irrelevant.

MOORE, G. E. *Ethics.* Chap. VI. London: Oxford University Press, 1912. The classic analysis of "could have done otherwise."

MORGENBESSER, S., and WALSH, J. *Free Will.* Englewood Cliffs, New Jersey: Prentice-Hall, 1962. Ancient and modern essays, pro and con free will.

PEARS, D., ed. *Freedom and the Will.* London: Macmillan, 1963. A debate among some contemporary British philosophers.

RANKIN, K. W. *Choice and Chance.* Oxford: Blackwell, 1961. An existentialist argument for libertarianism, based on considerations of ordinary language.

SARTRE, J. P. *Being and Nothingness.* Translated by H. Barnes. New York: Philosophical Library, 1956. The metaphysics of existential freedom.

SKINNER, B. F. *Beyond Freedom and Dignity.* New York: Knopf, 1971. Arguments of a distinguished psychologist that free will is illusory.

———. *Walden Two*. New York: Macmillan, 1948. A hard determinist's concept of utopia.

WHITE, A., ed. *The Philosophy of Action*. London: Oxford University Press, 1968. Contemporary essays on the role of causality in action.

WRIGHT, G. H., VON. *Causality and Determinism*. New York: Columbia University Press, 1974. A precise definition of causality suggesting that actions are not caused.

PART TWO

Epistemology

Chapter 5

Induction: Can We Learn from Experience?

There is a story about the ancient Greek philosopher Pyrrho of the third and fourth centuries B.C. It is said that when Pyrrho was out walking with his students and found himself approaching the edge of a cliff, he would refuse to change direction, so that his students had to restrain him by tugging at his cloak. When asked why he engaged in this apparently suicidal behavior, he would reply with another question: What good reason can you give me for thinking it any more likely that I will be killed if I walk over the edge of the cliff than if I do not?

Pyrrho was not mad. Judging from his longevity, it seems likely that he avoided cliffs when his students were not around to protect him. He was what is known as a philosophical skeptic, concerned with dramatizing a philosophical point. Most people would consider it a perfectly adequate answer to Pyrrho to point out that unsupported objects heavier than air have been observed invariably to fall; that a person walking off a cliff has no means of support, such as wings, and that falling from a great height against hard ground has always been found to result in serious injury or death. But it is characteristic of the philosophical skeptic not to be satisfied with such commonsensical answers. Pyrrho was concerned precisely to question our complacent claims to knowledge. Why, he wanted to know, does the fact that certain things have been found to be associated in the past—for example, walking off a cliff and being injured or killed—give us reason for thinking it more likely than not that they will be so associated in the future? This is what has come to be called the "problem of induction."

Contemporary interest in the problem of induction stems mainly from the writings of David Hume, whose philosophical ideas were not fully appreciated in the eighteenth century but are very much alive today. Hume presented the problem of induction in the form of a dilemma: Extrapolation from past observation to cases as yet unobserved (to believe, as he put it, that "the future will be conformable to the past") is based either on *demonstrative* reasoning—the kind employed in logic and mathematics—or it is based on *experiential* reasoning—the kind employed in the natural sciences. As an example of experiential reasoning, Hume cites our finding a watch on a desert island and inferring that a human being must have been there. Now, Hume continues, demonstrative reasoning is characterized by the fact that its conclusions cannot be denied without contradiction. However, the "conformability of the future to the past" cannot be established by demonstrative reasoning since there is no contradiction in asserting that nature might change in just such a way as to falsify any, and perhaps even all, of our expectations. So it would seem that if the principle of induction is to be justified at all, that justification must be empirical or experiential in nature. But, Hume notes, when we examine the matter more closely, we find that all reasoning from experience is itself *based* on the assumption that generalizations derived from past observation hold equally for unobserved cases. Consequently any argument for the reliability of induction that is based on experience of its past successes would beg the question at issue. This consideration appears to leave inductive inference without any rational basis. As Hume himself put it:

Let the course of things be allowed hitherto ever so regular; that alone, without some new argument or inference, proves not that, for the future, it will continue so. In vain do you pretend to have learned the nature of bodies from your past experience. Their secret nature, and consequently all their effects and influence, may change, without any change in their sensible qualities. This happens sometimes, and with regard to some objects. Why may it not happen always, and with regard to all objects? What logic, what process of argument secures you against this supposition? My practice, you may say, refutes my doubts. But you mistake the purport of my question. As an agent, I am quite satisfied on this point; but as a philosopher, who has some share of curiosity, I will not say scepticism, I want to learn the foundation of this inference.

This, in essence, is Hume's argument, and it has offered a continuing challenge to all subsequent generations of philosophers.

Nowadays, if we were asked how we know that we will fall and be injured if we walk off a cliff, we might not appeal directly to past experience but might instead reply: It follows from the law of gravity that we would be bound to fall fast and hard. But it is clear on reflection that this sort of appeal to science would be no more successful in combating the philosophical problem of induction than the more naive answer available to Pyrrho's contemporaries. No doubt it is more satisfactory to be able to speak, as does Bertrand Russell, of "the laws of motion" and the like, rather than in terms of such crude exception-prone generalizations as "unsupported heavy bodies always fall." It is neater because the very same laws that explain why an apple falls to the ground can also be cited to explain an apparently dissimilar phenomenon such as a satellite remaining in orbit. And these abstract laws are not refuted by balloons, airplanes, and other such airborne objects. But all the same, our so called laws of nature are simply more precise generalizations that explain our cruder generalizations. Although they are more abstract in character, and although different laws may be logically interlocked in certain ways, they still rest ultimately on past observation. And we can ask about them just what Pyrrho and Hume asked about the generalizations of scientifically uneducated common sense: In spite of the fact that they have been found to hold for cases observed in the past, have we any reason to believe that they will hold for cases we have yet to encounter? If so, what is that reason?

Sometimes the appeal to science will take a somewhat different form from that which we have just considered. When encountering the problem of induction for the first time, people frequently react by pointing out the impressive achievements of modern science that result from the repeated drawing of inductive inferences. They conclude by remarking: So you see, we use induction because it works. It is indeed tempting to suppose that this very plausible answer somehow enables us to sidestep skeptical doubts. But a person who argues in this way falls straight into the trap that Hume and Russell have prepared. What can it mean to say that induction *works*? If it means that induction not only has been a successful method of inference up to now but will also continue to be successful in the future, then the argument clearly begs the question. For how can anyone know this except by using induction? If, on the other hand, it means only that induction has led to correct conclusions in the past, then the argument is correct but irrelevant, for what we want to know is whether induction will continue to yield correct conclusions. As Russell points out, to argue that because induction has worked before, it is reasonable to believe that it will continue to work is to use induction in trying to prove induction—what logicians call "circular reasoning." In Russell's vivid phraseology, only induction itself enables us to make the leap from the fact that past futures have resembled past pasts to the conclusion that future futures will resemble future pasts.

We said just now that laws of nature are themselves no more than generalizations that rest inductively on lower-level generalizations. But of course we have a quite different attitude toward statements such as "All American presidents are under seven feet tall" and statements such as "The boiling point of water declines with falling air pressure." Both are generalizations. Both are true as far as we know from experience. And, for all we know, both may remain true for future cases as well. But we feel that the first statement merely tells us what *happens* to be the case, whereas the second statement tells us what *has* to be the case as a matter of causal necessity. This notion of necessity tempts us to say, for example, not merely that someone who walks off a cliff will fall, but that he or she cannot avoid falling. We speak of being constrained by the laws of nature, as though by invisible chains. Indeed, it is perhaps just this metaphor of constraint that leads us to speak of "law" of nature. It is arguable that much of the hold that the conclusion of an inductive inference has on us is due to our conviction that past experience has taught us not merely how things have been and are but rather how they must be.

An attack on this concept of natural necessity forms a second strand in Hume's skepticism. Hume reasons as follows:

When we look about us towards external objects, and consider the operation of causes, we are never able, in a single instance, to discover any power or necessary connection, any quality, which binds the effect to the cause, and renders the one an infallible consequence of the other. We only find that the one does actually, in fact, follow the other. The impulse of one billiard ball is attended with motion in the second. This is the whole that appears to the *outward* senses. The mind feels no sentiment or *inward* impression from this succession of objects: consequently there is not, in any single particular instance of cause and effect, anything which can suggest the idea of power or necessary connection.

Hume goes on to argue that the same can be said about the evidence we gather from introspection: we choose to raise our arm and our arm moves, but all that we are aware of is the impulse of our will accompanied by our arm rising. We may say that our arm is made or caused to rise by our decision to raise it. But once again nothing in this situation seems to provide any ground for speaking here of a necessary connection between the decision and the arm's movement. Indeed, we can easily imagine the connection being severed in practice. Consider, for example, someone whose nervous system has been "rewired" and who has yet to adjust to the fact, so that whenever he decides to raise his arm he finds, say, his big toe wiggling instead. What Hume concludes from this absence of a perceptible or provable necessary connection between will and action is that the concept of causal necessity has no genuine reference to experience and that we have no reason to suppose that the world has any features to which this concept corresponds. What happens is merely that through the constant conjunction of events of type *A* with events of type *B,* we form the habit of expecting new instances of *A* to be followed by instances of *B.* Our concept of causal necessity amounts to no more than a mistaken projection onto the external world of this psychological habit.

A closely analogous view may be found in our selection from Jean-Paul Sartre's existentialist novel, *Nausea.* In the passage preceding the one we have chosen for this anthology, Roquentin, the main character, reflects on what he calls the "brute contingency of things." By this he means that there is ultimately no necessary reason for things being as they are or, in fact, existing at all. Things simply do exist and behave in certain regular ways. Indeed the "nausea" of the title turns out to be Roquentin's emotional response to this very bruteness of existence. That is why we find him complaining, in the pages we have selected, that nature has no laws, only habits, and that its habits may change at any moment. If there is no necessity in things having been the way they were up to now, then there is equally no necessity for them to continue thus. As Ludwig Wittgenstein once expressed it, belief in induction turns out to be mere superstition. In Roquentin's fantasies as to just how the world might suddenly begin to confound our most confident expectations, we find a perfect illustration of Hume's warning.

It is only fair to point out, however, that when Sartre speaks of the contingency or superfluousness of things, he has in mind not merely the absence of causal necessity in Hume's sense but also the absence of any ultimate meaning or purpose in things—the denial, for example, of the necessary-being argument considered in chapter 1 of this book. Sartre's philosophy is staunchly atheistic. And Roquentin's fantasy is an expression not merely of Humean skepticism about induction but also, and perhaps even more strongly, of the feeling that the world is "absurd," a favorite expression of existential writers. What he is imagining might seem grotesque, irrational, "absurd" if it should come to pass. But— and this is the main point Sartre is making here—when we regard that world dispassionately, would it really be any more (or less) absurd than the world as we actually find it? Even here there is an affinity with Hume and Russell. For all three writers seem to agree that our sense of reason or necessity in nature, which is so characteristic of our ordinary view of the world, is no more than an illusion fostered by sheer familiarity, an attitude engendered by finding our expectations repeatedly and reassuringly confirmed. The reader may have noticed a similar assault on our commonsense complacency by Zeno and Nagarjuna in chapter 2, an assault that led them, however, to somewhat different conclusions.

The article by Paul Edwards, a contemporary American philosopher, is an attempt to reinstate common sense. Although his arguments are primarily directed against Russell, Edwards challenges the assumptions common to all who demand a justification for induction. Russell and Hume both picture inductive inference as lacking in logical proof. They regard the step from observed cases to unobserved cases as a precarious leap that can only be justified, if at all, by means of some principle of induction, an unstated premise asserting the "uniformity of nature" or something of the kind. They then argue that, in the nature of the case, no valid justification of any such unstated premise or rule of inference is possible without a question-begging appeal to past experience.

Edwards argues, in reply, that inductive inferences simply do not need justification in terms of any such general principle. According to him, the reason Russell thinks they do is that Russell, like all the followers of Hume, has assumed the legitimacy of applying to inductive inferences the same standards of proof that apply to demonstrative or deductive arguments in mathematics. As they stand, inductive inferences do not, it is true, make the grade as instances of valid deductive reasoning. The premises (i.e., the supporting statements) of an inductive inference do not give us *logically conclusive* reasons for accepting their consequences as true or, perhaps, even as likely to be true. But then why, Edwards asks, should it follow from the fact that we do not have logically conclusive reasons that we do not have any good reasons whatsoever? We do not normally use the term "good reason" in so restrictive a manner. So why should it be thought appropriate or even relevant to demand that inductive inferences satisfy the criteria of validity we employ in evaluating deductive inferences? Why can it not be allowed that past observation provides perfectly good reasons for thinking it highly probable that the sun will rise tomorrow and that, in general, the laws of nature will continue to hold? Induction has its own standards that are, within their own domain, just as capable of distinguishing good inferences from bad ones as are those of deductive logic.

There is perhaps a strong side and also a weak side to Edwards's line of reasoning. It does seem to be an unargued assumption of Hume and Russell that it is legitimate to take deductive inference as our model for all reasoning. To be sure, neither Hume nor Russell actually said that for anything to count as justifying inductive reasoning it would have to be a deductive justification. Nevertheless, the gap between evidence and conclusion that Russell and Hume both claim to find in inductive inferences is pretty clearly perceived by them as a gap only because the are implicitly comparing inductive with deductive inferences. Here Edwards is on very strong ground.

But on the other hand, it is hardly enough to say that an inductive inference, while invalid when judged by deductive standards, may be valid when judged by its own standards; we must also agree on what those special inductive standards are and determine whether they are reasonable standards. Otherwise, the skeptic can always retort: If there are such inductive standards, what are they and why should we accept the conclusions of an argument that meets these standards?

In replying, Edwards appears to rely heavily on an appeal to facts about ordinary language. It follows, from what we ordinarily mean by "good reason," he argues, that the premises of an inductive inference provide good reasons for accepting its conclusion. The standard he implicitly invokes for justifying inductive reasoning seems to be the fact that people ordinarily apply the phrase "good reasons" to the premises of inductive arguments. So in denying that such premises are, by themselves, good enough reasons, skeptics, according to Edwards, are in effect redefining the notion of "good reason" in such a way that they are no longer using it in the normal sense. We are thus forced to admit that we do not, in the skeptics' peculiar sense of the term, have good reasons for accepting the conclusion of an inductive inference. But then, Edwards's argument goes, why should we care whether or not we have good reasons in this idiosyncratic and excessively narrow sense of the term?

Here, however, Edwards seems to ignore what we might call the "evaluative dimension" of the phrase "good reason." When we say of people that they have good reasons for accepting an inductive conclusion, we do not do so merely because their thought processes have the shape or form of an inductive inference but because, in addition to this fact, we also believe that inferences of this form are a generally *reliable* guide to truth. It may be misleading to claim, as Edwards does, that skeptics use the term "good reason" in a different sense from the rest of us. Skeptics may rather be questioning the assumption of reliability on which our normal usage is based.

An analogy might help to clarify this point. Suppose astrology was so well entrenched in our ordinary ways of thinking that whenever a person's horoscope indicated that a disaster would happen if he or she traveled on a certain day, most people accepted this automatically as a "good reason" for not traveling on that day. Then someone skeptical about astrology, who maintained that a horoscope reading did not provide genuinely good reasons for believing that travel would result in disaster, would be subject to Edwards's charge of using "good reason"

arily idiosyncratic sense. But that accusation would not
eptic's doubts were ill founded. From the mere fact that
call something a good reason, it by no means follows
reason, in the sense of really providing a reliable basis
ing a conclusion. To insist, with Edwards, that the observation
past regularities provides, *by definition,* a good reason for predicting
the continuation of such regularities in the future merely shifts the
skeptic's question to: Why should I believe a conclusion for which I
have "good reasons" in the sense you have just defined? As Abraham
Lincoln observed, calling a horse's tail a "leg" doesn't give the horse a
fifth leg.

Numerous "solutions" to the problem of induction have, at one time
or another, been proposed—some of them extremely ingenious. But they
all turn out, on reflection, to be vulnerable to more or less decisive objections; and indeed, attempts to solve the problem outright have by
now attained a status somewhat analogous to attempts to square the
circle. Critics of Hume more frequently take the view, nowadays, that
the so-called problem of induction is not so much a genuine problem as
a "pseudo-problem"—that its very statement involves some kind of conceptual error. (There seems to be something of this way of thinking in
Edwards's article.) But one cannot help wondering whether there is not,
in this attitude, at least an element of philosophical "sour grapes": if the
problem cannot be solved, then there must be something wrong with the
problem. If there *is* something wrong with the question Hume was asking, as yet no one has provided a convincing account of what it is that is
wrong.

Other philosophers, most notably Ayer, have come to see inductive
skepticism essentially as something that one must learn to live with, and
perhaps this is so. By and large, we find ourselves *believing* the conclu-
ions of inductive inferences, come what may. And if it offends our commonsense intuitions to be told that we ultimately have no justification
for such beliefs, that is not necessarily a reason for dismissing so seemingly dismal a conclusion. For it seems unlikely that, on these matters
at least, common sense itself has anything but induction to back it up.

TUESDAY AT BOUVILLE

Jean-Paul Sartre

Is this what freedom is? Below me, the gardens slope gently toward the town, and in each garden there stands a house. I see the sea, heavy, motionless, I see Bouville. It is a fine day.

I am free: I haven't a single reason for living left, all the ones I have tried have given way and I can't imagine any more. I am still quite young, I still have enough strength to start again. But what must I start again? Only now do I realize how much, in the midst of my greatest terror and nauseas, I had counted on Anny to save me. My past is dead, Monsieur de Rollebon is dead, Anny came back only to take all hope away from me. I am alone in this white street lined with gardens. Alone and free. But this freedom is rather like death.

Today my life comes to an end. Tomorrow I shall have left the town which stretches out at my feet, where I have lived so long. It will no longer be anything but a name, stolid, bourgeois, very French, a name in my memory which is not as rich as the names of Florence or Baghdad. A time will come when I shall wonder: "Whatever did I find to do all day long when I was at Bouville?" And of this sunshine, of this afternoon, nothing will remain, not even a memory.

My whole life is behind me. I can see it all, I can see its shape and the slow movements which have brought me this far. There is very little to say about it: it's a lost game, that's all. Three years ago I came to Bouville with a certain solemnity. I had lost the first round. I decided to play the second round and I lost again: I lost the whole game. At the same time, I learnt that you always lose. Only the bastards think they win. Now I'm going to do like Anny, I'm going to outlive myself. Eat, sleep. Sleep, eat. Exist slowly, gently, like these trees, like a puddle of water, like the red seat in the tram.

The Nausea is giving me a brief respite. But I know that it will come back: it is my normal condition. Only today my body is too exhausted to stand it. Sick people too have happy weaknesses which relieve them

FROM *Nausea,* translated by Lloyd Alexander. © 1964 by New Directions Publishing Corp. and reprinted with their permission.

for a few hours of the consciousness of their suffering. Now and then I give such a big yawn that tears roll down my cheeks. It is a deep, deep boredom, the deep heart of existence, the very matter I am made of. I don't let myself go, far from it: this morning I took a bath, I shaved. Only, when I think back over all those careful little actions, I can't understand how I could bring myself to perform them. They are so futile. It was my habits, probably, which performed them for me. They aren't dead, my habits, they go on bustling about, gently, insidiously weaving their webs, they wash me, dry me, dress me, like nursemaids. Was it they too who brought me up on this hill? I can't remember now how I came here. Up the escalier Dautry I suppose: did I really climb its one hundred and ten steps one by one? What is perhaps even more difficult to imagine, is that in a little while I'm going to go down them again. Yet I know that I am: before long I shall find myself at the bottom of the Coteau Vert, and if I raise my head I shall be able to see the windows of these houses which are so close to me now light up. In the distance. Above my head; and this moment now, from which I cannot emerge, which shuts me in and hems me in on every side, this moment of which I am made will be nothing more than a confused dream.

I look at the grey shimmering of Bouville at my feet. In the sun it looks like heaps of shells, of splinters of bone, of gravel. Lost in the midst of that debris, tiny fragments of glass or mica give little flashes from time to time. An hour from now, the trickles, the trenches, the thin furrows running between the shells will be streets, I shall be walking in those streets, between walls. Those little black dots which I can make out in the rue Boulibet—an hour from now I shall be one of them.

How far away from them I feel, up on this hill. It seems to me that I belong to another species. They come out of their offices after the day's work, they look at the houses and the squares with a satisfied expression, they think that it is *their* town. A "good solid town." They aren't afraid, they feel at home. They have never seen anything but the tamed water which runs out of the taps, the light which pours from the bulbs when they turn the switch, the half-breed, bastard trees which are held up with crutches. They are given proof, a hundred times a day, that everything is done mechanically, that the world obeys fixed, unchangeable laws. Bodies released in a vacuum all fall at the same speed, the municipal park is closed every day at four P.M. in winter, at six P.M. in summer, lead melts at 335° C., the last tram leaves the Town Hall at 11:05 P.M. They are peaceable, a little morose, they think about Tomorrow, in other words simply about another today; towns have only one day at their disposal which comes back exactly the same every morning. They barely tidy it up a little on Sundays. The idiots. It horrifies me to think that I am going to see their thick, self-satisfied faces again. They make laws, they write Populist novels, they get married, they commit the supreme folly of having children. And meanwhile, vast, vague Nature has slipped into their town, it has infiltrated everywhere, into their houses, into their offices, into themselves. It doesn't move, it lies low, and they are right inside it, they breathe it, and they don't see it, they imagine that it is outside, fifty miles away. I *see* it, that Nature, I *see* it . . . I know that its submissiveness is laziness, I know that it has no laws, that what they consider its constancy doesn't exist. It has nothing but habits and it may change those tomorrow.

What if something were to happen? What if all of a sudden it started palpitating? Then they would notice that it was there and they would think that their hearts were going to burst. What use would their dykes and ramparts and power-houses and furnaces and pile-drivers be to them then? That may happen at any time, straight away perhaps: the omens are there. For example, the father of a family may go for a walk, and he will see a red rag coming toward him across the street, as if the wind were blowing it. And when the rag gets close to him, he will see that it is a quarter of rotten meat, covered with dust, crawling and hopping along, a piece of tortured flesh rolling in the gutters and spasmodically shooting out jets of blood. Or else a mother may look at her child's cheek and ask him: "What's that—a pimple?" And she will see the flesh puff up slightly, crack and split open, and at the bottom of the split a third eye, a laughing eye, will appear. Or else they will feel something gently brushing against their bodies, like the caresses reeds give swimmers in a river. And they will realize that their clothes have become living things. And somebody else will feel something scratching inside his mouth. And he will go to a mirror, open his mouth: and his tongue will have become a huge living centipede, rubbing its legs together and scraping his palate. He will try to spit it out, but the centipede will be part of himself and he will have to tear it out with his hands. And hosts of things will appear for which people will have to find new names—a stone-eye, a big three-cornered arm, a toe-crutch, a spider-jaw, and somebody who has gone to sleep in his comfortable bed, in his quiet, warm bedroom, will wake up naked on a bluish patch of earth, in a forest of rustling pricks, rising all red and white towards the sky like the chimneys of Jouxtebouville, with big testicles half way out of the ground, hairy and bulbous, like onions. And birds will flutter around these pricks and peck at them with their beaks and make them bleed. Sperm will flow slowly, gently, from these wounds, sperm mingled with blood, warm and vitreous with little bubbles. Or else nothing like that will happen, no appreciable change will take place, but one morning when people open their blinds they will be surprised by a sort of horrible feeling brooding heavily over things and giving the impression of waiting. Just that: but if it lasts a little while, there will be hundreds of suicides. Well, yes, let things change a little, just to see, I ask for nothing better. Then we shall see other people suddenly plunged into solitude. Men all alone, entirely alone, with horrible monstrosities, will run through the streets, will go clumsily past me, their eyes staring, fleeing from their ills and carrying them with them, open-mouthed, with their tongue-insect beating its wings. Then I shall burst out laughing, even if my own body is covered with filthy, suspicious-looking scabs blossoming into fleshy flowers, violets and buttercups. I shall lean against a wall and as they go by I shall shout to them: "What have you done with your science? What have you done with your humanism? Where is your dignity as a thinking reed?" I shan't be afraid—or at least no more than I am now. Won't it still be existence, variations on existence? All those eyes which will slowly eat up a face— no doubt they will be superfluous, but no more superfluous than the first two. Existence is what I am afraid of.

Dusk is falling, the first lights are going on in the town. Good Lord, how *natural* the town looks in spite of all its geometric patterns, how crushed by the evening it seems. It's so . . . so obvious from here; is it possible that I should be the only one to see it? Is there nowhere another Cassandra on the top of a hill, looking down at a town engulfed in the depths of Nature? But what does it matter to me? What could I possibly tell her?

My body turns very gently toward the east, wobbles slightly and starts walking.

THE PROBLEM OF
JUSTIFYING INDUCTION

Bertrand Russell

We are all convinced that the sun will rise tomorrow. Why? Is this belief a mere blind outcome of past experience, or can it be justified as a reasonable belief? It is not easy to find a test by which to judge whether a belief of this kind is reasonable or not, but we can at least ascertain what sort of general beliefs would suffice, if true, to justify the judgement that the sun will rise tomorrow, and the many other similar judgements upon which our actions are based.

It is obvious that if we are asked why we believe that the sun will rise tomorrow, we shall naturally answer, "Because it always has risen every day." We have a firm belief that it will rise in the future, because it has risen in the past. If we are challenged as to why we believe that it will continue to rise as heretofore, we may appeal to the laws of motion: the earth, we shall say, is a freely rotating body, and such bodies do not cease to rotate unless something interferes from outside, and there is nothing outside to interfere with the earth between now and tomorrow. Of course it might be doubted whether we are quite certain that there is nothing outside to interfere, but this is not the interesting doubt. The interesting doubt is as to whether the laws of motion will remain in operation until tomorrow. If this doubt is raised, we find ourselves in the same position as when the doubt about the sunrise was first raised.

The *only* reason for believing that the laws of motion will remain in operation is that they have operated hitherto, so far as our knowledge of the past enables us to judge. It is true that we have a greater body of evidence from the past in favor of the laws of motion than we have in favor of the sunrise, because the sunrise is merely a particular case of fulfillment of the laws of motion, and there are countless other particular

FROM *The Problems of Philosophy,* chapter 6. Reprinted by permission of Oxford University Press.

cases. But the real question is: Do *any* number of cases of a law being fulfilled in the past afford evidence that it will be fulfilled in the future? If not, it becomes plain that we have no ground whatever for expecting the sun to rise tomorrow, or for expecting the bread we shall eat at our next meal not to poison us, or for any of the other scarcely conscious expectations that control our daily lives. It is to be observed that all such expectations are only *probable;* thus we have not to seek for a proof that they *must* be fulfilled, but only for some reason in favor of the view that they are *likely* to be fulfilled.

Now in dealing with this question we must, to begin with, make an important distinction, without which we should soon become involved in hopeless confusions. Experience has shown us that, hitherto, the frequent repetition of some uniform succession or coexistence has been a *cause* of our expecting the same succession or coexistence on the next occasion. Food that has a certain appearance generally has a certain taste, and it is a severe shock to our expectations when the familiar appearance is found to be associated with an unusual taste. Things which we see become associated, by habit, with certain tactile sensations which we expect if we touch them; one of the horrors of a ghost (in many ghost-stories) is that it fails to give us any sensations of touch. Uneducated people who go abroad for the first time are so surprised as to be incredulous when they find their native language not understood.

And this kind of association is not confined to men; in animals also it is very strong. A horse which has been often driven along a certain road resists the attempt to drive him in a different direction. Domestic animals expect food when they see the person who usually feeds them. We know that all these rather crude expectations of uniformity are liable to be misleading. The man who has fed the chicken every day throughout its life at last wrings its neck instead, showing that more refined views as to the uniformity of nature would have been useful to the chicken.

But in spite of the misleadingness of such expectations, they nevertheless exist. The mere fact that something has happened a certain number of times causes animals and men to expect that it will happen again. Thus our instincts certainly cause us to believe that the sun will rise tomorrow, but we may be in no better a position than the chicken which unexpectedly has its neck wrung. We have therefore to distinguish the fact that past uniformities *cause* expectations as to the future, from the question whether there is any reasonable ground for giving weight to such expectations after the question of their validity has been raised.

The problem we have to discuss is whether there is any reason for believing in what is called "the uniformity of nature." The belief in the uniformity of nature is the belief that everything that has happened or will happen is an instance of some general law to which there are *no* exceptions. The crude expectations which we have been considering are all subject to exceptions, and therefore liable to disappoint those who entertain them. But science habitually assumes, at least as a working hypothesis, that general rules which have exceptions can be replaced by general rules which have no exceptions. "Unsupported bodies in air fall" is a general rule to which balloons and airplanes are exceptions. But the laws of motion and the law of gravitation, which account for the fact that most bodies fall, also account for the fact that balloons and airplanes can rise; thus the laws of motion and the law of gravitation are not subject to these exceptions.

The belief that the sun will rise tomorrow might be falsified if the earth came suddenly into contact with a large body which destroyed its rotation; but the laws of motion and the law of gravitation would not be infringed by such an event. The business of science is to find uniformities, such as the laws of motion and the law of gravitation, to which, so far as our experience extends, there are no exceptions. In this search science has been remarkably successful, and it may be conceded that such uniformities have held hitherto. This brings us back to the question: Have we any reason, assuming that they have always held in the past, to suppose that they will hold in the future?

It has been argued that we have reason to know that the future will resemble the past, because what was the future has constantly become the past, and has always been found to resemble the past, so that we really have experience of the future, namely of times which were formerly future, which we may call past futures. But such an argument really begs the very question at issue. We have experience of past futures, but not of future futures, and the question is: Will future futures resemble past futures? This question is not to be answered by an argument which starts from past futures alone. We have therefore still to seek for some principle which shall enable us to know that the future will follow the same laws as the past.

The reference to the future in this question is not essential. The same question arises when we apply the laws that work in our experience to past things of which we have no experience—as, for example, in geology, or in theories as to the origin of the Solar System. The question we really have to ask is: "When two things have been found to be often associated, and no instance is known of the one occurring without the other, does the occurrence of one of the two, in a fresh instance, give any good ground for expecting the other?" On our answer to this question must depend the validity of the whole of our expectations as to the future, the whole of the results obtained by induction, and in fact practically all the beliefs upon which our daily life is based.

It must be conceded, to begin with, that the fact that two things have been found often together and never apart does not, by itself, suffice to *prove* demonstratively that they will be found together in the next case we examine. The most we can hope is that the oftener things are found together, the more probable it becomes that they will be found together another time, and that, if they have been found together often enough, the probability will amount *almost* to certainty. It can never quite reach certainty, because we know that in spite of frequent repetitions there sometimes is a failure at the last, as in the case of the chicken whose neck is wrung. Thus probability is all we ought to seek.

It might be urged, as against the view we are advocating, that we know all natural phenomena to be subject to the reign of law, and that sometimes, on the basis of observation, we can see that only one law can possibly fit the facts of the case. Now to this view there are two answers. The first is that, even if *some* law which has no exceptions applies to our case, we can never, in practice, be sure that we have discovered that law and not one to which there are exceptions. The second is that the reign of law would seem to be itself only probable, and that our belief that it will hold in the future, or in unexamined cases in the past, is itself based upon the very principle we are examining.

The principle we are examining may be called the *principle of induction,* and its two parts may be stated as follows:

1. When a thing of a certain sort A has been found to be associated with a thing of a certain other sort B, and has never been found dissociated from a thing of the sort B, the greater the number of cases in which A and B have been associated, the greater is the probability that they will be associated in a fresh case in which one of them is known to be present;
2. Under the same circumstances, a sufficient number of cases of association will make the probability of a fresh association nearly a certainty, and will make it approach certainty without limit.

As just stated, the principle applies only to the verification of our expectation in a single fresh instance. But we want also to know that there is a probability in favor of the general law that things of the sort A are *always* associated with things of the sort B, provided a sufficient number of cases of association are known, and no cases of failure of association are known. The probability of the general law is obviously less than the probability of the particular case, since if the general law is true, the particular case must also be true, whereas the particular case may be true without the general law being true. Nevertheless the probability of the general law is increased by repetitions, just as the probability of the particular case is. We may therefore repeat the two parts of our principle as regards the general law, thus:

1. The greater the number of cases in which a thing of the sort A has been found associated with a thing of the sort B, the more probable it is (if no cases of failure of association are known) that A is always associated with B;
2. Under the same circumstances, a sufficient number of cases of the association of A with B will make it nearly certain that A is always associated with B, and will make this general law approach certainty without limit.

It should be noted that probability is always relative to certain data. In our case, the data are merely the known cases of coexistence of A and B. There may be other data, which *might* be taken into account, which would gravely alter the probability. For example, a man who had seen a great many white swans might argue, by our principle, that on the data it was *probable* that all swans were white, and this might be a perfectly sound argument. The argument is not disproved by the fact that some swans are black, because a thing may very well happen in spite of the fact that some data render it improbable. In the case of the swans, a man might know that color is a very variable characteristic in many species of animals, and that, therefore, an induction as to color is peculiarly liable to error. But this knowledge would be a fresh datum, by no means proving that the probability relatively to our previous data had been wrongly estimated. The fact, therefore, that things often fail to fulfill our expectations is no evidence that our expectations will not *probably* be fulfilled in a given case or a given class of cases. Thus our inductive principle is at any rate not capable of being *disproved* by an appeal to experience.

The inductive principle, however, is equally incapable of being *proved* by an appeal to experience. Experience might conceivably confirm the inductive principle as regards the cases that have been already examined; but as regards unexamined cases, it is the inductive principle alone that can justify any inference from what has been examined to what has not been examined. All arguments which, on the basis of experience, argue as to the future or the unexperienced parts of the past or present, assume the inductive principle; hence we can never use experience to prove the inductive principle without begging the question. Thus we must either accept the inductive principle on the ground of its intrinsic evidence, or forgo all justification of our expectations about the future. If the principle is unsound, we have no reason to expect the sun to rise tomorrow, to expect bread to be more nourishing than a stone, or to expect that if we throw ourselves off the roof we shall fall. When we see what looks like our best friend approaching us, we shall have no reason to suppose that his body is not inhabited by the mind of our worst enemy or of some total stranger. All our conduct is based upon associations which have worked in the past, and which we therefore regard as likely to work in the future; and this likelihood is dependent for its validity upon the inductive principle.

The general principles of science, such as the belief in the reign of law, and the belief that every event must have a cause, are as completely dependent upon the inductive principle as are the beliefs of daily life. All such general principles are believed because mankind have found innumerable instances of their truth and no instances of their falsehood. But this affords no evidence for their truth in the future, unless the inductive principle is assumed.

Thus all knowledge which, on a basis of experience tells us something about what is not experienced, is based upon a belief which experience can neither confirm nor confute, yet which, at least in its more concrete applications, appears to be as firmly rooted in us as many of the facts of experience. The existence and justification of such beliefs raises some of the most difficult and most debated problems of philosophy.

BERTRAND RUSSELL'S DOUBTS ABOUT INDUCTION

Paul Edwards

I

A. In the celebrated chapter on induction in his *Problems of Philosophy,* Bertrand Russell asks the question: "Have we any reason, assuming that they (laws like the law of gravitation) have always held in the past, to suppose that these laws will hold in the future?" Earlier in the same chapter he raises the more specific question: "Do *any* number of cases of a law being fulfilled in the past afford evidence that it will be fulfilled in the future?" We may reformulate these questions in a way which lends itself more easily to critical discussion as follows:

1. Assuming that we possess n positive instances of a phenomenon, observed in extensively varied circumstances, and that we have not observed a single negative instance (where n is a large number), have we any reason to suppose that the $n + 1$st instance will also be positive?
2. Is there any number n of observed positive instances of a phenomenon which affords evidence that the $n + 1$st instance will also be positive?

It is clear that Russell uses "reason" synonymously with "good reason" and "evidence" with "sufficient evidence." I shall follow the same procedure throughout this article.

Russell asserts that unless we appeal to a nonempirical principle which he calls the "principle of induction," both of his questions must be answered in the negative. "Those who emphasized the scope of induction," he writes, "wished to maintain that all logic is empirical, and therefore could not be expected to realize that induction itself, their own darling, required a logical principle which obviously could not be proved inductively, and must therefore be *a priori* if it could be known at all." "We must either accept the inductive principle on the ground of its in-

FROM "Russell's Doubts about Induction," in *Mind,* vol. 58, no. 230 (April 1949). Reprinted by permission of Basil Blackwell Publisher.

trinsic evidence or forgo all justification of our expectations about the future."

In conjunction with the inductive principle, on the other hand, question (1) at least, he contends, can be answered in the affirmative. "Whether inferences from past to future are valid depends wholly, if our discussion has been sound, upon the inductive principle: if it is true, such inferences are valid." Unfortunately Russell does not make it clear whether in his opinion the same is true about question (2).

As against Russell, I shall try to show in this article that question (1) can be answered in the affirmative without in any way appealing to a nonempirical principle. I shall also attempt to show that, without in any way invoking a nonempirical principle, numbers of observed positive instances do frequently afford us evidence that unobserved instances of the same phenomenon are also positive. At the outset, I shall concentrate on question (1) since this is the more general question. Once we have answered question (1) it will require little further effort to answer question (2).

I want to emphasize here that, to keep this paper within manageable bounds, I shall refrain from discussing, at any rate explicitly, the questions "Are any inductive conclusions probable?" and "Are any inductive conclusions certain?" I hope to fill in this gap on another occasion.

It will be well to conduct our discussion in terms of a concrete example. Supposing a man jumps from a window on the fiftieth floor of the Empire State Building. Is there any reason to suppose that his body will move in the direction of the street rather than say in the direction of the sky or in a flat plane? There can be no doubt that any ordinary person and any philosophically unsophisticated scientist, would answer this question in the affirmative without in any way appealing to a nonempirical principle. He would say that there is an excellent reason to suppose that the man's body will move toward the street. This excellent reason, he would say, consists in the fact that whenever in the past a human being jumped out of a window of the Empire State Building his body moved in a downward direction; that whenever any human being anywhere jumped out of a house he moved in the direction of the ground; that, more generally, whenever a human body jumped or was thrown off an elevated locality in the neighbourhood of the earth, it moved downwards and not either upwards or at an angle of 180°; that the only objects which have been observed to be capable of moving upwards by themselves possess certain special characteristics which human beings lack; and finally in all the other observed confirmations of the theory of gravitation.

B. The philosophers who reject commonsense answers like the one just described, have relied mainly on three arguments. Russell himself explicitly employs two of them and some of his remarks make it clear that he also approves of the third. These three arguments are as follows: (a) Defenders of commonsense point to the fact that many inferences to unobserved events were subsequently, by means of direct observation, found to have resulted in true conclusions. However, any such appeal to observed results of inductive inferences is irrelevant. For the question at stake is: Have we ever a reason, assuming that all the large number of observed instances of a phenomenon are positive, to suppose that an instance which is still unobserved is also positive? The question is not: Have we ever a reason for supposing that instances which have by now been observed but were at one time unobserved are positive? In Russell's own words: "We have experience of past futures, but not of future futures, and the question is: Will future futures resemble past futures? This question is not to be answered by an argument which starts from past futures alone."

(b) Cases are known where at a certain time a large number of positive instances and not a single negative instance had been observed and where the next instance nevertheless turned out to be negative. "We know that in spite of frequent repetitions there sometimes is a failure at the last." The man, for instance, "who has fed the chicken every day throughout its life at last wrings its neck instead." Even in the case of the human being who is jumping out of the Empire State Building, "we may be in no better position than the chicken which unexpectedly has its neck wrung."

(c) The number of positive and negative necessary conditions for the occurrence of any event is infinite or at any rate too large to be directly observed by a human being or indeed by all human beings put together. None of us, for example, has explored every corner of the universe to make sure that there nowhere exists a malicious but powerful individual who controls the movements of the sun by means of wires which are too fine to be detected by any of our microscopes. None of us can be sure that there is no such Controller who, in order to play a joke with the human race, will prevent the sun from rising tomorrow. Equally, none of us can be sure that there is nowhere a powerful individual who can, if he wishes, regulate the movement of human bodies by means of ropes which are too thin to be detected by any of our present instruments. None of us therefore can be sure that when a man jumps out of the Empire State Building he will not be drawn skyward by the Controller of Motion. Hence we have no reason to suppose that the man's body will move in the direction of the street and not in the direction of the sky.

In connection with the last of these three arguments attention ought to be drawn to a distinction which Russell makes between what he calls the "interesting" and the "uninteresting" doubt about induction. The uninteresting doubt is doubt about the occurrence of a given event on the ground that not all the conditions which are known to be necessary are in fact known to be present. What Russell calls the interesting doubt is the doubt whether an event will take place although all the conditions known to be necessary are known to obtain. Russell's "interesting doubt," if I am not mistaken, is identical with Donald William's "tragic problem of induction."

II

As I indicated above, it is my object in this article to defend the commonsense answers to both of Russell's questions. I propose to show, in other words, that, without in any way calling upon a nonempirical principle for assistance, we often have a reason for supposing that a generalization will be confirmed in the future as it has been confirmed in the past. I also propose to show that numbers "of cases of a law being fulfilled in the past" do often afford evidence that it will be fulfilled in the future.

However, what I have to say in support of these answers is so exceedingly simple that I am afraid it will not impress the philosophers who are looking for elaborate and complicated theories to answer these questions. But I think I can make my case appear plausible even in the eyes of some of these philosophers if I describe at some length the general method of resolving philosophical puzzles which I shall apply to the problem of induction.

Let us consider a simple statement like "there are several thousand physicians in New York." We may call this a statement of commonsense, meaning thereby no more than that anybody above a certain very moderate level of instruction and intelligence would confidently give his assent to it.

The word "physician," as ordinarily used, is not entirely free from ambiguity. At times it simply means "person who possesses a medical degree from a recognized academic institution." At other times, though less often, it means the same as "person who possesses what is by ordinary standards a considerable skill in curing dieases." On yet other occasions when people say about somebody that he is a physician they mean both that he has a medical degree and that he possesses a skill in curing diseases which considerably exceeds that of the average layman.

Let us suppose that in the commonsense statement "there are several thousand physicians in New York" the word "physician" is used exclusively in the last-mentioned sense. This assumption will simplify our discussion, but it is not at all essential to any of the points I am about to make. It is essential, however, to realize that when somebody asserts in ordinary life that there are several thousand physicians in New York, he is using the word "physician" in one or other of the ordinary senses just listed. By "physician" he does not mean for example "person who can speedily repair bicycles" or "person who can cure any conceivable illness in less than two minutes."

Now, supposing somebody were to say "Really, there are no physicians at all in New York," in the belief that he was contradicting and refuting commonsense. Supposing that on investigation it turns out that by "physician" he does not mean "person who has a medical degree and who has considerably more skill in curing disease than the average layman." It turns out that by "physician" he means "person who has a medical degree and who can cure any conceivable illness in less than two minutes."

What would be an adequate reply to such an "enemy of commonsense"? Clearly it would be along the following lines: "What you say is true. There are no physicians in New York—in *your* sense of the word. There are no persons in New York who can cure any conceivable disease in less than two minutes. But this in no way contradicts the commonsense view expressed by "there are several thousand physicians in New York." For the latter asserts no more than that there are several thousand pople in New York who have a medical degree and who possess a skill in curing disease which considerably exceeds that of the average layman. You are guilty of *ignoratio elenchi* [irrelevant proof] since the proposition you refute is different from the proposition you set out to refute."

Our discussion from here on will be greatly simplified by introducing a few technical terms. Let us, firstly, call *"ignoratio elenchi* by *redefinition"* any instance of *ignoratio elenchi* in which (i) the same sentence expresses both the proposition which ought to be proved and the proposition which is confused with it and where (ii) in the latter employment of the sentence one or more of its parts are used in a sense which is different from their ordinary sense or senses. Secondly, let us refer to any redefinition of a word which includes all that the ordinary definition of the word includes but which includes something else as well as a *"high* redefinition"; and to the sense which is defined by a high redefinition we shall refer as a high sense of the word. Thus "person who has a medical degree and who is capable of curing any conceivable disease in less than two minutes" is a high redefinition of "physician" and anybody using the word in that fashion is using it in a high sense. Thirdly, we shall refer to a redefinition of a word which includes something but not all of what the ordinary definition includes and which includes nothing else as a *"low* redefinition"; and the sense which is defined by a low redefinition we shall call a low sense of the word. "Person capable of giving first aid" or "person who knows means of alleviating pain" would be low redefinitions of "physician." Finally, it will be convenient to call a statement in which a word is used in a high or in a low sense a *redefinitional statement*. If the word is used in a high sense we shall speak of a highdefinitional statement; if it is used in a low sense we shall speak of a lowdefinitional statement.

A short while ago, I pointed out that the man who says "there are no physicians in New York," meaning that there are no people in New York who have a medical degree and who can cure any conceivable illness in less than two minutes, is not really contradicting the commonsense view that there are physicians in New York. I pointed out that he would be guilty of what in our technical language is called an *ignoratio elenchi* by redefinition. Now, it seems to me that the relation between the assertion of various philosophers that past experience never constitutes a reason for prediction or generalization except perhaps in conjunction with a nonempirical principle and the commonsense view that past experience does often by itself constitute a reason for inferences to unobserved events has some striking resemblances to the relation between the redefinitional statement about physicians in New York and the commonsense view which this redefinitional statement fails to refute. And more generally, it strongly seems to me that almost all the bizarre pronouncements of philosophers—their "paradoxes," their "silly" theories—are in certain respects strikingly like the statement that there are no physicians in New York, made by one who means to assert that there are no people in New York who have medical degrees and who are capable of curing any conceivable disease in less than two minutes.

In making the last statement I do not mean to deny that there are also important differences between philosophical paradoxes and the highdefinitional statement about physicians. There are three differences in particular which have to be mentioned if my subsequent remarks are not to be seriously misleading. Firstly, many of the philosophical paradoxes are not without some point; they do often draw attention to likenesses and differences which ordinary usage obscures. Secondly, the redefinitions which are implicit in philosophical paradoxes do quite often, though by no means always, receive a certain backing from ordinary usage. Frequently, that is to say, there is a secondary sense or trend in ordinary usage which corresponds to the philosophical redefinition, the "real" sense of the word. Thirdly, philosophical paradoxes are invariably ambiguous in a sense in which the highdefinitional statement about the physicians is not ambiguous.

Now, while fully admitting all these (and other) differences, I wish to insist on the great likenesses between philosophical paradoxes and the redefinitional statement about the physicians. And in this article I am mainly concerned with the likenesses, not with the differences. My main object of course is to point out the likenesses between the highdefinitional statement "there are no physicians in New York" and the statement that past experience never by itself affords a reason for making inferences to unobserved events. However, my points there will be clearer if I first make them in connection with another celebrated paradox.

Following Plato, Berkeley argued in favor of the view that heat and cold are not really "in the object." Ordinary people would unhesitatingly say that water of e.g., 50° Centigrade is hot. Against this, Plato and Berkeley would point out that to a man who a moment before had held his hands in a jug of water with a temperature of 80° C., the water of 50° C. would appear cold. Similarly, to a race of individuals whose body-temperature was say 75° C., water of 50° would regularly appear cold. But the percepts of those to whom the water of 50° appears cold are just as genuine as the percepts of people to whom the water appears hot. Now, since it would be wrong to say that the water of 50° is really cold simply because of these genuine percepts of cold, it cannot any more rationally be said to be hot. The cold has "just as good a right to be considered real" as the hot; and therefore, "to avoid favoritism, we are compelled to deny that in itself" the water is either hot or cold.

It is not difficult to show that this argument is a case of *ignoratio elenchi* by redefinition. When an ordinary person says that water of 50° C. is hot all he means is that human beings, with their body temperature being what it is, would in *all ordinary circumstances* have sense-impressions of heat on coming into contact with such water. In saying that water of 50° is hot, is *really* hot, an ordinary person in no way denies that under certain *special* conditions a human being would have genuine sense-impressions of cold. He also in no way denies that to a race of individuals whose body temperature is 75° the water would genuinely appear cold. Pointing to these facts does therefore not refute the ordinary man. Berkeley is clearly guilty of a high redefinition of "hot" or "really hot." To him something is hot only if, in addition to appearing hot to human beings in ordinary circumstances, it also appears hot to them under special circumstances and if it appears hot to beings with a body temperature which is much greater than the actual body temperature of human beings.

However, this is not quite accurate since, like most other philosophical paradoxes, the paradox about heat and cold has a double meaning. It would be inaccurate simply to say that Berkeley is guilty of *ignoratio elenchi* by redefinition. On the other hand, without in any way being inaccurate, it can be said that Berkeley and Plato have laid themselves open to the following dilemma: "Either you mean by 'hot' what is ordinarily meant by it—if you do, then what you say is plainly false; or else you are using 'hot' in a high sense—if so what you say is true, but in that case you are guilty of *ignoratio elenchi* by redefinition. In either event you have failed to refute commonsense." Very similar answers can also be made to Berkeley's and Russell's arguments concerning colors, shapes, and the other qualities which commonsense believes to exist independently of being perceived.

At the same time it must be admitted that Berkeley's arguments have a certain value. In ordinary speech we make a fairly rigid distinction between "real" and "unreal" data. Among the unreal data we lump together both the percepts which we have under special conditions (and percepts which do and would appear to beings differently constituted from ourselves) and what we experience *e.g.,* in dreams and hallucinations. "Real" we call only those percepts which a normal observer has under certain standard conditions.

A classification of this sort obscures the many likenesses between the "real" percepts and percepts appearing under special conditions, while also hiding the many differences between the latter and data which are experienced in dreams and hallucinations.

The situation becomes quite clear if we divide data into three and not merely into two groups, as follows:

> the R-data: percepts appearing to a normal observer under standard conditions,
>
> the A-data: percepts appearing to a normal observer under special conditions or to an abnormal observer in certain normal or special circumstances, and
>
> the D-data: data appearing in dreams, hallucinations, etc.

It is unnecessary for our purposes to discuss exactly what are the likenesses between the R-data and the A-data. It is unnecessary, too, to discuss what exactly are the differences between the A-data and the D-data. It is sufficient to point out that while Berkeley is wrong in believing or suggesting that there are no differences between the R-data and the A-data, he is right in insisting that the differences between the R-data and the A-data are not nearly as great as ordinary speech suggests. In the case of colors, Berkeley's argument has the further merit of bringing out the fact that the expression "X's real color" has *two* perfectly proper senses. His argument helps one to realize that "X's real colors" may mean "the color which X exhibits to a normal observer under certain standard conditions" *as well as* "the color which X exhibits to a normal observer under a finer instrument than the human eye, e.g., a microscope."

III

A. Supposing a man, let us call him M, said to us "I have not yet found any physicians in New York." Suppose we take him to Park Avenue and introduce him to Brown, a man who has a medical degree and who has cured many people suffering from diseases of the car. Brown admits, however, that he has not been able to cure *all* the patients who ever consulted him. He also admits that many of his cures took a long time, some as long as eight years. On hearing this, M says "Brown certainly isn't a physician."

Supposing we next take M to meet Black who has a medical degree and who can prove to M's and to our satisfaction that he has cured every patient who ever consulted him. Moreover, none of Black's cures took more than three years. However, on hearing that some of Black's cures took as long as two years and ten months, M says "Black certainly isn't a physician either."

Finally we introduce M to White who has a medical degree and who has cured every one of his patients in less than six months. When M hears that some of White's cures took as long as five and a half months, he is adamant and exclaims "White—what a ridiculous error to call him a physician!"

At this stage, if not much sooner, all of us would impatiently ask M: What on earth do you mean by "physician"? And we would plainly be justified in adding: Whatever you may mean by "physician," in any sense in which we ever use the word, Black and Brown and White are physicians and very excellent ones at that.

Let us return now to Russell's doubt about the sun's rising tomorrow or about what would happen to a man who jumps out of the Empire State Building. Let us consider what Russell would say in reply to the following question: Supposing that the observed confirmatory instances for the theory of gravitation were a million or ten million times as extensive as they now are and that they were drawn from a very much wider field; would we then have a reason to suppose that the man will fall into the street and not move up into the sky? It is obvious that Russell and anybody taking his view would say "No." He would reply that though our *expectation* that the man's body will move in the direction of the street would be even stronger then than it is at present, we would still be without a *reason*.

Next, let us imagine ourselves to be putting the following question to Russell: Supposing the world were such that no accumulation of more than five hundred observed positive instances of a phenomenon has ever been found to be followed by a negative instance; supposing, for instance, that all the chickens who have ever been fed by the same man for 501 days in succession or more are still alive and that all the men too are still alive feeding the chickens every day—would the observed confirmations of the law of gravity in that case be a reason to suppose that the man jumping out of the Empire State Building will move in the direction of the street and not in the direction of the sky? I am not quite sure what Russell would say in reply to this question. Let us assume he would once again answer "No—past experience would not even then ever be a *reason*."

Thirdly and finally, we have to consider what Russell would say to the following question: Supposing we had explored every corner of the universe with instruments millions of times as fine and accurate as any we now possess and that we had yet failed to discover any Controller of the movements of human bodies—would we then in our predictions about the man jumping out of the Empire State Building be in a better position than the chicken is in predicting its meals? Would our past observations then be a reason for our prediction? Whatever Russell would in fact say to this, it is clear that his remarks concerning the "interesting" doubt about induction require him to answer our question in the negative. He would have to say something like this: "Our *expectation* that the man's body will move in a downward direction will be even stronger than it is now. However, without invoking a non-empirical principle, we shall not *really* be in a better position than the chicken. We should still fail to possess a *reason*."

As in the case of the man who refused to say that Brown, Black, and White were doctors, our natural response to all this will be to turn to Russell and say: What do you mean by "being in a better position"? What on earth do you mean by "a reason"? And, furthermore, why should anybody be interested in a reason in your sense of the word?

Russell's remarks about the need for a general principle like his principle of induction to serve as major premise in every inductive argument make it clear what he means by a reason: like the Rationalists and Hume (in most places), he means by "reason" a *logically conclusive* reason and by "evidence" *deductively conclusive* evidence. When "reason" is used in this sense, it must be admitted that past observations can never by themselves be a reason for any prediction whatsoever. But "reason" is not used in this sense when, in science or in ordinary life, people claim to have a reason for a prediction.

So far as I can see, there are three different trends in the ordinary usage of "reason for an inductive conclusion" and according to none of them does the word mean "logically conclusive reason." Among the three trends one is much more prominent than the others. It may fitly be called the main sense of the word. According to this main sense, what we mean when we claim that we have a reason for a prediction is that the past observation of this phenomenon or of analogical phenomena are of a certain kind: they are exclusively or predominantly positive, the number of the positive observations is at least fairly large, and they come from extensively varied sets of circumstances. This is of course a very crude formulation. But for the purposes of this article it is, I think, sufficient.

Next, there is a number of trends according to which we mean very much less than this. Occasionally, for instance, we simply mean that it is *reasonable* to infer the inductive conclusion. And clearly it may be reasonable to infer an inductive conclusion for which we have no reason in the main sense. Thus let us suppose I know that Parker will meet Schroeder in a game in the near future and that it is imperative for me not to suspend my judgment but to come to a conclusion as to who will win. Supposing I know nothing about their present form and nothing also about the type of court on which the match is to be played. All I know is that Parker and Schroeder have in the previous two seasons met six times, Parker scoring four victories to Schroeder's two. In these circumstances it would be reasonable for me to predict that Parker will win and unreasonable to predict that Schroeder will win. Clearly however, in the main sense of the word I have no reason for either prediction.

Again there is a trend according to which any positive instance of a phenomenon is *a* reason for concluding that the next instance of the phenomenon will be positive. Thus in the circumstances described in the preceding paragraph, it would be quite proper to say we have *more reason* for supposing that Parker will win than for predicting Schroeder's victory. It would be quite proper also to say that we have *some reason* for supposing that Schroeder will win. It would be proper to say this even if Schroeder had won only one of the six matches. To all these and similar trends in the ordinary usage of "reason for an inductive conclusion" I shall from now on refer as the second ordinary sense of the word.

There can be no doubt that in both these ordinary senses of the word, we frequently have a reason for an inductive conclusion. In these senses we have an excellent reason for supposing that the man jumping out of the Empire State Building will move in the direction of the street, that the sun will rise tomorrow and that Stalin will die before the year 2000. The answer to question (1) is therefore a firm and clear "Yes": in many domains we have a multitude of exclusively positive instances coming from extensively different circumstances.

The same is true if "reason" is used in the third ordinary sense.

However, . . . it will be convenient and, I think, not at all misleading to speak as if what I have called the main sense is the *only* ordinary sense of "reason for an inductive conclusion."

It should now be clear that, when Russell says that observed instances are never by themselves a reason for an inductive conclusion, he is guilty of an *ignoratio elenchi* by redefinition. His assertion that the premises of an inductive argument never by themselves constitute a *logically conclusive* reason for an inductive conclusion in no way contradicts the commonsense assertion that they frequently constitute a reason *in the ordinary sense of the word*. Russell's definition of "reason" is indeed in one respect not a redefinition since in certain contexts we do use "reason" to mean "deductively conclusive reason." However, it is a redefinition in that we never in ordinary life use "reason" in Russell's sense when we are talking about inductive arguments.

Moreover, if "reason" means "deductively conclusive reason," Russell's questions are no more genuinely questions than e.g., the sentence "Is a father a female parent?" For, since part of the definition of "inductive inference" is inference from something observed to something unobserved, it is a *contradiction* to say that an inference is both inductive and at the same time in the same respect deductively conclusive. Russell's "interesting" doubt, then, is no more sensible or interesting than the "doubt" whether we shall ever see something invisible or find an object which is a father and also female or an object which is a man but not a human being.

In a similar fashion, Russell's remarks about the future future which we quoted in Section 1B constitute an *ignoratio elenchi* by redefinition. If the word "future" is used in its ordinary sense in the statement "the future will resemble the past and the present in certain respects" then we have plenty of evidence to support it. For in the ordinary sense of the word, "future" simply means "period which has to the past and the present the relation of happening after it." In its ordinary sense, "future" does *not* mean "period which has to the past and the present the relation of happening after it *and* which can never itself be experienced *as a present*." The period which is referred to by "future" in its ordinary sense may very well one day be experienced as a present.

In the ordinary sense of the word "future" therefore, what Russell calls past futures *are* futures. They are futures in relation to certain other periods which preceded them. Now, the appeal to the fact that past futures resembled past pasts and past presents constitutes excellent inductive evidence for the conclusion that the future will resemble the past and the present. Stated fully, the argument is as follows: a period which has to the past and present the relation of happening after it will resemble the past and the present in certain respects because in the past periods which stood in the same temporal relation to other periods were found to resemble those periods in these respects.

It should be emphasized that in the conclusion of this argument "future" means "future future," as that phrase would normally be understood. It refers to a period which by the time at which the statement is made has not yet been experienced, i.e., has not yet become a present or a past.

The appeal to the resemblance between past futures and past pasts and presents is not to the point only if in the sentence "the future will resemble the past and the present" the word "future" means "period which has to the present the relation of occurring after it *and* which can never be experienced as a present." In that case, of course past futures are not really futures. For, when they were experienced they were experienced as presents. However, anybody who in ordinary life or in science says or implies that the future will resemble the past and the present does not use "future" in this sense. He means to assert something about a future which may one day be experienced as a present.

B. If Russell had answered in the affirmative any of the three questions which we imagined ourselves to be addressing to him, his question (1) would be a genuine question in the sense that it could then not be disposed of by an examination of definitions alone. But even then Russell would have been guilty of *ignoratio elenchi* by high redefinition. For in order to have a reason, in the ordinary sense of the word, for inferring that the next instance of a certain phenomenon is positive it is not necessary to observe all the positive and negative necessary conditions for the occurrence of this instance. Nor is it necessary that the collection of positive observed instances should be larger or taken from more extensively different circumstances than many we actually have. Nor, finally, is it necessary that breakdowns should never have occurred in *any* domain. All that is necessary in this connection is that there should have been no breakdowns in the same domain. Or if any did occur in the same domain they must have proved capable of correlation with certain special features which are known not to be present in the subject of the prediction.

Anybody who takes the trouble to observe the ordinary usage of the word "reason" in connection with inductive arguments can easily check up on these claims.

It may be interesting to return for a moment to the case of the chicken which finally had its neck wrung. If we had explored every corner of the universe with wonderfully fine instruments and failed to discover a Controller of human movements, then in any ordinary sense of "being in a better position" we should undoubtedly, be in a better position in the case of the man jumping out of the Empire State Building than the chicken in regard to its meals. If Russell even then denied that we are in a better position he is surely using the phrase "being in a better position" in a strange sense. Or else he is asserting a very plain falsehood. For to say that possession of one set of observed facts, say P, puts one in a better position with regard to a certain inductive conclusion, say c, than possession of another set of observed facts, say Q, simply means that P is a reason for c while Q is not, or that P is a better reason than Q.

Moreover, even without having explored every corner of the universe, we *are* in a very much better position in the case of predicting the sun's rising or the movement of a man jumping from the Empire State Building than the chicken is regarding its meals. The truth is that Russell's analogy, although it is not wholly pointless, is very weak indeed. Its only merit consists in bringing out the fact that neither we nor the chicken have explored every corner of the universe. On the other hand, there are two important differences which Russell obscures when he says that even in the case of our most trusted scientific theories we may be in no better a position than the chicken. Firstly, the number of observed instances supporting our prediction in a case like the man's jumping from the Empire State Building is obviously much greater than the number of positive instances observed by the chicken. And secondly, although we cannot definitely say that there is nowhere a Controller of human motions, we certainly have no reason whatsoever to suppose that one exists. We have no reason whatsoever to suppose that a living individual, in any ordinary sense of "control," controls the movements of human beings who jump out of a house. The chicken, on the other hand, if it knows anything, knows that it depends for its meals on another living object.

C. Let us now turn to question (2): Is there any number, *n,* of observed positive instances of a phenomenon which affords evidence that the *n +* 1st instance will also be positive? I have already mentioned the familiar fact that scientists as well as ordinary people of a certain level of intelligence do not rely for their inductive conclusions on the number of observed positive instances exclusively. However, it will be easier to discuss the question before us if we proceed on the assumption that according to commonsense the strength of the past experience as evidence depends on the number of observed positive instances and on nothing else. All important points can be made more easily if we proceed on this assumption.

Now, in two senses the answer to question (2) must be admitted to be a clear "No." Firstly, even if there were in every domain or in some domains a number of observed positive instances which constitutes the dividing line between evidence and non-evidence, or, as it is more commonly expressed, between sufficient and insufficient evidence, there is no reason whatsoever to suppose that the number would be the same for different domains. There is no reason to suppose that in the domain of animal learnings, for example, the number is the same as in the domain of the movements of the heavenly bodies. But, secondly, there is no such number in *any* domain. For we are here clearly faced with a case of what is sometimes called "continuous variation." There is no more *a* number dividing sufficient from insufficient evidence than there is a number dividing bald people from those who are not bald or poor people from people who are not poor.

These facts, however, imply nothing against commonsense. For, from the fact that there is no rigid division between sufficient and insufficient evidence it does not follow that there are no cases of sufficient evidence. From the fact that there is no number which constitutes the borderline between adequate collections of positive instances and those which are not adequate it does not follow that no number of positive instances is adequate. Although we cannot point to a number which divides bald people from people who are not bald, we can without any hesitation say that a man without a single hair on his head is bald while one with a million hairs on his head is not bald.

Furthermore, just as we can say about many people that they are bald and about many others that they are not bald although we have not counted the number of hairs on their heads and just as we can say that Rockefeller is rich although we cannot even approximately say what is the dollar-equivalent of his total possessions, so we can very often say *that* a number of observed instances constitutes sufficient evidence although we cannot say *what* this number is. The number of instances supporting the theory of gravitation which human beings have observed is for example more than sufficient evidence in any ordinary sense of the word—for supposing that the man jumping out of the Empire State Building will move in a downward direction. But nobody knows what this number is. Human beings simply do not bother to keep records of all instances which confirm the law of gravity.

Questions for Discussion

1. Sartre's character, Roquentin, reflects that people take as submissiveness on nature's part what is really only "laziness." "Nature," he says, "has no laws. . . . It has nothing but habits and these it may change tomorrow." What literal sense, if any, can be given to this assertion?

2. Suppose Roquentin's grotesque fantasy of a future that violates every-

one's expectations were to come about in fact. Would this vindicate the claim that induction is an unsound method of reasoning?

3. "All those eyes which will slowly eat up a face—no doubt they will be superfluous, but no more superfluous than the first two," reflects Sartre's Roquentin. What point is Sartre making here? Is it correct?

4. "The principle we are examining," says Russell, "may be stated as follows: When a thing of a certain sort A has been found to be associated with a certain other sort B, and has never been found dissociated from a thing of the sort B, the greater the number of cases in which A and B have been associated, the greater is the probability that they will be associated in a fresh case in which one of them is known to be present." Consider this problem: Your being alive at midnight has invariably been found by you to be associated with your being alive a day later. How might Russell meet the objection that, according to the above, the probability that you will continue to live should increase, the older you get?

5. Do you consider Russell guilty, as Edwards charges, of a "high redefinition" of the term "reason," making it mean "deductively conclusive reason"? If Russell is in fact using "reason" in its ordinary sense, can he escape the alternate objection that, far from being an "interesting doubt," it is then self-contradictory to deny that inductive evidence provides a reason for the inductive conclusion?

6. Something which constitutes a typical case of the sort of thing we call an F, which satisfies the accepted conditions for being an F, cannot be supposed not to be an F without doing violence to the very meaning of the term "F." Arguments of this form have come to be called "paradigm case arguments." It has been questioned whether such arguments are always sound. Edwards uses this type of argument against Russell, arguing that induction cannot be supposed to be unreasonable without doing violence to the meaning of "reasonable." Is this or is this not a valid application of the paradigm case argument?

7. (For very ambitious students) C. S. Peirce and Hans Reichenbach have argued for induction as follows: Any method at all for extrapolating from the observed to the unobserved would, if it were repeatedly successful, be one that a person would, on purely inductive grounds, be justified in employing. Thus it seems that induction is a method of arriving at predictions that can, as it were, cash in on the success of any method that proves successful, and hence cannot repeatedly fail where *any* method repeatedly succeeds. Does this constitute a justification of induction? If not, why not?

Selected Readings

AYER, A. J. *Probability and Evidence.* New York: Columbia University Press, 1972. A contemporary defense of the Humean outlook.

BARKER, S. *Induction and Hypothesis.* Ithaca, New York: Cornell University Press, 1957. Proposes solutions to puzzles of inductive reasoning.

BLACK, M. "Induction." In *Encyclopedia of Philosophy,* Vol. 4. edited by P. Edwards. New York: Macmillan, 1957. A concise overview of the subject.

———. *Problems of Analysis.* Ithaca, New York: Cornell University Press, 1954.

CARNAP, R. *The Logical Foundations of Probability.* Chicago: Chicago University Press, 1950. Offers a solution on deductive grounds.

EDWARDS, P. "Bertrand Russell's Doubts about Induction." *Mind* (1949). Offers a solution to the problem from the perspective of ordinary language.

GOODMAN, N. *Fact, Fiction and Forecast.* Cambridge, Massachusetts: Harvard University Press, 1955. New problems of inductive confirmation.

HUME, D. *An Enquiry Concerning Human Understanding.* Chaps. 4–6.

———. *A Treatise of Human Nature.* Book 1, Part III.
The classic statements of the problem of induction.

KATZ, J. *The Problem of Induction and Its Solution.* Chicago: University of Chicago Press, 1962. A linguistic approach.

KEYNES, J. M. *A Treatise on Probability.* London: Macmillan, 1963. A solution using deduction.

KNEALE, W. *Probability and Induction.* Oxford: Clarendon Press, 1949. An empiricist approach.

KYBURG, H., and NAGEL, E., eds. *Induction: Some Current Issues.* Middleton, Connecticut: Wesleyan University Press, 1963. Essays on the current state of the problem.

POPPER, K. *The Logic of Scientific Discovery.* London: Hutchinson, 1959. Rejects induction and offers another explanation of the method of science.

REICHENBACH, H. *Theory of Probability.* Berkeley: University of California Press, 1949. A technical attempt at an empirical solution.

RUSSELL, B. *Human Knowledge, Its Scope and Limits.* New York: Simon & Schuster, 1948.

———. *The Problems of Philosophy.* Oxford: Oxford University Press, 1912.
Modern Humean accounts of the problem.

SALMON, W. *The Foundations of Scientific Inference.* Pittsburgh: University of Pittsburgh Press, 1967. An analysis and empiricist solution of the problem.

STRAWSON, P. F. *Introduction to Logical Theory.* London: Methuen, 1952. Offers a solution by means of ordinary language analysis.

TOULMIN, S. *The Uses of Argument.* Cambridge: Cambridge University Press, 1958. A novel approach using ordinary language analysis.

WILL, F. "Will the Future Be Like the Past?" *Mind* (1947). A critique of Russell.

Chapter 6

Skepticism: Can We Know Anything?

The townspeople in Luigi Pirandello's comic masterpiece, *Right You Are . . .* are dying to know why Mr. Ponza, the new official, never allows his wife to leave the house. Laudisi, the skeptic, insists that their curiosity cannot possibly be satisfied: they will never find out the truth for the reason that there is no such thing as "the truth." Each person, he claims, has his or her own personal way of perceiving a situation that is as good as any other. Ponza's mother-in-law tells the group that Ponza keeps his wife a prisoner. Ponza later explains that his first wife died four years ago and that his mother-in-law, who is insane, will not face the fact that her daughter died and was succeeded by a second Mrs. Ponza. The mother-in-law then retorts that it is Ponza who is insane and who falsely believes her daughter is dead. Laudisi argues that Ponza and his mother-in-law are both right, but the other townspeople cannot understand how that could be possible. Can you? How can opposite accounts of the same facts be equally true? What can be meant by "true" in such a view?

Pirandello has distilled the essence of a familiar predicament we face in trying to understand ourselves and others. Who has not had the experience—as a juror at a trial, or as a parent or older brother or sister refereeing a dispute between children, or as a friend of two disputants—of listening to complaints from all sides, of believing first one person, then another, finally despairing of ever knowing the truth. There is an old story about a marriage counselor to whom a married couple brings their complaints about each other. The wife is accompanied by her mother. First the wife tells her side of the story. "You are absolutely right," intones the counselor. Then the husband tells his story. "You are right," declares the counselor. "Look here," the wife's mother interjects, "They can't both be right, can they?" The counselor smiles at her. "You too are right," says he.

Where human relations are concerned, so much is a matter of how we interpret our own and others' actions and motives that we may well despair of achieving reliable knowledge, in the sense of arriving at one true account of the matter, and we may feel that we must settle for a sympathetic appreciation of each person's point of view. Whether Ponza was mistreating his wife or protecting her depends, in part at least, on just how he perceives his situation, and that is up to him to say. But surely the "hard facts" about what has actually occurred, such as whether or not his first wife died, are objectively knowable, independently of anyone's interpretation. There must be tangible evidence, such as a death certificate in the files of the town hall, which can settle the matter. In the play, it turns out that all the records of the town from which the Ponzas came were destroyed in an earthquake. Does this show, as Laudisi suggests, that there is no truth to be known, or merely that it is difficult (perhaps impossible) to ascertain the truth in this particular case?

One important improvement that philosophical skepticism achieves over the rather unreflective skepticism of Laudisi is its shift of focus from truth to knowledge. We may rightly object to the suggestion that there is no such thing as objective truth or that the same assertion can be true for one person and false for another. The first suggestion denies a plain fact—that we apply the word "true" to some statements and "false" to others and that we often reach agreement on these matters. The second suggestion violates the principle of noncontradiction, the fundamental principle of logic, namely, that no statement can be both true and false. But what is really bothering Laudisi can be stated in a more precise and less objectionable way—in terms of knowledge, rather than truth—and that is what philosophical skepticism has done.

The earliest statement of skepticism was that of Protagoras, a Greek sophist of great renown in the fifth century B.C. The sophists were itinerant teachers of rhetoric, literature, and philosophy, whose social function seems to have been to educate merchants and to teach them to argue effectively in contractual disputes before the courts. Plato's *Theatetus,* a dialogue devoted to the problem of defining knowledge, contains a criticism by Socrates of the assertion by Protagoras that "man is the measure of all things." Socrates takes Protagoras to mean, like Pirandello's Laudisi, that each person has a right to his or her own opinion on any matter. "You see then," says Socrates to Theatetus, "that a doubt about the reality of sense is easily raised, since there may even be a doubt whether we are awake or in a dream. . . . Then my perception is true to me . . . and, as Protagoras says, to myself I am judge of what is and what is not to me." Socrates proceeds to ridicule this excessively democratic view of knowledge in a passage so witty that it is worth quoting at length:

> I wonder that he [Protagoras] did not begin his book on truth with a declaration that a pig or a dog-faced baboon, or some other yet stranger monster which has sensation, is the measure of all things; then he might have shown a magnificent contempt for our opinion of him by informing us at the outset that while we were reverencing him like a God for his wisdom he was no better than a tadpole, not to speak of his fellowmen—would this not have produced an overwhelming effect? For if truth is only sensation, and no man can discern another's feelings better than he, or has any superior right to determine whether his opinion is true or false, but each . . . is to himself the sole judge, and everything that he judges is true and right, why, my friend, should Protagoras be preferred . . . and deserve to be well paid, and we poor ignoramuses have to go to him, if each one is the measure of his own wisdom?

Socrates was attacking the claim that everyone's perceptions are equally true by showing that it leads to the notion that no one's beliefs are any better than those of a fool and is thus equivalent to the claim that everyone's beliefs are equally false. Later in the dialogue Socrates considers definitions of knowledge, first as true opinion and then as reasoned or well-substantiated opinion, and finds them faulty. The dialogue ends with the confession that no one knows what knowledge is, which would sound even more skeptical than Protagoras except that Socrates is doubtful not so much about the existence of knowledge as about our ability to define it with sufficient precision.

Although Socrates and his disciple, Plato, were not really skeptics but merely insisted that claims to knowledge must satisfy rigorous standards of precision and consistency, the Academy that Plato founded was later taken over by members of the Skeptical school. The leaders of this school, Pyrrho and then Carneades, taught that no beliefs are demonstrably true. Pyrrho concluded that there are no rational guides to action, so that we might as well do as we like without worrying about the consequences, which explains the story related in the previous chapter about his refusal to turn away from precipices. Carneades drew the more cautious conclusion that we should guide our actions by estimates of probability rather than waiting for unrealizable certitude.

In the modern age René Descartes revived the skeptical tradition by arguing, in his *Meditations* and *Discourse on Method,* that our perceptual judgments (i.e., the judgments we make about what we see, feel, etc.) are so much less precise and provable than our mathematical laws that the former do not deserve to be considered knowledge. For all we know, he reasoned, echoing the passage from Plato's *Theatetus* quoted above, everything we perceive may be an illusion or a dream. Descartes thought he was saved from skepticism by his proofs of the existence of a benevolent creator who would not allow him to be consistently deceived. Later philosophers, not convinced by his proofs of God, have naturally felt the need for some alternate means of salvation from skepticism.

John Locke took a further step toward Pyrrho's position by maintaining that only our own sensations are directly known to us through perception. Our beliefs in the existence of material objects and their properties, he claimed, are inferred from what our senses report. Failing to give any justification for such inferences, he provoked George Berkeley to conclude, as we saw in chapter 2, that they are in fact mistaken. Berkeley, in turn, thought, like Descartes, that he could save himself from the precipice of skepticism by appealing to God as the guarantor of our knowledge of objective reality; but David Hume, as we have seen, soon closed off that avenue of retreat in his *Dialogues Concerning Natural Religion*.

This skeptical tradition is the target of Norman Malcolm's attack, in our selection from his influential book, *Knowledge and Certainty*. Malcolm is one of the foremost disciples of Ludwig Wittgenstein, who inspired the contemporary school of thought known as "ordinary language philosophy." Wittgenstein's approach to philosophical problems was to try to dissolve them, rather than solve them, by showing that the problems arise out of our tendency to misuse key words like "cause" or "reality," stretching them beyond their proper bounds. Thus, Malcolm tries to show that skepticism, in rejecting our ordinary examples of knowledge, violates the implicit rules of use of the word "know."

Malcolm distinguishes two uses of "know" in everyday discourse, a "weak" use and a "strong" use. In the weak use, we say we know that something is the case if we have sufficient evidence for it, even though we recognize that new evidence may turn up that will refute our claim, which we are then prepared to withdraw. When we claim to know in the strong sense of "know," we do *not* admit the possibility of ever being proved mistaken. The case is closed, as far as we are concerned. Malcolm's examples of weak knowledge claims are that 92 times 16 equals 1,472 and that the sun is about 90 million miles away. His examples of strong knowledge claims are that 2 plus 2 equals 4 and that there is an inkwell on his desk that he is now perceiving.

In criticizing a contention of British philosopher H. A. Prichard, that, on reflection, we can always recognize the difference between genuine knowledge and mere belief, Malcolm points out that Prichard failed to note the difference between the strong and weak uses of "know"; it is precisely this oversight, he contends, which provides the opening for skepticism. You can properly say "I know the gorge won't be dry" if you saw water in it recently. Yet the gorge may in fact have dried out in the meantime, in which case you did not really know but only believed. When "know" is used in this weak sense, we cannot distinguish knowledge from belief by reflection alone. To be sure of the difference, we must also know (in the strong sense of "know") whether the knowledge claim is, in fact, true (i.e., provable by some experience, in this case). Nevertheless, even if a knowledge claim made in the weak sense turns out to be false, it was not a misuse of "know" to have made the claim, although in the light of its falsity one must withdraw the claim. So Prichard was right in maintaining that reflection alone enables us to judge that we have the *right* to claim we know, although only when we claim knowledge in the strong sense do we also have the right to refuse to recognize the possibility of being proved wrong. The skeptic, in common with Prichard, confuses the strong and irrevocable knowledge claim with the weak and revocable claim and then, unlike Prichard, argues that since we may always turn out to be mistaken, we *never* have a logical right to say we know anything. In reply to the skeptic, Malcolm argues that he has a right to claim he knows commonsense facts and simple mathematical truths—such as that there is an inkwell on his desk and that 2 plus 2 equals 4—in the strong irrevocable sense, because it is inconceivable that any evidence could turn up to prove him mistaken.

The contemporary American philosopher Peter Unger, in his recent book, *Ignorance,* revives the skeptical tradition on the basis of current theories in linguistics. In the chapter from which our selection is taken, he seizes on Malcolm's argument as a good example of the dogmatism involved in the belief that we ever know anything. Unger brushes aside Malcolm's weak sense of "know," contending that only the strong sense conforms to ordinary usage, on the ground that "I know that p" (p meaning any proposition) entails the truth of p, so that if p turns out to be false, it *must* have been wrong to have claimed to know that p. Yet any proposition, Unger claims, can conceivably be false, even "2 plus 2 equals 4" and "Here is an inkwell." Consequently, there is no weak sense of "know," and the strong sense is never justifiably employed. Whenever we say we know, we express a dogmatic and unreasonable attitude for we imply we cannot be mistaken, and this is never so, according to Unger.

Thus, the commonsense realism of Malcolm and the radical skepticism of Unger disagree on the answers to three questions: (1) Do all claims to knowledge imply that the claimant cannot possibly be mistaken, as Unger contends, or is "know" often used in the weak sense defined by Malcolm, that is correctly employed if one has good, but not necessarily irrefutable, evidence. (2) Is there a strong use of "know" that leads to the conclusion that nothing could count as disproof of one's claim? And (3) Is this strong use unjustifiable and dogmatic?

On the first question, there can be no doubt that we do often say we know without feeling any discomfort when events prove us wrong (e.g., regarding weather forecasts). Unger recognizes this, but attributes it to sloppy, though common, thinking or speaking. We should not, he maintains, use "know" in this way, for we misinform others and even ourselves. For if we can be mistaken, we do not know. Otherwise, we could be said to know what is not the case, and that is absurd. On the second question, Malcolm and Unger agree that there is a strong sense of "know." However, they disagree on whether it is ever justifiable to say "I know" in so strong a sense. It is not obvious that normal people ever mean to imply that nothing would induce them to reassess their claim. The alleged "strong sense" of "know" may express an over-confidence verging on fanaticism. Perhaps Malcolm means only that we sometimes cannot *imagine* being proved wrong. Unger insists on a stronger implication of "know," that it is *impossible* to be wrong. One who makes the latter claim would be vulnerable to Unger's charge of dogmatism. Thus the answer to whether a strong sense of "know" is ever justifiable depends on whether we mean that we cannot imagine being proved wrong, or that it is impossible to be proved wrong. In the first case the answer seems to be yes, and in the second case, no. Unger is right in maintaining that it is logically possible for any knowledge claim to be mistaken. Does it follow that Malcolm must be wrong in holding that when he says he knows there is an inkwell on his desk, he cannot imagine any evidence that might prove him to be mistaken? Does the mere *logical* possibility of contrary evidence, as pointed out by Unger, discredit Malcolm's refusal to consider such evidence as a *real* possibility? Does it show Malcolm's attitude to be unreasonably dogmatic? Compare this case with the commonsense attitude toward miracles. Miracles are presumably logically possible, in the sense that assertions of their occurrence are not self-contradictory. But does it follow that we should admit that miracles really might happen, as we do not *know* that they will not? Hume, for all his philosophical skepticism, did not accept this conclusion in his well-known discussion of miracles. Perhaps further analysis of the concepts of possibility and knowledge is needed to resolve this issue.

RIGHT YOU ARE . . .

Luigi Pirandello

[*There is a knock at the door and the* BUTLER *enters*]

BUTLER. Callers, madam!

AMALIA. Who is it, please?

BUTLER. Signor Sirelli, and the Signora with another lady, madam.

AMALIA. Very well, show them in.

[*The* BUTLER *bows and withdraws*]

[SIRELLI, SIGNORA SIRELLI, SIGNORA CINI *appear in the doorway, rear.*

[SIRELLI, *also a man of about forty, is a bald, fat gentleman with some pretensions to stylish appearance that do not quite succeed: the over-dressed provincial.*

[SIGNORA SIRELLI, *his wife, plump, petite, a faded blonde, still young and girlishly pleasing. She, too, is somewhat overdressed with the provincial's fondness for display. She has the aggressive curiosity of the small-town gossip. She is chiefly occupied in keeping her husband in his place.*

[SIGNORA CINI *is the old provincial lady of affected manners, who takes malicious delight in the failings of others, all the while affecting innocence and inexperience regarding the waywardness of mankind*]

AMALIA [*as the visitors enter, and taking* SIGNORA SIRELLI'S *hands effusively*]. Dearest! Dearest!

SIGNORA SIRELLI. I took the liberty of bringing my good friend, Signora Cini, along. She was so anxious to know you!

AMALIA. So good of you to come, Signora! Please make yourself at home! My daughter Dina, Signora Cini, and this is my brother, Lamberto Laudisi.

SIRELLI [*bowing to the ladies*]. Signora, Signorina.

[*He goes over and shakes hands with* LAUDISI]

SIGNORA SIRELLI. Amalia dearest, we have come here as to the fountain of knowledge. We are two pilgrims athirst for the truth!

FROM "Right You Are! (If You Think So)," translated by A. Livingston, in *Dramas of Modernism and Their Forerunners*, edited by M. Moses. Reprinted by permission of E. P. Dutton.

AMALIA. The truth? Truth about what?

SIGNORA SIRELLI. Why . . . about this blessed Mr. Ponza of ours, the new secretary at the prefecture. He is the talk of the town, take my word for it, Amalia.

SIGNORA CINI. And we are all just dying to find out!

AMALIA. But we are as much in the dark as the rest of you, I assure you, madam.

SIRELLI [*to his wife*]. What did I tell you? They know no more about it than I do. In fact, I think they know less about it than I do. Why is it this poor woman is not allowed to see her daughter? Do you know the reason, you people, the real reason?

AMALIA. Why, I was just discussing the matter with my brother.

LAUDISI. And my view of it is that you're all a pack of gossips!

DINA. The reason is, they say, that Ponza will not allow her to.

SIGNORA CINI. Not a sufficient reason, if I may say so, Signorina.

SIGNORA SIRELLI. Quite insufficient! There's more to it than that!

SIRELLI. I have a new item for you, fresh, right off the ice: he keeps her locked up at home!

AMALIA. His mother-in-law?

SIRELLI. No, no, his wife!

SIGNORA CINI. Under lock and key?

DINA. There, Nunky, what have you to say to that? And you've been trying to defend him all along!

SIRELLI [*staring in astonishment at* LAUDISI]. Trying to defend that man? Really . . .

LAUDISI. Defending him? No! I am not defending anybody. All I'm saying, if you ladies will excuse me, is that all this gossip is not worthy of you. More than that, you are just wasting your breath; because, as far as I can see, you're not getting anywhere at all.

SIRELLI. I don't follow you, sir!

LAUDISI. You're getting nowhere, my charming ladies!

SIGNORA CINI. But we're trying to get somewhere—we are trying to find out!

LAUDISI. Excuse me, what can you find out? What can we really know about other people—who they are—what they are—what they are doing, and why they are doing it?

SIGNORA SIRELLI. How can we know? Why not? By asking, of course! You tell me what you know, and I tell you what I know.

LAUDISI. In that case, madam, you ought to be the best informed person in the world. Why, your husband knows more about what others are doing than any other man—or woman, for that matter—in this neighborhood.

SIRELLI [*deprecatingly but pleased*]. Oh I say, I say . . .

SIGNORA SIRELLI [*to her husband*]. No, dear, he's right, he's right. [*Then turning to* AMALIA] The real truth, Amalia, is this: for all my husband says he knows, I never manage to keep posted on anything!

SIRELLI. And no wonder! The trouble is—that woman never trusts me! The moment I tell her something she is convinced it is not *quite* as I say. Then, sooner or later, she claims that it *can't* be as I say. And at last she is certain it is the exact opposite of what I say!

SIGNORA SIRELLI. Well, you ought to hear all he tells me!

LAUDISI [*laughing aloud*]. Hah! Hah! Hah! Hah! Hah! Hah! Hah! May I speak, madam? Let me answer your husband. My dear Sirelli, how do you expect your wife to be satisfied with things as you explain them to her, if you, as is natural, represent them as they seem to you?

SIGNORA SIRELLI. And that means—as they cannot possibly be!

LAUDISI. Why no, Signora, now you are wrong. From your husband's point of view things are, I assure you, exactly as he represents them.

SIRELLI. As they are in reality!

SIGNORA SIRELLI. Not at all! You are always wrong.

SIRELLI. No, not a bit of it! It is you who are always wrong. I am always right.

LAUDISI. The fact is that neither of you is wrong. May I explain? I will prove it to you. Now here you are, you, Sirelli, and Signora Sirelli, your wife, there; and here I am. You see me, don't you?

SIRELLI. Well . . . er . . . yes.

LAUDISI. Do you see me, or do you not?

SIRELLI. Oh, I'll bite! Of course I see you.

LAUDISI. So you see me! But that's not enough. Come here!

SIRELLI [*smiling, he obeys, but with a puzzled expression on his face as though he fails to understand what* LAUDISI *is driving at*]. Well, here I am!

LAUDISI. Yes! Now take a better look at me . . . Touch me! That's it —that's it! Now you are touching me, are you not? And you see me! You're sure you see me?

SIRELLI. Why, I should say . . .

LAUDISI. Yes, but the point is, you're sure! Of course you're sure! Now if you please, Signora Sirelli, you come here—or rather . . . no . . . [*gallantly*] it is my place to come to you! [*He goes over to* SIGNORA SIRELLI *and kneels chivalrously on one knee*] You see me, do you not, madam? Now that hand of yours . . . touch me! A pretty hand, on my word! [*He pats her hand*]

SIRELLI. Easy! Easy!

LAUDISI. Never mind your husband, madam! Now, you have touched me, have you not? And you see me? And you are absolutely sure about me, are you not? Well now, madam, I beg of you; do not tell your husband, nor my sister, nor my niece, nor Signora Cini here, what you think of me; because, if you were to do that, they would all tell you that you are completely wrong. But, you see, you are really right; because I am really what you take me to be; though, my dear madam, that does not prevent me from also being really what your husband, my sister, my niece, and Signora Cini take me to be— because they also are absolutely right!

SIGNORA SIRELLI. In other words you are a different person for each of us.

LAUDISI. Of course I'm a different person! And you, madam, pretty as you are, aren't you a different person, too?

SIGNORA SIRELLI [*hastily*]. No siree! I assure you, as far as I'm concerned, I'm always the same, always, yesterday, today, and forever!

LAUDISI. Ah, but so am I, from my point of view, believe me! And, I would say that you are all mistaken unless you see me as I see myself; but that would be an inexcusable presumption on my part—as it would be on yours, my dear madam!

SIRELLI. And what has all this rigmarole got to do with it, may I ask?

LAUDISI. What has it got to do with it? Why . . . I find all you people here at your wits' ends trying to find out who and what other people are; just as though other people had to be this, or that, and nothing else.

SIGNORA SIRELLI. All you are saying is that we can never find out the truth! A dreadful idea!

SIGNORA CINI. I give up! I give up! If we can't believe even what we see with our eyes and feel with our fingers . . .

LAUDISI. But you must understand, madam! Of course you can believe what you see with *your* eyes and feel with *your* fingers. All I'm saying is that you should show some respect for what other people see with their eyes and feel with their fingers, even though it be the exact opposite of what you see and feel.

SIGNORA SIRELLI. The way to answer you is to refuse to talk with you. See, I turn my back on you! I am going to move my chair around and pretend you aren't in the room. Why, you're driving me crazy, crazy!

LAUDISI. Oh, I beg your pardon. Don't let me interfere with your party. Please go on! Pray continue your argument about Signora Frola and Signora Ponza—I promise not to interrupt again!

AMALIA. You're right for once, Lamberto; and I think it would be even better if you should go into the other room.

DINA. Serves you right, Nunky! Into the other room with you, into the other room!

LAUDISI.   No, I refuse to budge! Fact is, I enjoy hearing you gossip; but I promise not to say anything more, don't fear! At the very most, with your permission, I shall indulge in a laugh or two.

SIGNORA SIRELLI.   How funny . . . and our idea in coming here was to find out . . . But really, Amalia, I thought this Ponza man was your husband's secretary at the Provincial building.

AMALIA.   He is his secretary—in the office. But here at home what authority has Agazzi over the fellow?

SIGNORA SIRELLI.   Of course! I understand! But may I ask . . . haven't you even tried to see Signora Frola, next door?

DINA.   Tried? I should say we had! Twice, Signora!

SIGNORA CINI.   Well . . . so then . . . you have probably talked to her . . .

DINA.   We were not *received,* if you please!

SIGNORA SIRELLI, SIRELLI, SIGNORA CINI [*in chorus*].   Not received? Why! Why! Why!

DINA.   This very forenoon!

AMALIA.   The first time we waited fully fifteen minutes at the door. We rang and rang and rang, and no one came. Why, we weren't even able to leave our cards! So we went back today . . .

DINA [*throwing up her hands in an expression of horror*].   And *he* came to the door.

SIGNORA SIRELLI.   Why yes, with that face of his . . . you can tell by just looking at the man . . . Such a face! Such a face! You can't blame people for talking! And then, with that black suit of his . . . Why, they all dress in black. Did you ever notice? Even the old lady? And the man's eyes, too! . . .

SIRELLI [*with a glance of pitying disgust at his wife*].   What do you know about his eyes? You never saw his eyes! And you never saw the woman. How do you know she dresses in black? *Probably* she dresses in black . . . By the way, they come from a little town in the next county. Had you heard that? A village called Marsica?

AMALIA.   Yes, the village that was destroyed a short time ago.

SIRELLI.   Exactly! By an earthquake! Not a house left standing in the place.

DINA.   And all their relatives were lost, I have heard. Not one of them left in the world!

SIGNORA CINI [*impatient to get on with the story*].   Very well, very well, so then . . . he came to the door . . .

AMALIA.   Yes . . . And the moment I saw him in front of me with that weird face of his I had hardly enough gumption left to tell him that we had just come to call on his mother-in-law, and he . . . well . . . not a word, not a word . . . not even a "thank you," if you please!

DINA. That is not quite fair, mama: . . . he did bow!

AMALIA. Well, yes, a bow . . . if you want to call it that. Something like this! . . .

DINA. And his eyes! You ought to see his eyes—the eyes of a devil, and then some! You never saw a man with eyes like that!

SIGNORA CINI. Very well, what did he say, finally?

DINA. He seemed quite taken aback.

AMALIA. He was all confused like; he hitched about for a time; and at last he said that Signora Frola was not feeling well, but that she would appreciate our kindness in having come; and then he just stood there, and stood there, apparently waiting for us to go away.

DINA. I never was more mortified in my life!

SIRELLI. A boor, a plain boor, I say! Oh, it's his fault, I am telling you. And . . . who knows? Perhaps he has got the old lady also under lock and key.

SIGNORA SIRELLI. Well, I think something should be done about it! . . . After all, you are the wife of a superior of his. You can *refuse* to be treated like this.

AMALIA. As far as that goes, my husband did take it rather badly— as a lack of courtesy on the man's part; and he went straight to the prefect with the matter, insisting on an apology.

[SIGNOR AGAZZI, *commendatore and provincial councillor, appears in the doorway rear*]

DINA. Oh goody, here's papa now!

[AGAZZI *is well on toward fifty. He has the harsh, authoritarian manner of the provincial of importance. Red hair and beard, rather unkempt: gold-rimmed eyeglasses*]

AGAZZI. Oh, Sirelli, glad to see you!

[*He steps forward and bows to the company*]

AGAZZI. Signora! . . . [*He shakes hands with* SIGNORA SIRELLI]

AMALIA [*introducing* SIGNORA CINI]. My husband, Signora Cini!

AGAZZI [*with a bow and taking her hand*]. A great pleasure, madam! [*Then turning to his wife and daughter in a mysterious voice*] I have come back from the office to give you some real news! Signora Frola will be here shortly.

SIGNORA SIRELLI [*clapping her hands delightedly*]. Oh, the mother-in-law! She is coming? Really? Coming here?

SIRELLI [*going over to* AGAZZI *and pressing his hand warmly as an expression of admiration*]. That's the talk, old man, that's the talk! What's needed here is some show of authority.

AGAZZI. Why I had to, you see, I had to! . . . I can't let a man treat my wife and daughter that way! . . .

SIRELLI.   I should say not! I was just expressing myself to that effect right here.

SIGNORA SIRELLI.   And it would have been entirely proper to inform the prefect also . . .

AGAZZI [*anticipating*].   . . . of all the talk that is going around on this fine gentleman's account? Oh, leave that to me! I didn't miss the opportunity.

SIRELLI.   Fine! Fine!

SIGNORA CINI.   And such talk!

AMALIA.   For my part, I never heard of such a thing. Why, do you know, he has them both under lock and key!

DINA.   No, mama, we are not *quite* sure of that. We are not *quite* sure about the old lady, yet.

AMALIA.   Well, we know it—about his wife, anyway.

SIRELLI.   And what did the prefect have to say?

AGAZZI.   Oh the prefect . . . well, the prefect . . . he was very much impressed, *very* much impressed with what I had to say.

SIRELLI.   I should hope so!

AGAZZI.   You see, some of the talk had reached his ears already. And he agrees that it is better, as a matter of his own official prestige, for all this mystery in connection with one of his assistants to be cleared up, so that once and for all we shall know the truth.

LAUDISI.   Hah, hah, hah, hah, hah, hah, hah!

AMALIA.   That is Lamberto's usual contribution. He laughs!

AGAZZI.   And what is there to laugh about?

SIGNORA SIRELLI.   Why he says that no one can ever know the truth.

[*The* BUTLER *appears at the door in back set*]

THE BUTLER.   Excuse me, Signora Frola!

SIRELLI.   Ah, here she is now!

AGAZZI.   Now we'll see if we can settle it!

SIGNORA SIRELLI.   Splendid! Oh, I am so glad I came.

AMALIA [*rising*].   Shall we have her come in?

AGAZZI.   Wait, you keep your seat, Amalia! Let's have her come right in here. [*Turning to the* BUTLER]. Show her in!

[*Exit* BUTLER]

[*A moment later all rise as* SIGNORA FROLA *enters, and* AMALIA *steps forward, holding out her hand in greeting.*

[SIGNORA FROLA *is a slight, modestly but neatly dressed old lady, very eager to talk and apparently fond of people. There is a world of sadness in her eyes, tempered, however, by a gentle smile that is constantly playing about her lips*]

AMALIA.   Come right in, Signora Frola! [*She takes the old lady's hand*

and begins the introductions] Mrs. Sirelli, a good friend of mine; Signora Cini; my husband; Mr. Sirelli; and this is my daughter, Dina; my brother Lamberto Laudisi. Please take a chair, Signora!

SIGNORA FROLA.   Oh, I am so very, very sorry! I have come to excuse myself for having been so negligent of my social duties. You, Signora Agazzi, were so kind, so very kind, to have honored me with a first call—when really it was my place to leave my card with you!

AMALIA.   Oh, we are just neighbors, Signora Frola! Why stand on ceremony? I just thought that you, being new in town and all alone by yourself, would perhaps like to have a little company.

SIGNORA FROLA.   Oh, how very kind of you it was!

SIGNORA SIRELLI.   And you are quite alone, aren't you?

SIGNORA FROLA.   Oh no! No! I have a daughter, married, though she hasn't been here very long, either.

SIRELLI.   And your daughter's husband is the new secretary at the prefecture, Signor Ponza, I believe?

SIGNORA FROLA.   Yes, yes, exactly! And I hope that Signor Agazzi, as his superior, will be good enough to excuse me—and him, too!

AGAZZI.   I will be quite frank with you, madam! I was a bit put out.

SIGNORA FROLA [*interrupting*].   And you were quite right! But I do hope you will forgive him. You see, we are still—what shall I say—still so upset by the terrible things that have happened to us . . .

AMALIA.   You went through the earthquake, didn't you?

SIGNORA SIRELLI.   And you lost all your relatives?

SIGNORA FROLA.   Every one of them! All our family—yes, madam. And our village was left just a miserable ruin, a pile of bricks and stones and mortar.

SIRELLI.   Yes, we heard about it.

SIGNORA FROLA.   It wasn't so bad for me, I suppose. I had only one sister and her daughter, and my niece had no family. But my poor son-in-law had a much harder time of it. He lost his mother, two brothers, and their wives, a sister and her husband, and there were two little ones, his nephews.

SIRELLI.   A massacre!

SIGNORA FROLA.   Oh, one doesn't forget such things! You see, it sort of leaves you with your feet off the ground.

AMALIA.   I can imagine.

SIGNORA SIRELLI.   And all overnight with no warning at all! It's a wonder you didn't go mad.

SIGNORA FROLA.   Well, you see, we haven't quite gotten our bearings yet; and we do things that may seem impolite without in the least intending to. I hope you understand!

AGAZZI. Oh please, Signora Frola, of course!

AMALIA. In fact it was partly on account of your trouble that my daughter and I thought we ought to go to see you first.

SIGNORA SIRELLI [*literally writhing with curiosity*]. Yes, of course, since they saw you all alone by yourself, and yet . . . excuse me, Signora Frola . . . if the question doesn't seem impertinent . . . how is it that when you have a daughter here in town and after a disaster like the one you have been through . . . I should think you people would all stand together, that you would need one another.

SIGNORA FROLA. Whereas I am left here all by myself?

SIRELLI. Yes, exactly. It does seem strange, to tell the honest truth.

SIGNORA FROLA. Oh, I understand—of course! But you know, I have a feeling that a young man and a young woman who have married should be left a good deal to themselves.

LAUDISI. Quite so, quite so! They should be left to themselves. They are beginning a life of their own, a life different from anything they have led before. One should not interfere in these relations between a husband and a wife!

SIGNORA SIRELLI. But there are limits to everything, Laudisi, if you will excuse me! And when it comes to shutting one's own mother out of one's life . . .

LAUDISI. Who is shutting her out of the girl's life? Here, if I have understood the lady, we see a mother who understands that her daughter cannot and must not remain so closely associated with her as she was before, for now the young woman must begin a new life on her own account.

SIGNORA FROLA [*with evidence of keen gratitude and relief*]. You have hit the point exactly, sir. You have said what I would like to have said. You are exactly right! Thank you!

SIGNORA CINI. But your daughter, I imagine, often comes to see you . . .

SIGNORA FROLA [*hesitating, and manifestly ill at ease*]. Why yes . . . I . . . I . . . we do see each other, of course.

SIRELLI [*quickly pressing the advantage*]. But your daughter never goes out of her house! At least no one in town has ever seen her.

SIGNORA CINI. Oh, she probably has her little ones to take care of.

SIGNORA FROLA [*speaking up quickly*]. No, there are no children yet, and perhaps there won't be any now. You see, she has been married seven years. Oh, of course, she has a lot to do about the house; but that is not the reason, really. You know, we women who come from the little towns in the country—we are used to staying indoors much of the time.

AGAZZI. Even when your mothers are living in the same town, but not in your house? You prefer staying indoors to going and visiting your mother?

AMALIA. But it's Signora Frola probably who visits her daughter.

SIGNORA FROLA [*quickly*]. Of course, of course, why not! I go there once or twice a day.

SIRELLI. And once or twice a day you climb all those stairs up to the fifth story of that tenement, eh?

SIGNORA FROLA [*growing pale and trying to conceal under a laugh the torture of that cross-examination*]. Why . . . er . . . to tell the truth, I don't go up. You're right, five flights would be quite too much for me. No, I don't go up. My daughter comes out on the balcony in the courtyard and . . . well . . . we see each other . . . and we talk!

SIGNORA SIRELLI. And that's all, eh? How terrible! You never see each other more intimately than that?

DINA. I have a mamma and certainly I wouldn't expect her to go up five flights of stairs to see me, either; but at the same time I could never stand talking to her that way, shouting at the top of my lungs from a balcony on the fifth story. I am sure I should want a kiss from her occasionally, and feel her near me, at least.

SIGNORA FROLA [*with evident signs of embarrassment and confusion*]. And you're right! Yes, exactly . . . quite right! I must explain. Yes . . . I hope you people are not going to think that my daughter is something she really is not. You must not suspect her of having so little regard for me and for my years, and you mustn't believe that I, her mother, am . . . well . . . five, six, even more stories to climb would never prevent a real mother, even if she were as old and infirm as I am, from going to her daughter's side and pressing her to her heart with a real mother's love . . . oh no!

SIGNORA SIRELLI [*triumphantly*]. There you have it, there you have it, just as we were saying!

SIGNORA CINI. But there must be a reason, there must be a reason!

AMALIA [*pointedly to her brother*]. Aha, Lamberto, now you see, there is a reason, after all!

SIRELLI [*insisting*]. Your son-in-law, I suppose?

SIGNORA FROLA. Oh please, please, please, don't think badly of *him*. He is such a very good boy. Good is no name for it, my dear sir. You can't imagine all he does for me! Kind, attentive, solicitous for my comfort, everything! And as for my daughter—I doubt if any girl ever had a more affectionate and well-intentioned husband. No, on that point I am proud of myself! I could not have found a better man for her.

SIGNORA SIRELLI. Well then . . . What? What? *What?*

SIGNORA CINI.   So your son-in-law is not the reason?

AGAZZI.   I never thought it was his fault. Can you imagine a man forbidding his wife to call on her mother, or preventing the mother from paying an occasional visit to her daughter?

SIGNORA FROLA.   Oh, it's not a case of forbidding! Who ever dreamed of such a thing! No, it's we, Commendatore, I and my daughter, that is. Oh, please, believe me! We refrain from visiting each other of our own accord, out of consideration for him, you understand.

AGAZZI.   But excuse me . . . how in the world could he be offended by such a thing? I *don't* understand.

SIGNORA FROLA.   Oh, please don't be angry, Signor Agazzi. You see it's a . . . what shall I say . . . a feeling . . . that's it, a feeling, which it would perhaps be very hard for anyone else to understand; and yet, when you do understand it, it's all so simple, I am sure . . . so simple . . . and believe me, my dear friends, it is no slight sacrifice that I am making, and that my daughter is making, too.

AGAZZI.   Well, one thing you will admit, madam. This is a very, very unusual situation.

SIRELLI.   Unusual, indeed! And such as to justify a curiosity even more persistent than ours.

AGAZZI.   It is not only unusual, madam. I might even say it is suspicious.

SIGNORA FROLA.   Suspicious? You mean you suspect Signor Ponza? Oh please, Commendatore, don't say that. What fault can you possibly find with him, Signor Agazzi?

AGAZZI.   I didn't say just that. . . . Please don't misunderstand! I said simply that the situation is so very strange that people might legitimately suspect . . .

SIGNORA FROLA.   Oh, no, no, no! What could they suspect? We are in perfect agreement, all of us; and we are really quite happy, very happy, I might even say . . . both I and my daughter.

SIGNORA SIRELLI. Perhaps it's a case of jealousy?

SIGNORA FROLA.   Jealousy of me? It would be hardly fair to say that, although . . . really . . . oh, it is so hard to explain! . . . You see, he is in love with my daughter . . . so much so that he wants her whole heart, her every thought, as it were, for himself; so much so that he insists that the affections which my daughter must have for me, her mother—he finds that love quite natural of course, why not? Of course he does!—should reach me through him—that's it, through him—don't you understand?

AGAZZI.   Oh, that is going pretty strong! No, I don't understand. In fact it seems to me a case of downright cruelty!

SIGNORA FROLA.   Cruelty? No, no, please don't call it cruelty, Commendatore. It is something else, believe me. You see it's so hard for me to explain the matter. Nature, perhaps . . . but no, that's hardly the word. What shall I call it? Perhaps a sort of disease. It's a fullness of love, of a love shut off from the world. There, I guess that's it . . . a fullness . . . a completeness of devotion in which his wife must live without ever departing from it, and into which no other person must ever be allowed to enter.

DINA.   Not even her mother, I suppose?

SIRELLI.   It is the worst case of selfishness I ever heard of, if you want my opinion!

SIGNORA FROLA.   Selfishness? Perhaps! But a selfishness, after all, which offers itself wholly in sacrifice. A case where the selfish person gives all he has in the world to the one he loves. Perhaps it would be fairer to call me selfish; for selfish it surely is for me to be always trying to break into this closed world of theirs, break in by force if necessary; when I know that my daughter is really so happy, so passionately adored—you ladies understand, don't you? A true mother should be satisfied when she knows her daughter is happy, oughtn't she? Besides I'm not completely separated from my daughter, am I? I see her and I speak to her. [*She assumes a more confidential tone*] You see, when she lets down the basket there in the courtyard I always find a letter in it—a short note, which keeps me posted on the news of the day; and I put in a little letter that I have written. That is some consolation, a great consolation indeed, and now, in course of time, I've grown used to it. I am resigned, there! Resignation, that's it. And I've ceased really to suffer from it at all.

AMALIA.   Oh well then, after all, if you people are satisfied, why should . . .

SIGNORA FROLA [*rising*].   Oh yes, yes! But remember, I told you he is such a good man! Believe me, he couldn't be better, really! We all have our weaknesses in this world, haven't we! And we get along best by having a little charity, a little indulgence, for one another. [*She holds out her hand to* AMALIA] Thank you for calling, madam. [*She bows to* SIGNORA SIRELLI, SIGNORA CINI, *and* DINA; *then turning to* AGAZZI, *she continues*] And I do hope you have forgiven me!

AGAZZI.   Oh, my dear madam, please, please! And we are extremely grateful for your having come to call on us.

SIGNORA FROLA [*offering her hand to* SIRELLI *and* LAUDISI *and again turning to* AMALIA, *who has risen to show her out*].   Oh no, please, Signora Agazzi, please stay here with your friends! Don't put yourself to any trouble!

AMALIA.   No, no, I will go with you; and believe me, we were very, very glad to see you!

[*Exit* SIGNORA FROLA *with* AMALIA *showing her the way.* AMALIA *returns immediately*]

SIRELLI. Well, there you have the story, ladies and gentlemen! Are you satisfied with the explanation?

AGAZZI. An explanation, you call it? So far as I can see she has explained nothing. I tell you there is some big mystery in all this business.

SIGNORA SIRELLI. That poor woman! Who knows what torment she must be suffering?

DINA. And to think of that poor girl!

SIGNORA CINI. She could hardly keep in her tears as she talked.

AMALIA. Yes, and did you notice when I mentioned all those stairs she would have to climb before really being able to see her daughter?

LAUDISI. What impressed me was her concern, which amounted to a steadfast determination, to protect her son-in-law from the slightest suspicion.

SIGNORA SIRELLI. Not at all, not at all! What could she say for him? She couldn't really find a single word to say for him.

SIRELLI. And I would like to know how anyone could condone such violence, such downright cruelty!

THE BUTLER [*appearing again in the doorway*]. Beg pardon, sir! Signor Ponza calling.

SIGNOR SIRELLI. The man himself, upon my word!

[*An animated ripple of surprise and curiosity, not to say of guilty self-consciousness, sweeps over the company*]

AGAZZI. Did he ask to see me?

BUTLER. He asked simply if he might be received. That was all he said.

SIGNORA SIRELLI. Oh please, Signor Agazzi, please let him come in! I am really afraid of the man; but I confess the greatest curiosity to have a close look at the monster.

AMALIA. But what in the world can he be wanting?

AGAZZI. The way to find that out is to have him come in. [*To the* BUTLER] Show him in, please.

[*The* BUTLER *bows and goes out. A second later* PONZA *appears, aggressively, in the doorway*]

[PONZA *is a short, thick set, dark complexioned man of a distinctly unprepossessing appearance; black hair, very thick and coming down low over his forehead; a black mustache upcurling at the ends, giving his face a certain ferocity of expression. He is dressed entirely in black. From time to time he draws a black-bordered handkerchief and wipes the perspiration from his brow. When he speaks his eyes are invariably hard, fixed, sinister*]

AGAZZI. This way please, Ponza, come right in! [*Introducing him*] Signor Ponza, our new provincial secretary; my wife; Signora Sirelli; Signora Cini; my daughter Dina. This is Signor Sirelli; and here is Laudisi, my brother-in-law. Please join our party, won't you, Ponza?

PONZA. So kind of you! You will pardon the intrusion. I shall disturb you only a moment, I hope.

AGAZZI. You had some private business to discuss with me?

PONZA. Why yes, but I could discuss it right here. In fact, perhaps as many people as possible should hear what I have to say. You see it is a declaration that I owe, in a certain sense, to the general public.

AGAZZI. Oh my dear Ponza, if it is that little matter of your mother-in-law's not calling on us, it is quite all right; because you see . . .

PONZA. No, that was not what I came for, Commendatore. It was not to apologize for her. Indeed I may say that Signora Frola, my wife's mother, would certainly have left her cards with Signora Agazzi, your wife, and Signorina Agazzi, your daughter, long before they were so kind as to honor her with their call, had I not exerted myself to the utmost to prevent her coming, since I am absolutely unable to consent to her paying or receiving visits!

AGAZZI [*drawing up into an authoritative attitude and speaking with some severity*]. Why? If you will be so kind as to explain, Ponza?

PONZA [*with evidence of increasing excitement in spite of his efforts to preserve his self-control*]. I suppose my mother-in-law has been talking to you people about her daughter, my wife. Am I mistaken? And I imagine she told you further that I have forbidden her entering my house and seeing her daughter intimately.

AMALIA. Oh not at all, not at all, Signor Ponza! Signora Frola had only the nicest things to say about you. She could not have spoken of you with greater respect and kindness.

DINA. She seems to be very fond of you indeed.

AGAZZI. She says that she refrains from visiting your house of her own accord, out of regard for feelings of yours which we frankly confess we are unable to understand.

SIGNORA SIRELLI. Indeed, if we were to express our honest opinion . . .

AGAZZI. Well, yes, why not be honest? We think you are extremely harsh with the woman, extremely harsh, perhaps cruel would be an exacter word.

PONZA. Yes, that is what I thought; and I came here for the express purpose of clearing the matter up. The condition this poor woman is in is a pitiable one indeed—not less pitiable than my own perhaps; because, as you see, I am compelled to come here and make apologies —a public declaration—which only such violence as has just been used upon me could ever bring me to make in the world . . . [*He stops and looks about the room. Then he says slowly with emphatic emphasis on the important syllables*] My mother-in-law, Signora Frola, is not in her right mind! She is insane!

THE COMPANY.   Insane! A lunatic! Oh my! Really! No! Impossible!

PONZA.   And she has been insane for four years.

SIGNORA SIRELLI.   Dear me, who would ever have suspected it! She doesn't show it in the least.

AGAZZI.   Insane? Are you sure?

PONZA.   She doesn't show it, does she? But she is insane, nevertheless; and her delusion consists precisely in believing that I am forbidding her to see her daughter. [*His face takes on an expression of cruel suffering mingled with a sort of ferocious excitement*] What daughter, for God's sake? Why her daughter died four years ago! [*A general sensation*]

EVERYONE AT ONCE.   Died? She is dead? What do you mean? Oh, really? Four years ago? Why! Why!

PONZA.   Four years ago! In fact it was the death of the poor girl that drove her mad.

SIRELLI.   Are we to understand that the wife with whom you are now living . . .

PONZA.   Exactly! She is my second wife. I married her two years ago.

AMALIA.   And Signora Frola believes that her daughter is still living, that she is your wife still?

PONZA.   Perhaps it was best for her that way. She was in charge of a nurse in her own room, you see. Well, when she chanced to see me passing by inadvertence on her street one day, with this woman, my second wife, she suddenly began to laugh and cry and tremble all over in an extreme of happiness. She was sure her daughter, whom she had believed dead, was alive and well; and from a condition of desperate despondency which was the first form of her mental disturbance, she entered on a second obsession, believing steadily that her daughter was not dead at all; but that I, the poor girl's husband, am so completely in love with her that I want her wholly for myself and will not allow anyone to approach her. She became otherwise quite well, you might say. Her nervousness improved, and her powers of reasoning returned quite clear. Judge for yourself, ladies and gentlemen! You have seen her and talked with her. You would never suspect in the world that she is crazy.

AMALIA.   Never in the world! Never!

SIGNORA SIRELLI.   And the poor woman says she is so happy, so happy!

PONZA.   That is what she says to everybody; and for that matter she really has a wealth of affection and gratitude for me; because, as you may well suppose, I do my very best, in spite of the sacrifices entailed, to keep up this beneficial illusion in her. The sacrifices you can readily understand. In the first place I have to maintain two homes on my small salary. Then it is very hard on my wife, isn't it? But she, poor thing, does the very best she can to help me out! She comes to the window when the old lady appears. She talks to her from the balcony. She writes letters to her. But you people will understand that there are limits to what I can ask of my poor wife. Signora Frola, meanwhile, lives practically in confinement. We have to keep a pretty close watch on her. We have to lock her up, virtually. Otherwise, some fine day she would be walking right into my house. She is of a gentle, placid disposition fortunately; but you understand that my wife, good 'as she is, could never bring herself to accepting caresses intended for another woman, a dead woman! That would be a torment beyond conception.

AMALIA.   Oh, of course! Poor woman. Just imagine!

SIGNORA SIRELLI.   And the old lady herself consents to being locked up all the time?

PONZA.   You, Commendatore, will understand that I couldn't permit her calling here except under absolute constraint.

AGAZZI.   I understand perfectly, my dear Ponza, and you have my deepest sympathy.

PONZA.   When a man has a misfortune like this fall upon him he must not go about in society; but of course when, by complaining to the prefect, you practically compelled me to have Signora Frola call, it was my duty to volunteer this further information; because, as a public official, and with due regard for the post of responsibility I occupy, I could not allow any discredible suspicions to remain attached to my reputation. I could not have you good people suppose for a moment that, out of jealousy or for any other reason, I could ever prevent a poor suffering mother from seeing her own daughter. [*He rises*] Again my apologies for having intruded my personal troubles upon your party. [*He bows*] My compliments, Commendatore. Good afternoon, good afternoon! Thank you!

[*Bowing to* LAUDISI, SIRELLI, *and the others in turn, he goes out through the door, rear*]

AMALIA [*with a sigh of sympathy and astonishment*].   Uhh! Crazy! What do you think of that?

SIGNORA SIRELLI.   The poor old thing! But you wouldn't have believed it, would you?

DINA.   I always knew there was something under it all.

SIGNORA CINI.   But who could ever have guessed . . .

AGAZZI.   Oh, I don't know, I don't know! You could tell from the way she talked . . .

LAUDISI.   You mean to say that you thought . . . ?

AGAZZI. No, I can't say that. But at the same time, if you remember, she could never quite find her words.

SIGNORA SIRELLI. How could she, poor thing, out of her head like that?

SIRELLI. And yet, if I may raise the question, it seems strange to me that an insane person . . . oh, I admit that she couldn't really talk rationally . . . but what surprises me, is her trying to find a reason to explain why her son-in-law should be keeping her away from her daughter. This effort of hers to justify it and then to adapt herself to excuses of her own invention . . .

AGAZZI. Yes, but that is only another proof that she's insane. You see, she kept offering excuses for Ponza that really were not excuses at all.

AMALIA. Yes, that's so. She would say a thing without really saying it, taking it back almost in the next words.

AGAZZI. But there is one more thing. If she weren't a downright lunatic, how could she or any other woman ever accept such a situation from a man? How could she ever consent to talk with her own daughter only by shouting up from the bottom of a well five stories deep?

SIRELLI. But if I remember rightly she has you there! Notice, she doesn't accept the situation. She says she is resigned to it. That's different! No, I tell you, there is still something funny about this business. What do you say, Laudisi?

LAUDISI. Why, I say nothing, nothing at all!

THE BUTLER [*appearing at the door and visibly excited*]. Beg pardon, Signora Frola is here again!

AMALIA [*with a start*]. Oh dear me, again? Do you suppose she'll be pestering us all the time now?

SIGNORA SIRELLI. I understand how you feel now that you know she's a lunatic.

SIGNORA CINI. My, my, what do you suppose she is going to say now?

SIRELLI. For my part I'd really like to hear what she's got to say.

DINA. Oh, yes, mamma, don't be afraid! Ponza, said she was quite harmless. Let's have her come in.

AGAZZI. Of course, we can't send her away. Let's have her come in; and, if she makes any trouble, why . . .

[*Turning to the* BUTLER] Show her in.

[*The* BUTLER *bows and withdraws*]

AMALIA. You people stand by me, please! Why, I don't know what I am ever going to say to her now!

[SIGNORA FROLA *appears at the door.* AMALIA *rises and steps forward to welcome her. The others look on in astonished silence*]

SIGNORA FROLA. May I please . . . ?

AMALIA. Do come in, Signora Frola, do come in! You know all these ladies. They were here when you came before.

SIGNORA FROLA [*with an expression of sadness on her features, but still smiling gently*]. How you all look at me— and even you, Signora Agazzi! I am sure you think I am a lunatic, don't you!

AMALIA. My dear Signora Frola, what in the world are you talking about?

SIGNORA FROLA. But I am sure you will forgive me if I disturb you for a moment. [*Bitterly*] Oh, my dear Signora Agazzi, I wish I had left things as they were. It was hard to feel that I had been impolite to you by not answering the bell when you called that first time; but I could never have supposed that you would come back and force me to call upon you. I could foresee the consequences of such a visit from the very first.

AMALIA. Why, not at all, not at all! I don't understand. Why?

DINA. What consequences could you foresee, madam?

SIGNORA FROLA. Why, my son-in-law, Signor Ponza, has just been here, hasn't he?

AGAZZI. Why, yes, he was here! He came to discuss certain office matters with me . . . just ordinary business, you understand!

SIGNORA FROLA [*visibly hurt and quite dismayed*]. Oh, I know you are saying that just to spare me, just in order not to hurt my feelings.

AGAZZI. Not at all, not at all! That was really why he came.

SIGNORA FROLA [*with some alarm*]. But he was quite calm, I hope, quite calm?

AGAZZI. Calm? As calm as could be! Why not? Of course!

[*The members of the company all nod in confirmation*]

SIGNORA FROLA. Oh, my dear friends, I am sure you are trying to reassure me; but as a matter of fact I came to set you right about my son-in-law.

SIGNORA SIRELLI. Why no, Signora, what's the trouble?

AGAZZI. Really, it was just a matter of politics we talked about . . .

SIGNORA FROLA. But I can tell from the way you all look at me . . . Please excuse me, but it is not a question of me at all. From the way you all look at me I can tell that he came here to prove something that I would never have confessed for all the money in the world. You will all bear me out, won't you? When I came here a few moments ago you all asked me questions that were very cruel questions to me, as I hope you will understand. And they were questions that I couldn't answer very well; but anyhow I gave an explanation of our manner of living which can be satisfactory to nobody, I am well aware. But how could I give you the real reason? How could I tell you people, as he's doing, that my daughter has been dead for four years and that I'm a poor, insane mother who believes that her daughter is still living and that her husband will not allow me to see her?

AGAZZI [*quite upset by the ring of deep sincerity he finds in* SIGNORA FROLA's *manner of speaking*]. What do you mean, your daughter?

SIGNORA FROLA [*hastily and with anguished dismay written on her features*]. You know that's so. Why do you try to deny it? He did say that to you, didn't he?

SIRELLI [*with some hesitation and studying her features warily*]. Yes . . . in fact . . . he did say that.

SIGNORA FROLA. I know he did; and I also know how it pained him to be obliged to say such a thing of me. It is a great pity, Commendatore! We have made continual sacrifices, involving unheard of suffering, I assure you; and we could endure them only by living as we are living now. Unfortunately, as I well understand, it must look very strange to people, seem even scandalous, arouse no end of gossip! But after all, if he is an excellent secretary, scrupulously honest, attentive to his work, why should people complain? You have seen him in the office, haven't you? He is a good worker, isn't he?

AGAZZI. To tell the truth, I have not watched him particularly, as yet.

SIGNORA FROLA. Oh he really is, he really is! All the men he ever worked for say he's most reliable; and I beg of you, please don't let this other matter interfere. And why then should people go tormenting him with all this prying into his private life, laying bare once more a misfortune which he has succeeded in mastering and which, if it were widely talked about, might upset him again personally, and even hurt him in his career?

AGAZZI. Oh no, no, Signora, no one is trying to hurt him. It is nothing to his disgrace that I can see. Nor would we hurt you either.

SIGNORA FROLA. But, my dear sir, how can you help hurting me when you force him to give almost publicly an explanation which is quite absurd—ridiculous I might even say! Surely people like you can't seriously believe what he says? You can't possibly be taking me for a lunatic? You don't really think that this woman is his second wife? And yet it is all so necessary! He needs to have it that way. It is the only way he can pull himself together; get down to his work again . . . the only way . . . the only way! Why he gets all wrought up, all excited, when he is forced to talk of this other matter; because he knows himself how hard it is for him to say certain things. You may have noticed it . . .

AGAZZI. Yes, that is quite true. He did seem very much excited.

SIGNORA SIRELLI. Well, well, well, so then it's he!

SIRELLI [*triumphantly*]. I always said it was he.

AGAZZI. Oh, I say! Is that really possible? [*He motions to the company to be quiet*]

SIGNORA FROLA [*joining her hands beseechingly*]. My dear friends, what are you really thinking? It is only on this subject that he is a little queer. The point is, you must simply not mention this particular matter to him. Why, really now, you could never suppose that I would leave my daughter shut up with him all alone like that? And yet, just watch him at his work and in the office. He does everything he is expected to do and no one in the world could do it better.

AGAZZI. But this is not enough, madam, as you will understand. Do you mean to say that Signor Ponza, your son-in-law, came here and made up a story out of whole cloth?

SIGNORA FROLA. Yes sir, yes sir, exactly . . . only I will explain. You must understand—you must look at things from his point of view.

AGAZZI. What do you mean? Do you mean that your daughter is not dead?

SIGNORA FROLA. God forbid! Of course she is not dead!

AGAZZI. Well, then, he is the lunatic!

SIGNORA FROLA. No, no, look, look! . . .

SIRELLI. I always said it was he! . . .

SIGNORA FROLA. No, look, look, not that, not that! Let me explain . . . You have noticed him, haven't you? Fine, strong looking man. Well, when he married my daughter you can imagine how fond he was of her. But alas, she fell sick with a contagious disease; and the doctors had to separate her from him. Not only from him of course, but from all her relatives. They're all dead now, poor things, in the earthquake, you understand. Well, he just refused to have her taken to the hospital; and he got so over-wrought that they actually had to put him under restraint; and he broke down nervously as the result of it all and he was sent to a sanatorium. But my daughter got better very soon, while he got worse and worse. He had a sort of obsession that his wife had died in the hospital, that perhaps they had killed her there; and you couldn't get that idea out of his head.

Just imagine when we brought my daughter back to him quite recovered from her illness—and a pretty thing she was to look at, too—he began to scream and say, no, no, no, she wasn't his wife, his wife was dead! He looked at her: No, no, no, not at all! She wasn't the woman! Imagine, my dear friends, how terrible it all was. Finally he came up close to her and for a moment it seemed that he was going to recognize her again; but once more it was "No, no, no, she is not my wife!" And do you know, to get him to accept my daughter at all again, we were obliged to pretend having a second wedding, with the collusion of his doctors and his friends, you understand!

SIGNORA SIRELLI.   Ah, so that is why he says that . . .

SIGNORA FROLA.   Yes, but he doesn't really believe it, you know; and he hasn't for a long time, I am sure. But he seems to feel a need for maintaining the pretense. He can't do without it. He feels surer of himself that way. He is seized with a terrible fear from time to time, that this little wife he loves may be taken from him again. [*Smiling and in a low, confidential tone*] So he keeps her locked up at home where he can have her all for himself. But he worships her— he worships her; and I am really quite convinced that my daughter is one of the happiest women in the world. [*She gets up*] And now I must be going. You see, my son-in-law is in a terrible state of mind at present. I wouldn't like to have him call, and find me not at home. [*With a sigh, and gesturing with her joined hands*] Well, I suppose we must get along as best we can; but it is hard on my poor girl. She has to pretend all along that she is not herself, but another, his second wife; and I . . . oh, as for me, I have to pretend that I am a lunatic when he's around, my dear friends; but I'm glad to, I'm glad to really, so long as it does him some good. [*The ladies rise as she steps nearer to the door*] No, no, don't let me interrupt your party. I know the way out! Good afternoon! Good afternoon!

[*Bowing and smiling, she goes out through the rear door. The others stand there in silence, looking at each other with blank astonishment on their faces*]

LAUDISI [*coming forward*].   So you want the truth, eh? The truth! The truth! Hah! hah! hah! hah! hah! hah! hah!

CURTAIN

KNOWLEDGE AND BELIEF

Norman Malcolm

"We must recognize that when we know something we either do, or by reflecting, can know that our condition is one of knowing that thing, while when we believe something, we either do or can know that our condition is one of believing and not of knowing: so that we cannot mistake belief for knowledge or vice versa."

This remark is worthy of investigation. Can I discover *in myself* whether I know something or merely believe it?

Let us begin by studying the ordinary usage of "know" and "believe." Suppose, for example, that several of us intend to go for a walk and that you propose that we walk in Cascadilla Gorge. I protest that I should like to walk beside a flowing stream and that at this season the gorge is probably dry. Consider the following cases:

(1) You say "I believe that it won't be dry although I have no particular reason for thinking so." If we went to the gorge and found a flowing stream we should not say that you *knew* that there would be water but that you thought so and were right.

(2) You say "I believe that it won't be dry because it rained only three days ago and usually water flows in the gorge for at least that long after a rain." If we found water we should be inclined to say that you knew that there would be water. It would be quite natural for you to say "I knew that it wouldn't be dry"; and we should tolerate your remark. This case differs from the previous one in that here you had a *reason*.

(3) You say "I know that it won't be dry" and give the same reason as in (2). If we found water we should have very little hesitation in saying that you knew. Not only had you a reason, but you *said* "I know" instead of "I believe." It may seem to us that the latter should not make a difference—but it does.

(4) You say "I know that it won't be dry" and give a stronger reason, e.g., "I saw a lot of water flowing in the gorge when I passed it

FROM "Knowledge and Belief," in *Mind,* vol. 61, no. 242 (April 1952). Reprinted by permission of Basil Blackwell Publisher.

this morning." If we went and found water, there would be no hesitation at all in saying that you knew. If, for example, we later met someone who said "Weren't you surprised to see water in the gorge this afternoon?" you would reply "No, I *knew* that there would be water; I had been there earlier in the day." We should have no objection to this statement.

(5) Everything happens as in (4), except that upon going to the gorge you find it to be dry. We should not say that you knew, but that you *believed* that there would be water. And this is true even though you declared that you knew, and even though your evidence was the same as it was in case (4) in which you did know.

I wish to make some comments on the usage of "know," "knew," "believe," and "believed," as illustrated in the preceding cases:

(*a*) Whether we should say that you knew, depends in part on whether you had grounds for your assertion and on the strength of those grounds. There would certainly be less hesitation to say that you knew in case (4) than in case (3), and this can be due only to the difference in the strength of the grounds.

(*b*) Whether you should say that you knew, depends in part on how *confident* you were. In case (2), if you had said "It rained only three days ago and usually water flows in the gorge for at least that long after a rain; but, of course, I don't feel absolutely sure that there will be water," then we should *not* have said that you knew that there would be water. If you lack confidence that *p* is true then others do not say that you know that *p* is true, even though *they* know that *p* is true. Being confident is a necessary condition for knowing.

(*c*) Prichard says that if we reflect we cannot mistake belief for knowledge. In case (4) you knew that there would be water, and in case (5) you merely believed it. Was there any way that you could have discovered by reflection, in case (5), that you did not know? It would have been useless to have reconsidered your grounds for saying that there would be water, because in case (4), where you *did* know, your grounds were identical. They could be at fault in (5) only if they were at fault in (4), and they were not at fault in (4). Cases (4) and (5) differ in only one respect—namely, that in one case you did subsequently find water and in the other you did not. Prichard says that we can determine by reflection whether we know something or merely believe it. But where, in these cases, is the material that reflection would strike upon? There is none.

There is only one way that Prichard could defend his position. He would have to say that in case (4) you did *not* know that there would be water. And it is obvious that he would have said this. But this is false. It is an enormously common usage of language to say, in commenting upon just such an incident as (4), "He knew that the gorge would be dry because he had seen water flowing there that morning." It is a usage that all of us are familiar with. We so employ "know" and "knew" every day of our lives. We do not think of our usage as being loose or incorrect—and it is not. As philosophers we may be surprised to observe that it *can* be that the knowledge that *p* is true should differ from the belief that *p* is true only in the respect that in one case *p* is true and in the other false. But that is the fact.

There is an argument that one is inclined to use as a proof that you did not know that there would be water. The argument is the following: It could have turned out that you found no water, if it had so turned out you would have been mistaken in saying that you would find water; therefore you could have been mistaken; but if you could have been mistaken then you did not know.

Now it certainly *could* have turned out that the gorge was quite dry when you went there, even though you saw lots of water flowing through it only a few hours before. This does not show, however, that you did not know that there would be water. What it shows is that *although you knew you could have been mistaken.* This would seem to be a contradictory result; but it is not. It seems so because our minds are fixed upon another usage of "know" and "knew"; one in which "It could have turned out that I was mistaken," implies "I did not know."

When is "know" used in this sense? I believe that Prichard uses it in this sense when he says that when we go through the proof of the proposition that the angles of a triangle are equal to two right angles we *know* that the proposition is true. He says that if we put to ourselves the question: Is our condition one of knowing this, or is it only one of being convinced of it? then "We can only answer 'Whatever may be our state on other occasions, here we are knowing this.' And this statement is an expression of our *knowing* that we are knowing; for we do not *believe* that we are knowing this, we know that we are." He goes on to say that if someone were to object that we might be making a mistake "because for all we know we can later on discover some fact which is incompatible with a triangle's having angles that are equal to two right angles, we can answer that we *know* that there can be no such fact, for in knowing that a triangle must have such angles we also know that nothing can exist which is incompatible with this fact."

It is easy to imagine a nonphilosophical context in which it would have been natural for Prichard to have said "I know that the angles of a triangle are equal to two right angles." Suppose that a young man just beginning the study of geometry was in doubt as to whether that proposition is true, and had even constructed an ingenious argument that appeared to prove it false. Suppose that Prichard was unable to find any error in the argument. He might have said to the young man: "There must be an error in it. I know that the angles of a triangle are equal to two right angles."

When Prichard says that "nothing can exist which is incompatible with" the truth of that proposition, is he prophesying that no one will ever have the ingenuity to construct a flawless-looking argument against it? I believe not. When Prichard says that "we" *know* (and implies that *he* knows) that the proposition is true and *know* that nothing can exist that is incompatible with its being true, he is not making any *prediction* as to what the future will bring in the way of arguments or measurements. On the contrary, he is asserting that *nothing* that the future might bring could ever count as evidence against the proposition. He is implying that he would not *call* anything "evidence" against it. He is using "know" in what I shall call its "strong" sense. "Know" is used in this sense when a person's statement "I know that *p* is true" implies that the person who makes the statement would look upon nothing whatever as evidence that *p* is false.

It must not be assumed that whenever "know" is used in connection with mathematical propositions it is used in the strong sense. A great many people have *heard* of various theorems of geometry, e.g., the Pythagorean. These theorems are a part of "common knowledge." If a schoolboy doing his geometry assignment felt a doubt about the Pythagorean theorem, and said to an adult "Are you *sure* that it is true?" the latter might reply "Yes, I know that it is." He might make this reply even though he could not give proof of it and even though he had never gone through a proof of it. If subsequently he was presented with a "demonstration" that the theorem is false, or if various persons reputed to have a knowledge of geometry soberly assured him that it is false, he might be filled with doubt or even be convinced that he was mistaken. When he said "Yes, I know that it is true," he did not pledge himself to hold to the theorem through thick and thin. He did not absolutely exclude the possibility that something could prove it to be false. I shall say that he used "know" in the "weak" sense.

Consider another example from mathematics of the difference between the strong and weak senses of "know." I have just now rapidly calculated that 92 times 16 is 1472. If I had done this in the commerce of daily life where a practical problem was at stake, and if someone had asked "Are you sure that $92 \times 16 = 1472$?" I might have answered "I *know* that it is; I have just now calculated it." But also I might have answered "I know that it is; but I will calculate it again to *make sure*." And here my language points to a distinction. I say that I *know* that $92 \times 16 = 1472$. Yet I am willing to *confirm* it—that is, there is something that I should *call* "making sure"; and, likewise, there is something that I should *call* "finding out that it is false." If I were to do this calculation again and obtain the result that $92 \times 16 = 1372$, and if I were to carefully check this latter calculation without finding any error, I should be disposed to say that I was previously mistaken when I declared that $92 \times 16 = 1472$. Thus when I say that I know that $92 \times 16 = 1472$, I allow for the possibility of a *refutation;* and so I am using "know" in its weak sense.

Now consider propositions like $2 + 2 = 4$ and $7 + 5 = 12$. It is hard to think of circumstances in which it would be natural for me to say that I know that $2 + 2 = 4$, because no one ever questions it. Let us try to suppose, however, that someone whose intelligence I respect argues that certain developments in arithmetic have shown that $2 + 2$ does not equal 4. He writes out a proof of this in which I can find no flaw. Suppose that his demeanor showed me that he was in earnest. Suppose that several persons of normal intelligence became persuaded that his proof was correct and that $2 + 2$ does not equal 4. What would be my reaction? I should say "I can't see what is wrong with your proof; but it *is* wrong, because I *know* that $2 + 2 = 4$." Here I should be using "know" in its strong sense. I should not admit that any argument or any future development in mathematics could show that it is false that $2 + 2 = 4$.

The propositions $2 + 2 = 4$ and $92 \times 16 = 1472$ do not have the same status. There *can* be a demonstration that $2 + 2 = 4$. But a demonstration would be for me (and for any average person) only a curious exercise, a sort of *game*. We have no serious interest in proving that proposition. It does not *need* a proof. It stands without one, and would not fall if a proof went against it. The case is different with the proposition that $92 \times 16 = 1472$. We take an interest in the demonstration (calculation) because that proposition *depends* upon its demonstration. A calculation may lead me to reject it as false. But $2 + 2 = 4$ does *not* depend on its demonstration. It does not depend on anything! And in the calculation that proves that $92 \times 16 = 1472$, there are steps that do not depend on any calculation (e.g., $2 \times 6 = 12$; $5 + 2 = 7$; $5 + 9 = 14$).

There is a correspondence between this dualism in the logical status of mathematical propositions and the two senses of "know." When I use "know" in the weak sense I am prepared to let an investigation (demonstration, calculation) determine whether the something that I claim to know is true or false. When I use "know" in the strong sense I am not prepared to look upon anything as an *investigation;* I do not concede that anything whatsoever could prove me mistaken; I do not regard the matter as open to any *question;* I do not admit that my proposition could turn out to be false, that any future investigation *could* refute it or cast doubt on it.

We have been considering the strong sense of "know" in its application to mathematical propositions. Does it have application anywhere in the realm of *empirical* propositions—for example, to propositions that assert or imply that certain physical things exist? Descartes said that we have a "moral assurance" of the truth of some of the latter propositions but that we lack a "metaphysical certainty." Locke said that the perception of the existence of physical things is not "so certain as our intuitive knowledge, or the deductions of our reason" although "it is an assurance that deserves the name of knowledge." Some philosophers have held that when we make judgments of perception such as that there are peonies in the garden, cows in the field, or dishes in the cupboard, we are "taking for granted" that the peonies, cows, and dishes exist, but not knowing it in the "strict" sense. Others have held that all empirical propositions, including judgments of perception, are merely hypotheses. The thought behind this exaggerated mode of expression is that any empirical proposition whatever *could* be refuted by future experience—that is, it *could* turn out to be false. Are these philosophers right?

Consider the following propositions:

i. The sun is about ninety million miles from the earth.
ii. There is a heart in my body.
iii. Here is an ink bottle.

In various circumstances I should be willing to assert of each of these propositions that I know it to be true. Yet they differ strikingly. This I see when, with each, I try to imagine the possibility that it is false.

(i) If in ordinary conversation someone said to me "The sun is about twenty million miles from the earth, isn't it?" I should reply "No, it is about ninety million miles from us." If he said "I think that you are confusing the sun with Polaris," I should reply, "I *know* that ninety million miles is roughly the sun's distance from the earth." I might invite him to verify the figure in an encyclopedia. A third person who overheard our conversation could quite correctly report that I knew the distance to the sun, whereas the other man did not. But this knowledge of mine is little better than hearsay. I have seen that figure mentioned in a few books. I know nothing about the observations and calculations that led astronomers to accept it. If tomorrow a group of eminent astronomers announced that a great error had been made and that the correct figure is twenty million miles, I should not insist that they were wrong. It would surprise me that such an enormous mistake could have been made. But I should no longer be willing to say that I *know* that ninety million is the correct figure. Although I should *now* claim that I know the distance to be about ninety million miles, it is easy for me to envisage the possibility that some future investigation will prove this to be false.

(ii) Suppose that after a routine medical examination the excited doctor reports to me that the X-ray photographs show that I have no heart. I should tell him to get a new machine. I should be inclined to say that the fact that I have a heart is one of the few things that I can count on as absolutely certain. I can feel it beat. I know it's there. Furthermore, how could my blood circulate if I didn't have one? Suppose that later on I suffer a chest injury and undergo a surgical operation. Afterwards the astonished surgeons solemnly declare that they searched my chest cavity and found no heart, and that they made incisions and looked about in other likely places but found it not. They are convinced that I am without a heart. They are unable to understand how circulation can occur or what accounts for the thumping in my chest. But they are in agreement and obviously sincere, and they have clear photographs of my interior spaces. What would be my attitude? Would it be to insist that they were all mistaken? I think not. I believe that I should eventually accept their testimony and the evidence of the photographs. I should consider to be false what I now regard as an absolute certainty.

(iii) Suppose that as I write this paper someone in the next room were to call out to me "I can't find an ink bottle; is there one in the house?" I should reply "Here is an ink bottle." If he said in a doubtful tone "Are you sure? I looked there before," I should reply "Yes, I know there is; come and get it."

Now could it turn out to be false that there is an ink bottle directly in front of me on this desk? Many philosophers have thought so. They would say that many things could happen of such a nature that if they did happen it would be proved that I am deceived. I agree that many extraordinary things could happen, in the sense that there is no logical absurdity in the supposition. It could happen that when I next reach for this ink bottle my hand should seem to pass *through* it and I should not feel the contact of any object. It could happen that in the next moment the ink bottle will suddenly vanish from sight; or that I should find myself under a tree in the garden with no ink bottle about; or that one or more persons should enter this room and declare with apparent sincerity that they see no ink bottle on this desk; or that a photograph taken now of the top of the desk should clearly show all of the objects on it except the ink bottle. Having admitted that these things *could happen,* am I compelled to admit that if they did happen then it would be proved that there is no ink bottle here *now?* Not at all! I could say that when my hand seemed to pass through the ink bottle I should *then* be suffering from hallucination; that if the ink bottle suddenly vanished it would have miraculously ceased to exist; that the other persons were conspiring to drive me mad, or were themselves victims of remarkable concurrent hallucinations; that the camera possessed some strange flaw or that there was trickery in developing the negative. I admit that in the next moment I could find myself under a tree or in the bathtub. But this is not to admit that it could be revealed in the next moment that I am now dreaming. For what I admit is that I might be instantaneously transported to the garden, but not that in the next moment I might *wake up* in the garden. There is nothing that could happen to me in the next moment that I should call "waking up"; and therefore nothing that could happen to me in the next moment would be accepted by me now as proof that I now dream.

Not only do I not *have* to admit that these extraordinary occurrences would be evidence that there is no ink bottle here; the fact is that I *do not* admit it. There is nothing whatever that could happen in the next moment or the next year that would by me be called *evidence* that there is not an ink bottle here now. No future experience or investigation could prove to me that I am mistaken. Therefore, if I were to say "I know that there is an ink bottle here," I should be using "know" in the strong sense.

It will appear to some that I have adopted an *unreasonable* attitude toward that statement. There is, however, nothing unreasonable about it. It seems so because one thinks that the statement that here is an ink bottle *must* have the same status as the statements that the sun is ninety million miles away and that I have a heart and that there will be water in the gorge this afternoon. But this is a *prejudice*.

In saying that I should regard nothing as evidence that there is no ink bottle here now, I am not *predicting* what I should do if various astonishing things happened. If other members of my family entered this room and, while looking at the top of this desk, declared with apparent sincerity that they see no ink bottle, I might fall into a swoon or become mad. I *might* even come to believe that there is not and has not been an ink bottle here. I cannot foretell with certainty how I should react. But if it is *not* a prediction, what is the meaning of my assertion that I should regard nothing as evidence that there is no ink bottle here?

That assertion describes my *present* attitude toward the statement that here is an ink bottle. It does not prophesy what my attitude *would* be if various things happened. My present attitude toward that statement is radically different from my present attitude toward those other statements (i.e., that I have a heart). I do *now* admit that certain future occurrences would disprove the latter. Whereas no imaginable future occurrence would be considered by me *now* as proving that there is not an ink bottle here.

These remarks are not meant to be autobiographical. They are meant to throw light on the common concepts of evidence, proof, and disproof. Every one of us upon innumerable occasions of daily life takes this same attitude toward various statements about physical things, e.g., that here is a torn page, that this dish is broken, that the thermometer reads 70, that no rug is on the floor. Furthermore, the concepts of proof, disproof, doubt, and conjecture *require* us to take this attitude. In order for it to be possible that any statements about physical things should *turn out to be false* it is necessary that some statements about physical things *cannot* turn out to be false.

This will be made clear if we ask ourselves the question, When do we *say* that something turned out to be false? When do we use those words? Someone asks you for a dollar. You say "There is one in this drawer." You open the drawer and look, but it is perfectly empty. Your statement turned out to be false. This can be said because you *discovered* an empty drawer. It could not be said if it were only probable that the drawer is empty or were still open to question. Would it make sense to say "I had better make sure that it is empty; perhaps there is a dollar in it after all?" Sometimes; but not always. Not if the drawer lies open before your eyes. That remark is the prelude to a search. What search can there be when the emptiness of the drawer confronts you? In certain circumstances there is nothing that you would call "making sure" that the drawer is empty; and likewise nothing that you would call "its turning out to be false" that the drawer is empty. You *made* sure that the drawer is empty. One statement about physical things *turned out to be false* only because you *made sure* of another statement about physical things. The two concepts cannot exist apart. Therefore it is impossible that *every* statement about physical things *could* turn out to be false.

In a certain important respect some a priori statements and some empirical statements possess the same logical character. The statements that $5 \times 5 = 25$ and that here is an ink bottle, both lie beyond the reach of doubt. On both, my judgment and reasoning *rests*. If you could somehow undermine my confidence in either, you would not teach me *caution*. You would fill my mind with chaos! I could not even make *conjectures* if you took away those fixed points of certainty; just as a man cannot *try* to climb whose body has no support. A conjecture implies an understanding of what certainty would be. If it is not a certainty that $5 \times 5 = 25$ and that here is an ink bottle, then I do not understand what it is. You cannot make me doubt either of these statements or treat them as hypotheses. You cannot persuade me that future experience could refute them. With both of them it is perfectly unintelligible to me to speak of a "possibility" that they are false. This is to say that I know both of them to be true, in the strong sense of "know." And I am inclined to think that the strong sense of "know" is what various philosophers have had in mind when they have spoken of "perfect," "metaphysical," or "strict certainty."

It will be thought that I have confused a statement about my "sensations," or my "sense-data," or about the way something *looks* or *appears* to me, with a statement about physical things. It will be thought that the things that I have said about the statement "Here is an ink bottle" could be true only if that statement is interpreted to mean something like "There appears to me to be an ink bottle here," i.e., interpreted so as not to assert or imply that any physical thing exists. I wish to make it clear that my statement "Here is an ink bottle" is *not* to be interpreted in that way. It would be utterly fantastic for me in my present circumstances to say "There appears to me to be an ink bottle here."

If someone were to call me on the telephone and say that he urgently needed an ink bottle I should invite him to come here and get this one. If he said that it was extremely urgent that he should obtain one immediately and that he could not afford to waste time going to a place where there might not be one, I should tell him that it is an absolute certainty that there is one here, that nothing could be more certain, that it is something I absolutely guarantee. But if my statement "There is an ink bottle here" were a statement about my "sensations" or "sense-data," or if it meant that there *appears* to me to be an ink bottle here or that something here *looks* to me like an ink bottle, and if that is all that I meant by it—then I should react quite differently to his urgent request. I should say that there is probably an ink bottle here but that I could not *guarantee* it, and that if he needs one very desperately and at once then he had better look elsewhere. In short, I wish to make it clear that my statement "Here is an ink bottle" is strictly about physical things and not about "sensations," "sense-data," or "appearances."

Let us go back to Prichard's remark that we can determine by reflection whether we know something or merely believe it. Prichard would think that "knowledge in the weak sense" is mere belief and not knowledge. This is wrong. But if we let ourselves speak this way, we can then see some justification for Prichard's remark. For then he would be asserting, among other things, that we can determine by reflection whether we know something in the strong sense or in the weak sense. This is not literally true; however, there is this truth in it—that reflection can make us realize that we are *using* "I know it" in the strong (or weak) sense in a particular case. Prichard says that reflection can show us that "our condition is one of knowing" a certain thing, or instead that "our condition is one of believing and not of knowing" that thing. I do not understand what could be meant here by "our condition." The way I should put it is that reflection on *what we should think* if certain things were to happen may make us realize that we should (or should not) call those things "proof" or "evidence" that what we claim to know is not so. I have tried to show that the distinction between strong and weak knowledge does not run parallel to the distinction between a priori and empirical knowledge but cuts across it, i.e., these two kinds of knowledge may be distinguished *within* a priori knowledge and *within* empirical knowledge.

Reflection can make me realize that I am using "know" in the strong sense; but can reflection show me that I *know* something in the strong sense (or in the weak)? It is not easy to state the logical facts here. On the one hand, if I make an assertion of the form "I know that *p*" it does not follow that *p,* whether or not I am using "know" in the strong sense. If I have said to someone outside my room "Of course, I know that Freddie is in here," and I am speaking in the strong sense, it does not *follow* that Freddie is where I claim he is. This logical fact would not be altered even if I *realized* that I was using "know" in the strong sense. My reflection on what I should say if . . . , cannot show me that I *know* something. From the fact that I should not call anything "evidence" that Freddie is not here, it does not follow that he *is* here; therefore, it does not follow that I *know* he is here.

On the other hand, in an actual case of my using "know" in the strong sense, I cannot envisage a possibility that what I say to be true should turn out to be not true. If I were speaking of *another person's* assertion about something, I *could* think both that he is using "know" in the strong sense and that nonetheless what he claims he knows to be so might turn out to be not so. But *in my own case* I cannot have this conjunction of thoughts, and this is a logical and not a psychological fact. When *I* say that I know something to be so, using "know" in the strong sense, it is unintelligible *to me* (although perhaps not to others) to suppose that anything could prove that it is not so and, therefore, that I do not know it.

IGNORANCE:
A CASE FOR SKEPTICISM

Peter Unger

What Attitude Is Involved in One's Being Absolutely Certain?

I will now, at last, begin to argue for the idea that to be absolutely certain of something is, owing to a certain feature of personal certainty, to be *dogmatic* in the matter of whether that thing is so. It is because of this dogmatic feature that there is always *something* wrong with being absolutely certain. . . . My argument for the idea that this feature ensures this dogmatism falls naturally into two parts. The first part, which will occupy us in this present section . . . is aimed at specifying the feature. . . . Thus, we will argue here that one's being absolutely certain of something involves one in having a certain severely negative *attitude* in the matter of whether that thing is so. . . . It is, at least roughly, the attitude that *no* new information, evidence, or experience will now be seriously considered by one to be *at all* relevant to any possible change in how certain one should be in the matter; no matter what new experience I may have, I will be no less certain but that *p*. . . . What can we say for the idea that one's being absolutely certain entails one's having such an absolutely severe attitude, or approach, or frame of mind?

The thought that such an absolutely severe attitude should be essential to one's knowing is hardly novel with me. Indeed, philosophers who are quite plainly anti-skeptical proclaim just this attitude as essential to one's knowing. Thus Norman Malcolm, a good representative, thinks himself to know that there is an ink bottle before him, and describes what he takes to be implicit in this knowledge of his:

Not only do I not *have* to admit that (those) extraordinary occurrences would be evidence that there is no ink bottle here; the fact is that I *do not* admit it. There is nothing whatever that could happen in the next moment that would by me be called *evidence* that there is not an ink bottle here now. No future experience or investigation could prove to me that I am mistaken. . . .

It will appear to some that I have adopted an *unreasonable* attitude toward that statement. There is, however, nothing unreasonable about it.

In saying that I should regard nothing as evidence that there is no ink bottle here now, I am not *predicting* what I should do if various astonishing things happened. . . .

That assertion describes my *present* attitude toward the statement that here is an ink bottle.

Now Malcolm, it is true, aligns himself with the idea that there are two (or more) senses of "know" to be found in sentences like "John *knows* that there is an ink bottle before him." But, while this idea is not correct, it is not essential to his position in these passages. We already have argued, . . . that this idea is not correct. That this incorrect idea is not essential to the main thrust of Malcolm's quoted remarks is, I think, equally clear. For he allows that there is at least *a* sense of "know" where knowing entails one's having the extreme attitude he characterizes. Presumably, that sense, at least, is just the sense where knowing entails being absolutely certain. Now, in that anti-skeptical philosophers think that when one knows the attitude of certainty is not only present but quite all right, their thinking that the attitude is to be characterized in such severe negative terms is some indirect evidence for thinking so. For an attitude which is so severely negative as this might well *not* be one which is very often justified. The point is that even if one wants to *avoid* skepticism, one may have a concern for the truth about what attitude, regarding possible new experience, is involved in someone's being *certain* and in his *knowing*. This laudable concern seems to make an absolutely severe characterization quite unavoidable.

The attitude of certainty concerns *any* sequence of experience or events (which could consistently be presented to the sentient subject, and which does not prejudge the issue, i.e., is not like "the experience of realizing that, after all, not-*p*"). Thus, one is certain that there is an ink bottle before one only if one's attitude is this: No matter how things may seem to appear, *I will not count* as contrary evidence such extraordinary sequences as these:

When I next reach for this ink bottle my hand should seem to pass *through* it and I should not feel the contact of any object. . . . In the next moment the ink bottle will suddenly vanish from sight; . . . I should find myself under a tree in the garden with no ink bottle about; . . . one or more persons should enter this room and declare that they see no ink bottle on this desk; . . . a photograph taken now of the top of the desk should clearly show all of the objects on it except the ink bottle.

Now, however certain one may be that some or all of these sequences will not occur, that is of course not the same thing as being certain that there is an ink bottle before one. But, though there may be many differences between the two, perhaps the one which should most clearly be focused on is this: If one is really certain of the ink bottle, and not just of other things however related, then one's attitude is that *even if one should* seem to find oneself in a contrary garden, one *would disregard* this experience as irrelevant to the question of whether, at the time in question, there is or was an ink bottle before one. One might resist this characterization, but then, I think, one would lose one's proper focus on what it is of which one is certain.

Here is a line of resistance to our characterization of being certain. Suppose, in contrast, one's attitudes were these: *If* strange things seemed to happen, then perhaps I would change my mind; I just might. But, I am absolutely certain that no strange things will ever happen to speak against there being an ink bottle. Might not these attitudes be those of a man who was *absolutely* certain *that there is an ink bottle before him?* Might not he be certain of the ink bottle, not in or by having a completely exclusionary attitude on that matter itself, but, rather, indirectly, so to speak, in or by having just such an attitude toward the possibility of apparently contrary appearances.

This suggestion, this line of resistance, is an interesting one, but it is neither correct nor of any use even if it were correct. First, let us notice that at least almost invariably when one is even quite close to being absolutely certain of something, one is not nearly so certain that no contrary appearances will turn up. For example, you may be quite sure that I am married. But, you will not be quite so sure that no appearances to the contrary might show up: I may be married but say to you "No, I'm not really married. Mary and I don't believe in such institutions. We only sent out announcements to see the effect—and, of course, it's easier to have most people believe that you are." I might, at a certain point, say these things to you and get a few other people to say apparently confirmatory things. All of this, and some more if need be, should and would, I think, incline you to be at least a bit less certain that I am married. Thus, at least with things where one is *quite* certain, the matter seems to be quite the *opposite* of what was suggested: one will not be so certain that nothing strangely contradictory will turn up—but one will reject at least almost any such thing even if it does turn up. We may plausibly project that things work even more strongly in this direction in situations where someone is absolutely certain (if there really are any such).

Let us now take something of which you are as certain as anything, say, that one and one are two. Suppose that you are very sure that your favorite mathematician will never say something false to you about any such simple sum. Imagine that he, or God, tells you and insists that one and one are three, and not two. Or, you may be told that this proposition is *not* true because, according to the *correct* ontology, there are no numbers at all. If your attitude is that he, or He, is still to be trusted or, at least, that you would no longer be quite so sure of the sum, then you are *not* absolutely certain that one and one are two. If you *are absolutely certain* of this sum, then, I submit, your attitude will be to reject entirely the message from the mathematician or God. In this simple arithmetical matter, you are to give it, perhaps unlike other messages from the same source, no weight at all in your thinking. It seems, then, that this line of resistance is not faithful to the idea of being certain of a particular thing. But would it be of any use in countering skepticism, or the skeptic's charge of dogmatism, even if it were right?

It seems to me that it is *at least as dogmatic* to take the approach that one will count nothing as even appearing to speak against one's position than to take the approach that any such appearances which might show up will be entirely rejected. What about appearances to the effect that some contrary appearances, their precise nature left open as yet, are likely to show up in the future? If one is absolutely certain that the latter sort of appearances won't ever show up, one would, presumably, have the attitude of rejecting entirely the indication of the former appearances. One's attitude of rejection gets pushed farther back from the matter itself. Perhaps according to our line of resistance, this may go on indefinitely. But each retreat, and the consequent new place for rejection, only makes a man look more and more striking in his dogmatism and unreasonableness about the whole affair. Even going back no farther than the second level, so to speak, only a quite foolhardy man would, it seems to me, reject any suggestion that some things might be brought forth to appear to speak against his position. If anything, it is better for him to allow that they may and to be ready to reject them. If *anything,* that would represent a *less* dogmatic approach or attitude. So, even if our line of resistance had presented us with a case of being certain, such an "indirect" way of being certain would hardly help us to avoid the skeptical charge. That is quite surely no way for being perfectly certain to be perfectly all right.

It is important to stress very hard that a clause like "I will regard nothing as evidence that there is no ink bottle now" must be regarded as the expression of a man's *current attitude,* and not as expressing any prediction of what he will do under certain future circumstances. Thus, one may allow that a sentence like the following is indeed consistent: "He is absolutely *certain* that there are automobiles, but he *may* change his mind should certain evidence come up." That is, because even if his present attitude is that he will not, things may not happen in accordance with his attitude. For example, things might happen to him which *cause* him to become uncertain. Or, his attitude might just evaporate, so to speak, the new evidence then effecting him in the unwanted way; and so on. Such conditions as these give us a consistent interpretation for the foregoing sentence, even if not a very ordinary one. A sentence which will still appear to express an inconsistency, on the other hand, is obtained once we make sure that our severely negative clause is embedded so that it is clear that the man's current attitude is the point. Thus, in contrast with the foregoing, it still seems always inconsistent to say, "He is absolutely *certain* that there are automobiles, but *his attitude* is that he really *may* change his mind should certain evidence come up." A proper assessment of the direct linguistic evidence supports the idea that the attitude of certainty is thus absolutely severe.

Even this reference to the attitude may not be enough, however, to ensure that an inconsistency is actually expressed. There is the possibility of what we might call the motivational problem, the problem of the subject being certain of the thing but not caring that much about whether he is right in the matter. . . . You might be certain of a particular thing, say, that there is a lamp-post on the north-east corner of 19th St. and 6th Ave., but you may not care to clutter up your mind with such trivial information (trivial, that is, for your presumed purposes). In such a case, you may not wish to exert any effort to make sure that you will continue to be right about whether there is a lamp-post at that particular street location, and you may have a weak attitude in respect of new experiences here, to accord with this lack of desire. The attitude of certainty, however, seems to require a more positive approach on your part toward making such an effort should contrary appearances arise. Thus, it might be concluded, while you *are now certain* there is a lamp-post right there, you attitude is *not* this: no matter what new experiences may show up to suggest that no lamp-post is (or was) there, I will not be any less certain that there is (or was) a lamp-post on the north-east corner of 19th St. and 6th Ave.

As I said when this idea was first introduced, I am not sure that it presents a coherent description of any person's mental states and attitudes. But, again, it may do so. In any event, to accommodate the possibility that it does, we may redescribe the attitude with an appropriate initial clause about caring enough about being right: *Insofar as I care about being right in the matter,* no matter what new experiences may show up to suggest that no lamp-post is (or was) there, I will not be any less certain that there is (or was) a lamp-post on the north-east corner of 19th St. and 6th Ave. If there is no coherent possibility here described, this initial clause may always be dropped in favor of the simpler description. The point for us to bear in mind now is this. The initial clause does nothing to make the described attitude any less dogmatic than it would be without the clause's being applicable. For if a man is not at least a bit open to new experience, his caring about being correct will not save him from the charge of dogmatism.

If one thinks that some such qualifying clause is needed, and if one was previously inclined to accept the idea that an absolutely severe attitude was entailed in being certain, one may now have second thoughts about the whole matter. Here is how those thoughts may run: You can satisfy even the strongest desire to be right about a matter just by believing correctly, by believing what is true. Being *certain* does nothing extra for you here. So why is being certain at all important for this desire, for this motivation? Perhaps our apparently upsetting examples, about the lamp-post and so on, had best be taken as upsetting our whole account of certainty, and not as requiring us only to qualify that account by an appropriate motivational clause.

These thoughts present no direct criticism of our account. But they do ask for a rationale for our motivational clause, for our idea that the concept of personal certainty entails such a severe attitude, and even for our having such a concept in our language. I think we can meet these requests in terms of the following natural considerations. If one cares about being right, one does not just want to be right for the moment. One cares about continuing to be right. Not knowing what may lie in store for one, one wants to have, not just a correct belief, but a belief or some other such attitudinal state which, other things being equal, or in most situations, will withstand the sorts of things which might get one to change ones mind in the matter, or get one to lose the belief or state in some other way. Thus, other things being equal, a stronger belief is better for one's purposes here than a weaker one. The stronger the belief, the less one will accept as evidence sufficient for suitably lessening its strength, and eventually, for abandoning it. The best state for one to be in, then, will be one of absolute certainty. For here, other things being equal, one will be in the least danger of coming to be no longer right. I think that this, or something very like it, lies behind our idea of personal certainty. (I would not be surprised if those who got the idea of certainty into our language, or into an ancestor of it, thought along just such lines.) The way which we would describe cases where other things are not equal bears out the idea that we have now been talking about our actual concept of certainty. Suppose that you believed that an eccentric deity was going to get everyone who was certain that there were automobiles to lose his certainty and, indeed, to stop even being right in the matter. Being a mind-reader, he would of course operate by selective tampering. If you cared most about being right, you might first tamper with yourself so as to avoid selection by him. But our feeling is that this is a special case, where the threats to one's position come from things which must be dealt with separately and specially. No simple state or attitude, like believing or being certain, can be expected to handle such a danger. But, the normal dangers, and most dangers, would best be thwarted by one's being *certain* that there were automobiles. Accordingly, so long as we do not restrict its temporal application too near to the present moment, our clause about caring about being right seems, no *ad hoc* device, but just what we need in describing our attitude of certainty.

Granting that the clause about caring must be added, we have the task of explaining why our sentences without it do sound inconsistent, like the sentence, "He is absolutely *certain* that there are automobiles, but his *attitude* is that he really *may* change his mind should certain evidence come up." Perhaps the reason is simply that the sorts of considerations which (at least allegedly) allow a consistent interpretation are themselves so far from our minds when we think of matters of certainty that we would not ordinarily consider them. This would be in line with our explanation of why certain normative sentences *sound* inconsistent event if without qualification they may actually express a thought which is consistent: "He really *knows* that there are automobiles, but he *shouldn't* be absolutely *certain* of it." That too *sounds* inconsistent, but without a clause like, "even if no overriding (consideration or) considerations make(s) it not even all right," the sentence actually will express a consistent idea. Now, the clause with "even if" rules out certain cases. But these are all cases which don't ordinarily come to mind when thinking of knowledge and certainty. So, the addition of that clause won't have any opportunity to effect the way the sentence sounds to us. The cases involved require so elaborate a description that linguistic intuition has no chance to operate there. Likewise with our present sentences: the clause about caring about being right rules out only bizarre and remote cases; it rules out none which would normally come to mind, or which would fit only simple descriptions. Accordingly, just as the *apparent* inconsistency of the normative sentence with "knows" provides *some* support for the idea that knowing, if it obtains, is an extraordinarily strong justifying state or condition, so the *apparent* inconsistency of these newer sentences gives *some* support for our simpler description of the attitude. We may say, I think, that the first appearance *equally* supports a premise about knowing without our "providing" clause and also one with that clause. Further considerations are needed to decide in favor of the latter, more complex alternative; and they do that. And, we may also say that the latter appearance *equally* supports a description without the initial "caring" clause and also one with that clause, thus giving some positive support to each of these. Again, further considerations are needed to decide in favor of one or the other. As I have just suggested, it may well be true that, in the latter case too, the further considerations will decide in favor of the more complex but essentially similar description. The key point here remains this: However the further decisions go, in both of these cases, the direct linguistic evidence gives some good support to a central idea which is much wanted by a skeptic.

Questions for Discussion

1. In *Right You Are . . .*, does Laudisi's claim that there is no objective truth of the matter depend on the accidental fact that all records of the Ponzas were destroyed in an earthquake? Suppose a record of the death of Ponza's first wife had been found. What could the mother-in-law have said in order to explain away such a document? In general, can documents ever conclusively prove any historical fact? In Malcolm's "strong" sense of knowledge, do we ever *know* what happened in the distant past?

2. Discuss the question of whether there are two established uses of "know." Are there more than two? Consider: "I know I had my wallet when I left the house"; "He knows very well that I wouldn't cheat him"; "Do you know what you want?"; "I know that Columbus discovered America"; and "I know that I am not dreaming." Which of Malcolm's two senses of "know" is employed in each case?

3. Malcolm claims that when he says that nothing in the future would count for him *now* as evidence against there being an inkwell on his desk, he is describing his attitude, not making a prediction. What, if anything, is the difference?

4. What does Unger mean by "dogmatic"? Is it always wrong to be dogmatic in this way? Can you describe cases in which it would be abnormal *not* to be dogmatic? (Consider: A husband refuses to say that he *knows* his wife is faithful to him, although he has no reason to suspect her.)

5. The classical empiricist tradition, from John Locke to Bertrand Russell, searched for an indubitable foundation for knowledge in the simple data of the senses, such as reports of colors, shapes, sounds, and so forth. Can a person conceivably be mistaken even in reporting "I see a bluish, rectangular patch," or "I feel hot"? If so, how? If not, do such cases provide counterexamples to Unger's absolute skepticism?

6. Can we be mistaken in believing that 2 plus 2 equals 4? What kind of evidence would show us to be mistaken? Descartes suggested that an evil demon might be deceiving us to believe that 2 plus 2 equals 4 when it really equals 5, and Unger, in his book, agrees with Descartes. But what

would the real world have to be like in order for 2 plus 2 to equal 5?
7. What does "real" mean in question 6? (See chap. 2.)

Selected Readings

AYER, A. J. *The Problem of Knowledge.* Baltimore: Pelican, 1956. The problem of the external world considered as unsolved.

CHISHOLM, R. *Perceiving.* Ithaca, New York: Cornell University Press, 1957.

———. *Theory of Knowledge.* Englewood Cliffs, New Jersey: Prentice-Hall, 1966.
Solutions to skepticism about perceptual knowledge.

FLEW, A. *Hume's Philosophy of Belief.* New York: Humanities Press, 1961. Exposition and criticism of Hume's skepticism.

HUME, D. *An Enquiry Concerning Human Understanding.* Chaps. 4, 12.

———. *A Treatise of Human Nature.* Book I, Part IV.
The main sources of modern skepticism.

MALCOLM, N. *Knowledge and Certainty.* Englewood Cliffs, New Jersey: Prentice-Hall, 1963. A critique of skepticism using ordinary language analysis.

MOORE, G. E. *Philosophical Papers.* London: Allen & Unwin, 1959. A defense of perceptual knowledge.

NAGEL, E., and BRANDT, R., eds. *Meaning and Knowledge.* New York: Harcourt Brace Jovanovich, 1965. An anthology of essays on the limits of knowledge.

RUSSELL, B. *Human Knowledge, Its Scope and Limits.* New York: Simon & Schuster, 1948. A qualified form of skepticism.

———. *Our Knowledge of the External World.* London: Allen & Unwin, 1925.

SANTAYANA, G. *Skepticism and Animal Faith.* New York: Scribner's, 1923. Attempts a pragmatic solution to skepticism.

SEXTUS EMPIRICUS. *Skepticism, Man and God.* Translated by S. Etheridge. Middletown, Connecticut: Wesleyan University Press, 1964. The main source of information about ancient skepticism.

STRAWSON, P. F. *Individuals.* Chaps. 1–2. London: Methuen, 1959. Argues that skepticism cannot be coherently stated.

STROLL, A., ed. *Epistemology.* New York: Harper & Row, 1967. A representative anthology on problems of knowledge.

UNGER, P. *Ignorance.* Oxford: Clarendon Press, 1974. Arguments for total skepticism based on linguistic considerations.

WITTGENSTEIN, L. *On Certainty.* Translated by D. Paul and G. E. M. Anscombe. New York: Harper & Row, 1969. A critique of Moore as well as of skepticism in terms of ordinary language philosophy.

PART THREE

Ethics

Chapter 7

Rules and Consequences: What Is Morally Right?

We all pride ourselves on knowing right from wrong. Indeed, someone who does not know the difference is considered to be legally insane. But sometimes a situation arises that presents us with an agonizing moral dilemma in which even the wisest and sanest among us is hard pressed to say what course of action is right. Such was the case in the court-martial of Billy Budd, in American writer Herman Melville's extraordinary novel, which is excerpted in our first selection. Melville possessed a Manichean sense of the unending struggle between good and evil and the cunning with which each can take on the appearance of the other. At the end of the story it is difficult to say which force has prevailed.

The British naval ship *Bellipotent,* commanded by Captain Starry Vere, becomes the scene of a psychological duel between Claggart, the satanic master-at-arms, and Billy Budd, a naively trusting, inarticulate, but lovable sailor. Claggart hates Billy just because Billy is kind and well liked, and persecutes him, finally accusing him of plotting mutiny. Billy can only express his shock and indignation by striking Claggart, who dies from the blow. Captain Vere than appoints three officers to preside over the court-martial and decide whether Billy Budd should be hanged. They know that Billy was innocent of any evil intention, but they agree that Billy must be hanged. The question is: Are they right?

The officers question Billy and establish that he did not intend to injure Claggart but merely wanted to express in a physical way his indignation at Claggart's false accusation. However, Billy admits that he knowingly and intentionally struck an officer, which is a capital offense. Captain Vere points out that under naval law Billy's innocent motives are irrelevant to the issue of punishment. "At the last Assizes," he declares poignantly, "Billy Budd will be acquitted, but our military duty is to hang him." The captain thus places military duty above moral duty, which is highly questionable, but he fortifies his position with a second argument. If Billy Budd should be acquitted of the act of striking an officer, the news of his acquittal would inspire many other mutinous acts, and naval discipline, already perilously weak, would collapse altogether. For the good of England, Billy Budd must be sacrificed. Thus, Captain Vere's main argument for hanging a morally innocent man is an appeal to the harmful consequences of failing to enforce the law. This kind of appeal raises the philosophical question: Is morally right action to be decided in terms of consistency with moral rules or in terms of beneficial and harmful consequences?

Utilitarianism (and its offspring, pragmatism) answers this question in terms of consequences, while formalism (which Immanuel Kant espoused) rests on adherence to universal moral rules. For the late eighteenth- and early nineteenth-century British philosopher Jeremy Bentham, we ought always to act so as to maximize benefit or minimize harm; for Kant, a German thinker of the eighteenth century, we ought always to act according to a rule that we can will to be followed by everyone.

Bentham's reason for judging rightness in terms of pleasurable and painful consequences is that it is a law of animal nature to seek pleasure and avoid pain. "Nature hath placed mankind under the governance of two masters, *pain* and *pleasure*," he declared. Consequently, there is no other basis on which we *can* act. How then, we may wonder, can anyone act imprudently? Bentham's answer is that it is all too easy to misjudge the consequences of our acts because of the variety of dimensions or factors of pleasure (benefit) involved. He therefore offered a "felicific calculus" as a method for comparing the weights of the various factors so as to arrive at an exact and informed judgment.

Bentham's calculus is a list of seven factors with respect to which pleasure and pain, or "benefit" and "disbenefit," can be "measured" (roughly, of course, since he was perfectly aware that we cannot measure benefit as precisely as weight or volume). Using this calculus, we can sum up (again, only roughly or intuitively) our particular results with regard to each factor and thereby judge the total long-range consequences of our alternative choices. The first four factors—intensity, duration, propinquity, and certainty—apply to objects between which we wish to make a reasonable choice. The next two, purity and fecundity, apply to self-regarding actions (actions that affect only oneself) in addition to the first four. The last, extent, is to be considered when our actions affect the interests of others.

Despite the criticisms, often voiced, that pleasure and pain are subjective states that vary with the individual and even for the same person from one time to another, and that the pleasure or displeasure of one kind of experience (such as eating a meal) is difficult, if not impossible, to compare with that of a very different kind (such as playing tennis or engaging in conversation), Bentham's analysis has a certain common-sense plausibility. When deciding between two alternatives, we do, in fact, often deliberate as to which will give us more intense satisfaction, which will have more lasting benefits, which is closer at hand, which is more likely to prove really satisfying, which involves a painful cost (such as overeating), which will help produce other pleasant experiences (as in the case of getting a college degree), and what will be the effect on others. The fact that we cannot assign numerical values to such considerations, as Bentham seems to suggest we do (although he may very well not have meant this literally), should not blind us to the fact that when we weigh alternatives, these are the kinds of considerations that we bear in mind in our most prudent moments.

A more serious objection may be raised to Bentham's assumption that pleasure and benefit amount to the same thing. We seem to strain the meaning of "pleasure" when we say, for example, of a mother who saves her child's life at the expense of her own that she was aiming either at her own pleasure or at that of her child; yet it would not be at all strained to say that her child's safety was, for her, of greater value or benefit to herself than even her own life. The same point could be made with respect to other "higher values," such as the advancement of science or of art or of social reform. Nevertheless, to be fair to utilitarian ethics, we should not hold it to the hedonistic limitation Bentham imposed on it by his choice of the term "pleasure" but rather consider it in its broader form, as advising us to determine the rightness of an action in terms of its likely benefits.

Bentham's seventh factor, "extent," moves us from the area of judgments of self-interest into the area of judgments of morally right action. An action that affects only oneself is prudentially right if it can reasonably be expected to maximize one's own benefit, while an action that affects more than one person is morally right if it maximizes the total benefits of all concerned. From this standpoint, if Captain Vere's estimate of the harmful consequences to the entire British navy of sparing Billy Budd's life was correct, then hanging the innocent lad was justified.

Despite its initial plausibility, two difficulties confront this view. First, if the rightness of an act is a mattter of its expected benefits, then how can we ever say that we deliberately and willfully do something wrong?

Will we not, if we have any ingenuity and know we are being judged by utilitarian standards, explain to our judges that, in our estimation, the action we chose to perform, grotesquely vicious though it may have been, seemed likely to produce maximum total benefit for all concerned? It may have cost the life of another person, one who had little to expect from life (as in Raskolnikov's case in the excerpt we chose from *Crime and Punishment* in the next chapter) but it seemed to promise so much happiness as to outweigh by far the inconvenience to the victim. No doubt a utilitarian could say that we were wrong in our estimation of the benefits and disbenefits involved, but could the utilitarian fault us *morally* and say that we were evil? It would seem 'that we had committed only an error of judgment, and if we were to be convicted morally for errors of judgment, we would all wind up, if not in hell, at least in jail. If, on the other hand, the utilitarian maintains that it is easy to judge our sincerity in claiming that we believed our action would maximize total benefit for all concerned, and that the case of murder is one where it is clear that we were insincere, then the objection may be raised that far too heavy a burden is being placed on the ability of people to judge the motivation of others and that people are notoriously unreliable, even in judging their own cases. Since these considerations seem to lead us back to the problem of free will in chapter 4, we shall let the matter rest there.

A second, and perhaps fatal, difficulty—one that the proponent of an ethics of rules such as Kant would be quick to raise—is that actions aimed solely at maximizing benefit would often be so obviously unjust that morally sensitive people could not possibly condone them. A frequently mentioned example is the case of the district attorney in a racist community who has every good reason to believe that if he or she does not frame an innocent black person for a crime, that person will be lynched and a race riot will ensue causing many more innocent deaths. Falsely accusing and then executing an innocent person cannot be justified, even by such powerful considerations of general benefit.

Utilitarians have sometimes tried to blunt the edge of this objection by agreeing that the action would be wrong but maintaining that it can be shown to be wrong on utilitarian grounds. They argue that the injustice involved is unacceptable because such injustices do more harm to the social fabric in the long run than even a race riot would produce. But this reply is convincing only in cases where the act of injustice would become known to others besides the district attorney, so that the public would then lose faith in the system of justice. If we could be assured that no one else would ever know that an innocent person had been framed and executed, the utilitarian counterargument seems to lose its force.

In direct opposition to utilitarianism (or, as it is sometimes called, "consequentialism"), Immanuel Kant maintained that the moral rightness of an act must be determined independently of any results achieved by means of it. An action is morally right only if it is performed out of duty—that is, obedience to a moral rule—rather than out of desire for its consequences. The storekeeper who charges a fair price for the sake of keeping her customers deserves no moral credit for honesty. Only if sh refrains from overcharging as a matter of duty, even when it is clearly to her advantage to overcharge (e.g., when everyone else is doing it, so that there is no reason to fear loss of customers) should we think of her action as morally right.

Duty, Kant asserts, is "respect for law," by which he clearly means moral law, not statutory law. But just which rules of conduct qualify as genuine moral laws that are worthy of such respect? Is our moral code dependent on the customs and traditions of our society, or on our personal taste, or is there just one set of laws for all? Kant's answer is that there is only one set of rules of conduct that qualify as moral laws. That set holds independently of time, place, custom, or personal preference and defines our moral duties. To determine just which rules are the moral laws, Kant suggested a fundamental principle of morality: Act so that the maxim of your conduct can be willed as a universal law (in other words. do unto others not only as you would have them do unto you, but as you would have them do to people in general). This principle has since been called the "universalizability criterion" of morality. A rule is a moral rule if and only if it makes sense to want everyone to obey it. Such rules are "categorical imperatives" (i.e., unconditional commands) rather than "hypothetical" (or conditional) admonitions because they hold independently of the goals anyone happens to pursue. Kant's ethics is also often described as "formalistic" because it is concerned only with the logical structure of rules and not with their pragmatic value in achieving personal or social benefit.

Kant offers three reasons for defining moral right in this formalistic way. First, the function of morality cannot be to promote happiness, as consequentialists maintain, since we are annoyed rather than glad when evil people enjoy happy lives. Second, Kant believes that moral duties are universally binding, whereas rules that serve as guides to satisfying our desires (hypothetical imperatives) apply only under some conditions. Exceptions can be made to hypothetical rules such as "Save your money for a rainy day" since they imply conditions such as that you expect to live long enough to benefit from your savings. But moral laws are categorical imperatives; they permit no exceptions. One is never justified in making a false promise or in deliberately taking a human life. Third, moral laws have the binding force of quasi-legal necessity (i.e., we feel we *must* obey them), whereas prudential or hypothetical rules do not have to be followed if we are prepared to take the risks involved. You ought to save some money, in the sense that it would be wise to do so. But you need not and should not feel compelled to do so. In fact, such compulsion would be pathological, a sign of mental illness. However, it is not pathological but rational to feel compelled to tell the truth. The sense of "ought" in this case is much stronger.

The Kantian view clearly escapes the two difficulties we found in utilitarianism, namely, that it seems to make moral evil an intellectual fault for which we do not normally blame a person, and that it tends to support cases of unacceptable injustice. However, Kant's formalistic or, as it is often technically called, "deontological" ethics faces difficulties of its own.

In the first place, Kant's ethics assumes that everyone is bound to want to universalize exactly the same rules, such as "Tell the truth," "Do not kill except in self-defense," and so forth. But the fact is that many people have tried to impose on others all sorts of rules that were ultimately, if not immediately, rejected. For example, people have tried to persuade others to conform to the rules "Never submit to surgical operations, but put your trust in God," "Always give a tenth of your income to the poor," and even "Superior people should be recognized to have privileges over inferior people." Either a deontologist must grant that even the craziest code is an acceptable moral code providing only that those who hold it are willing to have it practiced universally, even if they themselves suffer as a result; or else the deontologist must somehow prove that only certain rules can be willed universally with both logical and psychological consistency. Kant took the latter course, but it is highly questionable whether he succeeded. Indeed, critics claim that some of his arguments to show that only the duties he describes can be consistently universalized depend on utilitarian considerations. For example, he argues that we cannot consistently will that people may make false promises when it suits their purposes because such a rule would destroy our faith in each other's promises and thus subvert the very practice of making and believing promises. This does indeed look very suspiciously like a utilitarian argument with an eye on the consequences of the act.

A second difficulty for the deontologist is the problem of how to resolve conflicts between universal rules. We accept the rule that we should try to save human life and also the rule that we should not lie. But what should we do in a situation where it is necessary to tell a lie to save a life? Kant held that even in such a situation we should not lie because telling the truth is a strict duty, while saving lives is, according to him, only a "meritorious" duty—one that need not always be performed. There is a grain of truth in Kant's distinction between the two types of duty, but it does not follow that a strict duty must always take precedence over a meritorious duty. Few would agree that, in the case at hand, the value of truth takes precedence over that of life. In addition, there are countless situations where even strict duties are in conflict, such as the duty of a priest to protect the confidence of a criminal who has confessed to him and his duty to society to aid in the prevention of crime. The selection from Sartre in the next chapter describes a particularly agonizing conflict of a young man between duty to his mother and duty to society, which leads Sartre to reject Kantian ethics.

Although it seems impossible in view of the complexity of life to avoid conflicts between moral rules, the deontological position can perhaps be somewhat modified to take account of this tragic feature of the human condition without surrendering its basic insight. Where two moral rules are in conflict, it could be granted that one must be sacrificed, perhaps the one whose violation does the lesser harm. But the deontologist could nevertheless point out that, in such cases, a morally sensitive person would not, and should not, feel easy about such an action; he or she would and should feel, if not remorse, at least regret. The doctor who lies to his frightened patient about the patient's incurable condition should at least be sorry that he has to lie. Otherwise, we have a right to suspect that lying has become a habitual practice on his part.

Perhaps the most sinister aspect of utilitarian ethics is that it tends to encourage a frightening kind of moral complacency in people who do terrible things to others sincerely convinced that their actions will produce more benefit than harm in the long run. Political leaders who undertake wars, revolutions, counterrevolutions, and other policies that involve widespread suffering for the sake of some real or imagined higher cause are prone to this kind of complacency. "Reasons of state," "national security," "making the world safe for democracy," "a classless society," "fiscal responsibility,"—such considerations, it must be granted, often do require actions that cause considerable suffering for some in order to ensure benefits for others. On the utilitarian view, if such actions are in fact necessary, then they are right and we should admire those who have the toughness to carry them out. On the deontological view, they may be less wrong than their alternatives, but they are nonetheless wrong in that they violate moral rules. They should be done reluctantly and with regret—perhaps even in some appropriate way expiated, such as the victor nation rebuilding a territory it has devastated during a war.

It is not immediately clear how Kant's deontological view applies to the problem of Billy Budd. Since what is morally right must be decided, on Kant's view, by rules alone, it could be argued that no exception should be made to the legal rule prescribing hanging for striking an officer. This, in fact, was Captain Vere's first argument. But such an interpretation would confuse Kant's principle of respect for *moral* law with a much more dubious principle of respect for *statutory* law. Kant seems to have committed this mistake himself at times because he assumed that the first principle implies the second, but we need not accept this assumption. Since Billy Budd was, by unanimous agreement, *morally* innocent, a Kantian could argue that hanging Billy Budd for the purpose of avoiding unpleasant consequences such as mutiny would be a violation of the moral duty not to punish an innocent man. Captain Vere's second and more persuasive argument was a utilitarian appeal to consequences, and such an argument is unacceptable on Kantian grounds.

Our discussion thus far has brought to light a peculiar and very puzzling feature of moral reasoning. We often subject a rule of conduct to the test of consequences. For example, if someone claims that parents should always let their children make their own decisions, others object to this rule on the ground that following it would have disastrous results, as when a child decides not to go to school or to subsist on a diet of cake and candy. On the other hand, we often disregard undesirable consequences for the sake of consistency with a rule, as when a doctor says "I shall have to tell you the truth although you will find it painful," or when a judge reluctantly dismisses a case against a notorious criminal for lack of evidence. To resolve this dilemma of choosing between rules and consequences, philosophy tries to explain which type of consideration should take precedence. Bentham's answer is consequences. Kant's answer is consistency with rule. Since both positions have support from our moral experience, how are we to decide?

The stalemate between a morality of rules and a morality of consequences seems to call for some kind of compromise or synthesis. Many such compromises have been offered, such as Aristotle's ethics of virtuous character ("Act the way a man of good character would act") and the ideal utilitarianism of G. E. Moore and C. D. Broad ("So act as to maximize good"). Perhaps the most influential compromise nowadays is the "rule utilitarianism" of J. O. Urmson, John Rawls, Richard Brandt, and others, who argue that the morally right action is that which conforms to a universal rule, but the rule itself must be justified by the generally beneficial consequences of everyone following that rule. We leave it to the reader to explore these suggested syntheses further.

BILLY BUDD

Herman Melville

Who in the rainbow can draw the line where the violet tint ends and the orange tint begins? Distinctly we see the difference of the colors, but where exactly does the one first blendingly enter into the other? So with sanity and insanity. In pronounced cases there is no question about them. But in some supposed cases, in various degrees supposedly less pronounced, to draw the exact line of demarcation few will undertake, though for a fee becoming considerate some professional experts will. There is nothing namable but that some men will, or undertake to, do it for pay.

Whether Captain Vere, as the surgeon professionally and privately surmised, was really the sudden victim of any degree of aberration, every one must determine for himself by such light as this narrative may afford.

That the unhappy event which has been narrated could not have happened at a worse juncture was but too true. For it was close on the heel of the suppressed insurrections, an aftertime very critical to naval authority, demanding from every English sea commander two qualities not readily interfusable—prudence and rigor. Moreover, there was something crucial in the case.

In the jugglery of circumstances preceding and attending the event on board the *Bellipotent,* and in the light of that martial code whereby it was formally to be judged, innocence and guilt personified in Claggart and Budd in effect changed places. In a legal view the apparent victim of the tragedy was he who had sought to victimize a man blameless; and the indisputable deed of the latter, navally regarded, constituted the most heinous of military crimes. Yet more. The essential right and wrong involved in the matter, the clearer that might be, so much the worse for the responsibility of a loyal sea commander, inasmuch as he was not authorized to determine the matter on that primitive basis.

Small wonder then that the *Bellipotent's* captain, though in general a man of rapid decision, felt that circumspectness not less than promptitude was necessary. Until he could decide upon his course, and in each detail; and not only so, but until the concluding measure was upon the point of being enacted, he deemed it advisable, in view of all the circumstances, to guard as much as possible against publicity. Here he may or may not have erred. Certain it is, however, that subsequently in the confidential talk of more than one or two gun rooms and cabins he was not a little criticized by some officers, a fact imputed by his friends and vehemently by his cousin Jack Denton to professional jealousy of Starry Vere. Some imaginative ground for invidious comment there was. The maintenance of secrecy in the matter, the confining all knowledge of it for a time to the place where the homicide occurred, the quarterdeck cabin; in these particulars lurked some resemblance to the policy adopted in those tragedies of the palace which have occurred more than once in the capital founded by Peter the Barbarian.

The case indeed was such that fain would the *Bellipotent's* captain have deferred taking any action whatever respecting it further than to keep the foretopman a close prisoner till the ship rejoined the squadron and then submitting the matter to the judgment of his admiral.

But a true military officer is in one particular like a true monk. Not with more of self-abnegation will the latter keep his vows of monastic obedience than the former his vows of allegiance to martial duty.

Feeling that unless quick action was taken on it, the deed of the foretopman, so soon as it should be known on the gun decks, would tend to awaken any slumbering embers of the Nore among the crew, a sense of the urgency of the case overruled in Captain Vere every other consideration. But though a conscientious disciplinarian, he was no lover of authority for mere authority's sake. Very far was he from embracing opportunities for monopolizing to himself the perils of moral responsibility, none at least that could properly be referred to an official superior or shared with him by his official equals or even subordinates. So thinking, he was glad it would not be at variance with usage to turn the matter over to a summary court of his own officers, reserving to himself, as the one on whom the ultimate accountability would rest, the right of maintaining a supervision of it, or formally or informally interposing at need. Accordingly a drumhead court was summarily convened, he electing the individuals composing it: the first lieutenant, the captain of marines, and the sailing master.

In associating an officer of marines with the sea lieutenant and the sailing master in a case having to do with a sailor, the commander perhaps deviated from general custom. He was prompted thereto by the circumstance that he took that soldier to be a judicious person, thoughtful, and not altogether incapable of grappling with a difficult case unprecedented in his prior experience. Yet even as to him he was not without some latent misgiving, for withal he was an extremely good-natured man, an enjoyer of his dinner, a sound sleeper, and inclined to obesity—a man who though he would always maintain his manhood in battle might not prove altogether reliable in a moral dilemma involving aught of the tragic. As to the first lieutenant and the sailing master, Captain Vere could not but be aware that though honest natures, of approved gallantry upon occasion, their intelligence was mostly confined to the matter of active seamanship and the fighting demands of their profession.

The court was held in the same cabin where the unfortunate affair had taken place. This cabin, the commander's, embraced the entire area under the poop deck. Aft, and on either side, was a small stateroom, the one now temporarily a jail and the other a dead-house, and a yet smaller compartment, leaving a space between expanding forward into a goodly oblong of length coinciding with the ship's beam. A skylight of moderate dimension was overhead, and at each end of the oblong space were two sashed porthole windows easily convertible back into embrasures for short carronades.

All being quickly in readiness, Billy Budd was arraigned, Captain Vere necessarily appearing as the sole witness in the case, and as such temporarily sinking his rank, though singularly maintaining it in a matter apparently trivial, namely, that he testified from the ship's weather side, with that object having caused the court to sit on the lee side. Concisely he narrated all that had led up to the catastrophe, omitting nothing in Claggart's accusation and deposing as to the manner in which the prisoner had received it. At this testimony the three officers glanced with no little surprise at Billy Budd, the last man they would have suspected either of the mutinous design alleged by Claggart or the undeniable deed he himself had done. The first lieutenant, taking judicial primacy and turning toward the prisoner, said, "Captain Vere has spoken. Is it or is it not as Captain Vere says?"

In response came syllables not so much impeded in the utterance as might have been anticipated. They were these: "Captain Vere tells the truth. It is just as Captain Vere says, but it is not as the master-at-arms said. I have eaten the King's bread and I am true to the King."

"I believe you, my man," said the witness, his voice indicating a suppressed emotion not otherwise betrayed.

"God will bless you for that, your honor!" not without stammering said Billy, and all but broke down. But immediately he was recalled to self-control by another question, to which with the same emotional difficulty of utterance he said, "No, there was no malice between us.

I never bore malice against the master-at-arms. I am sorry that he is dead. I did not mean to kill him. Could I have used my tongue I would not have struck him. But he foully lied to my face and in presence of my captain, and I had to say something, and I could only say it with a blow, God help me!"

In the impulsive aboveboard manner of the frank one the court saw confirmed all that was implied in words that just previously had perplexed them, coming as they did from the testifier to the tragedy and promptly following Billy's impassioned disclaimer of mutinous intent—Captain Vere's words, "I believe you, my man."

Next it was asked of him whether he knew of or suspected aught savoring of incipient trouble (meaning mutiny, though the explicit term was avoided) going on in any section of the ship's company.

The reply lingered. This was naturally imputed by the court to the same vocal embarrassment which had retarded or obstructed previous answers. But in main it was otherwise here, the question immediately recalling to Billy's mind the interview with the afterguardsman in the forechains. But an innate repugnance to playing a part at all approaching that of an informer against one's own shipmates—the same erring sense of uninstructed honor which had stood in the way of his reporting the matter at the time, though as a loyal man-of-war's man it was incumbent on him, and failure so to do, if charged against him and proven, would have subjected him to the heaviest of penalties; this, with the blind feeling now his that nothing really was being hatched, prevailed with him. When the answer came it was a negative.

"One question more," said the officer of marines, now first speaking and with a troubled earnestness. "You tell us that what the master-at-arms said against you was a lie. Now why should he have so lied, so maliciously lied, since you declare there was no malice between you?"

At that question, unintentionally touching on a spiritual sphere wholly obscure to Billy's thoughts, he was nonplused, evincing a confusion indeed that some observers, such as can readily be imagined, would have construed into involuntary evidence of hidden guilt. Nevertheless, he strove some way to answer, but all at once relinquished the vain endeavor, at the same time turning an appealing glance toward Captain Vere as deeming him his best helper and friend. Captain Vere, who had been seated for a time, rose to his feet, addressing the interrogator. "The question you put to him comes naturally enough. But how can he rightly answer it?—or anybody else, unless indeed it be he who lies within there," designating the compartment where lay the corpse. "But the prone one there will not rise to our summons. In effect, though, as it seems to me, the point you make is hardly material. Quite aside from any conceivable motive actuating the master-at-arms, and irrespective of the provocation to the blow, a martial court must needs in the present case confine its attention to the blow's consequence, which consequence justly is to be deemed not otherwise than as the striker's deed."

This utterance, the full significance of which it was not at all likely that Billy took in, nevertheless caused him to turn a wistful interrogative look toward the speaker, a look in its dumb expressiveness not unlike that which a dog of generous breed might turn upon his master, seeking in his face some elucidation of a previous gesture ambiguous to the canine intelligence. Nor was the same utterance without marked effect upon the three officers, more especially the soldier. Couched in it seemed to them a meaning unanticipated, involving a prejudgment on the speaker's part. It served to augment a mental disturbance previously evident enough.

The soldier once more spoke, in a tone of suggestive dubiety addressing at once his associates and Captain Vere: "Nobody is present —none of the ship's company, I mean—who might shed lateral light, if any is to be had, upon what remains mysterious in this matter."

"That is thoughtfully put," said Captain Vere; "I see your drift. Ay, there is a mystery; but, to use a scriptural phrase, it is a 'mystery of iniquity,' a matter for psychologic theologians to discuss. But what has a military court to do with it? Not to add that for us any possible investigation of it is cut off by the lasting tongue-tie of—him—in yonder," again designating the mortuary stateroom. "The prisoner's deed—with that alone we have to do."

To this, and particularly the closing reiteration, the marine soldier, knowing not how aptly to reply, sadly abstained from saying aught. The first lieutenant, who at the outset had not unnaturally assumed primacy in the court, now overrulingly instructed by a glance from Captain Vere, a glance more effective than words, resumed that primacy. Turning to the prisoner, "Budd," he said, and scarce in equable tones, "Budd, if you have aught further to say for yourself, say it now."

Upon this the young sailor turned another quick glance toward Captain Vere; then, as taking a hint from that aspect, a hint confirming his own instinct that silence was now best, replied to the lieutenant, "I have said all, sir."

The marine—the same who had been the sentinel without the cabin door at the time that the foretopman, followed by the master-at-arms, entered it—he, standing by the sailor throughout these judicial proceedings, was now directed to take him back to the after compartment originally assigned to the prisoner and his custodian. As the twain disappeared from view, the three officers, as partially liberated from some inward constraint associated with Billy's mere presence, simultaneously stirred in their seats. They exchanged looks of troubled indecision, yet feeling that decide they must and without long delay. For Captain Vere, he for the time stood—unconsciously with his back toward them, apparently in one of his absent fits—gazing out from a sashed porthole to windward upon the monotonous blank of the twilight sea. But the court's silence continuing, broken only at moments by brief consultations, in low earnest tones, this served to arouse him and energize him. Turning, he to-and-fro paced the cabin athwart; in the returning ascent to windward climbing the slant deck in the ship's lee roll, without knowing it symbolizing thus in his action a mind resolute to surmount difficulties even if against primitive instincts strong as the wind and the sea. Presently he came to a stand before the three. After scanning their faces he stood less as mustering his thoughts for expression than as one only deliberating how best to put them to well-meaning men not intellectually mature, men with whom it was necessary to demonstrate certain principles that were axioms to himself. Similar impatience as to talking is perhaps one reason that deters some minds from addressing any popular assemblies.

When speak he did, something, both in the substance of what he said and his manner of saying it, showed the influence of unshared studies modifying and tempering the practical training of an active career. This, along with his phraseology, now and then was suggestive of the grounds whereon rested that imputation of a certain pedantry socially alleged against him by certain naval men of wholly practical cast, captains who nevertheless would frankly concede that His Majesty's navy mustered no more efficient officer of their grade than Starry Vere.

What he said was to this effect: "Hitherto I have been but the witness, little more; and I should hardly think now to take another tone, that of your coadjutor for the time, did I not perceive in you— at the crisis too—a troubled hesitancy, proceeding, I doubt not, from the clash of military duty with moral scruple—scruple vitalized by compassion. For the compassion, how can I otherwise than share it? But, mindful of paramount obligations, I strive against scruples that may tend to enervate decision. Not, gentlemen, that I hide from myself that the case is an exceptional one. Speculatively regarded, it well might be referred to a jury of casuists. But for us here, acting not as casuists or moralists, it is a case practical, and under martial law practically to be dealt with.

"But your scruples: do they move as in a dusk? Challenge them. Make them advance and declare themselves. Come now; do they import something like this: If, mindless of palliating circumstances, we are bound to regard the death of the master-at-arms as the prisoner's deed, then does that deed constitute a capital crime whereof the penalty is a mortal one. But in natural justice is nothing but the prisoner's overt act to be considered? How can we adjudge to summary and shameful death a fellow creature innocent before God, and whom we feel to be so?—Does that state it aright? You sign sad assent. Well, I too feel that, the full force of that. It is Nature. But do these buttons that we wear attest that our allegiance is to Nature? No, to the King. Though the ocean, which is inviolate Nature primeval, though this be the element where we move and have our being as sailors, yet as the King's officers lies our duty in a sphere correspondingly natural? So little is that true, that in receiving our commissions we in the most important regards ceased to be natural free agents. When war is declared are we the commissioned fighters previously consulted? We fight at command. If our judgments approve the war, that is but co-incidence. So in other particulars. So now. For suppose condemnation to follow these present proceedings. Would it be so much we ourselves that would condemn as it would be martial law operating through us? For that law and the rigor of it, we are not responsible. Our vowed responsibility is in this: That however pitilessly that law may operate in any instances, we nevertheless adhere to it and administer it.

"But the exceptional in the matter moves the hearts within you. Even so too is mine moved. But let not warm hearts betray heads that should be cool. Ashore in a criminal case, will an upright judge allow himself off the bench to be waylaid by some tender kinswoman of the accused seeking to touch him with her tearful plea? Well, the heart here, sometimes the feminine in man, is as that piteous woman, and hard though it be, she must here be ruled out."

He paused, earnestly studying them for a moment; then resumed.

"But something in your aspect seems to urge that it is not solely the heart that moves in you, but also the conscience, the private conscience. But tell me whether or not, occupying the position we do, private conscience should not yield to that imperial one formulated in the mode under which alone we officially proceed?"

Here the three men moved in their seats, less convinced than agitated by the course of an argument troubling but the more the spontaneous conflict within.

Perceiving which, the speaker paused for a moment; then abruptly changing his tone, went on.

"To steady us a bit, let us recur to the facts.—In wartime at sea a man-of-war's man strikes his superior in grade, and the blow kills. Apart from its effect the blow itself is, according to the Articles of War, a capital crime, Furthermore————"

"Ay, sir," emotionally broke in the officer of marines, "in one sense it was. But surely Budd purposed neither mutiny nor homicide."

"Surely not, my good man. And before a court less arbitrary and more merciful than a martial one, that plea would largely extenuate. At the Last Assizes it shall acquit. But how here? We proceed under the law of the Mutiny Act. In feature no child can resemble his father more than that Act resembles in spirit the thing from which it derives—War. In His Majesty's service—in this ship, indeed—there are Englishmen forced to fight for the King against their will. Against their conscience, for aught we know. Though as their fellow creatures some of us may appreciate their position, yet as navy officers what reck we of it? Still less recks the enemy. Our impressed men he would fain cut down in the same swath with our volunteers. As regards the enemy's naval conscripts, some of whom may even share our own abhorrence of the regicidal French Directory, it is the same on our side. War looks but to the frontage, the appearance. And the Mutiny Act, War's child, takes after the father. Budd's intent or non-intent is nothing to the purpose.

"But while, put to it by those anxieties in you which I cannot but respect, I only repeat myself—while thus strangely we prolong proceedings that should be summary—the enemy may be sighted and an engagement result. We must do; and one of two things must we do—condemn or let go."

"Can we not convict and yet mitigate the penalty?" asked the sailing master, here speaking, and falteringly, for the first.

"Gentlemen, were that clearly lawful for us under the circumstances, consider the consequences of such clemency. The people" (meaning the ship's company) "have native sense; most of them are familiar with our naval usage and tradition; and how would they take it? Even could you explain to them—which our official position forbids—they, long molded by arbitrary discipline, have not that kind of intelligent responsiveness that might qualify them to comprehend and discriminate. No, to the people the foretopman's deed, however it be worded in the announcement, will be plain homicide committed in a flagrant act of mutiny. What penalty for that should follow, they know. But it does not follow. *Why?* they will ruminate. You know what sailors are. Will they not revert to the recent outbreak at the Nore? Ay. They know the well-founded alarm—the panic it struck throughout England. Your clement sentence they would account pusillanimous. They would think that we flinch, that we are afraid of them—afraid of practicing a lawful rigor singularly demanded at this juncture, lest it should provoke new troubles. What shame to us such a conjecture on their part, and how deadly to discipline. You see then, whither, prompted by duty and the law, I steadfastly drive. But I beseech you, my friends, do not take me amiss. I feel as you do for this unfortunate boy. But did he know our hearts, I take him to be of that generous nature that he would feel even for us on whom this military necessity so heavy a compulsion is laid."

With that, crossing the deck he resumed his place by the sashed porthole, tacitly leaving the three to come to a decision. On the cabin's opposite side the troubled court sat silent. Loyal lieges, plain and practical, though at bottom they dissented from some points Captain Vere had put to them, they were without the faculty, hardly had the inclination, to gainsay one whom they felt to be an earnest man, one too not less their superior in mind than in naval rank. But it is not improbable that even such of his words as were not without influence over them, less came home to them than his closing appeal to their instinct as sea officers: in the forethought he threw out as to the practical consequences to discipline, considering the unconfirmed tone of the fleet at the time, should a man-of-war's man's violent killing at sea of a superior in grade be allowed to pass for aught else than a capital crime demanding prompt infliction of the penalty.

Not unlikely they were brought to something more or less akin to that harassed frame of mind which in the year 1842 actuated the commander of the U.S. brig-of-war *Somers* to resolve, under the so-called Articles of War, Articles modeled upon the English Mutiny Act, to resolve upon the execution at sea of a midshipman and two sailors as mutineers designing the seizure of the brig. Which resolution was carried out though in a time of peace and within not many days' sail of home. An act vindicated by a naval court of inquiry subsequently convened ashore. History, and here cited without comment. True, the circumstances on board the *Somers* were different from those on board the *Bellipotent*. But the urgency felt, well-warranted or otherwise, was much the same.

Says a writer whom few know, "Forty years after a battle it is easy for a noncombatant to reason about how it ought to have been fought. It is another thing personally and under fire to have to direct the fighting while involved in the obscuring smoke of it. Much so with respect to other emergencies involving considerations both practical and moral, and when it is imperative promptly to act. The greater the fog the more it imperils the steamer, and speed is put on though at the hazard of running somebody down. Little ween the snug card players in the cabin of the responsibilities of the sleepless man on the bridge."

In brief, Billy Budd was formally convicted and sentenced to be hung at the yardarm in the early morning watch, it being now night. Otherwise, as is customary in such cases, the sentence would forthwith have been carried out. In wartime on the field or in the fleet, a mortal punishment decreed by a drumhead court—on the field sometimes decreed by but a nod from the general—follows without delay on the heel of conviction, without appeal.

THE PRINCIPLE OF UTILITY

Jeremy Bentham

Of the Principle of Utility

Nature has placed mankind under the governance of two sovereign masters, *pain* and *pleasure*. It is for them alone to point out what we ought to do, as well as to determine what we shall do. On the one hand the standard of right and wrong, on the other the chain of causes and effects, are fastened to their throne. They govern us in all we do, in all we say, in all we think; every effort we can make to throw off our subjection, will serve but to demonstrate and confirm it. In words a man may pretend to abjure their empire: but in reality he will remain subject to it all the while. The *principle of utility* recognizes the subjection, and assumes it for the foundation of that system, the object of which is to rear the fabric of felicity by the hands of reason and of law. Systems which may attempt to question it, deal in sounds instead of sense, in caprice instead of reason, in darkness instead of light.

But enough of metaphor and declamation: it is not by such means that moral science is to be improved.

The principle of utility is the foundation of the present work; it will be proper therefore at the outset to give an explicit and determinate account of what is meant by it. By the principle of utility is meant that principle which approves or disapproves of every action whatsoever, according to the tendency which it appears to have to augment or diminish the happiness of the party whose interest is in question; or, what is the same thing in other words, to promote or to oppose that happiness. I say of every action whatsoever; and therefore not only of every action of a private individual, but of every measure of government.

By utility is meant that property in any object, whereby it tends to produce benefit, advantage, pleasure, good, or happiness (all this in

FROM *The Principles of Morals and Legislations,* chapters 1 and 4. First printed in 1780.

the present case comes to the same thing) or (what comes again to the same thing) to prevent the happening of mischief, pain, evil, or unhappiness to the party whose interest is considered: if that party be the community in general, then the happiness of the community: if a particular individual, then the happiness of that individual.

The interest of the community is one of the most general expressions that can occur in the phraseology of morals: no wonder that the meaning of it is often lost. When it has a meaning, it is this. The community is a fictitious *body,* composed of the individual persons who are considered as constituting as it were its *members.* The interest of the community then is, what?—the sum of the interests of the several members who compose it.

It is in vain to talk of the interest of the community, without understanding what is the interest of the individual. A thing is said to promote the interest, or to be *for* the interest, of an individual, when it tends to add to the sum total of his pleasures: or, what comes to the same thing, to diminish the sum total of his pains.

An action then may be said to be conformable to the principle of utility, or, for shortness' sake, to utility (meaning with respect to the community at large) when the tendency it has to augment the happiness of the community is greater than any it has to diminish it.

A measure of government (which is but a particular kind of action, performed by a particular person or persons) may be said to be conformable to or dictated by the principle of utility, when in like manner the tendency which it has to augment the happiness of the community is greater than any which it has to diminish it.

When an action, or in particular a measure of government is supposed by a man to be conformable to the principle of utility, it may be convenient, for the purposes of discourse, to imagine a kind of law or dictate, called a law or dictate of utility: and to speak of the action in question, as being conformable to such law or dictate.

A man may be said to be a partisan of the principle of utility, when the approbation or disapprobation he annexes to any action, or to any measure, is determined by and proportioned to the tendency which he conceives it to have to augment or to diminish the happiness of the community: or in other words, to its conformity or unconformity to the laws or dictates of utility.

Of an action that is conformable to the principle of utility, one may always say either that it is one that ought to be done, or at least that it is not one that ought not to be done. One may say also, that it is right it should be done; at least that it is not wrong it should be done: that it is right action; at least that it is not a wrong action. When thus interpreted, the words *ought,* and *right* and *wrong,* and others of that stamp, have a meaning: when otherwise they have none.

Has the rectitude of this principle been ever formally contested? It should seem that it had, by those who have not known what they have been meaning. Is it susceptible of any direct proof? It should seem not, for that which is used to prove everything else, cannot itself be proved; a chain of proofs must have their commencement somewhere. To give such proof is as impossible as it is needless.

Not that there is or ever has been that human creature breathing, however stupid or perverse, who has not on many, perhaps on most occasions of his life, deferred to it. By the natural constitution of the human frame, on most occasions of their lives men in general embrace this principle, without thinking of it; if not for the ordering of their own actions, yet for the trying of their own actions, as well as of those of other men. There have been, at the same time, not many, perhaps, even of the most intelligent, who have been disposed to embrace it purely and without reserve. There are even few who have not taken some occasion or other to quarrel with it, either on account of their not understanding always how to apply it, or on account of some prejudice or other which they were afraid to examine into, or could not bear to part with. For such is the stuff that man is made of: in principle and in practice, in a right track and in a wrong one, the rarest of all human qualities is consistency.

When a man attempts to combat the principle of utility, it is with reason drawn, without his being aware of it, from that very principle itself. His arguments, if they prove anything, prove not that the principle is *wrong,* but that, according to the applications he supposes to be made of it, it is *misapplied* Is it possible for a man to move the earth? Yes; but he must first find out another earth to stand upon.

To disprove the propriety of it by arguments is impossible; but, from the causes that have been mentioned, or from some confused or partial view of it, a man may happen to be disposed not to relish it. Where this is the case, if he thinks the settling of his opinions on such a subject worth the trouble, let him take the following steps, and at length, perhaps, he may come to reconcile himself to it.

1. Let him settle with himself, whether he would wish to discard this principle altogether; if so, let him consider what it is that all his reasonings (in matters of politics especially) can amount to?

2. If he would, let him settle with himself, whether he would judge and act without any principle, or whether there is any other he would judge and act by?

3. If there be, let him examine and satisfy himself whether the

principle he thinks he has found, is really any separate intelligible principle; or whether it be not a mere principle in words, a kind of phrase, which at bottom expresses neither more nor less than the mere averment of his own unfounded sentiments; that is, what in another person he might be apt to call caprice?

4. If he is inclined to think that his own approbation or disapprobation, annexed to the idea of an act, without any regard to its consequences, is a sufficient foundation for him to judge and act upon, let him ask himself whether his sentiment is to be a standard of right and wrong, with respect to every other man, or whether every man's sentiment has the same privilege of being a standard to itself?

5. In the first case, let him ask himself whether his principle is not despotical, and hostile to all the rest of the human race?

6. In the second case, whether it is not anarchical, and whether at this rate there are not as many different standards of right and wrong as there are men? and whether even to the same man, the same thing, which is right today, may not (without the least change in its nature) be wrong tomorrow? and whether the same thing is not right and wrong in the same place at the same time? and in either case, whether all argument is not at an end? and whether, when two men have said, "I like this," and "I don't like it," they can (upon such principle) have anything more to say?

7. If he should have said to himself, No: for that the sentiment which he proposes as a standard must be grounded on reflection, let him say on what particulars the reflection is to turn? if on particulars having relation to the utility of the act, then let him say whether this is not deserting his own principle and borrowing assistance from that very one in opposition to which he sets it up: or if not on those particulars, on what other particulars?

8. If he should be for compounding the matter, and adopting his own principle in part, and the principle of utility in part, let him say how far he will adopt it?

9. When he has settled with himself where he will stop, then let him ask himself how he justifies to himself the adopting it so far? and why he will not adopt it any farther?

10. Admitting any other principle than the principle of utility to be a right principle, a principle that it is right for a man to pursue; admitting (what is not true) that the word *right* can have a meaning without reference to utility, let him say whether there is any such thing as a *motive* that a man can have to pursue the dictates of it: if there is, let him say what that motive is, and how it is to be distinguished from those which enforce the dictates of utility: if not, then lastly let him say what it is this other principle can be good for?

Value of a Lot of Pleasure or Pain, How to Be Measured

Pleasures then, and the avoidance of pains, are the *ends* which the legislator has in view: it behooves him therefore to understand their *value*. Pleasures and pains are the *instruments* he has to work with: it behooves him therefore to understand their force, which is again, in other words, their value.

To a person considered by *himself,* the value of a pleasure or pain considered *by itself,* will be greater or less, according to the four following circumstances.

1. Its *intensity.*
2. Its *duration.*
3. Its *certainty* or *uncertainty.*
4. Its *propinquity* or *remoteness.*

These are the circumstances which are to be considered in estimating a pleasure or a pain considered each of them by itself. But when the value of any pleasure or pain is considered for the purpose of estimating the tendency of any *act* by which it is produced, there are two other circumstances to be taken into account; these are,

5. Its *fecundity,* or the chance it has of being followed by sensations of the *same* kind: that is, pleasures, if it be a pleasure: pains, if it be a pain.

6. Its *purity,* or the chance it has of *not* being followed by sensations of the *opposite* kind: that is, pains if it be a pleasure: pleasures if it be a pain.

These two last, however, are in strictness scarcely to be deemed properties of the pleasures or the pain itself; they are not, therefore, in strictness to be taken into the account of the value of that pleasure or that pain. They are in strictness to be deemed properties only of the act, or other event, by which such pleasure or pain has been produced; and accordingly are only to be taken into the account of the tendency of such an act or such event.

To a *number* of persons, with reference to each of whom the value of a pleasure or pain is considered, it will be greater or less, according to seven circumstances: to wit, the six preceding ones; *viz.*

1. Its *intensity.*
2. Its *duration.*
3. Its *certainty* or *uncertainty.*
4. Its *propinquity* or *remoteness.*
5. Its *fecundity.*
6. Its *purity.*

And one other, to wit:

7. Its *extent;* that is, the number of persons to whom it *extends;* or (in other words) who are affected by it.

To take an exact account then of the general tendency of any act, by which the interests of a community are affected, proceed as follows. Begin with any one person of those whose interests seem most immediately to be affected by it: and take an account.

1. Of the value of each distinguishable *pleasure* which appears to be produced by it in the *first* instance.

2. Of the value of each *pain* which appears to be produced by it in the *first* instance.

3. Of the value of each pleasure which appears to be produced by it *after* the first. This constitutes the *fecundity* of the first *pleasure* and the *impurity* of the first *pain.*

4. Of the value of each *pain* which appears to be produced by it after the first. This constitutes the *fecundity* of the first *pain,* and the impurity of the first pleasure.

5. Sum up all the values of all the *pleasures* on the one side, and those of all the pains on the other. The balance, if it be on the side of pleasure, will give the *good* tendency of the act upon the whole, with respect to the interest of that *individual* person; if on the side of pain, the *bad* tendency of it upon the whole.

6. Take an account of the *number* of persons whose interests appear to be concerned; and repeat the above process with respect to each. *Sum up* the numbers expressive of the degrees of *good* tendency, which the act has, with respect to each individual, in regard to whom the tendency of it is *good* upon the whole: do this again with respect to each individual, in regard to whom the tendency of it is *bad* upon the whole. Take the *balance;* which, if on the side of *pleasure,* will give the general *good tendency* of the act, with respect to the total number of community of individuals concerned; if on the side of pain, the general *evil tendency* with respect to the same community.

It is not to be expected that this process should be strictly pursued previously to every moral judgment, or to every legislative or judicial operation. It may, however, be always kept in view: and as near as the process actually pursued on these occasions approaches to it, so near will such process approach to the character of an exact one.

The same process is alike applicable to pleasure and pain in whatever shape they appear: and by whatever denomination they are distinguished: to pleasure, whether it be called *good* (which is properly the cause or instrument of pleasure), or *profit* (which is distant pleasure, or the cause or instrument of distant pleasure), or *convenience,* or *advantage, benefit, emolument, happiness,* and so forth: to pain, whether it be called *evil* (which corresponds to *good*), or *mischief,* or *inconvenience,* or *disadvantage,* or *loss,* or *unhappiness,* and so forth.

Nor is this a novel and unwarranted, any more than it is a useless theory. In all this there is nothing but what the practice of mankind, wheresoever they have a clear view of their own interest, is perfectly conformable to. An article of property, and estate in land, for instance, is valuable, on what account? On account of the pleasures of all kinds which it enables a man to produce, and what comes to the same thing, the pains of all kinds which it enables him to avert. But the value of such an article of property is universally understood to rise or fall according to the length or shortness of the time which a man has in it: the certainty or uncertainty of its coming into possession: and the nearness or remoteness of the time at which, if at all, it is to come into possession. As to the *intensity* of the pleasures which a man may derive from it, this is never thought of, because it depends upon the use which each particular person may come to make of it; which cannot be estimated till the particular pleasures he may come to derive from it, or the particular pains he may come to exclude by means of it, are brought to view. For the same reason, neither does he think of the *fecundity* or *purity* of those pleasures.

THE CATEGORICAL IMPERATIVE

Immanuel Kant

Part One

Nothing in the world—indeed nothing even beyond the world—can possibly be conceived which could be called good without qualification except a *good will*. Intelligence, wit, judgment, and the other talents of the mind, however they may be named, or courage, resoluteness, and perseverance as qualities of temperament are doubtless in many respects good and desirable. But they can become extremely bad and harmful if the will, which is to make use of these gifts of nature and which in its special constitution is called character, is not good. It is the same with the gifts of fortune. Power, riches, honor, even health, general well-being, and the contentment with one's condition which is called happiness make for pride and even arrogance if there is not a good will to correct their influence on the mind and on its principles of action, so as to make it universally conformable to its end. It need hardly be mentioned that the sight of a being adorned with no feature of a pure and good will yet enjoying uninterrupted prosperity can never give pleasure to a rational impartial observer. Thus the good will seems to constitute the indispensable condition even of worthiness to be happy.

Some qualities seem to be conducive to this good will and can facilitate its action, but, in spite of that, they have no intrinsic unconditional worth. They rather presuppose a good will, which limits the high esteem which one otherwise rightly has for them, and prevents their being held to be absolutely good. Moderation in emotions and passions, self-control, and calm deliberation not only are good in many respects but even seem to constitute a part of the inner worth of the person. But however unconditionally they were esteemed by the ancients, they are far from being good without qualification. For, without the principles of a good will, they can become extremely bad, and the coolness of a

FROM *Foundations of the Metaphysics of Morals,* translated by L. W. Beck. Copyright © 1959 by Liberal Arts Press, Inc. Reprinted by permission of the Liberal Arts Division of the Bobbs-Merrill Company, Inc.

villain makes him not only far more dangerous but also more directly abominable in our eyes than he would have seemed without it.

The good will is not good because of what it effects or accomplishes or because of its adequacy to achieve some proposed end; it is good only because of its willing, i.e., it is good of itself. And, regarded for itself, it is to be esteemed incomparably higher than anything which could be brought about by it in favor of any inclination or even of the sum total of all inclinations. Even if it should happen that, by a particularly unfortunate fate or by the niggardly provision of a stepmotherly nature, this will should be wholly lacking in power to accomplish its purpose, and if even the greatest effort should not avail it to achieve anything of its end, and if there remained only the good will (not as a mere wish but as the summoning of all the means in our power), it would sparkle like a jewel with its own light, as something that had its full worth in itself. Usefulness or fruitlessness can neither diminish nor augment this worth. Its usefulness would be only its setting, as it were, so as to enable us to handle it more conveniently in commerce or to attract the attention of those who are not yet connoisseurs, but not to recommend it to those who are experts or to determine its worth.

But there is something so strange in this idea of the absolute worth of the will alone, in which no account is taken of any use, that, notwithstanding the agreement even of common sense, the suspicion must arise that perhaps only high-flown fancy is its hidden basis, and that we may have misunderstood the purpose of nature in its appointment of reason as the ruler of our will. We shall therefore examine this idea from this point of view.

In the natural constitution of an organized being, i.e., one suitably adapted to life, we assume as an axiom that no organ will be found for any purpose which is not the fittest and best adapted to that purpose. Now if its preservation, welfare—in a word, its happiness—were the real end of nature in a being having reason and will, then nature would have hit upon a very poor arrangement in appointing the reason of the creature to be the executor of this purpose. For all the actions which the creature has to perform with this intention, and the entire rule of its conduct, would be dictated much more exactly by instinct, and that end would be far more certainly attained by instinct than it ever could be by reason. And if, over and above this, reason should have been granted to the favored creature, it would have served only to let it contemplate the happy constitution of its nature, to admire it, to rejoice in it, and to be grateful for it to its beneficent cause. But reason would not have been given in order that the being should subject its faculty of desire to that weak and delusive guidance and to meddle with the purpose of nature. In a word, nature would have taken care that reason did not break forth into practical use nor have the presumption, with its weak insight, to think out for itself the plan of happiness and the means of attaining it. Nature would have taken over not only the choice of ends but also that of the means and with wise foresight would have intrusted both to instinct alone.

And in fact, we find that the more a cultivated reason deliberately devotes itself to the enjoyment of life and happiness, the more the man falls short of true contentment. From this fact there arises in many persons, if only they are candid enough to admit it, a certain degree of misology, hatred of reason. This is particularly the case with those who are most experienced in its use. After counting all the advantages which they draw—I will not say from the invention of the arts of common luxury—from the sciences (which in the end seem to them to be also a luxury of the understanding), they nevertheless find that they have actually brought more trouble on their shoulders instead of gaining in happiness; they finally envy, rather than despise, the common run of men who are better guided by mere natural instinct and who do not permit their reason much influence on their conduct. And we must at least admit that a morose attitude or ingratitude to the goodness with which the world is governed is by no means always found among those who temper or refute the boasting eulogies which are given of the advantages of happiness and contentment with which reason is supposed to supply us. Rather their judgment is based on the idea of another and far more worthy purpose of their existence for which, instead of happiness, their reason is properly intended, this purpose, therefore, being the supreme condition to which the private purposes of men must for the most part defer.

Reason is not, however, competent to guide the will safely with regard to its objects and the satisfaction of all our needs (which it in part multiplies), and to this end an innate instinct would have led with far more certainty. But reason is given to us as a practical faculty, i.e., one which is meant to have an influence on the will. As nature has elsewhere distributed capacities suitable to the functions they are to perform, reason's proper function must be to produce a will good in itself and not one good merely as a means, for to the former reason is absolutely essential. This will must indeed not be the sole and complete good and the condition of all others, even of the desire for happiness. In this case it is entirely compatible with the wisdom of nature that the cultivation of reason, which is required for the former unconditional purpose, at least in this life restricts in many ways—indeed can reduce to less than nothing—the achievement of the latter conditional purpose, happiness. For one perceives that nature here does not proceed unsuitably to its purpose, because reason, which recognizes its highest practical vocation in the establishment of a good will, is capable only of a contentment of its own kind, i.e., one that springs from the attainment of a purpose, which in turn is determined by reason, even though this injures the ends of inclination.

We have, then, to develop the concept of a will which is to be esteemed as good of itself without regard to anything else. It dwells already in the natural sound understanding and does not need so much to be taught as only to be brought to light. In the estimation of the entire worth of our actions it always takes first place and is the condition of everything else. In order to show this, we shall take the concept of duty. It contains that of a good will, though with certain subjective restrictions and hindrances; but these are far from concealing it and making it unrecognizable, for they rather bring it out by contrast and make it shine forth all the brighter.

I here omit all actions which are recognized as opposed to duty, even though they may be useful in one respect or another, for with these the question does not arise at all as to whether they may be done *from* duty, since they conflict with it. I also pass over the actions which are really in accordance with duty and to which one has no direct inclination, rather doing them because impelled to do so by another inclination. For it is easily decided whether an action in accord with duty is done from duty or for some selfish purpose. It is far more difficult to note this difference when the action is in accordance with duty and, in addition, the subject has a direct inclination to do it. For example, it is in fact in accordance with duty that a dealer should not overcharge an inexperienced customer, and wherever there is much business the prudent merchant does not do so, having a fixed price for everyone, so that a child may buy of him as cheaply as any other. Thus the customer is honestly served. But this is far from sufficient to justify the belief that the merchant has behaved in this way from duty and principles of honesty. His own advantage required this behavior; but it cannot be assumed that over and above that he had a direct inclination to the purchaser and that, out of love, as it were, he gave none an advantage in price over another. Therefore the action was done neither from duty nor from direct inclination but only for a selfish purpose.

On the other hand, it is a duty to preserve one's life, and moreover everyone has a direct inclination to do so. But for that reason, the often anxious care which most men take of it has no intrinsic worth, and the maxim of doing so has no moral import. They preserve their lives according to duty, but not from duty. But if adversities and hopeless sorrow completely take away the relish for life; if an unfortunate man, strong in soul, is indignant rather than despondent or dejected over his fate and wishes for death, and yet preserves his life without loving it and from neither inclination nor fear but from duty—then his maxim has a moral import.

To be kind where one can is a duty, and there are, moreover, many persons so sympathetically constituted that without any motive of vanity or selfishness they find an inner satisfaction in spreading joy and rejoice in the contentment of others which they have made possible. But I say that, however dutiful and amiable it may be, that kind of action has no true moral worth. It is on a level with other inclinations, such as the inclination to honor, which, if fortunately directed to what in fact accords with duty and is generally useful and thus honorable, deserve praise and encouragement but no esteem. For the maxim lacks the moral import of an action done not from inclination but from duty. But assume that the mind of that friend to mankind was clouded by a sorrow of his own which extinguished all sympathy with the lot of others and that he still had the power to benefit others in distress, but that their need left him untouched because he was preoccupied with his own need. And now suppose him to tear himself, unsolicited by inclination, out of this dead insensibility and to do this action only from duty and without any inclination—then for the first time his action has genuine moral worth. Furthermore, if nature has put little sympathy in the heart of a man, and if he, though an honest man, is by temperament cold and indifferent to the sufferings of others perhaps because he is provided with special gifts of patience and fortitude, and expects or even requires that others should have the same—and such a man would certainly not be the meanest product of nature—would not he find in himself a source from which to give himself a far higher worth than he could have got by having a good-natured temperament? This is unquestionably true even though nature did not make him philanthropic, for it is just here that the worth of the character is brought out, which is morally and incomparably the highest of all: he is beneficent not from inclination but from duty.

To secure one's own happiness is at least indirectly a duty, for discontent with one's condition under pressure from many cares and amid unsatisfied wants could easily become a great temptation to transgress duties. But, without any view to duty, all men have the strongest and deepest inclination to happiness, because in this idea all inclinations are summed up. But the precept of happiness is often so formulated that it definitely thwarts some inclinations, and men can make no definite and certain concept of the sum of satisfaction of all inclinations, which goes under the name of happiness. It is not to be wondered at, therefore, that a single inclination, definite as to what it promises and as to the time at which it can be satisfied, can outweigh a fluctuating idea, and that, for example, a man with the gout can choose to enjoy what he likes and to suffer what he may, because according to his calculations at least on this occasion he has not sacrificed the enjoyment of the present moment to a perhaps groundless expectation of a happiness supposed to lie in health. But, even in this case, if the universal inclination to happiness did not determine his will, and if health were not at least for him a necessary factor in these calculations, there yet would remain, as in all other cases, a law that he ought to promote his happiness, not from inclination but from duty. Only from this law would his conduct have true moral worth.

It is in this way, undoubtedly, that we should understand those passages of Scripture which command us to love our neighbor and even our enemy, for love as an inclination cannot be commanded. But beneficence from duty, also when no inclination impels it and even when it is opposed by a natural and unconquerable aversion, is practical love, not pathological love; it resides in the will and not in the propensities of feeling, in principles of action and not in tender sympathy; and it alone can be commanded.

[Thus the first proposition of morality is that to have moral worth an action must be done from duty.] The second proposition is: An action done from duty does not have its moral worth in the purpose which is to be achieved through it but in the maxim by which it is determined. Its moral value, therefore, does not depend on the reality of the object of the action but merely on the principle of volition by which the action is done without any regard to the objects of the faculty of desire. From the preceding discussion it is clear that the purposes we may have for our actions and their effects as ends and incentives of the will cannot give the actions any unconditional and moral worth. Wherein, then, can this worth lie, if it is not in the will in relation to its hoped-for effect? It can lie nowhere else than in the principle of the will irrespective of the ends which can be realized by such action. For the will stands, as it were, at the crossroads halfway between its a priori principle which is formal and its a posteriori incentive which is material. Since it must be determined by something, if it is done from duty, it must be determined by the formal principle of volition as such, since every material principle has been withdrawn from it.

The third principle, as a consequence of the two preceding, I would express as follows: Duty is the necessity of an action done from respect for the law. I can certainly have an inclination to the object as an effect of the proposed action, but I can never have respect for it precisely because it is a mere effect and not an activity of a will. Similarly, I can have no respect for any inclination whatsoever, whether my own or that of another; in the former case I can at most approve of it and in the latter I can even love it, i.e., see it as favorable to my own advantage.

But that which is connected with my will merely as ground and not as consequence, that which does not serve my inclination but overpowers it or at least excludes it from being considered in making a choice—in a word, the law itself—can be an object of respect and thus a command. Now as an act from duty wholly excludes the influence of inclination and therewith every object of the will, nothing remains which can determine the will objectively except the law and subjectively except pure respect for this practical law. This subjective element is the maxim that I should follow such a law even if it thwarts all my inclinations.

Thus the moral worth of an action does not lie in the effect which is expected from it or in any principle of action which has to borrow its motive from this expected effect. For all these effects (agreeableness of condition, indeed even the promotion of the happiness of others) could be brought about through other causes and would not require the will of a rational being, while the highest and unconditional good can be found only in such a will. Therefore, the pre-eminent good can consist only in the conception of the law in itself (which can be present only in a rational being) so far as this conception and not the hoped-for effect is the determining ground of the will. This pre-eminent good, which we call moral, is already present in the person who acts according to this conception, and we do not have to expect it first in the result.

But what kind of a law can that be, the conception of which must determine the will without reference to the expected result? Under this condition alone the will can be called absolutely good without qualifications. Since I have robbed the will of all impulses which could come to it from obedience to any law, nothing remains to serve as a principle of the will except universal conformity of its action to law as such. That is, I should never act in such a way that I could not will that my maxim should be a universal law. Mere conformity to law as such (without assuming any particular law applicable to certain actions) serves as the principle of the will, and it must serve as such a principle if duty is not to be a vain delusion and chimerical concept. The common reason of mankind in its practical judgments is in perfect agreement with this and has this principle constantly in view.

Let the question, for example, be: May I, when in distress, make a promise with the intention not to keep it? I easily distinguish the two meanings which the question can have, viz., whether it is prudent to make a false promise, or whether it conforms to my duty. Undoubtedly the former can often be the case, though I do see clearly that it is not sufficient merely to escape from the present difficulty by this expedient, but that I must consider whether inconveniences much greater than the present one may not later spring from this lie. Even with all my supposed cunning, the consequences cannot be so easily foreseen. Loss of credit might be far more disadvantageous than the misfortune I now seek to avoid, and it is hard to tell whether it might not be more prudent to act according to a universal maxim and to make it a habit not to promise anything without intending to fulfill it. But it is soon clear to me that such a maxim is based only on an apprehensive concern with consequences.

To be truthful from duty, however, is an entirely different thing from being truthful out of fear of disadvantageous consequences, for in the former case the concept of the action itself contains a law for me, while in the latter I must first look about to see what results for me may be connected with it. For to deviate from the principle of duty is certainly bad, but to be unfaithful to my maxim of prudence can sometimes be very advantageous to me, though it is certainly safer to abide by it. The shortest but most infallible way to find the answer to the question as to whether a deceitful promise is consistent with duty is to ask myself: Would I be content that my maxim (of extricating myself from difficulty by a false promise) should hold as a universal law for myself as well as for others? And could I say to myself that everyone may make a false promise when he is in a difficulty from which he otherwise cannot escape? I immediately see that I could will the lie but not a universal law to lie. For with such a law there would be no promises at all inasmuch as it would be futile to make a pretense of my intention in regard to future actions to those who would not believe this pretense or—if they overhastily did so—who would pay me back in my own coin. Thus my maxim would necessarily destroy itself as soon as it was made a universal law.

I do not, therefore, need any penetrating acuteness in order to discern what I have to do in order that my volition may be morally good. Inexperienced in the course of the world, incapable of being prepared for all its contingencies, I only ask myself: Can I will that my maxim become a universal law? If not, it must be rejected, not because of any disadvantage accruing to myself or even to others, but because it cannot enter as a principle into a possible universal legislation, and reason extorts from me an immediate respect for such legislation. I do not as yet discern on what it is grounded (a question the philosopher may investigate), but I at least understand that it is an estimation of the worth which far outweighs all the worth of whatever is recommended by the inclinations, and that the necessity of my actions from pure respect for the practical law constitutes duty. To duty every other motive must give place, because duty is the condition of a will good in itself, whose worth transcends everything.

Thus within the moral knowledge of common human reason we have attained its principle. To be sure, common human reason does not think it abstractly in such a universal form, but it always has it in view and uses it as the standard of its judgments. It would be easy to show how common human reason, with this compass, knows well how to distinguish what is good, what is bad, and what is consistent or inconsistent with duty. Without in the least teaching common reason anything new, we need only to draw its attention to its own principle, in the manner of Socrates, thus showing that neither science nor philosophy is needed in order to know what one has to do in order to be honest and good, and even wise and virtuous. We might have conjectured beforehand that the knowledge of what everyone is obliged to do and thus also to know would be within the reach of everyone, even the most ordinary man. Here we cannot but admire the great advantages which the practical faculty of judgment has over the theoretical in ordinary human understanding. In the theoretical, if ordinary reason ventures to go beyond the laws of experience and perceptions of the senses, it falls into sheer inconceivabilities and self-contradictions, or at least into a chaos of uncertainty, obscurity, and instability. In the practical, on the other hand, the power of judgment first shows itself to advantage when common understanding excludes all sensuous incentives from practical laws. It then becomes even subtle, quibbling with its own conscience or with other claims to what should be called right, or wishing to determine correctly for its own instruction the worth of certain actions. But the most remarkable thing about ordinary reason in its practical concern is that it may have as much hope as any philosopher of hitting the mark. In fact, it is almost more certain to do so than the philosopher, because he has no principle which the common understanding lacks, while his judgment is easily confused by a mass of irrelevant considerations, so that it easily turns aside from the correct way. Would it not, therefore, be wiser in moral matters to acquiesce in the common rational judgment, or at most to call in philosophy in order to make the system of morals more complete and comprehensible and its rules more convenient for use (especially in disputation) than to steer the common understanding from its happy simplicity in practical matters and to lead it through philosophy into a new path of inquiry and instruction?

Innocence is indeed a glorious thing, but, on the other hand, it is very sad that it cannot well maintain itself, being easily led astray. For this reason, even wisdom—which consists more in acting than in knowing—needs science, not so as to learn from it but to secure admission and permanence to its precepts. Man feels in himself a powerful counterpoise against all commands of duty which reason presents to him as so deserving of respect; this counterpoise is his needs and inclinations, the complete satisfaction of which he sums up under the name of happiness. Now reason issues inexorable commands without promising anything to the inclinations. It disregards, as it were, and holds in contempt those claims which are so impetuous and yet so plausible, and which will not allow themselves to be abolished by any command. From this a natural dialectic arises, i.e., a propensity to argue against the stern laws of duty and their validity, or at least to place their purity and strictness in doubt and, where possible, to make them more accordant with our wishes and inclinations. This is equivalent to corrupting them in their very foundations and destroying their dignity—a thing which even common practical reason cannot ultimately call good.

In this way common human reason is impelled to go outside its sphere and to take a step into the field of practical philosophy. But it is forced to do so not by any speculative need, which never occurs to it so long as it is satisfied to remain merely healthy reason; rather, it is so impelled on practical grounds in order to obtain information and clear instruction respecting the source of its principle and the correct determination of this principle in its opposition to the maxims which are based on need and inclination. It seeks this information in order to escape from the perplexity of opposing claims and to avoid the danger of losing all genuine moral principles through the equivocation in which it is easily involved. Thus when practical common reason cultivates itself, a dialectic surreptitiously ensues, which forces it to seek aid in philosophy, just as the same thing happens in the theoretical use of reason. In this case, as in the theoretical, it will find rest only in a thorough critical examination of our reason. . . .

Part Two

Everything in nature works according to laws. Only a rational being has the capacity of acting according to the conception of laws, i.e., according to principles. This capacity is will. Since reason is required for the derivation of actions from laws, will is nothing else than practical reason. If reason infallibly determines the will, the actions which such a being recognizes as objectively necessary are also subjectively necessary. That is, the will is a faculty of choosing only that which reason, independently of inclination, recognizes as practically necessary, i.e., as good. But if reason of itself does not sufficiently determine the will, and if the will is subjugated to subjective conditions (certain incentives) which do not always agree with objective conditions; in a word, if the will is not of itself in complete accord with reason (the actual case of men), then the actions which are recognized as objectively necessary are subjectively contingent, and the determination of such a will according to objective laws is constraint. That is, the relation of objective laws to a will which is not completely good is conceived as the determination of the will of a rational being by principles of reason to which this will is not by nature necessarily obedient.

The conception of an objective principle, so far as it constrains a will, is a command (of reason), and the formula of this command is called an *imperative*.

All imperatives are expressed by an "ought" and thereby indicate the relation of an objective law of reason to a will which is not in its subjective constitution necessarily determined by this law. This relation is that of constraint. Imperatives say that it would be good to do or to refrain from doing something, but they say it to a will which does not always do something simply because it is presented to it as a good thing to do. Practical good is what determines the will by means of the conception of reason and hence not by subjective causes but, rather, objectively, i.e., on grounds which are valid for every rational being as such. It is distinguished from the pleasant, as that which has an influence on the will only by means of a sensation from merely subjective causes, which hold only for the senses of this or that person and not as a principle of reason which holds for everyone.

A perfectly good will, therefore, would be equally subject to objective laws (of the good), but it could not be conceived as constrained by them to act in accord with them, because, according to its own subjective constitution, it can be determined to act only through the conception of the good. Thus no imperatives hold for the divine will or, more generally, for a holy will. The "ought" is here out of place, for the volition of itself is necessarily in unison with the law. Therefore imperatives are only formulas expressing the relation of objective laws of volition in general to the subjective imperfection of the will of this or that rational being, e.g., the human will.

All imperatives command either hypothetically or categorically. The former present the practical necessity of a possible action as a means to achieving something else which one desires (or which one may possibly desire). The categorical imperative would be one which presented an action as of itself objectively necessary, without regard to any other end.

Since every practical law presents a possible action as good and thus as necessary for a subject practically determinable by reason, all imperatives are formulas of the determination of action which is necessary by the principle of a will which is in any way good. If the action is good only as a means to something else, the imperative is hypothetical; but if it is thought of as good in itself, and hence as necessary in a will which of itself conforms to reason as the principle of this will, the imperative is categorical.

The imperative thus says what action possible to me would be good, and it presents the practical rule in relation to a will which does not forthwith perform an action simply because it is good, in part because the subject does not always know that the action is good and in part (when it does know it) because his maxims can still be opposed to the objective principles of practical reason.

The hypothetical imperative, therefore, says only that the action is good to some purpose, possible or actual. In the former case it is a problematical, in the latter an assertorical, practical principle. The categorical imperative, which declares the action to be of itself objectively necessary without making any reference to a purpose, i.e., without having any other end, holds as an apodictical (practical) principle.

We can think of that which is possible through the mere powers of some rational being as a possible purpose of any will. As a consequence, the principles of action, in so far as they are thought of as necessary to attain a possible purpose which can be achieved by them, are in reality infinitely numerous. All sciences have some practical part which consists of problems of some end which is possible for us and of imperatives as to how it can be reached. These can therefore generally be called imperatives of skill. Whether the end is reasonable and good is not in question at all, for the question is only of what must be done in order to attain it. The precepts to be followed by a physician in order to cure his patient and by a poisoner in order to bring about certain death are of equal value in so far as each does that which will perfectly accomplish his purpose. Since in early youth we do not know what ends may occur to us in the course of life, parents seek to let their children learn a great many things and provide for skill in the use of means to all sorts of arbitrary ends, among which they cannot determine whether any one of them may later become an actual purpose of their pupil, though it is possible that he may someday have it as his actual purpose. And this anxiety is so great that they commonly neglect to form and correct their judgment on the worth of things which they make their ends.

There is one end, however, which we may presuppose as actual in all rational beings so far as imperatives apply to them, i.e., so far as they are dependent beings; there is one purpose not only which they *can* have but which we can presuppose that they all *do* have by a necessity of nature. This purpose is happiness. The hypothetical imperative which represents the practical necessity of action as means to the promotion of happiness is an assortorial imperative. We may not expound it as merely necessary to an uncertain and a merely possible purpose, but as necessary to a purpose which we can a priori and with assurance assume for everyone because it belongs to his essence. Skill in the choice of means to one's own highest welfare can be called prudence in the narrowest sense. Thus the imperative which refers to the choice of means to one's own happiness, i.e., the precept of prudence, is still only hypothetical; the action is not absolutely commanded but commanded only as a means to another end.

Finally, there is one imperative which directly commands a certain conduct without making its condition some purpose to be reached by it. This imperative is categorical. It concerns not the material of the action and its intended result but the form and the principle from which it results. What is essentially good in it consists in the intention, the result being what it may. This imperative may be called the imperative of morality.

Volition according to these three principles is plainly distinguished by dissimilarity in the constraint to which they subject the will. In order to clarify this dissimilarity, I believe that they are most suitably named if one says that they are either rules of skill, counsels of prudence, or commands (laws) of morality, respectively. For law alone implies the concept of an unconditional and objective and hence universally valid necessity, and commands are laws which must be obeyed, even against inclination. Counsels do indeed involve necessity, but a necessity that can hold only under a subjectively contingent condition, i.e., whether this or that man counts this or that as part of his happiness; but the categorical imperative, on the other hand, is restricted by no condition. As absolutely, though practically, necessary it can be called a command in the strict sense. We could also call the first imperative technical (belonging to art), the second pragmatic (belonging to welfare), and the third moral (belonging to free conduct as such, i.e., to morals).

If I think of a hypothetical imperative as such, I do not know what it will contain until the condition is stated (under which it is an imperative). But if I think of a categorical imperative, I know immediately what it contains. For since the imperative contains besides the law only the necessity of the maxim of acting in accordance with this law, while the law contains no condition to which it is restricted, there is nothing remaining in it except the universality of law as such to which the maxim of the action should conform; and in effect this conformity alone is represented as necessary by the imperative.

There is, therefore, only one categorical imperative. It is: Act only according to that maxim by which you can at the same time will that it should become a universal law.

Now if all imperatives of duty can be derived from this one imperative as a principle, we can at least show what we understand by the concept of duty and what it means, even though it remain undecided whether that which is called duty is an empty concept or not.

We shall now enumerate some duties, adopting the usual division of them into duties to ourselves and to others and into perfect and imperfect duties.

1. A man who is reduced to despair by a series of evils feels a weariness with life but is still in possession of his reason sufficiently to ask whether it would not be contrary to his duty to himself to take his own life. Now he asks whether the maxim of his action could become a universal law of nature. His maxim, however, is: For love of myself, I make it my principle to shorten my life when by a longer duration it threatens more evil than satisfaction. But it is questionable whether this principle of self-love could become a universal law of nature. One immediately sees a contradiction in a system of nature, whose law would be to destroy life by the feeling whose special office is to impel the improvement of life. In this case it would not exist as nature; hence that maxim cannot obtain as a law of nature, and thus it wholly contradicts the supreme principle of all duty.

2. Another man finds himself forced by need to borrow money. He well knows that he will not be able to repay it, but he also sees that nothing will be loaned him if he does not firmly promise to repay it at a certain time. He desires to make such a promise, but he has enough conscience to ask himself whether it is not improper and opposed to duty to relieve his distress in such a way. Now, assuming he does decide to do so, the maxim of his action would be as follows: When I believe myself to be in need of money, I will borrow money and promise to repay it, although I know I shall never do so. Now this principle of self-love or of his own benefit may very well be compatible with his whole future welfare, but the question is whether it is right. He changes the pretension of self-love into a universal law and then puts the question: How would it be if my maxim became a universal law? He immediately sees that it could never hold as a universal law of nature and be consistent with itself; rather it must necessarily contradict itself. For the universality of a law which says that anyone who believes himself to be in need could promise what he pleased with the intention of not fulfilling it would make the promise itself and the end to be accomplished by it impossible; no one would believe what was promised to him but would only laugh at any such assertion as vain pretense.

3. A third finds in himself a talent which could, by means of some cultivation, make him in many respects a useful man. But he finds himself in comfortable circumstances and prefers indulgence in pleasure to troubling himself with broadening and improving his fortunate natural

gifts. Now, however, let him ask whether his maxim of neglecting his gifts, besides agreeing with his propensity to idle amusement, agrees also with what is called duty. He sees that a system of nature could indeed exist in accordance with such a law, even though man (like the inhabitants of the South Sea Islands) should let his talents rust and resolve to devote his life merely to idleness, indulgence, and propagation—in a word, to pleasure. But he cannot possibly will that this should become a universal law of nature or that it should be implanted in us by a natural instinct. For, as a rational being, he necessarily wills that all his faculties should be developed, inasmuch as they are given to him for all sorts of possible purposes.

4. A fourth man, for whom things are going well, sees that others (whom he could help) have to struggle with great hardships, and he asks, "What concern of mine is it? Let each one be as happy as heaven wills, or as he can make himself; I will not take anything from him or even envy him but to his welfare or to his assistance in time of need I have no desire to contribute." If such a way of thinking were a universal law of nature, certainly the human race could exist, and without doubt even better than in a state where everyone talks of sympathy and good will or even exerts himself occasionally to practice them while, on the other hand, he cheats when he can and betrays or otherwise violates the rights of man. Now although it is possible that a universal law of nature according to that maxim could exist, it is nevertheless impossible to will that such a principle should hold everywhere as a law of nature. For a will which resolved this would conflict with itself, since instances can often arise in which he would need the love and sympathy of others, and in which he would have robbed himself, by such a law of nature springing from his own will, of all hope of the aid he desires.

The foregoing are a few of the many actual duties, or at least of duties we hold to be real, whose derivation from the one stated principle is clear. We must be able to will that the maxim of our action become a universal law; this is the canon of the moral estimation of our action generally. Some actions are of such a nature that their maxim cannot even be *thought* as a universal law of nature without contradiction, far from it being possible that one could will that it should be such. In others this internal impossibility is not found, though it is still impossible to *will* that their maxim should be raised to the universality of a law of nature, because such a will would contradict itself. We easily see that the former maxim conflicts with the stricter or narrower (imprescriptible) duty, the latter with broader (meritorious) duty. Thus all duties, so far as the kind of obligation (not the object of their action) is concerned, have been completely exhibited by these examples in their dependence on the one principle.

Questions for Discussion

1. Is it really clear, in the Billy Budd case, that an acquittal would seriously impair the effectiveness of the British navy, even if it were publicly declared that the death of Claggart was accidental? Is it good for military morale to hold men and woman responsible for the unforeseeable consequences of their instinctual responses to severe provocation? Why or why not?

2. Does the professional duty of a military officer, a doctor, or a judge take precedence over his or her general moral duties toward others? If so, is this because the lives and health of others depend on his or her performance of professional duties more than on his or her moral judgment? In the light of your answer, does it follow that it was unjust to convict Nazi officers for having committed atrocities in obedience to military orders?

3. If Bentham is right that our actions are always governed by desire for pleasure or fear of pain for ourselves, then how can he expect us to be guided by the moral factor of extent, when that requires sacrificing our own benefit for the sake of a greater benefit to others?

4. Kant's reason for holding that a "good will" or virtuous character is more desirable than happiness is that we do not like to see others who are immoral and happy. But what about ourselves? Is it natural not to want to profit from our own misdeeds? Are our judgments of others more reliable evidence as to what is desirable than our judgments of ourselves? Discuss.

5. According to Kant, a person who is suffering from an incurable disease deserves moral credit for resisting the temptation to take his or her own life. Do you agree? Does it depend on whether or not he or she is a burden to others? Kant maintains that we have the same duties to ourselves as to others. What reason could he give for this claim?

6. What would a Benthamite say concerning the officer in the lifeboat who throws a few people overboard to save the rest? What would a Kantian say? What do you say?

7. It has been suggested that utilitarianism tends to encourage moral complacency. Is this criticism fair? Is complacency or self-satisfaction better or worse than self-doubt about one's difficult moral decisions?

Selected Readings

BAIER, K. *The Moral Point of View.* Ithaca, New York: Cornell University Press, 1958. Combines formalism and consequentialism.

BAYLES, M., ed. *Contemporary Utilitarianism.* Garden City: Anchor, 1968. A useful anthology of essays on aspects of utilitarianism.

BENTHAM, J. *An Introduction to the Principles of Morals and Legislation.* New York: Hafner, 1948. The major source of utilitarian theory.

BRANDT, R. *Ethical Theories.* Englewood Cliffs, New Jersey: Prentice-Hall, 1959. A strong defense of rule utilitarianism.

BROAD, C. D. *Five Types of Ethical Theory*. New York: Harcourt Brace Jovanovich, 1934. Supports ideal utilitarianism.

DEWEY, J. *A Theory of Valuation*. Chicago: University of Chicago Press, 1939. A pragmatic defense of consequentialism.

GERT, B. *The Moral Rules*. New York: Harper & Row, 1973. Argues for rule utilitarianism.

HARE, R. M. *Freedom and Reason*. New York: Oxford University Press, 1965. A synthesis of deontology and utilitarianism.

———. *The Language of Morals*. Oxford:. Oxford University Press, 1952.

HUME, D. *An Enquiry Concerning the Principles of Morals*. Combines subjectivism and utilitarianism.

KANT, I. *Foundations of the Metaphysics of Morals*. Translated by L. Beck. New York: Liberal Arts Press, 1959. The classic statement of deontological ethics.

LYONS, D. *The Forms and Limits of Utilitarianism*. Oxford: Clarendon Press, 1965. A critique of rule utilitarianism.

MAYO, B. *Ethics and the Moral Life*. London: Macmillan, 1958. A contemporary form of Kantian ethics.

MELDIN, A., ed. *Essays in Moral Philosophy*. Seattle: Washington University Press, 1958. Contemporary essays for and against consequentialism.

MILL, J. S. *Utilitarianism*. Indianapolis, Indiana: Bobbs-Merrill, 1971. Adds qualifications to Bentham's crude hedonism.

MOORE, G. E. *Ethics*. Oxford: Oxford University Press, 1912.

———. *Principia Ethica*. Cambridge: Cambridge University Press, 1903. Ideal utilitarianism.

NARVESON, J. *Morality and Utility*. Baltimore: Johns Hopkins Press, 1967. A careful study of the problems of utilitarianism.

PLATO. *Republic*. Books 1, 2, 9, 10. In *The Dialogues of Plato*. Translated by B. Jowett. Attempts to show the convergence of moral rules and beneficial consequences.

PRICHARD, H. *Moral Obligation*. Oxford: Clarendon Press, 1949. A contemporary Kantian view.

ROSS, W. D. *The Right and the Good*. Oxford: Clarendon Press, 1930. Kantian morality plus intuition.

SIDGWICK, H. *The Methods of Ethics*. London: Macmillan, 1962. Intuitionistic utilitarianism.

SINGER, M. *Generalization in Ethics*. New York: Knopf, 1961. An analytical exploration of the problems involved in Kant's principle of the universal applicability of moral principles.

SMART, J. J. C. *An Outline of a System of Utilitarian Ethics*. Carlton, Australia: Melbourne University Press, 1961. Argues persuasively for act utilitarianism.

SMART, J. J. C., and WILLIAMS, B. O. A. *Utilitarianism, For and Against*. Cambridge: Cambridge University Press, 1973. A classic debate.

TOULMIN, S. *An Examination of the Place of Reason in Ethics*. Cambridge: Cambridge University Press, 1950. Combines appeals to language with utilitarianism.

Chapter 8

Morality and Self-Interest: Why Be Moral?

"Why should I be moral?" wonders Raskolnikov, in Fyodor Dostoyevsky's *Crime and Punishment*. Not finding a satisfactory answer, he proceeds to commit robbery and murder. By the end of the novel, he is convinced he has found the answer—God. Was he right? Let us take a closer look.

Raskolnikov is an impoverished student, threatened with the termination of his studies unless his sister marries a man she dislikes. The only way out of his predicament, as he sees it, is to rob and kill an old woman, a greedy and relentless pawnbroker, notorious for her cruelty toward her gentle sister. As Raskolnikov reasons, great men must be above conventional morality. They cannot afford to let the needs of inferior people stand in their way. The old pawnbroker is an inferior, indeed a worthless, creature, undeserving of the consideration she denies to others including her sister. To rid the world of her and at the same time profit from the act may be immoral in the eyes of society, but it is the most rational course of action.

Our selection narrates Raskolnikov's murder of the old woman, Alyona Ivanovna, and then, to avoid detection, the reluctant murder of her sister, Lizaveta. The novel concludes with his discovering, through love, that he is not above morality. He becomes a devout Christian.

Dostoyevsky rather dubiously assumes that at the bottom of everyone's soul lurks a natural morality, based on religious belief, that will prevent one from ever achieving happiness at the expense of others.

Plato took a somewhat similar view in the *Republic*, but without the religious ground. His view was more like that of modern psychiatrists who argue that morality leads to psychic health and happiness, rather than to heaven. It was Plato who gave the first clear formulation of the philosophical problem of why we should be moral. The reader can see why, allowing some license for literary overstatement, the contemporary philosopher Alfred North Whitehead wrote that the history of philosophy is a series of footnotes to Plato.

In Book II of the *Republic,* Plato's older brother, Glaucon, challenges Socrates to show why it is better to be just than unjust even when one would surely profit from injustice. Glaucon cites the story of a shepherd named Gyges who, upon acquiring a ring that made him invisible, began to steal, rape, and murder his way to fame, fortune, and royal power. Glaucon wants to know how Socrates can show that Gyges should not have followed his immoral course of action, even though the gods themselves are believed to admire successful injustice as long as they are bribed by a share of the loot:

On what principle, then, shall we any longer choose justice rather than the worst injustice, when, if we only unite the latter with a deceitful regard to appearances, we shall fare to our mind both with gods and men, in life and after death, as the most numerous and the highest authorities tell us. . . . And therefore I say, not only prove to us that justice is better than injustice, but show what either of them does to the possessor of them, which makes the one to be a good and the other an evil, whether seen or unseen by gods and men.

It is not until Book IX that Socrates directly replies to this question. His answer is that the political tyrant, whom he compares to the evil person whose desires "tyrannize" over reason, is, despite wealth and influence, the most pitiful of creatures, because his soul is in a state of discord; as we say in our medical and psychiatric age, he is "sick, sick, sick."

Thus Plato argues that we should be moral because it is in our self-interest to be moral. This kind of answer prompts an objection that was most forcefully stated by the British Kantian philosopher H. A. Prichard in a well-known essay, "Does Moral Philosophy Rest on a Mistake?" He maintained that the attempt to support morality in terms of self-interest is a profound mistake that has infected philosophy ever since Plato and was only avoided by Kant. Prichard argues that anyone who demands to know what he or she "can get out of" morality before following it is guilty of immorality. To be genuinely moral, as Kant insisted, is to follow morality for its own sake, not for the sake of self-interest.

If the question "Why should I be moral?" necessarily meant "What's in it for me?" or "How will being moral bring me power, fame, and fortune?" then it is clear that the question is a mistake. It is perfectly obvious, first, that being moral is unlikely to produce such benefits, and, more importantly, as Prichard argued, such concerns are not what morality is all about. However, it is not likely that Plato meant anything so crude as that morality is to be followed because it is profitable. Rather he suggested that it be followed because it is the way to be a healthy and happy human being, that is, morality is the fulfillment of our human nature. True self-interest and morality, in the last analysis, are identical.

But how could anyone justify this claim? All around us we find moral people losing out and immoral people raking in the chips. Can appearances be as deceiving as all that? We shall consider three ethical views that, at first glance, seem to distinguish self-interest from morality and to set them at odds but, on closer inspection, turn out to be different explanations of why Socrates was right after all to identify the two. Each view, therefore, provides us with an explanation of why it is reasonable to be moral. Each, in a way, assures us that it is beneficial to us to be moral, but not in the crude way that Prichard criticized.

We begin with the nineteenth-century German philosopher Friedrich Nietzsche, who is often denounced as the archenemy of morality, the anti-Christ (as he defiantly called himself), who advises us to subvert the Ten Commandments and the Golden Rule and to assert ourselves and our worst instincts. Nietzsche liked to shock his readers. He described his writings as "philosophizing with a hammer." Many of his remarks, when taken out of context, do sound like invitations to aggressive self-aggrandizement. But when considered in the context of the many quite different-sounding things he said, we must either accuse him of frequent inconsistencies or, more sympathetically and fairly, as we shall see, interpret his call to self-assertion in a more subtle way.

In *The Genealogy of Morals* Nietzsche argues that values did not arise out of considerations of personal or social utility but out of the free choices of the leaders and born rulers of society. Their values were natural expressions of confidence in their superiority, which showed itself in their virtues of courage, pride, honor, and self-discipline. The Buddhist, Judaic, and Christian religions overthrew and subverted these ancient natural values in favor of the character traits of natural slaves, such as humility, charity, timidity, patience, and obedience, which then came to prevail in the modern world. In order to be safe from their cruelties, the weak somehow persuaded the strong to value weakness over strength. Nietzsche commends the British "psychologists" (Thomas Hobbes, Bernard de Mandeville, John Locke, and David Hume) for recognizing once again that it is natural and reasonable to be motivated by self-interest, but he derides their vulgar concept of self-interest, somewhat as Plato exposed the folly in the average person's idea of happiness.

Does all this signify that Nietzsche would approve of Gyges and of Raskolnikov? Only on the most superficial and careless reading. Nietzsche maintains that only superior people, the natural aristocrats, are able to assert their self-interest. But how are these superior aristocratic people? What is the measure of their superiority? Clearly, it cannot be brute physical strength since there were plenty of muscular slaves in the ancient world, the "beasts of burden," as Nietzsche calls them. Nor can it be the capacity for brutality since he celebrates the aristocratic Count Mirabeau of the French revolutionary era as kind and forgiving, and asserts that only such superior people are capable of "the real 'love of one's enemies'." Of course, Nietzsche also celebrates "the magnificent *blond brute,* avidly rampant for spoil and victory," referring to the ancient Teutonic tribes that engaged in "murder, arson, rape and torture, with bravado and a moral equanimity." But we should bear in mind that he is comparing them, perhaps a bit effusively, with the resentful slaves and their religious leaders in the ancient world, who also killed and tortured those whom they could not convert, and did so, according to Nietzsche, with vindictiveness and unrelenting hatred. Whether he is right about the historical facts need not concern us. The point is that he is not placing the self-interest of the average person above what he considers *true* morality, but the self-interest of the superior aristocratic person above what he considers to be slavish obedience to the Judeo-Christian code (which is, for him, a false morality).

Returning to the question of Nietzsche's measure of superiority, it would seem from his description of the aristocratic virtues that by "superiority" he means moral superiority, and by "aristocrat," not a social aristocrat but a natural or moral aristocrat. But then what does he mean by moral? It is not at all clear. We might conclude that his entire view is circular, that virtue is defined by strength and real strength in turn defined by virtue. One escape from this circle is that he means to stress the importance of character in contrast with the conventional stress on obedience to rules. We know that very good people sometimes break rules, and we feel that they are right to do so. We find attractive rather than ill-mannered, the cultivated person who seems to know how to eat chicken with her fingers at a formal dinner, while most of us would not dare chance so grievous a violation of the rules. Nietzsche seems to be saying, not implausibly, that the morally superior person is superior to any rigid set of rules. Rules are attempts to describe what the morally superior person does intuitively, and they never quite succeed in that attempt because such a person is creative, while the rules are mechanical.

When, in fairness to Nietzsche, all this is granted, it still seems to be true that we generally identify the morally superior person by the fact that he or she *usually* follows the rules that we want everyone to follow and only occasionally breaks them. Moreover, it is also true, to recall our discussion of Kant in the previous chapter, that when a person rightly breaks a rule, what makes him or her right is that there is some *other* rule followed that seems to take precedence. Perhaps Nietzsche would answer that the new rule is one that had never been explicitly recognized, and the moral leader's creative insight has enabled us to formulate it for the first time (as when Jesus broke the Sabbath to cure a sick man). In a sense, then, the moral innovator "creates" the rule, or the value. But in another, equally reasonable sense, it can be argued, he or she brings to our attention only what was already there. We cannot hope to settle here the issue of whether morality has more to do with rules or with personal qualities, or equally with both. What seems clear is that, in identifying proper self-interest with the aims of the morally superior and creative person, Nietzsche does not mean to set self-interest —in the sense of fulfillment of one's own purposes—above morality, but to identify the two.

The contemporary Australian philosopher Kurt Baier offers a contrasting point of view in his recent book, *The Moral Point of View*. Rather than quarrel with the ordinary person's idea of self-interest, he instead attempts to refute the common assumption that self-interest and morality are, on the whole, incompatible. Baier revives the arguments of the early seventeenth-century English philosopher Thomas Hobbes that a universal moral code is indispensable to the existence of any kind of society, without which human life would be, as Hobbes put it, "solitary, poor, nasty, brutish and short." Baier reasons that it is in the long-range interest of everyone that they bind themselves by mutually acceptable rules of conduct that will, on some occasions, require a sacrifice of immediate self-interest. The point seems to be that long-range self-interest coincides with the dictates of morality, although immediate self-interest frequently does not, in which case it must be overridden. In Baier's words, "Moralities are systems of principles whose acceptance by everyone as overruling the dictates of self-interest is in the interest of everyone alike, though following the rules of a morality is not of course identical with following self-interest."

Baier adds that his argument applies only to societies in which there is a widely accepted code of behavior that most people can be reasonably expected to follow. In a society like that of Nazi Germany (if it can even be regarded as a genuine society rather than what Hobbes called a "state of nature," that is, a jungle), there was no acceptable code of behavior that people could be relied upon to follow. In such a case, the individual has no good reason to obey moral rules but is free to resort to tooth and claw.

It is not clear that Baier's analysis provides us with an answer as to why, in any *particular* case, we should sacrifice our self-interest for the sake of a moral rule. Gyges could argue that he, like Baier, is perfectly in favor of people generally sacrificing their self-interest for morality when the two collide, but he insists on making an exception in his own case. As long as *other* people can be relied upon to follow the moral rules, Gyges might reason, his own violations will not seriously disturb the social harmony that all benefit by, including himself. So, why not continue on his merry course?

The problem is that once we follow Baier in granting that immediate self-interest often collides with morality, it becomes difficult, perhaps impossible, to explain why morality should take precedence. Baier makes an effort to explain this, but it is questionable whether he succeeds. "It is better for everyone that there should be a morality generally observed," Baier maintains, "than that the principle of self-interest should be acknowledged as supreme." He cites this consideration as the reason for holding that "Moral rules are not designed to serve the agent's interest directly. Hence it would be quite inappropriate for him to break them whenever he discovers that they do not serve his interest." But it is doubtful that Baier's conclusion really follows from his premise. Gyges could have heartily endorsed the premise that self-interest should not be acknowledged as a "supreme principle," since it suited his purposes for others to be moral. Nonetheless, he did not find it at all "inappropriate," to use Baier's word, to break the rules himself. What then can Baier mean by "inappropriate," except, perhaps, immoral. But then he would be saying, in effect, that breaking a moral rule is immoral— hardly a convincing refutation of Gyges.

Baier successfully explains why we need and want a system of morality in society. Thus, he has answered the question: Why should *we* (society) be moral? It is not equally clear that he has answered the question: Why should *I* (Gyges) be moral? The reason may be that Baier accepts, without further analysis, an inadequate, although all too common, concept of self-interest—a concept that Jean-Paul Sartre, in our next selection, attacks.

Like Nietzsche, Sartre, the existentialist, appears to denounce morality and proclaim self-interest. Yet when the smoke of rhetoric has cleared away. we find morality reenthroned, although now wrapped in the mantle of a higher form of self-interest.

Sartre's pamphlet, "Existentialism Is a Humanism," is the transcript of a lecture he gave shortly after World War II. In the work, Sartre explains the philosophy of existentialism and defends it against critics, particularly against the communists who considered Sartre's arguments for absolute freedom a threat to the Marxist doctrine of economic determinism. Sartre is mainly concerned to prove two theses in defense of existentialism: (1) that its celebration of human freedom does not lead to social irresponsibility; and (2) that it does not, after all, undermine sound moral values.

Sartre speaks, like Nietzsche, of the individual creating his or her own values, and he also speaks, in an unusual way, of creating *oneself*. "Creating values," as we noted in our discussion of Nietzsche, is a hyperbolic figure of speech, not to be taken too literally. Neither Nietzsche nor Sartre means to say that people mold things called values out of clay. They do speak of replacing God as creator with humankind as creator, which suggests creation out of nothing. But this again is clearly a metaphor, since it is unlikely that they take the notion of creation out of nothing seriously. What they obviously mean by "creating values" is that our decisions are not imposed on us either by a coercive agent, God, or by causal necessity (determinism). Both writers probably go too far in the conclusions they draw from these initial convictions by suggesting that, as Sartre favorably quotes from Dostoyevsky, "Since God does not exist, everything is permitted." Perhaps they mean that everything is permitted in the innocent sense that nobody and no thing can compel us to do anything, but we should be on guard against misinterpreting them to mean that there are no objective standards of right and wrong—that we can make anything right by merely asserting that it is right. This is a subjectivist muddle that existentialists tend to fall into and then struggle valiantly to get out of. Let us avoid the trap from the start and save time and trouble.

Sartre's notion of self-creation is more difficult to understand and more crucial to his view. A person, he tells us, "is nothing else but that which he makes of himself"—a "project" toward which he aspires, rather than a finished object. And it is to this projected or self-created self that a person must be faithful in order to become "authentic," an honest risk taker rather than a self-deceptive coward pretending to be an inert object. It sounds as if Sartre is assuring us that we have a perfect right to "define ourselves" by aiming at any project we like, even the vicious projects of Gyges and Raskolnikov. But he soon deprives us of any such license to crime by pointing out that the isolated "I" of the Cartesian *cogito* is not a genuine person, but a philosophical abstraction. The self that a person creates through decision and action is a self *among other selves,* so that "nothing can be better for us unless it is better for all. . . . In fashioning myself I fashion man." His point is that there are certain objective limitations to the rules or policies of action we can consistently frame, limitations imposed by being a free human being capable of rational choice. These limitations provide a universal and objective moral framework for action. Those who violate such limitations, like the fascists in World War II, may rightfully be condemned as "scum." Sartre seems to have achieved a synthesis of the moral absolutism of Kant with the individualism of Nietzsche, and perhaps he has discovered how to retain the best of both worlds, a free world and a moral world—a feat that, as we found in chapter 1, even God may not have been able to perform.

Arguably, Sartre may place too much weight on an arbitrary definition of the self as a project involving all other selves in such a way that what one chooses for oneself one chooses for all. A cynic like Gyges or like Raskolnikov (before he found religion) might retort: "You wooly-headed sentimentalists can go ahead and identify yourselves with others as much as you like, but as for me, I identify myself with Number One, and other people are mere instruments for or obstacles to my purposes." Nietzsche, no doubt, would not even deign to reason with such scoundrels. But both Baier and Sartre might point out to them that they want to achieve fame and fortune to enjoy with other people. Would even the worst scoundrel be willing to destroy the rest of humanity to achieve purely selfish ends? Without the comforts of family and friends and the secure sense that they are reasonably safe from the violence of others, without the admiration, even the envy, of neighbors toward one's palatial home, and of onlookers toward one's expensive clothes and vehicles, without reasonably trustworthy tradespeople to supply one with goods, what value can wealth and power have? What good is it if mere instruments and obstacles admire the scoundrel, rather than persons whom he or she respects? How can a person have any sense of self at all without recognizing what Sartre calls the "subjectivity" of others, the fact that their interests are also worthy of consideration? We are not isolated atoms colliding randomly with each other but social and rational beings with common interests as well as competing desires. Perhaps we would not convince Gyges with this argument, but at least we would have tried, before reaching for our gun.

WHY NOT MURDER?

Fyodor Dostoyevsky

Later on, Raskolnikov happened to find out why the huckster and his wife had invited Lizaveta. It was a very ordinary matter and there was nothing exceptional about it. A family who had come to the town and been reduced to poverty were selling their household goods and clothes, all women's things. As the things would have fetched little in the market, they were looking for a dealer. This was Lizaveta's business. She undertook such jobs and was frequently employed, as she was very honest and always fixed a fair price and stuck to it. She spoke as a rule little and, as we have said already, she was very submissive and timid.

But Raskolnikov had become superstitious of late. The traces of superstition remained in him long after, and were almost ineradicable. And in all this he was always afterwards disposed to see something strange and mysterious, as it were the presence of some peculiar influences and coincidences. In the previous winter a student he knew called Pokorev, who had left for Harkov, had chanced in conversation to give him the address of Alyona Ivanovna, the old pawnbroker, in case he might want to pawn anything. For a long while he did not go to her, for he had lessons and managed to get along somehow. Six weeks ago he had remembered the address; he had two articles that could be pawned: his father's old silver watch and a little gold ring with three red stones, a present from his sister at parting. He decided to take the ring. When he found the old woman he had felt an insurmountable repulsion for her at the first glance, though he knew nothing special about her. He got two roubles from her and went into a miserable little tavern on his way home. He asked for tea, sat down and sank into deep thought. A strange idea was pecking at his brain like a chicken in the egg, and very, very much absorbed him.

Almost beside him at the next table there was sitting a student whom he did not know and had never seen, and with him a young officer. They had played a game of billiards and began drinking tea. All at once

FROM *Crime and Punishment,* part I, chapters 6 and 7, translated by Constance Garnett. Published by Random House, Inc.

he heard the student mention to the officer the pawnbroker Alyona Ivanovna and give him her address. This of itself seemed strange to Raskolnikov; he had just come from her and here at once heard her name. Of course it was a chance, but he could not shake off a very extraordinary impression, and here some one seemed to be speaking expressly for him; the student began telling his friend various details about Alyona Ivanovna.

"She is first rate," he said. "You can always get money from her. She is as rich as a Jew, she can give you five thousand roubles at a time and she is not above taking a pledge for a rouble. Lots of our fellows have had dealings with her. But she is an awful old harpy. . . ."

And he began describing how spiteful and uncertain she was, how if you were only a day late with your interest the pledge was lost; how she gave a quarter of the value of an article and took five and even seven percent a month on it and so on. The student chattered on, saying that she had a sister Lizaveta, whom the wretched little creature was continually beating, and kept in complete bondage like a small child, though Lizaveta was at least six feet high.

"There's a phenomenon for you," cried the student and he laughed.

They began talking about Lizaveta. The student spoke about her with a peculiar relish and was continually laughing and the officer listened with great interest and asked him to send Lizaveta to do some mending for him. Raskolnikov did not miss a word and learned everything about her. Lizaveta was younger than the old woman and was her half-sister, being the child of a different mother. She was thirty-five. She worked day and night for her sister, and besides doing the cooking and the washing, she did sewing and worked as a charwoman and gave her sister all she earned. She did not dare to accept an order or job of any kind without her sister's permission. The old woman had already made her will, and Lizaveta knew of it, and by this will she would not get a farthing; nothing but the movables, chairs and so on; all the money was left to a monastery in the province of N———, that prayers might be said for her in perpetuity. Lizaveta was of lower rank than her sister, unmarried and awfully uncouth in appearance, remarkably tall with long feet that looked as if they were bent outwards. She always wore battered goatskin shoes, and was clean in her person. What the student expressed most surprise and amusement about was the fact that Lizaveta was continually with child.

"But you say she is hideous?" observed the officer.

"Yes, she is so dark-skinned and looks like a soldier dressed up, but you know she is not at all hideous. She has such a good-natured face and eyes. Strikingly so. And the proof of it is that lots of people are attracted by her. She is such a soft, gentle creature, ready to put up with anything, always willing, willing to do anything. And her smile is really very sweet."

"You seem to find her attractive yourself," laughed the officer.

"From her queerness. No, I'll tell you what. I could kill that damned old woman and make off with her money, I assure you, without the faintest conscience-prick," the student added with warmth. The officer laughed again while Raskolnikov shuddered. How strange it was!

"Listen, I want to ask you a serious question," the student said hotly. "I was joking of course, but look here; on one side we have a stupid, senseless, worthless, spiteful, ailing, horrid old woman, not simply useless but doing actual mischief, who has not an idea what she is living for herself, and who will die in a day or two in any case. You understand? You understand?"

"Yes, yes, I understand," answered the officer, watching his excited companion attentively.

"Well, listen then. On the other side, fresh young lives thrown away for want of help and by thousands, on every side! A hundred thousand good deeds could be done and helped, on that old woman's money which will be buried in a monastery! Hundreds, thousands perhaps, might be set on the right path; dozens of families saved from destitution, from ruin, from vice, from the Lock hospitals—and all with her money. Kill her, take her money and with the help of it devote oneself to the service of humanity and the good of all. What do you think, would not one tiny crime be wiped out by thousands of good deeds? For one life thousands would be saved from corruption and decay. One death, and a hundred lives in exchange—it's simple arithmetic! Besides, what value has the life of that sickly, stupid, ill-natured old woman in the balance of existence? No more than the life of a louse, of a black beetle, less in fact because the old woman is doing harm. She is wearing out the lives of others; the other day she bit Lizaveta's finger out of spite; it almost had to be amputated."

"Of course she does not deserve to live," remarked the officer, "but there it is, it's nature."

"Oh well, brother, but we have to correct and direct nature, and, but for that, we should drown in an ocean of prejudice. But for that, there would never have been a single great man. They talk of duty, conscience—I don't want to say anything against duty and conscience;—but the point is what do we mean by them. Stay, I have another question to ask you. Listen!"

"No, you stay, I'll ask you a question. Listen!"

"Well!"

"You are talking and speechifying away, but tell me, would you kill the old woman *yourself?*"

"Of course not! I was only arguing the justice of it. . . . It's nothing to do with me. . . ."

"But I think, if you would not do it yourself, there's no justice about it. . . . Let us have another game."

Raskolnikov was violently agitated. Of course, it was all ordinary youthful talk and thought, such as he had often heard before in different forms and on different themes. But why had he happened to hear such a discussion and such ideas at the very moment when his own brain was just conceiving . . . *the very same ideas?* And why, just at the moment when he had brought away the embryo of his idea from the old woman, had he dropped at once upon a conversation about her? This coincidence always seemed strange to him. This trivial talk in a tavern had an immense influence on him in his later action; as though there had really been in it something preordained, some guiding hint. . . .

On returning from the Hay Market he flung himself on the sofa and sat for a whole hour without stirring. Meanwhile it got dark; he had no candle and, indeed, it did not occur to him to light up. He could never recollect whether he had been thinking about anything at that time. At last he was conscious of his former fever and shivering, and he realised with relief that he could lie down on the sofa. Soon heavy, leaden sleep came over him, as it were crushing him.

He slept an extraordinarily long time and without dreaming. Nastasya, coming into his room at ten o'clock the next morning, had difficulty in rousing him. She brought him in tea and bread. The tea was again the second brew and again in her own teapot.

"My goodness, how he sleeps!" she cried indignantly. "And he is always asleep."

He got up with an effort. His head ached, he stood up, took a turn in his garret and sank back on the sofa again.

"Going to sleep again," cried Nastasya. "Are you ill, eh?"

He made no reply.

"Do you want some tea?"

"Afterwards," he said with an effort, closing his eyes again and turning to the wall.

Nastasya stood over him.

"Perhaps he really is ill," she said, turned and went out. She came in again at two o'clock with soup. He was lying as before. The tea stood untouched. Nastasya felt positively offended and began wrathfully rousing him.

"Why are you lying like a log?" she shouted, looking at him with repulsion.

He got up, and sat down again, but said nothing and stared at the floor.

"Are you ill or not?" asked Nastasya and again received no answer. "You'd better go out and get a breath of air," she said after a pause. "Will you eat it or not?"

"Afterwards," he said weakly. "You can go."

And he motioned her out.

She remained a little longer, looked at him with compassion and went out.

A few minutes afterwards, he raised his eyes and looked for a long while at the tea and the soup. Then he took the bread, took up a spoon and began to eat.

He ate a little, three or four spoonfuls, without appetite, as it were mechanically. His head ached less. After his meal he stretched himself on the sofa again, but now he could not sleep; he lay without stirring, with his face in the pillow. He was haunted by day-dreams and such strange day-dreams; in one, that kept recurring, he fancied that he was in Africa, in Egypt, in some sort of oasis. The caravan was resting, the camels were peacefully lying down; the palms stood all round in a complete circle; all the party were at dinner. But he was drinking water from a spring which flowed gurgling close by. And it was so cool, it was wonderful, wonderful, blue, cold water running among the parti-colored stones and over the clean sand which glistened here and there like gold. . . . Suddenly he heard a clock strike. He started, roused himself, raised his head, looked out of the window, and seeing how late it was, suddenly jumped up wide awake as though some one had pulled him off the sofa. He crept on tiptoe to the door, stealthily opened it and began listening on the staircase. His heart beat terribly. But all was quiet on the stairs as if every one was asleep. . . . It seemed to him strange and monstrous that he could have slept in such forgetfulness from the previous day and had done nothing, had prepared nothing yet. . . . And meanwhile perhaps it had struck six. And his drowsiness and stupefaction were followed by extraordinary, feverish, as it were, distracted, haste. But the preparations to be made were few. He concentrated all his energies on thinking of everything and forgetting nothing; and his heart kept beating and thumping so that he could hardly breathe. First he had to make a noose and sew it into his overcoat—a work of a moment. He rummaged under his pillow and picked out amongst the things stuffed away under it, a worn out, old unwashed shirt. From its rags he tore a long strip, a couple of inches wide and about sixteen inches long. He folded this strip in two, took off his wide, strong summer overcoat of some stout cotton material (his only outer garment) and began sewing the two ends of the rag on the inside, under the left armhole. His hands shook as he sewed, but he did it successfully so that nothing showed outside when he put the coat on again. The needle and thread he had got ready long before and they lay on his table in a piece of paper. As for the noose, it was a very ingenious device of his own; the noose was intended for the axe. It was impossible for him to carry the axe through the street in his hands. And if hidden under his coat he would still have had to support it with his hand, which would have been noticeable. Now he had only to put the head of the axe in the noose, and it would hang quietly under his arm on the inside. Putting his hand in his coat pocket, he could hold the end of the handle all the way, so that it did not swing; and as the coat was very full, a regular sack in fact, it could not be seen from outside that he was holding something with the hand that was in the pocket. This noose, too, he had designed a fortnight before.

When he had finished with this, he thrust his hand into a little opening between his sofa and the floor, fumbled in the left corner and drew out the *pledge,* which he had got ready long before and hidden there. This pledge was, however, only a smoothly planed piece of wood the size and thickness of a silver cigarette case. He picked up this piece of wood in one of his wanderings in a courtyard where there was some sort of a workshop. Afterwards he had added to the wood a thin smooth piece of iron, which he had also picked up at the same time in the street. Putting the iron which was a little the smaller on the piece of wood, he fastened them very firmly, crossing and recrossing the thread round them; then wrapped them carefully and daintily in clean, white paper and tied up the parcel so that it would be very difficult to untie it. This was in order to divert the attention of the old woman for a time, while she was trying to undo the knot, and so to gain a moment. The iron strip was added to give weight, so that the woman might not guess the first minute that the "thing" was made of wood. All this had been stored by him beforehand under the sofa. He had only just got the pledge out when he heard someone suddenly shout in the yard.

"It struck six long ago."

"Long ago! My God!"

He rushed to the door, listened, caught up his hat and began to descend his thirteen steps cautiously, noiselessly, like a cat. He had still the most important thing to do—to steal the axe from the kitchen. That the deed must be done with an axe he had decided long ago. He had also a pocket pruning-knife, but he could not rely on the knife and still less on his own strength, and so resolved finally on the axe. We may note in passing one peculiarity in regard to all the final resolutions taken by him in the matter; they had one strange characteristic; the more final they were, the more hideous and the more absurd they at once became in his eyes. In spite of all his agonizing inward struggle, he never for a single instant all that time could believe in the carrying out of his plans.

And, indeed, if it had ever happened that everything to the least point could have been considered and finally settled, and no uncertainty of any kind had remained, he would, it seems, have renounced it all as something absurd, monstrous and impossible. But a whole mass of unsettled points and uncertainties remained. As for getting the axe, that trifling business cost him no anxiety, for nothing could be easier. Nastasya was continually out of the house, especially in the evenings; she would run in to the neighbors or to a shop, and always left the door ajar. It was the one thing the landlady was always scolding her about. And so when the time came, he would only have to go quietly into the kitchen and to take the axe, and an hour later (when everything was over) go in and put it back again. But these were doubtful points. Supposing he returned an hour later to put it back, and Nastasya had come back and was on the spot. He would of course have to go by and wait till she went out again. But supposing she were in the meantime to miss the axe, look for it, make an outcry—that would mean suspicion or at least grounds for suspicion.

But those were all trifles which he had not even begun to consider, and indeed he had no time. He was thinking of the chief point, and put off trifling details, until he *could believe in it all*. But that seemed utterly unattainable. So it seemed to himself at least. He could not imagine, for instance, that he would sometime leave off thinking, get up and simply go there. . . . Even his late experiment (*i.e.,* his visit with the object of a final survey of the place) was simply an attempt at an experiment, far from being the real thing, as though one should say "come, let us go and try it—why dream about it!"—and at once he had broken down and had run away cursing, in a frenzy with himself. Meanwhile it would seem, as regards the moral question, that his analysis was complete; his casuistry had become keen as a razor, and he could not find rational objections in himself. But in the last resort he simply ceased to believe in himself, and doggedly, slavishly sought arguments in all directions, fumbling for them, as though some one were forcing and drawing him to it.

At first—long before indeed—he had been much occupied with one question; why almost all crimes are so badly concealed and so easily detected, and why almost all criminals leave such obvious traces? He had come gradually to many different and curious conclusions, and in his opinion the chief reason lay not so much in the material impossibility of concealing the crime, as in the criminal himself. Almost every criminal is subject to a failure of will and reasoning power by a childish and phenomenal heedlessness, at the very instant when prudence and caution are most essential. It was his conviction that this eclipse of reason and failure of will power attacked a man like a disease, developed gradually and reached its highest point just before the perpetration of the crime, continued with equal violence at the moment of the crime and for longer or shorter time after, according to the individual case, and then passed off like any other disease. The question whether the disease gives rise to the crime, or whether the crime from its own peculiar nature is always accompanied by something of the nature of disease, he did not yet feel able to decide.

When he reached these conclusions, he decided that in his own case there could not be such a morbid reaction, that his reason and will would remain unimpaired at the time of carrying out his design, for the single reason that his design was "not a crime. . . ." We will omit all the process by means of which he arrived at this last conclusion; we have run too far ahead already. . . . We may add only that the practical, purely material difficulties of the affair occupied a secondary position in his mind. "One has but to keep all one's will power and reason to deal with them, and they will all be overcome at the time when once one has familiarized oneself with the minutest details of the business. . . ." But this preparation had never been begun. His final decisions were what he came to trust least, and when the hour struck, it all came to pass quite differently, as it were accidentally and unexpectedly.

One trifling circumstance upset his calculations, before he had even left the staircase. When he reached the landlady's kitchen, the door of which was open as usual, he glanced cautiously in to see whether, in Nastasya's absence, the landlady herself was there, or if not, whether the door to her own room was closed, so that she might not peep out when he went in for the axe. But what was his amazement when he suddenly saw that Nastasya was not only at home in the kitchen, but was occupied there, taking linen out of a basket and hanging it on a line. Seeing him, she left off hanging the clothes, turned to him and stared at him all the time he was passing. He turned away his eyes, and walked past as though he noticed nothing. But it was the end of everything; he had not the axe! He was overwhelmed.

"What made me think," he reflected, as he went under the gateway. "What made me think that she would be sure not to be at home at that moment! Why, why, why did I assume this so certainly?"

He was crushed and even humiliated. He could have laughed at himself in his anger. . . . A dull animal rage boiled within him.

He stood hesitating in the gateway. To go into the street, to go for a walk for appearance' sake was revolting; to go back to his room, even more revolting. "And what a chance I have lost for ever!" he muttered, standing aimlessly in the gateway, just opposite the porter's little dark room, which was also open. Suddenly he started. From the porter's room, two paces away from him, something shining under the bench to the right caught his eye. . . . He looked about him—nobody. He approached the room on tiptoe, went down two steps into it and in a faint voice called the porter. "Yes, not at home! Somewhere near though, in the yard, for the door is wide open." He dashed to the axe (it was an axe) and pulled it out from under the bench, where it lay between two chunks of wood; at once, before going out, he made it fast in the noose, he thrust both hands into his pockets and went out of the room; no one had noticed him! "When reason fails, the devil helps!" he thought with a strange grin. This chance raised his spirits extraordinarily.

He walked along quietly and sedately, without hurry, to avoid awakening suspicion. He scarcely looked at the passers-by, tried to escape looking at their faces at all, and to be as little noticeable as possible. Suddenly he thought of his hat. "Good heavens! I had the money the day before yesterday and did not get a cap to wear instead!" A curse rose from the bottom of his soul.

Glancing out of the corner of his eye into a shop, he saw by a clock on the wall that it was ten minutes past seven. He had to make haste and at the same time to go some way round, so as to approach the house from the other side. . . .

When he had happened to imagine all this beforehand, he had sometimes thought that he would be very much afraid. But he was not very much afraid now, was not afraid at all, indeed. His mind was even occupied by irrelevant matters, but by nothing for long. As he passed the Yusupov garden, he was deeply absorbed in considering the building of great fountains, and of their refreshing effect on the atmosphere in all the squares. By degrees he passed to the conviction that if the summer garden were extended to the field of Mars, and perhaps joined to the garden of the Mihailovsky Palace, it would be a splendid thing and a great benefit to the town. Then he was interested by the question why in all great towns men are not simply driven by necessity, but in some peculiar way inclined to live in those parts of the town where there are no gardens nor fountains; where there is most dirt and smell and all sorts of nastiness. Then his own walks through the Hay Market came back to his mind, and for a moment he waked up to reality. "What nonsense!" he thought, "better think of nothing at all!"

"So probably men led to execution clutch mentally at every object that meets them on the way," flashed through his mind, but simply flashed, like lightning; he made haste to dismiss this thought. . . . And by now he was near; here was the house, here was the gate. Suddenly a clock somewhere struck once. "What! can it be half-past seven? Impossible, it must be fast!"

Luckily for him, everything went well again at the gates. At that very moment, as though expressly for his benefit, a huge wagon of hay had just driven in at the gate, completely screening him as he passed under the gateway, and the wagon had scarcely had time to drive through into the yard, before he had slipped in a flash to the right. On the other side of the wagon he could hear shouting and quarreling; but no one noticed him and no one met him. Many windows looking into that huge quadrangular yard were open at that moment, but he did not raise his head—he had not the strength to. The staircase leading to the old woman's room was close by, just on the right of the gateway. He was already on the stairs. . . .

Drawing a breath, pressing his hand against his throbbing heart, and once more feeling for the axe and setting it straight, he began softly and cautiously ascending the stairs, listening every minute. But the stairs, too, were quite deserted; all the doors were shut; he met no one. One flat indeed on the second floor was wide open and painters were at work in it, but they did not glance at him. He stood still, thought a minute and went on. "Of course it would be better if they had not been here, but . . . it's two stories above them."

And here was the fourth story, here was the door, here was the flat opposite, the empty one. The flat underneath the old woman's was apparently empty also; the visiting card nailed on the door had been torn off—they had gone away! . . . He was out of breath. For one instant the thought floated through his mind "Shall I go back?" But he made no answer and began listening at the old woman's door, a dead silence. Then he listened again on the staircase, listened long and intently . . . then looked about him for the last time, pulled himself together, drew himself up, and once more tried the axe in the noose. "Am I very pale?" he wondered. "Am I not evidently agitated? She is mistrustful. . . . Had I better wait a little longer . . . till my heart leaves off thumping?"

But his heart did not leave off. On the contrary, as though to spite him, it throbbed more and more violently. He could stand it no longer, he slowly put out his hand to the bell and rang. Half a minute later he rang again, more loudly.

No answer. To go on ringing was useless and out of place. The old woman was, of course, at home, but she was suspicious and alone. He had some knowledge of her habits . . . and once more he put his ear to the door. Either his senses were peculiarly keen (which it is difficult to suppose), or the sound was really very distinct. Anyway, he suddenly heard something like the cautious touch of a hand on the lock and the rustle of a skirt at the very door. Some one was standing stealthily close to the lock and just as he was doing on the outside was secretly listening within, and seemed to have her ear to the door. . . .

He moved a little on purpose and muttered something aloud that he might not have the appearance of hiding, then rang a third time, but quietly, soberly and without impatience. Recalling it afterwards, that moment stood out in his mind vividly, distinctly, forever; he could not make out how he had had such cunning, for his mind was as it were clouded at moments and he was almost unconscious of his body. . . . An instant later he heard the latch unfastened.

. . . .

The door was as before opened a tiny crack, and again two sharp and suspicious eyes stared at him out of the darkness. Then Raskolnikov lost his head and nearly made a great mistake.

Fearing the old woman would be frightened by their being alone, and not hoping that the sight of him would disarm her suspicions, he took hold of the door and drew it towards him to prevent the old woman from attempting to shut it again. Seeing this she did not pull the door back, but she did not let go the handle so that he almost dragged her out with it on to the stairs. Seeing that she was standing in the doorway not allowing him to pass, he advanced straight upon her. She stepped back in alarm, tried to say something, but seemed unable to speak and stared with open eyes at him.

"Good evening, Alyona Ivanovna," he began, trying to speak easily, but his voice would not obey him, it broke and shook. "I have come . . . I have brought something . . . but we'd better come in . . . to the light. . . ."

And leaving her, he passed straight into the room uninvited. The old woman ran after him; her tongue was unloosed.

"Good heavens! What is it? Who is it? What do you want?"

"Why, Alyona Ivanovna, you know me . . . Raskolnikov . . . here, I brought you the pledge I promised the other day . . ." and he held out the pledge.

The old woman glanced for a moment at the pledge, but at once stared in the eyes of her uninvited visitor. She looked intently, maliciously and mistrustfully. A minute passed; he even fancied something like a sneer in her eyes, as though she had already guessed everything. He felt that he was losing his head, that he was almost frightened, so frightened that if she were to look like that and not say a word for another half minute, he thought he would have run away from her.

"Why do you look at me as though you did not know me?" he said suddenly, also with malice. "Take it if you like, if not I'll go elsewhere, I am in a hurry."

He had not even thought of saying this, but it was suddenly said of itself. The old woman recovered herself, and her visitor's resolute tone evidently restored her confidence.

"But why, my good sir, all of a minute. . . . What is it?" she asked, looking at the pledge.

"The silver cigarette case; I spoke of it last time, you know."

She held out her hand.

"But how pale you are, to be sure . . . and your hands are trembling too? Have you been bathing, or what?"

"Fever," he answered abruptly. "You can't help getting pale . . . if you've nothing to eat," he added, with difficulty articulating the words.

His strength was failing him again. But his answer sounded like the truth; the old woman took the pledge.

"What is it?" she asked once more, scanning Raskolnikov intently and weighing the pledge in her hand.

"A thing . . . cigarette case. . . . Silver. . . . Look at it."

"It does not seem somehow like silver. . . . How he has wrapped it up!"

Trying to untie the string and turning to the window, to the light (all her windows were shut, in spite of the stifling heat), she left him altogether for some seconds and stood with her back to him. He unbuttoned his coat and freed the axe from the noose, but did not yet take it out altogether, simply holding it in his right hand under the coat. His hands were fearfully weak, he felt them every moment growing more numb and more wooden. He was afraid he would let the axe slip and fall. . . . A sudden giddiness came over him.

"But what has he tied it up like this for?" the old woman cried with vexation and moved towards him.

He had not a minute more to lose. He pulled the axe quite out, swung it with both arms, scarcely conscious of himself, and almost without effort, almost mechanically, brought the blunt side down on her head. He seemed not to use his own strength in this. But as soon as he had once brought the axe down, his strength returned to him.

The old woman was as always bare-headed. Her thin, light hair, streaked with grey, thickly smeared with grease, was plaited in a rat's tail and fastened by a broken horn comb which stood out on the nape of her neck. As she was so short, the blow fell on the very top of her skull. She cried out, but very faintly, and suddenly sank all of a heap on the floor, raising her hands to her head. In one hand she still held "the pledge." Then he dealt her another and another blow with the blunt side and on the same spot. The blood gushed as from an overturned glass, the body fell back. He stepped back, let it fall, and at once bent over her face; she was dead. Her eyes seemed to be starting out of their sockets, the brow and the whole face were drawn and contorted convulsively.

He laid the axe on the ground near the dead body and felt at once in her pocket (trying to avoid the streaming blood)—the same right hand pocket from which she had taken the key on his last visit. He was in full possession of his faculties, free from confusion or giddiness, but his hands were still trembling. He remembered afterwards that he had been particularly collected and careful, trying all the time not to get smeared with blood. . . . He pulled out the keys at once, they were all, as before, in one bunch on a steel ring. He ran at once into the bedroom with them. It was a very small room with a whole shrine of holy images. Against the other wall stood a big bed, very clean and covered with a silk patchwork wadded quilt. Against a third wall was a chest of drawers. Strange to say, so soon as he began to fit the keys into the chest, so soon as he heard their jingling, a convulsive shudder passed over him. He suddenly felt tempted again to give it all up and go away. But that was only for an instant; it was too late to go back. He positively smiled at himself, when suddenly another terrifying idea occurred to his mind. He suddenly fancied that the old woman might be still alive and might recover her senses. Leaving the keys in the chest, he ran back to the body, snatched up the axe and lifted it once more over the old woman, but did not bring it down. There was no doubt that she was dead. Bending down and examining her again more closely, he saw clearly that the skull was broken and even battered in on one side. He was about to feel it with his finger, but drew back his hand and indeed it was evident without that. Meanwhile there was a perfect pool of blood. All at once he noticed a string on her neck; he tugged at it, but the string was strong and did not snap and besides, it was soaked with blood. He tried to pull it out from the front of the dress, but something held it and prevented its coming. In his impatience he raised the axe again to cut the string from above on the body, but did not dare, and with difficulty, smearing his hand and the axe in the blood, after two minutes' hurried effort, he cut the string and took it off without touching the body with the axe; he was not mistaken—it was a purse. On the string were two crosses, one of Cyprus wood and one of copper, and an image in silver filigree, and with them a small greasy chamois leather purse with a steel rim and ring. The purse was stuffed very full; Raskolnikov thrust it in his pocket without looking at it, flung the crosses on the old woman's body and rushed back into the bedroom, this time taking the axe with him.

He was in terrible haste, he snatched the keys, and began trying them again. But he was unsuccessful. They would not fit in the locks. It was not so much that his hands were shaking, but that he kept making mistakes; though he saw for instance that a key was not the right one and would not fit, still he tried to put it in. Suddenly he remembered and realized that the big key with the deep notches, which was hanging there with the small keys could not possibly belong to the chest of drawers, (on his last visit this had struck him) but to some strong box, and that everything perhaps was hidden in that box. He left the chest of drawers, and at once felt under the bedstead, knowing that old women usually keep boxes under their beds. And so it was; there was a good-sized box under the bed, at least a yard in length, with an arched lid covered with red leather and studded with steel nails. The notched key fitted at once and unlocked it. At the top, under a white sheet, was a coat of red brocade lined with hareskin; under it was a silk dress, then a shawl and it seemed as though there was nothing below but clothes. The first thing he did was to wipe his blood-stained hands on the red brocade. "It's red, and on red blood will be less noticeable," the thought passed through his mind; then he suddenly came to himself. "Good God, am I going out of my senses?" he thought with terror.

But no sooner did he touch the clothes than a gold watch slipped from under the fur coat. He made haste to turn them all over. There turned out to be various articles made of gold among the clothes— probably all pledges, unredeemed or waiting to be redeemed—bracelets, chains, earrings, pins and such things. Some were in cases, others simply wrapped in newspaper, carefully and exactly folded, and tied round with tape. Without any delay, he began filling up the pockets of his trousers and overcoat without examining or undoing the parcels and cases; but he had not time to take many. . . .

He suddenly heard steps in the room where the old woman lay. He stopped short and was still as death. But all was quiet, so it must have been his fancy. All at once he heard distinctly a faint cry, as though some one had uttered a low broken moan. Then again dead silence for a minute or two. He sat squatting on his heels by the box and waited holding his breath. Suddenly he jumped up, seized the axe and ran out of the bedroom.

In the middle of the room stood Lizaveta with a big bundle in her arms. She was gazing in stupefaction at her murdered sister, white as a sheet and seeming not to have the strength to cry out. Seeing him run out of the bedroom, she began faintly quivering all over, like a leaf, a shudder ran down her face; she lifted her hand, opened her mouth, but still did not scream. She began slowly backing away from him into the corner, staring intently, persistently at him, but still uttered no sound, as though she could not get breath to scream. He rushed at her with the axe; her mouth twitched piteously, as one sees babies' mouths, when they begin to be frightened, stare intently at what frightens them and are on the point of screaming. And this hapless Lizaveta was so simple and had been so thoroughly crushed and scared that she did not even raise a hand to guard her face, though that was the most necessary and natural action at the moment, for the axe was raised over her face. She only put up her empty left hand, but not to her face, slowly holding it out before her as though motioning him away. The axe fell with the sharp edge just on the skull and split at one blow all the top of the head. She fell heavily at once. Raskolnikov completely lost his head, snatched up her bundle, dropped it again and ran into the entry.

Fear gained more and more mastery over him, especially after this second, quite unexpected murder. He longed to run away from the place as fast as possible. And if at that moment he had been capable of seeing and reasoning more correctly, if he had been able to realize all the difficulties of his position, the hopelessness, the hideousness and the absurdity of it, if he could have understood how many obstacles and, perhaps, crimes he had still to overcome or to commit, to get out of that place and to make his way home, it is very possible that he would have flung up everything, and would have gone to give himself up, and not from fear, but from simple horror and loathing of what he had done. The feeling of loathing especially surged up within him and grew stronger every minute. He would not now have gone to the box or even into the room for anything in the world.

But a sort of blankness, even dreaminess had begun by degrees to take possession of him; at moments he forgot himself, or rather forgot what was of importance and caught at trifles. Glancing, however, into the kitchen and seeing a bucket half full of water on a bench, he bethought him of washing his hands and the axe. His hands were sticky with blood. He dropped the axe with the blade in the water, snatched a piece of soap that lay in a broken saucer on the window, and began washing his hands in the bucket. When they were clean, he took out the axe, washed the blade and spent a long time, about three minutes, washing the wood where there were spots of blood, rubbing them with soap. Then he wiped it all with some linen that was hanging to dry on a line in the kitchen and then he was a long while attentively examining the axe at the window. There was no trace left on it, only the wood was still damp. He carefully hung the axe in the noose under his coat. Then as far as was possible, in the dim light in the kitchen, he looked over his overcoat, his trousers and his boots. At the first glance there seemed to be nothing but stains on the boots. He wetted the rag and rubbed the boots. But he knew he was not looking thoroughly, that there might be something quite noticeable that he was overlooking. He stood in the middle of the room, lost in thought. Dark agonizing ideas rose in his mind—the idea that he was mad and that at that moment he was incapable of reasoning, of protecting himself, that he ought perhaps to be doing something utterly different from what he was now doing. "Good God!" he muttered, "I must fly, fly," and he rushed into the entry. But here a shock of terror awaited him such as he had never known before.

He stood and gazed and could not believe his eyes: the door, the outer door from the stairs, at which he had not long before waited and rung, was standing unfastened and at least six inches open. No lock, no bolt, all the time, all that time! The old woman had not shut it after him perhaps as a precaution. But, good God! Why, he had seen Lizaveta afterwards! And how could he, how could he have failed to reflect that she must have come in somehow! She could not have come through the wall!

He dashed to the door and fastened the latch.

"But no, the wrong thing again I must get away, get away. . . ."

He unfastened the latch, opened the door and began listening on the staircase.

He listened a long time. Somewhere far away, it might be in the gateway, two voices were loudly and shrilly shouting, quarreling and scolding. "What are they about?" He waited patiently. At last all was still, as though suddenly cut off; they had separated. He was meaning to go out, but suddenly, on the floor below, a door was noisily opened and some one began going downstairs humming a tune. "How is it they all make such a noise!" flashed through his mind. Once more he closed the door and waited. At last all was still, not a soul stirring. He was just taking a step towards the stairs when he heard fresh footsteps.

The steps sounded very far off, at the very bottom of the stairs, but he remembered quite clearly and distinctly that from the first sound he began for some reason to suspect that this was some one coming *there,* to the fourth floor, to the old woman. Why? Were the sounds somehow peculiar, significant? The steps were heavy, even and unhurried. Now *he* had passed the first floor, now he was mounting higher, it was growing more and more distinct! He could hear his heavy breathing. And now the third story had been reached. Coming here! And it seemed to him all at once that he was turned to stone, that it was like a dream in which one is being pursued, nearly caught and will be killed, and is rooted to the spot and cannot even move one's arms.

At last when the unknown was mounting to the fourth floor, he suddenly started, and succeeded in slipping neatly and quickly back into the flat and closing the door behind him. Then he took the hook and softly, noiselessly, fixed it in the catch. Instinct helped him. When he had done this, he crouched holding his breath, by the door. The unknown visitor was by now also at the door. They were now standing opposite one another, as he had just before been standing with the old woman, when the door divided them and he was listening.

The visitor panted several times. "He must be a big, fat man," thought Raskolnikov, squeezing the axe in his hand. It seemed like a dream indeed. The visitor took hold of the bell and rang loudly.

As soon as the tin bell tinkled, Raskolnikov seemed to be aware of something moving in the room. For some seconds he listened quite seriously. The unknown rang again, waited and suddenly tugged violently and impatiently at the handle of the door. Raskolnikov gazed in horror at the hook shaking in its fastening, and in blank terror expected every minute that the fastening would be pulled out. It certainly did seem possible, so violently was he shaking it. He was tempted to hold the fastening, but he might be aware of it. A giddiness came over him again. "I shall fall down" flashed through his mind, but the unknown began to speak and he recovered himself at once.

"What's up? Are they asleep or murdered? D-damn them!" he bawled in a thick voice. "Hey, Alyona Ivanovna, old witch! Lizaveta Ivanovna, hey, my beauty! open the door! Oh, damn them! Are they asleep or what?"

And again, enraged, he tugged with all his might a dozen times at the bell. He must certainly be a man of authority and an intimate acquaintance.

At this moment light hurried steps were heard not far off, on the stairs. Some one else was approaching. Raskolnikov had not heard them at first.

"You don't say there's no one at home," the newcomer cried in a cheerful ringing voice, addressing the first visitor who still went on pulling the bell. "Good-evening, Koch."

"From his voice he must be quite young," thought Raskolnikov.

"Who the devil can tell? I've almost broken the lock," answered Koch. "But how do you come to know me?"

"Why! The day before yesterday I beat you three times running at billiards at Gambrinus'."

"Oh!"

"So they are not at home? That's queer? It's awfully stupid though. Where could the old woman have gone? I've come on business."

"Yes; and I have business with her, too."

"Well, what can we do? Go back, I suppose. Aie—aie! And I was hoping to get some money!" cried the young man.

"We must give it up, of course, but what did she fix this time for? The old witch fixed the time for me to come herself. It's out of my way. And where the devil she can have got to, I can't make out. She sits here from year's end to year's end, the old hag; her legs are bad and yet here all of a sudden she is out for a walk!"

"Hadn't we better ask the porter?"

"What?"

"Where she's gone and when she'll be back."

"H'm . . . Damn it all! . . . We might ask. . . . But you know she never does go anywhere."

And he once more tugged at the door-handle.

"Damn it all. There's nothing to be done, we must go!"

"Stay!" cried the young man suddenly. "Do you see how the door shakes if you pull it?"

"Well?"

"That shows it's not locked, but fastened with the hook! Do you hear how the hook clanks?"

"Well?"

'Why, don't you see? That proves that one of them is at home. If they were all out, they would have locked the door from outside with the key and not with the hook from inside. There, do you hear how the hook is clanking? To fasten the hook on the inside they must be at home, don't you see. So there they are sitting inside and don't open the door!"

"Well! And so they must be!" cried Koch, astonished. "What are they about in there!" And he began furiously shaking the door.

"Stay!" cried the young man again. "Don't pull at it! There must be something wrong. . . . Here, you've been ringing and pulling at the door and still they don't open! So either they've both fainted or . . ."

"What?"

"I tell you what. Let's go and fetch the porter, let him wake them up."

"All right."

Both were going down.

"Stay. You stop here while I run down for the porter."

"What for?"

"Well, you'd better."

"All right."

"I'm studying the law you see! It's evident, e-vi-dent there's something wrong here!" the young man cried hotly, and he ran downstairs.

Koch remained. Once more he softly touched the bell which gave one tinkle, then gently, as though reflecting and looking about him, began touching the door-handle pulling it and letting it go to make sure once more that it was only fastened by the hook. Then puffing and panting he bent down and began looking at the keyhole: but the key was in the lock on the inside and so nothing could be seen.

Raskolnikov stood keeping tight hold of the axe. He was in a sort of delirium. He was even making ready to fight when they should come in. While they were knocking and talking together, the idea several times occurred to him to end it all at once and shout to them through the door. Now and then he was tempted to swear at them, to jeer at them, while they could not open the door! "Only make haste!" was the thought that flashed through his mind.

"But what he devil is he about? . . ." Time was passing, one minute, and another—no one came. Koch began to be restless.

"What the devil?" he cried suddenly and in impatience deserting his sentry duty, he, too, went down, hurrying and thumping with his heavy boots on the stairs. The steps died away.

"Good heavens! What am I to do?"

Raskolnikov unfastened the hook, opened the door—there was no sound. Abruptly, without any thought at all, he went out, closing the door as thoroughly as he could, and went downstairs.

He had gone down three flights when he suddenly heard a loud noise below—where could he go! There was nowhere to hide. He was just going back to the flat.

"Hey there! Catch the brute!"

Somebody dashed out of a flat below, shouting, and rather fell than ran down the stairs, bawling at the top of his voice:

"Mitka! Mitka! Mitka! Mitka! Mitka! Blast him!"

The shout ended in a shriek; the last sounds came from the yard; all was still. But at the same instant several men talking loud and fast began noisily mounting the stairs. There were three or four of them. He distinguished the ringing voice of the young man. "They!"

Filled with despair he went straight to meet them, feeling "come what must!" If they stopped him—all was lost; if they let him pass— all was lost too; they would remember him. They were approaching; they were only a flight from him—and suddenly deliverance! A few steps from him on the right, there was an empty flat with the door wide open, the flat on the second floor where the painters had been at work, and which, as though for his benefit, they had just left. It was they, no doubt, who had just run down, shouting. The floor had only just been painted, in the middle of the room stood a pail and a broken pot with paint and brushes. In one instant he had whisked in at the open door and hidden behind the wall and only in the nick of time; they had already reached the landing. Then they turned and went on up to the fourth floor, talking loudly. He waited, went out on tiptoe and ran down the stairs.

No one was on the stairs, nor in the gateway. He passed quickly through the gateway and turned to the left in the street.

He knew, he knew perfectly well that at that moment they were at the flat, that they were greatly astonished at finding it unlocked, as the door had just been fastened, that by now they were looking at the bodies, that before another minute had passed they would guess and completely realize that the murderer had just been there, and had succeeded in hiding somewhere, slipping by them and escaping. They would guess most likely that he had been in the empty flat, while they were going upstairs. And meanwhile he dared not quicken his pace much, though the next turning was still nearly a hundred yards away. "Should he slip through some gateway and wait somewhere in an unknown street? No, hopeless! Should be fling away the axe? Should he take a cab? Hopeless, hopeless!"

At last he reached the turning. He turned down it more dead than alive. Here he was half-way to safety, and he understood it; it was less risky because there was a great crowd of people, and he was lost in it like a grain of sand. But all he had suffered had so weakened him that he could scarcely move. Perspiration ran down him in drops, his neck was all wet. "My word, he has been going it!" some one shouted at him when he came out on the canal bank.

He was only dimly conscious of himself now, and the farther he went the worse it was. He remembered however, that on coming out on to the canal bank, he was alarmed at finding few people there and so being more conspicuous, and he had thought of turning back. Though he was almost falling from fatigue, he went a long way round so as to get home from quite a different direction.

He was not fully conscious when he passed through the gateway of his house; he was already on the staircase before he recollected the axe. And yet he had a very grave problem before him, to put it back and to escape observation as far as possible in doing so. He was of course incapable of reflecting that it might perhaps be far better not to restore the axe at all, but to drop it later on in somebody's yard. But it all happened fortunately, the door of the porter's room was closed but not locked, so that it seemed most likely that the porter was at home. But he had so completely lost all power of reflection that he walked straight to the door and opened it. If the porter had asked him "What do you want?" he would perhaps have simply handed him the axe. But again the porter was not at home, and he succeeded in putting the axe back under the bench and even covering it with the chunk of wood as before. He met no one, not a soul, afterwards on the way to his room; the landlady's door was shut. When he was in his room, he flung himself on the sofa just as he was—he did not sleep, but sank into blank forgetfulness. If any one had come into his room then, he would have jumped up at once and screamed. Scraps and shreds of thoughts were simply swarming in his brain, but he could not catch at one, he could not rest on one, in spite of all his efforts. . . .

THE GENEALOGY OF MORALS

Friedrich Nietzsche

Those English psychologists, who up to the present are the only philosophers who are to be thanked for any endeavor to get as far as a
history of the origin of morality—these men, I say, offer us in their
own personalities no paltry problem—they even have, if I am to be
quite frank about it, in the capacity of living riddles, an advantage
over their books—*they themselves are interesting!* These English psychologists—what do they really mean? We always find them voluntarily
or involuntarily at the same task of pushing to the front the *partie
honteuse* [shameful part] of our inner world, and looking for the efficient, governing, and decisive principle in that precise quarter where
the intellectual self-respect of the race would be the most reluctant to
find it (for example, in the *vis inertia* of habit, or in forgetfulness, or in
a blind and fortuitous mechanism and association of ideas, or in some
factor that is purely passive, reflex, molecular, or fundamentally stupid)
—what is the real motive power which always impels these psychologists
in precisely *this* direction? Is it an instinct for human disparagement
somewhat sinister, vulgar, and malignant, or perhaps in comprehensible
even to itself? or perhaps a touch of pesssimistic jealousy, the mistrust
of disillusioned idealists who have become gloomy, poisoned, and
bitter? or a petty subconscious enmity and rancor against Christianity
(and Plato), that has conceivably never crossed the threshold of consciousness? or just a vicious taste for those elements of life which are
bizarre, painfully paradoxical, mystical, and illogical? or, as a final
alternative, a dash of each of these motives—a little vulgarity, a little
gloominess, a little anti-Christianity, a little craving for the necessary
piquancy?

But I am told that it is simply a case of old frigid and tedious frogs
crawling and hopping around men and inside men, as if they were as
thoroughly at home there, as they would be in a *swamp.*

I am opposed to this statement, nay, I do not believe it; and if, in

FROM *The Genealogy of Morals.* Reprinted by permission of George Allen &
Unwin Ltd.

the impossibility of knowledge, one is permitted to wish, so do I wish from my heart that just the converse metaphor should apply, and that these analysts with their psychological microscopes should be, at bottom, brave, proud, and magnanimous animals who know how to bridle both their hearts and their smarts, and have specifically trained themselves to sacrifice what is desirable to what is true, *any* truth in fact, even the simple, bitter, ugly, repulsive, unchristian, and immoral truths—for there are truths of that description.

All honor, then, to the noble spirits who would fain dominate these historians of morality. But it is certainly a pity that they lack the *historical sense* itself, that they themselves are quite deserted by all the beneficent spirits of history. The whole train of their thought runs, as was always the way of old-fashioned philosophers, on *thoroughly* unhistorical lines, there is no doubt on this point. The crass ineptitude of their genealogy of morals is immediately apparent when the question arises of ascertaining the origin of the idea and judgment of "good." "Man had originally," so speaks their decree, "praised and called 'good' altruistic acts from the standpoint of those on whom they were conferred, that is, those to whom they were *useful;* subsequently the origin of this praise was *forgotten,* and altruistic acts, simply because, as a sheer matter of habit, they were praised as good, came also to be felt as good—as though they contained in themselves some intrinsic goodness." The thing is obvious—this initial derivation contains already all the typical and idiosyncratic traits of the English psychologists—we have "utility," "forgetting," "habit," and finally "error," the whole assemblage forming the basis of a system of values, on which the higher man has up to the present prided himself as though it were a kind of privilege of man in general. This pride *must* be brought low, this system of values *must* lose its values: is that attained?

Now the first argument that comes ready to my hand is that the real homestead of the concept "good" is sought and located in the wrong place: the judgment "good" did *not* originate among those to whom goodness was shown. Much rather has it been the good themselves, that is, the aristocratic, the powerful, the high-stationed, the high-minded, who have felt that they themselves were good, and that their actions were good, that is to say of the first order, in contradistinction to all the low, the low-minded, the vulgar, and the plebian. It was out of this pathos of distance that they first arrogated the right to create values for their own profit, and to coin the names of such values: what had they to do with utility? The standpoint of utility is as alien and as inapplicable as it could possibly be, when we have to deal with so volcanic an effervescence of supreme values, creating and demarcating as they do a hierarchy within themselves: it is at this juncture that one arrives at an appreciation of the contrast to that tepid temperature, which is the presupposition on which every combination of worldly wisdom and every calculation of practical expediency is always based—and not for one occasional, not for one exceptional instance, but chronically. The pathos of nobility and distance, as I have said, the chronic and despotic *esprit de corps* and fundamental instinct of a higher dominant race coming into association with a meaner race, an "under race," this is the origin of the antithesis of good and bad.

(The masters' right of giving names goes so far that it is permissible to look upon language itself as the expression of the power of the masters: they say "this *is* that, and that," they seal finally every object and every event with a sound, and thereby at the same time take possession of it.) It is because of this origin that the word "good" is far from having any necessary connection with altruistic acts, in accordance with the superstitious belief of these moral philosophers. On the contrary, it is on the occasion of the *decay* of aristocratic values, that the antitheses between "egoistic" and "altruistic" press more and more heavily on the human conscience—it is, to use my own language, the *herd instinct* which finds in this antithesis an expression in many ways. And even then it takes a considerable time for this instinct to become sufficiently dominant, for the valuation to be inextricably dependent on this antithesis (as is the case in contemporary Europe); for today the prejudice is predominant, which, acting even now with all the intensity of an obsession and brain disease, holds that "moral," "altruistic," and *"désintéressé"* [disinterest] are concepts of equal value. . . .

The revolt of the slaves in morals begins in the very principle of *resentment* becoming creative and giving birth to values—a resentment experienced by creatures who, deprived as they are of the proper outlet of action, are forced to find their compensation in an imaginary revenge. While every aristocratic morality springs from a triumphant affirmation of its own demands, the slave morality says "no" from the very outset to what is "outside itself," "different from itself," and "not itself": and this "no" is its creative deed. This volte-face of the valuing standpoint—this *inevitable* gravitation to the objective instead of back to the subjective—is typical of "resentment": the slave-morality requires as the condition of its existence an external and objective world, to employ physiological terminology, it requires objective stimuli to be capable of action at all—its action is fundamentally a reaction. The contrary is the case when we come to the aristocrat's system of values: it acts and grows spontaneously, it merely seeks its antithesis in order to pronounce a more grateful and exultant "yes" to its own self—its negative conception, "low," "vulgar," "bad," is merely a pale late-born foil in comparison with its positive and fundamental conception (saturated as it is with life and passion), of "we aristocrats, we good ones, we beautiful ones, we happy ones."

When the aristocratic morality goes astray and commits sacrilege on reality, this is limited to that particular sphere with which it is *not* sufficiently acquainted—a sphere, in fact, from the real knowledge of which it disdainfully defends itself. It misjudges, in some cases, the sphere which it despises, the sphere of the common vulgar man and the low people: on the other hand, due weight should be given to the consideration that in any case the mood of contempt, of disdain, of superciliousness, even on the supposition that it *falsely* portrays the object of its contempt, will always be far removed from that degree of falsity which will always characterize the attacks—in effigy, of course —of the vindictive hatred and revengefulness of the weak in onslaughts on their enemies. In point of fact, there is in contempt too strong an admixture of nonchalance, of casualness, of boredom, of impatience, even of personal exultation, for it to be capable of distorting its victim into a real caricature or a real monstrosity. Attention again should be paid to the almost benevolent *nuances* which, for instance, the Greek nobility imports into all the words by which it distinguishes the common people from itself; note how continuously a kind of pity, care, and consideration imparts its honeyed *flavor,* until at last almost all the words which are applied to the vulgar man survive finally as expressions for "unhappy," "worthy of pity" . . . and how, conversely, "bad," "low," "unhappy" have never ceased to ring in the Greek ear with a tone in which "unhappy" is the predominant note: this is a heritage of the old noble aristocratic morality, which remains true to itself even in contempt. . . . The "well-born" simply *felt* themselves the "happy"; they did not have to manufacture their happiness artificially through looking at their enemies, or in cases to talk and lie themselves into happiness (as is the custom with all resentful men); and similarly, complete men as they were, exuberant with strength, and consequently *necessarily* energetic, they were too wise to dissociate happiness from action—activity becomes in their minds necessarily counted as happiness . . . all in sharp contrast to the "happiness" of the weak and the oppressed, with their festering venom and malignity, among whom happiness appears essentially as a narcotic, a deadening, a quietude, a peace, a "Sabbath," an enervation of the mind and relaxation of the limbs—in short, a purely *passive* phenomenon. While the aristocratic man lived in confidence and openness with himself, . . . the resentful man, on the other hand, is neither sincere nor naive, nor honest and candid with himself. His soul *squints;* his mind loves hidden crannies, tortuous paths and backdoors, everything secret appeals to him as *his* word, *his* safety, *his* balm; he is past master in silence, in not forgetting, in waiting, in provisional self-depreciation and self-abasement. A race of such *resentful* men will of necessity eventually prove more *prudent* than any aristocratic race, it will honor prudence on quite a distinct scale, as, in fact, a paramount condition of existence, while prudence among aristocratic men is apt to be tinged with a delicate flavor of luxury and refinement; so among them it plays nothing like so integral a part as that complete certainty of function of the governing *unconscious* instincts, or as indeed a certain lack of prudence, such as a vehement and valiant charge, whether against danger or the enemy, or as those ecstatic bursts of rage, love, reverence, gratitude, by which at all times noble souls have recognized each other. When the resentment of the aristocratic man manifests itself, it fulfills and exhausts itself in an immediate reaction, and consequently instills no *venom:* on the other hand, it never manifests itself at all in countless instances, when in the case of the feeble and weak it would be inevitable. An inability to take seriously for any length of time their enemies, their disasters, their *misdeeds*—that is the sign of the full strong natures who possess a superfluity of moulding plastic force, that heels completely and produces forgetfulness: a good example of this in the modern world is Mirabeau, who had no memory for any insults and meannesses which were practiced on him, and who was only incapable of forgiving because he forgot. Such a man indeed shakes off with a shrug many a worm which would have buried itself in another; it is only in characters like these that we see the possibility (supposing, of course, that there is such a possibility in the world) of the real "*love* of one's enemies." What respect for his enemies is found, forsooth, in an aristocratic man—and such a reverence is already a bridge to love! He insists on having his enemy to himself as his distinction. He tolerates no other enemy but a man in whose character there is nothing to despise and *much* to honor! On the other hand, imagine the "enemy" as the resentful man conceives him—and it is here exactly that we see his work, his creativeness; he has conceived "the evil enemy," the "evil one," and indeed that is the root idea from which he now evolves as a contrasting and corresponding figure a "good one," himself—his very self!

The method of this man is quite contrary to that of the aristocratic man, who conceives the root idea "good" spontaneously and straight away, that is to say, out of himself, and from that material then creates for himself a concept of "bad"! This "bad" of aristocratic origin and that "evil" out of the cauldron of unsatisfied hatred—the former an imitation, an "extra," an additional nuance; the latter, on the other hand, the original, the beginning, the essential act in the conception of a slave-morality—these two words "bad" and "evil," how great a difference do they mark, in spite of the fact that they have an identical contrary in the idea "good." But the idea "good" is *not* the same: much rather let the question be asked, "Who is really evil according to the meaning of the morality of resentment?" In all sternness let it be answered thus —*just* the good man of the other morality, just the aristocrat, the powerful one, the one who rules, but who is distorted by the venomous eye of resentfulness, into a new color, a new signification, a new appearance. This particular point we would be the last to deny: the man who learned to know those "good" ones only as enemies, learned at the same time not to know them only as *"evil enemies,"* and the same men who *inter pares* [among equals] were kept so rigorously in bounds through convention, respect, custom, and gratitude, though much more through mutual vigilance and jealousy *inter pares,* these men who in their relations with each other find so many new ways of manifesting consideration, self-control, delicacy, loyalty, pride, and friendship, these men are in reference to what is outside their circle (where the foreign element, a *foreign* country, begins), not much better than beasts of prey, which have been let loose. They enjoy there freedom from all social control, they feel that in the wilderness they can give vent with impunity to that tension which is produced by enclosure and imprisonment in the peace of society, they *revert* to the innocence of the beast-of-prey conscience, like jubilant monsters, who perhaps come from a ghostly bout of murder, arson, rape, and torture, with bravado and a moral equanimity, as though merely some wild student's prank had been played, perfectly convinced that the poets have now an ample theme to sing and celebrate. It is impossible not to recognize at the core of all these aristocratic races the beast of prey; the magnificent *blond brute,* avidly rampant for spoil and victory; this hidden core needed an outlet from time to time, the beast must get loose again, must return into the wilderness—the Roman, Arabic, German, and Japanese nobility, the Homeric heroes, the Scandinavian Vikings, are all alike in this need. It is the aristocratic races who have left the idea "Barbarian" on all the tracks in which they have marched; nay, a consciousness of this very barbarianism, and even a pride in it, manifests itself even in their highest civilization (for example, when Pericles says to his Athenians in that celebrated funeral oration, "Our audacity has forced a way over land and sea, rearing everywhere imperishable memorials of itself for *good* and for *evil*"). This audacity of aristocratic races, mad, absurd, and spasmodic as may be its expression; the incalculable and fantastic nature of their enterprises—Pericles sets in special relief the glory of the Athenians, their nonchalance and contempt for safety, body, life, and comfort, their awful joy and intense delight in all destruction, in all the ecstasies of victory and cruelty—all these features become crystalized, for those who suffered thereby in the picture of the "barbarian," of the "evil enemy," perhaps of the "Goth" and of the "Vandal." The profound, icy mistrust which the German provokes, as soon as he arrives at power—even at the present time—is always still an aftermath of that inextinguishable horror with which for whole centuries Europe has regarded the wrath of the blond Teuton beast (although between the old Germans and ourselves there exists scarcely a psychological, let alone a physical, relationship). I have once called attention to the embarrassment of Hesiod, when he conceived the series of social ages, and endeavored to express them in gold, silver, and bronze. He could only dispose of the contradiction, with which he was confronted, by the Homeric world, an age magnificent indeed, but at the same time so awful and so violent, by making two ages out of one, which he henceforth placed one behind the other—first, the age of the heroes and demigods, as that world had remained in the memories of the aristocratic families, who found therein their own ancestors; secondly, the bronze age, as that corresponding age appeared to the descendants of the oppressed, spoiled, ill-treated, exiled, enslaved; namely, as an age of bronze, as I have said, hard, cold, terrible, without feelings and without conscience, crushing everything, and bespattering everything with blood. Granted the truth of the theory now believed to be true, that the very *essence of all civilization* is to *train* out of man, the beast of prey, a tame and civilized animal, a domesticated animal, it follows indubitably that we must regard as the real *tools of civilization* all those instincts of reaction and resentment, by the help of which the aristocratic races, together with their ideals, were finally degraded and overpowered; though that has not yet come to be synonymous with saying that the bearers of those tools also *represented* the civilization. It is rather the contrary that is not only probable—nay, it is *palpable* today; these bearers of vindictive instincts that have to be bottled up, these descendants of all European and non-European slavery, especially of the pre-Aryan population—these people, I say, represent the *decline* of humanity! These "tools of civilization" are a disgrace to humanity, and constitute in reality more of an argument against civilization, more of a reason why civilization should be suspected. One may be perfectly justified in being always afraid of the blonde beast that lies at the core of all aristocratic races, and in being on one's guard: but who would not a hundred times prefer to be afraid, when one at the same time admires, then to be immune from fear, at the cost of being perpetually obsessed with the loathsome spectacle of the distorted, the dwarfed, the stunted, the envenomed? And is that not our fate? What produces today our repulsion toward "man"?—for we *suffer* from "man," there is no doubt about it. It is not fear; it is rather that we have nothing more to fear from men; it is that the worm "man" is in the foreground and pullulates; it is that the "tame man," the wretched mediocre and unedifying creature, has learned to consider himself a goal and a pinnacle, an inner meaning, an historic principle, a "higher man"; yes, it is that he has a certain right so to consider himself, in so far as he feels that in contrast to that excess of deformity, disease, exhaustion, and effeteness whose odor is beginning to pollute present-day Europe, he at any rate has achieved a relative success, he at any rate still says "yes" to life.

I cannot refrain at this juncture from uttering a sigh and one last hope. What is it precisely which I find intolerable? That which I alone cannot get rid of, which makes me choke and faint? Bad air! Bad air! That something misbegotten comes near me; that I must inhale the odor of the entrails of a misbegotten soul!—That excepted, what can one not endure in the way of need, privation, bad weather, sickness, toil, solitude? In point of fact, one manages to get over everything, born as one is to a burrowing and battling existence; one always returns once again to the light, one always lives again one's golden hour of victory— and then one stands as one was born, unbreakable, tense, ready for something more difficult, for something more distant, like a bow stretched but the tauter by every strain. But from time to time do ye grant me—assuming that "beyond good and evil" there are goddesses who can grant—one glimpse, grant me but one glimpse only, of something perfect, fully realized, happy, mighty, triumphant, of something that still gives cause for fear! A glimpse of a man that justifies the existence of man, a glimpse of an incarnate human happiness that realizes and redeems, for the sake of which one may hold fast to *the belief in man!* For the position is this: in the dwarfing and leveling of the European man lurks *our* greatest peril, for it is this outlook which fatigues— we see today nothing which wishes to be greater, we surmise that the process is always still backwards, still backwards toward something more attenuated, more inoffensive, more cunning, more comfortable, more mediocre, more indifferent, more Chinese, more Christian—man, there is no doubt about it, grows always "better"—the destiny of Europe lies even in this—that in losing the fear of man, we have also lost the hope in man, yea, the will to be man. The sight of man now fatigues.— What is present-day Nihilism if it is not *that?*—We are tired of *man*.

But let us come back to it; the problem of *another* origin of the good —of the good, as the resentful man has thought it out—demands its solution. It is not surprising that the lambs should bear a grudge against the great birds of prey, but that is no reason for blaming the great birds of prey for taking the little lambs. And when the lambs say among themselves, "Those birds of prey are evil, and he who is as far removed from being a bird of prey, who is rather its opposite, a lamb—is he not good?" then there is nothing to cavil at in the setting up of this ideal, though it may also be that the birds of prey will regard it a little sneeringly, and perchance say to themselves, *"We* bear no grudge against them, these good lambs, we even like them: nothing is tastier than a tender lamb." To require of strength that it should *not* express itself as strength, that it should not be a wish to overpower, a wish to overthrow, a wish to become master, a thirst for enemies and antagonisms and triumphs, is just as absurd as to require of weakness that it should express itself as strength. A quantum of force is just such a quantum of movement, will, action—rather it is nothing else than just those very phenomena of moving, willing, acting, and can only appear otherwise in the misleading errors of language (and the fundamental fallacies of reason which have become petrified therein), which understands, and understands wrongly, all working as conditioned by a worker, by a "subject." And just exactly as the people separate the lightning from its flash, and interpret the latter as a thing done, as the working of a subject which is called lightning, so also does the popular morality separate strength from the expression of strength, as though behind the strong man there existed some indifferent neutral *substratum,* which enjoyed *a caprice and option* as to whether or not it should express strength. But there is no such *substratum,* there is no "being" behind doing, working, becoming; "the doer" is a mere appanage to the action. The action is everything. In point of fact, the people duplicate the doing, when they make the lightning lighten, that is a "doing-doing"; they make the same phenomenon first a cause, and then, secondly, the effect of that cause. The scientists fail to improve matters when they say, "Force moves, force causes," and so on. Our whole science is still, in spite of all its coldness, of all its freedom from passion, a dupe of the tricks of language, and has never succeeded in getting rid of that superstitious changeling "the subject" (the atom, to give another instance, is such a changeling, just as the Kantian "Thing-in-itself"). What wonder, if the suppressed and stealthily simmering passions of revenge and hatred exploit for their own advantage their belief, and indeed hold no belief with a more steadfast enthusiasm than this—"that the strong has the *option* of being weak, and the bird of prey of being a lamb." Thereby do they win for themselves the right of attributing to the birds of prey the *responsibility* for being birds of prey: when the oppressed, downtrodden, and overpowered say to themselves with the vindictive guile of weakness, "Let us be otherwise than the evil, namely, good! and good is every one who does not oppress, who hurts no one, who does not attack, who does not pay back, who hands over revenge to God, who holds himself, as we do, in hiding; who goes out of the way of evil, and demands, in short, little from life; like ourselves the patient, the meek, the just"—yet all this, in its cold and unprejudiced interpretation, means nothing more than "once for all, the weak are weak; it is good to do *nothing for which we are not strong enough"*; but this dismal state of affairs, this prudence of the lowest order, which even insects possess (which in a great danger are fain to sham death so as to avoid doing "too much"), has, thanks to the counterfeiting and self-deception of weakness, come to masquerade in the pomp of an ascetic, mute, and expectant virtue, just as though the *very* weakness of the weak—that is, forsooth, its *being,* its working, its whole unique inevitable inseparable reality—were a voluntary result, something wished, chosen, a deed, an act of *merit.* This kind of man finds the belief in a neutral, free-choosing "subject" *necessary* from an instinct of self-preservation, of self-assertion, in which every lie is fain to sanctify itself. The subject (or, to use popular language, the *soul*) has perhaps proved itself the best dogma in the world simply because it rendered possible to the horde of mortal, weak, and oppressed individuals of every kind, that most sublime specimen of self-deception, the interpretation of weakness as freedom, of being this, or being that, as *merit.*

Will any one look a little into—right into—the mystery of how *ideals* are *manufactured* in this world? Who has the courage to do it? Come!

Here we have a vista opened into these grimy workshops. Wait just a moment, dear Mr. Inquisitive and Foolhardy; your eye must first grow accustomed to this false changing light—Yes! Enough! Now speak! What is happening below down yonder? Speak out! Tell what you see, man of the most dangerous curiosity—for now *I* am the listener.

"I see nothing, I hear the more. It is a cautious, spiteful, gentle whispering and muttering together in all the corners and crannies. It seems to me that they are lying; a sugary softness adheres to every sound. Weakness is turned to *merit,* there is no doubt about it—it is just as you say."

Further!

"And the impotence which requites not, is turned to 'goodness,' craven baseness to meekness, submission to those whom one hates, to obedience (namely, obedience to one of whom they say that he ordered this submission—they call him God). The inoffensive character of the weak, the very cowardice in which he is rich, his standing at the door, his forced necessity of waiting, gain here fine names, such as 'patience,' which is also called 'virtue'; not being able to avenge one's self, is called not wishing to avenge one's self, perhaps even forgiveness (for *they* know not what they do—we alone know what they do). They also talk of the 'love of their enemies' and sweat thereby."

Further!

"They are miserable, there is no doubt about it, all these whisperers and counterfeiters in the corners, although they try to get warm by crouching close to each other, but they tell me that their misery is a favor and distinction given to them by God, just as one beats the dogs one likes best; that perhaps this misery is also a preparation, a probation, a training; that perhaps it is still more something which will one day be compensated and paid back with a tremendous interest in gold, nay in happiness. This they call 'Blessedness'."

Further!

"They are now giving me to understand, that not only are they better men than the mighty, the lords of the earth, whose spittle they have got to lick (*not* out of fear, not at all out of fear! But because God ordains that one should honor all authority)—not only are they better men, but that they also have a 'better time,' at any rate, will one day have a 'better time.' But enough! Enough! I can endure it no longer. Bad air! Bad air! These workshops *where ideals are manufactured*—verily they reek with the crassest lies."

Nay. Just one minute! You are saying nothing about the masterpieces of these virtuosos of black magic, who can produce whiteness, milk, and innocence out of any black you like: have you not noticed what a pitch of refinement is attained by their *chef d'oeuvre,* their most audacious, subtle, ingenious, and lying artist-trick? Take care! These cellar-beasts, full of revenge and hate—what do they make, forsooth, out of their revenge and hate? Do you hear these words? Would you suspect, if you trusted only their words, that you are among men of resentment and nothing else?

"I understand, I prick my ears up again (ah! ah! ah! and I hold my nose). Now do I hear for the first time that which they have said so often: 'We good, *we are the righteous*'—what they demand they call not revenge but 'the triumph of *righteousness*'; what they hate is not their enemy, no, they hate 'unrighteousness,' 'godlessness'; what they believe in and hope is not the hope of revenge, the intoxication of sweet revenge (—'sweeter than honey,' did Homer call it?), but the victory of God, of the *righteous God* over the 'godless'; what is left for them to love in this world is not their brothers in hate, but their 'brothers in love,' as they say, all the good and righteous on the earth."

And how do they name that which serves them as a solace against all the troubles of life—their phantasmagoria of their anticipated future blessedness?

"How? Do I hear right? They call it 'the last judgment,' the advent of *their* kingdom, 'the kingdom of God'—but *in the meanwhile* they live 'in faith,' 'in love,' 'in hope'."

Enough! Enough!

WHY SHOULD WE BE MORAL?

Kurt Baier

The Supremacy of Moral Reasons

Are moral reasons really superior to reasons of self-interest as we all
believe? Do we really have reason on our side when we follow moral
reasons against self-interest? What reasons could there be for being
moral? Can we really give an answer to "Why should we be moral?" It is
obvious that all these questions come to the same thing. When we ask,
"Should we be moral?" or "Why should we be moral?" or "Are moral
reasons superior to all others?" we ask to be given a reason for regarding moral reasons as superior to all others. What is this reason?

Let us begin with a state of affairs in which reasons of self-interest
are supreme. In such a state everyone keeps his impulses and inclinations in check when and only when they would lead him into behavior
detrimental to his own interest. Everyone who follows reason will discipline himself to rise early, to do his exercises, to refrain from excessive
drinking and smoking, to keep good company, to marry the right sort
of girl, to work and study hard in order to get on, and so on. However,
it will often happen that people's interests conflict. In such a case, they
will have to resort to ruses or force to get their own way. As this becomes known, men will become suspicious, for they will regard one
another as scheming competitors for the good things in life. The universal supremacy of the rules of self-interest must lead to what Hobbes
called the state of nature. At the same time, it will be clear to everyone
that universal obedience to certain rules overriding self-interest would
produce a state of affairs which serves everyone's interest much better
than his unaided pursuit of it in a state where everyone does the same.
Moral rules are universal rules designed to override those of self-interest
when following the latter is harmful to others. "Thou shalt not kill,"
"Thou shalt not lie," "Thou shalt not steal" are rules which forbid the

FROM *The Moral Point of View,* chapter 7. Copyright 1958 by Cornell University
Press. Reprinted by permission of Cornell University Press and Random House, Inc.

inflicting of harm on someone else even when this might be in one's interest.

The very *raison d'être* of a morality is to yield reasons which overrule the reasons of self-interest in those cases when everyone's following self-interest would be harmful to everyone. Hence moral reasons are superior to all others.

"But what does this mean?" it might be objected. "If it merely means that we do so regard them, then you are of course right, but your contention is useless, a mere point of usage. And how could it mean any more? If it means that we not only do so regard them, but *ought* so to regard them, then there must be *reasons* for saying this. But there could not be any reasons for it. If you offer reasons of self-interest, you are arguing in a circle. Moreover, it cannot be true that it is always in my interest to treat moral reasons as superior to reasons of self-interest. If it were, self-interest and morality could never conflict, but they notoriously do. It is equally circular to argue that there are moral reasons for saying that one ought to treat moral reasons as superior to reasons of self-interest. And what other reasons are there?"

The answer is that we are now looking at the world from the point of view of *anyone*. We are not examining particular alternative courses of action before this or that person; we are examining two alternative worlds, one in which moral reasons are always treated by everyone as superior to reasons of self-interest and one in which the reverse is the practice. And we can see that the first world is the better world, because we can see that the second world would be the sort which Hobbes describes as the state of nature.

This shows that I ought to be moral, for when I ask the question "What ought I to do?" I am asking, "Which is the course of action supported by the best reasons?" But since it has just been shown that moral reasons are superior to reasons of self-interest, I have been given a reason for being moral, for following moral reasons rather than any other, namely, they are better reasons than any other.

But is this always so? Do we have a reason for being moral whatever the conditions we find ourselves in? Could there not be situations in which it is not true that we have reasons for being moral, that, on the contrary, we have reasons for ignoring the demands of morality? Is not Hobbes right in saying that in a state of nature the laws of nature, that is, the rules of morality, bind only *in foro interno* [subjectively]?

Hobbes argues as follows.

(i) To live in a state of nature is to live outside society. It is to live in conditions in which there are no common ways of life and, therefore, no reliable expectations about other people's behavior other than that they will follow their inclination or their interest.

(ii) In such a state reason will be the enemy of co-operation and mutual trust. For it is too risky to hope that other people will refrain from protecting their own interests by the preventive elimination of probable or even possible dangers to them. Hence reason will counsel everyone to avoid these risks by preventive action. But this leads to war.

(iii) It is obvious that everyone's following self-interest leads to a state of affairs which is desirable from no one's point of view. It is, on the contrary, desirable that everybody should follow rules overriding self-interest whenever that is to the detriment of others. In other words, it is desirable to bring about a state of affairs in which all obey the rules of morality.

(iv) However, Hobbes claims that in the state of nature it helps nobody if a single person or a small group of persons begins to follow the rules of morality, for this could only lead to the extinction of such individuals or groups. In such a state, it is therefore contrary to reason to be moral.

(v) The situation can change, reason can support morality, only when the presumption about other people's behavior is reversed. Hobbes thought that this could be achieved only by the creation of an absolute ruler with absolute power to enforce his laws. We have already seen that this is not true and that it can also be achieved if people live in a society, that is, if they have common ways of life, which are taught to all members and somehow enforced by the group. Its members have reason to expect their fellows generally to obey its rules, that is, its religion, morality, customs, and law, even when doing so is not, on certain occasions, in their interest. Hence they too have reason to follow these rules.

Is this argument sound? One might, of course, object to step (i) on the grounds that this is an empirical proposition for which there is little or no evidence. For how can we know whether it is true that people in a state of nature would follow only their inclinations or, at best, reasons of self-interest, when nobody now lives in that state or has ever lived in it?

However, there is some empirical evidence to support this claim. For in the family of nations, individual states are placed very much like individual persons in a state of nature. The doctrine of the sovereignty of nations and the absence of an effective international law and police force are a guarantee that nations live in a state of nature, without commonly accepted rules that are somehow enforced. Hence it must be granted that living in a state of nature leads to living in a state in which individuals act either on impulse or as they think their interest dictates. For states pay only lip service to morality. They attack their hated neighbors when the opportunity arises. They start preventive wars in order to destroy the enemy before he can deliver his knockout blow. Where interests conflict, the stronger party usually has his way, whether his claims are justified or not. And where the relative strength of the parties is not obvious, they usually resort to arms in order to determine "whose side God is on." Treaties are frequently concluded but, morally speaking, they are not worth the paper they are written on. Nor do the partners regard them as contracts binding in the ordinary way, but rather as public expressions of the belief of the governments concerned that for the time being their alliance is in the interest of the allies. It is well understood that such treaties may be canceled before they reach their predetermined end or simply broken when it suits one partner. In international affairs, there are very few examples of *Nibelungentreue,* although statesmen whose countries have kept their treaties in the hope of profiting from them usually make such high moral claims.

It is, moreover, difficult to justify morality in international affairs. For suppose a highly moral statesman were to demand that his country adhere to a treaty obligation even though this meant its ruin or possibly its extinction. Suppose he were to say that treaty obligations are sacred and must be kept whatever the consequences. How could he defend such a policy? Perhaps one might argue that someone has to make a start in order to create mutual confidence in international affairs. Or one might say that setting a good example is the best way of inducing others to follow suit. But such a defense would hardly be sound. The less skeptical one is about the genuineness of the cases in which nations have adhered to their treaties from a sense of moral obligation, the more skeptical one must be about the effectiveness of such examples of virtue in effecting a change of international practice. Power politics still govern in international affairs.

We must, therefore, grant Hobbes the first step in his argument and admit that in a state of nature people, as a matter of psychological fact, would not follow the dictates of morality. But we might object to the next step that knowing this psychological fact about other people's behavior constitutes a reason for behaving in the same way. Would it not still be immoral for anyone to ignore the demands of morality even though he knows that others are likely or certain to do so, too? Can we offer as a justification for morality the fact that no one is entitled to do wrong just because someone else is doing wrong? This argument begs the question whether it *is* wrong for anyone in this state to disregard the demands of morality. It cannot be wrong to break a treaty or make preventive war if we have no reason to obey the moral rules. For to say that it is wrong to do so is to say that we ought not to do so. But if we have no reason for obeying the moral rule, then we have no reason overruling self-interest, hence no reason for keeping the treaty when keeping it is not in our interest, hence it is not true that we have a reason for keeping it, hence not true that we ought to keep it, hence not true that it is wrong not to keep it.

I conclude that Hobbes's argument is sound. Moralities are systems of principles whose acceptance by everyone as overruling the dictates of self-interest is in the interest of everyone alike, though following the rules of a morality is not of course identical with following self-interest. If it were, there could be no conflict between a morality and self-interest and no point in having moral rules overriding self-interest. Hobbes is also right in saying that the application of this system of rules is in accordance with reason only under social conditions, that is, when there are well-established ways of behavior.

The answer to our question "Why should we be moral?" is therefore as follows. We should be moral because being moral is following rules designed to overrule reasons of self-interest whenever it is in the interest of everyone alike that such rules should be generally followed. This will be the case when the needs and wants and aspirations of individual agents conflict with one another and when, in the absence of such overriding rules, the pursuit of their ends by all concerned would lead to the attempt to eliminate those who are in the way. Since such rules will always require one of the rivals to abandon his pursuit in favor of the other, they will tend to be broken. Since, ex hypothesi it is in everyone's interest that they should be followed, it will be in everyone's interest that they should not only be taught as "superior to" other reasons but also adequately enforced, in order to reduce the temptation to break them. A person instructed in these rules can acknowledge that such reasons are superior to reasons of self-interest without having to admit that he is always or indeed ever attracted or moved by them.

But is it not self-contradictory to say that it is in a person's interest to do what is contrary to his interest? It certainly would be if the two expressions were used in exactly the same way. But they are not. We have already seen that an enlightened egoist can acknowledge that a certain course of action is in his enlightened long-term, but contrary to his narrow short-term interest. He can infer that it is "in his interest" and according to reason to follow enlightened long-term interest, and "against his interest" and contrary to reason to follow short-term interest. Clearly, "in his interest" and "against his interest" here are used in new ways. For suppose it is discovered that the probable long-range consequences and psychological effects on others do not work out as predicted. Even so we need not admit that, in this new and extended sense, the line of action followed merely seemed but really was not in his interest. For we are now considering not merely a single action but a policy.

All the same, we must not make too much of this analogy. There is an all-important difference between the two cases. The calculations of the enlightened egoist properly allow for "exceptions in the agent's favor." After all, his calculus is designed to promote his interest. If he has information to show that in his particular circumstances it would pay to depart from a well-established general canon of enlightened self-interest, then it is proper for him to depart from it. It would not be a sign of the enlightened self-interest of a building contractor, let us say, if he made sacrifices for certain subcontractors even though he knew that they would or could not reciprocate, as subcontractors normally do. By contrast, such information is simply irrelevant in cases where moral reasons apply. Moral rules are not designed to serve the agent's interest directly. Hence it would be quite inappropriate for him to break them whenever he discovers that they do not serve his interest. They are designed to adjudicate primarily in cases where there is a conflict of interests so that from their very nature they are bound to be contrary to the interest of one of the persons affected. However, they are also bound to serve the interest of the other person, hence his interest in the other's observing them. It is on the assumption of the likelihood of a reversal of roles that the universal observation of the rule will serve everyone's interest. The principle of justice and other principles which we employ in improving the moral rules of a given society help to bring existing moralities closer to the ideal which is in the interest of everyone alike. Thus, just as following the canons of enlightened self-interest is in one's interest only if the assumptions underlying it are correct, so following the rules of morality is in everyone's interest only if the assumptions underlying it are correct, so following the rules of morality is in everyone's interest only if the assumptions underlying it are correct, that is, if the moral rules come close to being true and are generally observed. Even then, to say that following them is in the interest of everyone alike means only that it is better for everyone that there should be a morality generally observed than that the principle of self-interest should be acknowledged as supreme. It does not of course mean that a person will not do better for himself by following self-interest than by doing what is morally right, when others are doing what is right. But of course such a person cannot *claim* that he is following a superior reason.

It must be added to this, however, that such a system of rules has the support of reason only where people live in societies, that is, in conditions in which there are established common ways of behavior.

Outside society, people have no reason for following such rules, that is, for being moral. In other words, outside society, the very distinction between right and wrong vanishes.

Why Should We Follow Reason?

But someone might now ask whether and why he should follow reason itself. He may admit that moral reasons are superior to all others, but doubt whether he ought to follow reason. He may claim that this will have to be proved first, for if it is not true that he ought to follow reason, then it is not true that he ought to follow the strongest reason either.

What is it to follow reason? It involves two tasks, the theoretical, finding out what it would be in accordance with reason to do in a certain situation, what contrary to reason, and the practical task, to act accordingly. . . . We must also remind ourselves that there are many different ways in which what we do or believe or feel can be contrary to reason. It may be *irrational,* as when, for no reason at all, we set our hand on fire or cut off our toes one by one, or when, in the face of conclusive evidence to the contrary, someone *believes* that her son killed in the war is still alive, or when someone is *seized by fear* as a gun is pointed at him although he knows for certain that it is not loaded. What we do, believe, or feel is called irrational if it is the case not only that there are conclusive or overwhelming reasons against doing, believing, or feeling these things, but also that we must know there are such reasons and we still persist in our action, belief, or feeling.

Or it may be *unreasonable,* as when we make demands which are excessive or refuse without reason to comply with requests which are reasonable. We say of demands or requests that they are excessive if, though we are entitled to make them, the party against whom we make them has good reasons for not complying, as when the landlord demands the immediate vacation of the premises in the face of well-supported pleas of hardship by the tenant.

Being unreasonable is a much weaker form of going counter to reason than being irrational. The former applies in cases where there is a conflict of reasons and where one party does not acknowledge the obvious force of the case of the other or, while acknowledging it, will not modify his behavior accordingly. A person is irrational only if he flies in the face of reason, if, that is, all reasons are on one side and he acts contrary to it when he either acknowledges that this is so or, while refusing to acknowledge it, has no excuse for failing to do so.

Again, someone may be *inconsistent,* as when he refuses a Jew admission to a club although he has always professed strong positive views on racial equality. Behavior or remarks are inconsistent if the agent or author professes principles adherence to which would require him to say or do the opposite of what he says or does.

Or a person may be *illogical,* as when he does something which, as anyone can see, cannot or is not at all likely to lead to success. Thus when I cannot find my glasses or my fountain pen, the logical thing to do is to look for them where I can remember I had them last or where I usually have them. It would be illogical of me to look under the bed or in the oven unless I have special reason to think they might be there. To say of a person that he is a logical type is to say that he always does what, on reflection, anyone would agree is most likely to lead to success. Scatterbrains, people who act rashly, without thinking, are the opposite of logical.

When we speak of following reason, we usually mean "doing what is supported by the best reasons because it is so supported" or perhaps "doing what we think (rightly or wrongly) is supported by the best reasons because we think it is so supported." It might, then, occur to someone to ask, "Why should I follow reason?" During the last hundred years or so, reason has had a very bad press. Many thinkers have sneered at it and have recommended other guides, such as the instincts, the unconscious, the voice of the blood, inspiration, charisma, and the like. They have advocated that one should not follow reason but be guided by these other forces.

However, in the most obvious sense of the question "Should I follow reason?" this is a tautological question like "Is a circle a circle?"; hence the advice "You should not follow reason" is as nonsensical as the claim "A circle is not a circle." Hence the question "Why should I follow reason?" is as silly as "Why is a circle a circle?" We need not, therefore, take much notice of the advocates of unreason. They show by their advocacy that they are not too clear on what they are talking about.

How is it that "Should I follow reason?" is a tautological question like "Is a circle a circle?" Questions of the form "Shall I do this?" or "Should I do this?" or "Ought I do this?" are . . . requests to someone (possibly oneself) to deliberate on one's behalf. That is to say, they are requests to survey the facts and weigh the reasons for and against this course of action. These questions could therefore be paraphrased as follows. "I wish to do what is supported by the best reasons. Tell me whether this is so supported." As already mentioned "following reason" means "doing what is supported by the best reasons." Hence the question "Shall (should, ought) I follow reason?" must be paraphrased as "I wish to do what is supported by the best reasons. Tell me whether doing what is supported by the best reasons is doing what is supported by the best reasons." It is, therefore, not worth asking.

The question "*Why* should I follow reason?" simply does not make sense. Asking it shows complete lack of understanding of the meaning of "why questions." "Why should I do this?" is a request to be given the reason for saying that I should do this. It is normally asked when someone has already said, "You should do this" and answered by giving the reason. But since "Should I follow reason?" means "Tell me whether doing what is supported by the best reasons is doing what is supported by the best reasons," there is simply no possibility of adding "Why?" For the question now comes to this, "Tell me the reason why doing what is supported by the best reasons is doing what is supported by the best reasons." It is exactly like asking, "Why is a circle a circle?"

However, it must be admitted that there is another possible interpretation to our question according to which it makes sense and can even be answered. "Why should I follow reason?" may not be a request for a reason in support of a tautological remark, but a request for a reason why one should enter on the theoretical task of deliberation. As already explained, following reason involves the completion of two tasks, the theoretical and the practical. The point of the theoretical is to give guidance in the practical task. We perform the theoretical only because we wish to complete the practical task in accordance with the outcome of the theoretical. On our first interpretation, "Should I follow reason?" meant "Is the practical task completed when it is completed in accordance with the outcome of the theoretical task?" And the answer to this is obviously "Yes," for that is what we mean by "completion of the practical task." On our second interpretation, "Should I follow reason?" is not a question about the practical but about the theoretical task. It is not a question about whether, given that one is prepared to perform both these tasks, they are properly completed in the way indicated. It is a question about whether one should enter on the whole performance at all, whether the "game" is worth playing. And this is a meaningful question. It might be better to "follow inspiration" than to "follow reason," in this sense: better to close one's eyes and wait for an answer to flash across the mind.

But while, so interpreted, "Should I follow reason?" makes sense, it seems to me obvious that the answer to it is "Yes, because it pays." Deliberation is the only reliable method. Even if there were other reliable methods, we could only tell whether they were reliable by checking them against this method. Suppose some charismatic leader counsels, "Don't follow reason, follow me. My leadership is better than that of reason"; we would still have to check his claim against the ordinary methods of reason. We would have to ascertain whether in following his advice we were doing the best thing. And this we can do only by examining whether he has advised us to do what is supported by the best reasons. His claim to be better than reason can in turn only be supported by the fact that he tells us precisely the same as reason does.

Is there any sense, then, in his claim that his guidance is preferable to that of reason? There may be, for working out what is supported by the best reasons takes a long time. Frequently, the best thing to do is to do something quickly now rather than the most appropriate thing later. A leader may have the ability to "see," to "intuit," what is the best thing to do more quickly than it is possible to work this out by the laborious methods of deliberation. In evaluating the qualities of leadership of such a person, we are evaluating *his ability to perform correctly the practical task of following reason* without having to go through the lengthy operations of the theoretical. Reason is required to tell us whether anyone has qualities of leadership better than ordinary, in the same way that pencil and paper multiplications are required to tell us whether a mathematical prodigy is genuine or a fraud.

Lastly, it must be said that sometimes it may be better even for an ordinary person without charisma not to follow reason but to do something at once, for quick action may be needed.

EXISTENTIALISM IS A HUMANISM

Jean-Paul Sartre

My purpose here is to offer a defense of existentialism against several reproaches that have been laid against it.

First, it has been reproached as an invitation to people to dwell in quietism of despair. For if every way to a solution is barred, one would have to regard any action in this world as entirely ineffective, and one would arrive finally at a contemplative philosophy. Moreover, since contemplation is a luxury, this would be only another bourgeois philosophy. This is, especially, the reproach made by the Communists.

From another quarter we are reproached for having underlined all that is ignominious in the human situation, for depicting what is mean, sordid or base to the neglect of certain things that possess charm and beauty and belong to the brighter side of human nature: for example, according to the Catholic critic, Mlle. Mercier, we forget how an infant smiles. Both from this side and from the other we are also reproached for leaving out of account the solidarity of mankind and considering man in isolation. And this, say the Communists, is because we base our doctrine upon pure subjectivity—upon the Cartesian "I think"; which is the moment in which solitary man attains to himself; a position from which it is impossible to regain solidarity with other men who exist outside of the self. The *ego* cannot reach them through the *cogito*.

From the Christian side, we are reproached as people who deny the reality and seriousness of human affairs. For since we ignore the commandments of God and all values prescribed as eternal, nothing remains but what is strictly voluntary. Everyone can do what he likes, and will be incapable, from such a point of view, of condemning either the point of view or the action of anyone else.

It is to these various reproaches that I shall endeavor to reply today; that is why I have entitled this brief exposition "Existentialism Is a Hu-

FROM "Existentialism Is a Humanism," a pamphlet translated by P. Mairet. Reprinted by permission of Sanford J. Greenburger Associates.

manism." Many may be surprised at the mention of humanism in this connection, but we shall try to see in what sense we understand it. In any case, we can begin by saying that existentialism, in our sense of the word, is a doctrine that does render human life possible; a doctrine, also, which affirms that every truth and every action imply both an environment and a human subjectivity. The essential charge laid against us is, of course, that of over-emphasis upon the evil side of human life. I have lately been told of a lady who, whenever she lets slip a vulgar expression in a moment of nervousness, excuses herself by exclaiming, "I believe I am becoming an existentialist." So it appears that ugliness is being identified with existentialism. That is why some people say we are "naturalistic," and if we are, it is strange to see how much we scandalize and horrify them, for no one seems to be much frightened or humiliated nowadays by what is properly called naturalism. Those who can quite well keep down a novel by Zola such as *La Terre* are sickened as soon as they read an existentialist novel. Those who appeal to the wisdom of the people—which is a sad wisdom—find ours sadder still. And yet, what could be more disillusioned than such sayings as "Charity begins at home" or "Promote a rogue and he'll sue you for damage, knock him down and he'll do you homage?" We all know how many common sayings can be quoted to this effect, and they all mean much the same— that you must not oppose the powers-that-be; that you must not fight against superior force; must not meddle in matters that are above your station. Or that any action not in accordance with some tradition is mere romanticism; or that any undertaking which has not the support of proven experience is foredoomed to frustration; and that since experience has shown men to be invariably inclined to evil, there must be firm rules to restrain them, otherwise we shall have anarchy. It is, however, the people who are forever mouthing these dismal proverbs and, whenever they are told of some more or less repulsive action, say "How like human nature!"—it is these very people, always harping upon realism, who complain that existentialism is too gloomy a view of things. Indeed their excessive protests make me suspect that what is annoying them is not so much our pessimism, but, much more likely, our optimism. For at bottom, what is alarming in the doctrine that I am about to try to explain to you is—is it not?—that it confronts man with a possibility of choice. To verify this, let us review the whole question upon the strictly philosophic level. What, then, is this that we call existentialism?

Most of those who are making use of this word would be highly confused if required to explain its meaning. For since it has become fashionable, people cheerfully declare that this musician or that painter is "existentialist." A columnist in *Clartés* signs himself "The Existentialist," and, indeed, the word is now so loosely applied to so many things that it no longer means anything at all. It would appear that, for the lack of any novel doctrine such as that of surrealism, all those who are eager to join in the latest scandal or movement now seize upon this philosophy in which, however, they can find nothing to their purpose. For in truth this is of all teachings the least scandalous and the most austere: it is intended strictly for technicians and philosophers. All the same, it can easily be defined.

The question is only complicated because there are two kinds of existentialists. There are, on the one hand, the Christians, among whom I shall name Jaspers and Gabriel Marcel, both professed Catholics; and on the other the existential atheists, amongst whom we must place Heidegger as well as the French existentialists and myself. What they have in common is simply the fact that they believe that *existence* comes before *essence*—or, if you will, that we must begin from the subjective. What exactly do we mean by that?

If one considers an article of manufacture—as, for example, a book or a paper-knife—one sees that it has been made by an artisan who had a conception of it; and he has paid attention, equally, to the conception of a paper-knife and to the pre-existent technique of production which is a part of that conception and is, at bottom, a formula. Thus the paper-knife is at the same time an article producible in a certain manner and one which, on the other hand, serves a definite purpose, for one cannot suppose that a man would produce a paper-knife without knowing what it was for. Let us say, then, of the paper-knife that its essence—that is to say the sum of the formulae and the qualities which made its production and its definition possible—precedes its existence. The presence of such-and-such a paper-knife or book is thus determined before my eyes. Here, then, we are viewing the world from a technical standpoint, and we can say that production precedes existence.

When we think of God as the creator, we are thinking of him, most of the time, as a supernal artisan. Whatever doctrine we may be considering, whether it be a doctrine like that of Descartes, or of Leibniz himself, we always imply that the will follows, more or less, from the understanding or at least accompanies it, so that when God creates he knows precisely what he is creating. Thus, the conception of man in the mind of God is comparable to that of the paper-knife in the mind of the artisan: God makes man according to a procedure and a conception, exactly as the artisan manufactures a paper-knife, following a definition and a formula. Thus each individual man is the realization of a certain conception which dwells in the divine understanding. In the philosophic atheism of the eighteenth century, the notion of God is suppressed, but not, for all that, the idea that essence is prior to existence; something of that idea we still find everywhere, in Diderot, in Voltaire and even in Kant. Man possesses a human nature; that "human nature," which is the conception of human being, is found in every man; which means that each man is a particular example of a universal conception, the conception of Man. In Kant, this universality goes so far that the wild man of the woods, man in the state of nature and the bourgeois are all contained in the same definition and have the same fundamental qualities. Here again, the essence of man precedes that historic existence which we confront in experience.

Atheistic existentialism, of which I am a representative, declares with greater consistency that if God does not exist there is at least one being whose existence comes before its essence, a being which exists before it can be defined by any conception of it. That being is man or, as Heidegger has it, the human reality. What do we mean by saying that existence precedes essence? We mean that man first of all exists, encounters himself, surges up in the world—and defines himself afterwards. If man as the existentialist sees him is not definable, it is because to begin with he is nothing. He will not be anything until later, and then he will be what he makes of himself. Thus, there is no human nature, because there is no God to have a conception of it. Man simply is. Not that he is simply what he conceives himself to be, but he is what he wills, and as he conceives himself after already existing—as he wills to be after that leap toward existence. Man is nothing else but that which he makes of himself. That is the first principle of existentialism. And this is what people call its "subjectivity," using the word as a reproach against us. But what do we mean to say by this, but that man is of a greater dignity than a stone or a table? For we mean to say that man primarily exists—that man is, before all else, something which propels itself towards a future and is aware that it is doing so. Man is, indeed, a project which possesses a subjective life, instead of being a kind of moss, or a fungus or a cauliflower. Before that projection of the self nothing exists; not even in the heaven of intelligence: man will only attain existence when he is what he purposes to be. Not, however, what he may wish to be. For what we usually understand by wishing or willing is a conscious decision taken—much more often than not—after we have made ourselves what we are. I may wish to join a party, to write a book or to marry—but in such a case what is usually called my will is probably a manifestation of a prior and more spontaneous decision. If however, it is true that existence is prior to essence, man is responsible for what he is. Thus, the first effect of existentialism is that it puts every man in possession of himself as he is, and places the entire responsibility for his existence squarely upon his own shoulders. And, when we say that man is responsible for himself, we do not mean that he is responsible only for his own individuality, but that he is responsible for all men. The word "subjectivism" is to be understood in two senses, and our adversaries play upon only one of them. Subjectivism means, on the one hand, the freedom of the individual subject and, on the other, that man cannot pass beyond human subjectivity. It is the latter which is the deeper meaning of existentialism. When we say that man chooses himself, we do mean that every one of us must choose himself; but by that we also mean that in choosing for himself he chooses for all men. For in effect, of all the actions a man may take in order to create himself as he wills to be, there is not one which is not creative, at the same time, of an image of man such as he believes he ought to be. To choose between this or that is at the same time to affirm the value of that which is chosen; for we are unable ever to choose the worse. What we choose is always the better; and nothing can be better for us unless it is better for all. If, moreover, existence precedes essence and we will to exist at the same time as we fashion our image, that image is valid for all and for the entire epoch in which we find ourselves. Our responsibility is thus much greater than we had supposed, for it concerns mankind as a whole. If I am a worker, for instance, I may choose to join a Christian rather than a Communist trade union. And if, by that membership, I choose to signify that resignation is, after all, the attitude that best becomes a man, that man's kingdom is not upon this earth, I do not commit myself alone to that view. Resignation is my will for everyone, and my action is, in consequence, a commitment on behalf of all mankind. Or if, to take a more personal case, I decide to marry and to have children, even though this decision proceeds simply from my situation, from my passion or my desire, I am thereby committing not only myself, but humanity as a whole, to the practice of monogamy. I am thus responsible for myself and for all men, and I am creating a certain image of man as I would have him to be. In fashioning myself I fashion man.

This may enable us to understand what is meant by such terms—perhaps a little grandiloquent—as anguish, abandonment and despair. As you will soon see, it is very simple. First, what do we mean by anguish? The existentialist frankly states that man is in anguish. His meaning is as follows—When a man commits himself to anything, fully realizing that he is not only choosing what he will be, but is thereby at the same time a legislator deciding for the whole of mankind—in such a moment a man cannot escape from the sense of complete and profound responsibility. There are many, indeed, who show no such anxiety. But we affirm that they are merely disguising their anguish or are in flight from it. Certainly, many people think that in what they are doing they commit no one but themselves to anything: and if you ask them, "What would happen if everyone did so?" they shrug their shoulders and reply, "Everyone does not do so." But in truth, one ought always to ask oneself what would happen if everyone did as one is doing; nor can one escape from that disturbing thought except by a kind of self-deception. The man who lies in self-excuse, by saying "Everyone will not do it" must be ill at ease in his conscience, for the act of lying implies the universal value which it denies. By its very disguise his anguish reveals itself. This is the anguish that Kierkegaard called "the anguish of Abraham." You know the story: An angel commanded Abraham to sacrifice his son: and obedience was obligatory, if it really was an angel who had appeared and said, "Thou, Abraham, shalt sacrifice thy son." But anyone in such a case would wonder, first, whether it was indeed an angel and secondly, whether I am really Abraham. Where are the proofs? A certain mad woman who suffered from hallucinations said that people were telephoning to her, and giving her orders. The doctor asked, "But who is it that speaks to you?" She replied: "He says it is God." And what, indeed, could prove to her that it was God? If an angel appears to me, what is the proof that it is an angel; or, if I hear voices, who can prove that they proceed from heaven and not from hell, or from my own subconsciousness or some pathological condition? Who can prove that they are really addressed to me?

Who, then, can prove that I am the proper person to impose, by my own choice, my conception of man upon mankind? I shall never find any proof whatever; there will be no sign to convince me of it. If a voice speaks to me, it is still I myself who must decide whether the voice is or is not that of an angel. If I regard a certain course of action as good, it is only I who choose to say that it is good and not bad. There is nothing to show that I am Abraham: nevertheless I also am obliged at every instant to perform actions which are examples. Everything happens to every man as though the whole human race had its eyes fixed upon what he is doing and regulated its conduct accordingly. So every man ought to say, "Am I really a man who has the right to act in such a manner that humanity regulates itself by what I do." If a man does not say that, he is dissembling his anguish. Clearly, the anguish with which we are concerned here is not one that could lead to quietism or inaction. It is anguish pure and simple, of the kind well known to all those who have borne responsibilities. When, for instance, a military leader takes upon himself the responsibility for an attack and sends a number of men to their death, he chooses to do it and at bottom he alone chooses. No doubt he acts under a higher command, but its orders, which are more general, require interpretation by him and upon that interpretation depends the life of ten, fourteen or twenty men. In making the decision, he cannot but feel a certain anguish. All leaders know that anguish. It does not prevent their acting, on the contrary it is the very condition of their action, for the action presupposes that there is a plurality of possibilities, and in choosing one of these, they realize that it has value only because it is chosen. Now it is anguish of that kind which existentialism describes, and moreover, as we shall see, makes explicit through direct responsibility toward other men who are concerned. Far from being a screen which could separate us from action, it is a condition of action itself.

And when we speak of "abandonment"—a favorite word of Heidegger—we only mean to say that God does not exist, and that it is necessary to draw the consequences of his absence right to the end. The existentialist is strongly opposed to a certain type of secular moralism which seeks to suppress God at the least possible expense. Toward 1880, when the French professors endeavored to formulate a secular morality, they said something like this—God is a useless and costly hypothesis, so we will do without it. However, if we are to have morality, a society and a law-abiding world, it is essential that certain values should be taken seriously; they must have an *a priori* existence ascribed to them. It must be considered obligatory *a priori* to be honest, not to lie, not to beat one's wife, to bring up children and so forth; so we are going to do a little work on this subject, which will enable us to show that these values exist all the same, inscribed in an intelligible heaven although, of course, there is no God. In other words—and this is, I believe, the purport of all that we in France call radicalism—nothing will be changed if God does not exist; we shall rediscover the same norms of honesty, progress and humanity, and we shall have disposed of God as an out-of-date hypothesis which will die away quietly of itself. The existentialist, on the contrary, finds it extremely embarrassing that God does not exist, for there disappears with Him all possibility of finding values in an intelligible heaven. There can no longer be any good *a priori,* since there is no infinite and perfect consciousness to think it. It is nowhere written that "the good" exists, that one must be honest or must not lie, since we are now upon the plane where there are only men. Dostoyevsky once wrote "If God did not exist, everything would be permitted"; and that, for existentialism, is the starting point. Everything is indeed permitted if God does not exist, and man is in consequence forlorn, for he cannot find anything to depend upon either within or outside himself. He discovers forthwith, that he is without excuse. For if indeed existence precedes essence, one will never be able to explain one's action by reference to a given and specific human nature; in other words, there is no determinism—man is free, man *is* freedom. Nor, on the other hand, if God does not exist, are we provided with any values or commands that could legitimize our behavior. Thus we have neither behind us, nor before us in a luminous realm of values, any means of justification or excuse. We are left alone, without excuse. That is what I mean when I say that man is condemned to be free. Condemned, because he did not create himself, yet is nevertheless at liberty, and from the moment that he is thrown into this world he is responsible for everything he does. The existentialist does not believe in the power of passion. He will never regard a grand passion as a destructive torrent upon which a man is swept into certain actions as by fate, and which, therefore, is an excuse for them. He thinks that man is responsible for his passion. Neither will an existentialist think that a man can find help through some sign being vouchsafed upon earth for his orientation: for he thinks that the man himself interprets the sign as he chooses. He thinks that every man, without any support or help whatever, is condemned at every instant to invent man. As Ponge has written in a very fine article, "Man is the future of man." That is exactly true. Only, if one took this to mean that the future is laid up in Heaven, that God knows what it is, it would be false, for then it would no longer even be a future. If, however, it means that, whatever man may now appear to be, there is a future to be fashioned, a virgin future that awaits him—then it is a true saying. But in the present one is forsaken.

As an example by which you may the better understand this state of abandonment, I will refer to the case of a pupil of mine, who sought me out in the following circumstances. His father was quarreling with his mother and was also inclined to be a "collaborator"; his elder brother had been killed in the German offensive of 1940 and this young man, with a sentiment somewhat primitive but generous, burned to avenge him. His mother was living alone with him, deeply afflicted by the semi-treason of his father and by the death of her eldest son, and her one consolation was in this young man. But he, at this moment, had the choice between going to England to join the Free French Forces or of staying near his mother and helping her to live. He fully realized that this woman lived only for him and that his disappearance—or perhaps his death—would plunge her into despair. He also realized that, concretely and in fact, every action he performed on his mother's behalf would be sure of effect in the sense of aiding her to live, whereas anything he did in order to go and fight would be an ambiguous action which might vanish like water into sand and serve no purpose. For instance, to set out for England he would have to wait indefinitely in a Spanish camp on the way through Spain; or, on arriving in England or in Algiers he might be put into an office to fill up forms. Consequently, he found himself confronted by two very different modes of action; the one concrete, immediate, but directed toward only one individual; and the other action addressed to an end infinitely greater, a national collectivity, but for that very reason ambiguous—and it might be frustrated on the way. At the same time, he was hesitating between two kinds of morality; on the one side the morality of sympathy, of personal devotion and, on the other side, a morality of wider scope but of more debatable validity. He had to choose between these two. What could help him to choose? Could the Christian doctrine? No. Christian doctrine says: Act with charity, love your neighbor, deny yourself for others, choose the way which is hardest, and so forth. But which is the harder road? To whom does one owe the more brotherly love, the patriot or the mother? Which is the more useful aim, the general one of fighting in and for the whole community, or the precise aim of helping one particular person to live? Who can give an answer to that *a priori?* No one. Nor is it given in any ethical scripture. The Kantian ethic says, Never regard another as a means, but always as an end. Very well; if I remain with my mother, I shall be regarding her as the end and not as a means: but by the same token I am in danger of treating as means those who are fighting on my behalf; and the converse is also true, that if I go to the aid of the combatants I shall be treating them as the end at the risk of treating my mother as a means.

If values are uncertain, if they are still too abstract to determine the particular, concrete case under consideration, nothing remains but to trust in our instincts. That is what this young man tried to do; and when I saw him he said, "In the end, it is feeling that counts; the direction in which it is really pushing me is the one I ought to choose. If I feel that I love my mother enough to sacrifice everything else for her—my will to be avenged, all my longings for action and adventure—then I stay with her. If, on the contrary, I feel that my love for her is not enough, I go." But how does one estimate the strength of a feeling? The value of his feeling for his mother was determined precisely by the fact that he was standing by her. I may say that I love a certain friend enough to sacrifice such or such a sum of money for him, but I cannot prove that unless I have done it. I may say, "I love my mother enough to remain with her," if actually I have remained with her. I can only estimate the strength of this affection if I have performed an action by which it is defined and ratified. But if I then appeal to this affection to justify my action, I find myself drawn into a vicious circle.

Moreover, as Gide has very well said, a sentiment which is play-acting and one which is vital are two things that are hardly distinguishable one from another. To decide that I love my mother by staying beside her, and to play a comedy the upshot of which is that I do so—these are nearly the same thing. In other words, feeling is formed by the deeds that one does; therefore I cannot consult it as a guide to action. And that is to say that I can neither seek within myself for an authentic impulse of action, nor can I expect, from some ethic, formulae that will enable me to act. You may say that the youth did, at least, go to a professor to ask for advice. But if you seek counsel—from a priest, for example—you have selected that priest; and at bottom you already knew, more or less, what he would advise. In other words, to choose an adviser is nevertheless to commit oneself by that choice. If you are a Christian, you will say, Consult a priest; but there are collaborationists, priests who are resisters and priests who wait for the tide to turn: which will you choose? Had this young man chosen a priest of the resistance, or one of the collaboration, he would have decided beforehand the kind of advice he was to receive. Similarly, in coming to me, he knew what advice I should give him, and I had but one reply to make. You are free, therefore choose—that is to say, invent. No rule of general morality can show you what you ought to do: no signs are vouchsafed in this world. The Catholics will reply, "Oh, but they are!" Very well; still, it is I myself, in every case, who have to interpret the signs. While I was imprisoned, I made the acquaintance of a somewhat remarkable man, a Jesuit, who had become a member of that order in the following manner. In his life he had suffered a succession of rather severe setbacks. His father had died when he was a child, leaving him in poverty, and he had been awarded a free scholarship in a religious institution, where he had been made continually to feel that he was accepted for charity's sake, and, in consequence, he had been denied several of those distinctions and honors which gratify children. Later, about the age of eighteen, he came to grief in a sentimental affair; and finally, at twenty-two—this was a trifle in itself, but it was the last drop that overflowed his cup—he failed in his military examination. This young man, then, could regard himself as a total failure: it was a sign—but a sign of what? He might have taken refuge in bitterness or despair. But he took it—very cleverly for him—as a sign that he was not intended for secular successes, and that only attainments of religion, those of sanctity and of faith, were accessible to him. He interpreted his record as a message from God, and became a member of the Order. Who can doubt but that this decision as to the meaning of the sign was his, and his alone? One could have drawn quite different conclusions from such a series of reverses—as, for example, that he had better become a carpenter or a revolutionary. For the decipherment of the sign, however, he bears the entire responsibility. That is what "abandonment" implies, that we ourselves decide our being. And with this abandonment goes anguish.

As for "despair," the meaning of this expression is extremely simple. It merely means that we limit ourselves to a reliance upon that which is within our wills, or within the sum of the probabilities which render our action feasible. Whenever one wills anything, there are always these elements of probability. If I am counting upon a visit from a friend, who may be coming by train or by tram, I presuppose that the train will arrive at the appointed time, or that the tram will not be derailed. I remain in the realm of possibilities; but one does not rely upon any possibilities beyond those that are strictly concerned in one's action. Beyond the point at which the possibilities under consideration cease to affect my action, I ought to disinterest myself. For there is no God and no prevenient design, which can adapt the world and all its possibilities to my will. When Descartes said, "Conquer yourself rather than the world," what he meant was, at bottom, the same—that we should act without hope.

Marxists, to whom I have said this, have answered: "Your action is limited, obviously, by your death; but you can rely upon the help of others. That is, you can count both upon what the others are doing to help you elsewhere, as in China and in Russia, and upon what they will do later, after your death, to take up your action and carry it forward to its final accomplishment which will be the revolution. Moreover you must rely upon this; not to do so is immoral." To this I rejoin, first, that I shall always count upon my comrades-in-arms in the struggle, in so far as they are committed, as I am, to a definite, common cause; and in the unity of a party or a group which I can more or less control—that is, in which I am enrolled as a militant and whose movements at every moment are known to me. In that respect, to rely upon the unity and the will of the party is exactly like my reckoning that the train will run to time or that the tram will not be derailed. But I cannot count upon men whom I do not know, I cannot base my confidence upon human goodness or upon man's interest in the good of society, seeing that man is free and that there is no human nature which I can take as foundational. I do not know where the Russian revolution will lead. I can admire it and take it as an example in so far as it is evident, today, that the proletariat plays a part in Russia which it has attained in no other nation. But I cannot affirm that this will necessarily lead to the triumph of the proletariat: I must confine myself to what I can see. Nor can I be sure that comrades-in-arms will take up my work after my death and carry it to the maximum perfection, seeing that those men are free agents and will freely decide, tomorrow, what man is then to be. Tomorrow, after my death, some men may decide to establish Fascism, and the others may be so cowardly or so slack as to let them do so. If so, Fascism will then be the truth of man, and so much the worse for us. In reality, things will be such as men have decided they shall be. Does that mean that I should abandon myself to quietism? No. First I ought to commit myself and then act my commitment, according to the time-honored formula that "one need not hope in order to undertake one's work." Nor does this mean that I should not belong to a party, but only that I should be without illusion and that I should do what I can. For instance, if I ask myself "Will the social ideal as such, ever become a reality?" I cannot tell, I only know that whatever may be in my power to make it so, I shall do; beyond that, I can count upon nothing.

Quietism is the attitude of people who say, "let others do what I cannot do." The doctrine I am presenting before you is precisely the opposite of this, since it declares that there is no reality except in action. It goes further, indeed, and adds, "Man is nothing else but what he purposes, he exists only in so far as he realizes himself, he is therefore nothing else but the sum of his actions, nothing else but what his life is." Hence we can well understand why some people are horrified by our teaching. For many have but one resource to sustain them in their misery, and that is to think, "Circumstances have been against me, I was worthy to be something much better than I have been. I admit I have never had a great love or a great friendship; but that is because I never met a man or a woman who were worthy of it; if I have not written any very good books, it is because I had not the leisure to do so; or, if I have had no children to whom I could devote myself it is because I did not find the man I could have lived with. So there remains within me a wide range of abilities, inclinations and potentialities, unused but perfectly viable, which endow me with a worthiness that could never be inferred from the mere history of my actions." But in reality and for the existentialist, there is no love apart from the deeds of love; no potentiality of love other than that which is manifested in loving; there is no genius other than that which is expressed in works of art. The genius of Proust is the totality of the works of Proust; the genius of Racine is the series of his tragedies, outside of which there is nothing. Why should we attribute to Racine the capacity to write yet another tragedy when that is precisely what he did not write? In life, a man commits himself, draws his own portrait and there is nothing but that portrait. No doubt this thought may seem comfortless to one who has not made a success of his life. On the other hand, it puts everyone in a position to understand that reality alone is reliable; that dreams, expectations and hopes serve to define a man only as deceptive dreams, abortive hopes, expectations unfulfilled; that is to say, they define him negatively, not positively. Nevertheless, when one says, "You are nothing else but what you live," it does not imply that an artist is to be judged solely by his works of art, for a thousand other things contribute no less to his definition as a man. What we mean to say is that a man is no other than a series of undertakings, that he is the sum, the organization, the set of relations that constitute these undertakings.

In the light of all this, what people reproach us with is not, after all, our pessimism, but the sternness of our optimism. If people condemn our works of fiction, in which we describe characters that are base, weak, cowardly and sometimes even frankly evil, it is not only because those characters are base, weak, cowardly or evil. For suppose that, like Zola, we showed that the behavior of these characters was caused by their heredity, or by the action of their environment upon them, or by determining factors, psychic or organic. People would be reassured, they would say, "You see, that is what we are like, no one can do anything about it." But the existentialist, when he portrays a coward, shows him as responsible for his cowardice. He is not like that on account of a cowardly heart or lungs or cerebrum, he has not become like that through his physiological organism; he is like that because he has made himself into a coward by his actions. There is no such thing as a cowardly temperament. There are nervous temperaments; there is what is called impoverished blood, and there are also rich temperaments. But the man whose blood is poor is not a coward for all that, for what produces cowardice is the act of giving up or giving way; and a temperament is not an action. A coward is defined by the deed that he has done. What people feel obscurely, and with horror, is that the coward as we present him is guilty of being a coward. What people would prefer would be to be born either a coward or a hero. One of the charges most often laid against the *Chemins de la Liberté* is something like this—"But, after all, these people being so base, how can you make them into heroes?" That objection is really rather comic, for it implies that people are born heroes: and that is, at bottom, what such people would like to think. If you are born cowards, you can be quite content, you can do nothing about it and you will be cowards all your lives whatever you do; and if you are born heroes you can again be quite content; you will be heroes all your lives, eating and drinking heroically. Whereas the existentialist says that the coward makes himself cowardly, the hero makes himself heroic; and that there is always a possibility for the coward to give up cowardice and for the hero to stop being a hero. What counts is the total commitment, and it is not by a particular case or particular action that you are committed altogether.

We have now, I think, dealt with a certain number of the reproaches against existentialism. You have seen that it cannot be regarded as a philosophy of quietism since it defines man by his action; nor as a pessimistic description of man, for no doctrine is more optimistic, the destiny of man is placed within himself. Nor is it an attempt to discourage man from action since it tells him that there is no hope except in his action, and that the one thing which permits him to have life is the deed. Upon this level therefore, what we are considering is an ethic of action and self-commitment. However, we are still reproached, upon these few data, for confining man within his individual subjectivity. There again people badly misunderstand us.

Our point of departure is, indeed, the subjectivity of the individual, and that for strictly philosophic reasons. It is not because we are bourgeois, but because we seek to base our teaching upon the truth, and not upon a collection of fine theories, full of hope but lacking real foundations. And at the point of departure there cannot be any other truth than this, *I think, therefore I am,* which is the absolute truth of consciousness as it attains to itself. Every theory which begins with man, outside of this moment of self-attainment, is a theory which thereby suppresses the truth, for outside of the Cartesian *cogito,* all objects are no more than probable, and any doctrine of probabilities which is not attached to a truth will crumble into nothing. In order to define the probable one must possess the true. Before there can be any truth whatever, then, there must be an absolute truth, and there is such a truth which is simple, easily attained and within the reach of everybody; it consists in one's immediate sense of one's self.

In the second place, this theory alone is compatible with the dignity of man, it is the only one which does not make man into an object. All kinds of materialism lead one to treat every man including oneself as an object—that is, as a set of pre-determined reactions, in no way different from the patterns of qualities and phenomena which constitute a table, or a chair or a stone. Our aim is precisely to establish the human kingdom as a pattern of values in distinction from the material world. But the subjectivity which we thus postulate as the standard of truth is no narrowly individual subjectivism, for as we have demonstrated, it is not only one's own self that one discovers in the *cogito,* but those of others too. Contrary to the philosophy of Descartes, contrary to that of Kant, when we say "I think" we are attaining to ourselves in the presence of the other, and we are just as certain of the other as we are of ourselves. Thus the man who discovers himself directly in the *cogito* also discovers all the others, and discovers them as the condition of his own existence. He recognizes that he cannot be anything (in the sense in which one says one is spiritual, or that one is wicked or jealous) unless others recognize him as such. I cannot obtain any truth whatsoever about myself, except through the mediation of another. The other is indispensable to my existence, and equally so to any knowledge I can have of myself. Under these conditions, the intimate discovery of myself is at the same time the revelation of the other as a freedom which confronts mine, and which cannot think or will without doing so either for or against me. Thus, at once, we find ourselves in a world which is, let us say, that of "inter-subjectivity." It is in this world that man has to decide what he is and what others are.

Furthermore, although it is impossible to find in each and every man a universal essence that can be called human nature, there is nevertheless a human universality of *condition*. It is not by chance that the thinkers of today are so much more ready to speak of the condition than of the nature of man. By this condition they understand, with more or less clarity, all the *limitations* which *a priori* define man's fundamental situation in the universe. His historical situations are variable: man may be born a slave in a pagan society, or may be a feudal baron, or a proletarian. But what never vary are the necessities of being in the world, of having to labor and to die there. These limitations are neither subjective nor objective, or rather there is both a subjective and an objective aspect of them. Objective, because we meet with them everywhere and they are everywhere recognizable; and subjective because they are *lived* and are nothing if man does not live them—if, that is to say, he does not freely determine himself and his existence in relation to them. And, diverse though man's purposes may be, at least none of them is wholly foreign to me, since every human purpose presents itself as an attempt either to surpass these limitations, or to widen them, or else to deny or to accommodate oneself to them. Consequently every purpose, however individual it may be, is of universal value. Every purpose, even that of a Chinese, an Indian or a Negro, can be understood by a European. To say it can be understood, means that the European of 1945 may be striving out of a certain situation toward the same limitations in the same way, and that he may reconceive in himself the purpose of the Chinese, of the Indian or the African. In every purpose there is universality, in this sense that every purpose is comprehensible to every man. Not that this or that purpose defines man for ever, but that it may be entertained again and again. There is always some way of understanding an idiot, a child, a primitive man or a foreigner if one has sufficient information. In this sense we may say that there is a human universality, but it is not something given; it is being perpetually made. I make this universality in choosing myself; I also make it by understanding the purpose of any other man, of whatever epoch. This absoluteness of the act of choice does not alter the relativity of each epoch.

What is at the very heart and center of existentialism, is the absolute character of the free commitment, by which every man realizes himself in realizing a type of humanity—a commitment always understandable to no matter whom in no matter what epoch—and its bearing upon the relativity of the cultural pattern which may result from such absolute commitment. One must observe equally the relativity of Cartesianism and the absolute character of the Cartesian commitment. In this sense you may say, if you like, that every one of us makes the absolute by breathing, by eating, by sleeping or by behaving in any fashion whatsoever. There is no difference between free being—being as self-committal, as existence choosing its essence—and absolute being. And there is no difference whatever between being as an absolute, temporarily localized—that is, localized in history—and universally intelligible being.

This does not completely refute the charge of subjectivism. Indeed that objection appears in several other forms, of which the first is as follows. People say to us, "Then it does not matter what you do," and they say this in various ways. First they tax us with anarchy; then they say, "You cannot judge others, for there is no reason for preferring one purpose to another"; finally, they may say, "Everything being merely voluntary in this choice of yours, you give away with one hand what you pretend to gain with the other." These three are not very serious objections. As to the first, to say that it does not matter what you choose is not correct. In one sense choice is possible, but what is not possible is not to choose. I can always choose, but I must know that if I do not choose, that is still a choice. This, although it may appear merely formal, is of great importance as a limit to fantasy and caprice. For, when I confront a real situation—for example, that I am a sexual being, able to have relations with a being of the other sex and able to have children —I am obliged to choose my attitude to it, and in every respect I bear the responsibility of the choice which, in committing myself, also commits the whole of humanity. Even if my choice is determined by no *a priori* value whatever, it can have nothing to do with caprice: and if anyone thinks that this is only Gide's theory of the *acte gratuit* over again, he has failed to see the enormous difference between this theory and that of Gide. Gide does not know what a situation is, his "act" is one of pure caprice. In our view, on the contrary, man finds himself in an organized situation in which he is himself involved: his choice involves mankind in its entirety, and he cannot avoid choosing. Either he must remain single, or he must marry without having children, or he must marry and have children. In any case, and whichever he may choose, it is impossible for him, in respect of this situation, not to take complete responsibility. Doubtless he chooses without reference to any pre-established values, but it is unjust to tax him with caprice. Rather let us say that the moral choice is comparable to the construction of a work of art.

But here I must at once digress to make it quite clear that we are not propounding an aesthetic morality, for our adversaries are disingenuous enough to reproach us even with that. I mention the work of art only by way of comparison. That being understood, does anyone reproach an artist, when he paints a picture, for not following rules established *a priori?* Does one ever ask what is the picture that he ought to paint? As everyone knows, there is no pre-defined picture for him to make; the artist applies himself to the composition of a picture, and the picture that ought to be made is precisely that which he will have made. As everyone knows, there are no aesthetic values *a priori,* but there are values which will appear in due course in the coherence of the picture, in the relation between the will to create and the finishd work. No one can tell what the painting of tomorrow will be like; one cannot judge a painting until it is done. What has that to do with morality? We are in the same creative situation. We never speak of a work of art as irresponsible; when we are discussing a canvas by Picasso, we understand very well that the composition became what it is at the time when he was painting it, and that his works are part and parcel of his entire life.

It is the same upon the plane of morality. There is this in common between art and morality, that in both we have to do with creation and invention. We cannot decide *a priori* what it is that should be done. I think it was made sufficiently clear to you in the case of that student who came to see me, that to whatever ethical system he might appeal, the Kantian or any other, he could find no sort of guidance whatever; he was obliged to invent the law for himself. Certainly we cannot say that this man, in choosing to remain with his mother—that is, in taking sentiment, personal devotion and concrete charity as his moral foundations—would be making an irresponsible choice, nor could we do so if he preferred the sacrifice of going away to England. Man makes himself; he is not found ready-made; he makes himself by the choice of his morality, and he cannot but choose a morality, such is the pressure of circumstances upon him. We define man only in relation to his commitments; it is therefore absurd to reproach us for irresponsibility in our choice.

In the second place, people say to us, "You are unable to judge others." This is true in one sense and false in another. It is true in this sense, that whenever a man chooses his purpose and his commitment in all clearness and in all sincerity, whatever that purpose may be, it is impossible for him to prefer another. It is true in the sense that we do not believe in progress. Progress implies amelioration; but man is always the same, facing a situation which is always changing, and choice remains always a choice in the situation. The moral problem has not changed since the time when it was a choice between slavery and anti-slavery—from the time of the war of Secession, for example, until the present moment when one chooses between the M.R.P. [*Mouvement Républicain Populaire*] and the Communists.

We can judge, nevertheless, for, as I have said, one chooses in view of others, and in view of others one chooses himself. One can judge, first—and perhaps this is not a judgment of value, but it is a logical judgment—that in certain cases choice is founded upon an error, and in others upon the truth. One can judge a man by saying that he deceives himself. Since we have defined the situation of man as one of free choice, without excuse and without help, any man who takes refuge behind the excuse of his passions, or by inventing some deterministic doctrine, is a self-deceiver. One may object: "But why should he not choose to deceive himself?" I reply that it is not for me to judge him morally, but I define his self-deception as an error. Here one cannot avoid pronouncing a judgment of truth. The self-deception is evidently a falsehood, because it is a dissimulation of man's complete liberty of commitment. Upon this same level, I say that it is also a self-deception if I choose to declare that certain values are incumbent upon me; I am in contradiction with myself if I will these values and at the same time say that they impose themselves upon me. If anyone says to me, "And what if I wish to deceive myself?" I answer, "There is no reason why you should not, but I declare that you are doing so, and that the attitude of strict consistency alone is that of good faith." Furthermore, I can pronounce a moral judgement. For I declare that freedom, in respect of concrete circumstances, can have no other end and aim but itself; and when once a man has seen that values depend upon himself, in that state of forsakenness he can will only one thing, and that is freedom as the foundation of all values. That does not mean that he wills it in the abstract; it simply means that the actions of men of good faith have, as their ultimate significance, the quest of freedom itself as such. A man who belongs to some communist or revolutionary society wills certain concrete ends, which imply the will to freedom, but that freedom is willed in community. We will freedom for freedom's sake, in and through particular circumstances. And in this willing freedom, we discover that it depends entirely upon the freedom of others and that the freedom of others depends upon our own. Obviously, freedom as the definition of a man does not depend upon others, but as soon as there is a commitment, I am obliged to will the liberty of others at the same time as my own. I cannot make liberty my aim unless I make that of others equally my aim. Consequently, when I recognize, as entirely authentic, that man is a being whose existence precedes his essence, and that he is a free being who cannot, in any circumstances, but will his freedom, at the same time I realize that I cannot not will the freedom of others. Thus, in the name of that will to freedom which is implied to freedom itself, I can form judgments upon those who seek to hide from themselves the wholly voluntary nature of their existence and its complete freedom. Those who hide from this total freedom, in a guise of solemnity or with deterministic excuses, I shall call cowards. Others, who try to show that their existence is necessary, when it is merely an accident of the appearance of the human race on earth—I shall call scum. But neither cowards nor scum can be identified except upon the plane of strict authenticity. Thus, although the content of morality is variable, a certain form of this morality is universal. Kant declared that freedom is a will both to itself and to the freedom of others. Agreed: but he thinks that the formal and the universal suffice for the contitution of a morality. We think, on the contrary, that principles that are too abstract break down when we come to defining action. To take once again the case of that student; by what authority, in the name of what golden rule of morality, do you think he could have decided, in perfect peace of mind, either to abandon his mother or to remain with her? There are no means of judging. The content is always concrete, and therefore unpredictable; it has always to be invented. The one thing that counts, is to know whether the invention is made in the name of freedom.

Let us, for example, examine the two following cases, and you will see how far they are similar in spite of their difference. Let us take *The Mill on the Floss*. We find here a certain young woman, Maggie Tulliver, who is an incarnation of the value of passion and is aware of it. She is in love with a young man, Stephen, who is engaged to another, an insignificant young woman. This Maggie Tulliver, instead of heedlessly seeking her own happiness, chooses in the name of human solidarity to sacrifice herself and to give up the man she loves. On the other hand, La Sanseverina in Stendahl's *Chartreuse de Parme,* believing that it is passion which endows man with his real value, would have declared that a grand passion justifies its sacrifices, and must be preferred to the banality of such conjugal love as would unite Stephen to the little goose he was engaged to marry. It is the latter that she would have chosen to sacrifice in realizing her own happiness, and, as Stendhal shows, she would also sacrifice herself upon the plane of passion if life made that demand upon her. Here we are facing two clearly opposed moralities; but I claim that they are equivalent, seeing that in both cases the overruling aim is freedom. You can imagine two attitudes exactly similar in effect, in that one girl might prefer, in resignation, to give up her lover while the other preferred, in fulfillment of sexual desire, to ignore the prior engagement of the man she loved; and, externally, these two cases might appear the same as the two we have just cited, while being in fact entirely different. The attitude of La Sanseverina is much nearer to that of Maggie Tulliver than to one of careless greed. Thus, you see, the second objection is at once true and false. One can choose anything, but only if it is upon the plane of free commitment.

The third objection, stated by saying, "You take with one hand what you give with the other," means, at bottom, "your values are not serious, since you choose them yourselves." To that I can only say that I am very sorry that it should be so; but if I have excluded God the Father, there must be somebody to invent values. We have to take things as they are. And moreover, to say that we invent values means neither more nor less than this; that there is no sense in life *a priori*. Life is nothing until it is lived; but it is yours to make sense of, and the value of it is nothing else but the sense that you choose. Therefore, you can see that there is a possibility of creating a human community. I have been reproached for suggesting that existentialism is a form of humanism: people have said to me, "But you have written in your *Nausée* that the humanists are wrong, you have even ridiculed a certain type of humanism, why do you now go back upon that?" In reality, the word humanism has two very different meanings. One may understand by humanism a theory which upholds man as the end-in-itself and as the supreme value. Humanism in this sense appears, for instance, in Cocteau's story *Round the World in 80 Hours,* in which one of the characters declares, because he is flying over mountains in an airplane, "Man is magnificent!" This signifies that although I, personally, have not built airplanes I have the benefit of those particular inventions and that I personally, being a man, can consider myself responsible for, and honored by, achievements that are peculiar to some men. It is to assume that we can ascribe value to man according to the most distinguished deeds of certain men. That kind of humanism is absurd, for only the dog or the horse would be in a position to pronounce a general judgment upon man and declare that he is magnificent, which they have never been such fools as to do—at least, not as far as I know. But neither is it admissible that a man should pronounce judgment upon Man. Existentialism dispenses with any judgment of this sort: an existentialist will never take man as the end, since man is still to be determined. And we have no right to believe that humanity is something to which we could set up a cult, after the manner of Auguste Comte. The cult of humanity ends in Comtian humanism, shut-in upon itself, and—this must be said—in Fascism. We do not want a humanism like that.

But there is another sense of the word, of which the fundamental meaning is this: Man is all the time outside of himself: it is in projecting and losing himself beyond himself that he makes man to exist; and, on the other hand, it is by pursuing transcendent aims that he himself is able to exist. Since man is thus self-surpassing, and can grasp objects only in relation to his self-surpassing, he is himself the heart and center of his transcendence. There is no other universe except the human universe, the universe of human subjectivity. This relation of transcendence as constitutive of man (not in the sense that God is transcendent, but in the sense of self-surpassing) with subjectivity (in such a sense that man is not shut up in himself but forever present in a human universe)—it is this that we call existential humanism. This is humanism, because we remind man that there is no legislator but himself; that he himself, thus abandoned, must decide for himself; also because we show that it is not by turning back upon himself, but always by seeking, beyond himself, an aim which is one of liberation or of some particular realization, that man can realize himself as truly human.

You can see from these few reflections that nothing could be more unjust than the objections people raise against us. Existentialism is nothing else but an attempt to draw the full conclusions from a consistently atheistic position. Its intention is not in the least that of plunging men into despair. And if by despair one means—as the Christians do—any attitude of unbelief, the despair of the existentialists is something different. Existentialism is not atheist in the sense that it would exhaust itself in demonstrations of the non-existence of God. It declares, rather, than even if God existed that would make no difference from its point of view. Not that we believe God does exist, but we think that the real problem is not that of His existence; what man needs is to find himself again and to understand that nothing can save him from himself, not even a valid proof of the existence of God. In this sense existentialism is optimistic. It is a doctrine of action, and it is only by self-deception, by confusing their own despair with ours that Christians can describe us as without hope.

Questions for Discussion

1. Raskolnikov overhears the following in *Crime and Punishment:* "Kill her, take her money and with the help of it devote oneself to the service of humanity and the good of all. What do you think, would not one tiny crime be wiped out by thousands of good deeds?" Do you think, in the light of the previous chapter, that a utilitarian like Bentham would have to agree with this argument? Why or why not?

2. Nietzsche claims that morality originated from the decrees of ancient aristocrats who arrogated to themselves "the right to create values for their own profit, and to coin the names of such values." Does calling

something good make it good? Is Nietzsche saying, like Humpty Dumpty in *Alice in Wonderland,* that it is a matter of "who is to be master—we or the words?" Explain.

3. Comment on this passage of Nietzsche: "To require of strength that it should not express itself as strength, that it should not be a wish to overpower, a wish to overthrow, a wish to become master . . . is just as absurd as to require of weakness that it should express itself as strength." Is he right that the strong can no more control their strength than the weak can control their weakness? If he is right, does it follow that there is no free will?

4. Does Nietzsche present convincing evidence for his claim that the religious virtues of humility, charity, and gentleness originated out of the resentment of the weak for the strong? In your answer, consider whether such a historical conjecture could ever be adequately proved or disproved.

5. Was it possible for Hitler to have committed genocide out of what Sartre calls a "project" by which a person "defines himself"? If so, can Sartre rationally justify the condemnation of Hitler's actions as morally evil?

6. Comment on Baier's assertion that "in the family of nations, individual states are placed very much like individual persons in a state of nature." Is this analogy between nations and individuals sound? Baier suggests that it would be difficult to justify a nation keeping to a treaty at its own expense. Does it follow, from his analogy, that it would be equally understandable for a person to break a firm promise when keeping it would be against his or her interests? Why or why not?

7. Baier claims that "no one wants to become mad. . . . Our conclusion must be that there is a correct use of the word 'mad'." But Freud and Sartre have argued that people who go mad want to go mad to escape their troubles, and psychologist R. D. Laing has even claimed that going mad is often the best thing to do under the circumstances. If they are right, would that defeat Baier's conclusion that "there is a correct use of the word 'mad' "? Explain.

8. Sartre says we are "condemned to be free." But he also asserts that "We [revolutionaries] will freedom for freedom's sake." It there any point in willing something (freedom) to which we are condemned and thus cannot possibly escape? If not, then what is the revolutionary really willing? Is he or she willing Sartrian metaphysical freedom of the will, or rather some sort of political freedom?

9. "I am in contradiction with myself if I will these values and at the same time say that they impose themselves upon me," writes Sartre. Is this a genuine contradiction? Compare: We cannot hold our breath indefinitely, since breathing is "imposed" on us by our biological nature, but isn't it true nevertheless that we want or "will" to breathe?

10. Sartre compares morality with art as "having to do with creation and invention." How sound is this comparison? Does it follow that morality is a matter of individual taste, or rather that artistic value is a matter of objective and universal standards?

Selected Readings

ABELSON, R. *Persons.* Chap. 8. London: Macmillan, 1977. Argues for the convergence of morality and self-interest.

BAIER, K. *The Moral Point of View.* Chaps. 11–12. Ithaca, New York: Cornell University Press, 1958. Morality is claimed to be in accordance with enlightened self-interest.

BRANDT, R. *Ethical Theories.* Chap 14. Englewood Cliffs, New Jersey: Prentice-Hall, 1959. Surveys the problem and argues for the rationality of morality.

CARRITT, E. *The Theory of Morals.* London: Oxford University Press, 1928. A critique of egoism in moral matters.

FOOT, P. "Moral Beliefs." *Proceedings of the Aristotalian Society,* 59 (1959). Argues that morality must promote self-interest.

FRANKENA, W. *Ethics.* Chap 6. Englewood Cliffs, New Jersey: Prentice-Hall, 1963. Defends the compatibility of morality and self-interest.

GAUTHIER, D., ed. *Morality and Rational Self-Interest.* Englewood Cliffs, New Jersey: Prentice-Hall, 1970. An anthology of contemporary views.

GERT, B. *The Moral Rules.* Chap. 10. New York: Harper & Row, 1973. Argues that the problem of morality and self-interest is insoluble.

HOBBES, T. *Leviathan.* London: Penguin, 1975. Maintains that morality is purely for self-interest.

HOSPERS, J. *Human Conduct.* Chap. 4. New York: Harcourt Brace Jovanovich, 1972. Argues that morality is rational.

NAGEL, T. *The Possibility of Altruism.* Oxford: Clarendon Press, 1970. Argues that altruism is more reasonable than egoism.

NARVESON, J. *Morality and Utility.* Baltimore: Johns Hopkins Press, 1967. A criticism of egoism.

NIETZSCHE, F. *Thus Spake Zarathustra.* Translated by T. Common. *The Genealogy of Morals.* Translated by H. Samuel. *Beyond Good and Evil.* Translated by H. Zimmern. In *The Philosophy of Nietzsche.* New York: Modern Library, 1927. A spirited defense of the right of self-assertion.

OLSON, R. *The Morality of Self Interest.* New York: Harcourt Brace Jovanovich, 1965. A persuasive defense of egoism.

PEPPER, S. *Ethics.* Chap. 5. New York: Appleton-Century-Crofts, 1960. A critique of egoism.

PLATO, *Republic,* Books 2, 9. In *The Dialogues of Plato.* Translated by B. Jowett. London: Methuen, 1892. Defends a convergence of morality and self-interest.

PRICHARD, H. *Moral Obligation.* Oxford: Clarendon Press, 1949. Denies the validity of the question.

RAND, A. *The Virtue of Selfishness.* New York: New American Library, 1964. A contemporary Nietzschean.

SARTRE, J. P. "Existentialism Is a Humanism." Translated by P. Mairet. London: Methuen, 1949. Deduces morality from the concept of self.

PART FOUR

Political
Philosophy

Chapter 9

The State and the Individual: How Should We Be Governed?

Our ancestors were so stupid and short-sighted that when the first reformers came along . . . they wouldn't have anything to do with them. . . . Sleep teaching was actually prohibited in England. There was something called liberalism. Parliament, if you know what that was, passed a law against it. The records survive. Speeches about liberty of the subject. Liberty to be inefficient and miserable. Freedom to be a round peg in a square hole. . . . Or the Caste System. Constantly proposed, constantly rejected. There was something called democracy. As though men were more than physicochemically equal.

So speaks Mustapha Mond, World Controller in twentieth-century author Aldous Huxley's fantasy of the future, *Brave New World*. The form of society he advocates in Huxley's novel is not likely to find much favor with the contemporary reader, for it is authoritarian, elitist, antidemocratic, paternalist and philistine. But then, Huxley intended the portrayal to evoke feelings of revulsion in us. The ideal city-state described by Socrates in Plato's *Republic* is also all of these things, except that Plato's utopia is one that he would actually wish to see brought into being. Both works, however, present us with a serious philosophical challenge, for, faced with the arguments advanced by Plato's Socrates and Huxley's Mustapha Mond, we may find it surprisingly difficult to justify our dislike of the social systems they advocate. It is by no means easy to explain just why democracy and personal freedom deserve to be highly valued or even to say just what we mean by "democracy" and "freedom" in the first place.

The classic defense of the liberal democratic view is offered by nine-teenth-century philosopher and political economist John Stuart Mill, an extract from whose famous work *On Liberty* is included in this section. It may be helpful here to summarize some of the key features of the societies envisaged by Plato and Huxley, and then to consider them in the light of Mill's philosophy.

Plato's ideal city-state and Huxley's society of the future represent extreme embodiments of the principle of the division of labor. Both writers portray societies in which people are divided into classes or castes according to the functions they perform. Both societies are undemocratic, because only members of the highest class are allowed any role or voice in government. What is perhaps most striking about Huxley's vision is the part played by technology in bringing about and maintaining the caste system. Huxley, like Plato, foresees the possibility of state-con-trolled eugenics, that is, the practice of improving human offspring. But whereas in Plato's *Republic* the stock from which the ruling elite is to be drawn is preserved and enhanced by selective breeding, Huxley's society has perfected a technique for producing "test-tube babies" with the required genetic characteristics. In *Brave New World,* human beings of given potential can literally be produced to order. A lab technician decides whether a person is to have the degree of intelligence appropriate to an Alpha, Beta, Gamma, Delta or Epsilon (categories inspired by the Oxford and Cambridge grading system). After being born (or rather "decanted"), a child in Huxley's society is immediately subjected to a precisely controlled program of conditioning, designed both to supply the knowledge and skills appropriate to the societal niche the child is to occupy and to instill a set of psychological attitudes that will render him or her content to occupy that position. For instance, those who are going to work underground are conditioned to dislike flowers and the open air. All are made to consider themselves highly fortunate to belong to their respective castes. This conditioning, in the case of a Beta, say, consists in part of hearing in one's sleep a soft voice encouraging one to feel contempt for the stupidity of the lower castes and to feel thankful for not having to endure the burdens and responsibilities of the Alphas.

In Huxley's case, this division of humankind represents mainly a pro-jection into the future of the trend toward ever-increasing specialization that he observed in the Britain of the 1930s. For Plato, who clearly considered that society would benefit from a greater specialization than Athenian society allowed, the notion had a somewhat deeper philo-sophical foundation.

Plato's purpose in the *Republic* was to analyze the Greek concept of *dikaiosune,* which is usually (though somewhat misleadingly) translated as "justice." According to Plato, society was merely the individual writ large, and analogous things could be said of each. Thus for Plato, a just individual (and therefore a just society) is one whose parts work harmoniously for the good of the whole. Plato thought of the soul as being composed of three fundamental elements: reason, spirit (by which he meant the will and the higher emotions), and finally appetite. Correspondingly, he held that people themselves could be assigned to different categories, depending on which of these three elements played the major role in their personalities. Plato argued that, just as in an individual reason should be master of the appetites, so in society only the wisest should rule. In the ideal society, men and women of reason, in whom the virtue of wisdom would be found in greatest abundance, would accordingly be Rulers; and people of spirit, whose primary virtue is courage, would be Auxiliaries, assisting the Rulers in the capacities of warriors and police. The remainder of the populace—artisans, farmers, business people, and so on—would have no say whatever in the administration of the state. Because of their total subordination to the Guardians—Plato's collective term for Rulers and Auxiliaries—this ideal society would possess its third cardinal virtue of temperance or discipline.

Plato, like Huxley, envisaged the very greatest care being taken, in his projected society, to ensure that personalities and occupations were properly matched. Potential Guardians would be sought among the common people as well as the higher castes, and the offspring of Guardians relegated to common positions if they failed to possess the qualities requisite for Guardianship. Those judged to be suitable would be put through an exceedingly rigorous education, intended both to discover and develop their natural talents. This education would proceed until students were no longer able to handle the curriculum, at which point they would be assigned positions appropriate to their qualifications. The few who managed to prolong their education until the age of fifty, by which time they would have progressed to the very highest reaches of philosophy, would then be given the role of Rulers, or "Philosopher Kings." According to Plato, they would assume this mantle reluctantly, much preferring to occupy their time in philosophic contemplation; but Plato considered that those cast unwillingly in the role of rulers were likely to make far better ones than those who achieved office in consequence of a positive ambition for power. Here, as elsewhere, *Brave New World* bears the stamp of Platonic influence. Huxley's World Controller, Mustapha Mond, is, in a sense, Plato's Philosopher King. In the passage included here, he reveals himself as a politically unambitious man, whose first love was theoretical physics, but who reluctantly agreed to train for the position of World Controller when faced with the choice of doing that or going into permanent exile.

The forms of government envisaged by Plato and Huxley both constitute examples of what is known as *meritocracy*. Perhaps the closest that we come to meritocracy in our own system of government is the civil service, where admission and promotion both depend upon one's performance in a competitive examination. But, in our society, the role of the civil service is essentially to give advice, and to administer policies and decisions made by others; we prefer to vest real power in men and women who are popularly elected. A system which assigned individuals to positions of power strictly on the basis of their ability to pass certain tests, and the assessment made of them by people of established expertise, would typically be deplored as "elitist." But what is wrong with elitism? It is obvious that some people are far better endowed than others with intelligence, worldly wisdom, relevant experience, moral sensitivity, leadership, initiative, or whatever other attributes enable a person to govern wisely and effectively. So it would seem that any rational person ought to prefer a system whereby people's selection for high political office was dependent on their possessing these qualities, rather than on the vagaries of public opinion.

Plato's distaste for democracy, and corresponding preference for a meritocratic form of government, was due, in large part, to his own disillusioning experience of Athenian democracy. It was, after all, a democratic Athens that ordered the execution of his friend and mentor, Socrates. Athens had a system of direct participatory democracy; in the principle legislative body, the *Ecclesia* or Assembly, every freeborn male adult citizen was entitled to speak and cast his vote. But the Assembly tended in practice to become dominated by demagogues; and most political offices were allocated either by ballot or by a lottery which effectively bypassed all considerations of individual ability. This, then, was what Plato was specifically reacting against. But it seems unlikely that his response to modern parliamentary democracy would have been substantially different. Those who attain positions of power in contemporary democracies may have greater drive and personal ambition than the bulk of the populace; but by and large they are not, in other respects, particularly outstanding. In short, the situation today does not seem to differ significantly from that which Plato observed in ancient Athens, when, comparing society to a beehive, he likened the mass of the citizens to drones, and their leaders to drones with stings.

From this standpoint, Plato's advocacy of a system in which people are appointed to positions of political power on the basis of merit rather than being democratically elected can come to seem eminently reasonable. Yet, as Mill pointed out, there are serious flaws in Plato's argument. In the first place, whatever sort of education, training, or experience we required an office holder to have, it is unrealistic to think that it could guarantee the honesty or competence of that person. In view of its corrupting tendency, it is essential that political power be subject to some sort of check. Mill saw this as a strong argument for some form of democratic control; for of all systems of government, democracy provides what is surely the most effective safeguard against oppressive or incompetent rule. Even if people at large cannot be relied upon to elect leaders who are outstandingly good, it is at least less likely that outstandingly bad leaders will long remain in office or be allowed to persist with disastrous policies if those on the receiving end have the power of recall.

Plato himself was by no means oblivious to the dangers of corrupt leadership. But his own approach to the problem seems open to obvious objections. He believed, for instance, that power would not corrupt leaders if they were properly educated in virtue. That belief stemmed from his conviction that virtue is a form of knowledge—that a person only has to see clearly in order to act rightly. This view seems not only excessively optimistic, but to involve a fundamental misconception as to the very nature of virtue. Plato also thought that the danger of corruption could be reduced by depriving the Guardians of traditionally corrupting influences, such as family, wealth and possessions. The problem with this recommendation, however, is that it would prevent leaders from ever becoming acquainted at first hand with the interests and aspirations so vital to the majority of the governed—something that is hardly conducive to informed or sympathetic government.

Mill was no more inclined than Plato to think that the masses or their elected representatives constituted any particular mine of wisdom. Nevertheless, Mill saw several virtues in popular government which would be largely lost were meritocratic proposals such as Plato's to be put into practice. For one thing, he believed that the welfare of the community could not be adequately served unless there was some route whereby the views, needs, wishes and problems of people at large could at least be forced to the government's attention. In the large nation-state, representative democracy is, arguably, the most effective means yet devised for bringing this about.

There is another consideration which greatly impressed Mill. However much we may lament the comparative incapacity of ordinary people, as they are at present, to make informed, intelligent and independent judgments on social and political matters, actually involving them in the processes of political decision making is bound to be educational. Speaking of the extension of the vote to the working class, still largely disenfranchised in Mill's day, Mill argued that it would be "conducive to progress, because the appeals constantly made to the less instructed classes, the exercise given to their mental powers, and the exertions which the more instructed are obliged to make for enlightening their judgment and ridding them of errors and prejudices, are powerful stimulants to their advance in intelligence." For similar reasons, Mill had high hopes for the effect that granting women the vote would have in "raising their political consciousness," as we would now say, and was himself an active campaigner in this cause.

In addition to defending democracy, Mill was also a staunch advocate of individual freedom. But "freedom," as we remarked earlier, is not an easy term to define. In the excerpt from *On Liberty* used in this chapter, Mill seems, for the most part, to be presupposing a definition of "freedom" according to which people are free so long as they are not hindered from doing what they want by the actions of others. Freedom as the absence of coercion or externally imposed constraints has been dubbed "negative freedom" by one contemporary writer, Sir Isaiah Berlin. Now it is obvious that no society, except possibly one composed of like-minded saints, could function at all without some laws or regulations which placed limits on the negative freedom of its members. Mill's concern is to articulate a principle indicating where these limits should be drawn. The principle he states is the following:

The sole end for which mankind are warranted, individually or collectively, in interfering with the liberty of action of any of their number, is self-protection. . . . The only purpose for which power can be rightfully exercised over any member of a civilized community, against his will, is to prevent harm to others.

The question, of course, is how, for the purposes of this principle, we are to understand the word "harm." A broad interpretation could be used to justify an extremely repressive form of society, whereas a narrow interpretation might be used to justify virtual anarchy. Mill seems to have had in mind such things as physical injury and damage to a person's property, livelihood, or reputation, when these arise as a fairly direct consequence of another individual's behavior. The fact that people engage in homosexual practices may create in some feelings of extreme disgust and moral repugnance, causing psychological distress. But this is precisely *not* the sort of harmful effect that Mill thought would justify making homosexual activity between consenting adults a criminal offense.

Mill though that by applying his principle, a "region of liberty" for the individual member of society could be clearly demarcated—a region within which no one has the right to interfere. For Mill this includes first and foremost the liberty of thought and conscience, a corollary of which, he argues, is the "liberty of expressing and publishing opinions." The latter is clearly infringed by Plato's notorious recommendation that classical poetry and drama be banned in his utopia, on the grounds that the manner in which the gods and ancient heroes are presented in these works is liable to undermine faith in divine perfection and encourage moral weakness. In *Brave New World* Mustapha Mond advocates a similar ban on great works of literature, since they threaten to seduce people away from the laboriously established new order. In the society of *Brave New World,* serious artistic endeavor has been ousted in favor of such things as the utterly banal and propagandistic "community songs" and the "feelies," films that enable the audience actually to experience the sensuous pleasures portrayed by the actors, but in which passion and romance have no place. When Helmholtz Watson, a chief "Emotional Engineer," turns his hand to writing real poetry instead of the mindless rhymes and jingles that are expected of him, he comes perilously close to losing his job.

The holding in check of people's freedom of expression is, in *Brave New World,* by no means confined to the arts. Science also is regarded as "a public danger," "a menace to stability," potentially subversive." So scientific research is carefully restricted. Having himself, in his youth, come into conflict with the authorities for toying with new theories in physics, Mustapha Mond regretfully scrawls "Not to be published" on an ingenious work giving a mathematical treatment of the concept of purpose, and orders its author to be closely watched.

In addition to advocating virtually unrestricted freedom of speech, Mill also insists that his principle "requires liberty of tastes and pursuits; of framing the plan of our life to suit our own character." This, too, is infringed in Plato's and Huxley's imaginary societies. Plato's Guardians, for example, are constrained to live a life of Spartan simplicity in communal barracks. (Impressed by Spartan discipline, Plato actually took Sparta as the model for many of his proposals.) More striking still, sexual relations are, in the *Republic,* carefully regulated, members of the Guardian class being permitted to engage in sexual intercourse only at special "marriage festivals," and then only with state-approved partners.

Though there is doubtless an element of sheer puritanism in Plato's thinking here, he seems primarily to have been influenced by the eugenic considerations alluded to earlier. In *Brave New World,* where the population is constantly replenished from the laboratory and contraceptive devices are freely available, the demands of eugenics can be met while at the same time people are positively encouraged to be sexually promiscuous. What is forbidden, in Huxley's society, is for a person to become too attached to any one sexual partner, since it is felt that such romantic entanglements are liable both to be emotionally unsettling and to undermine a proper communal spirit. Bernard Marx (who, in our chosen excerpt, has been brought, together with Helm-holtz Watson and John Savage, to face judgment at the hands of the World Controller) is denounced in an earlier chapter for "the scandal-ous unorthodoxy of his sex-life," "his heretical views on sport and *soma*" (a universal narcotic "at once less harmful and more pleasure-giving than gin or heroin"), and "his refusal to obey the teachings of Our Ford" (Henry Ford, now prophet of a religion of mass consumption).

We have been considering thus far fairly straightforward limitations on freedom, involving control of people's behavior through the simple exercise of superior authority (backed by threats). We have said little as yet about the subtler means whereby the powers that be in Huxley's society manipulate people's actions and even their inner thoughts. Be-havioral conditioning, hypnopaedia (that is, sleep suggestions), drugs, propaganda: do these constitute a violation of people's freedom? In *Brave New World,* we are certainly made to think so. But if this is the correct way to conceive of them, then the concept of freedom with which we have so far been working—that a person is free when un-hindered by others from realizing his or her desires—seems seriously inadequate. By using drugs, by submitting people to conditioning in their infancy, by carefully slanting their education in childhood, by feed-ing them propaganda in their sleep, by determining what opinions they encounter, what they read in their newspapers, see at the movies, hear on the radio, the World Controllers have produced a race of men and women who have just those desires that the Controllers wish them to have. But these desires and aspirations are ones that society can and does satisfy. As Mustapha Mond says, by and large "people get what they want and never want what they can't get."

The members of Huxley's society do not think of the state as placing obstacles in their path. And indeed, why should they? There are no obstacles to the satisfaction of the desires they actually have. Accord-ing to our earlier "negative" conception of freedom, then, they are not only free, but a great deal freer than any of us. This is pretty clearly an unacceptable consequence of the definition. We would not call the society of *Brave New World* or its citizens "free," even if there were no such misfits as Bernard Marx or Helmholtz Watson, whose behavior had to be held in check by conventional coercive means. It would seem, therefore, that our definition of freedom needs to be enlarged in some way. But how?

Some philosophers have suggested that we stretch the notion of co-ercion to include conditioning, the use of propaganda, and the like. But this would surely be a mistake. "Coercion" has a reasonably clear and circumscribed sense when what is meant is preventing people from doing what they want to do, or making them do things they do not want to do. To insist that people can be coerced when their desires are neither being frustrated nor opposed is, in contrast, both to engender a gratuitous air of paradox, and also to run the danger of making the concept so all-embracing as to be philosophically valueless. A better approach is to expand one's conception of freedom. We should recognize that freedom not only has a negative aspect—the absence of constraints—but a positive one as well—the ability to be one's own master, to act from reasons of one's own choosing, rather than merely in response to external forces—to be, in Berlin's words, "the instrument of my own, not of other men's acts of will." It is, one may argue, this latter concept of freedom as *self-mastery*—"positive freedom," as Berlin calls it—that is violated by the mind-shaping techniques of *Brave New World*.

However, the problem is that it is very plausible, from a certain point of view, to argue that this whole notion of self-mastery is really a myth. We may feel that there is something especially ignominious, if not positively sinister, in the idea that our actions are a product of the will of other people. But are our actions not bound to depend ultimately on external factors of some kind, if only on the sum of environmental forces interacting with our genetic endowment? And is this not just as incompatible with positive freedom, or self-mastery, as would be a deliberate program of behavioral conditioning? As Berlin says " 'I am a slave to no man' . . . but may I not be a slave to nature?"

This is the argument that B. F. Skinner advances in *Walden Two,* discussed in chapter 4. Skinner contends that freedom is an illusion anyway, so one might just as well settle for a benign and rational manipulation of one's behavior. After all, behavioral conditioning only accomplishes in a more efficient manner what education and the random impact of environmental stimuli achieve imperfectly, with less efficiency and more pain.

But this reasoning is fallacious, resting on a combination of concepts that can and should be kept distinct. First, freedom, in a social or political sense—even positive freedom—should not be confused with the metaphysical notion of free will; a society can be classified as relatively free or unfree without ever going into the free will versus determinism controversy. Second, there is a difference in kind between education or moral instruction on the one hand and behavioral conditioning on the other—a difference not captured by saying merely that the one is more effective or scientific than the other.

It may, indeed, be true to say that we are all in one way or another products of the societies in which we have been brought up; nature and nurture may, for all we know, have combined to make us what we are. But regardless of whether determinism of this kind is tenable, it is of crucial importance how society shapes the character and attitudes of its members, and what sort of people it produces. The point about conditioning, drugs, propaganda, and so forth—the key feature that makes them seem to us at least potentially antithetical to freedom—is that they are essentially nonrational processes. They neither call upon, nor do they help to foster, the faculty of human reason. This is where they differ, at least in theory, from education. As Joseph Wood Krutch has observed, in a critique of Skinner's utopia, "Conditioning is achieved by methods which by-pass or, as it were, short circuit, those very reasoning faculties which education proposes to cultivate and exercise." Education is actually conducive to self-mastery. For ideally it makes people aware of alternatives, acquaints them with facts that are germane to making reasoned choices, and renders them less vulnerable to the "hidden persuaders" of the advertising industry, say, or the political establishment, by enhancing their capacity to engage in rational and informed thought.

The very concept of behavioral conditioning is, of course, a comparatively modern one with which Mill would not have been familiar. But there are other ways in which reason can be bypassed, choice inhibited, and people blinded to the existence of alternatives. Mill followed de Tocqueville in seeing as one of the greatest threats to freedom in Western democracies the tendency towards a "tyranny of the majority": a tyranny whose sanction is not so much the law as public opinion, and whose driving force is, in the main, simply the fear of seeming different from one's neighbor. Modern societies are full of subtle pressures towards conformity; persons whose attitudes or life-styles set them apart from the majority are, at best, regarded as jokes—"harmless eccentrics" —and at worst as social outcasts. In such a world it is all too easy simply to take one's cue from one's fellow men and women, relinquishing the autonomous exercise of rational choice in favor of an unthinking submission to the attitudes and mores of the society in which one moves.

As will become apparent, the benefits that Mill sees as deriving from negative freedom do so, according to him, by way of social and psychological mechanisms for which a diversity of opinions and life-styles, and the capacity to exercise reason in the evaluation of the latter, are both prerequisites. So for this reason alone Mill is, for the sake of consistency, bound to defend what he calls "individuality" against the "tyranny of custom." As he points out,

The human faculties of perception, judgment, discriminative feeling, mental activity, and even moral preference, are exercised only in making a choice. He who does anything because it is the custom makes no choice. He gains no practice either in discerning or in desiring what is best. The mental and moral, like the muscular faculties, are improved only by being used. The faculties are called into no exercise by doing a thing because others do it, no more than by believing a thing because others believe it. . . . He who lets the world decide for him has no use for any faculty other than the ape-like one of imitation.

But then why should it matter if these higher cognitive faculties atrophy or fail to develop if the welfare of society can be served without their aid? Mustapha Mond would simply insist that hypnopaedia, conditioning, drugs, propaganda, and so on are sufficient to produce happy, stable, socially integrated human beings. Given these techniques, he would say, such qualities as rationality, moral discernment, and the capacity to make informed choices become utterly useless, if not counterproductive.

Mill, in effect, anticipates such a response. He admits that

It is possible that [a person] might be guided in some good path, and kept out of harm's way, without any of these things. But what will be his comparative worth as a human being? It really is of importance, not only what men do, but also what manner of men they are that do it. Human nature is not a machine to be built after a model, and set to do exactly the work prescribed for it, but a tree, which requires to grow and develop itself on all sides, according to the tendency of the inward forces which make it a living thing. . . . One whose desires and impulses are not his own has no character, no more than a steam engine has a character.

Here it becomes quite clear that Mill in fact regards positive freedom or self-mastery as intrinsically good, something which has value, not merely as an instrument to some more fundamental end, but as an end in its own right.

It is important to note that both Plato (at least at the time when he wrote the *Republic*) and Mill subscribed to what has come to be known as the "greatest happiness principle"—the principle that the right action or right policy is that which leads to "the greatest happiness of the greatest number." In his introduction to *Brave New World* Huxley makes it clear that he intended his futuristic society to be one which takes this principle to its logical conclusion. Philosophers who accept this principle are known as utilitarians. In the hands of philosophers, however, happiness has turned out to be a somewhat slippery notion. When the savage in *Brave New World* renounces the grotesquely conformist but also highly hedonistic society that Huxley describes, his choice is portrayed as the deliberate—and hence seemingly perverse—decision to be unhappy. Yet according to Mill, "Where, not the person's own character, but the traditions or customs of other people are the rule of conduct, there is wanting one of the principal ingredients of human happiness . . ."

Whether this is in fact a useful way to conceive of positive freedom and the exercise of cognitive faculties, or whether these are better regarded—as Huxley seems to have regarded them—as distinct goods to be valued alongside or in addition to happiness, and to which happiness should sometimes give way, is a question which, important though it is, we shall not attempt to decide.

Mill's main argument is, in any case, of a fairly straightforward utilitarian character. It may be approached indirectly via a consideration of one fundamental feature that both Plato's ideal city state and Huxley's imaginary society have in common. "Community, Identity, Stability"—this is the slogan in Huxley's *Brave New World,* and it is one which Plato would probably have applauded. But if there is one notion which is lacking here, it is that of progress. The concept of progress is altogether alien to the societies described by Plato and Huxley, and necessarily so. For progress means change for the better. Judged by the social and political ideals, the logical consequences of which they are intended to illustrate (albeit, in Huxley's case, for the purposes of showing these consequences to be repugnant), the societies of the *Republic* and *Brave New World* are already virtually flawless. So to the extent that Plato's Philosopher Kings or Huxley's World Controllers approve of these ideals, they cannot but see their task as principally that of sustaining in being the status quo; from their point of view any substantial change would be either pointless or retrograde. Hence we find Mustapha Mond (in the extract chosen for this volume) saying quite explicitly: "We don't want to change." And the only change that Plato envisages for his own projected society is a gradual degeneration, culminating in tyranny.

It is thus no accident that the utopian visions with which Plato and Huxley present us are essentially static. As Karl Popper points out in *The Open Society and Its Enemies,* the sort of utopianism for which Plato stands seems tacitly to presuppose that there is "one absolute and unchanging ideal" such that "(a) there are rational methods to determine once and for all what this ideal is, and (b) what the best methods of its realization are." Mill's defense of personal liberty is intimately bound up with his implicit rejection of this brand of utopianism. Mill would hold, with Popper, that any substantive set of social and political ideals can only be provisional, that it is always liable to prove incomplete, always open to revision. In social and ethical matters, as in matters of scientific knowledge, it is always possible to become more enlightened. And even where we feel reasonably confident as to our principles, it is only by a constant and continuing process of practical experiment, trial and error, thought, discussion, and observation that we can learn how best to translate these principles into practice. The implications are evident. Once the idea of a *perfect* society is dismissed as chimerical, then we see that the *good* society must, among other things, be one that is conducive to the intellectual, material, and moral advancement of its members, both individually and collectively. And for this, Mill argues, a large measure of personal freedom is indispensable. As he puts it, "the only permanent and unfailing source of improvement is liberty, since by it there are as many independent centers of improvement as there are individuals."

It is along these lines that Mill makes out a case for freedom of opinion and expression. Mill takes it to be quite evident that we simply do know better, on all kinds of matters—moral, practical, intellectual— than even our most eminent forbears. Asking why this is so, he answers that it is because people have the capacity constantly to revise their opinions, not only in the light of experience, but also as a result of reasoned discussion—by continually bringing their own views into confrontation with those of others. Any person or group who would stifle the expression of opinions to which they do not themselves subscribe will thus be inhibiting a vital factor in the moral and intellectual development of society. For the opinions suppressed may in fact be valid and of potential benefit to society, and without discussion people are unable to form a rational judgment one way or the other. They are in the position of a jury that has heard only one side of the case. Moreover, it is only by constant exposure to contrary opinions that the truth remains living and dynamic, not something that people pay occasional lip service to, but otherwise ignore. Hence Mill insists that we must "keep the lists open" and discover whether our views stand up to opposition. And not only our views; for Mill adds that likewise there should be experiments in *living,* that "free scope should be given to varieties of character, short of injury to others, and that the worth of different modes of life should be proved practically."

Mill qualifies his principle of free speech by confining it to "that stage in the development of mankind at which it is capable of being improved by free and equal discussion." He was firmly of the opinion that Western society had reached this stage and that, in such a society, freedom of expression and diversity of views do, in general, lead to truth and that whatever leads to truth, also leads to progress. Both claims are questionable. The first is perhaps ambiguous: Just whose acquisition of the truth is at issue? The so-called advance of human knowledge is for the most part something that takes place, in the first instance, among a comparatively small academic elite; advances at this level may be only very indirectly reflected, if at all, in the society at large (and even then with a considerable element of time lag). Now the pursuit of truth in a given area by experts in the field almost certainly is greatly assisted by free discussion and the open exchange of diverse opinions. But present most people with a diversity of views on a given topic, and one is as likely to engender sheer confusion as to stimulate them into making intelligent, reasoned, informed assessments. Not because they are stupid, necessarily; but because on so many issues the making of such assessments will call for knowledge, understanding, or a degree of intellectual sophistication that they have simply not acquired. Moreover, many people who are capable of choosing between different views in an informed, reasoned manner will fail to exercise this capacity; there is a persistent tendency to believe things because to do so is somehow attractive, because others believe them, because it makes the world seem more exciting or comforting, or because to have such beliefs fits in with one's image of oneself (as, for example, a left-wing radical, or an arch cynic). It is arguable that the presence of a great diversity of views often has the effect of so overtaxing average peoples' capacity for rational choice that they are positively encouraged to fall back on largely irrational criteria. Also, the very fact that a view is allowed widespread publicity may lend it a spurious air of respectability in the eyes of the less well-educated or more gullible members of the community. Regardless of how ill-founded it may be, just by virtue of being very widely canvassed a view tends to become a serious candidate for belief—as witnessed by the popular credence given to such things as newspaper horoscopes, reincarnation, flying saucers, and the like.

Mill rejects the assumption that truth will always triumph over persecution. "It is," he rightly observes "a piece of idle sentimentality that truth, merely as truth, has any inherent power denied to error of prevailing against the dungeon or the stake." But, as Karl Britton points out, "it is no less sentimental to suppose that truth must prevail over . . . ridicule, slander, provocation, bogus philosophizing, and vituperation." Much as we may applaud the ideal of a free marketplace of ideas, we must be leary of either overestimating the discernment of the customer, or of underestimating the cunning of the salesman.

Finally, there is the question of how far the acquisition of truth does, in general, conduce to social progress; to what extent the promotion of truth within society will—at least in the long run—benefit its members, from a utilitarian standpoint. Religious belief is a case in point. Mustapha Mond is of the opinion that there probably is a God, but that people are better off believing that there is not. This may sound perverse. But the converse is frequently argued. Many people who do not themselves believe in God nevertheless maintain that religion has been of considerable social value, helping to foster desirable codes of conduct, providing a source of comfort and reassurance to the individual, and in general making for a more cohesive society—and correspondingly attribute the contemporary prevalance of antisocial behavior, the decline in standards of honesty, increasing alienation, and so forth, to a falling off in religious belief. Assuming them to be right, it does not automatically follow, of course, that utilitarian ends would be furthered by a policy of suppressing criticism of traditional religious views through control of the media and the educational process. But Mill's own arguments for opposing any attempt on such grounds as these to curb religious dissent seem, nevertheless, most unsatisfactory. He argues, first, that the question of whether a given view is useful or beneficial is no more a matter on which those in a position of authority can claim infallible knowledge than is its truth; so this also must be allowed to be decided in the open court of free discussion. But Mill here seems to have forgotten that, according to his own arguments, it is the truth of a view, not its utility, that is supposed ultimately to enable it to win out in open discussion. So no one who (agreeing with Mill on this point) believed truth and utility to diverge—say, in the case of religious doctrines—would think that utility was going to be well served by exposing them to free and open debate.

Doubtless there are many people who would not wish their lives to be founded on a lie, even if they knew that it would make them happier. They would perhaps agree with Bertrand Russell when he says, "There is something feeble, and a little contemptible, about a man who cannot face the perils of life without the help of comfortable myths." But much as we may sympathize with these sentiments, it must be stressed that they cannot consistently be given much weight by a philosopher who, like Mill, wishes to adhere to the greatest happiness principle.

Mill seems ultimately to rest his case on an almost providentialist conviction that truth and utility will not diverge, at least in the long run. "In the opinion, not of bad, but of the best men," he declares, "no belief which is contrary to truth can be really useful." It must be pointed out here that even if this last assertion of Mill's could be sustained, it still would not follow that the truth is never harmful. This is of crucial importance, since it raises a vital question—which Mill never considered—concerning the wisdom of allowing the scientist's quest for truth to proceed unchecked. Few of us, probably, would be prepared to countenance the measures endorsed by Mustapha Mond in suppressing scientific discoveries whose irresponsible application might threaten the stability or even the survival of society as we know it. But his arguments can scarcely fail to give us pause. We have now come to recognize, as

Mill apparently did not, that truth, at least in the scientific sphere, is a decidedly double-edged weapon. Hence our current hesitation in allowing experiments in genetic "engineering" to go ahead, lest their results prove to be as far-reaching and as potentially destructive as the discovery of nuclear fission a generation ago.

Marxist philosophy has not, thus far, figured at all in our discussion of the good society. Yet its dominance in the contemporary world, both in the political and in the intellectual realm, is such that we can scarcely afford to overlook it in the present volume. The passages we have chosen from Karl Marx and John Strachey (an English communist theoretician of the 1930s) are intended to provide a glimpse of how Marxian socialists regard the issues we have been discussing. Philosophers in the Marxist tradition tend to view the conception of freedom which Mill and other liberals espouse as radically inadequate, typically dismissing it (in terminology ultimately derived from Hegel) as "purely formal" or "mere negativity"; and it is important to grasp the basis of this attitude.

To avoid possible confusion, it must be stressed at the outset that it would, as we mentioned earlier, be quite wrong to suppose that Mill, in *On Liberty,* was concerned merely with "negative freedom," in Sir Isaiah Berlin's sense of that term. It is clear, in fact, that one reason why Mill placed such emphasis on the limitations that must be placed on the power of an individual or group to interfere in the lives of others was that he saw these limitations as indispensable to the promotion of what he called "self-development." Contrary to what Marxist writers would sometimes have us believe, it is thus not true that liberals invariably conceive of freedom in a way that overlooks those more positive aspects of freedom that Marx refers to as "self-realization" (*selbstwirklicheit*) or "mastery over ourselves." What is true, however, is that Marxian socialists have a very different concept of the conditions under which self-development, self-mastery, or self-realization may be achieved. And this, in turn, is in part due to their having a substantially different concept of the self—a concept that leads them to evaluate contemporary society in a very different manner from Mill.

For Marx, humans are essentially social animals; only in voluntary, creative activity that brings them into a cooperative relationship with others are they capable, Marx maintains, of finding true fulfillment. Yet the very structure of modern bourgeois society, as Marx sees it, stands in the way of this. Here, as elsewhere, Marx was greatly influenced by Hegel. Marx follows Hegel in using the term "civil society" (*die burgerliche Gesellschaft*) to designate the pattern of concrete relationships and transactions between individuals that form the substance of a functioning community; and it is evident, in the passage we have selected, that Marx fully endorses the description of civil society in its bourgeois form offered by Hegel in his *Philosophy of Right*. It is, says Hegel, a

battlefield where everybody's private interest meets everyone else's. . . . In civil society each member is his own end, everything else is nothing to him. But except in contact with others he cannot attain the whole compass of his ends and therefore these others are means to the end of the particular member.

In short, it is a sphere of mutual exploitation, where universal egoism reigns supreme.

According to Hegel and Marx, the liberal concept of freedom—as embodied in the constitutions, bills of rights, and so forth that are so characteristic a product of the American and French revolutions—constitutes a moral and political response to an emergent bourgeois society which has, and is seen as having, essentially the features that Hegel describes. The original apostles of the liberal state took for granted that a person is egoistic and society atomistic. So, wishing to liberate economic enterprise from the residual constraints of an outdated feudal mode of political organization, they sought to provide each individual with the maximum room for maneuver in seeking to compass his or her own (largely selfish) ends, that was compatible with similar pursuits by others. As Marx so graphically expresses it (in words very reminiscent of Mill), the law then came to be viewed as a kind of fence, marking out for each an area in which he or she may act unhindered, but upon which others are forbidden to encroach.

Neither Marx nor Strachey wishes to deny that such "political emancipation" constitutes an important step forward. Marx says quite explicitly that it "at least represents important progress." But in taking it to be "the last form of human emancipation generally," the liberal has, in Marx's estimation, failed to locate the really fundamental source of human oppression. As Marx puts it,

Political democracy . . . regards man—not merely one but every man—as *sovereign* and supreme. But this means man in his uncivilized and unsocial aspect, in his fortuitous existence and just as he is, corrupted by the entire organization of our society, lost and alienated from himself, oppressed by inhuman relations and elements . . .

What people really need to be liberated from is the very system of economic relations, of production and exchange, capital and distribution—brilliantly described by eighteenth-century economist Adam Smith in his classic treatise on economics, *The Wealth of Nations*—which places people in these mutually antagonistic roles, prevents them from identifying creatively with the products of their own labor, and reduces them, as labor, to the status of commodities. Where liberal thinking has gone astray is in taking this atomized society of egoistic individuals as an unyielding fact, rather than perceiving it as merely one stage of historical development, the product of an economic system which has outlived its usefulness, has become spiritually as well as economically enslaving, and is now ripe for transformation. The sense in which the liberal conception of freedom is, from an Hegelian or Marxist standpoint, "negative" is that, taking totally for granted a form of society which in reality distorts a person's "true" nature, it embodies a purely negative view of the role of other people *vis à vis* the freedom of the individual. As Marx puts it, "It allows every man to find in other men not the realization but rather the *limitation* of his own freedom."

In Marx's view, a person's social self (he uses the terms "generic man" or "species-being") is systematically frustrated under bourgeois civil society. And in a sense the political emancipation, for which he expresses qualified approval, actually contributes to this. For the very withdrawal of the political tentacles from a person's material and spiritual life, which comes with freedom of religion, freedom of ownership, freedom of speech, and freedom to dispose of the fruits of one's labor, actually serves to diminish the communal aspect of human existence. An individual's status as citizen, that is, as a member of the political community, becomes increasingly abstract, while the concrete realities of that person's life as *bourgeois,* that is, as a member of civil society, becomes increasingly asocial. In this "unsocial social existence," people's religion, financial transactions, political opinions, and the like become private matters that serve to separate them from, rather than unite them with, the community as a whole.

Here Marx's philosophy represents a fundamental departure from Hegel's. Hegel saw the modern political state as the ultimate embodiment of a kind of Rousseauesque general will, in identification with which a person's freedom as a social being could at last find full expression. Marx, in contrast, saw the state as merely an abstract externalization of people's social essence—providing, at best, a thin substitute for the social fulfillment denied by the day-to-day, concrete realities of civil society. The state, for Marx, is an external objectification of one's generic being, the effect of which is to divide people from themselves. According to Marx:

Where the political state has achieved its full development, man leads a double life . . . not only in thought or consciousness but in *actuality*. In the *political community* he regards himself as a *communal being;* but in *civil society* he is active as a *private individual,* treats other men as means, reduces himself to a means, and becomes the plaything of alien powers.

True emancipation will come only when political or communal life is absorbed back into civil society—a state of affairs that only a revolution will bring about. Not that this revolution can be expected to achieve total emancipation at a stroke. According to Marx, society will first have to pass through a transitional phase, the so-called dictatorship of the proletariat, during which even some liberal freedoms will temporarily have to be curtailed in order to prevent entrenched bourgeois interests from reasserting themselves.

Philosophical theses that are couched, as is Marx's, in terms of "true man" or "human essence"—where the latter are to be distinguished from the "inauthentic man" or "merely empirical" human manifestations encountered in actual contemporary society—are exceedingly resistant to rational assessment. For it is very difficult to see what would count as evidence for or against the claim that people were "naturally" or "essentially" communal beings, rather than the egoistic creatures they more often appear to be in society as we know it. When we attempt, in the imagination, to abstract human beings totally from their material circumstances we find, in effect, that there remains nothing of substance to evaluate. And yet if it is claimed that certain types of material circumstance "distort" people's nature, while others tend rather to realize or fulfill their nature, then we must ask, "On what basis is one entitled to assert that one kind of influence, social or economic, is distorting, and another not?" Clearly, the concept of alienation, which Marx inherited from Hegel, is intended to provide an answer to this question. But the very notion of alienation is embedded in an intricate metaphysical web that we cannot begin to disentangle here. We shall therefore restrict ourselves, by way of comment, to a few rather obvious remarks.

First, there is something decidedly farfetched in Marx's claim that the competitive and self-centered nature of individuals in modern society is merely, or even predominantly, a reflection of the underlying pattern of economic relations. Egoism is scarcely a bourgeois invention. It is far easier to believe that it is the other way around, that the structure of capitalist society is rather a reflection of people's natural egoism.

On the other hand, there seems no obvious reason to deny that it may be possible, eventually, to bring into being a vastly more cooperative mode of social and economic organization, in which men and women find gratification in the thought that their labor is satisfying a communal need (and not merely filling their purses). The People's Republic of China seems, indeed, to have moved a substantial distance toward the accomplishment of this goal. And yet there is, to Western eyes, something very disturbing about the uniformity of dress, culture and social mores which Communist societies exhibit. Is this just a bourgeois prejudice on our part? Perhaps. But there is ample evidence in his writings that even Marx would have preferred a society in which Mill's "individuality"—spontaneous, original creativity, even to the point of eccentricity—played a vastly greater role than any present Communist government allows. Marx often employs the model of the artist when speaking of "unalienated labor"; yet, ironically, artistic creation is the activity that thrives least in those societies that claim to embody Marxist principles. Marx himself, and Marxian socialists in general, are exceedingly coy as to just how communal and individual life are supposed to converge under communism; and one cannot help but wonder whether there may not be an intrinsic and irresolvable contradiction in what Marx was trying to envisage.

However, one does not really need to accept Marx's conception of future society, or to wrestle with the finer points of his quasi-Hegelian metaphysics, in order to understand and perhaps agree with much of the Marxist critique of contemporary social and economic arrangements. First of all, as Marx points out, while it may be true in the liberal state that no one (in theory at least) receives any special political privileges on the basis of private property, the enslaving power of property remains within civil society at large. And this has vast consequences when we come to consider the average citizen's capacity effectively to exercise the negative freedom which we discussed earlier. Marx's analysis of "alienated labor" is particularly perceptive. In an earlier age, one's labor was essentially one's own: people would grow their own crops or exercise their particular crafts in a manner largely of their own choosing—subject, of course, to the demands of the marketplace. But in modern industrial society the very means of production are, for the most part, the exclusive possession of a privileged few—with the result that most citizens are obliged to contract out their labor. What they then produce is largely decided for them by others; they have little say in what becomes of it; and they frequently have little responsibility for, or awareness of, the finished product. To be sure, they can, within limits, choose their jobs. But then, as a contemporary Marxist, Herbert Marcuse, has remarked in another context, free election by slaves of their masters would scarcely constitute the abolition of slavery.

More generally, and this is the burden of Strachey's argument, it is a limitation in Mill's discussion of liberty that he sees governmental or societal interference as detracting from individual freedom, but does not see economic constraint in the same light. Yet, as Strachey points out, few desires can be satisfied without at least minimal financial or material resources; and a person's lack of the resources requisite to the pursuit of some activity, when society is so structured as to make their attainment impossible, is, for that person, as genuine a constraint as would be a law forbidding the activity in question. Under such conditions, the "freedom" to perform the activity in question is indeed "purely formal," if not empty.

In summary, the existence within society of substantial economic inequalities implies, for the less privileged, a relative lack both of negative and positive freedom. For poverty constrains actions, and simultaneously limits self-mastery, insofar as it cannot but place one at the mercy of the economically more privileged—who are, in their turn, if Marx is to be believed, subject to a subtler form of enslavement.

It would be out of place here to draw any specific political moral from these considerations. But experience teaches us that we should at least be wary of trading in, for the "economic freedom" that a more equitable distribution of material resources might bring, those political freedoms for which Mill argued so vigorously. It has too often proved, in practice, a costly bargain.

BRAVE NEW WORLD

Aldous Huxley

The room into which the three were ushered was the Controller's study.

"His fordship will be down in a moment." The Gamma Butler left them to themselves.

Helmholtz laughed aloud.

"It's more like a caffeine-solution party than a trial," he said, and let himself fall into the most luxurious of the pneumatic armchairs. "Cheer up, Bernard," he added, catching sight of his friend's green unhappy face. But Bernard would not be cheered; without answering, without even looking at Helmholtz, he went and sat down on the most uncomfortable chair in the room, carefully chosen in the obscure hope of somehow deprecating the wrath of the higher powers.

The Savage meanwhile wandered restlessly round the room, peering with a vague superficial inquisitiveness at the books in the shelves, at the sound-track rolls and the reading-machine bobbins in their num-bered pigeon-holes. On the table under the window lay a massive volume bound in limp black leather-surrogate, and stamped with large golden Ts. He picked it up and opened it. *My Life and Work, by Our Ford.* The book had been published at Detroit by the Society for the Propa-gation of Fordian Knowledge. Idly he turned the pages, read a sentence here, a paragraph there, and had just come to the conclusion that the book didn't interest him, when the door opened, and the Resident World Controller for Western Europe walked briskly into the room.

Mustapha Mond shook hands with all three of them; but it was to the Savage that he addressed himself. "So you don't much like civiliza-tion, Mr. Savage," he said.

The Savage looked at him. He had been prepared to lie, to bluster, to remain sullenly unresponsive; but, reassured by the good-humored intelligence of the Controller's face, he decided to tell the truth, straight-forwardly. "No." He shook his head.

Bernard started and looked horrified. What would the Controller think? To be labeled as the friend of a man who said that he didn't like civilization—said it openly and, of all people, to the Controller—it was terrible. "But John," he began. A look from Mustapha Mond reduced him to an abject silence.

"Of course," the Savage went on to admit, "there are some very nice things. All that music in the air, for instance . . ."

"Sometimes a thousand twangling instruments will hum about my ears, and sometimes voices."

The Savage's face lit up with a sudden pleasure. "Have you read it too?" he asked. "I thought nobody knew about that book here, in England."

"Almost nobody. I'm one of the very few. It's prohibited, you see. But as I make the laws here, I can also break them. With impunity, Mr. Marx," he added, turning to Bernard. "Which I'm afraid you *can't* do."

Bernard sank into a yet more hopeless misery.

"But why is it prohibited?" asked the Savage. In the excitement of meeting a man who had read Shakespeare he had momentarily forgotten everything else.

The Controller shrugged his shoulders. "Because it's old; that's the chief reason. We haven't any use for old things here."

"Even when they're beautiful?"

"Particularly when they're beautiful. Beauty's attractive, and we don't want people to be attracted by old things. We want them to like the new ones."

"But the new ones are so stupid and horrible. Those plays, where there's nothing but helicopters flying about and you *feel* the people kissing." He made a grimace. "Goats and monkeys!" Only in Othello's words could he find an adequate vehicle for his contempt and hatred.

"Nice tame animals, anyhow," the Controller murmured parenthetically.

"Why don't you let them see *Othello* instead?"

"I've told you; it's old. Besides, they couldn't understand it."

Yes, that was true. He remembered how Helmholtz had laughed at *Romeo and Juliet.* "Well, then," he said, after a pause, "something new that's like *Othello,* and that they could understand."

"That's what we've all been wanting to write," said Helmholtz, breaking a long silence.

"And it's what you never will write," said the Controller. "Because, if it were really like *Othello* nobody could understand it, however new it might be. And if it were new, it couldn't possibly be like *Othello.*"

"Why not?"

"Yes, why not?" Helmholtz repeated. He too was forgetting the unpleasant realities of the situation. Green with anxiety and apprehension, only Bernard remembered them; the others ignored him. "Why not?"

"Because our world is not the same as Othello's world. You can't make flivvers without steel—and you can't make tragedies without social instability. The world's stable now. People are happy; they get what they want, and they never want what they can't get. They're well off; they're safe; they're never ill; they're not afraid of death; they're blissfully ignorant of passion and old age; they're plagued with no mothers or fathers; they've got no wives, or children, or loves to feel strongly about; they're so conditioned that they practically can't help behaving as they ought to behave. And if anything should go wrong, there's *soma*. Which you go and chuck out of the window in the name of liberty, Mr. Savage. *Liberty!*" He laughed. "Expecting Deltas to know what liberty is! And now expecting them to understand *Othello!* My good boy!"

The Savage was silent for a little. "All the same," he insisted obstinately, *"Othello's* good, *Othello's* better than those feelies."

"Of course it is," the Controller agreed. "But that's the price we have to pay for stability. You've got to choose between happiness and what people used to call high art. We've sacrificed the high art. We have the feelies and the scent organ instead."

"But they don't mean anything."

"They mean themselves; they mean a lot of agreeable sensations to the audience."

"But they're . . . they're told by an idiot."

The Controller laughed. "You're not being very polite to your friend Mr. Watson. One of our most distinguished Emotional Engineers . . ."

"But he's right," said Helmholtz gloomily. "Because it *is* idiotic. Writing when there's nothing to say . . ."

"Precisely. But that requires the most enormous ingenuity. You're making flivvers out of the absolute minimum of steel—works of art out of practically nothing but pure sensation."

The Savage shook his head. "It all seems to me quite horrible."

"Of course it does. Actual happiness always looks pretty squalid in comparison with the over-compensations for misery. And, of course, stability isn't nearly so spectacular as instability. And being contented has none of the glamour of a good fight against misfortune, none of the picturesqueness of a struggle with temptation, or a fatal overthrow by passion or doubt. Happiness is never grand."

"I suppose not," said the Savage after a silence. "But need it be quite so bad as those twins?" He passed his hand over his eyes as though he were trying to wipe away the remembered image of those long rows of identical midgets at the assembling tables, those queued-up twin-herds at the entrance to the Brentford monorail station, those human maggots swarming round Linda's bed of death, the endlessly repeated face of his assailants. He looked at his bandaged left hand and shuddered. "Horrible!"

"But how useful! I see you don't like our Bokanovsky Groups; but, I assure you, they're the foundation on which everything else is built. They're the gyroscope that stabilizes the rocket plane of state on its unswerving course." The deep voice thrillingly vibrated; the gesticulating hand implied all space and the onrush of the irresistible machine; Mustapha Mond's oratory was almost up to synthetic standards.

"I was wondering," said the Savage, "why you had them at all—seeing that you can get whatever you want out of those bottles. Why don't you make everybody an Alpha-Double-Plus while you're about it?"

Mustapha Mond laughed. "Because we have no wish to have our throats cut," he answered. "We believe in happiness and stability. A society of Alphas couldn't fail to be unstable and miserable. Imagine a factory staffed by Alphas—that is to say by separate and unrelated individuals of good heredity and conditioned so as to be capable (within limits) of making a free choice and assuming responsibilities. Imagine it!" he repeated.

The Savage tried to imagine it, not very successfully.

"It's an absurdity. An Alpha-decanted, Alpha-conditioned man would go mad if he had to do Epsilon Semi-Moronwork—go mad, or start smashing things up. Alphas can be completely socialized—but only on condition that you make them do Alpha work. Only an Epsilon can be expected to make Epsilon sacrifices, for the good reason that for him they aren't sacrifices; they're the line of least resistance. His conditioning has laid down rails along which he's got to run. He can't help himself; he's foredoomed. Even after decanting, he's still inside a bottle —an invisible bottle of infantile and embryonic fixations. Each one of us, of course," the Controller meditatively continued, "goes through life inside a bottle. But if we happen to be Alphas, our bottles are, relatively speaking, enormous. We should suffer acutely if we were confined in a narrower space. You cannot pour upper-caste champagne-surrogate into lower-caste bottles. It's obvious theoretically. But it has also been proved in actual practice. The result of the Cyprus experiment was convincing."

"What was that?" asked the Savage.

Mustapha Mond smiled. "Well, you can call it an experiment in re-bottling if you like. It began in A.F.473. The Controllers had the island of Cyprus cleared of all its existing inhabitants and re-colonized with a specially prepared batch of twenty-two thousand Alphas. All agricultural and industrial equipment was handed over to them and they were left to manage their own affairs. The result exactly fulfilled all the theoretical predictions. The land wasn't properly worked; there were strikes in all the factories; the laws were set at naught, orders disobeyed; all the people detailed for a spell of low-grade work were perpetually intriguing for high-grade jobs, and all the people with high-grade jobs were counter-intriguing at all costs to stay where they were. Within six years they were having a first class civil war. When nineteen out of the twenty-two thousand had been killed, the survivors unanimously petitioned the World Controllers to resume the government of the island. Which they did. And that was the end of the only society of Alphas that the world has ever seen."

The Savage sighed, profoundly.

"The optimum population," said Mustapha Mond, "is modeled on the iceberg—eight-ninths below the water line, one-ninth above."

"And they're happy below the water line?"

"Happier than above it. Happier than your friends here, for example." He pointed.

"In spite of that awful work?"

"Awful? *They* don't find it so. On the contrary, they like it. It's light, it's childishly simple. No strain on the mind or the muscles. Seven and a half hours of mild, unexhausting labor, and then the *soma* ration and games and unrestricted copulation and the feelies. What more can they ask for? True," he added, "they might ask for shorter hours. And of course we could give them shorter hours. Technically, it would be perfectly simple to reduce all lower-caste working hours to three or four a day. But would they be any the happier for that? No, they wouldn't. The experiment was tried, more than a century and a half ago. The whole of Ireland was put on to the four-hour day. What was the result? Unrest and a large increase in the consumption of *soma;* that was all. Those three and a half hours of extra leisure were so far from being a source of happiness, that people felt constrained to take a holiday from them. The Inventions Office is stuffed with plans for labor-saving processes. Thousands of them." Mustapha Mond made a lavish gesture. "And why don't we put them into execution? For the sake of the laborers; it would be sheer cruelty to afflict them with excessive leisure. It's the same with agriculture. We could synthesize every morsel of food, if we wanted to. But we don't. We prefer to keep a third of the population on the land. For their own sakes—because it takes *longer* to get food out of the land than out of a factory. Besides, we have our stability to think of. We don't want to change. Every change is a menace to stability. That's another reason why we're so chary of applying new inventions. Every discovery in pure science is potentially subversive; even science must sometimes be treated as a possible enemy. Yes, even science."

Science? The Savage frowned. He knew the word. But what it exactly signified he could not say. Shakespeare and the old men of the pueblo had never mentioned science, and from Linda he had only gathered the vaguest hints: science was something you made helicopters with, something that caused you to laugh at the Corn Dances, something that prevented you from being wrinkled and losing your teeth. He made a desperate effort to take the Controller's meaning.

"Yes," Mustapha Mond was saying, "that's another item in the cost of stability. It isn't only art that's incompatible with happiness; it's also science. Science is dangerous; we have to keep it most carefully chained and muzzled."

"What?" said Helmholtz, in astonishment. "But we're always saying that science is everything. It's a hypnopaedic platitude."

"Three times a week between thirteen and seventeen," put in Bernard.

"And all the science propaganda we do at the College . . ."

"Yes; but what sort of science?" asked Mustapha Mond sarcastically. "You've had no scientific training, so you can't judge. I was a pretty good physicist in my time. Too good—good enough to realize that all our science is just a cookery book, with an orthodox theory of cooking that nobody's allowed to question, and a list of recipes that mustn't be added to except by special permission from the head cook. I'm the head cook now. But I was an inquisitive young scullion once. I started doing a bit of cooking on my own. Unorthodox cooking, illicit cooking. A bit of real science, in fact." He was silent.

"What happened?" asked Helmholtz Watson.

The Controller sighed. "Very nearly what's going to happen to you young men. I was on the point of being sent to an island."

The words galvanized Bernard into a violent and unseemly activity. "Send *me* to an island?" He jumped up, ran across the room, and stood gesticulating in front of the Controller. "You can't send *me*. I haven't done anything. It was the others. I swear it was the others." He pointed accusingly to Helmholtz and the Savage. "Oh, please don't send me to Iceland. I promise I'll do what I ought to do. Give me another chance. Please give me another chance." The tears began to flow. "I tell you, it's their fault," he sobbed. "And not to Iceland. Oh, please, your fordship, please . . ." And in a paroxysm of abjection he threw himself on his knees before the Controller. Mustapha Mond tried to make him get up; but Bernard persisted in his groveling; the stream of words poured out inexhaustibly. In the end the Controller had to ring for his fourth secretary.

"Bring three men," he ordered, "and take Mr. Marx into a bedroom.

Give him a good *soma* vaporization and then put him to bed and leave him."

The fourth secretary went out and returned with three green-uniformed twin footmen. Still shouting and sobbing, Bernard was carried out.

"One would think he was going to have his throat cut," said the Controller, as the door closed. "Whereas, if he had the smallest sense, he'd understand that his punishment is really a reward. He's being sent to an island. That's to say, he's being sent to a place where he'll meet the most interesting set of men and women to be found anywhere in the world. All the people who, for one reason or another, have got too self-consciously individual to fit into community-life. All the people who aren't satisfied with orthodoxy, who've got independent ideas of their own. Everyone, in a word, who's anyone. I almost envy you, Mr. Watson."

Helmholtz laughed. "Then why aren't you on an island yourself?"

"Because, finally, I preferred this," the Controller answered. "I was given the choice: to be sent to an island, where I could have got on with my pure science, or to be taken on to the Controller's Council with the prospect of succeeding in due course to an actual Controllership. I chose this and let the science go." After a little silence, "Sometimes," he added, "I rather regret the science. Happiness is a hard master— particularly other people's happiness. A much harder master, if one isn't conditioned to accept it unquestioningly, than truth." He sighed, fell silent again, then continued in a brisker tone. "Well, duty's duty. One can't consult one's own preferences. I'm interested in truth. I like science. But truth's a menace, science is a public danger. As dangerous as it's been beneficent. It has given us the stablest equilibrium in history. China's was hopelessly insecure by comparison; even the primitive matriarchies weren't steadier than we are. Thanks, I repeat, to science. But we can't allow science to undo its own good work. That's why we so carefully limit the scope of its researches—that's why I almost got sent to an island. We don't allow it to deal with any but the most immediate problems of the moment. All other inquiries are most sedulously discouraged. It's curious," he went on after a little pause, "to read what people in the time of Our Ford used to write about scientific progress. They seem to have imagined that it could be allowed to go on indefinitely, regardless of everything else. Knowledge was the highest good, truth the supreme value; all the rest was secondary and subordinate. True, ideas were beginning to change even then. Our Ford himself did a great deal to shift the emphasis from truth and beauty to comfort and happiness. Mass production demanded the shift. Universal happiness keeps the wheels steadily turning; truth and beauty can't. And, of course, whenever the masses seized political power, then it was happiness rather than truth and beauty that mattered. Still, in spite of everything, unrestricted scientific research was still permitted. People still went on talking about truth and beauty as though they were the sovereign goods. Right up to the time of the Nine Years' War. *That* made them change their tune all right. What's the point of truth or beauty or knowledge when the anthrax bombs are popping all around you? That was when science first began to be controlled—after the Nine Years' War. People were ready to have even their appetites controlled then. Anything for a quiet life. We've gone on controlling ever since. It hasn't been very good for truth, of course. But it's been very good for happiness. One can't have something for nothing. Happiness has got to be paid for. You're paying for it, Mr. Watson—paying because you happen to be too much interested in beauty. I was too much interested in truth; I paid too."

"But *you* didn't go to an island," said the Savage, breaking a long silence.

The Controller smiled. "That's how I paid. By choosing to serve happiness. Other people's—not mine. It's lucky," he added, after a pause, "that there are such a lot of islands in the world. I don't know what we should do without them. Put you all in the lethal chamber, I suppose. By the way, Mr. Watson, would you like a tropical climate? The Marquesas, for example; or Samoa? Or something rather more bracing?"

Helmholtz rose from his pneumatic chair. "I should like a thoroughly bad climate," he answered. "I believe one would write better if the climate were bad. If there were a lot of wind and storms for example . . ."

The Controller nodded his approbation. "I like your spirit, Mr. Watson. I like it very much indeed. As much as I officially disapprove of it." He smiled. "What about the Falkland Islands?"

"Yes, I think that will do," Helmholtz answered. "And now, if you don't mind, I'll go and see how poor Bernard's getting on."

. . . .

"Art, science—you seem to have paid a fairly high price for your happiness," said the Savage, when they were alone. "Anything else?"

"Well, religion, of course," replied the Controller. "There used to be something called God—before the Nine Years' War. But I was forgetting; you know all about God, I suppose."

"Well . . ." The Savage hesitated. He would have liked to say something about solitude, about night, about the mesa lying pale under the moon, about the precipice, the plunge into shadowy darkness, about death. He would have liked to speak; but there were no words. Not even in Shakespeare.

The Controller, meanwhile, had crossed to the other side of the room and was unlocking a large safe set into the wall between the bookshelves. The heavy door swung open. Rummaging in the darkness within, "It's a subject," he said, "that has always had a great interest for me." He pulled out a thick black volume. "You've never read this, for example."

The Savage took it. *"The Holy Bible, containing the Old and New Testaments,"* he read aloud from the title-page.

"Nor this." It was a small book and had lost its cover.

"The Imitation of Christ."

"Nor this." He handed out another volume.

"The Varieties of Religious Experience. By William James."

"And I've got plenty more," Mustapha Mond continued, resuming his seat. "A whole collection of pornographic old books. God in the safe and Ford on the shelves." He pointed with a laugh to his avowed library—to the shelves of books, the racks full of reading-machine bobbins and sound-track rolls.

"But if you know about God, why don't you tell them?" asked the Savage indignantly. "Why don't you give them these books about God?"

"For the same reason as we don't give them *Othello:* they're old; they're about God hundreds of years ago. Not about God now."

"But God doesn't change."

"Men do, though."

"What difference does that make?"

"All the difference in the world," said Mustapha Mond. He got up again and walked to the safe. "There was a man called Cardinal Newman," he said. "A cardinal," he exclaimed parentheticlly, "was a kind of Arch-Community-Songster."

" 'I, Pandulph, of fair Milan cardinal.' I've read about them in Shakespeare."

"Of course you have. Well, as I was saying, there was a man called Cardinal Newman. Ah, here's the book." He pulled it out. "And while I'm about it I'll take this one too. It's by a man called Maine de Biran. He was a philosopher, if you know what that was."

"A man who dreams of fewer things than there are in heaven and earth," said the Savage promptly.

"Quite so. I'll read you one of the things he *did* dream of in a moment. Meanwhile, listen to what this old Arch-Community-Songster said." He opened the book at the place marked by a slip of paper and began to read. " 'We are not our own any more than what we possess is our own. We did not make ourselves, we cannot be supreme over ourselves. We are not our own masters. We are God's property. Is it not our happiness thus to view the matter? Is it any happiness, or any comfort, to consider that we *are* our own? It may be thought so by the young and prosperous. These may think it a great thing to have every-thing, as they suppose, their own way—to depend on no one—to have to think of nothing out of sight, to be without the irksomeness of con-tinual acknowledgement, continual prayer, continual reference of what they do to the will of another. But as time goes on, they, as all men, will find that independence was not made for man—that it is an unnatural state—will do for a while, but will not carry us on safely to the end. . . .' " Mustapha Mond paused, put down the first book and, picking up the other, turned over the pages. "Take this, for example," he said, and in his deep voice once more began to read: " 'A man grows old; he feels in himself that radical sense of weakness, of listlessness, of discomfort, which accompanies the advance of age; and, feeling thus, imagines himself merely sick, lulling his fears with the notion that this distressing condition is due to some particular cause, from which, as from an illness, he hopes to recover. Vain imaginings! That sickness is old age; and a horrible disease it is. They say that it is the fear of death and of what comes after death that makes men turn to religion as they advance in years. But my own experience has given me the conviction that, quite apart from any such terrors or imaginings, the religious sentiment tends to develop as we grow older; to develop because, as the passions grow calm, as the fancy and sensibilities are less excited and less excitable, our reason becomes less troubled in its working, less obscured by the images, desires and distractions, in which it used to be absorbed; whereupon God emerges as from behind a cloud; our soul feels, sees, turns toward the source of all light; turns naturally and in-evitably; for now that all that gave to the world of sensations its life and charm has begun to leak away from us, now that phenomenal existence is no more bolstered up by impressions from within or from without, we feel the need to lean on something that abides, something that will never play us false—a reality, an absolute and everlasting truth. Yes, we inevitably turn to God; for this religious sentiment is of its nature so pure, so delightful to the soul that experiences it, that it makes up to us for all our other losses.' " Mustapha Mond shut the book and leaned back in his chair. "One of the numerous things in heaven and earth that these philosophers didn't dream about was this" (he waved his hand), "us, the modern world. 'You can only be independent of God while you've got youth and prosperity; independence won't take you safely to the end.' Well, we've now got youth and prosperity right up to the end. What follows? Evidently, that we can be independent of God. 'The reli-gious sentiment will compensate us for all our losses.' But there aren't any losses for us to compensate; religious sentiment is superfluous. And why should we go hunting for a substitute for youthful desires, when youthful desires never fail? A substitute for distractions, when we go on enjoying all the old fooleries to the very last? What need have we of repose when our minds and bodies continue to delight in activity? of consolation, when we have *soma?* of something immovable, when there is the social order?"

"Then you think there is no God?"

"No, I think there quite probably is one."

"Then why? . . ."

Mustapha Mond checked him. "But he manifests himself in different ways to different men. In pre-modern times he manifested himself as the being that's described in these books. Now . . ."

"How does he manifest himself now?" asked the Savage.

"Well, he manifests himself as an absence; as though he weren't there at all."

"That's your fault."

"Call it the fault of civilization. God isn't compatible with machinery and scientific medicine and universal happiness. You must make your choice. Our civilization has chosen machinery and medicine and happiness. That's why I have to keep these books locked up in the safe. They're smut. People would be shocked if . . ."

The Savage interrupted him. "But isn't it *natural* to feel there's a God?"

"You might as well ask if it's natural to do up one's trousers with zippers," said the Controller sarcastically. "You remind me of another of those old fellows called Bradley. He defined philosophy as the finding of bad reasons for what one believes by instinct. As if one believed anything by instinct! One believes things because one has been conditioned to believe them. Finding bad reasons for what one believes for other bad reasons—that's philosophy. People believe in God because they've been conditioned to believe in God."

"But all the same," insisted the Savage, "it is natural to believe in God when you're alone—quite alone, in the night, thinking about death . . ."

"But people never are alone now," said Mustapha Mond. "We make them hate solitude; and we arrange their lives so that it's almost impossible for them ever to have it."

The Savage nodded gloomily. At Malpais he had suffered because they had shut him out from the communal activities of the pueblo; in civilized London he was suffering because he could never escape from those communal activities, never be quietly alone.

"Do you remember that bit in *King Lear?*" said the Savage at last: " 'The gods are just, and of our pleasant vices make instruments to plague us; the dark and vicious place where thee he got cost him his eyes,' and Edmund answers—you remember, he's wounded, he's dying—

'Thou hast spoken right; 'tis true. The wheel is come full circle; I am here.' What about that, now? Doesn't there seem to be a God managing things, punishing, rewarding?"

"Well, does there?" questioned the Controller in his turn. "You can indulge in any number of pleasant vices with a freemartin and run no risks of having your eyes put out by your son's mistress. 'The wheel is come full circle; I am here.' But where would Edmund be nowadays? Sitting in a pneumatic chair, with his arm round a girl's waist, sucking away at his sex-hormone chewing-gum and looking at the feelies. The gods are just. No doubt. But their code of law is dictated, in the last resort, by the people who organize society; Providence takes its cue from men."

"Are you sure?" asked the Savage. "Are you quite sure that the Edmund in that pneumatic chair hasn't been just as heavily punished as the Edmund who's wounded and bleeding to death? The gods are just. Haven't they used his pleasant vices as an instrument to degrade him?"

"Degrade him from what position? As a happy, hard-working, goods-consuming citizen he's perfect. Of course, if you choose some other standard than ours, then perhaps you might say he was degraded. But you've got to stick to one set of postulates. You can't play Electro-magnetic Golf according to the rules of Centrifugal Bumble-puppy."

"But value dwells not in particular will," said the Savage. "It holds his estimate and dignity as well wherein 'tis precious of itself as in the prizer."

"Come, come," protested Mustapha Mond, "that's going rather far, isn't it?"

"If you allowed yourself to think of God, you wouldn't allow yourselves to be degraded by pleasant vices. You'd have a reason for bearing things patiently, for doing things with courage. I've seen it with the Indians."

"I'm sure you have," said Mustapha Mond. "But then we aren't Indians. There isn't any need for a civilized man to bear anything that's seriously unpleasant. And as for doing things—Ford forbid that he should get the idea into his head. It would upset the whole social order if men started doing things on their own."

"What about self-denial, then? If you had a God, you'd have a reason for self-denial."

"But industrial civilization is only possible when there's no self-denial. Self-indulgence up to the very limits imposed by hygiene and economics. Otherwise the wheels stop turning."

"You'd have a reason for chastity!" said the Savage, blushing a little as he spoke the words.

" But chastity means passion, chastity means neurasthenia. And passion and neurasthenia mean instability. And instability means the end of civilization. You can't have a lasting civilization without plenty of pleasant vices."

"But God's the reason for everything noble and fine and heroic. If you had a God . . ."

"My dear young friend," said Mustapha Mond, "civilization has absolutely no need of nobility or heroism. These things are symptoms of political inefficiency. In a properly organized society like ours, nobody has any opportunities for being noble or heroic. Conditions have got to be thoroughly unstable before the occasion can arise. Where there are wars, where there are divided allegiances, where there are temptations to be resisted, objects of love to be fought for or defended —there, obviously, nobility and heroism have some sense. But there aren't any wars nowadays. The greatest care is taken to prevent you from loving anyone too much. There's no such thing as a divided allegiance; you're so conditioned that you can't help doing what you ought to do. And what you ought to do is on the whole so pleasant, so many of the natural impulses are allowed free play, that there really aren't any temptations to resist. And if ever, by some unlucky chance, anything unpleasant should somehow happen, why, there's always *soma* to give you a holiday from the facts. And there's always *soma* to calm your anger, to reconcile you to your enemies, to make you patient and long-suffering. In the past you could only accomplish these things by making a great effort and after years of hard moral training. Now, you swallow two or three half-gram tablets, and there you are. Anybody can be virtuous now. You can carry at least half your morality about in a bottle. Christianity without tears—that's what *soma* is."

"But the tears are necessary. Don't you remember what Othello said? 'If after every tempest come such calms, may the winds blow till they have wakened death.' There's a story one of the old Indians used to tell us, about the Girl of Mátsaki. The young men who wanted to marry her had to do a morning's hoeing in her garden. It seemed easy; but there were flies and mosquitoes, magic ones. Most of the young men simply couldn't stand the biting and stinging. But the one that could—he got the girl."

"Charming! But in civilized countries," said the Controller, "you can have girls without hoeing for them; and there aren't any flies or mosquitoes to sting you. We got rid of them all centuries ago."

The Savage nodded, frowning. "You got rid of them. Yes, that's just like you. Getting rid of everything unpleasant instead of learning to put up with it. Whether 'tis nobler in the mind to suffer the slings and arrows of outrageous fortune, or to take arms against a sea of troubles and by opposing end them. . . . But you don't do either. Neither suffer nor oppose. You just abolish the slings and arrows. It's too easy."

He was suddenly silent, thinking of his mother. In her room on the thirty-seventh floor, Linda had floated in a sea of singing lights and perfumed caresses—floated away, out of space, out of time, out of the prison of her memories, her habits, her aged and bloated body. And Tomakin, ex-Director of Hatcheries and Conditioning, Tomakin was still on holiday—on holiday from humiliation and pain, in a world where he could not hear those words, that derisive laughter, could not see that hideous face, feel those moist and flabby arms round his neck, in a beautiful world . . .

"What you need," the Savage went on, "is something *with* tears for a change. Nothing costs enough here."

("Twelve and a half million dollars," Henry Foster had protested when the Savage told him that. "Twelve and a half million—that's what the new Conditioning Center cost. Not a cent less.")

"Exposing what is mortal and unsure to all that fortune, death and danger dare, even for an egg-shell. Isn't there something in that?" he asked, looking up at Mustapha Mond. "Quite apart from God—though of course God would be a reason for it. Isn't there something in living dangerously?"

"There's a great deal in it," the Controller replied. "Men and women must have their adrenals stimulated from time to time."

"What?" questioned the Savage, uncomprehending.

"It's one of the conditions of perfect health. That's why we've made the V.P.S. treatments compulsory."

"V.P.S.?"

"Violent Passion Surrogate. Regularly once a month. We flood the whole system with adrenalin. It's the complete physiological equivalent of fear and rage. All the tonic effects of murdering Desdemona and being murdered by Othello, without any of the inconveniences."

"But I like the inconveniences."

"We don't," said the Controller. "We prefer to do things comfortably."

"But I don't want comfort. I want God, I want poetry, I want real danger, I want freedom, I want goodness. I want sin."

"In fact," said Mustapha Mond, "you're claiming the right to be unhappy."

"All right, then," said the Savage defiantly, "I'm claiming the right to be unhappy."

"Not to mention the right to grow old and ugly and impotent; the right to have syphilis and cancer; the right to have too little to eat;

the right to be lousy; the right to live in constant apprehension of what may happen tomorrow; the right to catch typhoid; the right to be tortured by unspeakable pains of every kind."

There was a long silence.

"I claim them all," said the Savage at last.

Mustapha Mond shrugged his shoulders. "You're welcome," he said.

THE IDEAL STATE

Plato

Here Adeimantus interposed a question: How would you answer, Socrates, said he, if a person were to say that you are not making these men very happy, and that they are themselves to blame; the city in fact belongs to them, but they reap no advantage from it; whereas other men acquire lands, and build large and handsome houses, and have everything handsome about them, offering sacrifices to the gods on their own account, and practicing hospitality; moreover, they have the gold and silver which you have just mentioned, and all that is usual among the favorites of fortune; but our poor citizens are no better than mercenaries who are quartered in the city and are always mounting guard?

Yes, I said; and you may add that they are only fed, and not paid in addition to their food like other men; and therefore they cannot, if they would, take a private journey abroad; they have no money to spend on a mistress or any other luxurious fancy, which, as the world goes, is thought to be happiness; and many other accusations of the same nature might be added.

But, said he, let us suppose all this to be included in the charge.

You mean to ask, I said, what will be our answer?

Yes.

If we proceed along the old path, my belief, I said, is that we shall find the answer. And our answer will be that, even as they are, our guardians may very likely be the happiest of men; but that our aim in founding the State was not the disproportionate happiness of any one class, but the greatest happiness of the whole; we thought that in a State which is ordered with a view to the good of the whole we should be most likely to find justice, and in the worst-ordered State injustice; and, having found them, we might then decide upon the answer to our first question. At present, I take it, we are fashioning the happy State, not piecemeal, or with a view of making a few happy citizens, but as a whole; and by-and-by we will proceed to view the opposite kind of State.

FROM "The Republic," Book IV, in *The Dialogues of Plato*, translated by Benjamin Jowett (1892).

Suppose that we were painting a statue, and someone came up to us and said, Why do you not put the most beautiful colors on the most beautiful parts of the body—the eyes ought to be purple, but you have made them black—to him we might fairly answer, "Sir, you would not surely have us beautify the eyes to such a degree that they are no longer eyes; consider rather whether, by giving this and the other features their due proportion, we make the whole beautiful." And so I say to you, do not compel us to assign to the guardians a sort of happiness which will make them no guardians at all; for we too can clothe our husband-men in royal apparel, and set crowns of gold on their heads, and bid them till the ground as much as they like, and no more. Our potters also might be allowed to repose on couches, and feast by the fireside, passing round the winecup, while their wheel is conveniently at hand, so that they may make a few pots when they feel inclined; in this way we might make every class happy—and then, as you imagine, the whole State would be happy. But do not put this idea into our heads; for, if we listen to you, the husbandman will be no longer a husbandman, the potter will cease to be a potter, and no one will have the character of any distinct class in the State. Now this is not of much consequence where the corruption of society, and pretension to be what you are not, is confined to cobblers; but when the guardians of the laws and of the government are only seeming and not real guardians, then see how they turn the State upside down; and on the other hand they alone have the power of giving order and happiness to the State. We mean our guardians to be true saviors and not the destroyers of the State, whereas our opponent is thinking of peasants at a festival, who are enjoying a life of revelry, not of citizens who are doing their duty to the State. But, if so, we mean different things, and he is speaking of something which is not a State. And therefore we must consider whether in appointing our guardians we look to their greatest happiness individually, or whether our aim is not to ensure that happiness appears in the State as a whole. What these guardians or auxiliaries must be compelled or induced to do (and the same may be said of every other trade), is to become as expert as possible in their professional work. And thus the whole State will grow up in a noble order, and the several classes will receive the proportion of happiness which nature assigns to them.

I think that you are quite right.

I wonder whether you will agree with another remark which occurs to me.

What may that be?

There seem to be two causes of the deterioration of the arts.

What are they?

Wealth, I said, and poverty.

How do they act?

The process is as follows: When a potter becomes rich, will he, think you, any longer take the same pains with his art?

Certainly not.

He will grow more and more indolent and careless?

Very true.

And the result will be that he becomes a worse potter?

Yes; he greatly deteriorates.

But, on the other hand, if he has no money and cannot provide himself with tools or other requirements of his craft, his own work will not be equally good, and he will not teach his sons or apprentices to work equally well.

Certainly not.

Then, under the influence either of poverty or of wealth, workmen and their work are equally liable to degenerate?

That is evident.

Here then is a discovery of new evils, I said, against which the guardians will have to watch, or they will creep into the city unobserved.

What evils?

Wealth, I said, and poverty; the one is the parent of luxury and indolence, and the other of meanness and viciousness, and both of a revolutionary spirit.

That is very true, he replied; but still I should like to know, Socrates, how our city will be able to go to war, especially against an enemy who is rich and powerful, if deprived of the sinews of war.

Evidently it would be difficult, I replied, to wage war with one such enemy; but it will be easier where there are two of them.

How so? he asked.

In the first place, I said, if we have to fight, our side will be trained warriors fighting against an army of rich men.

That is true, he said.

And do you not suppose, Adeimantus, that a single boxer who was perfect in his art would easily be a match for two stout and well-to-do gentlemen who were not boxers?

Hardly, if they came upon him at once.

What, not, I said, if he were able to run away and then turn and strike at the one who first came up? And supposing he were to do this several times under the heat of a scorching sun, might he not, being an expert, overturn more than one stout personage?

Certainly, he said, there would be nothing wonderful in that.

And yet rich men probably have more instruction in the science and practice of boxing than they have in military science.

Likely enough.

Then we may assume that our athletes will be able to fight with two or three times their own number?

I will accept that, for I think you right.

And suppose that, before engaging, our citizens send an embassy to one of the two cities, telling them what is the truth: "Silver and gold we neither have nor are permitted to have, but you may; do you therefore come and help us in war, and take the spoils of the other city." Who, on hearing these words; would choose to fight against lean wiry dogs, rather than, with the dogs on their side, against fat and tender sheep?

That is not likely; and yet there might be a danger to the poor State if the wealth of many States were to be gathered into one.

But how simple of you to think that the term State is applicable at all to any but our own!

Why so?

You ought to speak of other States in the plural number; not one of them is a city, but many cities, as they say in the game. Each will contain not less than two divisions, one the city of the poor, the other of the rich, which are at war with one another; and within each there are many smaller divisions. You would be altogether beside the mark if you treated these as a single State; but if you deal with them as many, and give the wealth or power or persons of the one to the others, you will always have a great many friends and not many enemies. And your State, while the wise order which has now been prescribed continues to prevail in her, will be the greatest of States, I do not mean to say in reputation or appearance, but in deed and truth, though she number not more than a thousand defenders. A single State of that size you will hardly find, either among Hellenes or barbarians, though many that appear to be as great and many times greater.

That is most true, he said.

Hence, I said, it can be seen what will be the best limit for our rulers to fix when they are considering the size of the State and the amount of territory which they are to include, and beyond which they will not go.

What limit would you propose?

I would allow the State to increase so far as is consistent with unity; that, I think, is the proper limit.

Very good, he said.

Here then, I said, is another order which will have to be conveyed to our guardians: Let them guard against our city becoming small, or great only in appearance. It must attain an adequate size, but it must remain one.

And perhaps, said he, you do not think this is a very severe order?

And here is another, said I, which is lighter still—I mean the duty, of which some mention was made before, of degrading the offspring of the guardians when inferior, and of elevating into the rank of guardians the offspring of the lower classes, when naturally superior. The intention was that, in the case of the citizens generally, each individual should be put to the use for which nature intended him, one to one work, and then every man would do his own business, and become one and not many; and so the whole city would be one and not many.

Yes, he said; that is not so difficult.

The regulations which we are prescribing, my good Adeimantus, are not, as might be supposed, a number of great principles, but trifles all, if care be taken, as the saying is, of the one great thing—a thing, however, which I would rather call, not great, but sufficient for our purpose.

What may that be? he asked.

Education, I said, and nurture: if our citizens are well educated, and grow into sensible men, they will easily see their way through all these, as well as other matters which I omit; such, for example, as marriage, the possession of women and the procreation of children, which will all follow the general principle that friends have all things in common, as the proverb says.

That will be the best way of settling them.

Also, I said, the State, if once started well, moves with accumulating force like a wheel. For where good nurture and education are maintained, they implant good constitutions, and these good constitutions taking root in a good education improve more and more, and this improvement affects the breed in man as in other animals.

Very possibly, he said.

Then to sum up: This is the principle to which our rulers should cling throughout, taking care that neglect does not creep in—that music and gymnastic be preserved in their original form, and no innovation made. They must do their utmost to maintain them intact. And when anyone says that

> Mankind most regard the newest song which the singers have

they will be afraid that he may be praising, not new songs, but a new kind of song; and this ought not to be praised, or conceived to be the meaning of the poet; for any musical innovation is to be shunned, as likely to bring danger to the whole State. So Damon tells me, and I can quite believe him—he says that when modes of music change, the fundamental laws of the State always change with them.

Yes, said Adeimantus; and you may add my suffrage to Damon's and your own.

Then, I said, our guardians must lay the foundations of their fortress in music?

Yes, he said; the lawlessness of which you speak too easily steals in.

Yes, I replied, in the form of amusement, and as though it were harmless.

Why, yes, he said, and harmless it would be; were it not that little by little this spirit of license, finding a home, imperceptibly penetrates into manners and customs; whence issuing with greater force it invades contracts between man and man, and from contracts goes on to laws and constitutions, in utter recklessness, ending at last, Socrates, by an overthrow of all rights, private as well as public.

Is that true? I said.

That is my belief, he replied.

Then, as I was saying, our boys should be trained from the first in a stricter system, for if childish amusement becomes lawless, it will produce lawless children, who can never grow up into well-conducted and virtuous citizens.

Very true, he said.

And when boys who have made a good beginning in play, have later gained the habit of good order through music, then this habit accompanies them in all their actions and is a principle of growth to them, and is able to correct anything in the State which had been allowed to lapse. It is the reverse of the picture I have just drawn.

Very true, he said.

Thus educated, they will discover for themselves any lesser rules which their predecessors have altogether neglected.

What do you mean?

I mean such things as these—when the young are to be silent before their elders; how they are to show respect to them by standing and making them sit; what honor is due to parents; what garments or shoes are to be worn; the mode of dressing the hair; deportment and manners in general. You would agree with me?

Yes.

But there is, I think, small wisdom in legislating about such matters— precise written enactments cannot create these observances, and are not likely to make them lasting.

Impossible.

It would seem, Adeimantus, that the direction in which education starts a man will determine his future life. Does not like always attract like?

To be sure.

Until some one grand result is reached which may be good, and may be the reverse of good?

That is not to be denied.

And for this reason, I said, I, for my part, should not attempt to extend legislation to such details.

Naturally enough, he replied.

Well, and about the business of the agora, and the ordinary dealings between man and man, or again about agreements with artisans; about insult and injury, or the commencement of actions, and the appointment of juries, what would you say? there may also arise questions about any impositions and exactions of market and harbor dues which may be required, and in general about the regulations of markets, police, harbors, and the like. But, oh heavens! shall we condescend to legislate on any of these particulars?

No, he said, it is unseemly to impose laws about them on good men; what regulations are necessary they will find out soon enough for themselves.

Yes, I said, my friend, if God will only preserve to them the laws which we have given them.

And without divine help, said Adeimantus, they will go on for ever making and mending their laws and their lives in the hope of attaining perfection.

You would compare them, I said, to those invalids who, having no self-restraint, will not leave off their habits of intemperance?

Exactly.

Yes, I said; and what a delightful life they lead! they are always doctoring their disorders, with no result except to increase and complicate them, and always fancying that they will be cured by any nostrum which anybody advises them to try.

Such cases are very common, he said, with invalids of this sort.

Yes, I replied; and the charming thing is that they deem him their worst enemy who tells them the truth, which is simply that, unless they give up gorging and drinking and wenching and idling, neither drug nor cautery nor amputation nor spell nor amulet nor any other remedy will avail.

Charming? he replied. I see nothing charming in going into a passion with a man who tells you what is right.

These gentlemen, I said, do not seem to be in your good graces.

Asuredly not.

Nor would you approve if a whole State behaves in this way, and that brings me back to my point. For when, in certain ill-ordered States, the citizens are forbidden under pain of death to alter the constitution; and yet he who most sweetly courts those who live under this regime and indulges them and fawns upon them and is skillful in anticipating and gratifying their humors is honored as a great and good statesman— do not these States resemble the persons whom I was describing?

Yes, he said; the fault is the same; and I am very far from approving it.

But what of these ready and eager ministers of political corruption? I said. Do you not admire their coolness and dexterity?

Yes, he said, I do; but not of all of them, for there are some whom the applause of the multitude has deluded into the belief that they are really statesmen.

What do you mean? I said; you should have more feeling for them. When a man cannot measure, and a great many others who cannot measure declare that he is four cubits high, can he help believing what they say?

Nay, he said, certainly not in that case.

Well, then, do not be angry with them; for are they not as good as a play, trying their hand at paltry reforms such as I was describing; they are always fancying that by legislation they will make an end of frauds in contracts, and the other rascalities which I was mentioning, not knowing that they are in reality cutting off the heads of a hydra?

Yes, he said; that is just what they are doing.

I conceive, I said, that the true legislator will not trouble himself with this class of enactments whether concerning laws or the constitution either in an ill-ordered or in a well-ordered State; for in the former they are quite useless, and in the latter they will either be of a kind which anyone can devise, or will naturally flow out of our previous regulations.

What, then, he said, is still remaining to us of the work of legislation?

Nothing to us, I replied; but to Apollo, the god of Delphi, there remains the ordering of the greatest and noblest and chiefest things of all.

Which are they? he said.

The institution of temples and sacrifices, and the entire service of gods, demigods, and heroes; also the ordering of the repositories of the dead, and the rites which have to be observed by him who would propitiate the inhabitants of the world below. These are matters of which we are ignorant ourselves, and as founders of a city we should be unwise in trusting them to any interpreter but the ancestral one. For it is Apollo who, sitting at the navel of the earth, is the ancestral interpreter of such observances to all mankind.

You are right, and we will do as you propose.

So now the foundation of your city, son of Ariston, is finished. What comes next? Provide yourself with a bright light and search, and get your brother and Polemarchus and the rest of our friends to help, and let us see where in it we can discover justice and where injustice, and in what they differ from one another, and which of them the man who would be happy should have for his portion, whether seen or unseen by gods and men.

Nonsense, said Glaucon: did you not promise to search yourself, saying that for you not to help justice in her need would be an impiety?

Your reminder is true, and I will be as good as my word; but you must join.

We will, he replied.

Well, then, I hope to make the discovery in this way; I mean to begin with the assumption that our State, if rightly ordered, is perfect. That is most certain.

And being perfect, is therefore wise and valiant and temperate and just.

That is likewise clear.

And whichever of these qualities we first find in the State, the one which is not yet found will be the residue?

Very good.

If in some other instance there were four things, in one of which we were most interested, the one sought for might come to light first, and there would be no further trouble; or if we came to know the other three first, we should thereby attain the object of our search, for it must clearly be the part remaining.

Very true, he said.

And is not a similar method to be pursued about the virtues, which are also four in number?

Clearly.

First among the virtues found in the State, wisdom comes into view, and in this I detect a certain peculiarity.

What is that?

The State which we have been describing has, I think, true wisdom. You would agree that it is good in counsel?

Yes.

And this good counsel is clearly a kind of knowledge, for not by ignorance, but by knowledge, do men counsel well?

Clearly.

And the kinds of knowledge in a State are many and diverse?

Of course.

There is the knowledge of the carpenter; but is that the sort of knowledge which gives a city the title of wise and good in counsel?

Certainly not; that would only give a city the reputation of skill in carpentering.

Then a city is not to be called wise because possessing a knowledge which counsels for the best about wooden implements?

Certainly not.

Nor by reason of a knowledge which advises about brazen pots, he said, nor as possessing any other similar knowledge?

Not by reason of any of them, he said.

Nor yet by reason of a knowledge which cultivates the earth; that would give the city the name of agricultural?

Yes.

Well, I said, and is there any knowledge in our recently founded State among any of the citizens which advises not about any particular thing in the State, but about the whole, and considers how it can best conduct itself in relation with itself and with other States?

There certainly is.

And what is this knowledge, and among whom is it found? I asked.

It is the knowledge of guarding, he replied, and is found in those rulers whom we were just now describing as perfect guardians.

And what is the name which the city derives from the possession of this sort of knowledge?

The name of good in counsel and truly wise.

And will there be in our city more of these true guardians or more smiths?

The smiths, he replied, will be far more numerous.

Will not the guardians probably be the smallest of all the classes who receive a name from the profession of some kind of knowledge?

Much the smallest.

And so by reason of the smallest part or class, and of the knowledge which resides in this presiding and ruling part of itself, the whole State, being thus constituted according to nature, will be wise; and this, which can claim a share in the only knowledge worthy to be called wisdom, has been ordained by nature to be of all classes the least.

Most true.

Thus, then, I said, the nature and place in the State of one of the four virtues has somehow or other been discovered.

And, in my humble opinion, very satisfactorily discovered, he replied.

Again, I said, there is no difficulty in seeing the nature of courage, and in what part that quality resides which gives the name of courageous to the State.

How do you mean?

Why, I said, everyone who calls any State courageous or cowardly, will be thinking of the part which fights and goes out to war on the State's behalf.

No one, he replied, would ever think of any other.

The rest of the citizens may be courageous or may be cowardly, but their courage or cowardice will not, as I conceive, have the effect of making the city either the one or the other.

No.

The city will be courageous also by one part of herself, in which resides the power to preserve under all circumstances that opinion about the nature and description of things to be feared in which our legislator educated them; and this is what you term courage.

I should like to hear what you are saying once more, for I do not think that I perfectly understand you.

I mean that courage is a kind of preservation.

Preservation of what kind?

Of the opinion respecting things to be feared, what they are and of what nature, which the law implants through education; and I mean by the words "under all circumstances" to intimate that in pleasure or in pain, or under the influence of desire or fear, a man preserves and does not lose this opinion. Shall I give you an illustration?

If you please.

You know, I said, that dyers, when they want to dye wool for making the true sea-purple, begin by choosing the white from among all the colors available; this they prepare and dress with much care and pains, in order that the white ground may take the purple hue in full perfection. The dyeing then proceeds; and whatever is dyed in this manner becomes a fast color, and no washing either with lyes or without them can take away the bloom. But, when the ground has not been duly prepared, you will have noticed how poor is the look either of purple or of any other color.

Yes, he said; I know that they have a washed-out and ridiculous appearance.

Then now, I said, you will understand that our object in selecting our soldiers, and educating them in music and gymnastic, was very similar; we were contriving influences which would prepare them to take the dye of the laws in perfection, and the color of their opinion about dangers and of every other opinion was to be indelibly fixed by their nurture and training, not to be washed away by such potent lyes as pleasure—mightier agent far in washing the soul than any soda or lye—or by sorrow, fear, and desire, the mightiest of all other solvents. And this sort of universal saving power of true opinion in conformity with law about real and false dangers I call and maintain to be courage, unless you disagree.

But I agree, he replied; for I suppose that you mean to exclude mere right belief about dangers when it has grown up without instruction, such as that of a wild beast or of a slave—this, in your opinion, is something not quite in accordance with law, which in any case should have another name than courage.

Most certainly.

Then I concede courage to be such as you describe.

Excellent, said I, and if you add the words "of a citizen," you will not be far wrong—hereafter, if you agree, we will carry the examination of courage further, but at present we are seeking not for courage but justice; and for the purpose of our inquiry we have said enough.

You are right, he replied.

Two virtues remain to be discovered in the State—first, temperance, and then justice which is the end of our search.

Very true.

Now, can we find justice without troubling ourselves about temperance?

I do not know how that can be accomplished, he said, nor do I desire that justice should be brought to light and temperance lost sight of; and therefore I wish that you would do me the favor of considering temperance first.

Certainly, I replied, I should not be justified in refusing your request.

Then consider, he said.

Yes, I replied; I will; and as far as I can at present see, temperance has more of the nature of harmony and symphony than have the preceding virtues.

How so? he asked.

Temperance, I replied, is the ordering or controlling of certain pleasures and desires; this is curiously enough implied in the saying of "a man being his own master"; and and other traces of the same notion may be found in language, may they not?

No doubt, he said.

There is something ridiculous in the expression "master of himself"; for the master must also be the servant and the servant the master, since in all these modes of speaking the same person is denoted.

Certainly.

The meaning of this expression is, I believe, that there is within the man's own soul a better and also a worse principle; and when the better has the worse under control, then he is said to be master of himself; and this is a term of praise: but when, owing to evil education or association, the better principle, which is also the smaller, is overwhelmed by the greater mass of the worse—in this case he is blamed and is called the slave of self and dissolute.

Yes, there is reason in that.

And now, I said, look at our newly created State, and there you will find one of these two conditions realized; for the State, as you will acknowledge, may be justly called master of itself, if the words "temperance" and "self-mastery" truly express the rule of the better part over the worse.

On looking, he said, I see that what you say is true.

Let me further note that the manifold and complex pleasures and desires and pains are generally found in children and women and servants, and in the freemen so called who are of the lowest and more numerous class.

Certainly, he said.

Whereas the simple and moderate desires, which follow reason and are under the guidance of mind and true opinion, are to be found only in a few, and those the best born and best educated.

Very true.

These too, as you may perceive, have a place in your State; and the meaner desires of the many are held down by the desires and wisdom of the more virtuous few.

That I perceive, he said.

Then if there be any city which may be described as master of its own pleasures and desires, and master of itself, ours may claim such a designation?

Certainly, he replied.

It may also for all these reasons be called temperate?

Yes.

And if there be any State in which rulers and subjects will be agreed as to the question who are to rule, that again will be our State? Do you think so?

I do, emphatically.

And the citizens being thus agreed among themselves, in which class will temperance be found—in the rulers or in the subjects?

In both, as I should imagine, he replied.

Do you observe that we were not badly inspired in our guess that temperance bore some resemblance to harmony?

Why so?

Why, because temperance is unlike courage and wisdom, each of which resides in a part only, the one making the State wise and the other valiant; not so temperance, which extends to the whole, and runs through all the notes of the scale, and produces a unison of the weaker and the stronger and the middle class, whether you suppose them to be stronger or weaker in wisdom or power or numbers or wealth, or anything else you please. Most truly then may we deem this unity of mind to be temperance, an agreement of the naturally superior and inferior as to the right of rule of either both in states and individuals.

I entirely agree with you.

And so, I said, we may consider three out of the four virtues to have been discovered in our State. What remainder is there of qualities which make a state virtuous? For this, it is evident, must be justice.

The inference is obvious.

The time then has arrived, Glaucon, when, like huntsmen, we should surround the cover, and look sharp that justice does not steal away, and pass out of sight and escape us; for beyond a doubt she is somewhere in this country: watch therefore and strive to catch a sight of her, and if you see her first, let me know.

Would that I could! but you will do right to regard me rather as a follower who has just eyes enough to see what you show him.

Offer up a prayer with me and follow.

I will, but you must show me the way.

Here is no path, I said, and the wood is dark and perplexing; still we must push on.

Let us push on.

Here I saw something: Halloo! I said, I begin to perceive a track, and I believe that the quarry will not escape.

Good news, he said.

Truly, I said, we are stupid fellows.

Why so?

Why, my dear friend, far back from the beginning of our inquiry, justice has been lying at our feet, and we never saw her; nothing could be more ridiculous. Like people who go about looking for what they have in their hands, we looked not at what we were seeking, but at what was far off in the distance; and that, I suppose, was how we missed her.

What do you mean?

I mean to say that for a long time past we have been talking or hearing of justice, and yet have failed to recognize that we were in some sense actually describing it.

I grow impatient at the length of your exordium.

Well then, tell me, I said, whether I am right or not: You remember the original principle which we laid down at the foundation of the State; we decided, and more than once insisted, that one man should practice one occupation only, that to which his nature was best adapted —now justice, in my view, either is this principle or is some form of it.

Yes, we did.

Further, we affirmed that justice was doing one's own business, and not being a busybody; we said so again and again, and many others have said the same to us.

Yes, we said so.

Then to attend to one's own business, in some form or another, may be assumed to be justice. Do you know my evidence for this?

No, but I should like to be told.

Because I think that this is the virtuous quality which remains in the State when the other virtues of temperance and courage and wisdom are abstracted; and that this not only made it possible for them to appear, but is also their preservative as long as they remain; and we were saying that if the three were discovered by us, justice would be the fourth or remaining one.

That follows of necessity.

If we are asked to determine which of these four qualities by its presence will contribute most to the excellence of our State, whether the agreement of rulers and subjects, or the preservation in the soldiers of the opinion which the law ordains about the true nature of dangers, or wisdom and watchfulness in the rulers, or this other which is found in children and women, slave and freeman, artisan, ruler, subject (I mean the quality of every one doing his own work, and not being a busybody), the decision is not so easy.

Certainly, he replied, there would be a difficulty in saying which.

Then the attention of each individual to his own work appears to be a quality rivaling wisdom, temperance, and courage, with reference to the excellence of the State.

Yes, he said.

And the only virtue which, from that point of view, is of equal importance with them, is justice?

Exactly.

Let us look at the question also in this way: Are not the rulers in a State those to whom you would entrust the office of determining suits at law?

Certainly.

In the decision of such suits will any principle be prior to this, that a man may neither take what is another's nor be deprived of what is his own?

No.

Because it is a just principle?

Yes.

Then on this view also justice will be admitted to be the having and doing what is a man's own, and belongs to him?

Very true.

Think, now, and say whether you agree with me or not. Suppose a carpenter sets out to do the business of a cobbler, or a cobbler that of a carpenter; and suppose them to exchange their implements or social position, or the same person to try to undertake the work of both, or whatever be the change; do you think that any great harm would result to the State?

Not much.

But when the cobbler or any other man whom nature designed to be a trader, having his heart lifted up by wealth or strength or the number of his followers or any like advantage, attempts to force his way into the class of warriors, or a warrior into that of legislators and guardians, to which he ought not to aspire, and when these exchange their implements and their social position with those above them; or when one man would be trader, legislator, and warrior all in one, then I think you will agree with me in saying that this interchange and this meddling of one with another is the ruin of the State.

Most true.

Seeing then, I said, that there are three distinct classes, any meddling of one with another, or the change of one into another, is the greatest harm to the State, and may be most justly termed evil-doing?

Precisely.

And the greatest degree of evil-doing to one's own city would be termed by you injustice?

Certainly.

This then is injustice; and on the other hand when the three main classes, traders, auxiliaries, and guardians, each do their own business, that is justice, and will make the city just.

I agree with you.

We will not, I said, be over-positive as yet; but if, on trial, this conception of justice be verified in the individual as well as in the State, there will be no longer any room for doubt; if it be not verified, we must have a fresh inquiry. First let us complete the old investigation, which we began, as you remember, under the impression that, if we could previously examine justice on the larger scale, there would be less difficulty in discerning her in the individual. That larger example appeared to be the State, and accordingly we constructed as good a one as we could, knowing well that in the good State justice would be found. Let the discovery which we made be now applied to the individual—if they agree, we shall be satisfied; or, if there be a difference in the individual, we will come back to the State and have another trial of the theory. The friction of the two when rubbed together may possibly strike the light of justice, from which we can kindle a steady flame in our souls.

That will be in regular course; let us do as you say.

I proceeded to ask: When two things, a greater and less, are called by the same name, are they like or unlike in so far as they are called the same?

Like, he replied.

The just man then, if we regard the idea of justice only, will be like the just State?

He will.

And a State was thought by us to be just when the three classes in the State severally did their own business; and also thought to be temperate and valiant and wise by reason of certain other affections and qualities of these same classes?

True, he said.

And so of the individual: we may assume that he has the same three principles in his own soul which are found in the State; and he may be rightly described in the same terms, because he is affected in the same manner?

Certainly, he said.

Once more then, O my friend, we have alighted upon an easy question—whether the soul has these three principles or not?

An easy question? Nay, rather, Socrates, the proverb holds that hard is the good.

Very true, I said; and I must impress upon you, Glaucon, that in my opinion our present methods of argument are not at all adequate to the accurate solution of this question; the true method is another and a longer one. Still we may arrive at a solution not below the level of the previous inquiry.

May we not be satisfied with that? he said—under the circumstances, I am quite content.

I too, I replied, shall be extremely well satisfied.

Then faint not in pursuing the speculation, he said.

Must we not perforce acknowledge, I said, that in each of us there are the same principles and habits which there are in the State; for it is from the individual that the State derives them. Take the quality of passion or spirit—it would be ridiculous to imagine that this quality, when found in States, is not derived from the individuals who are supposed to possess it, e.g., the Thracians, Scythians, and in general the northern nations; and the same may be said of the love of knowledge, which may be claimed as the special characteristic of our part of the world, or of the love of money, which may, with equal truth, be attributed to the Phoenicians and Egyptians.

Exactly so, he said.

This is a fact, and there is no difficulty in perceiving it.

None whatever.

But the question is not quite so easy when we proceed to ask whether these principles are three or one; whether, that is to say, we learn with one part of our nature, are angry with another, and with a third part desire the satisfaction of our natural appetites; or whether the whole soul comes into play in each sort of action—to determine that is the difficulty.

Yes, he said; there lies the difficulty.

Then let us now try and determine whether they are the same or different.

How?

Clearly the same thing cannot act or be acted upon in the same part or in relation to the same thing at the same time, in contrary ways; and therefore whenever this contradiction occurs in things apparently the same, we know that they are really not the same, but different.

Good.

For example, I said, can the same thing be at rest and in motion at the same time in the same part?

Impossible.

Now, I said, let us have still more precise understanding, lest we should hereafter fall out by the way. Imagine the case of a man who is standing and also moving his hands and his head, and suppose a person to say that one and the same person is in motion and at rest at the same moment—to such a mode of speech we should object, and should rather say that one part of him is in motion while another is at rest.

Very true.

And suppose the objector to refine still further, and to draw the nice distinction that not only parts of tops, but whole tops, when they spin round with their pegs fixed on the spot, are at rest and in motion at the same time (and he may say the same of anything which revolves in the same spot), his objection would not be admitted by us, because in such cases things are not at rest and in motion in the same parts of themselves; we should rather say that they have both an axis and a circumference; and that the axis stands still, for there is no deviation from the perpendicular; and that the circumference goes round. But if, while revolving, the axis inclines either to the right or left, forwards or backwards, then in no point of view can they be at rest.

That is the correct mode of describing them, he replied.

Then none of these objections will confuse us, or incline us to believe that the same thing at the same time, in the same part or in relation to the same thing, can be contrary or act or be acted upon in contrary ways.

Certainly not, according to my way of thinking.

Yet, I said, that we may not be compelled to examine all such objections, and prove at length that they are untrue, let us assume their absurdity, and go forward on the understanding that hereafter, if this assumption turn out to be untrue, all the consequences which follow from it shall be withdrawn.

Yes, he said, that will be the best way.

Well, I said, would you not allow that assent and dissent, desire and aversion, attraction and repulsion, are all of them opposites, whether they are regarded as active or passive (for that makes no difference in the fact of their opposition)?

Yes, he said, they are opposites.

Well, I said, and hunger and thirst, and the desires in general, and again willing and wishing—all these you would refer to the classes already mentioned. You would say—would you not—that the soul of him who desires is either seeking after the object of desire; or is drawing toward herself the thing which she wishes to possess; or again—for she may merely consent that something should be offered to her—intimates her wish to have it by a nod of assent, as if she had been asked a question?

Very true.

And what would you say of unwillingness and dislike and the absence of desire; should not these be referred to the opposite class of repulsion and rejection?

Certainly.

Admitting this to be true of desire generally, let us suppose a particular class of desires, and out of these we will select hunger and thirst, as they are termed, which are the most obvious of them?

Let us take that class, he said.

The object of one is food, and of the other drink?

Yes.

And here comes the point: is not thirst the desire which the soul has of drink, and of drink only, not of drink qualified by anything else; for example, warm or cold, or much or little, or, in a word, drink of any particular sort? But if there is heat additional to the thirst, it will bring with it the desire of cold drink; or, if cold, then that of warm drink. And again, if the thirst is qualified by abundance or by smallness, it will become a desire for much or little drink, as the case may be: but thirst pure and simple will desire drink pure and simple, which is the natural satisfaction of thirst, as food is of hunger?

Yes, he said; the simple desire is, as you say, in every case of the simple object, and the qualified desire of the qualified object.

But here a confusion may arise; and I should wish to guard against an opponent starting up and saying that no man desires drink only, but good drink, or food only, but good food; for good is the universal object of desire, and if thirst be a desire, it will necessarily be thirst after good drink (or whatever its object is); and the same is true of every other desire.

Yes, he replied, the opponent might seem to be talking sense.

Nevertheless I should still maintain that of relatives some have a quality attached to either term of the relation; others are simple and have their correlatives simple.

I do not know what you mean.

Well, you know of course that the greater is relative to the less?

Certainly.

And the much greater to the much less?

Yes.

And the sometime greater to the sometime less, and the greater that is to be to the less that is to be?

Certainly, he said.

And so of more and less, and of other correlative terms, such as the double and the half, or again, the heavier and the lighter, the swifter and the slower; and of hot and cold, and of any other relatives—is not this true of all of them?

Yes.

And does not the same principle hold in the sciences? The object of science is knowledge (assuming that to be the true definition), but the object of a particular science is a particular kind of knowledge; I mean, for example, that the science of house-building is a kind of knowledge which is defined and distinguished from other kinds and is therefore termed architecture.

Certainly.

Because it has a particular quality which no other has?

Yes.

And it has this particular quality because it has an object of a particular kind; and this is true of the other arts and sciences?

Yes.

Now, then, if I have made myself clear, you will understand my original meaning in what I said about relatives. My meaning was, that if one term of a relation is taken alone, the other is taken alone; if one term is qualified, the other is also qualified. I do not mean to say that relative terms must possess all the same qualities as their correlates; that the science of health is healthy, or that of disease necessarily diseased, or that the sciences of good and evil are therefore good and evil; but only that, when the term science is no longer used absolutely, but has a qualified object which in this case is the nature of health and disease, it becomes defined, and is hence called not merely science, but the science of medicine.

I quite understand, and I think as you do.

Would you not say that thirst is one of these essentially relative terms, having clearly a relation——

Yes, thirst is relative to drink.

And a certain kind of thirst is relative to a certain kind of drink; but thirst taken alone is neither of much nor little, nor of good nor bad, nor of any particular kind of drink, but of drink only?

Certainly.

Then the soul of the thirsty one, in so far as he is thirsty, desires only drink; for this she yearns, and for this she strives?

That is plain.

And if you suppose something which pulls a thirsty soul away from drink, that must be different from the thirsty principle which draws him like a beast to drink; for, as we were saying, the same thing cannot at the same time with the same part of itself act in contrary ways about the same.

Impossible.

No more than you can say that the hands of the archer push and pull the bow at the same time, but what you say is that one hand pushes and the other pulls.

Exactly so, he replied.

Now are there times when men are thirsty, and yet unwilling to drink?

Yes, he said, it constantly happens.

And in such a case what is one to say? Would you not say that there was something in the soul bidding a man to drink, and something else forbidding him, which is other and stronger than the principle which bids him?

I should say so.

And the prohibition in such cases is derived from reasoning, whereas the motives which lead and attract proceed from passions and diseases?

Clearly.

Then we may fairly assume that they are two, and that they differ from one another; the one with which a man reasons, we may call the rational principle of the soul, the other, with which he loves and hungers and thirsts and feels the flutterings of any other desire, may be termed the irrational or appetitive, the ally of sundry pleasures and satisfactions?

Yes, he said, we may fairly assume them to be different.

So much, then, for the definition of two of the principles existing in the soul. And what now of passion, or spirit? Is it a third, or akin to one of the preceding?

I should be inclined to say—akin to desire.

Well, I said, there is a story which I remember to have heard, and in which I put faith. The story is, that Leontius, the son of Aglaion, coming up one day from the Piraeus, under the north wall on the outside, observed some dead bodies lying on the ground at the place of execution. He felt a desire to see them, and also a dread and abhorrence of them; for a time he struggled and covered his eyes, but at length the desire got the better of him; and forcing them open, he ran up to the dead bodies, saying, Look, ye wretches, take your fill of the fair sight.

I have heard the story myself, he said.

The moral of the tale is that anger at times goes to war with desire, as though they were two distinct things.

Yes; that is the meaning, he said.

And are there not many other cases in which we observe that when a man's desires violently prevail over his reason, he reviles himself, and is angry at the violence within him, and that in this struggle, which is like the struggle of factions in a State, his spirit is on the side of his reason—but for the passionate or spirited element to take part with the desires when reason decides that she should not be opposed, is a sort of thing which I believe that you never observed occurring in yourself, nor, as I should imagine, in anyone else?

Certainly not.

Suppose that a man thinks he has done a wrong to another, the nobler he is the less able is he to feel indignant at any suffering, such as hunger, or cold, or any other pain which the injured person may inflict upon him—these he deems to be just, and, as I say, his spirit refuses to be excited by them.

True, he said.

But when a man thinks that he is the sufferer of the wrong, then the spirit within him boils and chafes, and is on the side of what it believes to be justice; and though it suffers hunger of cold or other pain, it is only the more determined to persevere and conquer. Such a noble spirit will not be quelled until it has achieved its object or been slain, or until it has been recalled by the reason within, like a dog by the shepherd?

The illustration is perfect, he replied; and in our State, as we were saying, the auxiliaries were to be dogs, and to hear the voice of the rulers, who are their shepherds.

Yes, I said, you understand me admirably; there is, however, a further point which I wish you to consider.

What point?

You remember that passion or spirit appeared at first sight to be a kind of desire, but now we should say quite the contrary; for in the conflict of the soul spirit is arrayed on the side of the rational principle.

Most assuredly.

But a further question arises: Is passion different from reason also, or only a kind of reason; in which latter case, instead of three principles in the soul, there will only be two, the rational and the concupiscent? or rather, as the State was composed of three classes, traders, auxiliaries, counsellors, so may there not be in the individual soul a third element which is passion or spirit, and when not corrupted by bad education is the natural auxiliary of reason?

Yes, he said, there must be a third.

Yes, I replied, if passion, which has already been shown to be different from desire, turn out also to be different from reason.

But that is easily proved—We may observe even in young children that they are full of spirit almost as soon as they are born, whereas some of them never seem to attain to the use of reason, and most of them late enough.

Excellent, I said, and you may see passion equally in brute animals, which is a further proof of the truth of what you are saying. And we may once more appeal to the words of Homer, which have been already quoted by us,

He smote his breast, and thus rebuked his heart

for in this verse Homer has clearly supposed the power which reasons about the better and worse to be different from the unreasoning anger which is rebuked by it.

Very true, he said.

And so, after much tossing, we have reached land, and are fairly agreed that the same principles which exist in the State exist also in the individual, and that they are three in number.

Exactly.

Must we not then infer that the individual is wise in the same way and in virtue of the same quality which makes the State wise?

Certainly.

Also that the State is brave in the same way and by the same quality as an individual is brave, and that there is the same correspondence in regard to the other virtues?

Assuredly.

Therefore the individual will be acknowledged by us to be just in the same way in which the State has been found just?

That follows of course.

We cannot but remember that the justice of the State consisted in each of the three classes doing the work of its own class?

I do not think we have forgotten, he said.

We must now record in our memory that the individual in whom the several components of his nature do their own work will be just, and will do his own work?

Yes, he said, we must record that important fact.

First, it is proper for the rational principle, which is wise, and has the care of the whole soul, to rule, and for the spirit to be the subject and ally?

Certainly.

And, as we were saying, the blending of music and gymnastic will bring them into accord, nerving and sustaining the reason with noble words and lessons, and moderating and soothing and civilizing the wildness of passion by harmony and rhythm?

Quite true, he said.

And these two, thus nurtured and educated, and having learned truly to know their own functions, will rule over the concupiscent, which in each of us is the largest part of the soul and by nature most insatiable of gain; over this they will keep guard, lest, waxing great and strong with the fullness of bodily pleasures, as they are termed, the concupiscent soul, no longer confined to her own sphere, should attempt to enslave and rule those who are not her natural-born subjects, and overturn the whole life of man?

Very true, he said.

Both together will they not be the best defenders of the whole soul and the whole body against attacks from without; the one counseling, and the other going out to fight as the leader directs, and courageously executing his commands and counsels?

True.

Likewise it is by reference to spirit that an individual man is deemed courageous, because his spirit retains in pleasure and in pain the commands of reason about what he ought or ought not to fear?

Right, he replied.

And we call him wise on account of that little part which rules, and which proclaims these commands; the part in which is situated the knowledge of what is for the interest of each of the three parts and of the whole?

Assuredly.

And would you not say that he is temperate who has these same elements in friendly harmony, in whom the one ruling principle of reason, and the two subject ones of spirit and desire, are equally agreed that reason ought to rule, and do not rebel?

Certainly, he said, that is a precise account of temperance whether in the State or individual.

And, finally, I said, a man will be just in that way and by that quality which we have often mentioned.

That is very certain.

And is justice dimmer in the individual, and is her form different, or is she the same which we found her to be in the State?

There is no difference in my opinion, he said.

Because, if any doubt is still lingering in our minds, a few commonplace instances will satisfy us of the truth of what I am saying.

What sort of instances do you mean?

If the case is put to us, must we not admit that the just State, or the man of similar nature who has been trained in the principles of such a State, will be less likely than the unjust to make away with a deposit of gold or silver? Would any one deny this?

No one, he replied.

Will such a man ever be involved in sacrilege or theft, or treachery either to his friends or to his country?

Never.

Neither will he ever, for any reason, break faith where there have been oaths or agreements?

Impossible.

No one will be less likely to commit adultery, neglect his father and mother, or fail in his religious duties?

No one.

And the reason for all this is that each part of him is doing its own business, whether in ruling or being ruled?

Exactly so.

Are you satisfied then that the quality which makes such men and such states is justice, or do you hope to discover some other?

Not I, indeed.

Then our dream has been realized, and the suspicion which we expressed that, at the beginning of our work of construction, some divine power must have conducted us to a primary form of justice, has now been verified?

Yes, certainly.

And the division of labor which required the carpenter and the shoemaker and the rest of them to devote himself to the work for which he is naturally fitted, and to do nothing else, was a shadow of justice, and for that reason it was of use?

Clearly.

And in reality justice was such as we were describing, being concerned however, not with a man's external affairs, but with an inner relationship in which he himself is more truly concerned; for the just man does not permit the several elements within him to interfere with one another, or any of them to do the work of others—he sets in order his own inner life, and is his own master and his own law, and at peace with himself; and when he has bound together the three principles within him, which may be compared to the higher, lower, and middle notes of the scale, and any that are intermediate between them—when he has bound all these together, and is no longer many, but has become one entirely temperate and perfectly adjusted nature, then he proceeds to act, if he has to act, whether in a matter of property, or in the treatment of the body, or in some affair of politics or private business; always thinking and calling that which preserves and cooperates with this harmonious condition, just and good action, and the knowledge which presides over it, wisdom, and that which at any time impairs this condition, he will call unjust action, and the opinion which presides over it ignorance.

You have said the exact truth, Socrates.

Very good; and if we were to affirm that we had discovered the just man and the just State, and the nature of justice in each of them, we should not be far from the truth?

Most certainly not.

May we say so, then?

Let us say so.

And now, I said, injustice has to be considered.

Clearly.

Must not injustice be a strife which arises among the same three principles—a meddlesomeness, and interference, and rising up of a part of the soul against the whole, an assertion of unlawful authority, which is made by a rebellious subject against a true prince, of whom he is the natural vassal—what is all this confusion and delusion but injustice and intemperance and cowardice and ignorance, and, in short, every form of vice?

Exactly so.

And if the nature of justice and injustice is known, then the meaning of acting unjustly and being unjust, or again of acting justly, is now also perfectly clear?

How so? he said.

Why, I said, they are like disease and health; being in the soul just what disease and health are in the body.

How so? he said.

Why, I said, that which is healthy causes health, and that which is unhealthy causes disease.

Yes.

And just actions cause justice, and unjust actions cause injustice?

That is certain.

And the creation of health is the institution of a natural order and government of one by another in the parts of the body; and the creation of disease is the production of a state of things at variance with this natural order?

True.

And is not the creation of justice the institution of a natural order and government of one by another in the parts of the soul, and the creation of injustice the production of a state of things at variance with the natural order?

Exactly so, he said.

Then virtue is the health and beauty and well-being of the soul, and vice the disease and weakness and deformity of the same?

True.

And how are virtue and vice acquired—is it not by good and evil practices?

Assuredly.

The time has come, then, to answer the final question of the comparative advantage of justice and injustice: Which is the more profitable, to be just and act justly and honorably, whether one's character is or is not known, or to be unjust and act unjustly, if one is unpunished, that is to say unreformed?

In my judgment, Socrates, the question has now become ridiculous. We know that, when the bodily constitution is gone, life is no longer endurable, though pampered with all kinds of meats and drinks, and having all wealth and all power; and shall we be told that when the natural health of our vital principle is undermined and corrupted, life is still worth having to a man, if only he be allowed to do whatever he likes, except to take steps to acquire justice and virtue and escape from injustice and vice; assuming them both to be such as we have described?

Yes, I said, the question is, as you say, ridiculous. Still, as we are near the spot at which we may see the truth in the clearest manner with our eyes, let us not faint by the way.

Certainly not, he replied.

Come here, then, I said, and behold the various forms of vice, those of them, I mean, which are worth looking at.

I am following you, he replied: proceed.

I said, The argument seems to have reached a height from which, as from some tower of speculation, a man may look down and see that virtue is one, but that the forms of vice are innumerable; there being four special ones which are deserving of note.

What do you mean? he said.

I mean, I replied, that there appear to be as many forms of the soul as there are distinct forms of the State.

How many?

There are five of the State, and five of the soul, I said.

What are they?

The first, I said, is that which we have been describing, and which may be given either of two names, monarchy or aristocracy, according as rule is exercised by one man distinguished among the ruling class or by more.

True, he replied.

But I regard the two names as describing one form only; for whether the government is in the hands of one or many, if the governors have been bred and trained in the manner which we have supposed, the fundamental laws of the State will not be disturbed.

Probably not, he replied.

ON LIBERTY

John Stuart Mill

Introduction

In England, from the peculiar circumstances of our political history, though the yoke of opinion is perhaps heavier, that of law is lighter, than in most other countries of Europe; and there is considerable jealousy of direct interference, by the legislative or the executive power, with private conduct; not so much from any just regard for the independence of the individual, as from the still subsisting habit of looking on the government as representing an opposite interest to the public. The majority have not yet learned to feel the power of the government their power, or its opinions their opinions. When they do so, individual liberty will probably be as much exposed to invasion from the government, as it already is from public opinion. But, as yet, there is a considerable amount of feeling ready to be called forth against any attempt of the law to control individuals in things in which they have not hitherto been accustomed to be controlled by it; and this with very little discrimination as to whether the matter is, or is not, within the legitimate sphere of legal control; insomuch that the feeling, highly salutary on the whole, is perhaps quite as often misplaced as well grounded in the particular instances of its application. There is, in fact, no recognized principle by which the propriety or impropriety of government interference is customarily tested. People decide according to their personal preferences. Some, whenever they see any good to be done, or evil to be remedied, would willingly instigate the government to undertake the business; while others prefer to bear almost any amount of social evil, rather than add one to the departments of human interests amenable to government control. And men range themselves on one or the other side in any particular case, according to this general direction of their sentiments; or according to the degree of interest which they feel in the particular thing which it is proposed that the government should do, or according to the belief they entertain that the govern-

FROM *On Liberty*, first printed in 1859.

ment would, or would not, do it in the manner they prefer; but very rarely on account of any opinion to which they consistently adhere, as to what things are fit to be done by a government. And it seems to me that in consequence of this absence of rule or principle, one side is at present as often wrong as the other: the interference of government is, with about equal frequency, improperly invoked and improperly condemned.

The object of this essay is to assert one very simple principle, as entitled to govern absolutely the dealings of society with the individual in the way of compulsion and control, whether the means used be physical force in the form of legal penalties, or the moral coercion of public opinion. That principle is, that the sole end for which mankind are warranted, individually or collectively, in interfering with the liberty of action of any of their number, is self-protection. That the only purpose for which power can be rightfully exercised over any member of a civilized community, against his will, is to prevent harm to others. His own good, either physical or moral, is not a sufficient warrant. He cannot rightfully be compelled to do or forbear because it will be better for him to do so, because it will make him happier, because, in the opinions of others, to do so would be wise, or even right. These are good reasons for remonstrating with him, or reasoning with him, or persuading him, or entreating him, but not for compelling him, or visiting him with any evil in case he do otherwise. To justify that, the conduct from which it is desired to deter him must be calculated to produce evil to someone else. The only part of the conduct of anyone, for which he is amenable to society, is that which concerns others. In the part which merely concerns himself, his independence is, of right, absolute. Over himself, over his own body and mind, the individual is sovereign.

It is perhaps hardly necessary to say that this doctrine is meant to apply only to human beings in the maturity of their faculties. We are not speaking of children, or of young persons below the age which the law may fix as that of manhood of womanhood. Those who are still in a state to require being taken care of by others, must be protected against their own actions as well as against external injury. For the same reason, we may leave out of consideration those backward states of society in which the race itself may be considered as in its nonage. The early difficulties in the way of spontaneous progress are so great, and there is seldom any choice of means for overcoming them; and a ruler full of the spirit of improvement is warranted in the use of any expedients that will attain an end, perhaps otherwise unattainable. Despotism is a legitimate mode of government in dealing with barbarians, provided the end be their improvement, and the means justified by actually effecting that end. Liberty, as a principle, has no application to any state of things anterior to the time when mankind have become capable of being improved by free and equal discussion. Until then, there is nothing for them but implicit obedience to an Akbar or a Charlemagne, if they are so fortunate as to find one. But as soon as mankind have attained the capacity of being guided to their own improvement by conviction or persuasion (a period long since reached in all nations with whom we need here concern ourselves), compulsion, either in the direct form or in that of pains and penalties for non-compliance, is no longer admissible as a means to their own good, and justifiable only for the security of others.

It is proper to state that I forego any advantage which could be derived to my argument from the idea of abstract right, as a thing independent of utility. I regard utility as the ultimate appeal on all ethical questions; but it must be utility in the largest sense, grounded on the permanent interests of a man as a progressive being. Those interests, I contend, authorized the subjection of individual spontaneity to external control, only in respect to those actions of each which concern the interests of other people. If anyone does an act hurtful to others, there is a *prima facie* case for punishing him, by law, or, where legal penalties are not safely applicable, by general disapprobation. There are also many positive acts for the benefit of others, which he may rightfully be compelled to perform: such as to give evidence in a court of justice; to bear his fair share in the common defense, or in any other joint work necessary to the interest of the society of which he enjoys the protection; and to perform certain acts of individual beneficence, such as saving a fellow-creature's life, or interposing to protect the defenseless against ill-usage, things which whenever it is obviously a man's duty to do, he may rightfully be made responsible to society for not doing. A person may cause evil to others not only by his actions but by his inaction, and in either case he is justly accountable to them for the injury. . . .

But there is a sphere of action in which society, as distinguished from the individual, has, if any, only an indirect interest; comprehending all that portion of a person's life and conduct which affects only himself, or if it also affects others, only with their free, voluntary, and undeceived consent and participation. When I say only himself, I mean directly, and in the first instance; for whatever affects himself, may affect others through himself; and the objection which may be grounded on this contingency, will receive consideration in the sequel. This, then, is the appropriate region of human liberty. It comprises, *first,* the inward domain of consciousness; demanding liberty of conscience in the most comprehensive sense; liberty of thought and feeling; absolute freedom of opinion and sentiment on all subjects, practical or speculative, scientific, moral, or theological. The liberty of expressing and publishing opinions may seem to fall under a different principle, since it belongs to that part of the conduct of an individual which concerns other people; but, being almost of as much importance as the liberty of thought itself, and resting in great part on the same reasons, is practically inseparable from it. *Secondly,* the principle requires liberty of tastes and pursuits; of framing the plan of our life to suit our own character; of doing as we like, subject to such consequences as may follow: without impediment from our fellow-creatures, so long as what we do does not harm them, even though they should think our conduct foolish, perverse, or wrong. *Thirdly,* from this liberty of each individual, follows the liberty, within the same limits, of combination among individuals; freedom to unite, for any purpose not involving harm to others: the persons combining being supposed to be of full age, and not forced or deceived.

No society in which these liberties are not, on the whole, respected, is free, whatever may be its form of government; and none is completely free in which they do not exist absolute and unqualified. The only freedom which deserves the name, is that of pursuing our own good in our own way, so long as we do not attempt to deprive others of theirs, or impede their efforts to obtain it. Each is the proper guardian of his own health, whether bodily, or mental and spiritual. Mankind are greater gainers by suffering each other to live as seems good to themselves, than by compelling each to live as seems good to the rest. . . .

Of the Liberty of Thought and Discussion

The time, it is to be hoped, is gone by, when any defense would be necessary of the "liberty of the press" as one of the securities against corrupt or tyrannical government. No argument, we may suppose, can now be needed against permitting a legislature or an executive, not identified in interest with the people, to prescribe opinions to them, and determine what doctrines or what arguments they shall be allowed to hear. This aspect of the question, besides, has been so often and so triumphantly enforced by preceding writers, that it need not be specially insisted on in this place. Though the law of England, on the subject of the press, is as servile to this day as it was in the time of the Tudors, there is little danger of its being actually put in force against political discussion, except during some temporary panic, when fear of insurrection drives ministers and judges from their propriety; and, speaking generally, it is not, in constitutional countries, to be apprehended that the government, whether completely responsible to the people or not, will often attempt to control the expression of opinion, except when in doing so it makes itself the organ of the general intolerance of the public. Let us suppose, therefore, that the government is entirely at one with the people, and never thinks of exerting any power of coercion unless in agreement with what it conceives to be their voice. But I deny the right of the people to exercise such coercion, either by themselves or by their government. The power itself is illegitimate. The best government has no more title to it than the worst. It is as noxious, or more noxious, when exerted in accordance with public opinion, than when in opposition to it. If all mankind minus one were of one opinion, and only one person were of the contrary opinion, mankind would be no more justified in silencing that one person, than he, if he had the power, would be justified in silencing mankind. Were an opinion a personal possession of no value except to the owner; if to be obstructed in the enjoyment of it were simply a private injury, it would make some difference whether the injury was inflicted only on a few persons or on many. But the peculiar evil of silencing the expression of an opinion is, that it is robbing the human race: posterity as well as the existing generation; those who dissent from the opinion, still more than those who hold it. If the opinion is right, they are deprived of the opportunity of exchanging error for truth; if wrong, they lose, what is almost as great a benefit, the clearer perception and livelier impression of truth, produced by its collision with error.

It is necessary to consider separately these two hypotheses, each of which has a distinct branch of the argument corresponding to it. We can never be sure that the opinion we are endeavoring to stifle is a false opinion; and if we were sure, stifling it would be an evil still.

First: the opinion which it is attempting to suppress by authority may possibly be true. Those who desire to suppress it, of course deny its truth; but they are not infallible. They have no authority to decide the question for all mankind, and exclude every other person from the means of judging. To refuse a hearing to an opinion, because they are sure that it is false, is to assume that *their* certainty is the same thing as *absolute* certainty. All silencing of discussion is an assumption of infallibility. Its condemnation may be allowed to rest on this common argument, not the worse for being common. . . .

The objection likely to be made to this argument would probably take some such form as the following. There is no greater assumption of infallibility in forbidding the propagation of error, than in any other thing which is done by public authority on its own judgment and responsibility. Judgment is given to men that they may use it. Because it may be used erroneously, are men to be told that they ought not to use it at all? To prohibit what they think pernicious, is not claiming exemption from error, but fulfilling the duty incumbent on them, although fallible, of acting on their conscientious conviction. If we were never to act on our opinions, because those opinions may be wrong, we should leave all our interests uncared for, and all our duties unperformed. . . . Men, and governments, must act to the best of their ability. There is no such thing as absolute certainty, but there is assurance sufficient for the purposes of human life. We may, and must, assume our opinion to be true for the guidance of our own conduct: and it is assuming no more when we forbid bad men to pervert society by the propagation of opinions which we regard as false and pernicious.

I answer that it is assuming very much more. There is the greatest difference between presuming an opinion to be true because, with every opportunity for contesting it, it has not been refuted, and assuming its truth for the purpose of not permitting its refutation. Complete liberty of contradicting and disproving our opinion is the very condition which justifies us in assuming its truth for purposes of action; and on no other terms can a being with human faculties have any rational assurance of being right.

When we consider either the history of opinion, or the ordinary conduct of human life, to what is it to be ascribed that the one and the other are no worse than they are? Not certainly to the inherent force of the human understanding; for, on any matter not self-evident, there are ninety-nine persons totally incapable of judging of it for one who is capable; and the capacity of the hundredth person is only comparative: for the majority of the eminent men of every past generation held many opinions now known to be erroneous, and did or approved numerous things which no one will now justify. Why is it, then, that there is on the whole a preponderance among mankind of rational opinions and rational conduct? If there really is this preponderance—which there must be unless human affairs are, and have always been, in an almost desperate state—it is owing to a quality of the human mind, the source of everything respectable in man either as an intellectual or as a moral being, namely, that his errors are corrigible. He is capable of rectifying his mistakes, by discussion and experience. Not by experience alone. There must be discussion, to show how experience is to be interpreted. Wrong opinions and practices gradually yield to fact and argument; but facts and arguments, to produce any effect on the mind, must be brought before it. Very few facts are able to tell their own story, without comments to bring out their meaning. The whole strength and value, then, of human judgment, depending on the one property, that it can be set right when it is wrong, reliance can be placed on it only when the means of setting it right are kept constantly at hand. In the case of any person whose judgment is really deserving of confidence, how has it become so? Because he has kept his mind open to criticism of his opinions and conduct. Because it has been his practice to listen to all that could be said against him; to profit by as much of it as was just, and expound to himself, and upon occasion to others, the fallacy of what was fallacious. Because he has felt that the only way in which a human being can make some approach to knowing the whole of a subject, is by hearing what can be said about it by persons of every variety of opinion, and studying all modes in which it can be looked at by every character of mind. No wise man ever acquired his wisdom in any mode but this; nor is it in the nature of human intellect to become wise in any other manner. The steady habit of correcting and completing his own opinion by collating it with those of others, so far from causing doubt and hesitation in carrying it into practice, is the only stable foundation for a just reliance on it: for, being cognizant of all that can, at least obviously, be said against him, and having taken up his position against all gainsayers—knowing that he has sought for objections and difficulties, instead of avoiding them, and has shut out no light which can be thrown upon the subject from any quarter—he has a right to think his judgment better than that of any person, or any multitude, who have not gone through a similar process.

. . . The beliefs which we have most warrant for, have no safeguard to rest on but a standing invitation to the whole world to prove them unfounded. If the challenge is not accepted, or is accepted and the attempt fails, we are far enough from certainty still; but we have done the best that the existing state of human reason admits of; we have neglected nothing that could give the truth a chance of reaching us: if the lists are kept open, we may hope that if there be a better truth, it will be found when the human mind is capable of receiving it; and in the meantime we may rely on having attained such approach to truth as is possible in our own day. This is the amount of certainty attainable by a fallible being, and this the sole way of attaining it. . . .

In the present age—which has been described as "destitute of faith, but terrified at scepticism—in which people feel sure, not so much that their opinions are true, as that they should not know what to do without them—the claims of an opinion to be protected from public attack are rested not so much on its truth, as on its importance to society. There are, it is alleged, certain beliefs so useful, not to say indispensable, to well-being that it is as much the duty of governments to uphold those beliefs, as to protect any other of the interests of society. In a case of such necessity, and so directly in the line of their duty, something less than infallibility may, it is maintained, warrant, and even bind, governments to act on their own opinion, confirmed by the general opinion of mankind. It is also often argued, and still oftener thought, that none but bad men would desire to weaken these salutary beliefs; and there can be nothing wrong, it is thought, in restraining bad men, and prohibiting what only such men would wish to practice. This mode of thinking makes the justification of restraints on discussion not a question of the truth of doctrines, but of their usefulness; and flatters itself by that means to escape the responsibility of claiming to be an infallible judge of opinions. But those who thus satisfy themselves, do not perceive that the assumption of infallibility is merely shifted from one point to another. The usefulness of an opinion is itself a matter of opinion: as disputable, as open to discussion, and requiring discussion as much as the opinion itself. There is the same need of an infallible judge of opinions to decide an opinion to be noxious, as to decide it to be false, unless the opinion condemned has full opportunity to defending itself. And it will not do to say that the heretic may be allowed to maintain the utility or harmlessness of his opinion, though forbidden to maintain its truth. The truth of an opinion is part of its utility. If we would know whether or not it is desirable that a proposition should be believed, is it possible to exclude the consideration of whether or not it is true? In the opinion, not of bad men, but of the best men, no belief which is contrary to truth can be really useful: and can you prevent such men from urging that plea, when they are charged with culpability for denying some doctrine which they are told is useful, but which they believe to be false? . . .

Let us now pass to the second division of the argument, and dismissing the supposition that any of the received opinions may be false, let us assume them to be true, and examine into the worth of the manner in which they are likely to be held, when their truth is not freely and openly canvassed. However unwillingly a person who has a strong opinion may admit the possibility that his opinion may be false, he ought to be moved by the consideration that, however true it may be, if it is not fully, frequently, and fearlessly discussed, it will be held as a dead dogma, not a living truth.

There is a class of persons (happily not quite so numerous as formerly) who think it enough if a person assents undoubtingly to what they think true, though he has no knowledge whatever of the grounds of the opinion, and could not make a tenable defense of it against the most superficial objections. Such persons, if they can once get their creed taught from authority, naturally think that no good, and some harm, comes of its being allowed to be questioned. Where their influence prevails, they make it nearly impossible for the received opinion to be rejected wisely and considerately, though it may still be rejected rashly and ignorantly; for to shut out discussion entirely is seldom possible, and when it once gets in, beliefs not grounded on conviction are apt to give way before the slightest semblance of an argument. Waiving, however, this possibility—assuming that the true opinion abides in the mind, but abides as a prejudice, a belief independent of, and proof against, argument—this is not the way in which truth ought to be held by a rational being. This is not knowing the truth. Truth, thus held, is but one superstition the more, accidentally clinging to the words which enunciate a truth. . . .

. . . The greatest orator, save one, of antiquity, has left it on record that he always studied his adversary's case with as great, if not still greater, intensity than even his own. What Cicero practiced as the means of forensic success requires to be imitated by all who study any subject in order to arrive at the truth. He who knows only his own side of the case, knows little of that. His reasons may be good, and no one may have been able to refute them. But if he is equally unable to refute the reasons on the opposite side; if he does not so much as know what they are, he has no ground for preferring either opinion. The rational position for him would be suspension of judgment, and unless he contents himself with that, he is either led by authority, or adopts, like the generality of the world, the side to which he feels most inclination. Nor is it enough that he should hear the arguments of adversaries from his own teachers, presented as they state them, and accompanied by what they offer as refutations. That is not the way to do justice to the arguments, or bring them into real contact with his own mind. He must be able to hear them from persons who actually believe them; who defend them in earnest, and do their very utmost for them. He must know them in their most plausible and persuasive form; he must feel the whole force of the difficulty which the true view of the subject has to encounter and dispose of; else he will never really possess himself of the portion of truth which meets and removes that difficulty. Ninety-nine in a hundred of what are called educated men are in this condition; even of those who can argue fluently for their opinions. Their conclusion may be true, but it might be false for anything they know: they have never thrown themselves into the mental position of those who think differently from them, and considered what such persons may have to say; and consequently they do not, in any proper sense of the word, know the doctrine which they themselves profess. They do not know those parts of it which explain and justify the remainder; the considerations which show that a fact which seemingly conflicts with another is reconcilable with it, or that, of two apparently strong reasons, one and not the other ought to be preferred. All that part of the truth which turns the scale, and decides the judgment of a completely informed mind, they are strangers to; nor is it ever really known but to those who have attended equally and impartially to both sides, and endeavored to see the reasons of both in the strongest light. . . .

If, however, the mischievous operation of the absence of free discussion, when the received opinions are true, were confined to leaving men ignorant of the grounds of those opinions, it might be thought that this, if an intellectual, is no moral evil, and does not affect the worth of the opinions, regarded in their influence on the character. The fact, however is that not only the grounds of the opinion are forgotten in the absence of discussion, but too often the meaning of the opinion itself. The words which convey it cease to suggest ideas, or suggest only a small portion of those they were originally employed to communicate. Instead of a vivid conception and a living belief, there remain only a few phrases retained by rote; or, if any part, the shell and husk only of the meaning is retained, the finer essence being lost. . . .

. . . When the mind is no longer compelled, in the same degree as at first, to exercise its vital powers on the questions which its belief presents to it, there is a progressive tendency to forget all of the belief except the formularies, or to give it a dull and torpid assent, as if accepting it on trust dispensed with the necessity of realizing it in consciousness, or testing it by personal experience, until it almost ceases to connect itself at all with the inner life of the human being. Then are seen the cases, so frequent in this age of the world as almost to form the majority, in which the creed remains as it were outside the mind, incrusting and petrifying it against all other influences addressed to the higher parts of our nature; manifesting its power by not suffering any fresh and living conviction to get in, but itself doing nothing for the mind or heart, except standing sentinel over them to keep them vacant. . . .

. . . All languages and literatures are full of general observations on life, both as to what it is, and how to conduct oneself in it; observations which everybody knows, which everybody repeats, or hears with acquiescence, which are received as truisms, yet of which most people first truly learn the meaning when experience, generally of a painful kind, has made it a reality to them. How often, when smarting under some unforeseen misfortune or disappointment, does a person call to mind some proverb or common saying, familiar to him all his life, the meaning of which, if he had ever before felt it as he does now, would have saved him from the calamity. There are indeed reasons for this, other than the absence of discussion; there are many truths of which the full meaning *cannot* be realized until personal experience has brought it home. But much more of the meaning even of these would have been understood, and what was understood would have been far more deeply impressed on the mind, if the man had been accustomed to hear it argued *pro* and *con* by people who did understand it. The fatal tendency of mankind to leave off thinking about a thing when it is no longer doubtful, is the cause of half their errors. A contemporary author has well spoken of "the deep slumber of a decided opinion." . . .

. . . We have hitherto considered only two possibilities: that the received opinion may be false, and some other opinion consequently true; or that, the received opinion being true, a conflict with the opposite error is essential to a clear apprehension and deep feeling of its truth. But there is a commoner case than either of these; when the conflicting doctrines, instead of being one true and the other false, share the truth between them; and the nonconforming opinion is needed to supply the remainder of the truth, of which the received doctrine embodies only a part. Popular opinions, on subjects not palpable to sense, are often true, but seldom or never the whole truth. They are a part of the truth; sometimes a greater, sometimes a smaller part, but exaggerated, distorted, and disjointed from the truths by which they ought to be accompanied and limited. Heretical opinions, on the other hand, are generally some of these suppressed and neglected truths, bursting the bonds which kept them down, and either seeking reconciliation with the truth contained in the common opinion, or fronting it as enemies, and setting themselves up, with similar exclusiveness, as the whole truth. The latter case is hitherto the most frequent, as, in the human mind, one-sidedness has always been the rule, and many-sidedness the exception. Hence, even in revolutions of opinion, one part of the truth usually sets while another rises. Even progress, which ought to superadd, for the most part only substitutes, one partial and incomplete truth for another; improvement consisting chiefly in this, that the new fragment of truth is more wanted, more adapted to the needs of the time, than that which it displaces. Such being the partial character of prevailing opinions, even when resting on a true foundation, every opinion which embodies somewhat of the portion of truth which the common opinion omits, ought to be considered precious, with whatever amount of error and confusion that truth may be blended. No sober judge of human affairs will feel bound to be indignant because those who force on our notice truths which we should otherwise have overlooked, overlook some of those which we see. Rather, he will think that so long as popular truth is one-sided, it is more desirable than otherwise that unpopular truth should have one-sided asserters too; such being usually the most energetic, and the most likely to compel reluctant attention to the fragment of wisdom which they proclaim as if it were the whole. . . .

I do not pretend that the most unlimited use of the freedom of enunciating all possible opinions would put an end to the evils of religious or philosophical sectarianism. Every truth which men of narrow capacity are in earnest about, is sure to be asserted, inculcated, and in many ways even acted on, as if no other truth existed in the world, or at all events none that could limit or qualify the first. I acknowledge that the tendency of all opinions to become sectarian is not cured by the freest discussion, but is often heightened and exacerbated thereby; the truth which ought to have been, but was not, seen, being rejected all the more violently because proclaimed by persons regarded as opponents. But it is not on the impassioned partisan, it is on the calmer and more disinterested bystander, that this collision of opinions works its salutary effect. Not the violent conflict between parts of the truth, but the quiet suppression of half of it, is the formidable evil; there is always hope when people are forced to listen to both sides; it is when they attend only to one that errors harden into prejudices, and truth itself ceases to have the effect of truth, by being exaggerated into falsehood. And since there are few mental attributes more rare than that judicial faculty which can sit in intelligent judgment between two sides of a question, of which only one is represented by an advocate before it, truth has no chance but in proportion as every side of it, every opinion which embodies any fraction of the truth, not only finds advocates, but is so advocated as to be listened to.

We have now recognized the necessity to the mental well-being of mankind (on which all their other well-being depends) of freedom of opinion, and freedom of the expression of opinion, on four distinct grounds; which we will now briefly recapitulate.

First, if any opinion is compelled to silence, that opinion may, for aught we can certainly know, be true. To deny this is to assume our own infallibility.

Secondly, though the silenced opinion be an error, it may, and very commonly does, contain a portion of truth; and since the general or prevailing opinion on any subject is rarely or never the whole truth, it is only by the collision of adverse opinions that the remainder of the truth has any chance of being supplied.

Thirdly, even if the received opinion be not only true, but the whole truth; unless it is suffered to be, and actually is, vigorously and earnestly contested, it will, by most of those who receive it, be held in the manner of a prejudice, with little comprehension or feeling of its rational grounds. And not only this, but, fourthly, the meaning of the doctrine itself will be in danger of being lost, or enfeebled, and deprived of its vital effect on the character and conduct: the dogma becoming a mere formal profession, inefficacious for good, but cumbering the ground, and preventing the growth of any real and heartfelt conviction, from reason or personal experience. . . .

Of Individuality As One of the Elements of Well-being

Such being the reasons which make it imperative that human beings should be free to form opinions, and to express their opinions without reserve; and such the baneful consequences to the intellectual, and through that to the moral nature of man, unless this liberty is either conceded, or asserted in spite of prohibition; let us next examine whether the same reasons do not require that men should be free to act upon their opinions—to carry these out in their lives, without hindrance, either physical or moral, from their fellow-men, so long as it is at their own risk and peril. This last proviso is of course indispensable. No one pretends that actions should be as free as opinions. On the contrary, even opinions lose their immunity when the circumstances in which they are expressed are such as to constitute their expression a positive instigation to some mischievous act. An opinion that corn-dealers are starvers of the poor, or that private property is robbery, ought to be unmolested when simply circulated through the press, but may justly incur punishment when delivered orally to an excited mob assembled before the house of a corn-dealer, or when handed about among the same mob in the form of a placard. Acts, of whatever kind, which without justifiable cause do harm to others, may be, and in the more important cases absolutely require to be, controlled by the unfavorable sentiments, and, when needful, by the active interference of mankind. The liberty of the individual must be thus far limited; he must not make himself a nuisance to other people. But if he refrains from molesting others in what concerns them, and merely acts according to his own inclination and judgment in things which concern himself, the same reasons which show that opinion should be free, prove also that he should be allowed, without molestation, to carry his opinions into practice at his own cost. That mankind are not infallible; that their truths, for the most part, are only half-truths; that unity of opinion, unless resulting from the fullest and freest comparison of opposite opinions, is not desirable, and diversity not an evil, but a good, until mankind are much more capable than at present of recognizing all sides of the truth, are principles applicable to men's modes of action, not less than to their opinions. As it is useful that while mankind are imperfect there should be different opinions, so it is that there should be different experiments of living; that free scope should be given to varieties of character, short of injury to others; and that the worth of different modes of life should be proved practically, when anyone thinks fit to try them. It is desirable, in short, that in things which do not primarily concern others, individuality should assert itself. Where not the person's own character, but the traditions or customs of other people are the rule of conduct, there is wanting one of the principal ingredients of human happiness, and quite the chief ingredient of individual and social progress.

. . . The majority, being satisfied with the ways of mankind as they now are (for it is they who make them what they are), cannot comprehend why those ways should not be good enough for everybody; and what is more, spontaneity forms no part of the ideal of the majority of moral and social reformers, but is rather looked on with jealousy, as a troublesome and perhaps rebellious obstruction to the general acceptance of what these reformers, in their own judgment, think would be best for mankind. Few persons, out of Germany, even comprehend the meaning of the doctrine which Wilhelm von Humboldt, so eminent both as a *savant* and as a politician, made the text of a treatise—that "the end of man, or that which is prescribed by the eternal or immutable dictates of reason, and not suggested by vague and transient desires, is the highest and most harmonious development of his powers to a complete and consistent whole"; that, therefore, the object "toward which every human being must ceaselessly direct his efforts, and on which especially those who design to influence their fellow-men must ever keep their eyes, is the individuality of power and development"; that for this there are two requisites, "freedom, and variety of situations"; and that from the union of these arise "individual vigor and manifold diversity," which combine themselves in "originality."

. . . The human faculties of perception, judgment, discriminative feeling, mental activity, and even moral preference, are exercised only in making a choice. He who does anything because it is the custom makes no choice. He gains no practice either in discerning or in desiring what is best. The mental and moral, like the muscular powers, are improved only by being used. The faculties are called into no exercise by doing a thing merely because others do it, no more than by believing a thing only because others believe it. If the grounds of an opinion are not conclusive to the person's own reason, his reason cannot be strengthened, but is likely to be weakened, by his adopting it; and if the inducements to an act are not such as are consentaneous to his own feelings and character (where affection or the rights of others, are not concerned) it is so much done toward rendering his feelings and character inert and torpid, instead of active and energetic.

He who lets the world, or his own portion of it, choose his plan of life for him, has no need of any other faculty than the ape-like one of imitation. He who chooses his plan for himself, employs all his faculties. He must use observation to see, reasoning and judgments to foresee, activity to gather materials for decision, discrimination to decide, and when he has decided, firmness and self-control to hold to his deliberate decision. And these qualities he requires and exercises exactly in proportion as the part of his conduct which he determines according to his own judgment and feelings is a large one. It is possible that he might be guided in some good path, and kept out of harm's way, without any of these things. But what will be his comparative worth as a human being? It really is of importance, not only what men do, but also what manner of men they are that do it. Among the works of man which human life is rightly employed in perfecting and beautifying, the first in importance surely is man himself. Supposing it were possible to get houses built, corn grown, battles fought, causes tried, and even churches erected and prayers said, by machinery—by automatons in human form—it would be a considerable loss to exchange for these automatons even the men and women who at present inhabit the more civilized parts of the world, and who assuredly are but starved specimens of what nature can and will produce. Human nature is not a machine to be built after a model, and set to do exactly the work prescribed for it, but a tree, which requires to grow and develop itself on all sides, according to the tendency of the inward forces which make it a living thing. . . .

. . . It will not be denied by anybody that originality is a valuable element in human affairs. There is always need of persons not only to discover new truths, and point out when what were once truths are true no longer, but also to commence new practices, and set the example of more enlightened conduct, and better taste and sense in human life. This cannot well be gainsaid by anybody who does not believe that the world has already attained perfection in all its ways and practices. It is true that this benefit is not capable of being rendered by everybody alike: there are but few persons, in comparison with the whole of mankind, whose experiments, if adopted by others, would be likely to be any improvement on established practice. But these few are the salt of the earth; without them, human life would become a stagnant pool. Not only is it they who introduce good things which did not before exist; it is they who keep the life in those which already exist. . . . Persons of genius, it is true, are, and are always likely to be, a small minority; but in order to have them, it is necessary to preserve the soil in which they grow. Genius can only breathe freely in an *atmosphere* of freedom. Persons of genius are . . . more individual than any other people— less capable, consequently, of fitting themselves, without hurtful compression, into any of the small number of molds which society provides in order to save its members the trouble of forming their own character. If from timidity they consent to be forced into one of these molds, and to let all that part of themselves which cannot expand under the pressure remain unexpanded, society will be little the better for their genius. . . .

I insist thus emphatically on the importance of genius, and the necessity of allowing it to unfold itself freely both in thought and in practice, being well aware that no one will deny the position in theory, but knowing also that almost everyone, in reality, is totally indifferent to it. People think genius a fine thing if it enables a man to write an exciting poem, or paint a picture. But in its true sense, that of originality in thought and action, though no one says that it is not a thing to be admired, nearly all, at heart, think that they can do very well without it. Unhappily this is too natural to be wondered at. Originality is the one thing which unoriginal minds cannot feel the use of. They cannot see what it is to do for them: how should they? If they could see what it would do for them, it would not be originality. The first service which originality has to render them, is that of opening their eyes: which being once fully done, they would have a chance of being themselves original. Meanwhile, recollecting that nothing was ever yet done which someone was not the first to do, and that all good things which exist are the fruits of originality, let them be modest enough to believe that there is something still left for it to accomplish, and assure themselves that they are more in need of originality, the less they are conscious of the want. . . .

I have said that it is important to give the freest scope possible to uncustomary things, in order that it may in time appear which of these are fit to be converted into customs. But independence of action, and disregard of custom, are not solely deserving of encouragement for the chance they afford that better modes of action, and customs more worthy of general adoption, may be struck out; nor is it only persons of decided mental superiority who have a just claim to carry on their lives in their own way. There is no reason that all human existence should be constructed on some one or some small number of patterns. If a person possesses any tolerable amount of common sense and experience, his own mode of laying out his existence is the best, not because it is the best in itself, but because it is his own mode. Human beings are not like sheep; and even sheep are not undistinguishably alike. A man cannot get a coat or a pair of boots to fit him unless they are either made to his measure, or he has a whole warehouseful to choose from: and is it easier to fit him with a life than with a coat, or are human beings more like one another in their whole physical and spiritual conformation than in the shape of their feet? If it were only that people have diversities of taste, that is reason enough for not attempting to shape them all after one model. But different persons also require different conditions for their spiritual development; and can no more exist healthily in the same moral, than all the variety of plants can in the same physical, atmosphere and climate. The same things which are helps to one person toward the cultivation of his higher nature are hindrances to another. The same mode of life is a healthy excitement to one, keeping all his faculties of action and enjoyment in their best order, while to another it is a distracting burden, which suspends or crushes all internal life. Such are the differences among human beings in their sources of pleasure, their susceptibilities of pain, and the operation on them of different physical and moral agencies, that unless there is a corresponding diversity in their modes of life, they neither obtain their fair share of happiness, nor grow up to the mental, moral, and aesthetic stature of which their nature is capable. . . .

Of the Limits to the Authority of Society over the Individual

What, then, is the rightful limit to the sovereignty of the individual over himself? Where does the authority of society begin? How much of human life should be assigned to individuality, and how much to society?

Each will receive its proper share, if each has that which more particularly concerns it. To individuality should belong the part of life in which it is chiefly the individual that is interested; to society, the part which chiefly interests society.

Though society is not founded on a contract, and though no good purpose is answered by inventing a contract in order to deduce social obligations from it, everyone who receives the protection of society owes a return for the benefit, and the fact of living in society renders it indispensable that each should be bound to observe a certain line of conduct toward the rest. This conduct consists, *first,* in not injuring the interests of one another; or rather certain interest, which, either by express legal provision or by tacit understanding, ought to be considered as rights; and *secondly,* in each person's bearing his share (to be fixed on some equitable principle) of the labors and sacrifices incurred for defending the society or its members from injury and molestation. These conditions society is justified in enforcing, at all costs to those who endeavor to withhold fulfillment. Nor is this all that society may do. The acts of an individual may be hurtful to others, or wanting in due consideration for their welfare, without going to the length of violating any of their constituted rights. The offender may then be justly punished by opinion, though not by law. As soon as any part of a person's conduct affects prejudicially the interests of others, society has jurisdiction over it, and the question whether the general welfare will or will not be promoted by interfering with it, becomes open to discussion. But there is no room for entertaining any such question when a person's conduct affects the interests of no persons besides himself, or need not affect them unless they like (all the persons concerned being of full age, and the ordinary amount of understanding). In all such cases, there should be perfect freedom, legal and social, to do the action and stand the consequences. . . .

I have reserved for the last place a large class of questions respecting the limits of government interference, which, though closely connected with the subject of this essay, do not, in strictness, belong to it. These are cases in which the reasons against interference do not turn upon the principle of liberty: the question is not about restraining the actions of individuals, but about helping them; it is asked whether the government should do, or cause to be done, something for their benefit, instead of leaving it to be done by themselves, individually or in voluntary combination.

The objections to government interference, when it is not such as to involve infringement of liberty, may be of three kinds.

The first is, when the thing to be done is likely to be better done by individuals than by the government. Speaking generally, there is no one so fit to conduct any business, or to determine how or by whom it shall be conducted, as those who are personally interested in it. This principle condemns the interferences, once so common, of the legislature, or the officers of government, with the ordinary processes of industry. But this part of the subject has been sufficiently enlarged upon by political economists, and is not particularly related to the principles of this essay.

The second objection is more nearly allied to our subject. In many cases, though individuals may not do the particular thing so well, on the average, as the officers of government, it is nevertheless desirable that it should be done by them rather than by the government, as a means to their own mental education—a mode of strengthening their active faculties, exercising their judgment, and giving them a familiar knowledge of the subjects with which they are thus left to deal. This is a principal, though not the sole, recommendation of jury trial (in cases not political); of free and popular local and municipal institutions; of the conduct of industrial and philanthropic enterprises by voluntary associations. These are not questions of liberty, and are connected with that subject only by remote tendencies; but they are questions of development. It belongs to a different occasion from the present to dwell on these things as parts of national education; as being, in truth, the peculiar training of a citizen, the practical part of the political education of a free people, taking them out of the narrow circle of personal and family selfishness, and accustoming them to the comprehension of joint interests, the management of joint concerns—habituating them to act from public or semi-public motives, and guide their conduct by aims which unite instead of isolating them from one another. Without these habits and powers, a free constitution can neither be worked nor preserved; as is exemplified by the too often transitory nature of political freedom in countries where it does not rest upon a sufficient basis of local liberties. The management of purely local business by the localities, and of the great enterprises of industry by the union of those who voluntarily supply the pecuniary means, is further recommended by all the advantages which have been set forth in this essay as belonging to individuality of development, and diversity of modes of action. Government operations tend to be everywhere alike. With individuals and voluntary associations, on the contrary, there are varied experiments, and endless diversity of experience. What the State can usefully do is to make itself a central depository, and active circulator and diffuser, of the experience resulting from many trials. Its business is to enable each experimentalist to benefit by the experiments of others, instead of tolerating no experiments but its own.

The third and most cogent reason for restricting the interference of government is the great evil of adding unnecessarily to its power. Every function superadded to those already exercised by the government causes its influence over hopes and fears to be more widely diffused, and converts, more and more, the active and ambitious part of the public into hangers-on of the government, or of some party which aims at becoming the government. If the roads, the railways, the banks, the insurance offices, the great joint-stock companies, the universities, and the public charities, were all of them branches of the government; if, in addition, the municipal corporations and local boards, with all that now devolves on them, became departments of the central administration; if the employees of all these different enterprises were appointed and paid by the government, and looked to the government for every rise in life; not all the freedom of the press and popular constitution of the legislature would make this or any other country free otherwise than in name. And the evil would be greater, the more efficiently and scientifically the administrative machinery was constructed—the more skillful the arrangements for obtaining the best qualified hands and heads with which to work it.

BOURGEOIS FREEDOM

Karl Marx

Let us consider for a moment the so-called rights of man, in fact the rights of man in their authentic shape, in the shape which they possess among their discoverers, the North Americans and the French. In part these rights of man are political rights, rights which are only exercised in the community with others. Participation in the affairs of the community, in fact of the political community, forms their substance. They come within the category of political freedom, of civil rights. . . . It remains to consider the other aspect of human rights, the *droits de l'homme* [rights of man] apart from the *droits du citoyen* [rights of the citizen].

Among them is to be found liberty of conscience, the right to practice any cult to one's liking. The privilege of belief is expressly recognized, either as a human right or as the consequence of a human right, of freedom.

Declaration of the rights of man and of citizenship, 1791, article 10: No penalty should attach to the holding of religious opinions. The right of every man to practice the religious cult to which he is attached is guaranteed by clause 1 of the Constitution of 1791.

The Declaration of the Rights of Man, etc., 1793, includes among human rights, article 7: The free practice of cults. With respect to the right to publish ideas and opinions and to assemble for the practice of a cult, it is even stated: The necessity for enunciating these rights presupposes either the presence or the recent memory of a despotism.

Constitution of Pennsylvania, article 9, paragraph 3: All men have received from Nature the imprescriptible right to worship the Almighty according to the dictates of their conscience, and nobody may legally be constrained to follow, to institute, or to support, against his will, any religious cult or ministry. In no case may any human authority interfere in questions of conscience and control the prerogatives of the soul.

Constitution of New Hampshire, articles 5 and 6: Among the number

FROM "On the Jewish Question," in *Selected Essays,* translated by H. J. Stenning.

of natural rights, some are inalienable by their nature, because nothing can take their place. Such are the rights of conscience. . . .

The rights of man as such are distinguished from the rights of the citizen. What is man apart from the citizen? Nothing else than a member of bourgeois society. Why is the member of bourgeois society called "man," and why are his rights called the rights of man? How do we explain this fact? From the relation of the political State to bourgeois society, from the meaning of political emancipation.

Above all we must record the fact that the so-called rights of man, as distinguished from the rights of the citizen, are nothing else than the rights of the member of bourgeois society, that is of the egoistic individual, of man separated from man and the community. The most radical constitution, the Constitution of 1793, may be cited:

Declaration of the rights of man and of the citizen. Article 2. These rights, etc. (natural and imprescriptible rights) are: equality, liberty, security, property.

Of what consists liberty? *Article 6. Liberty is the power which belongs to man to do everything which does not injure the rights of others.*

Freedom is therefore the right to do and perform that which injures none. The limits within which each may move without injuring others are fixed by the law, as the boundary between two fields is fixed by the fence. The freedom in question is the freedom of the individual as an isolated atom thrown back upon itself. . . . The right of man to freedom is not based upon the connection of man with man, but rather on the separation of man from man. It is the right to this separation, the right of the individual limited to himself.

The practical application of the right of man to freedom is the right of man to private property.

In what consists the right of man to private property?

Article 16 (Const. of 1793): The right to property is the right of every citizen to enjoy and dispose of as he likes his goods, his income, the fruit of his toil and of his industry.

The right of man to private property is therefore the right to enjoy and dispose of his property, at his will and pleasure, without regard for others, and independently of society: the right of self-interest. Each particular individual freedom exercised in this way forms the basis of bourgeois society. It leaves every man to find in other men not the realization, but rather the limits of his freedom. But it proclaims above all the right of man to enjoy and dispose of his property, his income, and the fruit of his toil and his industry according to his pleasure.

There still remain the other rights of man, equality and security.

Equality here in its non-political significance is nothing but the equality of the above described liberty, viz.: every individual is regarded as a uniform atom resting on its own bottom. Article 5 of the *Constitution of 1793* states: *Equality consists in the fact that the law is the same for all, whether it protects or whether it punishes.*

And security? *Article 8 of the Constitution of 1793: Security consists in the protection accorded by society to each of its members for the preservation of his person, his rights, and his property.*

Security is the supreme social conception of bourgeois society, the conception of the police, the idea that society as a whole only exists to guarantee to each of its members the maintenance of his person, his rights, and his property.

By the conception of security bourgeois society does not raise itself above its egoism. Security is rather the confirmation of its egoism.

None of the so-called rights of man, therefore, goes beyond the egoistic individual, beyond the individual as a member of bourgeois society, withdrawn into his private interests and separated from the community. Far from regarding the individual as a generic being, the generic life, Society itself, rather appears as an external frame for the individual, as a limitation of his original independence. The sole bond which connects him with his fellows is natural necessity, material needs and private interest, the preservation of his property and his egoistic person.

It is strange that a people who were just beginning to free themselves, to break down all the barriers between the various members of the community, to establish a political community, that such a people should solemnly proclaim the justification of the egoistic individual, separated from his fellows and from the community, and should even repeat this declaration at a moment when the most heroic sacrifice could alone save the nation and was therefore urgently required, at a moment when the sacrifice of all interests of bourgeois society was imperative, and egoism should have been punished as a crime. This fact is even stranger when we behold the political liberators degrading citizenship and the political community to the level of a mere means for the maintenance of these so-called rights of man, proclaiming the citizen to be the servant of the egoistic man, degrading the sphere in which the individual behaves as a social being below the sphere in which he behaves as a fractional being, and finally accepting as the true proper man not the individual as citizen, but the individual as bourgeois.

The aim of every political association is the preservation of the natural and imprescriptible rights of man. (Declaration of the rights, etc., of 1791, article 2.) The purpose of government is to assure to man the enjoyment of his natural and imprescriptible rights. (Declaration of 1793, art. 1.)

Thus even at the time when its enthusiasm was still fresh and kept at boiling point by the pressure of circumstances, the political life proclaimed itself to be a mere means whose end is the life of bourgeois society.

It is true that its revolutionary practice was in flagrant contradiction to its theory. While security, for example, was proclaimed to be a right of man, the violation of the secrecy of correspondence was publicly proposed.

While the indefinite liberty of the press (1793 Constitution, art. 122) was guaranteed as a consequence of the right of man to individual liberty, the freedom of the press was completely destroyed, for liberty of the press could not be permitted when it compromised public liberty. (Robespierre jeune, "Parliamentary History of the French Revolution." Buchez et Roux, p. 135.) This means that the right of man to liberty ceases to be a right as soon as it comes into conflict with the political life, whereas, according to theory, the political life is only the guarantee of the rights of man, and should therefore be surrendered as soon as its object contradicts these rights of man. But the practice is only the exception and the theory is the rule. If, however, we regard the revolutionary practice as the correct position of the relation, the riddle still remains to be solved, why the relationship was inverted in the consciousness of the political liberators, the end appearing as the means, and the means as the end. This optical illusion of their consciousness would still be the same riddle, although a psychological, a theoretical riddle.

The riddle admits of easy solution.

The political emancipation is at the same time the dissolution of the old society, upon which was based the civic society, or the rulership alienated from the people. The political revolution is the revolution of bourgeois society. What was the character of the old society? It can be described in one word. Feudality. The old civic society had a directly political character, that is, the elements of civic life, as for example property or the family, or the mode and kind of labor, were raised to the level of elements of the community in the form of landlordism, status, and corporation. In this form they determined the relation of the individual to the community, that is his political relation, his relationship of separation and exclusion from the other constituent parts of society. For the latter organization of popular life did not raise property or labor to the level of social elements, but rather completed their separation from the political whole and constituted them as special societies within society. Thus the vital functions and vital conditions of society continued to be political, although political in the sense of feudality, which means that they excluded the individual from the political whole, and transformed the special relation of his corporation to the political whole into his own general relation to the popular life. As a consequence of this organization, the political unity necessarily appears as the consciousness, the will and the activity of the political unity, and likewise the general State power as the special concern of a ruler and his servants sundered from the people.

The political revolution, which overthrew this domination and raised political affairs to the rank of popular affairs, which constituted the political State as a general concern, that is as a real State, necessarily shattered all Estates, corporations, guilds, privileges, which were just so many expressions of the separation of the people from their community. The political revolution thereby abolished the political character of civic society.

It dissolved civic society into its elemental parts, on the one hand, into the individuals, on the other hand, into the material and spiritual elements, which formed the vital content, the civic situation of these individuals. It released the political spirit, which was imprisoned in fragments in the various blind alleys of the feudal society; it collected all these dispersed parts of it, liberated it from its entanglement with the civic life, and constituted it as the sphere of the community, of the general popular concerns in ideal independence from its particular elements of civic life. The specific life activity and the specific life situation settled into a merely general significance. They no longer formed the general relation of the individual to the political whole. The public business as such became rather the general business of every individual and the political function became his general function.

But the completion of the idealism of the State was at the same time the completion of the materialism of civic society.

The throwing off of the political yoke was at the same time the throwing off of the bond which had curbed the egoistic spirit of civic society. The political emancipation was at the same time the emancipation of civic society from politics, from even the semblance of a general content.

Feudal society was resolved into its basic elements, its individual members. But into the individuals who really formed its basis, that is, the egoistic individual.

This individual, the member of civic society, is now the basis, the assumption of the political State. He is recognized as such in the rights of man.

The liberty of the egoistic individual and the recognition of this liberty are, however, tantamount to the recognition of the unbridled movement of the intellectual and material elements which inform him.

The individual was therefore not liberated from religion; he received religious freedom. He was not freed from property; he received freedom of property. He was not freed from the egoism of industry; he received industrial freedom.

The constitution of the political State and the dissolution of civic society into independent individuals—whose relation is right, as the relation of the members of Estates and of guilds was privilege—is accomplished in one and the same act. But the individual as a member of civic society, the unpolitical individual, necessarily appears as the natural individual. The rights of man appear as natural rights, for the self-conscious activity concentrates itself upon the political act. The egoistic individual is the sediment of the dissolved society, the object of immediate certitude, and therefore a natural object. The political revolution dissolves the civic society into its constituent parts without revolutionizing and subjecting to criticism those parts themselves. It regards bourgeois society, the world of needs, of labor, of private interests, as the foundation of its existence, as an assumption needing no proof, and therefore as its natural basis. Lastly, the individual as a member of bourgeois society counts as the proper individual, as the man in contradistinction to the citizen, because he is man in his sensual, individual, closest existence, whereas political man is only the abstract, artificial individual, the individual as an allegorical, moral person. The real man is only recognized in the shape of the egoistic individual, the true man is only recognized in the shape of the abstract citizen.

The abstraction of the political man was very well described by Rousseau:

He who dares undertake to give instructions to a nation ought to feel himself capable as it were of changing human nature; of transforming every individual who in himself is a complete and independent whole into part of a greater whole, from which he receives in some manner his life and his being; of altering man's constitution, in order to strengthen it; of substituting a social and moral existence for the independent and physical existence which we have all received from nature. In a word, it is necessary to deprive man of his native powers, in order to endow him with some which are alien to him, and of which he cannot make use without the aid of other people.

All emancipation leads back to the human world, to relationships, to men themselves.

Political emancipation is the reduction of man, on the one side, to the member of bourgeois society, to the egoistic, independent individual, on the other side, to the citizen, to the moral person.

Not until the real, individual man is identical with the citizen, and has become a generic being in his empirical life, in his individual work, in his individual relationships, not until man has recognized and organized his own capacities as social capacities, and consequently the social force is no longer divided by the political power, not until then will human emancipation be achieved.

SOCIALISM AND LIBERTY

John Strachey

The achievement of the maximum degree of human liberty is one way of stating the proper goal of all human endeavor. But we must reckon into the determination of how much liberty a man or a community enjoys, many factors [of] which are often wholly neglected. We must reckon, for example, such things as the number of hours which a man works, whether he is sure of being able to work and earn at all, and the degree of access to the culture of his age with which he is provided. These are clearly liberties of a different kind from the traditional liberties for which our forefathers struggled. We must disentangle these two kinds of liberties. In what, then, do the liberties which we possess, or claim to possess, in contemporary Britain and America, and those liberties which . . . it is a principal object of socialism to achieve, respectively consist?

Those civil liberties which exist, either in practice or in theory, in Britain and America today consist, primarily, of a series of provisions, built upon the foundation of a bill of rights, by which the State limits its own freedom of action in the coercion of its citizens. For example, the British and American States guarantee that a man shall be tried for a criminal offense by a jury of his peers and that he shall not be imprisoned without such trial. They further guarantee that citizens shall be free to meet for the discussion of any problem, that they shall be free to form associations for the promotion of any object not specifically declared illegal by statute, or by common law decision, and that they may print and publish any views and opinions not so declared illegal. These are extremely valuable liberties. They have, it is true, been perceptibly infringed upon both in Britain and America during recent years. Moreover, our now extreme class inequalities have served to change the character of some of the most important of them. They are a heritage imperfect and incomplete; nevertheless, they are precious.

FROM *Theory and Practice of Socialism*, chapter 18. Reprinted by permission of Victor Gollancz Ltd.

How can their existence be explained on the basis of the theory of the State which we have outlined above? For if the State is essentially the coercive instrument of the dominant capitalist class, why should that class have thus blunted the edge of its weapon? The answer to this question is, in part, that many of these liberties date from an epoch in which the capitalists were not the governing class in society. They date from an epoch in which, on the contrary, the capitalist class was often itself the victim of the State's apparatus of force. Hence it was to be expected that the young and struggling capitalists should attempt to limit the power of the State.

In a word, the establishment of our civil liberties was due to the same general causes as the establishment of democracy—of which they are in a sense a part. We instanced the obstinate resistance which Parliament, then as now the essential mouthpiece of the capitalists as a class, offered to the creation of a standing army as an example of the capitalists' efforts to prevent the creation of too effective an apparatus of coercion, so long as that apparatus might be used against them.

It was in the course of this same struggle that our original civil liberties were established. They were established in the interests of the rising capitalist class. But this does not mean that they were not, and are not now, of genuine value to the rest of the population. For the interests of a young, vigorous class, cleaving its way upward for the fulfillment of its historic mission, always coincide, on the whole, with the interests of the community. This is the explanation of how our existing civil liberties originally came into being in the seventeenth and eighteenth centuries. But it will not cover the considerable development of these liberties which took place in the nineteenth century. From 1832 onwards the British capitalists were in ever greater control of the State. How, then, do we account for the fact that for some decades the restrictions with which coercive State action was hedged about were increased? The explanation lies in the fact that the capitalists in their long and arduous struggle with the feudalists and semi-feudalists had had to call into political activity the classes lying below them. They had to set in motion both the lower middle class of petty traders and, in the early nineteenth century, the new class of industrial workers. It was these popular forces which won—usually in conflict with the capitalists, who were already becoming more and more conservative—our more recent civil liberties.

Today the capitalists have become wholly conservative. For their power is quite unchallenged from the now completely absorbed feudalists above them, and is increasingly challenged from the ever-growing working class below them. Naturally, therefore, they have come to have less and less use for liberties which have grown quite unnecessary to them for curbing the power of non-existent feudalists, and which hamper them before the growing menace of the workers. This is the explanation of why both the British and American capitalists are becoming more and more anti-libertarian. This is why they are making efforts to revoke those civil liberties which their ancestors played the leading part in establishing. In Britain and America these efforts have only recently begun. In Germany and Italy they have been disastrously successful.

It will be evident that those who take this view of the origin of our present liberties will not hesitate to fight for their retention by every possible means. For a knowledge of their origin and nature serves but to make us aware that these liberties are not only good in themselves but are also a vital asset to the workers in their struggle to abolish the more and more intolerably defective capitalist economic system. This is why communists and socialists are always ready to stand and to fight side by side with everyone, no matter what his other opinions may be, who is ready to defend our civil liberties.

Now let us look at the other side of the picture. Our existing civil liberties, however necessary it may be to prevent even them from being taken away from us, are, for the workers, poor, thin, and half-illusory things. . . .

[The socialist] conception of liberty is genuinely incomprehensible to most of those who set the tone of public discussion in Britain and America. Having never trembled because tomorrow they may lose their jobs, their homes or their food, they cannot conceive what such questions have to do with liberty. For them liberty is almost exclusively a matter of the absence of legal prohibitions against saying, writing or, more rarely, doing, things displeasing to the Government. But for by far the greater part of the population such liberty of prophesying is not, and cannot be, by any means the most important or valued liberty. . . . The liberty for which by far the greater part of the world's population is still fighting desperately is not the liberty to speak, but the liberty to eat.

The denial by their owners of access to those means of production without which a man cannot earn his livelihood is an incomparable oppression. Every other form of tyranny is but consequential to it. Nor is this oppression confined to those millions of the population to whom access to the means of production is wholly forbidden. The whole body of the employed workers are to a varying degree subjected to the irresponsible, invisible, and so partly unrealized, dictation of the owners of the means of production. For they are allowed to work and earn only upon conditions laid down by the wholly unchecked decision of the owners. Nor are these conditions confined to matters of wages and hours of work. They often extend, openly or tacitly, to the words and deeds of every employee. In many establishments to refrain from the expression of views, or the commission of acts, displeasing to the management is made into a condition of employment. No statute, bill of rights, or legal enactment whatsoever, can prevent those who neither own nor have independent access to the means of production from dependence upon those who have this ownership and access. Only a fortunate minority of those who have ever earned their living by selling their ability to work are likely to be unaware of this fact. For the great majority of workers have to adapt their actions, and in many cases their words, to the wishes of those who employ them.

But the spell cast by the ideas of the owners of the means of production (and *they* really do enjoy an admirable degree of liberty under capitalism) is so strong that only a minority of the workers ever reach a clear consciousness of the fact that the greater part of the liberty which the British and American Constitutions guarantee them has now been invisibly withdrawn from them by their ever more perfect exclusion from all independent opportunity to work and earn. The idea that this is why their actual situation does not correspond at all to the picture of a community of free citizens which is painted for them, by school textbook, newspaper and political leader, is only slowly and confusedly dawning upon them.

Another aspect of the communist and socialist conception of liberty is almost always incomprehensible to minds steeped in the ways of thinking developed in the epoch of capitalism. Liberty in the capitalist epoch has been conceived of almost exclusively as the absence of restraints; it is seldom thought of as the presence of opportunity. And yet for the mass of the population of any highly organized community the question of the provision of effective opportunity to speak and write, and to act, is the more important consideration. For example, the liberty which chiefly matters to the studious and ambitious is the availability of education, of books, of apparatus. A liberty which matters intensely, to take a simpler but only less important case, to the citizens of any great city is not merely that there should be no legal prohibitions against them amusing themselves, but that there should be enough playing-fields, enough, and cheap enough, transport to the country, enough, and cheap enough, cinema and theatre seats and the like. But the provision of these positive liberties to think, to learn, to speak, to play, and to do is not a matter of paper laws or decrees. It is a matter of the allocation of important economic resources. The provision of the educational opportunities now open to the children of the governing class in Britain to all children would necessitate, for example, the allocation, for this purpose, of substantial resources of production. The same thing is true of the provision, to all, of the opportunities for sport, amusement and travel now monopolized by about 10 per cent of the population.

The supply of economic resources is limited. Hence those who engross for themselves the whole supply available for the effective enjoyment of such fundamental liberties as those of self-improvement and recreation, deny these liberties to the rest of the population. No one who fails not merely to accept, but imaginatively to realize, the full implications of this truth has begun to understand the problem of the provision of liberty, not to a fortunate class, but to a whole community. Unless they really do see that an economic arrangement which reserves all, for example, of the available facilities for foreign travel to the governing class is almost (although, no doubt, never quite) as real a denial of liberty to the rest of the population as if men were legally forbidden to go more than so many miles from their homes, they are still under the capitalist hypnosis. Mr. and Mrs. Webb put the point thus:

There is, in any given place, at any given time, only a certain amount of opportunity open to the population in the aggregate. Anyone who takes to himself more than the appropriate amount and kind of opportunity that falls properly to his share, not only robs another of some or all of the opportunity that he might otherwise have enjoyed, but also, by increasing inequality, inevitably lessens the aggregate amount of individual freedoms within the community. The social organization which allows the British shipowner to treat himself and his family to a long and expensive holiday in Switzerland and Italy, whilst the hundreds of dock laborers who are unloading his ships, together with their families, get nothing more like a holiday than their wageless days of involuntary unemployment, not only injures them, but also diminishes the total aggregate of freedom within the community. Lenin is said once to have observed in his epigrammatic way: "It is true that liberty is precious—so precious that it must be rationed."

The rationing of liberty must necessarily seem a most deplorable thing to the unreflecting members of the capitalist class of Britain and America. For they now enjoy the almost unlimited supply of liberty, both in the sense of freedom from restraint and provision of opportunity, which their money can buy; nor have they cared to reflect that their present almost perfect liberty is only achieved by the almost equally perfect servitude to them of the rest of the population. They are careful never to become conscious of the fact (to return to Mr. and Mrs. Webb's example) that they can have unlimited holidays only because their workers can have no holidays at all. But the rationing, in the sense of the sharing out upon a just basis, of those opportunities without which liberty is little more than a name, will seem to every worker one of the most necessary and elementary acts of any socialist society.

An essential part of the communist and socialist conception of liberty is, then, the positive provision for the entire population of collective opportunity to work, to earn, and so to live, and also to improve and develop themselves by study, and to enjoy themselves. Until this has been done, liberty will remain for the greater part of men an aspiration, glorious but insubstantial. In fine, liberty cannot be effectively enjoyed, outside the ranks of the capitalist class, without that general plenty and security which socialism alone can provide.

Once this cardinal fact is realized, however, it is of importance to examine the question of that liberty of expression on which the attention of capitalist opinion is exclusively concentrated. For this is undoubtedly a very precious liberty. The question is, To what extent does the mass of the population possess this liberty under capitalism and socialism respectively?

Now the capitalists' ownership of the means of production includes the ownership of the means of production of opinion: it includes the ownership, that is to say, of the Press, the wireless, the cinema, and the control of the educational system. Yet today liberty of expression, if it is not to be illusory, must mean liberty of access to the Press, the wireless, and the cinema. It cannot become a reality for the mass of the population so long as those three methods of effective expression are in the exclusive possession of a limited ruling class. It is hardly too much to say that the worker under capitalism has the right of free speech —so long as there is no possibility of his making himself heard. In a socialist society the workers are not only free to speak; they are free to speak into the microphone, free to use the great printing presses, free to use the incomparable instrument of the cinema, to make articulate and visible their whole view of the world. In a word, it becomes apparent upon examination that effective liberty of expression is almost as closely bound up with the question of who is to own the means of production as is the basic question of the liberty to work and eat. If the means of production of opinion are in the hands of the capitalist class, they and they alone will enjoy effective liberty of expression; if they are in the hands of the workers, it is they who will enjoy this liberty.

This is the short answer to those who feel that the educational system, the Press, the cinema, and the wireless, in the existing socialist community, are in some sense unfree in which they are free in Britain and America. In order to get any significance out of this allegation we must at once ask the counter question—free to whom? For it is perfectly true that the Press of a socialist Britain and America will be as unfree to Messrs. Hearst and Howard, to Lords Rothermere and Beaverbrook [newspaper magnates], as it is now unfree to the mass of the population.

The mass of the population can only own the means of expression, to coin a generic term for Press, cinema, and wireless, through their own organizations—their Government, their Trade Unions, their political parties, their Co-operative Societies and the like. These are the organizations which own and control the Press of the Soviet Union, for example. Is it not remarkable that many quite sincere persons feel that such ownership constitutes a denial of the freedom of the Press, while the ownership of chains of newspapers by individual millionaires such as Mr. Hearst and Lord Rothermere constitutes the freedom of the Press? No doubt the fact which weighs with those who feel like this is that formally, legally, there is nothing to prevent any British citizen from establishing, say, a London daily newspaper in competition with Lord Rothermere's *Daily Mail,* or Lord Beaverbrook's *Daily Express,* or Mr. Elias' *Daily Herald*—nothing, that is to say, except the need to command at least one million pounds sterling. But this is an economic obstacle. And an economic obstacle seems to many people in some way not to count. Monopoly is not for them monopoly unless it is legally recognized. So long as our Press lords are content with the *fact* of monopolizing the effective expression of news and opinion, and do not lay claim to a legal title to this monopoly, they will not, it seems, be accused of even infringing the freedom of the Press. They will remain free to drench us with the news and the views, and those alone, which suit their interests: to select, to suppress, to distort, to harangue; to deafen and to madden the world with their campaigns and their crusades; to prevent us even from noticing, far less resenting, their exploitations; and finally to drive us into mutual slaughter to settle their accounts. And they will do all this in the sacred name of the freedom of the Press.

But let the democratically established organizations of the Russian working class put before the readers of the newspapers which they own the view of the world which the most responsible leaders of the community consider, after decades of reflection and of social experiment, to be the truth, so far as the human mind has yet apprehended it, and they are accused of using a kept Press for propaganda purposes! Certainly the workers' Press of the Soviet Union is full of propaganda. As Mr. and Mrs. Webb quietly remark, it is so full of propaganda that "it would be hard to decide whether there is, in the aggregate, more or less of it than in Great Britain and the United States." The difference is that in a socialist community the propaganda emanates from definite and democratically elected public bodies, which can be replaced at any time, from bodies which can scarcely have interests different from those of the mass of the population, from which they emanate; whilst in capitalist countries the propaganda emanates from some half a dozen totally irresponsible multi-millionaires, whose interests are often in deadly contradiction to those of the remainder of the community.

So much for the question of the liberty of expression respectively provided for the mass of the population by a capitalist and a socialist Press. The same considerations apply to such vital means of expression as the educational system, the wireless, and the cinema. To suppose that any of these means of expression can be free from propaganda—can fail, that is to say, to influence powerfully the minds of men—is a delusion. But if the capitalists own them, the propaganda which they will emit will be capitalist propaganda; if the workers own them, it will be socialist propaganda. And this is a very important difference.

Finally, we may notice a more subtle ground for the allegation that socialism will fail to maximize the liberty of expression of the individual man. We are sometimes told that, even if there will be no tyranny of legal coercion in a socialist community, there will be a tyranny of public opinion, an overmastering and all-pervading conformity which will stifle all idiosyncrasy or even individuality. In this case also it is necessary, in order to retain a sense of proportion, to envisage the degree of freedom for non-conformity which exists in capitalist communities. Just one hundred years ago the first great socialist which the English-speaking world ever produced wrote with insight and force on this point:

Some nations such as the British and their descendants, the population of the United States of North America, imagine that they now possess what they term civil and religious liberty; while both nations are in the very bondage of mental slavery, both civil and religious. Their civil and religious liberty consists in expressing within a small circle such thoughts and feelings as they know by experience will pass current within that circle. If they infringe these bounds they are likely to have lynch law in one country, and fine and imprisonment in the other. (Robert Owen, *The Book of the New Moral World*)

Neither self-satisfaction as an ingrained national characteristic, nor their differing methods of repression, seem to have changed much in Britain and America since Owen's day. Owen may be thought to have overstated his case somewhat. But it remains true that a united, identically educated and carefully trained governing class (such as the British, for example), which controls almost all access to the means of effective expression and employment, can and does impose its point of view upon a community to an extent which makes non-conformity difficult and usually dangerous.

The question is this: are the citizens of a socialist community likely to impose upon themselves an even more severe pressure toward conformity? Nothing would seem more unlikely. A community in which a genuine identity of interest between all citizens has been established will be able to afford to tolerate far more idiosyncrasy, salty variety, and even plain eccentricity, in its citizens than can a community which is maintaining the precarious eminence of a governing class. Again, the mere achievement of general plenty and security, the elimination of the fear that at any moment a man may be shut out from the opportunity to work and earn, will in itself foster an individuality which is totally impossible to the wage earning population today; an individuality which today can only exist amongst that tiny handful of the securely rich who have no such fears.

To sum up: nothing can prevent the capitalists from using the immense powers of coercion given them by their ownership of the means of production drastically to curtail every one of the liberties of the workers. The right of the capitalists to allow or to refuse the workers the possibility of earning their living is a power which, so long as it exists, transcends and overrides every constitution in the world. The initial act of dispossessing the capitalists creates at a stroke more liberty than has ever, or can ever, exist under capitalism, except for the capitalists. Neither constitutions nor bills of right, republics nor constitutional monarchies, can ever make men free so long as their livelihoods are at the mercy of a small class which holds sway over the means of life. In a socialist society alone those liberties, of which the workers of Britain and America possess little more than the shadow, can assume form and substance. In a socialist society the workers get, not merely the theoretical right, but also the practical, daily opportunity to use their liberties. They are enabled to live, and not merely to work. Under socialism work becomes a means to a free and good life. Under capitalism the life of the worker is preserved as a necessary means to the extraction of the maximum possible amount of work from him.

Questions for Discussion

1. Plato, Mill, and Huxley's World Controller all claim that the forms of social organization they respectively advocate will best ensure overall happiness. Do they all have the same concept of happiness? If not, how do they differ, and how do their differences affect their political conclusions?
2. Defining happiness in the way that seems to you most natural, do you think that happiness is the supreme value toward which social organization should be directed? If not, under what circumstances should happiness give way to other considerations, and what might such considerations be?

3. "Surely of all 'rights of man,' this right of the ignorant man to be guided by the wiser, to be, gently or forcibly, held in the true course by him, is the indisputablest," wrote historian Thomas Carlyle. How do you think Plato, Mill, and Marx, respectively, would have responded to this?
4. "Democracy substitutes election by the incompetent many for appointment by the corrupt few," said George Bernard Shaw. Can you suggest a way out of the implied dilemma?
5. Compare Mill's concept of self-fulfillment with that of Marx. What differences in their ideas of human nature are implicit in their respective concepts?
6. "They were happier when they were slaves," says a white racist of black people. Could one believe this and yet also approve of their liberation?
7. To what extent do you think that welfare-state liberalism represents a successful compromise between Mill's emphasis on personal liberty and Marx's principle "to each according to his needs"? Why or why not?
8. The contemporary American philosopher Robert Nozick has argued that taxation to provide welfare for the needy assaults the liberty of individuals, compelling them to be charitable against their will. To what extent would Mill have agreed or disagreed, and on what grounds?
9. There is a tendency among Marxists to think that Mill's concept of freedom corresponds only to what Isaiah Berlin, as indicated in the introduction to this chapter, calls "negative freedom," and that Marx's concept corresponds to what Berlin calls "positive freedom." To what extent is this true?

Selected Readings

ARENDT, H. *The Origins of Totalitarianism*. New York: Harcourt Brace Jovanovich, 1951. Discusses how tyranny results from disregard for liberties.

ARISTOTLE. *Politics*. Translated by E. Barker. Oxford: Clarendon Press, 1946. Presents an ideal compromise between authority and liberty.

BEDAU, H., ed. *Justice and Equality*. Englewood Cliffs, New Jersey: Prentice-Hall, 1971. Contemporary essays on social justice.

BERLIN, I. "Two Concepts of Liberty." Inaugural lecture. Oxford University, 1958. Distinguishes between positive and negative freedom.

BURNHAM, J. *The Machiavellians*. New York: John Day, 1943. Argues that political realism supports democracy.

COLLINGWOOD, R. *The New Leviathan*. Oxford: Clarendon Press, 1942. An idealist critique of political realism.

DE JOUVENAL, B. *Sovereignty*. Translated by J. Huntington. Chicago: University of Chicago Press, 1957. A classic study of politics and law.

DEWEY, J. *Freedom and Culture*. New York: Putnam, 1939. A pragmatic defense of social democracy.

HEGEL, G. W. F. *Philosophy of Right.* Translated by T. M. Knox. Oxford: Clarendon Press, 1942. The theory that the state is the realization of human freedom.

HOBBES, T. *De Cive.* New York: Appleton-Century-Crofts, 1947. A major source of both liberal and authoritarian views of the state.

———. *Leviathan.* New York: Liberal Arts Press, 1958.

HOBHOUSE, L. T. *The Metaphysical Theory of the State.* London: Allen & Unwin, 1918. A critique of Hegelianism.

HUXLEY, A. *Brave New World.* London: Chatto & Windus, 1932. A satire of the ideal of social engineering.

KAUTSKY, K. *Ethics and the Materialist Conception of History.* Translated by J. Askew. Chicago: Kerr, 1913. An argument for evolutionary socialism.

LENIN, V. I. *State and Revolution.* New York: International Publishers, 1932. Argues that the Communist Revolution is compatible with democracy.

LOCKE, J. *Two Treatises of Government.* Cambridge: Cambridge University Press, 1964. Presents a social contract theory based on natural rights.

MACHIAVELLI, N. *The Prince.* New York: Modern Library, 1940. The classic source of political realism.

MARCUSE, H. *An Essay on Liberation.* Boston: Beacon Press, 1969. Argues that democracy is impossible under capitalism.

———. *Reason and Revolution.* Boston: Beacon Press, 1966.

MARX, K. *Writings of the Young Marx.* Translated by L. Easton and K. Guddat. Garden City, New York: Doubleday, 1967. The main sources of Marxist political ethics.

MC PHERSON, C. B. *The Real World of Democracy.* Oxford: Clarendon Press, 1966. A powerful critique of capitalist democracy.

MILL, J. S. *Considerations on Representative Government.* New York: Dutton, 1962.

———. *On Liberty.* New York: Dutton, 1962. The classic defense of liberal democracy.

NOZICK, R. *Anarchy, State and Utopia.* Cambridge, Massachusetts: Harvard University Press, 1974. A well-argued case for laissez-faire democracy.

PLATO. *Republic.* Book 4. In *The Dialogues of Plato.* Translated by B. Jowett. London: Methuen, 1891. The main source of political authoritarianism.

POPPER, K. *The Open Society and Its Enemies.* Princeton, New Jersey: Princeton University Press, 1950. A strong criticism of Marxism as totalitarian.

RAWLS, J. *A Theory of Justice.* Cambridge, Massachusetts: Harvard University Press, 1971. A thorough elaboration of welfare state liberalism.

ROUSSEAU, J. J. *The Social Contract and Discourses.* New York: Everyman Books, 1947. A major source of both democratic and authoritarian political theory.

STRACHEY, J. *The Theory and Practice of Socialism.* New York: Random House, 1936. A forcefully argued defense of socialism as more democratic than capitalism.

TUCKER, R. C. *Philosophy and Myth in Karl Marx.* Cambridge: Cambridge University Press, 1972. Stresses the idealism of Marx's early writings.

PART FIVE

Aesthetics

Chapter 10

The Standards of Criticism: What Is Art?

"You know the thing is trash. How dare you praise it?" Alceste's words to Philinte, in Moliere's philosophical comedy, *The Misanthrope,* express the conviction that there are certain definite standards of artistic excellence on which all reasonable people should agree. Alceste insists that his friend Philinte has no *right* to praise the love poem of Oronte. Philinte, according to Alceste, is insincere in approving of Oronte's poem because he cannot fail to recognize that the poem is tasteless and trite, full of mannered conceits, unnatural and false. According to Alceste, it exemplifies the worst faults of their society and panders to the fashion of insincere hyperbole current in seventeenth-century France. Philinte, in contrast, sees merit in the elaborate construction of the poem and defends his approval on the ground that people are entitled to use whatever standards of artistic value they happen to prefer. There are no absolute, universal criteria of right or wrong in literary criticism. Which of these two views is correct?

If Alceste were writing nowadays for the Sunday *Times* or the *Saturday Review of Literature,* few would think well of Oronte's poem after reading Alceste's review of it. Art critics of prestigious journals have enormous influence on popular taste, which would indicate that most people believe that there are objective standards on these matters and that the critic knows them better than most of us. The fact that our schools offer courses in art appreciation and art criticism further supports the belief that aesthetic perception can be developed and refined with sufficient training and that the trained individual can recognize certain objective qualities in works of art that make them good or bad.

Nevertheless, and perhaps inconsistently, people are also quick to defend their right to judge for themselves and to stick to their preferences regardless of what critics say. They argue, plausibly, that what meets our standards at one time may be rejected at another time. They may point to the general rejection of early impressionist painting, followed later by a wave of critical enthusiasm. They may cite cases such as that of Marcel Duchamps, whose exhibition of a signed urinal shocked the art world, although the piece later came to be proudly displayed in the most renowned museums of fine art. Where then, they may ask, are these objective and eternally right standards of aesthetic excellence? Perhaps there are no standards at all. Perhaps it really is the case that "anything goes."

On reflection we often discover that we hold inconsistent beliefs about art. It seems possible to agree with Alceste's criticisms of Oronte's poem and yet also find merit in Philinte's defense of it. Philosophy of art reflects viewpoints of "objectivism" and "subjectivism," as the two opposing beliefs about art are called. Philosophers have run the gamut from those like Aristotle who maintain that there are universal standards of good art independent of personal taste to those like George Santayana who hold that anything that gives us aesthetic pleasure can reasonably be judged by us as good.

Aristotle's philosophy of art is presented in the *Poetics,* which is directly concerned with drama but may be generalized to apply to the other arts as well. The *Poetics* has had a greater influence on art criticism than any other philosophical work. Alceste, for example, defends the standards of seventeenth-century dramatists such as Racine and Corneille, who consciously modeled their work along Aristotelian lines. Moliere, like most of us, appreciated both the purity of strict rules and the creative freedom of artists who rebel against such rules. Thus he gives both Alceste and Philinte equally cogent arguments for their opposite points of view.

Aristotle insisted that art should be naturalistic, that is, true to life. Thus Alceste complains that people do not talk the way Oronte writes, especially to those they love. Aristotle held that dialogue and plot must be probable, that events must be causally linked, and that overall a play should be simple and unified in order to produce the aesthetic pleasure in the spectator that results from finding these standards fulfilled. Aristotle addressed himself mainly to tragic drama, which purges us of the emotions of pity and terror by portraying the inevitable downfall of a superior person whose tragic flaw is excessive pride. But, more generally, he suggested that all art is "imitation," or a depiction of life, and can be judged in terms of its success in revealing to us those general patterns that underlie the bewildering flux of appearances. He therefore argued that dialogue and plot should conform to our general knowledge of how people talk and act so that the spectator feels that the theme develops inevitably. Art, for Aristotle, is closer to science and metaphysics than to history, which he considered a mere chronicle of past events. History narrates events but reveals no general patterns or laws, while art reveals "the universal in the particular."

These Aristotelian principles may at first sight appear to be overthrown by modern art. In painting, sculpture, music, poetry, and theater, artists today may seem to revel in violating all rules, especially those suggested by Aristotle. But whether this is really so depends on how narrowly we interpret Aristotle's fundamental view. If we take him to mean not that art must be an exact naturalistic reproduction of its subject and theater an exact imitation of actual human conduct, but rather, as we have already suggested, that it should provide illuminating insights into the underlying reality of human life, then perhaps the best examples of contemporary art fulfill rather than contradict his notion. For example, Samuel Beckett's tragic comedy *Endgame,* though it seems bizarre and disunified, effectively reveals the loneliness and despair of many people when they confront their inability to communicate and to love.

In his influential essay, "What is Art?" Count Leo Tolstoy, a nineteenth-century Russian writer best known for his early novels, *Anna Karenina* and *War and Peace,* takes a considerably more subjectivist position toward art, although his religious commitment tempers his subjectivism. Tolstoy rejects any possibility of confining art within rules such as those of Aristotle that are presumed to be necessary conditions for the achievement of beauty. The perception of beauty, he holds, depends upon what gives us pleasure, which in turn depends upon what we happen to like. We cannot therefore define art as the creation of beauty according to formal rules but must look elsewhere for its essence. The direction he proposes is inward, toward the emotions that a work of art expresses. Artists produce works that inspire in others the emotions that they themselves feel. The most fundamental standards of aesthetic judgment, therefore, are to be found in the sincerity and intensity of the emotion conveyed by the work.

Although these standards enable us to distinguish art from trash, something more is needed, according to Tolstoy, to appreciate the greatest works of art and to explain why they stand out as monuments to the creative genius of the human spirit. Tolstoy maintains that good art is able to communicate its emotions to a wider range of spectators than poor art. Indeed, genuinely great art can be appreciated by all human beings. Tolstoy held that much of the art of his day, including his own early work, was inferior stuff because only a snobbish and frivolous elite could understand it. A poor peasant woman, struggling to keep her family alive, would not be able to feel the despair of Anna Karenina over the infidelity of her princely lover. Tolstoy's interpretation of Christianity as a humanistic love for all led him to the conviction that art, like social reform, should serve to promote brotherhood by conveying emotions that are universally shared. He found in the gospels a call for the elimination of the social inequalities that separate people from each other. He communicated his religious feeling to Gandhi in a series of letters that probably influenced Gandhi's later doctrine of achieving social reform through nonviolent passive resistance. The fundamental meaning of life, Tolstoy believed, is to achieve union with God, but for him this seems to amount to the realization of the brotherhood of humankind. Jesus had said in the gospels, "Whatsoever you do unto one of these, the least of my brethren, you do unto me." The role of great art is to lead people to the recognition of this brotherhood through the sympathetic sharing of experiences.

Tolstoy's account of the purpose of art as the communication of unifying emotions is a form of what has come to be called the "expressive" theory of art. This view, while held by many, faces at least two serious difficulties: (1) it overestimates the relevance of our knowledge of the artist's feelings; and (2) it fails to do justice to art that is contemplative rather than emotionally evocative.

Tolstoy's condemnation of insincerity in art is easy to agree with, but it is not so easy to explain what makes art insincere. He assumes too quickly that it is a lack of genuine feeling in the soul of the artist. But other thinkers, such as novelist Thomas Mann, argue plausibly that the artist gives up emotional involvement in life in order to achieve the cool detachment necessary for objective description of others. In his story *Tonio Kroger,* Mann maintained that artists are tragic figures because they heroically sacrifice their emotional life for their art. In any case, it seems practically impossible for us to know the feelings of artists about whom we know very little, such as the epic poet Homer or the sculptor Phidias or those who painted on the walls of their cave in prehistoric times, yet we seem to be able to appreciate their work and recognize its "sincerity" all the same. It is more likely, therefore, that artistic sincerity has to do with the truth of the artist's vision of things rather than with his or her emotional state.

The contemporary American philosopher Suzanne Langer has attempted to rescue the expressivist view in an ingenious manner. She has suggested that the emotions expressed by the artist and shared by the spectator are not real emotions but imagined or "virtual" emotions.

Artists merely have to imagine, rather than experience, the feelings they want to convey in their works and, because of certain formal similarities between works of art and the human face and body (e.g., sad sculptures have lines curving downward, as do sad faces), artists are able to stimulate us to imagine the same feelings. Sincerity would then presumably mean the accuracy of portrayal and the credibility of the feelings portrayed.

Although Langer's modified expressivism resolves the first difficulty, it may well founder, together with Tolstoy's, on the second, that it overemphasizes emotion in art. Unless we insist arbitrarily and fanatically that modern art is not genuine art, we must face up to the fact that expression of emotion plays less of a role as the arts become more abstract. Some might claim that the very *lack* of intense feeling conveyed by such genres as atonal music and abstract expressionist painting is meant to convey the sense of alienation from which people suffer in modern times. That claim fails as a defense of expressive art, however, because it confuses the theme or significance of a work with the mental state of the artist and the spectator.

One final criticism of Tolstoy's expressivism should be mentioned. Tolstoy's assertion that we can measure the value of works of art by the degree to which they evoke feelings of brotherhood and universal sympathy tends to reduce art to propaganda. Granted that this is propaganda of the noblest and least objectionable kind, it is nevertheless a debasement of art by making it an instrument for social reform.

Whereas Tolstoy considered but then rejected the definition of art as providing pleasure to the spectator, on the ground that it would lead to the subjectivist conclusion that "anything goes," George Santayana, an eminent Spanish-American writer of the early twentieth century, embraced this consequence cheerfully. Santayana holds that all our judgments of value, unlike scientific judgments of fact, are projections of the emotional state of the subject rather than true or false descriptions of the world. Here, he seems to support David Hume's claim that there is a logical gap between "is" and "ought to be," between fact and value, which cannot be bridged by reason but only by the arbitrary assertion of the person judging. All judgments are made on the basis of the pleasure or pain that the object being judged may give.

In order to distinguish works of art from other sources of pleasure such as a good meal, Santayana marks out a special type of pleasure, aesthetic pleasure, as distinct from the bodily or physical pleasure of scratching a mosquito bite or getting a good night's sleep. We are tempted, he thinks, to attribute our aesthetic pleasures to the properties of object enjoyed rather than to our own bodily sensations, because aesthetic pleasures do not call our attention to the organs of sensation through which we experience them. We do not, in listening to a Beethoven symphony, notice our auditory sensations but regard the pleasure of listening as due entirely to the beauty of the music. Beauty, for Santayana, is a pleasure objectified or projected into the external object and taken as a fact about the object rather than a psychological state of the spectator. "Beauty is an emotional element, a pleasure of ours, which nevertheless we regard as a quality of things."

Santayana does not consider aesthetic pleasure to be passively received by the spectator of the work of art. It is not only the artist who is creatively active but the aesthetic judge as well. The work of art is dead until the spectator resurrects it by infusing it with the vital force of his or her own experiences and capacity for joy. As Santayana puts it, "Not until I confound the impressions, and suffuse the symbols themselves with the emotions they arouse, and find joy and sweetness in the very words I hear, will the expressiveness constitute a beauty."

Although Santayana holds that beauty is valued only for the pleasure we feel in its contemplation, he does not crudely identify art with anything that gives us pleasure. He agrees with Aristotle that the very special kind of pleasure we take in works of art is more intellectual than are our bodily pleasures because it involves understanding and perceptual judgment.

Santayana's definition of aesthetic value as the pleasure of contemplating beauty seems at first glance to require art to be insipidly cheerful, like the cheap novels that must have happy endings. But on closer reading we find that he recognizes that great art is often tragic, biting, melancholy, even grotesque, insofar as it portrays these features of human experience with implacable truthfulness. But he argues that when art reveals the sordidness and horror of life, it does so with such clarity of form that it makes its subject bearable and transforms ugliness into beauty, presenting "the unlovely truth in a lovely form." Moreover, he maintains, although we take aesthetic pleasure only in beauty, we would not enjoy art if it were not mixed with the ugliness, sorrow, and despair that we know infects reality and without which art would become an escape into fantasy.

But Santayana's explanation of the presence of ugliness as well as beauty in art is not entirely convincing and may even undermine his subjectivism. He appears to be saying that we want the artist to throw in a bit of horror like a touch of vinegar, just to make the work believable, and he also seems to be saying, perhaps inconsistently, that we want the painful and ugly truth from art because we want art not merely to give us aesthetic pleasure but also to reveal truths, even unpleasant truths, about the world—a statement that sounds suspiciously like objectivism. He tries to avoid inconsistency by placing values other than beauty (e.g., values such as truth) outside the sphere of purely aesthetic value. He thus claims that beauty, or objectified pleasure, is the only distinctively *aesthetic* value. But this concept of aesthetic value does not correspond to much of what we actually look for in works of art.

Philosophers of art in our day have tended to move away from subjectivist views like those of Tolstoy and Santayana and have relocated the desirable features of art in the works themselves. The main line of argument is to reduce or entirely close the alleged gap between fact and value ("is" and "ought"). Marcia Cavell, a contemporary American philosopher, uses this line of argument. Cavell acknowledges some distinction between judgments of observable fact and judgments of value but notes that people often settle their disagreements about works of art rationally. She concludes from this that the fact-value "gap" does not necessarily lead to aesthetic subjectivism. In the essay we have chosen to close this chapter, Cavell cites numerous examples in which disputes concerning works of art are resolved on the basis of technical information about the features of the work being judged. For example, a critic may think that a musical composition is repetitious and then be persuaded that he or she was wrong when shown that the apparent repetition served an important purpose in the work.

Cavell argues that art appreciation and criticism involve informed perception of technical facts rather than just general approval or disapproval of the work, and that the final judgment of the value of a piece is usually agreed upon once the relevant facts are determined. Where it is not, nothing further can be said that would be worth dignifying as "aesthetic judgment." The art critic, she writes, "urges us away from standards and the demands of consistency, with which as moralists we must be concerned, but which in our experiences of works of art tend toward just what the artist hopes to free us from: rigidity of response." She therefore rejects the traditional philosophical search for an overall definition of the nature of art that would serve as a standard for evaluating works as good or bad. We need expert guidance in order to perceive what is in the work of art; the evaluation of the work's goodness or badness either follows naturally from what we perceive, or it is idiosyncratic and of no importance to anyone else.

Cavell maintains that the role of art criticism is to bring about a common way of perceiving artistic works. Accomplishing this requires many things, including "equal sensitivity to the medium, similar training in and experience with the medium, patience, intelligence, imagination, and often conversation itself."

Cavell's position reflects a paradoxical feature of contemporary art: in being freed of the rules imposed upon it by a social aristocracy, art is able to express the values and perceptions of any individual or group, yet it has become so technically complex that it is unintelligible to the unsophisticated observer. We must be what Cavell calls "qualified observers," with considerable information and training, to make reliable judgments of the kind that she considers worth making about works of art. But how many of us have that information and training? To appreciate the frescoes and statues of Michelangelo or the poetry of John Keats requires only a small amount of knowledge, but to appreciate abstract expressionist painting or atonal music requires a special expertise that few have in order to make a critical judgment. In the attempt to overcome subjectivism and its reduction of aesthetic value to mere opinion, Cavell appears to limit critical judgments to a cultural elite. If so, then what remains of the capacity of art, as Aristotle described it, to reveal the universal in the particular and to illuminate for us the underlying patterns of the world? If nothing remains, then why should art be of any importance to us? And if its significance depends only on whether we happen to be sufficiently interested in it to acquire the training of an expert critic, are we not making the value of art subjective after all? The perennial problems of philosophy, as we have seen throughout our journey, are not easily laid to rest.

THE MISANTHROPE

Molière

ORONTE, *to* ALCESTE   The servants told me at the door
That Éliante and Célimène were out,
But when I heard, dear Sir, that you were about,
I came to say, without exaggeration,
That I hold you in the vastest admiration,
And that it's always been my dearest desire
To be the friend of one I so admire.
I hope to see my love of merit requited,
And you and I in friendship's bond united.
I'm sure you won't refuse—if I may be frank—
A friend of my devotedness—and rank.

During this speech of ORONTE'S, ALCESTE *is abstracted, and seems
unaware that he is being spoken to. He only breaks off his reverie
when* ORONTE *says:*

It was for you, if you please, that my words were intended.
ALCESTE   For me, Sir?
ORONTE   Yes, for you. You're not offended?

ALCESTE   By no means. But this much surprises me . . .
          The honor comes most unexpectedly . . .
ORONTE   My high regard should not astonish you;
          The whole world feels the same. It is your due.
ALCESTE   Sir . . .
ORONTE   Why, in all the State there isn't one
          Can match your merits; they shine, Sir, like the sun.
ALCESTE   Sir . . .
ORONTE   You are higher in my estimation
          Than all that's most illustrious in the nation.
ALCESTE   Sir . . .
ORONTE   If I lie, may heaven strike me dead!
          To show you that I mean what I have said,
          Permit me, Sir, to embrace you most sincerely,
          And swear that I will prize our friendship dearly.
          Give me your hand. And now, Sir, if you choose,
          We'll make our vows.
ALCESTE   Sir . . .
ORONTE   What! You refuse?
ALCESTE   Sir, it's a very great honor you extend:
          But friendship is a sacred thing, my friend;
          It would be profanation to bestow
          The name of friend on one you hardly know.
          All parts are better played when well-rehearsed;
          Let's put off friendship, and get acquainted first.
          We may discover it would be unwise
          To try to make our natures harmonize.
ORONTE   By heaven! You're sagacious to the core;
          This speech has made me admire you even more.
          Let time, then, bring us closer day by day;
          Meanwhile, I shall be yours in every way.
          If, for example, there should be anything
          You wish at court, I'll mention it to the King.
          I have his ear, of course; it's quite well known
          That I am much in favor with the throne.
          In short, I am your servant. And now, dear friend,
          Since you have such fine judgment, I intend
          To please you, if I can, with a small sonnet
          I wrote not long ago. Please comment on it,
          And tell me whether I ought to publish it.
ALCESTE   You must excuse me, Sir; I'm hardly fit
          To judge such matters.
ORONTE   Why not?
ALCESTE   I am, I fear,
          Inclined to be unfashionably sincere.
ORONTE   Just what I ask; I'd take no satisfaction
          In anything but your sincere reaction.

I beg you not to dream of being kind.

ALCESTE   Since you desire it, Sir, I'll speak my mind.

ORONTE   *Sonnet. It's a sonnet . . . Hope . . .* The poem's addressed
  To a lady who wakened hopes within my breast.
  Hope . . . this is not the pompous sort of thing,
  Just modest little verses, with a tender ring.

ALCESTE   Well, we shall see.

ORONTE   *Hope . . .* I'm anxious to hear
  Whether the style seems properly smooth and clear,
  And whether the choice of words is good or bad.

ALCESTE   We'll see, we'll see.

ORONTE   Perhaps I ought to add
  That it took me only a quarter-hour to write it.

ALCESTE   The time's irrelevant, Sir: kindly recite it.

ORONTE, *reading*
  Hope comforts us awhile, 'tis true,
  Lulling our cares with careless laughter,
  And yet such joy is full of rue,
  My Phyllis, if nothing follows after.

PHILINTE   I'm charmed by this already; the style's delightful.

ALCESTE, *sotto voce, to* PHILINTE   How can you say that? Why, the thing is frightful.

ORONTE   *Your fair face smiled on me awhile,*
  But was it kindness so to enchant me?
  'Twould have been fairer not to smile,
  If hope was all you meant to grant me.

PHILINTE   What a clever thought! How handsomely you phrase it!

ALCESTE, *sotto voce, to* PHILINTE   You know the thing is trash. How dare you praise it?

ORONTE   *If it's to be my passion's fate*
  Thus everlastingly to wait,
  Then death will come to set me free:
  For death is fairer than the fair;
  Phyllis, to hope is to despair
  When one must hope eternally.

PHILINTE   The close is exquisite—full of feeling and grace.

ALCESTE, *sotto voce, aside*   Oh, blast the close; you'd better close your face
  Before you send your lying soul to hell.

PHILINTE   I can't remember a poem I've liked so well.

ALCESTE, *sotto voce, aside*   Good Lord!

ORONTE, *to* PHILINTE   I fear you're flattering me a bit.

PHILINTE   Oh, no!

ALCESTE, *sotto voce, aside*

What else d'you call it, you hypocrite?

ORONTE, *to* ALCESTE   But you, Sir, keep your promise now: don't shrink
From telling me sincerely what you think.

ALCESTE   Sir, these are delicate matters; we all desire
To be told that we've the true poetic fire.
But once, to one whose name I shall not mention,
I said, regarding some verse of his invention,
That gentlemen should rigorously control
That itch to write which often afflicts the soul;
That one should curb the heady inclination
To publicize one's little avocation;
And that in showing off one's works of art
One often plays a very clownish part.

ORONTE   Are you suggesting in a devious way
That I ought not . . .

ALCESTE   Oh, that I do not say.
Further, I told him that no fault is worse
Than that of writing frigid, lifeless verse,
And that the merest whisper of such a shame
Suffices to destroy a man's good name.

ORONTE   D'you mean to say my sonnet's dull and trite?

ALCESTE   I don't say that. But I went on to cite
Numerous cases of once-respected men
Who came to grief by taking up the pen.

ORONTE   And am I like them? Do I write so poorly?

ALCESTE   I don't say that. But I told this person, "Surely
You're under no necessity to compose;
Why you should wish to publish, heaven knows.
There's no excuse for printing tedious rot
Unless one writes for bread, as you do not.
Resist temptation, then, I beg of you;
Conceal your pastimes from the public view;
And don't give up, on any provocation,
Your present high and courtly reputation,
To purchase at a greedy printer's shop
The name of silly author and scribbling fop."
These were the points I tried to make him see.

ORONTE   I sense that they are also aimed at me;
But now—about my sonnet—I'd like to be told . . .

ALCESTE   Frankly, that sonnet should be pigeonholed.
You've chosen the worst models to imitate.
The style's unnatural. Let me illustrate:
For example, *Your fair face smiled on me awhile,*
Followed by, *'Twould have been fairer not to smile!*
Or this: *such joy is full of rue;*
Or this: *For death is fairer than the fair;*

Or, *Phyllis, to hope is to despair*
    When one must hope eternally!
This artificial style, that's all the fashion,
Has neither taste, nor honesty, nor passion;
It's nothing but a sort of wordy play,
And nature never spoke in such a way.
What, in this shallow age, is not debased?
Our fathers, though less refined, had better taste;
I'd barter all that men admire today
For one old love song I shall try to say:
If the King had given me for my own
Paris, his citadel,
And I for that must leave alone
Her whom I love so well,
I'd say then to the Crown,
Take back your glittering town;
My darling is more fair, I swear,
My darling is more fair.
The rhyme's not rich, the style is rough and old,
But don't you see that it's the purest gold
Beside the tinsel nonsense now preferred,
And that there's passion in its every word?
If the King had given me for my own
Paris, his citadel,
And I for that must leave alone
Her whom I love so well,
I'd say then to the Crown,
Take back your glittering town;
My darling is more fair, I swear,
My darling is more fair.
There speaks a loving heart. (*To* PHILINTE) You're laughing, eh?
Laugh on, my precious wit. Whatever you say,
I hold that song's worth all the bibelots
That people hail today with ah's and oh's.
ORONTE   And I maintain my sonnet's very good.
ALCESTE   It's not at all surprising that you should.
  You have your reasons; permit me to have mine
  For thinking that you cannot write a line.
ORONTE   Others have praised my sonnet to the skies.
ALCESTE   I lack their art of telling pleasant lies.
ORONTE   You seem to think you've got no end of wit.
ALCESTE   To praise your verse, I'd need still more of it.
ORONTE   I'm not in need of your approval, Sir.
ALCESTE   That's good; you couldn't have it if you were.
ORONTE   Come now, I'll lend you the subject of my sonnet;
  I'd like to see you try to improve upon it.
ALCESTE   I might, by chance, write something just as shoddy;

But then I wouldn't show it to everybody.

ORONTE   You're most opinionated and conceited.

ALCESTE   Go find your flatterers, and be better treated.

ORONTE   Look here, my little fellow, pray watch your tone.

ALCESTE   My great big fellow, you'd better watch your own.

PHILINTE, *stepping between them*   Oh, please, please, gentlemen!
This will never do.

ORONTE   The fault is mine, and I leave the field to you.
I am your servant, Sir, in every way.

ALCESTE   And I, Sir, am your most abject valet.

THE FORMAL UNITIES

Aristotle

There are six parts . . . of every tragedy, as a whole (that is) of such or such quality, viz. a Fable or Plot, Characters, Diction, Thought, Spectacle, and Melody; two of them arising from the means, one from the manner, and three from the objects of the dramatic imitation; and there is nothing else besides these six. Of these, its formative elements, then, not a few of the dramatists have made due use, as every play, one may say, admits of Spectacle, Character, Fable, Diction, Melody, and Thought.

The most important of the six is the combination of the incidents of the story. Tragedy is essentially an imitation not of persons but of action and life, of happiness and misery. All human happiness or misery takes the form of action; the end for which we live is a certain kind of activity, not a quality. Character gives us qualities, but it is in our actions—what we do—that we are happy or the reverse. In a play accordingly they do not act in order to portray the Characters; they include the Characters for the sake of the action. So that it is the action in it, i.e. its Fable or Plot, that is the end and purpose of the tragedy; and the end is everywhere the chief thing. Besides this, a tragedy is impossible without action, but there may be one without Character. The tragedies of most of the moderns are characterless—a defect common among poets of all kinds, and with its counterpart in painting in Zeuxis as compared with Polygnotus; for whereas the latter is strong in character, the work of Zeuxis is devoid of it. And again: one may string together a series of characteristic speeches of the utmost finish as regards Diction and Thought, and yet fail to produce the true tragic effect; but one will have much better success with a tragedy which, however inferior in these respects, has a Plot, a combination of incidents, in it. And again: the most powerful elements of attraction in Tragedy, the Peripeties and Discoveries, are parts of the Plot. A further proof is in the fact that beginners succeed earlier with the Diction and Characters than with the construction of

FROM *Poetics*, VI–VII, translated by Ingram Bywater. Reprinted by permission of Oxford University Press.

a story; and the same may be said of nearly all the early dramatists. We maintain, therefore, that the first essential, the life and soul, so to speak, of Tragedy is the Plot; and that the Characters come second—compare the parallel in painting, where the most beautiful colors laid on without order will not give one the same pleasure as a simple black-and-white sketch of a portrait. We maintain that Tragedy is primarily an imitation of action, and that it is mainly for the sake of the action that it imitates the personal agents. Third comes the element of Thought, i.e. the power of saying whatever can be said, or what is appropriate to the occasion. This is what, in the speeches in Tragedy, falls under the arts of Politics and Rhetoric; for the older poets make their personages discourse like statesmen, and the modern like rhetoricians. One must not confuse it with Character. Character in a play is that which reveals the moral purpose of the agents, i.e. the sort of thing they seek or avoid, where that is not obvious—hence there is no room for Character in a speech on a purely indifferent subject. Thought, on the other hand, is shown in all they say when proving or disproving some particular point, or enunciating some universal proposition. Fourth among the literary elements is the Diction of the personages, i.e., . . . the expression of their thoughts in words, which is practically the same thing with verse as with prose. As for the two remaining parts, the Melody is the greatest of the pleasurable accessories of Tragedy. The Spectacle, though an attraction, is the least artistic of all the parts, and has least to do with the art of poetry. The tragic effect is quite possible without a public performance and actors; and besides, the getting-up of the Spectacle is more a matter for the costumier than the poet.

Having thus distinguished the parts, let us now consider the proper construction of the Fable or Plot, as that is at once the first and the most important thing in Tragedy. We have laid it down that a tragedy is an imitation of an action that is complete in itself, as a whole of some magnitude; for a whole may be of no magnitude to speak of. Now a whole is that which has beginning, middle, and end. A beginning is that which is not itself necessarily after anything else, and which has naturally something else after it; an end is that which is naturally after something itself, either as its necessary or usual consequent, and with nothing else after it; and a middle, that which is by nature after one thing and has also another after it. A well-constructed Plot, therefore, cannot either begin or end at any point one likes; beginning and end in it must be of the forms just described. Again: to be beautiful, a living creature, and every whole made up of parts, must not only present a certain order in its arrangement of parts, but also be of a certain definite magnitude. Beauty is a matter of size and order, and therefore impossible either

(1) in a very minute creature, since our perception becomes indistinct as it approaches instantaneity; or (2) in a creature of vast size—one, say, 1,000 miles long—as in that case, instead of the object being seen all at once, the unity and wholeness of it is lost to the beholder. Just in the same way, then, as a beautiful whole made up of parts, or a beautiful living creature, must be of some size, but a size to be taken in by the eye, so a story or Plot must be of some length, but of a length to be taken in by the memory. As for the limit of its length, so far as that is relative to public performances and spectators, it does not fall within the theory of poetry. If they had to perform a hundred tragedies, they would be timed by water-clocks, as they are said to have been at one period. The limit, however, set by the actual nature of the thing is this: the longer the story, consistently with its being comprehensible as a whole, the finer it is by reason of its magnitude. As a rough general formula, "a length which allows of the hero passing by a series of proba-ble or necessary stages from misfortune to happiness, or from happiness to misfortune," may suffice as a limit for the magnitude of the story.

The Unity of a Plot does not consist, as some suppose, in its having one man as its subject. An infinity of things befall that one man, some of which it is impossible to reduce to unity; and in like manner there are many actions of one man which cannot be made to form one action. One sees, therefore, the mistake of all the poets who have written a *Heracleid,* a *Theseid,* or similar poems; they suppose that, because Heracles was one man, the story also of Heracles must be one story. Homer, however, evidently understood this point quite well, whether by art or instinct, just in the same way as he excels the rest in every other respect. In writing an *Odyssey,* he did not make the poem cover all that ever befell his hero—it befell him, for instance, to get wounded on Parnassus and also to feign madness at the time of the call to arms, but the two incidents had no necessary or probable connection with one another—instead of doing that, he took as the subject of the *Odyssey,* as also of the *Iliad,* an action with a Unity of the kind we are describing. The truth is that, just as in the other imitative arts one imitation is always of one thing, so in poetry the story, as an imitation of action, must repre-sent one action, a complete whole, with its several incidents so closely connected that the transposal or withdrawal of any one of them will dis-join and dislocate the whole. For that which makes no perceptible dif-ference by its presence or absence is no real part of the whole.

From what we have said it will be seen that the poet's function is to describe, not the thing that has happened, but a kind of thing that might happen, i.e. what is possible as being probable or necessary. The distinction between historian and poet is not in the one writing prose and the other verse—you might put the work of Herodotus into verse, and it would still be a species of history; it consists really in this, that the one describes the thing that has been, and the other a kind of thing that might be. Hence poetry is something more philosophic and of graver import than history, since its statements are of the nature rather of universals, whereas those of history are singulars. By a universal statement I mean one as to what such or such a kind of man will probably or necessarily say or do—which is the aim of poetry, though it affixes proper names to the characters; by a singular statement, one as to what, say, Alcibiades did or had done to him. In Comedy this has become clear by this time; it is only when their plot is already made up of probable incidents that they give it a basis of proper names, choosing for the purpose any names that may occur to them, instead of writing like the old iambic poets about particular persons. In Tragedy, however, they still adhere to the historic names; and for this reason: what convinces is the possible; now whereas we are not yet sure as to the possibility of that which has not happened, that which has happened is manifestly possible, else it would not have come to pass. Nevertheless even in Tragedy there are some plays with but one or two known names in them, the rest being inventions; and there are some without a single known name, e.g. Agathon's *Antheus,* in which both incidents and names are of the poet's invention; and it is no less delightful on that account. So that one must not aim at a rigid adherence to the traditional stories on which tragedies are based. It would be absurd, in fact, to do so, as even the known stories are only known to a few, though they are a delight none the less to all.

It is evident from the above that the poet must be more the poet of his stories or Plots than of his verses, inasmuch as he is a poet by virtue of the imitative element in his work, and it is actions that he imitates. And if he should come to take a subject from actual history, he is none the less a poet for that; since some historic occurrences may very well be in the probable and possible order of things; and it is in that aspect of them that he is their poet.

Of simple Plots and actions the episodic are the worst. I call a Plot episodic when there is neither probability nor necessity in the sequence of its episodes. Actions of this sort bad poets construct through their own fault, and good ones on account of the players. His work being for public performance, a good poet often stretches out a Plot beyond its capabilities, and is thus obliged to twist the sequence of incident.

Tragedy, however, is an imitation not only of a complete action, but also of incidents arousing pity and fear. Such incidents have the very greatest effect on the mind when they occur unexpectedly and at the same time in consequence of one another; there is more of the marvelous in them then than if they happened of themselves or by mere chance. Even matters of chance seem most marvelous if there is an appearance of design as it were in them; as for instance the statue of Mitys at Argos killed the author of Mitys' death by falling down on him when a looker-on at a public spectacle; for incidents like that we think to be not without a meaning. A Plot, therefore, of this sort is necessarily finer than others.

Plots are either simple or complex, since the actions they represent are naturally of this twofold description. The action, proceeding in the way defined, as one continous whole, I call simple, when the change in the hero's fortunes takes place without Peripety or Discovery; and complex, when it involves one or the other, or both. These should each of them arise out of the structure of the Plot itself, so as to be the consequence, necessary or probable, of the antecedents. There is a great difference between a thing happening *propter hoc* [because of something] and *post hoc* [after something].

A Peripety is the change of the kind described from one state of things within the play to its opposite, and that too in the way we are saying, in the probable or necessary sequence of events; as it is for instance in *Oedipus*: here the opposite state of things is produced by the Messenger, who, coming to gladden Oedipus and to remove his fears as to his mother, reveals the secret of his birth. And in *Lynceus*: just as he is being led off for execution, with Danaus at his side to put him to death, the incidents preceding this bring it about that he is saved and Danaus put to death. A Discovery is, as the very word implies, a change from ignorance to knowledge, and thus to either love or hate, in the personages marked for good or evil fortune. The finest form of Discovery is one attended by Peripeties, like that which goes with the Discovery in *Oedipus*. There are no doubt other forms of it; what we have said may happen in a way in reference to inanimate things, even things of a very casual kind; and it is also possible to discover whether some one has done or not done something. But the form most directly connected with the Plot and the action of the piece is the first-mentioned. This, with a Peripety, will arouse either pity or fear—actions of that nature being what Tragedy is assumed to represent; and it will also serve to bring about the happy or unhappy ending. The Discovery, then, being of persons it may be that of one party only to the other, the latter being already known; or both the parties may have to discover themselves. Iphigenia, for instance, was discovered to Orestes by sending the letter; and another Discovery was required to reveal him to Iphigenia.

Two parts of the Plot, then, Peripety and Discovery, are on matters of this sort. A third part is Suffering; which we may define as an action of a destructive or painful nature, such as murders on the stage, tortures, woundings, and the like. The other two have been already explained.

The parts of Tragedy to be treated as formative elements in the whole were mentioned in a previous Chapter. From the point of view, however, of its quantity, i.e. the separate sections into which it is divided, a tragedy has the following parts: Prologue, Episode, Exode, and a choral portion, distinguished into Parode and Stasimon; these two are common to all tragedies, whereas songs from the stage and *Commoe* are only found in some. The Prologue is all that precedes the Parode of the chorus; an Episode all that comes in between two whole choral songs; the Exode all that follows after the last choral song. In the choral portion the Parode is the whole first statement of the chorus; a Stasimon, a song of the chorus without anapests or trochees; a *Commos,* a lamentation sung by chorus and actor in concert. The parts of Tragedy to be used as formative elements in the whole we have already mentioned; the above are its parts from the point of view of its quantity, or the separate sections into which it is divided.

The next points after what we have said above will be these: (1) What is the poet to aim at, and what is he to avoid, in constructing his Plots? and (2) What are the conditions on which the tragic effect depends?

We assume that, for the finest form of Tragedy, the Plot must be not simple but complex; and further, that it must imitate actions arousing fear and pity, since that is the distinctive function of this kind of imitation. It follows, therefore, that there are three forms of Plot to be avoided. (1) A good man must not be seen passing from happiness to misery, or (2) a bad man from misery to happiness. The first situation is not fear-inspiring or piteous, but simply odious to us. The second is the most untragic that can be; it has no one of the requisites of Tragedy; it does not appeal either to the human feeling in us, or to our pity, or to our fears. Nor, on the other hand, should (3) an extremely bad man be seen falling from happiness into misery. Such a story may arouse the human feeling in us, but it will not move us to either pity or fear; pity is occasioned by undeserved misfortune, and fear by that of one like ourselves; so that there will be nothing either piteous or fear-inspiring in the situation. There remains, then, the intermediate kind of personage, a man not pre-eminently virtuous and just, whose misfortune, however, is brought upon him not by vice and depravity but by some error of judgement, of the number of those in the enjoyment of great reputation and prosperity; e.g. Oedipus, Thyestes, and the men of note of similar familes. The perfect Plot, accordingly, must have a single, and not (as some tell us) a double issue; the change in the hero's fortunes must be not from misery to happiness, but on the contrary from happiness to misery; and the cause of it must lie not in any depravity, but in some great error on his part; the man himself being either such as we have described, or better, not worse, than that. Fact also confirms our theory. Though the poets began by accepting any tragic story that came to hand, in these days the finest tragedies are always on the story of some few houses, on that of Alcmeon, Oedipus, Orestes, Meleager, Thyestes, Telephus, or any others that may have been involved, as either agents or sufferers, in some deed of horror. The theoretically best tragedy, then, has a Plot of this description. The critics, therefore, are wrong who blame Euripides for taking this line in his tragedies, and giving many of them an unhappy ending. It is, as we have said, the right line to take. The best proof is this: on the stage, and in the public performances, such plays, properly worked out, are seen to be the most truly tragic; and Euripides, even if his execution be faulty in every other point, is seen to be nevertheless the most tragic certainly of the dramatists. After this comes the construction of Plot which some rank first, one with a double story (like the *Odyssey*) and an opposite issue for the good and the bad personages. It is ranked as first only through the weakness of the audiences; the poets merely follow their public, writing as its wishes dictate. But the pleasure here is not that of Tragedy. It belongs rather to Comedy, where the bitterest enemies in the piece (e.g. Orestes and Aegisthus) walk off good friends at the end, with no slaying of any one by any one.

The tragic fear and pity may be aroused by the Spectacle; but they may also be aroused by the very structure and incidents of the play—which is the better way and shows the better poet. The Plot in fact should be so framed that, even without seeing the things take place, he who simply hears the account of them shall be filled with horror and pity at the incidents; which is just the effect that the mere recital of the story in *Oedipus* would have on one. To produce this same effect by means of the Spectacle is less artistic, and requires extraneous aid. Those, however, who make use of the Spectacle to put before us that which is merely monstrous and not productive of fear, are wholly out of touch with Tragedy; not every kind of pleasure should be required of a tragedy, but only its own proper pleasure.

The tragic pleasure is that of pity and fear, and the poet has to produce it by a work of imitation; it is clear, therefore, that the causes should be included in the incidents of his story. Let us see, then, what kinds of incident strike one as horrible, or rather as piteous. In a deed of this description the parties must necessarily be either friends, or enemies, or indifferent to one another. Now when enemy does it on enemy, there is nothing to move us to pity either in his doing or in his meditating the deed, except so far as the actual pain of the sufferer is concerned; and the same is true when the parties are indifferent to one another. Whenever the tragic deed, however, is done within the family—when murder or the like is done or meditated by brother on brother, by son on father, by mother on son, or son on mother—these are the situations the poet should seek after. The traditional stories, accordingly, must be kept as they are, e.g. the murder of Clytemnestra by Orestes and of Eriphyle by Alcmeon. At the same time even with these there is something left to the poet himself; it is for him to devise the right way of treating them. Let us explain more clearly what we mean by "the right way." The deed of horror may be done by the doer knowingly and consciously, as in the old poets, and in Medea's murder of her children in Euripides. Or he may do it, but in ignorance of his relationship, and discover that afterwards, as does the Oedipus in Sophocles. Here the deed is outside the play; but it may be within it, like the act of the Alemeon in Astydamas, or that of the Telegonus in *Ulysses Wounded.* A third possibility is for one meditating some deadly injury to another, in ignorance of his relaship, to make the discovery in time to draw back. These exhaust the possibilities, since the deed must necessarily be either done or not done, and either knowingly or unknowingly.

The worst situation is when the personage is with full knowledge on the point of doing the deed, and leaves it undone. It is odious and also (through the absence of suffering) untragic; hence it is that no one is made to act thus except in some few instances, e.g. Haemon and Creon in *Antigone*. Next after this comes the actual perpetration of the deed meditated. A better situation than that, however, is for the deed to be done in ignorance, and the relationship discovered afterwards, since there is nothing odious in it, and the Discovery will serve to astound us. But the best of all is the last; what we have in *Cresphontes,* for example, where Merope, on the point of slaying her son, recognizes him in time; in *Iphigenia,* where sister and brother are in a like position; and in *Helle,* where the son recognizes his mother, when on the point of giving her up to her enemy.

This will explain why our tragedies are restricted (as we said just now) to such a small number of families. It was accident rather than art that led the poets in quest of subjects to embody this kind of incident in their Plots. They are still obliged, accordingly, to have recourse to the families in which such horrors have occurred.

On the construction of the Plot, and the kind of Plot required for Tragedy, enough has now been said.

In the Characters there are four points to aim at. First and foremost, that they shall be good. There will be an element of character in the play, if (as has been observed) what a personage says or does reveals a certain moral purpose; and a good element of character, if the purpose so revealed is good. Such goodness is possible in every type of personage, even in a woman or a slave, though the one is perhaps an inferior, and the other a wholly worthless being. The second point is to make them appropriate. The Character before us may be, say, manly; but it is not appropriate in a female Character to be manly, or clever. The third is to make them like the reality, which is not the same as their being good and appropriate, in our sense of the term. The fourth is to make them consistent and the same throughout; even if inconsistency be part of the man before one for imitation as presenting that form of character, he should still be consistently inconsistent. We have an instance of baseness of character, not required for the story, in the Menelaus in *Orestes*; of the incongruous and unbefitting in the lamentation of Ulysses in *Scylla,* and in the (clever) speech of Melanippe; and of inconsistency in *Iphigenia at Aulis,* where Iphigenia the suppliant is utterly unlike the later Iphigenia. The right thing, however, is in the Characters just as in the incidents of the play to endeavor always after the necessary or the probable; so that whenever such-and-such a personage says or does such-and-such a thing, it shall be the necessary or probable outcome of his character; and whenever this incident follows on that, it shall be either the necessary or the probable consequence of it. From this one sees (to digress for a moment) that the Dénouement also should arise out of the plot itself, and not depend on a stage-artifice, as in *Medea,* or in the story of the (arrested) departure of the Greeks in the *Iliad*. The artifice must be reserved for matters outside the play—for past events beyond human knowledge, or events yet to come, which require to be foretold or announced; since it is the privilege of the Gods to know everything. There should be nothing improbable among the actual incidents. If it be unavoidable, however, it should be outside the tragedy, like the improbability in the *Oedipus* of Sophocles. But to return to the Characters. As Tragedy is an imitation of personages better than the ordinary man, we in our way should follow the example of good portrait-painters, who reproduce the distinctive features of a man, and at the same time, without losing the likeness, make him handsomer than he is. The poet in like manner, in portraying men quick or slow to anger, or with similar infirmities of character, must know how to represent them as such, and at the same time as good men, as Agathon and Homer have represented Achilles.

All these rules one must keep in mind throughout, and, further, those also for such points of stage-effect as directly depend on the art of the poet, since in these too one may often make mistakes. Enough, however, has been said on the subject in one of our published writings.

Discovery in general has been explained already. As for the species of Discovery, the first to be noted is (1) the least artistic form of it, of which the poets make most use through mere lack of invention, Discovery by signs or marks. Of these signs some are congenital, like the "lance-head which the Earth-born have on them," or "stars," such as Carcinus brings in his *Thyestes;* others acquired after birth—these latter being either marks on the body, e.g. scars, or external tokens, like necklaces, or (to take another sort of instance) the ark in the Discovery in *Tyro.* Even these, however, admit of two uses, a better and a worse; the scar of Ulysses is an instance; the Discovery of him through it is made in one way by the nurse and in another by the swineherds. A Discovery using signs as a means of assurance is less artistic, as indeed are all such as imply reflection; whereas one bringing them in all of a sudden, as in the *Bath-story,* is of a better order. Next after these are (2) Discoveries made directly by the poet; which are inartistic for that very reason; e.g. Orestes' Discovery of himself in *Iphigenia*: whereas his sister reveals who she is by the letter, Orestes is made to say himself what the poet rather than the story demands. This, therefore, is not far removed from the first-mentioned fault, since he might have presented certain tokens as well. Another instance is the "shuttle's voice" in the *Tereus* of Sophocles. (3) A third species is Discovery through memory, from a man's con-sciousness being awakened by something seen. Thus in *The Cyprioe of Dicaeogenes,* the sight of the picture makes the man burst into tears; and in the *Tale of Alcinous,* hearing the harper Ulysses is reminded of the past and weeps; the Discovery of them being the result. (4) A fourth kind is Discovery through reasoning, e.g. in *The Choephoroe;* "One like me is here; there is no one like me but Orestes; he, therefore, must be here." Or that which Polyidus the Sophist suggested for *Iphigenia*; since it was natural for Orestes to reflect: "My sister was sacrificed, and I am to be sacrified like her." Or that in the *Tydeus* of Theodectes: "I came to find a son, and am to die myself." Or that in *The Phinidae*: on seeing the place the women inferred their fate, that they were to die there, since they had also been exposed there. (5) There is, too, a composite Discovery arising from bad reasoning on the side of the other party. An instance of it is in *Ulysses the False Messenger*: he said he should know the bow—which he had not seen; but to suppose from that that he would know it again(as though he had once seen it) was bad reasoning. (6) The best of all Discoveries, however, is that arising from the incidents themselves, when the great surprise comes about through a probable incident, like that in the *Oedipus* of Sophocles; and also in *Iphigenia*; for it was not improbable that she should wish to have a letter taken home. These last are the only Discoveries independent of the artifice of signs and necklaces. Next after them come Discoveries through reasoning.

At the time when he is constructing his Plots, and engaged on the Diction in which they are worked out, the poet should remember (1) to put the actual scenes as far as possible before his eyes. In this way, seeing everything with the vividness of an eye-witness as it were, he will devise what is appropriate, and be least likely to overlook incongruities. This is shown by what was censured in Carcinus, the return of Amphiaraus from the sanctuary; it would have passed unnoticed, if it had not been actually seen by the audience; but on the stage his play failed, the incongruity of the incident offending the spectators. (2) As far as may be, too, the poet should even act his story with the very gestures of his personages. Given the same natural qualifications, he who feels the emotions to be described will be the most convincing; distress and anger, for instance, are portrayed most truthfully by one who is feeling them at the moment. Hence it is that poetry demands a man with a special gift for it, or else one with a touch of madness in him; the former can easily assume the required mood, and the latter may be actually beside himself with emotion. (3) His story, again, whether already made or of his own making, he should first simplify and reduce to a universal form, before proceeding to lengthen it out by the insertion of episodes. The following will show how the universal element in *Iphigenia,* for instance, may be viewed: A certain maiden having been offered in sacrifice, and spirited away from her sacrifices into another land, where the custom was to sacrifice all strangers to the Goddess, she was made there the priestess of this rite. Long after that the brother of the priestess happened to come; the fact, however, of the oracle having for a certain reason bidden him go thither, and his object in going, are outside the Plot of the play. On his coming he was arrested and about to be sacrified, when he revealed who he was—either as Euripides puts it, or (as suggested by Polyidus) by the not improbable exclamation, "So I too am doomed to be sacrificed, as my sister was"; and the disclosure led to his salvation. This done, the next thing, after the proper names have been fixed as a basis for the story, is to work in episodes or accessory incidents. One must mind, however, that the episodes are appropriate, like the fit of madness in Orestes, which led to his arrest, and the purifying, which brought about his salvation. In plays, then, the episodes are short; in epic poetry they serve to lengthen out the poem. The argument of the *Odyssey* is not a long one. A certain man has been abroad many years; Poseidon is ever on the watch for him, and he is all alone. Matters at home too have come to this, that his substance is being wasted and his son's death plotted by suitors to his wife. Then he arrives there himself after his grievous sufferings; reveals himself, and falls on his enemies; and the end is his salvation and their death. This being all that is proper to the *Odyssey,* everything else in it is episode.

(4) There is a further point to be borne in mind. Every tragedy is in part Complication and in part Dénouement; the incidents before the opening scene, and often certain also of those within the play, forming the Complication; and the rest the Dénouement. By Complication I mean all from the beginning of the story to the point just before the change in the hero's fortunes; by Dénouement, all from the beginning of the change to the end. In the *Lynceus* of Theodectes, for instance, the Complication includes, together with the presupposed incidents, the seizure of the child and that in turn of the parents; and the Dénouement all from the indictment for the murder to the end. Now it is right, when one speaks of a tragedy as the same or not the same as another, to do so on the ground before all else of their Plot, i.e. as having the same or not the same Complication and Dénouement. Yet there are many dramatists who, after a good Complication, fail in the Dénouement. But it is necessary for both points of construction to be always duly mastered. (5) There are four distinct species of Tragedy—that being the number of the constituents also that have been mentioned: first, the complex Tragedy, which is all Peripety and Discovery; second, the Tragedy of suffering, e.g. the *Ajaxes* and *Ixions;* third, the Tragedy of character, e.g. *The Phthiotides* and *Peleus.* The fourth constituent is that of "Spectacle," exemplified in *The Phorcides,* in *Prometheus,* and in all plays with the scene laid in the nether world. The poet's aim, then, should be to combine every element of interest, if possible, or else the more important and the major part of them. This is now especially necessary owing to the unfair criticism to which the poet is subjected in these days. Just because there have been poets before him strong in the several species of tragedy, the critics now expect the one man to surpass that which was the strong point of each one of his predecessors. (6) One should also remember what has been said more than once, and not write a tragedy on an epic body of incident (i.e. one with a plurality of stories in it), by attempting to dramatize, for instance, the entire story of the *Iliad.* In the epic owing to its scale every part is treated at proper length; with a drama, however, on the same story the result is very disappointing. This

is shown by the fact that all who have dramatized the fall of Ilium in its entirety, and not part by part, like Euripides, of the whole of the Niobe story, instead of a portion, like Aeschylus, either fail utterly or have but ill success on the stage; for that and that alone was enough to ruin even a play by Agathon. Yet in their Peripeties, as also in their simple plots, the poets I mean show wonderful skill in aiming at the kind of effect they desire—a tragic situation that arouses the human feeling in one, like the clever villain (e.g. Sisyphus) deceived, or the brave wrongdoer worsted. This is probable, however, only in Agathon's sense, when he speaks of the probability of even improbabilities coming to pass. (7) The Chorus too should be regarded as one of the actors; it should be an integral part of the whole, and take a share in the action—that which it has in Sophocles, rather than in Euripides. With the later poets, however, the songs in a play of theirs have no more to do with the Plot of that than of any other tragedy. Hence it is that they are now singing intercalary pieces, a practice first introduced by Agathon. And yet what real difference is there between singing such intercalary pieces, and attempting to fit in a speech, or even a whole act, from one play into another?

The Plot and Characters having been discussed, it remains to consider the Diction and Thought. As for the Thought, we may assume what is said of it in our Art of Rhetoric, as it belongs more properly to that department of inquiry. The Thought of the personages is shown in everything to be effected by their language—in every effort to prove or disprove, to arouse emotion (pity, fear, anger, and the like), or to maximize or minimize things. It is clear, also, that their mental procedure must be on the same lines in their actions likewise, whenever they wish them to arouse pity or horror, or to have a look of importance or probability. The only difference is that with the act the impression has to be made without explanation; whereas with the spoken word it has to be produced by the speaker, and result from his language. What, indeed, would be the good of the speaker, if things appeared in the required light even apart from anything he says?

As regards the Diction, one subject for inquiry under this head is the turns given to the language when spoken; e.g. the difference between command and prayer, simple statement and threat, question and answer, and so forth. The theory of such matters, however, belongs to Elocution and the professors of that art. Whether the poet knows these things or not, his art as a poet is never seriously criticized on that account. What fault can one see in Homer's "Sing of the wrath, Goddess"?—which Protagoras has criticized as being a command where a prayer was meant, since to bid one do or not do, he tells us, is a command. Let us pass over this, then, as appertaining to another art, and not to that of poetry.

WHAT IS ART?

Leo Tolstoy

There is no objective definition of beauty. The existing definitions
. . . amount only to one and the same subjective definition, which is
(strange as it seems to say so), that art is that which makes beauty
manifest, and beauty is that which pleases (without exciting desire).
Many aestheticians have felt the insufficiency and instability of such
a definition, and in order to give it a firm basis have asked themselves
why a thing pleases. And they have converted the discussion on beauty
into a question of taste, as did Hutcheson, Voltaire, Diderot, and others.
But all attempts to define what taste is must lead to nothing, as the
reader may see both from the history of aesthetics and experimentally.
There is and can be no explanation of why one thing pleases one man
and displeases another, or *vice versa;* so that the whole existing science
of aesthetics fails to do what we might expect from it as a mental
activity calling itself a science, namely, it does not define the qualities
and laws of art, or of the beautiful (if that be the content of art), or
the nature of taste (if taste decides the question of art and its merit),
and then on the basis of such definitions acknowledge as art those
productions which correspond to these laws and reject those which
do not come under them. But this science of aesthetics consists in first
acknowledging a certain set of productions to be art (because they
please us), and then framing such a theory of art as all these productions which please a certain circle of people can be fitted into. There
exists an art-canon according to which certain productions favored by
our circle are acknowledged as being art—the works of Phidias,
Sophocles, Homer, Titian, Raphael, Bach, Beethoven, Dante, Shakespeare, Goethe, and others—and the aesthetic laws must be such as
to embrace all these productions. In aesthetic literature you will constantly meet with opinions on the merit and importance of art, founded
not on any certain laws by which this or that is held to be good or bad,
but merely on consideration as to whether this art tallies with the art-
canon we have drawn up. . . .

FROM "What Is Art?" written in 1896, translated by Aylmer Maude in 1905.

So that the theory of art founded on beauty, expounded by aesthetics and in dim outline professed by the public, is nothing but the setting up as good of that which has pleased and pleases us, that is, pleases a certain class of people.

In order to define any human activity, it is necessary to understand its sense and importance; and in order to do this it is primarily necessary to examine that activity in itself, in its dependence on its causes and in connection with its effects, and not merely in relation to the pleasure we can get from it.

If we say that the aim of any activity is merely our pleasure and define it solely by that pleasure, our definition will evidently be a false one. But this is precisely what has occurred in the efforts to define art. . . .

What is art if we put aside the conception of beauty, which confuses the whole matter? The latest and most comprehensible definitions of art, apart from the conception of beauty, are the following—(1) *a,* Art is an activity arising even in the animal kingdom, and springing from sexual desire and the propensity to play (Schiller, Darwin, Spencer), and *b,* accompanied by a pleasurable excitement of the nervous system (Grant Allen). This is the physiological-evolutionary definition. (2) Art is the external manifestation, by means of lines, colors, movements, sounds, or words, of emotions felt by man (Véron). This is the experimental definition. According to the very latest definition (Sully), (3) Art is "the production of some permanent object or passing action which is fitted not only to supply an active enjoyment to the producer, but to convey a pleasurable impression to a number of spectators or listeners, quite apart from any personal advantage to be derived from it."

Notwithstanding the superiority of these definitions to the metaphysical definitions which depended on the conception of beauty, they are yet far from exact. The first, the physiological-evolutionary definition (1), *a,* is inexact, because instead of speaking about the artistic activity itself, which is the real matter in hand, it treats of the derivation of art. The modification of it, *b,* based on the physiological effects on the human organism, is inexact because within the limits of such definition many other human activities can be included, as has occurred in the neo-aesthetic theories which reckon as art the preparation of handsome clothes, pleasant scents, and even of victuals.

The experimental definition, (2), which makes art consist in the expression of emotions, is inexact because a man may express his emotions by means of lines, colors, sounds, or words and yet may not act on others by such expression—and then the manifestation of his emotions is not art.

The third definition (that of Sully) is inexact because in the production of objects or actions affording pleasure to the producer and a pleasant emotion to the spectators or hearers apart from personal advantage, may be included the showing of conjuring tricks or gymnastic exercises, and other activities which are not art. And further, many things the production of which does not afford pleasure to the producer and the sensation received from which is unpleasant, such as gloomy, heart-rending scenes in a poetic description or a play, may nevertheless be undoubted works of art.

The inaccuracy of all these definitions arises from the fact that in them all (as also in the metaphysical definitions) the object considered is the pleasure art may give, and not the purpose it may serve in the life of man and of humanity.

In order to define art correctly it is necessary first of all to cease to consider it as a means to pleasure, and to consider it as one of the conditions of human life. Viewing it in this way we cannot fail to observe that art is one of the means of intercourse between man and man.

Every work of art causes the receiver to enter into a certain kind of relationship both with him who produced or is producing the art, and with all those who, simultaneously, previously, or subsequently, receive the same artistic impression.

Speech transmitting the thoughts and experiences of men serves as a means of union among them, and art serves a similar purpose. The peculiarity of this latter means of intercourse, distinguishing it from intercourse by means of words, consists in this, that whereas by words a man transmits his thoughts to another, by art he transmits his feelings.

The activity of art is based on the fact that a man receiving through his sense of hearing or sight another man's expression of feeling, is capable of experiencing the emotion which moved the man who expressed it. To take the simplest example: one man laughs, and another who hears becomes merry, or a man weeps, and another who hears feels sorrow. A man is excited or irritated, and another man seeing him is brought to a similar state of mind. By his movements or by the sounds of his voice a man expresses courage and determination or sadness and calmness, and this state of mind passes on to others. A man suffers, manifesting his suffering by groans and spasms, and this suffering transmits itself to other people; a man expresses his feelings of admiration, devotion, fear, respect, or love, to certain objects, persons, or phenomena, and others are infected by the same feelings of admiration, devotion, fear, respect, or love, to the same objects, persons, or phenomena.

And it is on this capacity of man to receive another man's expression of feeling and to experience those feelings himself, that the activity of art is based.

If a man infects another or others directly, immediately, by his appearance or by the sounds he gives vent to at the very time he experiences the feeling; if he causes another man to yawn when he himself cannot help yawning, or to laugh or cry when he himself is obliged to laugh or cry, or to suffer when he himself is suffering—that does not amount to art.

Art begins when one person with the object of joining another or others to himself in one and the same feeling, expresses that feeling by certain external indications. To take the simplest example: a boy having experienced, let us say, fear on encountering a wolf, relates that encounter, and in order to evoke in others the feeling he has experienced, describes himself, his condition before the encounter, the surroundings, the wood, his own lightheartedness, and then the wolf's appearance, its movements, the distance between himself and the wolf, and so forth. All this, if only the boy when telling the story again experiences the feelings he had lived through, and infects the hearers and compels them to feel what he had experienced—is art. Even if the boy had not seen a wolf but had frequently been afraid of one, and if wishing to evoke in others the fear he had felt, he invented an encounter with a wolf and recounted it so as to make his hearers share the feelings he experienced when he feared the wolf, that also would be art. And just in the same way it is art if a man, having experienced either the fear of suffering or the attraction of enjoyment (whether in reality or in imagination), expresses these feelings on canvas or in marble so that others are infected by them. And it is also art if a man feels, or imagines to himself, feelings of delight, gladness, sorrow, despair, courage, or despondency, and the transition from one to another of these feelings, and expresses them by sounds so that the hearers are infected by them and experience them as they were experienced by the composer.

The feelings with which the artist infects others may be most various —very strong or very weak, very important or very insignificant, very bad or very good: feelings of love of one's country, self-devotion and submission to fate or to God expressed in a drama, raptures of lovers described in a novel, feelings of voluptuousness expressed in a picture, courage expressed in a triumphal march, merriment evoked by a dance, humor evoked by a funny story, the feeling of quietness transmitted by an evening landscape or by a lullaby, or the feeling of admiration evoked by a beautiful arabesque—it is all art.

If only the spectators or auditors are infected by the feelings which the author has felt, it is art.

To evoke in oneself a feeling one has once experienced and having evoked it in oneself then by means of movements, lines, colors, sounds, or forms expressed in words, so to transmit that feeling that others experience the same feeling—this is the activity of art.

Art is a human activity consisting in this, that one man consciously by means of certain external signs, hands on to others feelings he has lived through, and that others are infected by these feelings and also experience them.

Art is not, as the metaphysicians say, the manifestation of some mysterious Idea of beauty or God; it is not, as the aesthetic physiologists say, a game in which man lets off his excess of stored-up energy; it is not the expression of man's emotions by external signs; it is not the production of pleasing objects; and, above all, it is not pleasure; but it is a means of union among men joining them together in the same feelings, and indispensable for the life and progress toward well-being of individuals and of humanity.

As every man, thanks to man's capacity to express thoughts by words, may know all that has been done for him in the realms of thought by all humanity before this day, and can in the present, thanks to this capacity to understand the thoughts of others, become a sharer in their activity and also himself hand on to his contemporaries and descendants the thoughts he has assimilated from others as well as those that have arisen in himself; so, thanks to man's capacity to be infected with the feelings of others by means of art, all that is being lived through by his contemporaries is accessible to him, as well as the feelings experienced by men thousands of years ago, and he has also the possibility of transmitting his own feelings to others.

If people lacked the capacity to receive the thoughts conceived by men who preceded them and to pass on to others their own thoughts, men would be like wild beasts. . . .

And if men lacked this other capacity of being infected by art, people might be almost more savage still, and above all more separated from, and more hostile to, one another.

And therefore the activity of art is a most important one, as important as the activity of speech itself and as generally diffused.

As speech does not act on us only in sermons, orations, or books, but in all those remarks by which we interchange thoughts and experiences with one another, so also art in the wide sense of the word permeates our whole life, but it is only to some of its manifestations that we apply the term in the limited sense of the word.

We are accustomed to understand art to be only what we hear and see in theaters, concerts, and exhibitions; together with buildings, statues, poems, and novels. . . . But all this is but the smallest part of the art by which we communicate with one another in life. All human life is filled with works of art of every kind—from cradle-song, jest, mimicry, the ornamentation of houses, dress, and utensils, to church services, buildings, monuments, and triumphal processions. It is all artistic activity. So that by art, in the limited sense of the word, we do not mean all human activity transmitting feelings but only that part which we for some reason select from it and to which we attach special importance. . . .

There is one indubitable sign distinguishing real art from its counterfeit—namely, the infectiousness of art. If a man without exercising effort and without altering his standpoint, on reading, hearing, or seeing another man's work experiences a mental condition which unites him with that man and with others who are also affected by that work, then the object evoking that condition is a work of art. And however poetic, realistic, striking, or interesting, a work may be, it is not a work of art if it does not evoke that feeling (quite distinct from all other feelings) of joy and of spiritual union with another (the author) and with others (those who are also infected by it).

It is true that this indication is an *internal* one and that there are people who, having forgotten what the action of real art is, expect something else from art (in our society the great majority are in this state), and that therefore such people may mistake for this aesthetic feeling the feeling of diversion and a certain excitement which they receive from counterfeits of art. But though it is impossible to undeceive these people, just as it may be impossible to convince a man suffering from color-blindness that green is not red, yet for all that, this indication remains perfectly definite to those whose feeling for art is neither perverted nor atrophied, and it clearly distinguishes the feeling produced by art from all other feelings.

The chief peculiarity of this feeling is that the recipient of a truly artistic impression is so united to the artist that he feels as if the work were his own and not some one elses—as if what it expresses were just what he had long been wishing to express. A real work of art destroys in the consciousness of the recipient the separation between himself and the artist, and not that alone, but also between himself and all whose minds receive this work of art. In this freeing of our personality from its separation and isolation, in this uniting of it with others, lies the chief characteristic and the great attractive force of art.

If a man is infected by the author's condition of soul, if he feels this emotion and this union with others, then the object which has effected this is art; but if there be no such infection, if there be not this union with the author and with others who are moved by the same work— then it is not art. And not only is infection a sure sign of art, but the degree of infectiousness is also the sole measure of excellence in art.

The stronger the infection the better is the art, as art, speaking of it now apart from its subject-matter—that is, not considering the value of the feelings it transmits.

And the degree of the infectiousness of art depends on three conditions:

(1) On the greater or lesser individuality of the feeling transmitted; (2) on the greater or lesser clearness with which the feeling is transmitted; (3) on the sincerity of the artist, that is, on the greater or lesser force with which the artist himself feels the emotion he transmits.

The more individual the feeling transmitted the more strongly does it act on the recipient; the more individual the state of soul into which he is transferred the more pleasure does the recipient obtain and therefore the more readily and strongly does he join in it.

Clearness of expression assists infection because the recipient who mingles in consciousness with the author is the better satisfied the more clearly that feeling is transmitted which, as it seems to him, he has long known and felt and for which he has only now found expression.

But most of all is the degree of infectiousness of art increased by the degree of sincerity in the artist. As soon as the spectator, hearer, or reader, feels that the artist is infected by his own production and writes, sings, or plays, for himself, and not merely to act on others, this mental condition of the artist infects the recipient; and, on the contrary, as soon as the spectator, reader, or hearer, feels that the author is not writing, singing, or playing, for his own satisfaction—does not himself feel what he wishes to express, but is doing it for him, the recipient—resistance immediately springs up, and the most individual and the newest feelings and the cleverest technique not only fail to produce any infection but actually repel.

I have mentioned three conditions of contagion in art, but they may all be summed up into one, the last, sincerity; that is, that the artist should be impelled by an inner need to express his feeling. That condition includes the first; for if the artist is sincere he will express the feeling as he experienced it. And as each man is different from everyone else, his feeling will be individual for everyone else; and the more individual it is—the more the artist has drawn it from the depths of his nature—the more sympathetic and sincere will it be. And this same sincerity will impel the artist to find clear expression for the feeling which he wishes to transmit.

Therefore this third condition—sincerely—is the most important of the three. It is always complied with in peasant art, and this explains why such art always acts so powerfully; but it is a condition almost entirely absent from our upper-class art, which is continually produced by artists actuated by personal aims of covetousness or vanity.

Such are the three conditions which divide art from its counterfeits, and which also decide the quality of every work of art considered apart from its subject matter.

The absence of any one of these conditions excludes a work from the category of art and relegates it to that of art's counterfeits. If the work does not transmit the artist's peculiarity of feeling and is therefore not individual, if it is unintelligibly expressed, or if it has not proceeded from the author's inner need for expression—it is not a work of art. If all these conditions are present even in the smallest degree, then the work even if a weak one is yet a work of art.

The presence in various degrees of these three conditions: individuality, clearness, and sincerity, decides the merit of a work of art, apart from subject matter. All works of art take 'order of merit according to the degree in which they fulfill the first, the second, and the third, of these conditions. In one the individuality of the feeling transmitted may predominate; in another, clearness of expression; in a third, sincerity; while a fourth may have sincerity and individuality but be deficient in clearness; a fifth, individuality and clearness, but less sincerity; and so forth, in all possible degrees and combinations.

Thus is art divided from what is not art, and thus is the quality of art, as art, decided, independently of its subject matter, that is to say, apart from whether the feelings it transmits are good or bad. . . .

How in the subject matter of art are we to decide what is good and what is bad?

Art like speech is a means of communication and therefore of progress, that is, of the movement of humanity forward toward perfection. Speech renders accessible to men of the latest generation all the knowledge discovered by the experience and reflection both of preceding generations and of the best and foremost men of their own times; art renders accessible to men of the latest generations all the feelings experienced by their predecessors and also those felt by their best and foremost contemporaries. And as the evolution of knowledge proceeds by truer and more necessary knowledge dislodging and replacing what was mistaken and unnecessary, so the evolution of feeling proceeds by means of art—feelings less kind and less necessary for the well-being of mankind being replaced by others kinder and more needful for that end. That is the purpose of art. And speaking now of the feelings which are its subject matter, the more art fulfills that purpose the better the art, and the less it fulfills it the worse the art.

The appraisement of feelings (that is, the recognition of one or other set of feelings as more or less good, more or less necessary for the well-being of mankind) is effected by the religious perception of the age.

In every period of history and in every human society there exists an understanding of the meaning of life, which represents the highest level to which men of that society have attained—an understanding indicating the highest good at which that society aims. This understanding is the religious perception of the given time and society. And this religious perception is always clearly expressed by a few advanced men and more or less vividly perceived by members of the society generally. Such a religious perception and its corresponding expression always exists in every society. If it appears to us that there is no religious perception in our society, this is not because there really is none, but only because we do not wish to see it. And we often wish to see it because it exposes the fact that our life is inconsistent with that religious perception.

Religious perception in a society is like the direction of a flowing river. If the river flows at all it must have a direction. If a society lives, there must be a religious perception indicating the direction in which, more or less consciously, all its members tend.

And so there always has been, and is, a religious perception in every society. And it is by the standard of this religious perception that the feelings transmitted by art have always been appraised. It has always been only on the basis of this religious perception of their age, that men have chosen from amid the endlessly varied spheres of art that art which transmitted feelings making religious perception operative in actual life. And such art has always been highly valued and encouraged, while art transmitting feelings already outlived, flowing from the antiquated religious perceptions of a former age, has always been condemned and despised. All the rest of art transmitting those most diverse feelings by means of which people commune with one another was not condemned and was tolerated if only it did not transmit feelings contrary to religious perception. Thus for instance among the Greeks, art transmitting feelings of beauty, strength, and courage (Hesiod, Homer, Phidias) was chosen, approved, and encouraged, while art transmitting feelings of rude sensuality, despondency, and effeminacy, was condemned and despised. Among the Jews, art transmitting feelings of devotion and submission to the God of the Hebrews and to His will (the epic of Genesis, the prophets, the Psalms) was chosen and encouraged, while art transmitting feelings of idolatry (the Golden Calf) was condemned and despised. All the rest of art—stories, songs, dances, ornamentation of houses, of utensils, and of clothes— which was not contrary to religious perception, was neither distinguished nor discussed. Thus as regards its subject matter has art always and everywhere been appraised and thus it should be appraised, for this attitude toward art proceeds from the fundamental characteristics of human nature, and those characteristics do not change.

I know that according to an opinion current in our times religion is a superstition humanity has outgrown, and it is therefore assumed that no such thing exists as a religious perception common to us all by which art in our time can be appraised. I know that this is the opinion current in the pseudo-cultured circles of today. People who do not acknowledge Christianity in its true meaning because it undermines their social privileges, and who therefore invent all kinds of philosophic and aesthetic theories to hide from themselves the meaninglessness and wrongfulness of their lives, cannot think otherwise. These people intentionally, or sometimes unintentionally, confuse the notion of a religious cult with the notion of religious perception, and think that by denying the cult they get rid of the perception. But even the very attacks on religion and the attempts to establish an idea of life contrary to the religious perception of our times, most clearly demonstrate the existence of a religious perception condemning the lives that are not in harmony with it.

If humanity progresses, that is, moves forward, there must inevitably be a guide to the direction of that movement. And religions have always furnished that guide. All history shows that the progress of humanity is accomplished not otherwise than under the guidance of religion. But if the race cannot progress without the guidance of religion—and progress is always going on, and consequently goes on also in our own times—then there must be a religion of our times. So that whether it pleases or displeases the so-called cultured people of today, they must admit the existence of religion—not of a religious cult, Catholic, Protestant, or another, but of religious perception—which even in our times is the guide always present where there is any progress. And if a religious perception exists amongst us, then the feelings dealt with by our art should be appraised on the basis of that religious perception; and as has been the case always and everywhere, art transmitting feelings flowing from the religious perception of our time should be chosen from amid all the indifferent art, should be acknowledged, highly valued, and encouraged, while art running counter to that perception should be condemned and despised, and all the remaining, indifferent, art should neither be distinguished nor encouraged.

The religious perception of our time in its widest and most practical application is the consciousness that our well-being, both material and spiritual, individual and collective, temporal and eternal, lies in the growth of brotherhood among men—in their loving harmony with one another. This perception is not only expressed by Christ and all the best men of past ages, it is not only repeated in most varied forms and from most diverse sides by the best men of our times, but it already serves as a clue to all the complex labor of humanity, consisting as this labor does on the one hand in the destruction of physical and moral obstacles to the union of men, and on the other hand in establishing the principles common to all men which can and should unite them in one universal brotherhood. And it is on the basis of this perception that we should appraise all the phenomena of our life and among the rest our art also: choosing from all its realms and highly prizing and encouraging whatever transmits feelings flowing from this religious perception, rejecting whatever is contrary to it, and not attributing to the rest of art an importance that does not properly belong to it. . . .

Whatever the work may be and however it may have been extolled, we have first to ask whether this work is one of real art, or a counterfeit. Having acknowledged, on the basis of the indication of its infectiousness even to a small class of people, that a certain production belongs to the realm of art, it is necessary on this basis to decide the next question, Does this work belong to the category of bad exclusive art opposed to religious perception, or of Christian art uniting people? And having acknowledged a work to belong to real Christian art, we must then, according to whether it transmits feelings flowing from love of God and man, or merely the simple feelings uniting all men, assign it a place in the ranks of religious art, or in those of universal art.

Only on the basis of such verification shall we find it possible to select from the whole mass of what in our society claims to be art, those works which form real, important, necessary, spiritual food, and to separate them from all the harmful and useless art and from the counterfeits of art which surround us. Only on the basis of such verification shall we be able to rid ourselves of the pernicious results of harmful art and avail ourselves of that beneficent action which is the purpose of true and good art, and which is indispensable for the spiritual life of man and of humanity.

THE NATURE OF BEAUTY

George Santayana

It would be easy to find a definition of beauty that should give in a few words a telling paraphrase of the word. We know on excellent authority that beauty is truth, that it is the expression of the ideal, the symbol of divine perfection, and the sensible manifestation of the good. A litany of these titles of honor might easily be compiled, and repeated in praise of our divinity. Such phrases stimulate thought and give us a momentary pleasure, but they hardly bring any permanent enlightenment. A definition that should really define must be nothing less than the exposition of the origin, place, and elements of beauty as an object of human experience. We must learn from it, as far as possible, why, when, and how beauty appears, what conditions an object must fulfill to be beautiful, what elements of our nature make us sensible of beauty, and what the relation is between the constitution of the object and the excitement of our susceptibility. Nothing less will really define beauty or make us understand what aesthetic appreciation is. The definition of beauty in this sense will be the task of this whole book, a task that can be only very imperfectly accomplished within its limits.

The historical titles of our subject may give us a hint toward the beginning of such a definition. Many writers of the last century called the philosophy of beauty *Criticism,* and the word is still retained as the title for the reasoned appreciation of works of art. We could hardly speak, however, of delight in nature as criticism. A sunset is not criticized; it is felt and enjoyed. The word "criticism," used on such an occasion, would emphasize too much the element of deliberate judgment and of comparison with standards. Beauty, although often so described, is seldom so perceived, and all the greatest excellences of nature and art are so far from being approved of by a rule that they themselves furnish the standard and ideal by which critics measure inferior effects.

This age of science and of nomenclature has accordingly adopted a

FROM *The Sense of Beauty,* written in 1896.

more learned word. *Aesthetics,* that is, the theory of perception or of susceptibility. If criticism is too narrow a word, pointing exclusively to our more artificial judgments, aesthetics seems to be too broad and to include within its sphere all pleasures and pains, if not all perceptions whatsoever. Kant used it, as we know, for his theory of time and space as forms of all perception; and it has at times been narrowed into an equivalent for the philosophy of art.

If we combine, however, the etymological meaning of criticism with that of aesthetics, we shall unite two essential qualities of the theory of beauty. Criticism implies judgment, and esthetics perception. To get the common ground, that of perceptions with are critical, or judgments which are perceptions, we must widen our notion of deliberate criticism so as to include those judgments of value which are instinctive and immediate, that is, to include pleasures and pains; and at the same time we must narrow our notion of aesthetics so as to exclude all perceptions which are not appreciations, which do not find a value in their objects. We thus reach the sphere of critical or appreciative perception, which is, roughly speaking, what we mean to deal with. And retaining the word "aesthetics," which is now current, we may therefore say that aesthetics is concerned with the perception of values. The meaning and conditions of value are, then, what we must first consider.

Since the days of Descartes it has been a conception familiar to philosophers that every visible event in nature might be explained by previous visible events, and that all the motions, for instance, of the tongue in speech, or of the hand in painting, might have merely physical causes. If consciousness is thus accessory to life and not essential to it, the race of man might have existed upon the earth and acquired all the arts necessary for its subsistence without possessing a single sensation, idea, or emotion. Natural selection might have secured the survival of those automata which made useful reactions upon their environment. An instinct of self-preservation would have been developed, dangers would have been shunned without being feared, and injuries revenged without being felt.

In such a world there might have come to be the most perfect organization. There would have been what we should call the expression of the deepest interests and the apparent pursuit of conceived goods. For there would have been spontaneous and ingrained tendencies to avoid certain contingencies and to produce others; all the dumb show and evidence of thinking would have been patent to the observer. Yet there would surely have been no thinking, no expectation, and no conscious achievement in the whole process.

The onlooker might have feigned ends and objects of forethought, as we do in the case of the water that seeks its own level, or in that of the vacuum which nature abhors. But the particles of matter would have remained unconscious of their collocation, and all nature would have been insensible of their changing arrangement. We only, the possible spectators of that process, by virtue of our own interests and habits, could see any progress or culmination in it. We should see culmination where the result attained satisfied our practical or aesthetic demands, and progress wherever such a satisfaction was approached. But apart from ourselves, and our human bias, we can see in such a mechanical world no element of value whatever. In removing consciousness, we have removed the possibility of worth.

But it is not only in the absence of all consciousness that value would be removed from the world; by a less violent abstraction from the totality of human experience, we might conceive beings of a purely intellectual cast, minds in which the transformations of nature were mirrored without any emotion. Every event would then be noted, its relations would be observed, its recurrence might even be expected; but all this would happen without a shadow of desire, of pleasure, or of regret. No event would be repulsive, no situation terrible. We might, in a word, have a world of idea without a world of will. In this case, as if consciousness were absent altogether, all value and excellence would be gone. So that for the existence of good in any form it is not merely consciousness but emotional consciousness that is needed. Observation will not do, appreciation is required.

We may therefore at once assert this axiom, important for all moral philosophy and fatal to certain stubborn incoherences of thought, that there is no value apart from some appreciation of it, and no good apart from some preference of it before its absence or its opposite. In appreciation, in preference, lie the root and essence of all excellence. Or, as Spinoza clearly expresses it, we desire nothing because it is good, but it is good only because we desire it.

It is true that in the absence of an instinctive reaction we can still apply these epithets by an appeal to usage. We may agree that an action is bad or a building good, because we recognize in them a character which we have learned to designate by that adjective; but unless there is in us some trace of passionate reprobation or of sensible delight, there is no moral or aesthetic judgment. It is all a question of propriety of speech, and of the empty titles of things. The verbal and mechanical proposition, that passes for judgment of worth, is the great cloak of ineptitude in these matters. Insensibility is very quick in the conventional use of words. If we appealed more often to actual feelings, our judgments would be more diverse, but they would be more legitimate and instructive. Verbal judgments are often useful instruments of thought, but it is not by them that worth can ultimately be determined.

Values spring from the immediate and inexplicable reaction of vital impulse, and from the irrational part of our nature. The rational part is by its essence relative; it leads us from data to conclusions, or from parts to wholes; it never furnishes the data with which it works. If any preference or precept were declared to be ultimate and primitive, it would thereby be declared to be irrational, since mediation, inference, and synthesis are the essence of rationality. The idea of rationality is itself as arbitrary, as much dependent on the needs of a finite organization, as any other ideal. Only as ultimately securing tranquility of mind, which the philosopher instinctively pursues, has it for him any necessity. In spite of the verbal propriety of saying that reason demands rationality, what really demands rationality, what makes it a good and indispensable thing and gives it all its authority, is not its own nature, but our need of it both in safe and economical action and in the pleasures of comprehension.

It is evident that beauty is a species of value, and what we have said of value in general applies to this particular kind. A first approach to a definition of beauty has therefore been made by the exclusion of all intellectual judgments, all judgments of matter of fact or of relation. To substitute judgments of fact for judgments of value, is a sign of a pedantic and borrowed criticism. If we approach a work of art or nature scientifically, for the sake of its historical connections or proper classification, we do not approach it aesthetically. The discovery of its date or of its author may be otherwise interesting; it only remotely affects our aesthetic appreciation by adding to the direct effect certain associations. If the direct effect were absent, and the object in itself uninteresting, the circumstances would be immaterial. Molière's *Misanthrope* says to the court poet who commends his sonnet as written in a quarter of an hour, "The time's irrelevant, Sir," and so we might say to the critic that sinks into the archaeologist, show us the work, and let the date alone.

In an opposite direction the same substitution of facts for values makes its appearance, whenever the reproduction of fact is made the sole standard of artistic excellence. Many half-trained observers condemn the work of some naïve or fanciful masters with a sneer, because, as they truly say, it is out of drawing. The implication is that to be correctly copied from a model is the prerequisite of all beauty. Correctness is, indeed, an element of effect and one which, in respect to familiar objects, is almost indispensable, because its absence would cause a disappointment and dissatisfaction incompatible with enjoyment. We learn to value truth more and more as our love and knowledge of nature increase. But fidelity is a merit only because it is in this way a factor in our pleasure. It stands on a level with all other ingredients of effect. When a man raises it to a solitary pre-eminence and becomes incapable of appreciating anything else, he betrays the decay of aesthetic capacity. The scientific habit in him inhibits the artistic.

That facts have a value of their own, at once complicates and explains this question. We are naturally pleased by every perception, and recognition and surprise are particularly acute sensations. When we see a striking truth in any imitation we are therefore delighted, and this kind of pleasure is very legitimate, and enters into the best effects of all the representative arts. Truth and realism are therefore aesthetically good, but they are not all-sufficient, since the representation of everything is not equally pleasing and effective. The fact that resemblance is a source of satisfaction justifies the critic in demanding it, while the aesthetic insufficiency of such veracity shows the different value of truth in science and in art. Science is the response to the demand for information, and in it we ask for the whole truth and nothing but the truth. Art is the response to the demand for entertainment, for the stimulation of our senses and imagination, and truth enters into it only as it subserves these ends.

Even the scientific value of truth is not, however, ultimate or absolute. It rests partly on practical, partly on aesthetic interests. As our ideas are gradually brought into conformity with the facts by the painful process of selection—for intuition runs equally into truth and into error, and can settle nothing if not controlled by experience—we gain vastly in our command over our environment. This is the fundamental value of natural science, and the fruit it is yielding in our day. We have no better vision of nature and life than some of our predecessors, but we have greater material resources. To know the truth about the composition and history of things is good for this reason. It is also good because of the enlarged horizon it gives us, because the spectacle of nature is a marvelous and fascinating one, full of a serious sadness and large peace, which gives us back our birthright as children of the planet and naturalizes us upon the earth. This is the poetic value of the scientific *Weltanschauung* [world view]. From these two benefits, the practical and the imaginative, all the value of truth is derived.

Aesthetic and moral judgments are accordingly to be classed together in contrast to judgments intellectual; they are both judgments of value, while intellectual judgments are judgments of fact. If the latter have any value, it is only derivative, and our whole intellectual life has its only justification in its connection with our pleasures and pains.

The relation between aesthetic and moral judgments, between the spheres of the beautiful and the good, is close, but the distinction between them is important. One factor of this distinction is that while aesthetic judgments are mainly positive, that is, perceptions of good, moral judgments are mainly and fundamentally negative, or perceptions of evil. Another factor of the distinction is that whereas, in the perception of beauty, our judgment is necessarily intrinsic and based on the character of the immediate experience, and never consciously on the idea of an eventual utility in the object, judgments about moral worth, on the contrary, are always based, when they are positive, upon the consciousness of benefits probably involved. Both these distinctions need some elucidations.

Hedonistic ethics have always had to struggle against the moral sense of mankind. Earnest minds, that feel the weight and dignity of life, rebel against the assertion that the aim of right conduct is enjoyment. Pleasure usually appears to them as a temptation, and they sometimes go so far as to make avoidance of it a virtue. The truth is that morality is not mainly concerned with the attainment of pleasure; it is rather concerned, in all its deeper and more authoritative maxims, with the prevention of suffering. There is something artificial in the deliberate pursuit of pleasure, there is something absurd in the obligation to enjoy oneself. We feel no duty in that direction; we take to enjoyment naturally enough after the work of life is done, and the freedom and spontaneity of our pleasures are what is most essential to them.

The sad business of life is rather to escape certain dreadful evils to which our nature exposes us—death, hunger, disease, weariness, isolation, and contempt. By the awful authority of these things which stand like specters behind every moral injunction, conscience in reality speaks, and a mind which they have duly impressed cannot but feel, by contrast, the hopeless triviality of the search for pleasure. It cannot but feel that a life abandoned to amusement and to changing impulses must run unawares into fatal dangers. The moment, however, that society emerges from the early pressure of the environment and is tolerably secure against primary evils, morality grows lax. The forms that life will further assume are not to be imposed by moral authority, but are determined by the genius of the race, the opportunities of the moment, and the tastes and resources of individual minds. The reign of duty gives place to the reign of freedom, and the law and the covenant to the dispensation of grace.

The appreciation of beauty and its embodiment in the arts are activities which belong to our holiday life, when we are redeemed for the moment from the shadow of evil and the slavery to fear, and are following the bent of our nature where it chooses to lead us. The values, then, with which we here deal are positive; they were negative in the sphere of morality. The ugly is hardly an exception, because it is not the cause of any real pain. In itself it is rather a source of amusement. If its suggestions are vitally repulsive, its presence becomes a real evil toward which we assume a practical and moral attitude. And, correspondingly, the pleasant is never, as we have seen, the object of a truly moral injunction.

We have here, then, an important element of the distinction between aesthetic and moral values. It is the same that has been pointed to in the famous contrast between work and play. These terms may be used in different senses and their importance in moral classification differs with the meaning attached to them. We may call everything play which is useless activity, exercise that springs from the physiological impulse to discharge the energy which the exigencies of life have not called out. Work will then be all action that is necessary or useful for life. Evidently if work and play are thus objectively distinguished as useful and useless action, work is a eulogistic term and play a disparaging one. It would be better for us that all our energy should be turned to account, that none of it should be wasted in aimless motion. Play, in this sense, is a sign of imperfect adaptation. It is proper to childhood, when the body and mind are not yet fit to cope with the environment, but it is unseemly in manhood and pitiable in old age, because it marks an atrophy of human nature, and a failure to take hold of the opportunities of life.

Play is thus essentially frivolous. Some persons, understanding the term in this sense, have felt an aversion, which every liberal mind will share, to classifying social pleasures, art, and religion under the head of play, and by that epithet condemning them, as a certain school seems to do, to gradual extinction as the race approaches maturity. But if all the useless ornaments of our life are to be cut off in the process of adaptation, evolution would impoverish instead of enriching our nature. Perhaps that is the tendency of evolution, and our barbarous ancestors amid their toils and wars, with their flaming passions and mythologies, lived better lives than are reserved to our well-adapted descendants.

We may be allowed to hope, however, that some imagination may survive parasitically even in the most serviceable brain. Whatever course history may take—and we are not here concerned with prophecy—the question of what is desirable is not affected. To condemn spontaneous and delightful occupations because they are useless for self-preservation shows an uncritical prizing of life irrespective of its content. For such a system the worthiest function of the universe should be to establish perpetual motion. Uselessness is a fatal accusation to bring against any act which is done for its presumed utility, but those which are done for their own sake are their own justification.

At the same time there is an undeniable propriety in calling all the liberal and imaginative activities of man play, because they are spontaneous, and not carried on under pressure of external necessity or danger. Their utility for self-preservation may be very indirect and accidental, but they are not worthless for that reason. On the contrary, we may measure the degree of happiness and civilization which any race has attained by the proportion of its energy which is devoted to free and generous pursuits, to the adornment of life and the culture of the imagination. For it is in the spontaneous play of his faculties that man finds himself and his happiness. Slavery is the most degrading condition of which he is capable, and he is as often a slave to the niggardliness of the earth and the inclemency of heaven, as to a master or an institution. He is a slave when all his energy is spent in avoiding suffering and death, when all his action is imposed from without, and no breath or strength is left him for free enjoyment.

Work and play here take on a different meaning, and become equivalent to servitude and freedom. The change consists in the subjective point of view from which the distinction is now made. We no longer mean by work all that is done usefully, but only what is done unwillingly and by the spur of necessity. By play we are designating, no longer what is done fruitlessly, but whatever is done spontaneously and for its own sake, whether it have or not an ulterior utility. Play, in this sense, may be our most useful occupation. So far would a gradual adaptation to the environment be from making this play obsolete, that it would tend to abolish work, and to make play universal. For with the elimination of all the conflicts and errors of instinct, the race would do spontaneously whatever conduced to its welfare and we should live safely and prosperously without external stimulus or restraint. . . .

In this second and subjective sense, then, work is the disparaging term and play the eulogistic one. All who feel the dignity and importance of the things of the imagination, need not hesitate to adopt the classification which designates them as play. We point out thereby, not that they have no value, but that their value is intrinsic, that in them is one of the sources of all worth. Evidently all values must be ultimately intrinsic. The useful is good because of the excellence of its consequences; but these must somewhere cease to be merely useful in their turn, or only excellent as means; somewhere we must reach the good that is good in itself and for its own sake, else the whole process is futile, and the utility of our first object illusory. We here reach the second factor in our distinction, between aesthetic and moral values, which regards their immediacy. . . .

We have now separated with some care intellectual and moral judgments from the sphere of our subject, and found that we are to deal only with perceptions of value, and with these only when they are positive and immediate. But even with these distinctions the most remarkable characteristic of the sense of beauty remains undefined. All pleasures are intrinsic and positive values, but all pleasures are not perceptions of beauty. Pleasure is indeed the essence of that perception, but there is evidently in this particular pleasure a complication which is not present in others and which is the basis of the distinction made by consciousness and language between it and the rest. It will be instructive to notice the degrees of this difference.

The bodily pleasures are those least resembling perceptions of beauty. By bodily pleasures we mean, of course, more than pleasures with a bodily seat; for that class would include them all, as well as all forms and elements of consciousness. Aesthetic pleasures have physical conditions, they depend on the activity of the eye and the ear, of the memory and the other ideational functions of the brain. But we do not connect those pleasures with their seats except in physiological studies; the ideas with which aesthetic pleasures are associated are not the ideas of their bodily causes. The pleasures we call physical, and regard as low, on the contrary, are those which call our attention to some part of our own body, and which make no object so conspicuous to us as the organ in which they arise.

There is here, then, a very marked distinction between physical and aesthetic pleasure; the organs of the latter must be transparent, they must not intercept our attention, but carry it directly to some external object. The greater dignity and range of aesthetic pleasure is thus made very intelligible. The soul is glad, as it were, to forget its connection with the body and to fancy that it can travel over the world with the liberty with which it changes the objects of its thought. The mind passes from China to Peru without any conscious change in the local tensions of the body. This illusion of disembodiment is very exhilarating, while immersion in the flesh and confinement to some organ gives a tone of grossness and selfishness to our consciousness. The generally meaner associations of physical pleasures also help to explain their comparative crudity. . . .

There is, however, something more in the claim to universality in aesthetic judgments than the desire to generalize our own opinions. There is the expression of a curious but well-known psychological phenomenon, namely, the transformation of an element of sensation into the quality of a thing. If we say that other men should see the beauties we see, it is because we think those beauties *are in the object,* like its color, proportion, or size. Our judgment appears to us merely the perception and discovery of an external existence, of the real excellence that is without. But this notion is radically absurd and contradictory. Beauty, as we have seen, is a value; it cannot be conceived as an independent existence which affects our senses and which we consequently perceive. It exists in perception, and cannot exist otherwise. A beauty not perceived is a pleasure not felt, and a contradiction. But modern philosophy has taught us to say the same thing of every element of the perceived world—all are sensations and their grouping into objects imagined to be permanent and external—is the work of certain habits of our intelligence. We should be incapable of surveying or retaining the diffused experiences of life, unless we organized and classified them; and out of the chaos of impressions framed the world of conventional and recognizable objects.

How this is done is explained by the current theories of perception. External objects usually affect various senses at once, the impressions of which are thereby associated. Repeated experiences of one object are also associated on account of their similarity; hence a double tendency to merge and unify into a single percept, to which a name is attached, the group of those memories and reactions which in fact had one external thing for their cause. But this percept, once formed, is clearly different from those particular experiences out of which it grew. It is permanent, they are variable. They are but partial views and glimpses of it. The constituted notion therefore comes to be the reality, and the materials of it merely the appearance. The distinction between substance and quality, reality and appearance, matter and mind, has no other origin.

The objects thus conceived and distinguished from our ideas of them, are at first compacted of all the impressions, feelings, and memories, which offer themselves for association and fall within the vortex of the amalgamating imagination. Every sensation we get from a thing is originally treated as one of its qualities. Experiment, however, and the practical need of a simpler conception of the structure of objects lead us gradually to reduce the qualities of the object to a minimum, and to regard most perceptions as an affect of those few qualities upon us. These few primary qualities, like extension which we persist in treating as independently real and as the quality of a substance, are those which suffice to explain the order of our experiences. All the rest, like color, are relegated to the subjective sphere, as merely effects upon our minds, and apparent or secondary qualities of the object.

But this distinction has only a practical justification. Convenience and economy of thought alone determine what combination of our sensations we shall continue to objectify and treat as the cause of the rest. The right and tendency to be objective is equal in all, since they are all prior to the artifice of thought by which we separate the concept from its materials, the thing from our experiences.

The qualities which we now conceive to belong to real objects are for the most part images of sight and touch. One of the first classes of effects to be treated as secondary were naturally pleasures and pains, since it could commonly conduce very little to intelligent and successful action to conceive our pleasures and pains as resident in objects. But emotions are essentially capable of objectification, as well as impressions of sense; and one may well believe that a primitive and inexperienced consciousness would rather people the world with ghosts of its own terrors and passions than with projections of those luminous and mathematical concepts which as yet it could hardly have formed.

This animistic and mythological habit of thought still holds its own at the confines of knowledge, where mechanical explanations are not found. In ourselves, where nearness makes observation difficult, in the intricate chaos of animal and human life, we still appeal to the efficacy of will and ideas, as also in the remote night of cosmic and religious problems. But in all the intermediate realm of vulgar day, where mechanical science has made progress, the inclusion of emotional or passionate elements in the concept of the reality would be now an extravagance. Here our idea of things is composed exclusively of perceptual elements, of the ideas of form and of motion.

The beauty of objects, however, forms an exception to this rule. Beauty is an emotional element, a pleasure of ours, which nevertheless we regard as a quality of things. But we are now prepared to understand the nature of this exception. It is the survival of a tendency originally universal to make every effect of a thing upon us a constituent of its conceived nature. The scientific idea of a thing is a great abstraction from the mass of perceptions and reactions which that thing produces; the aesthetic idea is less abstract, since it retains the emotional reaction, the pleasure of the perception, as an integral part of the conceived thing.

Nor is it hard to find the ground of this survival in the sense of beauty of an objectification of feeling elsewhere extinct. Most of the pleasures which objects cause are easily distinguished and separated from the perception of the object: the object has to be applied to a particular organ, like the palate, or swallowed like wine, or used and operated upon in some way before the pleasure arises. The cohesion is therefore slight between the pleasure and the other associated elements of sense; the pleasure is separated in time from the perception, or it is localized in a different organ, and consequently is at once recognized as an effect and not as a quality of the object. But when the process of perception itself is pleasant, as it may easily be, when the intellectual operation, by which the elements of sense are associated and projected, and the concept of the form and substance of the thing produced, is naturally delightful, then we have a pleasure intimately bound up in the thing, inseparable from its character and constitution, the seat of which in us is the same as the seat of the perception. We naturally fail, under these circumstances, to separate the pleasure from the other objectified feelings. It becomes, like them, a quality of the object, which we distinguish from pleasures not so incorporated in the perception of things, by giving it the name of beauty.

We have now reached our definition of beauty, which, in the terms of our successive analysis and narrowing of the conception, is value positive, intrinsic, and objectified. Or, in less technical language, Beauty is pleasure regarded as the quality of a thing.

This definition is intended to sum up a variety of distinctions and identifications which should perhaps be here more explicitly set down. Beauty is a value, that is, it is not a perception of a matter of fact or of a relation: it is an emotion, an affection of our volitional and appreciative nature. An object cannot be beautiful if it can give pleasure to nobody: a beauty to which all men were forever indifferent is a contradiction in terms.

In the second place, this value is positive, it is the sense of the presence of something good, or (in the case of ugliness) of its absence. It is never the perception of a positive evil, it is never a negative value. That we are endowed with the sense of beauty is a pure gain which brings no evil with it. When the ugly ceases to be amusing or merely uninteresting and becomes disgusting, it becomes indeed a positive evil: but a moral and practical, not an aesthetic, one. In aesthetics that saying is true—often so disingenuous in ethics—that evil is nothing but the absence of good: for even the tedium and vulgarity of an existence without beauty is not itself ugly so much as lamentable and degrading. The absence of aesthetic goods is a moral evil: the aesthetic evil is merely relative, and means less of aesthetic good than was expected at the place and time. No form in itself gives pain, although some forms give pain by causing a shock of surprise even when they are really beautiful: as if a mother found a fine bull pup in her child's cradle, when her pain would not be aesthetic in its nature.

Further, this pleasure must not be in the consequence of the utility of the object or event, but in its immediate perception; in other words, beauty is an ultimate good, something that gives satisfaction to a natural function, to some fundamental need or capacity of our minds. Beauty is therefore a positive value that is intrinsic; it is a pleasure. These two circumstances sufficiently separate the sphere of aesthetics from that of ethics. Moral values are generally negative, and always remote. Morality has to do with the avoidance of evil and the pursuit of good: aesthetics only with enjoyment.

Finally, the pleasures of sense are distinguished from the perception of beauty, as sensation in general is distinguished from perception; by the objectification of the elements and their appearance as qualities rather of things than of consciousness. The passage from sensation to perception is gradual, and the path may be sometimes retraced: so it is with beauty and the pleasures of sensation. There is no sharp line between them, but it depends upon the degree of objectivity my feeling has attained at the moment whether I say "It pleases me," or "It is beautiful." If I am self-conscious and critical, I shall probably use one phrase; if I am impulsive and susceptible, the other. The more remote, interwoven, and inextricable the pleasure is, the more objective it will appear; and the union of two pleasures often makes one beauty. In Shakespeare's LIVth sonnet are these words:

> O how much more doth beauty beauteous seem
> By that sweet ornament which truth doth give!
> The rose looks fair, but fairer we it deem
> For that sweet odor which doth in it live.
> The canker-blooms have full as deep a dye
> As the perfumèd tincture of the roses,
> Hang on such thorns, and play as wantonly
> When summer's breath their maskèd buds discloses.
> But, for their beauty only is their show,
> They live unwooed and unrespected fade;
> Die to themselves. Sweet roses do not so:
> Of their sweet deaths are sweetest odors made.

One added ornament, we see, turns the deep dye, which was but show and mere sensation before, into an element of beauty and reality; and as truth is here the cooperation of perceptions, so beauty is the cooperation of pleasures. If color, form, and motion are hardly beautiful without the sweetness of the odor, how much more necessary would they be for the sweetness itself to become a beauty! If we had the perfume in a flask, no one would think of calling it beautiful: it would give us too detached and controllable a sensation. There would be no object in which it could be easily incorporated. But let it float from the garden, and it will add another sensuous charm to objects simultaneously recognized, and help to make them beautiful. Thus beauty is constituted by the objectification of pleasure. It is pleasure objectified.

We have found in the beauty of material and form the objectification of certain pleasures connected with the process of direct perception, with the formation, in the one case of a sensation, or quality, in the other of a synthesis of sensations or qualities. But the human consciousness is not a perfectly clear mirror, with distinct boundaries and clear-cut images, determinate in number and exhaustively perceived. Our ideas half emerge for a moment from the dim continuum of vital feeling and diffused sense, and are hardly fixed before they are changed and transformed, by the shifting of attention and the perception of new relations, into ideas of really different objects. This fluidity of the mind would make reflection impossible, did we not fix in words and other symbols certain abstract contents; we thus become capable of recognizing in one perception the repetition of another, and of recognizing in certain recurrences of impressions a persistent object. This discrimination and classification of the contents of consciousness is the work of perception and understanding, and the pleasures that accompany these activities make the beauty of the sensible world.

But our hold upon our thoughts extends even further. We not only construct visible unities and recognizable types, but remain aware of their affinities to what is not at the time perceived; that is, we find in them a certain tendency and quality, not original to them, a meaning and a tone, which upon investigation we shall see to have been the proper characteristics of other objects and feelings, associated with them once in our experience. The hushed reverberations of these associated feelings continue in the brain, and by modifying our present reaction, color the image upon which our attention is fixed. The quality thus acquired by objects through association is what we call their expression. Whereas in form or material there is one object with its emotional effect, in expression there are two, and the emotional effect belongs to the character of the second or suggested one. Expression may thus make beautiful by suggestion things in themselves indifferent, or it may come to heighten the beauty which they already possess.

Expression is not always distinguishable in consciousness from the value of material or form, because we do not always have a distinguishable memory of the related idea which the expressiveness implies. When we have such a memory, as at the sight of some once frequented garden, we clearly and spontaneously attribute our emotion to the memory and not to the present fact which it beautifies. The revival of a pleasure and its embodiment in a present object which in itself might have been indifferent, is here patent and acknowledged.

The distinctness of the analysis may indeed be so great as to prevent the synthesis; we may so entirely pass to the suggested object, that our pleasure will be embodied in the memory of that, while the suggestive sensation will be overlooked, and the expressiveness of the present object will fail to make it beautiful. Thus the mementos of a lost friend do not become beautiful by virtue of the sentimental associations which may make them precious. The value is confined to the images of the memory; they are too clear to let any of that value escape and diffuse itself over the rest of our consciousness, and beautify the objects which we actually behold. We say explicitly: I value this trifle for its associations. And so long as this division continues, the worth of the thing is not for us aesthetic.

But a little dimming of our memory will often make it so. Let the images of the past fade, let them remain simply as a halo and suggestion of happiness hanging about a scene; then this scene, however empty and uninteresting in itself, will have a deep and intimate charm; we shall be pleased by its very vulgarity. We shall not confess so readily that we value the place for its associations; we shall rather say: I am fond of this landscape; it has for me an ineffable attraction. The treasures of the memory have been melted and dissolved, and are now gilding the object that supplants them; they are giving this object expression. . . .

In all expression we may thus distinguish two terms: the first is the object actually presented, the word, the image, the expressive thing; the second is the object suggested, the further thought, emotion, or image evoked, the thing expressed.

These lie together in the mind, and their union constitutes expression. If the value lies wholly in the first term, we have no beauty of expression. The decorative inscriptions in Saracenic monuments can have no beauty of expression for one who does not read Arabic; their charm is wholly one of material and form. Or if they have any expression, it is by virtue of such thoughts as they might suggest, as, for instance, of the piety and oriental sententiousness of the builders and of the aloofness from us of all their world. And even these suggestions, being a wandering of our fancy rather than a study of the object, would fail to arouse a pleasure which would be incorporated in the present image. The scroll would remain without expression, although its presence might have suggested to us interesting visions of other things. The two terms would be too independent, and the intrinsic values of each would remain distinct from that of the other. There would be no visible expressiveness, although there might have been discursive suggestions.

Indeed, if expression were constituted by the external relation of object with object, everything would be expressive equally, indeterminately, and universally. The flower in the crannied wall would express the same thing as the bust of Caesar or the *Critique of Pure Reason*. What constitutes the individual expressiveness of these things is the circle of thoughts allied to each in a given mind; my words, for instance, express the thoughts which they actually arouse in the reader; they may express more to one man than to another, and to me they may have expressed more or less than to you. My thoughts remain unexpressed, if my words do not arouse them in you, and very likely your greater wisdom will find in what I say the manifestation of a thousand principles of which I never dreamed. Expression depends upon the union of two terms, one of which must be furnished by the imagination; and a mind cannot furnish what it does not possess. The expressiveness of everything accordingly increases with the intelligence of the observer.

But for expression to be an element of beauty, it must, of course, fulfill another condition. I may see the relations of an object, I may understand it perfectly, and may nevertheless regard it with entire indifference. If the pleasure fails, the very substance and protoplasm of beauty is wanting. Nor, as we have seen, is even the pleasure enough; for I may receive a letter full of the most joyous news, but neither the paper, nor the writing, nor the style, need seem beautiful to me. Not until I confound the impressions, and suffuse the symbols themselves with the emotions they arouse, and find joy and sweetness in the very words I hear, will the expressiveness constitute a beauty; as when they sing, *Gloria in excelsis Deo.*

The value of the second term must be incorporated in the first; for the beauty of expression is as inherent in the object as that of material or form, only it accrues to that object not from the bare act of perception, but from the association with it of further processes, due to the existence of former impressions. We may conveniently use the word "expressiveness" to mean all the capacity of suggestion possessed by a thing, and the word "expression" for the aesthetic modification which that expressiveness may cause in it. Expressiveness is thus the power given by experience to any image to call up others in the mind; and this expressiveness becomes an aesthetic value, that is, becomes expression, when the value involved in the associations thus awakened are incorporated in the present object.

That the noble associations of any object should embellish that object is very comprehensible. Homer furnishes us with a good illustration of the constant employment of this effect. The first term, one need hardly say, leaves with him little to be desired. The verse is beautiful. Sounds, images, and composition conspire to stimulate and delight. This immediate beauty is sometimes used to clothe things terrible and sad; there is no dearth of the tragic in Homer. But the tendency of his poetry is nevertheless to fill the outskirts of our consciousness with the trooping images of things no less fair and noble than the verse itself. The heroes are virtuous. There is none of importance who is not admirable in his way. The palaces, the arms, the horses, the sacrifices, are always excellent. The women are always stately and beautiful. The ancestry and the history of every one are honorable and good. The whole Homeric world is clean, clear, beautiful, and providential, and no small part of the perennial charm of the poet is that he thus immerses us in an atmosphere of beauty; a beauty not concentrated and reserved for some extraordinary sentiment, action, or person, but permeating the whole and coloring the common world of soldiers and sailors, war and craft, with a marvelous freshness and inward glow. There is nothing in the associations of life in this world or in another to contradict or disturb our delight. All is beautiful, and beautiful through and through.

Something of this quality meets us in all simple and idyllic compositions. There is, for instance, a popular demand that stories and comedies should "end well." The hero and heroine must be young and handsome; unless they die—which is another matter—they must not in the end be poor. The landscape in the play must be beautiful; the dresses pretty; the plot without serious mishap. A pervasive presentation of pleasure must give warmth and ideality to the whole. In the proprieties of social life we find the same principle; we study to make our surroundings, manner, and conversation suggest nothing but what is pleasing. We hide the ugly and disagreeable portion of our lives, and do not allow the least hint of it to come to light upon festive and public occasions. Whenever, in a word, a thoroughly pleasing effect is found, it is found by the expression, as well as presentation, of what is in itself pleasing—and when this effect is to be produced artificially, we attain it by the suppression of all expression that is not suggestive of something good.

If our consciousness were exclusively aesthetic, this kind of expression would be the only one allowed in art or prized in nature. We should avoid as a shock or an insipidity, the suggestion of anything not intrinsically beautiful. As there would be no values not aesthetic, our pleasure could never be heightened by any other kind of interest. But as contemplation is actually a luxury in our lives, and things interest us chiefly on passionate and practical grounds, the accumulation of values too exclusively aesthetic produces in our minds an effect of closeness and artificiality. So selective a diet cloys, and our palate, accustomed to much daily vinegar and salt, is surfeited by such unmixed sweet.

Instead we prefer to see through the medium of art—through the beautiful first term of our expression—the miscellaneous world which is so well known to us—perhaps so dear, and at any rate so inevitable, an object. We are more thankful for this presentation of the unlovely truth in a lovely form, than for the like presentation of an abstract beauty; what is lost in the purity of the pleasure is gained in the stimulation of our attention, and in the relief of viewing with aesthetic detachment the same things that in practical life hold tyrannous dominion over our souls. The beauty that is associated only with other beauty is therefore a sort of aesthetic dainty; it leads the fancy through a fairyland of lovely forms, where we must forget the common objects of our interest. The charm of such an idealization is undeniable; but the other important elements of our memory and will cannot long be banished. Thoughts of labor, ambition, lust, anger, confusion, sorrow, and death must needs mix with our contemplation and lend their various expressions to the objects with which in experience they are so closely allied. Hence the incorporation in the beautiful of values of other sorts, and the comparative rareness in nature or art of expressions the second term of which has only aesthetic value.

CRITICAL DIALOGUE

Marcia Cavell

Though I will be approaching it indirectly, my primary goal in this paper is to deny that aesthetic experience is in some radical sense "subjective" and to defend the position that critical remarks, or aesthetic ascriptions, can be challenged and defended. I will be discussing, then, the community appealed to in the making of such remarks and the nature of that appeal.

First, I want to make out a case for the notion of "the qualified observer" as the *only* subject relevant to the exchange of challenge and defense in aesthetic contexts. Second, I will argue that not only *can* aesthetic ascriptions be defended, but must be defensible to qualify, in given instances, as aesthetic ascriptions. And, finally, I shall suggest that explicit judgments of value, which have been the concern of aesthetics for so long, are not really at the center—though they typically seem to be—of critical disputes; that, in short, such disputes more generally derive from a disagreement about *what* is seen than about how it is to be valued. If this is so, then understanding the logic of aesthetic judgment is at least largely a matter of understanding the sort of remark with which I am here concerned.

By "critical remarks" or "aesthetic ascriptions" I mean propositions ascribing so-called "aesthetic properties" to an object. Recent attempts to delimit these properties by saying that they are "such that taste or perceptiveness is required in order to apply them" or that they are one sort of property which is not condition-governed are, I believe, in the first case unhelpful and in the second mistaken. So I shall simply say that I have in mind properties like "triteness," "grace," "balance," "harmoniousness," "garishness," and hope that an "etc." is not without suggestiveness. What the relationship is between such ascriptions and explicit evaluations does not concern me here; nor whether or not the ascriptions themselves have some evaluative force (though I think it is clear that they do: to the extent that an image in a poem is trite and is

FROM "Critical Dialogue," in *Journal of Philosophy,* vol. 67, no. 10 (May 28, 1970). Reprinted by permission.

judged to serve no artistic purpose in being so, its triteness would seem to be a good reason for saying that in this respect, at least, the poem fails). Rather, I am concerned with what is required for the making of them, that is, for the making of them to be meaningful in a given context.

What makes for the puzzle here is that aesthetic predicates refer to qualities or aspects of a work—if they are *in* or *of* the work—which can be "directly" experienced. That is, they are not inferred from what we perceive in the object, but are themselves perceived as qualifying the object. Though I may be moved by the fact that Beethoven's Opus 135 was written while the composer was deaf, I cannot *hear* his deafness in the music; whereas I can, presumably, hear its tensions, its grace or lack of grace, all of its many structural, melodic, and rhythmic qualities. To this extent, aesthetic ascriptions resemble descriptions of an object's color. But the latter can be said to be right or wrong, true or false, because we have a clear notion of "the normal observer" and "the normal circumstances of observation" by which to check what color an object appears to be against what it *really* is. And it is just these observers and conditions which seem to be lacking in relation to aesthetic qualities; so we are apparently forced to say that in the last analysis aesthetic ascriptions can only be statements about how the object looks to a particular person. And that as such, they are "subjective," *merely* expressions of personal idiosyncrasy or taste; justifiable only "within a coterie.". . .

The Normal Observer

But there are many things we say about how things look (sound, feel, etc.) which cannot be verified by "the normal observer" in the usual sense of this term, yet where the properties in question are in no way aesthetic and where the description or ascription is, we feel, as clearly challengeable, falsifiable, and supportable as when we say that an object is red; for example: "That looks like (has the look of) a mediaeval manuscript"; "The dog looks like an Afghan"; "The tumor looks cancerous"; etc. Each of these may be intended as a tentative claim about facts other than "the look" in question, but they may also be claims about how the thing does look. (This is the point behind the frequently made but very misleading claim that "aesthetic vision" has to do, as Vincent Tomas puts it, with the appearance, not the reality of things.) The tumor may truly look cancerous, yet turn out to be benign. The dog may truly look like an Afghan and be a first-class mongrel. But it's fairly obvious, I think, that the person who can sensibly claim that the dog looks like an Afghan must have more than 20/20 vision and an ability to discriminate reds and greens; he must also know about Afghans. Knowledge is required, and it's a knowledge that in fact makes a difference to what one looks for and, hence, perceives. (As Wittgenstein pointed out in *Philosophical Investigations,* the substratum of some experiences is the mastery of a technique.) Inquiring, then, whether or not a person is in a position to make a claim that presupposes knowledge or prior experience is one way of challenging that claim.

What qualifies someone to judge the color of an object is physical normality in certain respects; and most of us are in these respects physically normal. What qualifies someone to judge the look of a tumor is something in addition to good eyesight. Not a mysterious something; just a range of knowledge and experience that in fact many people have not had. In the one case, therefore, the qualified observer is apt to be the observer taken at random: standard and statistical norm coincide; but this is not so in the other.

In sum, "looks *x* to the normal observer" must in some cases be amended to "looks *x* to the qualified observer," or modified so as to acknowledge the fact that, normally, seeing the property in question may require more than good eyesight.

What I want to suggest is that "The fugue is tightly knit," "That visual design lacks balance," etc., are very much like "The manuscript looks medieval," etc. To the extent that they are statements about how the fugue sounds, the painting looks, etc., it is quite true that the implied audience is not the one with "normal" hearing and vision; but neither is it an audience chosen arbitrarily, or in accordance with the speaker's tastes. Rather, it is an audience that knows what fugues and visual designs are—a matter once again not only of knowing, but of hearing and seeing.

Are Aesthetic Ascriptions Defensible?

People say things about works of art for different reasons, in different contexts, playing different roles. In saying that a composition is tightly knit or elegant, someone might mean nothing more than that he likes it. But if this were the case, he would not be making, I contend, a genuine critical remark. It would become one, or reveal itself as one, only if it were capable of being defended. Or to put it another way: someone plays the critic's role if, when challenged, he is willing to look for supporting reasons.

In her article, "The Logic of Aesthetic Concepts," Isabel Hungerland contends that "it makes little difference whether we say . . . 'You look elegant' or 'You are elegant,' 'This color scheme looks gay' or

'This color scheme is gay' . . . because in neither case are we committing ourselves to supporting reasons."

I wonder if she would also say: "It makes little difference whether we say 'The composition is in A major' or 'The composition sounds as if it is in A major' "? There are, of course, many instances in which it is truly unclear what key a composition is in, if indeed it is in any key at all. But that's because there are many cases in which it is perfectly clear. Are such remarks about how the music is or about how it sounds? A funny question—because what the music "is" and how it sounds are obviously related; yet they are not identical. A composition might be in the key of A major and yet not sound as if it were, to anyone. Many people are musically well trained enough to be able to identify the key of a piece of music when they see the score, and to tell on hearing it whether it is in a major or a minor key; yet they are unable to identify the key when they hear it played. This might be universally the case. But at the same time, many people *can* hear, sometimes, what key a piece of music is in. And often a composition may sound, to someone who can hear the difference but who has listened carelessly, as if it were in A major, and on a second, more careful hearing, reveal itself as in the related minor, for example.

Hungerland's argument is: (a) that aesthetic ascriptions are, in the broad sense that I have also claimed for them, statements about how an object looks; (b) that since there is no equivalent to "the normal observer" with respect to aesthetic ascriptions, they rather resemble sentences like "The sweater looks red" than "The sweater is red"; and (c) that although for such sentences there are, in Strawson's sense, preconditions for my uttering them, it is not my experience that is being reported; nor is what I say supportable by reference to the experience of others.

But I have argued that there is a perfectly good parallel to "the normal observer" for aesthetic ascribings. And as for (c), I think Hungerland's analysis of what she considers a nonaesthetic analogy is mistaken. There is no usage of "The sweater looks red" for which it is the case both that its looking red to me is not a part of what I assert and that there can be no supporting reasons for my statement. This is an incomplete sentence and expands to a claim about how the object looks to me or would look to others under certain conditions. In either case, it can be challenged and defended, though, in *ordinary* cases, it is true that the only reason I could give for saying that it looks red to me is that it does. But that is partly because it is assumed that I have looked at the sweater and am not color-blind. For if either of these conditions has not been met, my claim is false.

The parallel failures in aesthetic experience are more complicated. If I talk about the visual aspects of a painting, it will also be assumed that I have looked at it. But suppose that I haven't looked at it in the way relevant to perceiving the quality in question—have only peered at a Seurat and, hence, have seen points rather than cones and arcs; haven't noticed the closing in of space in Van Gogh's painting of his room; haven't seen the formal elements in a Cézanne, but only the trees and mountains. In these cases, many claims that I might make about how the painting looks to me would be, if not simply false, certainly open to challenge; for have I, in fact, looked at the painting?

This suggests that not only is there an equivalent to "the normal observer" in relation to works of art, but also to "the normal conditions of observation." Daylight is normally the right condition in which to find out what color an object "really is." But often objects reveal the characteristics in which we are interested only under "abnormal" conditions. In *Sense and Sensibilia* John Austin asked us to:

Suppose that there is a species of fish which looks vividly multi-colored, slightly glowing, perhaps, at a depth of a thousand feet. I ask you what its real color is. So you catch a specimen and lay it out on the deck, making sure the condition of the light is just about normal, and you find that it looks a muddy sort of greyish white. Well, is *that* its real color? It's clear enough at any rate that we don't have to say so.

The "normal" conditions of viewing would not in this case reveal what might be considered the important characteristics. But it doesn't follow that the relevant conditions are abnormal in the sense that they yield an illusory or "merely personal" view of reality. The "right" perceptual viewpoint cannot be stipulated without regard to what is being asked; nor, it is important to note, prior to some knowledge of the object under consideration.

Finally, is it the case that remarks such as "The music sounds tightly knit" and "The music is tightly knit" are interchangeable? Surely not. For one thing, it is difficult to imagine a case in which I would say the first at all; but if I did, it would be to draw attention precisely to a discrepancy between the way the music sounds—in certain passages, played at a certain tempo, listened to with Bach rather than Schubert in mind—and the way it really is, however that would be determined (by looking at the score, perhaps). For another, on a second hearing—just as with my opening example, "It sounds to me as if it's in A major"— I may acknowledge my initial perception to have been mistaken.

And is it the case that the only reason I can give for saying that the music sounds loosely structured is that it does? Structure is, obviously, a function of the relations among a number of possible elements; in the case of music: voices, tonalities, rhythmic patterns, etc. Supporting a remark about its seeming structure would begin with more specific remarks about these elements. My point is not that any such elaboration might be final or conclusive. But only that if I were totally unable to give it, one would ordinarily say that I didn't know what I was talking about. In short, it seems that the one thing a remark like "The Beethoven E flat major piano sonata sounds tightly knit to me" cannot be is a first-person phenomenal report, on the order of "It tastes sweet to me" or "It looks red to me."

If a subjective experience is one describable in terms of myself, the red patch I see when I close my eyes tight, the pain in my left leg, the chill down my spine, the description of an aesthetic experience is at the same time an account of an object. Though of course it need not be. What I see when I look at Van Gogh's *Jacob Wrestling with the Angel* may be a scene from my childhood, and what I hear when I listen to Debussy's *La Mer* may be, simply, last summer's beach. Emma Bovary liked music because it "set her dreaming." We do sometimes use works of art as springboards for associations that have only incidentally to do with the work of art, functioning then as stimulus to response. In this sense, a description of my response need say nothing about the stimulus provoking it. And there can be no sense to asking me how I would justify my reaction. But there is another sense of "response" that has a different logic: here the description will probably take the form of an account of that to which I am responding—for example, in asking me what my response is to someone we have just met, you may expect something from me about how that person made me feel, but you will certainly expect me to say something about how I saw *him;* and you may also, then, ask me to justify that response—which I would prob- ably do by calling your attention to things he had said or done, gestures he had made, etc. In any case, however we answer it, the question of justification is certainly relevant. It is only in this second sense, then, that an account of one's response qualifies at the same time as an aesthetic ascription.

I should perhaps point out that implicit in my argument in this section is a rejection of any hard-and-fast distinction for aesthetic ascribings between preconditions and supporting reasons. What is assumed in the making of a remark in one situation may become the first line of de- fense in another. It depends on who is speaking, on where we are standing, and on whether or not we are on common ground.

The Function of Criticism

The claim that aesthetic ascriptions are not verifiable is, I hope to have shown, a mistaken claim if it is construed to mean that they are not verifiable to any degree and in any circumstances in which they are challenged. It is, however, a proper reminder that the critic does not so much prove to us the validity of what he says as show it to us, and the condition for this is our being able to understand the words he uses and the conventions to which he refers—"stretto," "key," "voice," "fugue," "sonata," "upbeat," "downbeat," etc. If we have been reading the first note in a musical composition as its initial pulse, the critic may, in certain clear cases, be able to prove to us that it functions rather as an upbeat. But his task isn't completed until he has shown us the importance of such a difference to the way we hear the music. To do this he may ask us to look more closely at the construction of the entire composition; he may ask us to conduct it or to dance it or to compare it to other compositions.

Suppose we have done all this, and we each seem to see, or hear, what the other sees; but we insist that the initial note really is, or should be played as, a downbeat. At this point, I claim that dialogue *about the music* is at an end. What sense could it make here for one of us to maintain that his is the right interpretation after all (unless this is an appeal to the composer's "intention")? That is, what might be conceived of as a resolution to such a dispute? That we cannot give meaning to the notion of "a resolution" here is related, I believe, to the fact that indeed there is no need of one. There may be a need for me to understand you. But then the focus of our conversation shifts from something presumably shared between us to each other, one consequence of which may be, of course, that we will be able to share the object after all.

I suggested at the beginning that the critic is typically more interested in the question, What do you see? than in the question, How do you defend your evaluation of what you see? He is interested in reformation, but of vision rather than value. Or if this is an unhelpful distinction, what I mean is that he urges us away from standards and the demands of consistency, with which as moralists we must be concerned, but which in our experience of works of art tend toward just what the artist hopes to free us from: rigidity of response. There is not even, so far as I can see, any real counterpart in aesthetics to moral principles. There are, of course, conventions. But these are more like the conventions that define what hospitality is in a given society than like those which rule for or against it.

In general, I suggest that what look like disagreements about the value of a work of art are usually disagreements about what the work of art is—in the broadest sense. Often, in fact, what we are unsure about is just the sort of thing that Sibley, for example, distinguishes from aesthetic ascriptions: whether or not a character in a novel functions as a character, whether or not a passage is a stretto, a fugue is a fugue, a rose is a rose. Of course the catch is that, though we may seem to be seeing the same thing, this may not be the case. So perhaps I should put my thesis in a positive form: so long as there is disagreement about the value of a work of art, one should presume that what is lacking is a shared perception of it, that there remains the possibility of meaningful (i.e., resolvable) dialogue, even though one may not be able to find the right key. (For two people from very different cultures to perceive an event, or a work of art, in the same way, may *in fact* in a given case not be possible. But there is no theoretical impossibility.)

I would also argue, then, that explicit value judgments are not usually the goal of criticism, but its starting point, functioning to provoke re-examination rather than, in the usual sense, defense. I imagine a dialogue, more sophisticated than the following, but for which it may serve as a model:

A: I didn't like that music at all. It was so repetitious.
B: Repetitious? I thought it extraordinarily inventive. What do you mean?
A: Well, just that one silly tune, all the way through, for example.
B: But the whole point was to invent variations on that tune. Didn't you like the third one, where it turned into a waltz? And then the marvelous fifth, where it became the second voice in the fugue?

Suppose that A acknowledges not having heard the waltz or the fugue. He will be forced to retreat. Which is not to say that B in turn might not be led to reconsider, to rehear, under the tutelage of a more equal opponent.

In ordinary conversation, the answer to "What an exciting play!" may well be, "I found it boring"; to "At least it's honest," "It's a lie"; to "Well, it was certainly skillfully done," "I think it was very sloppy." The ascription—or the remark—functions not so much as a move in a dialogue as in a duel, to which therefore no reasonable conclusion is possible. It is the experience of this kind of exchange that gives rise, I think, to the common belief that aesthetic ascriptions are really remarks not about an object, but about the subject making them; that they are hopelessly "subjective"; that the critic is simply another subject whose personal responses and evaluations have somehow received public sanction.

But there is another kind of exchange whose logic is quite different. One of the antonyms of "exciting" is "boring." But I don't answer your "It's exciting!" in this way unless we are—or I wish us to be—antagonists. When, on the other hand, we think of our relationship as mediated by an object, our exchange goes quite differently:

A: What an exciting play!
B: But it's an imitation of . . . and an inferior one at that.
A: At least it's honest.
B: But the portrayal of . . . is so sentimental.
A: Well, it certainly is skillfully done.
B: But the handling of the dialogue in the third act is out of character.

This is, of course, very sketchy. Each remark could—and in a real conversation would—be countered, expanded, in a variety of ways. Presumably A would not abandon his position so easily. He might respond by saying that B's claim is simply mistaken, or he might argue that, while it would be true if this work were to be construed in one way, it should be construed in another (for example, an event that is improbable in a realistic novel or play and therefore, perhaps, a weakness in the structure, may be improbable and *therefore* an integral part of the structure in an "absurdist" play). The point, however, is that the dialogue proceeds not by the countering of a predicate with its logical contrary, but obliquely, by the providing of ever more specific directions *into the work. There is no end* to the ways in which a play can fail to be exciting, honest, skillful. One can imagine this dialogue continuing, therefore, until someone gets tired or until it becomes clear that one person's reaction is highly idiosyncratic or until, finally, after this kaleidoscopic focusing and assembling of the parts, both people are satisfied that they are seeing pretty much the same thing.

The logic of the above conversation is such, then, that it comes to an end not with victory or defeat, but with a shared perception of the object at hand. Not, of course, that this is always, or often, attained. And it is almost certainly and nontrivially true that no two people ever see a work of art or experience an event in exactly the same ways. But communication often breaks down long before this ultimate limit is reached; for a sharing of an aesthetic experience requires many things: equal sensitivity to the medium, similar training in and experience with the medium, patience, intelligence, imagination, and often conversation itself.

If critical remarks, aesthetic ascriptions, are ever "objective," they must be intersubjectively verifiable. But I have been suggesting that this leaves open the questions: Which subjects? Under what conditions? And furthermore, *When?* What the critic says is tested not by how the objects looks *now* to the observer qualified to see what he is asked to see, but by how it *will* look when he has followed the critic's directions. The critic is certainly appealing to a community—a community, however, not achieved, but in the making. The critic's experience of the work of art may *in fact* be shared by no one. I take it that this is something of what Arnold Isenberg had in mind when he claimed, in "Critical Communication" that "it is a function of criticism *to bring about* communication at the level of the senses" (my emphasis).

This difference between construing aesthetic ascriptions like "It's exciting," ". . . honest," "well-constructed," as answerable by their logical contraries, on the one hand, and by a greater specificity in the direction indicated, on the other, provides a clue to an analysis of the so-called "criteria of value" for works of art; for example, those proposed by Monroe Beardsley: Unity, Complexity, and Intensity. The troubles with trying to establish any such criteria of value are well known and legion. For one, whether or not a work *is* unified is just as open to conflicts of opinion as whether or not it's good. For another, unless one construes "unity" so broadly as to render it useless, it is questionable whether every work we consider to be valuable we also consider to be unified. So it seems we must choose between construing an ascription of unity as unverifiable, and regarding it as verifiable but having little to do with the aesthetic experience and what makes it valuable.

The dilemma results, however, from taking: (a) "The work has unity" as a report, confirmed on finding the quality of unity in the work, disconfirmed if it is absent; (b) the conversation in which such a remark functions as an argument; and (c) the relationship between "The work has unity" and "The work is good" as that between premise and conclusion, or reason and verdict. Working backwards, suppose we construe (c) "The work is good" not as the conclusion to an argument, but, as I have suggested, as a very general directive to re-experience the work, to look at it again; (b) the conversation not as an argument *about* the work, but an investigation of it, a joint voyage into it (it is as if there were here a dialogue with three members: the work of art is not so much spoken *about,* as spoken *to,* addressed); and finally (a) unity, for example, not as a quality residing in some sense in the work of art, but as a vantage point from which to view it; that is, as indicating one of a great number of possible questions to put to it. Knowing which questions are indicated in any given case already requires knowing or learning something about, this particular work of art; which is why trying to define "unity," construed as a property, leads us to think that it is hopelessly ambiguous. Considering the unity in a work of art means considering the relationship of its parts to one another. I am unable to follow the instructions if, for example, I don't even know what to consider, to begin with, as the parts. The structural elements of a baroque fugue are not the same as those of a romantic symphony. And if I listen for the same elements and relations I am apt to make a muddle of one, if not both. In short, there are not so much criteria of value, as there are kinds of questions to be asked.

In conclusion: that we are not all equally qualified to talk about works of art; and that our various qualifications may make crucial differences to what we perceive, and hence, one would think, to how we feel, in the largest sense, about works of art, seems clear. It is even clear that, contrary to the arguments of Sibley and Hungerland, there are necessary conditions, and even occasionally sufficient conditions, for some aesthetic concepts. For example, it is a necessary condition for a painting to be "garish" that it not be monochromatically black, white, or pastel; it is a sufficient condition for a piece of music to be "well-constructed" that it be a fugue obeying the rules of counterpoint in Piston's *Elementary Harmony.* How then, have philosophers been led to deny the obvious? It's a question we often ask ourselves about philosophy in general, but it is particularly important, I think, in aesthetics, and I can only make a couple of suggestions here:

A. Responding to a work of art is not a matter of identifying it correctly as a four-part fugue, etc. But it follows neither: (a) that hearing it as a musical structure composed of voices in certain relations to one another is irrelevant to how I respond to it; nor (b) that learning about fugues, which involves learning to hear notes *as* voices, for one thing, is irrelevant to how I will eventually respond to it. Responding to a work of art which is a four-part fugue and which does make certain harmonic modulations, etc., is at its best—that is, most attentive, most responsive, least "subjective"—a matter of hearing those voices and those changes—though of course one may not be able to put a name to them. And this hearing inevitably involves certain responses in terms of feeling. Though it's not so much, I think, that the hearing produces the feeling, as that sometimes ways of hearing and seeing are themselves ways of feeling. (I have been talking about what is required in the way of skill and prior experience for the justification, or justifiability, of a critical remark. But equally important—thought a subject for another paper—is what is required in the way of feeling for the claim to have had "an aesthetic response" to be legitimate. I would say that unless one feels something like remorse—some species of pain—one cannot claim "to know" that he has wronged another. And something comparable is undoubtedly true of the claim—to put it very generally—to have "understood" a work of art.)

B. We identify the work of art with the work of genius; and genius is, in our mythology, mad, rule-defying, transcendent, unpredictable. It breaks all precedents. And isn't that just to say that there can be no conditions that the work of genius must satisfy? But it doesn't spring full-grown from its author's head. It is new and original in relation to a past; and what it transcends is the past as actual, taken as marking the limits of the possible. Any competent music student can write a "tightly-knit" fugue. There is no guarantee, and little hope, that it will also be inventive. But that's another matter. The difference between art and craft, genius and talent, may be enormous, but it's not categorical. Or if it is, the relation between the categories is that between originality and convention: originality "breaks" from convention in expanding it, playing with it, taking it somewhere new. The task of criticism is in part to reveal the old in the new and the new in the old, to trace the bridge between them. Which way it looks in any given case depends on what we have missed, or are likely to.

A final note: there is, I think, no class of judgment that can be set apart as requiring discrimination and sensitivity. It may require percep-tiveness to notice that a corner of the scarf is protruding from the magician's sleeve; that two lines are really the same length after all; even, depending on the weather and one's mood, that the sun is shining. Whether or not, and to what degree, perceptiveness is required is not a function of the predicate itself, but of the situation and the person perceiving. Noticing that the rhyming words of a poem form a significant sentence probably requires a little greater attentiveness than usual from most people and none at all from a Yeats. But even this depends on the particular poem.

Nor is there any class of judgment that can be set apart as eliciting or presupposing feeling. It is of the essence of art to challenge old ways of thinking and perceiving, and, as Dewey reminded us in *Art as Experience,* this is by nature a disruptive, sometimes even a painful, process. Art is more likely, therefore, to push us to the limits of awareness and to make more demands on us in all ways than other sorts of experience. It is also, therefore, more likely to force us to talking about what we see in new ways. But speaking metaphorically, as it were, is neither a matter of mere self-expression nor of pretending, but of seeing connec-tions to which our previous concerns did not call attention. The com-munity to which the work of art addresses itself may, then, in fact be very small. It is the critic's task to make it larger.

Questions for Discussion

1. Is Oronte's poem as bad as Alceste maintains? Do you think Moliere intended it to be really bad? Could Alceste's disapproval be related to the fact that Oronte wrote the poem to Celimène, the woman Alceste also loves?

2. The Roman philosopher Plotinus held that there is equal beauty in everything and that it is the task of the artist to reveal it. Was he right in claiming that all things are equally beautiful and, if so, does it follow that all works of art are equally good?

3. To what extent is it possible to value a work of art, the content of which is morally offensive, such as novels or paintings that favorably depict the subjection of women or that glorify crime?

4. Do you believe that artists must experience the emotions they portray? Must they be somewhat insane to describe insanity, or suicidal to portray despair, or criminally inclined to depict crime successfully?

5. Was Tolstoy right in criticizing his own novels as too remote from the experience of the peasantry? Must we have shared an artist's experience in order to understand and appreciate his or her work? Defend your position.

6. Tolstoy draws a distinction between fine art and merely playful activities such as conjuring tricks and gymnastics. The American pragmatist John Dewey maintained that art should move out of the museum and concert hall and into everyday life, so that any activity performed well and for enjoyment should be considered as art. Are these views compatible? If not, which is more sound?

7. Santayana holds that "in removing consciousness we have removed the possibility of worth." Does it follow that, if all human life were destroyed, a sunset would no longer be beautiful? Do you agree?

8. Is Santayana's assertion that most people insist on happy endings consistent with his statement that people want art to give beauty of form to the ugliness and horror of real life? Why or why not?

9. What does Cavell mean by a "qualified observer"? If one does not meet Cavell's qualifications of knowledge and training, is it possible to appreciate great art? Explain.

10. Cavell claims that the images and associations we form when we contemplate works of art "have only incidentally to do with the work." Santayana, on the other hand, maintains that it is essential for a work of art that it evoke in the spectator images and emotional associations. Is either of these positions sound? Are some images and associations more pertinent to a work of art than others? If so, what are they?

Selected Readings

ALDRICH, V. *Philosophy of Art*. Englewood Cliffs, New Jersey: Prentice-Hall, 1963. A good introduction to philosophy of art.

ARISTOTLE. *Poetica*. Translated by I. Bywater. Oxford: Oxford University Press, 1928. Art as imitation plus formal unity.

ARNHEIM, R. *Art and Visual Perception*. Berkeley: University of California Press, 1957. Psychological studies of art perception.

BEARDSLEY, M. *Aesthetics from Classical Greece to the Present.* New York: Macmillan, 1966. A clear and thorough historical study.

BELL, C. *Problems in Aesthetics.* New York: Macmillan, 1959. A modern objectivist account.

BOUWSMA, O. K. "The Expression Theory of Art." In *Philosophical Essays.* Lincoln: University of Nebraska Press, 1965. A powerful critique of the expressive theory of art.

CAVELL, M. "Critical Dialogue." *The Journal of Philosophy,* 67 (1970). An informed defense of the objectivity of aesthetic criticism.

DEWEY, J. *Art as Experience.* New York: Minton Balch, 1934. A pragmatic analysis of art as a type of experience.

GOMBRICH, E. H. *Art and Illusion.* Princeton, New Jersey: Princeton University Press, 1961. A critique of art as expression.

GOODMAN, N. *Languages of Art.* Indianapolis, Indiana: Bobbs-Merrill, 1968. An analysis of symbolic meaning in works of art.

HEGEL, G. W. F. *The Philosophy of Fine Art.* 4 vols. Translated by F. Osmaston. London: Bell, 1920. A difficult but rewarding account of art as the embodiment of absolute spirit.

HOOK, S., ed. *Art and Philosophy.* New York: New York University Press, 1966. Contemporary essays on the nature of art and art criticism.

LANGER, S. *Feeling and Form.* New York: Scribner's, 1953. A synthesis of symbolic expressionism and formalism.

MARGOLIS, J., ed. *Philosophy Looks at the Arts.* New York: Scribner's, 1962. An anthology of important contemporary essays.

PLATO, *Ion; Republic.* In *The Dialogues of Plato.* Translated by B. Jowett. London: Methuen, 1892. The imitation theory of art.

PLOTINUS. *Enneads.* Translated by A. Armstrong. Cambridge, Massachusetts: Harvard University Press, 1966. Identifies Platonic knowledge of forms with aesthetic perception.

RADER, M., ed. *A Modern Book of Aesthetics.* New York: Holt, Rinehart & Winston, 1960. A good anthology of essays, both classical and modern.

SANTAYANA, G. *The Sense of Beauty.* New York: Scribner's, 1936. A hedonistic account of art as the production of beauty.

TOLSTOY, L. *What is Art?* London: Oxford University Press, 1930. The expressive theory of art.

NAME INDEX

SUBJECT INDEX

Cause (*cont.*)
types of, 20, 68
unreality of, 83*f*
see also Determinism
Certainty, 40, 85, 203*f*, 407*f*, 410*f*
implied by "know," 410*f*
"metaphysical," 408
Choice, 56*f*, 172, 252*f*, 269*f*, 313*f*,
422–423, 518*f*, 616*f*
of self, 307*f*, 518*f*
rational, 57*f*, 422, 552
Christianity, 463, 499*f*, 514*f*, 644.
See also Jesus; Religion, Christian
Civil society, 554*f*, 624*f*
Civilization, 498
Cogito, 527*f*
Comedy, 641
Commitment, 528*f*
Common sense, 127*f*, 341–342,
356–357, 376
Compulsion. *See* Action, compul-
sive
Communism, 514*f*, 558, 631
Conditioning, 251*f*, 267*f*, 273*f*,
289*f*, 540
Consciousness, 306*f*, 544
continuity of, 182*f*, 214*f*, 223*f*,
237*f*, 305
of necessity, 314*f*
of negativity, 296*f*
reflective, 255–256, 302*f*
Conceivability, 39*f*, 59*f*, 76, 88,
151*f*, 176, 455
Consequentialism. *See* Utilitarian-
ism
Constraint, 315*f*, 323
Contingency, 20*f*, 53*f*, 240*f*
Conservatism, 629
Cosmological argument, 18*f*, 39*f*,
77
"crude" and "subtle," 47*f*
Courage, 584*f*
Creation, 17*f*
Criterion
of bodily identity, 237*f*
of explanation, 56

Criterion (*cont.*)
of personal identity, 184*f*, 211*f*,
225*f*, 237*f*
Criticism, 642, 647–648, 679, 697*f*
Culture, 10

Death, 228*f*. *See also* Immortality
Decision. *See* Choice
Definition, 359, 516*f*
of art, 669*f*
of beauty, 679*f*
of self, 469, 517*f*
see also Redefinition
Deism, 23
Democracy, 9, 539*f*
Denotation, 41*f*, 76–77
Deontology. *See* Formalism, moral
Design. *See* Teleological argument
Desire, 258*f*, 286*f*, 331, 449*f*, 586–
587, 592*f*
Determinism, 6, 90, 161*f*, 251*f*,
268*f*, 285*f*, 295*f*, 311*f*
"hard" and "soft," 252*f*
Dialectic, 199*f*
Divided line, 118*f*
Dogmatism, 376–377, 410*f*
Doubt. *See* Skepticism
Dreams, 206, 216, 406
Dualism, 174, 179*f*. *See also* Mind
and Body
Duty, 422*f*, 449*f*
military, 422, 461, 519
strict and meritorious, 426, 459*f*
to be happy, 450

Education, 541*f*, 580*f*
Egoism, 509, 555, 626*f*
Ekstasis, 299*f*
Eleatic School, 111. *See also* Par-
menides; Zeno
Emotion, 596*f*, 643*f*, 669*f*
religious, 25
tragic, 660*f*
"virtual," 644–645
Empiricism, 87, 89
Energy, 162*f*
Enlightenment, 180

Mind–Body, problem, 182*f*, 205*f*
Miracles, 26, 377
Monism, 161, 174*f*. *See also* Mysticism; Eleatic School
Morality, 7*f*, 421*f*, 493*f*, 504*f*, 522*f*, 684*f*
    "aesthetic," 529*f*
    and self-interest, 8, 422*f*, 463*f*, 493*f*, 504*f*, 522*f*
    "slave" and "master," 494*f*
Motion, 36*f*, 109*f*, 135*f*, 143*f*, 161*f*
    laws of, 349
Motive, 256, 286*f*, 297*f*, 306*f*, 465*f*. *See also* Desire
Music, 699*f*
Mysticism, 80, 84, 103*f*

Nagual, 81*f*
Naturalism, 642
Natural selection, 168*f*, 680
Nature, 36, 58, 60, 347, 369, 455
    human, 447*f*, 465*f*, 517*f*, 557, 617
    laws of, 54, 90, 155*f*, 181, 253, 285*f*, 356*f*, 460
    rationality of, 57, 347
    state of, 505*f*
    uniformity of, 155*f*, 350*f*, 356*f*
Necessary connection, 340*f*
Necessary being, 20*f*, 37*f*, 54*f*
Necessity, 20*f*, 311*f*, 657–659
    causal, 257, 286*f*, 340*f*
    logical, 49, 58*f*, 257
    moral, 425–426, 451*f*
Negativity, 257, 295*f*
Nihilism, 499
Nirvana, 83, 193*f*
Noncontradiction, principle of, 373

Objectivity, 455*f*
Occam's Razor, 159, 176
Occultism, 80*f*
Omnipotence, 17*f*, 57, 69
Omniscience, 69
Ontological argument, 18*f*, 39*f*, 76
Optimism and pessimism, 526

Paradox, 109*f*, 175, 360*f*
Perception. *See* Knowledge, perceptual
Perfection
    divine, 21*f*, 39*f*, 66
Person, 5, 6, 68, 179*f*, 211*f*, 256, 469, 525. *See also* Identity, personal
Philosophy
    analytic and synthetic, 2*f*, 12
    contrasted with theology, 1, 17
    ordinary language, 375
    scientific, 90
    subdivisions of, 3*f*
Physics, 12, 253*f*. *See also* Nature, laws of
Pity and terror, 660*f*
Pleasure, 114, 645
    aesthetic, 642, 645, 662, 668*f*, 686*f*
    and pain, 130*f*, 218, 221, 422–423, 439*f*, 461
Play, 685–686
Politics, 8–9, 539*f*
Positivism, 4
Possibility, 376–377, 524. *See also* Necessity
Potentiality and actuality, 36*f*, 110
Pragmatism, 91, 422
Praise and blame, 263, 323
Prediction, 6, 357*f*, 370, 406, 410
    of behavior, 255, 318, 325*f*
Prime mover, 19*f*, 37*f*, 266
Privileged access, 197*f*
Probability, 352*f*, 370, 523–524, 657–659
Project, 258, 297*f*, 517*f*
Providence, 23*f*
Psychoanalysis, 255, 317, 326, 535
Psychology, 1, 12, 52, 90, 172, 251, 268*f*, 273*f*, 465
Punishment, 270*f*, 285, 291, 323, 471, 605
Purpose, 52, 157*f*. *See also* Explanation, purposive

Qualified observer, 698*f*

Substance (*cont.*)
 See also Matter; Spirit
Substratum, 149*f*
Synthesis, 2, 11–12

Teleology. *See* Explanation, purposive
Teleological argument, 18*f*, 66, 68*f*, 77
Temperance, 586–587
Theology, 1, 11
 natural, 17*f*, 40*f*, 57, 65
 revealed, 17, 24, 65
Theory, in science, 54
Time, 109*f*, 175, 212, 445
Tonal. *See* Nagual
Totality, cosmic, 4–5, 46, 55, 73*f*, 157*f*
Tragedy, 655*f*
Transcendental, 103, 158, 166
Transcendence, 255, 299, 534
Truth
 duty toward, 451
 in art, 646*f*, 683*f*
 mathematical and empirical, 39, 48
 necessary, 203*f*
 problems of, 372*f*, 417
 value of, 551*f*, 607*f*

Unity, in art, 65*f*, 705
Universal, 643, 658
Universalizability, 425, 453*f*
Universe. *See* World
Use
 and mention, 41*f*

Use (*cont.*)
 of words, 41, 375, 399*f*, 417
Utilitarianism, 323, 422*f*, 439*f*, 461, 550, 605*f*
Utility, principle of, 439*f*. *See also* Happiness, "Greatest," principle of

Values, 465, 522*f*
 aesthetic, 530, 641*f*, 681*f*
 and facts, 645, 682*f*
 negative and positive, 690
Verifiability, 702
Virtue, 63, 113, 124, 251, 466, 502, 535, 541, 543, 660
 of state, 583*f*
Vision
 cosmic, 2*f*, 20
 mechanistic, 20
Volition, 72, 148, 170*f*, 206*f*, 254, 287*f*, 302*f*, 319*f*, 451, 458, 527*f*
Voluntarism. *See* Libertarianism

Welfare, 8
Will. *See* Volition; Freedom, of the will
Wisdom, 124, 541, 543, 583*f*
World
 eternity of, 58, 108
 possible, 55, 58
 soul of, 68*f*
 See also Totality, cosmic; Cause, first

Yoga, 67